DREAMS ACHIEVED AND DENIED

DREAMS ACHIEVED AND DENIED

MEXICAN INTERGENERATIONAL MOBILITY

ROBERT COURTNEY SMITH
WITH A FOREWORD BY MANUEL CASTRO

A Volume in the American Sociological Association's
Rose Series in Sociology

Russell Sage Foundation • New York

ROR: https://ror.org/02yh9se80
DOI: https://doi.org/10.7758/drwz9626

Library of Congress Cataloging in Publication Control Number: 2023059172
ISBN 9780871549419 (paperback) / 9781610449090 ISBN (ebook)

Cover art: *My walk to school* by Nathalie Bermejo. Watercolor. ©2024 Nathalie
Bermejo. Reprinted with permission.

The paper used in this publication meets the minimum requirements of
American National Standard for Information Sciences—Permanence of Paper
for Printed Library Materials. ANSI Z39.48-1992.

Text design by Suzanne Nichols. Front matter DOI: https://doi.org/10.7758
/drwz9626.7582

RUSSELL SAGE FOUNDATION
112 East 64th Street, New York, New York 10065
10 9 8 7 6 5 4 3 2 1

The Russell Sage Foundation

The Russell Sage Foundation, one of the oldest of America's general purpose foundations, was established in 1907 by Mrs. Margaret Olivia Sage for "the improvement of social and living conditions in the United States." The foundation seeks to fulfill this mandate by fostering the development and dissemination of knowledge about the country's political, social, and economic problems. While the foundation endeavors to assure the accuracy and objectivity of each book it publishes, the conclusions and interpretations in Russell Sage Foundation publications are those of the authors and not of the foundation, its trustees, or its staff. Publication by Russell Sage, therefore, does not imply foundation endorsement.

Previous Volumes
in the Series

American Memories: Atrocities and the Law
Joachim J. Savelsberg and Ryan D. King

America's Newcomers and the Dynamics of Diversity
Frank D. Bean and Gillian Stevens

Beyond the Boycott: Labor Rights, Human Rights, and Transnational Activism
Gay W. Seidman

Beyond College For All: Career Paths for the Forgotten Half
James E. Rosenbaum

Changing Rhythms of the American Family
Suzanne M. Bianchi, John Robinson, and Melissa Milkie

Collateral Damages: Landlords and the Urban Housing Crisis
Meredith J. Greif

*The Company We Keep: Interracial Friendships and Romantic Relationships
from Adolescence to Adulthood*
Grace Kao, Kara Joyner, and Kelly Stamper Balistreri

Counted Out: Same-Sex Relations and Americans' Definitions of Family
Brian Powell, Lala Carr Steelman, Catherine Bolzendahl,
and Claudi Giest

Divergent Social Worlds: Neighborhood Crime and the Racial-Spatial Divide
Ruth D. Peterson and Lauren J. Krivo

Egalitarian Capitalism: Jobs, Incomes, and Growth in Affluent Countries
Lane Kenworthy

*Ethnic Origins: History, Politics, Culture, and the Adaptation of Cambodian
and Hmong Refugees in Four American Cities*
Jeremy Hein

Family Consequences of Children's Disabilities
Denis Hogan

Golden Years? Social Inequality in Later Life
Deborah Carr

Forthcoming Titles

Chains of Discrimination
Reginald A. Byron and Vincent. J. Roscigno

The Great Dispersion: Geography, Diversity, and Opportunity among Hispanics in the United States
Emilio A. Parrado and Chenoa A. Flippen

Immigrant Growth Machines: Urban Growth Politics in Koreatown and Monterey Park
Angie Y. Chung and Jan Lin

The Journey to Adulthood in Uncertain Times
Robert Crosnoe and Shannon E. Cavanagh

Learning to Lead: The Intersectional Politics of the Second Generation
Veronica Terriquez

The Rose Series in Sociology

THE AMERICAN Sociological Association's Rose Series in Sociology publishes books that integrate knowledge and address controversies from a sociological perspective. Books in the Rose Series are at the forefront of sociological knowledge. They are lively and often involve timely and fundamental issues on significant social concerns. The series is intended for broad dissemination throughout sociology, across social science and other professional communities, and to policy audiences. The series was established in 1967 by a bequest to ASA from Arnold and Caroline Rose to support innovations in scholarly publishing.

JOANNA DREBY
AARON MAJOR
STEVEN F. MESSNER
KATHERINE TRENT

EDITORS

Contents

List of Illustrations   xv

About the Author   xviii

Foreword by Manuel Castro   xix

Acknowledgments   xxiii

CHAPTER 1   Introduction: Dreams Achieved and Denied   1

CHAPTER 2   Intergenerational Bequeathal of Dis/Advantage and the Immigrant Bargain: The Impact of Legal Status on the Intrafamily Mechanisms Promoting Upward Mobility   49

CHAPTER 3   How Did You Pick That School? Institutional Settings, Counterfactual Choices, Race, and Value Added (or Subtracted) in New York City High Schools   83

CHAPTER 4   Mentors: Boosting Adult Outcomes and Offering Paths Out of a Hard Life   114

CHAPTER 5   DACA: A Revocable Program That Can Unblock Mobility and Make Private the Stigma of Undocumented Status   139

CHAPTER 6   Second-Chance Mechanisms: Hitting the Reset Button for U.S. Citizens and the Derailment Button for Undocumented Americans   168

CHAPTER 7   Masculinities and Long-Term Outcomes: How Mexican Mobility Masculinity Promotes and Gang Masculinity Inhibits Mobility   194

CHAPTER 8   Friendship Strategies, White Contact, and
             Mexicanness as an Identity or a Status:
             Sequentially Constructing the Meaning of
             Mexicanness in Upwardly or Downwardly
             Mobile Contexts and Trajectories   227

CHAPTER 9   Conclusion: Empirical, Theoretical, and
             Policy Stories and Recommendations   261

             Guide to Online Appendixes   295

             Notes   303

             References   359

             Index   405

Illustrations

Figures

Figure 1.1   College Attainment or Higher of Mexican and
             U.S.-Born Men and Women Ages Twenty-Five
             and Older, 1990–2020   12
Figure 1.2   College Attainment of U.S.-Born Mexican Men
             Ages Twenty-Five and Older Relative to Other
             Same-Age U.S.-Born Men, 1990–2020   13
Figure 1.3   College Attainment of U.S.-Born Mexican Women
             Ages Twenty-Five and Older Relative to Other
             Same-Age U.S.-Born Women, 1990–2020   14
Figure 2.1   Family Earnings from Time 1 to Time 2 to Time 3
             for U.S.-Born, Category Changer, and
             Undocumented Participants   78
Figure 2.2   Income per Earner from Time 1 to Time 2 to
             Time 3 for U.S.-Born, Category Changer, and
             Undocumented Participants   79
Figure 2.3   Per Person Income from Time 1 to Time 2 to
             Time 3 for U.S.-Born, Category Changer, and
             Undocumented Participants   80
Figure 3.1   The New York City School Choice System and
             Educational Derailment Mechanisms in
             Students' Counterfactual Analyses   89
Figure 3.2   Counterfactual Proxy: Parallel Narrative Case
             Development for Esteban and Valerio   93
Figure 3.3   Family and Friendship Group Counterfactual
             Cases: Emmanuel   96
Figure 3.4   Family and Friendship Group Counterfactual
             Cases: Carmelita   97

Figure 3.5   The Absence of Counterfactuals in Framing
             School Choice: Skinny   98
Figure 3.6   A Category-Changing Counterfactual Case:
             Chucho   101
Figure 3.7   A Category-Changing Counterfactual Case:
             Vicky   107
Figure 4.1   Mentor Quality and Time 2 Outcomes   135
Figure 8.1   Friendship Strategies across Time and Adult
             Outcome Groups: Stuck Muddlers and
             Shallow Slopers versus College Graduates
             and High Fliers   237

Tables

Table 1.1   College Graduates among U.S.-Born and
            Foreign-Born Mexicans in the NYCOMP
            Study and in Other Studies   10
Table 1.2   Years of Education for U.S.- and Foreign-Born
            Mexican Men and Women, 1990–2020   304
Table 1.3   Number and Ratio of U.S.-Born and Foreign-Born
            Mexican Youth Ages Thirteen to Nineteen,
            2000–2021   305
Table 1.4   Comparison of Clustering Algorithms Based on
            Dependent Variables and Qualitative Typologies   307
Table 1.5   Expected versus Actual Time 2 (Average Age of
            Twenty-Eight) Outcome Categories   19
Table 1.6   The Legal Status of NYCOMP Participants
            over Time   39
Table 2.1   Associations between the Immigrant Bargain
            and Family History and Outcomes at Time 2   319
Table 2.2   Correlations between Keeping the Immigrant
            Bargain and Years of Education at Time 2   320
Table 2.3   Correlations between Keeping the Immigrant
            Bargain and Income at Time 2   321
Table 2.4   Correlations between Keeping the Immigrant
            Bargain and Being a College Graduate or
            High Flier at Time 2 and Time 3   322
Table 2.5   Family Earnings, Overall and per Earner and
            Member at Time 1, Time 2, and Time 3   323
Table 3.1   The Correlations of Institutional, Habitual, Legal,
            and Conjunctural Variables with Time 2 Outcomes:
            Proportion of College Graduates or High Fliers,
            Mean Years of Education, and Yearly Income   326

Table 3.2   Descriptive Statistics of Independent and
Dependent Variables   329

Table 3.3   Adjusted Coefficients of Legal Status History
Predicting Correlations with Time 2 Outcomes
(All Controls Added)   332

Table 3.4   Adjusted Coefficients of High School Quality
Predicting Correlations with Time 2 Outcomes
(All Controls Added)   334

Table 4.1   Dichotomous Measure of Positive Adult
Mentorship: Correlations with Overall
Outcomes, Years of Education, and Income   339

Table 4.2   Correlations between Having or Not Having
a Positive Adult Mentor and Having or Not Having
Positive Peer Mentors, Negative Peer Mentors,
Escalating Conflict, and Continuing Conflict
in the Teens and in Early and Middle Adulthood   339

Table 4.3   Mentor Quality and Time 2 Outcomes:
Distributions   340

Table 4.4   Mentor Quality and Time 2 Outcomes:
Predictive Models among U.S. Citizen
Participants Only   340

Table 4.5   Positive Adult Mentor Quality and Time 2
Outcome Distributions: U.S. Citizens and
Legal Permanent Residents   341

Table 4.6   Positive Adult Mentor Quality and Time 2
Outcome Distributions   341

Table 7.1   Masculinity Types and Time Use at Time 1
and Time 2 or Time 3   203

Table 7.2   Gang Membership and Time 2 Overall Life
Outcomes, Education, and Income   349

Table 8.1   Frequency of and Contexts for Substantive
White Relationships over Time   241

Table 8.2   Type of White Contact, Mobility, Work Setting,
and Meaning of Mexicanness   244

About the Author

Robert Courtney Smith ⊙ is professor of public and international affairs, Marxe School, Baruch College, and professor in the Sociology Department and Program in Social Welfare, Graduate Center, City University of New York.

Foreword

GROWING UP AS a young Mexican in New York City, I often found myself caught between two worlds. On one hand, the big city dreams, and on the other, being an undocumented immigrant. I remember walking the Brooklyn Bridge with my high school friends, sharing my dreams of going to college and becoming someone "important enough" to help my community. Yet there was always that reality (kept secret from my friends) of my undocumented status. The cruel irony was that the only city and country I could remember, the only home I had ever known, seemed to not want me or my family. It was a constant battle between my ambition to become *alguien* (someone) and the undocumented identity I didn't choose but had to embrace and turn into a source of strength. Ultimately, it was my identity, and this relentless struggle for survival that undocumented status imposed on me, that fueled my drive. This journey not only allowed me to "make it" but also empowered me to make a difference within my community.

As an immigrant, a lifelong immigrant rights activist, and now the New York City Commissioner for the Mayor's Office of Immigrant Affairs, I am pleased to write this preface. Not only does Professor Robert Courtney Smith's book tell a story that is important for policy makers, but it is also a story that I've lived. It is deeply personal. I am grateful to Professor Smith for dedicating so much time and care to capturing and sharing this story of immigrant youth like me.

I write this preface to offer my perspective, as I've had the unique opportunity to view the issues discussed in this book from various standpoints. These include my current role as a government official and previous roles as an executive director of an immigrant-serving nonprofit organization and an immigrant rights activist, and also as a student seeking a master's degree in public administration at the Marxe School, Baruch College, CUNY (where Professor Smith teaches), a program of study that deepened my academic knowledge of these topics. Yet at my core, my most profound connection to these issues stems from my experiences as a former undocumented immigrant and youth.

When I first met Professor Smith, I was seeking my way as a teenager, facing the realities of being an undocumented college student. Our conversations over the years breathed life into the struggles, dreams, and hopes of countless young Mexicans like me who were trying to shape an identity that would later be known as the "Dreamer," spawning a social movement. Professor Smith became a genuine ally to our cause and the mentor I deeply needed. Our bond deepened over the years as we collaborated on projects (promoting DACA applications and assessing the very positive impact of New York State's $2.1 billion Excluded Workers Fund, among other efforts). I continued to pursue the dream of helping immigrant communities, though it often seemed just out of reach. Professor Smith was always present, both in challenging times and in better moments, not only for me but also for so many in the community. Rob has been a good mentor.

It was through our work together that I came to appreciate the importance of Professor Smith's longitudinal academic work—following the same people for up to two decades to see how their lives turned out—and his constant search for ways to make his research and work of service to immigrants and immigrant communities. Professor Smith has had a unique vantage point through the relationships he developed with those in his study. He has intimately witnessed not only the journeys of youth immigrants as they transitioned from their formative teenage years into adulthood but also the challenges faced by adult immigrants, the children of these immigrants, and the broader community in their collective pursuit of recognition and opportunity. He has been in and with the community for decades and never said "no" when I asked him to help someone.

Professor Smith's findings in this book are important for policymakers. He documents that U.S.-born Mexicans in New York had one of the biggest single-generation jumps in mobility in our history. Most studies done in the last forty years show that 13 to 14 percent of U.S.-born second-generation Mexicans graduate from college, but his research and New York City census data show a much higher rate—42 percent for U.S.-born Mexican men and 49 percent for U.S.-born Mexican women. This increase is more remarkable considering that the income and education levels of his study participants' parents were low. He explains this mobility as the result of several things, including mobility-promoting family strategies and *ganas* (desire); the often unsung dedication and effectiveness of New York City public school teachers as mentors; pro-mobility, pro-family, and pro-immigrant policies and conditions in New York City and New York State; and the work of CUNY—of which I am a proud alum. Professor Smith's book shows how these and other factors helped the social mobility of U.S.-born second-generation Mexicans, their families, and their communities.

The book also illuminates a tragic side of immigrant life in New York City: lacking legal status blocks upward mobility for these "undocumented Americans" who are also New Yorkers, as Smith highlights to emphasize that their home is in this country and this city. Undocumented individuals and families who pursue the same pro-mobility strategies as their U.S.-born peers do not benefit from them. Mentors cannot open doors for undocumented mentees. U.S.-born younger children with undocumented older siblings do not benefit from the intrafamily learning and higher family income that occurs in families where U.S.-born or documented older siblings finish college, begin working, and live at home. These U.S.-born older siblings drive family mobility by increasing family income and helping their younger siblings navigate the schools, internships, and other resources that promote mobility.

In our conversations and work together, Professor Smith and I have always talked about how to combine research with action that helps immigrants or changes policy. His commitment here comes through in his classes, in his research, in his mentoring, and in his community work. His work has helped bring many community leaders and immigrant or second-generation students into CUNY. In this work, Professor Smith has helped CUNY keep its social bargain with the City of New York and with all New Yorkers, helping to make the city better. I applaud Smith and CUNY for this work. We need more of it.

This book looks into the hopes, dreams, and often heartbreaking realities of an immigrant community, set against the backdrop of a city that's always been a city of immigrants but that is now at the center of a humanitarian crisis driven by global mass migration and the arrival of over 100,000 asylum seekers in a short period of time. As waves of immigrants continue to seek refuge in our city, including tens of thousands of children and youth, this book couldn't be more timely.

It is through extended research like Professor Smith's, with an eye to public engagement and application, that we can gain insights into the impact of policymaking on individuals and entire communities. This book is a true achievement, and it holds significant relevance not only for understanding Mexican immigrants in New York but also for numerous other communities facing similar challenges, both in the present and in the future.

With gratitude and hope,

MANUEL CASTRO
COMMISSIONER, NEW YORK CITY MAYOR'S OFFICE OF IMMIGRANT AFFAIRS

Acknowledgments

Publishing this book feels a bit like watching my children launch into their own early adult lives. My children were born in 1997 (Liv) and 2000 (Liam), and being their dad and watching them move through the life-course stages and into adulthood, and sharing this with my wife Maura, has been a great and central joy in my life. This project was first funded in 1997 and since then has followed its own life course, from early research through three rounds of data collection, data analysis, and, in the last three years, several revisions of the manuscript. My wife, my family, and I moved together through our own life-course stages as the book developed—changing from a young family with small children and young parents into an older family with early adult children and late middle-aged parents. We haven't progressed quite to empty-nesterhood yet, as Liam has landed back with us post-college. Sending this book out into the world now feels as scary and satisfying as sending a kid off to college or moving them into their first apartment.

Working on such a long-term project, I've accrued many debts, and there are many I want to thank. I would first thank the American Sociological Association's Rose Committee (in its homes at both CUNY and then at SUNY) and the publications director of the Russell Sage Foundation (RSF), Suzanne Nichols, whose insights improved the manuscript. I also thank the production staff at RSF, including Jennifer Rappaport and copyeditor Cynthia Buck. The Rose Committee's critique of the book proposal and manuscript helped me rethink and develop the manuscript's central contributions and argumentation and to craft a cleaner through line. These discussions helped me sharpen the book's focus on explaining the processes and mechanisms that have promoted such strong intergenerational mobility for U.S.-born second-generation Mexicans in New York City and to juxtapose that positive story with the tragic slow-motion story of the derailment of the mobility of American youth who lack legal status, even when they and their families do the same "right" things as documented youth to promote their mobility. In particular, I thank Phil Kasinitz, Greg Smithsimon, Amy Adamczyk,

Richard Alba, Lynn Chancer, Nancy Foner, and Leslie Paik at the CUNY Graduate Center and Joanna Dreby, Aaron Major, Steven Messner, and Katherine Trent at SUNY Albany. Finally, I thank the participants in the Rose Series Seminar conducted for this book, as well as other scholars whose insights and conversations over the years have helped my thinking: Leisy Abrego, Jody Agius Vallejo, Liza Aranda, Amada Armenta, James Bachmeier, Frank Bean, Federico Besserer, Susan Brown, Dale Dannefer, Mitch Duneier, Jorge Durand, Laura Enriquez, David Fitzgerald, Herbert Gans, Angela Garcia, Roberto Gonzales, Jackie Hagan, Rubén Hernández-León, Tomás Jiménez, Jennifer Lee, Vivian Louie, David Martin-Cook, Doug Massey, Cecilia Menjívar, Caitlin Patler, Alex Portes, Charles Ragin, Wendy Roth, Rubén Rumbaut, Saskia Sassen, Carola and Marcelo Suárez-Orozco, Eddie Telles, Veronica Terriquez, the late Charles Tilly, Eli Vaquero, Jessica Vaquez-Tokos, Roger Waldinger, and Mary Waters.

I would also thank the many researchers who have worked on this book and become friends. (Their contributions are described more fully in the online appendixes.) First, I thank (now Dr.) Sara Guerrero-Mustafa (formerly Sara Guerrero-Rippberger), who did invaluable work in the first and second phases of the project, including conducting interviews, developing cases, and writing case narratives. Thank you, Sarita. Augustin Maestro and (now Dr.) Sandra Lara-Cinisomo did excellent interviews and case development in the first phase of data collection. I also thank student researchers Erika Flores, Katie Graves-Abe, Carolina Perez, Griscelda Perez, and Lisa Peterson. I thank Michelle Bialeck, Angelo Cabrera, Daisy Fuentes, Averi Guidicessi, Eduardo Torres, Karina Weinstein, and Maria Xique from the DACA Access Project. Specifically, I thank (now Dr.) Guillermo "Guille" Yrizar Barbosa, who created the analytical infrastructure for the variable-oriented database and did everything and anything needed for the project. I thank (now Dr.) Nico Legewie for his work on the set theoretical analysis and (now Dr.) Stephen Ruszczyk for his sage insights. Blanca Ibanez kept me and this project organized (improbably) for several key years. Thank you, Blanca. Thanks to (now Dr.) Dirk Witteveen, who thoughtfully discussed my causal thinking in combining case-oriented and statistical data and analyses, corrected slippages in my initial statistical runs, and produced the final versions you see in this book. Finally, thank you to Andrés Besserer Rayas, a CUNY doctoral student who read the whole manuscript twice and offered strong insights that helped clarify key points. I thank the Marxe School, Baruch College, CUNY, and the Sociology Department of the CUNY Graduate Center. David Birdsell, the Marxe School dean from 2005 to 2021, created a best-case scenario for my academic and publicly engaged scholarly work with immigrant communities.

Thank you, David, for your vision and support. I also thank colleagues who have commented on drafts of work presented in the Marxe Faculty Seminar, as well as faculty at Marxe and the Graduate Center who have offered thoughtful comments in conversation that helped me think through key points. At the Marxe School, these colleagues included: Nancy Aries, Sandy Korenman, Deborah Balk, Sherry Ryan, Ryan Smith, Neil Bennett, Hector Cordero-Guzman, Anna D'Souza, Sonia Jarvis, Nicole Marwell, Carla Robbins, and Cristina Balboa. At the Graduate Center, they include Phil Kasnitiz, Paul Attewell, John Mollenkopf, Van Tran, Mara Getz Sheftel, Mary Clare Lennon, Ryan Smith, and Richard Alba. For invaluable institutional help, I thank, at the Marxe School, Jessica Njoya, Rusudan Chitaia, Angelina Delgado, and Leticia Nunez, and at the Graduate Center, Rati Kashap (for organizing us all).

I thank the NYCOMPers, as I call participants in the New York Children of Migrants Project (NYCOMP). They shared their stories with me and my research team more than once and invited us into their lives, enabling us to follow them in school, at home, in Mexico, and in their social lives in New York. NYCOMPers included youth participants, but sometimes also their parents, siblings, and friends, which required a deeper level of trust on their part, and which I believe made the research stronger. Some NYCOMPers have read drafts of this book and given feedback on it, especially on the chapters featuring their stories. This book would have been impossible without their support, and I thank them all for it. I hope the book redeems their trust in me as they shared their stories and lives.

Many institutions have funded this project, from its inception to its completion, and I am grateful for their support. I thank the William T. Grant Foundation for grants on which I was the principal investigator, "Effects of Legal Status Change (DACA) on Individuals, within Families, and across Local Ecosystems," 2018–2014, and "Early Adulthood and Assimilation of Children of Immigrants," 2005–2010; I extend special thanks to foundation president Adam Gamoran and program officers Fabienne Doucet and Melissa Wooten, as well as to Sharon Brewster and Nancy Rivera-Torres. For other grants on which I was the principal investigator, I thank: Russell Sage Foundation, "Long-Term Effects of Legal Status and Deferred Action across Legal Status Categories and Institutional Ecosystems," 2016–2018; Institute for Mexicans Abroad, Mexican Consulate, "Mexican Initiative on Deferred Action," 2015–2016; and National Science Foundation, Social, Behavioral, and Economic Research Directorate, Sociology Section, "Strengthening Qualitative Research: Assimilation and the Transition to Early Adulthood for Mexican Americans," 2010–2012, and "Gender, Race, and Ethnicity and Social Organization: Determinants of Second-Generation Mexican American

Educational and Work Mobility in New York City," 1998–2000. I am also grateful to the John Simon Guggenheim Foundation for a fellowship; the Russell Sage Foundation Visiting Scholar Program for supporting my work on "Early Adulthood and Assimilation of Children of Immigrants," 2007–2008; the Rockefeller Foundation/Oral History Research Program, Columbia University, for a postdoctoral fellowship, 1999–2000; and the National Academy of Education for a Spencer Postdoctoral Fellowship, "Gendered Ethnicity at Three Strategic Sites: Explaining Variation in Second-Generation Mexican American Men and Women's Work and School Mobility," 1999–2000.

Finally, I thank the PSC-CUNY, the university's small grants program, which, in offering support to study new processes emerging in fieldwork or to finish analysis of collected data, has been a crucial support to my work. I am grateful for the following PSC-CUNY grants on which I was principal investigator: "Long-Term Research on Children of Immigrants"; "Case-Based Quantitative and Qualitative Research"; "America's Natural Experiments in Immigration"; "Thinking through Epistemology and Methods"; "Why Haven't More Youth Applied for DACA?"; "DACA and Special Visa Recipients or Applicants"; "Don't Call an Ambulance"; and "Legal Status, Locality, and Other Determinants."

Finally, I thank my family. What to say here? Liv and Liam, being your dad has been exhilarating, exhausting, joyful, and so much fun! Thank you. Maura, you have been the keel in my life for forty years, sharing our happiness and helping each other in harder times. How did I get so lucky?

Chapter 1

Introduction: Dreams Achieved and Denied

EMMANUEL'S GRADUATION party from law school in the 2010s was loud and happy, and I was delighted to be invited. I had known Emmanuel for over a decade and had admired both his work ethic and his ability to simultaneously navigate the complexities of his home on X Street and his place at Elite University.[1] I noted sadly the absence of the priest who had mentored him for sixteen years; he had died the year before. Brooklyn-born Emmanuel was an American success story straight from central casting. His undocumented single-parent mother, Lila, had worked hard, and his older brother, Thor, had quit school to work full-time to support their family while Emmanuel was still in school, helping his academic career. They still lived together, and Emmanuel now helped pay the rent. A U.S. citizen, Emmanuel had also gotten strong financial and other support in college and law school. At the party, his mother (still undocumented in 2020) hugged me and beamed happily at her son's success. I beamed too—who could not be happy for Emmanuel and his family?

Emmanuel understood his success to be at least partly due to the different path he had taken from his older siblings and friends. His brother and many friends had been active gang members, and he sometimes had hung out with them on the street. When I asked him, in his late twenties, where his life was now, he answered, "I am in my third year of law school and did not go to the same high school as my cousins." He drew a direct line from his high school choice to his adult success. After talking with his long-term mentor, the local parish priest, and with his mother's blessing, Emmanuel had chosen to go to a "Black" high school outside their neighborhood to avoid the problems and low academic performance of his friends, cousins, and siblings in their local zoned school. ("Black" here refers to the dominant youth culture, which also included Puerto Ricans and Dominicans.[2])

After his mentor, the priest, died, Emmanuel spoke of how he had cherished their key mentoring tradition: "We had a tradition—we hang

1

https://doi.org/10.7758/drwz9626.5060

out every month. We used to go out to eat together . . . [to] an Italian restaurant. . . . We used to go chat for hours, until they shut down the place." In what he called his "Black" high school, Emmanuel found academically successful Black students and connected with another mentor, Dr. Comer, a Black physician, whose mentoring helped him rethink his future possibilities. "The fact that he believed in me, that I could make it in there [Elite University]. I was like, you know, maybe I have a chance." As Emmanuel began to believe he had a brighter future, he increasingly avoided hanging out on X Street with his brother and friends, fearing that violence or police entanglements could endanger his future. He told them he needed to do homework.

"Don't look at me like that," Eddie said after seeing my shock that he had dropped out of high school, despite being an A student. His math teacher had gone to his house to see Eddie's mother and plead with him to stay in school, but he did not budge. He saw his widowed mother working fourteen-hour days, and his family needed the money. He described the scene this way:

> I still remember that day when I told her. I didn't, basically, tell her until my math teacher. . . . He came over to the house and had a talk with my mom. . . . Eventually she started crying. . . . She's like, "No! No! No!" Even my math teacher, my social studies teacher, they tried talking me back into continuing school. My math teacher, we were really close. When I did that [dropped out], I disappointed basically half my family. [For years after] I used to lay down on my bed and start thinking—if I continued school, I graduated and got my diploma. But what happens after? . . . If you don't have a green card in this country, you can't work, even if you're a professional.

Eddie was doing all the "right" things in high school to succeed, taking the same steps that propelled the upward mobility of his U.S. citizen peers. He always did his homework, never cut school, and declined invitations to join a gang, while maintaining good enough relationships with the gang members to keep them from harassing him. He had also developed close relationships with teachers, who sought to mentor him. But the benefit that his U.S. citizen peers enjoyed from making choices that promoted their mobility was blocked for Eddie by his legal status, which had itself been lost to a tragedy. Eddie came to the United States at age seven but was still undocumented in his thirties because his U.S. citizen grandfather, who had been sponsoring his and his mother's and sisters' green card applications, had died while they waited years for their visas.

Given these circumstances, Eddie felt that dropping out made more sense than staying in school. "It makes no sense for me to finish school. . . . You could be a professional," he said, but without papers, "they still . . . won't give you that [job]." After he dropped out, Eddie's mother did not talk to him for a year, while they were living together in a small New York City apartment.

The Obama administration's Deferred Action for Childhood Arrivals (DACA), a policy that gave some undocumented youth renewable but revokable work permits, Social Security numbers, and protection from deportation, began a decade after Eddie dropped out. After the DACA program began, I arranged free legal help for Eddie to apply (through a project I led at CUNY promoting DACA applications), but he repeatedly no-showed these meetings. His cousin told me that Eddie was too discouraged to apply: his grown-up responsibilities made college impossible, and he also feared that a Republican president could use his application information to deport him. Like so many long-term undocumented youth I have worked with over thirty years, Eddie feared that America would not give him a chance to become a full member of the only country he knew, in which he had grown up, and which he loved. Eddie's pessimistic calculus was right: like millions of others like him, Eddie was not given a chance by America to legalize or become a citizen.

"She is a joy!" Carla told me happily, describing her seven-month-old baby, Carolina. I had called her in early 2020 to discuss something in this book, but we mostly talked about our families. We laughed that she was then in the same place in her life—early to midthirties, with a young child—as I had been when I followed her around her high school for my research. Carla came to the United States without a visa and spent seven years as an undocumented girl before legalizing her status as a teenager via her parents, who had acquired U.S. citizenship through the 1986 Immigration Reform and Control Act (IRCA). Carla was what I call a legal-status Category Changer—a study participant who went from being undocumented to having permanent legal status, often during the course of the study. Legalizing their own status helped Carla's parents not only earn more money but also keep the immigrant family bargain, by enabling them to help their children gain permanent legal status, which then enabled their children to launch successfully into early adulthood and jobs commensurate with their college educations. In return, Carla and her sister Simone both felt a duty to be "obedient" to their parents (whom I also knew). Indeed, knowing how poor their mother's upbringing had been ("not even having shoes"), the daughters kept the immigrant bargain in turn by thinking of doing well in school as their "job" to make their parents' sacrifice worth it.

As a teen, Carla hung out with Mexican friends who went to DJ parties on weekends, but she avoided these friends in school. She chose a high school far away from her middle school and Mexican friends, and she identified with and emulated the "smart Black girls" in her AP classes. Carla became a socially "Black" Mexican (she "looked Mexican" phenotypically) by adopting a Black identity and having a school friendship group of academically successful Black students. These friends helped her succeed in high school, graduate from Elite University, and go on to a career in the nonprofit and private sectors. As an adult, she no longer identified as Black and described herself as Mexican. She eventually married her longtime boyfriend (a second-generation Mexican, employed in the finance industry), bought a house with her parents, and started her own family. Her family was rightly proud of the successes of Carla and her sister Simone.[3]

Carla and Simone had kept the immigrant bargain into established adulthood by continuing to live at home with their parents after finishing college and starting full-time work. Moreover, they drew on their understanding of the New York City public schools and colleges to help plot and support their little brother Kyle's path to upward mobility. Carla arranged for the family to buy a house in a neighborhood with better schools, and she and Simone paid the cost of Kyle's tutoring for AP classes, sports leagues, and other extracurricular lessons. Carla said: "I got them into this house. I made sure that they were okay making the monthly payments. And my sister and I split all the bills . . . gas, all the maintenance. . . . We pay for anything that Kyle needs—we arrange it. . . . Kyle has three mothers." By their late twenties, Carla and Simone had increased their family income to over $140,000 per year, compared to the $27,000 their parents earned when the sisters were in high school, giving Kyle a middle-class lifestyle that contrasted starkly with Carla and Simone's lean teen years. They were happy to give Kyle these opportunities, but the two sisters were only partly joking when they sometimes complained that he had become "spoiled."

These case sketches briefly convey two key findings from this long-term ethnographic project on children of Mexican immigrants in New York: first, that having or gaining legal status promotes mobility by enabling individual and family effort to be rewarded and by making efficacious the New York City and New York State policies and practices that support mobility; and second, that lacking legal status blocks mobility, even for those individuals and families engaging in the same strategies and practices, limiting the benefit derived from those mobility-promoting city and state policies and practices.

For over twenty years, I followed the lives of study participants, repeatedly interviewing them and hanging out with them in New York and Mexico, in school, with their families, and at community events. Some have sought advice or help from me or asked me to serve as a job reference. Some are now friends. Their generosity in inviting me into their lives enabled me to closely observe and trace the mechanisms by which they achieved strong and often impressive single-generation mobility and to understand how a lack of legal status cruelly derailed many upwardly mobile lives.

This study, the New York Children of Migrants Project (NYCOMP), differs from most in its length and depth. Large-scale panel studies follow the same people over years but have "thin" data, only on specific questions. Larger-scale interview studies often include more participants than this one, but do not follow people for years, interview them repeatedly, or follow them in person. Most ethnographic studies, especially long-term ones, focus on a relatively small number of people, generating "thick" data for fewer cases.[4] This study is an outlier in following an ethnographically large number of people (ninety-six) over a very long period of time and collecting and analyzing extensive data on them and their families. I have called this approach, half-jokingly, "life course ethnography": it combines ethnography's requirement to be in the field with people and life course studies' requirement to follow them as they move through the life course.

This book's first key finding is that U.S.-born Mexicans in New York City—and U.S.-born NYCOMP participants (NYCOMPers) as a group— have experienced strong and even exceptional single-generation mobility, made more impressive by the relatively low income and educational levels of their immigrant parents. NYCOMPers and their families who had legal status or were born in the United States became upwardly mobile via specific family and individual strategies whose efficacy was increased by specific policies, practices, and conditions in New York City and New York State, which treat immigrants and their families as fellow New Yorkers—as "us," not "them." Families who kept the immigrant bargain—the moral bargain whereby adult children redeem their parents' sacrifice through their own success and contributions to the family, especially by helping younger siblings—experienced great mobility as the older children became adults and dramatically increased family income and knowledge about American institutions, including the educational or financial systems. Mobility was strong for U.S.-born NYCOMPers who were planful—that is, who imagined and followed through on steps to their goals—and strategic in their choice of high school and friends and their model of masculinity, and who had strong extra-family mentoring, especially from New York City public school teachers. These youth also often skillfully navigated the complex relationship of Mexicanness and Blackness to education in the Mexican community in New York City in the late 1990s and early 2000s.[5]

This mobility suggests an emerging Mexican culture of mobility among the U.S.-born second generation in immigrant-friendly New York City that runs counter to most stories about Mexican mobility in decades of research and in public debate. Moreover, the mobility shown by my study participants fits with strong upward trajectories in the census data on educational attainment, suggesting that U.S.-born Mexicans in New York City have achieved one of the biggest one-generation jumps in mobility in American immigration history.

A quick caveat. Analyzing how family and individual strategies are fostering a Mexican culture of mobility in New York City does not imply that causes of group mobility are cultural—that others or anyone could just adopt those policies and prosper. Youth who do not know how to apply to, nor how to get into, the stronger, out-of-zone high schools that boost adult outcomes should not be held "culturally responsible" for the fact that their local school has low student outcomes. All schools should be good. Similarly, this emerging Mexican culture of mobility in New York city does not suggest the kind of "glass floor" that enables lower-achieving children of wealthier parents to live in safer places and go to stronger schools and thus replicate their wealthy lives as adults.[6] The paths to mobility traced in this book can be complex and precarious, even for high-achieving U.S.-borns. A minority culture of mobility helps youth navigate those paths, but alone it cannot explain who is mobile or not.

The second key finding is that the lives and mobility of "long-term undocumented Americans"—the term I use to refer to those who were brought to the United States as children but have been unable to legalize their status by adulthood—are blocked by their lack of legal status, even when engaging in *the same strategies and practices* as their upwardly mobile, U.S. citizen peers. Moreover, their lack of legal status blocked the positive impact that their U.S.-born peers experienced from many mobility-promoting New York City and New York State policies and practices.

These divergent trajectories underline the reality that, because Congress has been unable to make needed reforms to American immigration laws, structural inclusion or exclusion of immigrants and their children—that is, having or lacking legal status—has become an enduring feature of American life that affects intergenerational mobility and well-being.

I analyze how legal status affects mobility by comparing the steps in the trajectories of U.S.-born Americans and of long-term undocumented

Americans from adolescence and early adulthood into established adulthood, which I also call middle adulthood. More analytical leverage comes from examining how the mobility and lives of legal-status Category Changers—that is, undocumented Americans who later got permanent legal status, often during the study—who engaged in these same strategies and practices improved dramatically after they obtained legal status. ("Legal status" here refers to lawful permanent residency or some other visa, not to DACA, which gave renewable work permits and protection from deportation to some undocumented Americans. They remain undocumented. See chapter 5.) Thinking about how American immigration policies block mobility and harm families—in a country that sees itself as pro-family and pro-immigrant—made me think of the old Pogo cartoon quote: "We have met the enemy, and he is us."

These findings engage common theories and public beliefs about Mexican immigrants and their later-generation descendants in the United States, many of which seek to explain why, compared to Whites, Mexican immigrants' incomes, education levels, and life outcomes are lower on average. A first such theory is the discredited "problematic Mexicans" theory, a zombie theory, in the economist Paul Krugman's memorable phrase, that lives on without empirical support. This theory posits Mexican or Hispanic culture as the cause of persistent poverty or outcome disparities among later-generation Mexicans, making a "culture of poverty" argument. Other twentieth-century zombie theories attributed such differences to genetic or other group traits.[7] The "problematic Mexicans" narrative persists, especially in public and political speech.[8]

Second, "racial exclusion" theory posits that racial discrimination against Mexican immigrants and their children is a main blocker of long-term intergenerational mobility.[9] That many strong empirical studies find minimal to nil intergenerational mobility helps make this study a strategic case, because it reports higher average mobility overall and large variation in mobility among study participants.

Third, modern assimilation theories analyze how newcomers integrate into American society. "Second-generation advantage" theory posits that strategically adopting elements from the parents' home-country culture and from American culture helps the second generation advance.[10] "Two-way assimilation" theory posits that decreases in "social and cultural distance from the mainstream" enable "life chances [to] align with the dominant group."[11] "Segmented assimilation" theory posits that differences in individual, family, and community traits foster upward mobility, or downward mobility via reactive ethnicity.[12] "Mexican culture of mobility" theory analyzes how middle-class U.S.-born Mexicans increase their mobility and argues that scholars must analyze intra-ethnic differences in the Mexican population.[13] "Origins and destinations" theory argues that research should strive to explain cross- and intra-group variation in outcomes in the United States by considering not only individual and family traits and experiences in the United States but also variation in home-country contexts.[14] "Replenishment and home-land dissimilation" theories consider the impacts of a constant flow of newcomers and of social and temporal distance from Mexico as key factors in evaluating assimilation.[15]

Finally, "legal exclusion" theory posits that a lack of legal status, more than race or ethnicity, has blocked integration and intergenerational mobility, though it has less often focused on mobility promoting mechanisms analyzed in this study.[16]

This book engages these prior theories by intensively analyzing the "mechanisms" or "processes" (terms I use interchangeably), conditions, and policies that promoted or inhibited upward mobility for the ninety-six NYCOMP participants, who were all children of Mexican immigrants in New York City. Some factors, such as having legal status or lacking it, are staples of immigration research. Others, such as mentors, are missing or understudied in this research. Finally, factors such as seeking out high-achieving Black schools and friends, or models of masculinity, are new in the literature.

Eddie's inability to get legal status—a structural condition imposed by federal immigration law—derailed his promising academic career, leading him to drop out to help his widowed mother by working full-time. Eddie had public school teachers who cared about him and wanted to mentor him, he did his homework, and he rejected offers to join a Mexican gang. But his teachers' arguments could not defeat his clear-eyed assessment of his grim prospects and his family's dire need. His mother had moved to New York to give her children better opportunities, but by dropping out of high school, Eddie broke the immigrant bargain with her. That his mother, despite so much hard work, could not give Eddie legal status—the key condition he needed to launch into a successful young adulthood—meant she also had not kept the immigrant bargain. Eddie had done all the right things, and his mother had worked fourteen-hour days, but the structural condition of being undocumented blocked his mobility and his family's ability to keep the immigrant bargain and made that unkept bargain even more bitter for their family.

Conversely, Carla's lack of legal status for seven years did not derail her ambitions because, as she told me, she knew she would be legalized through her parents, who had, after decades of being undocumented, become lawful permanent residents and later U.S. citizens via IRCA. Carla and Emmanuel navigated a social world and time (the mid-1990s to the mid-2000s) in which being "Mexican" in school was linked to the fates of the mostly undocumented and numerically predominant Mexican teen migrants who often left high school without graduating—or never registered in the first place—and very few of whom went to college.[17] Both Carla and Emmanuel chose to avoid the high schools where their Mexican friends went and instead attended what they saw as "Black" high schools, where they became friends with academically successful Black students. Most of the successful students in their high schools, which had few Whites, were Black or Hispanic. This association between Blackness and upward mobility, which was strong among NYCOMPers, runs counter to the long-standing domain assumption in American sociology that upward mobility is linked to Whiteness.[18] NYCOMP participants' association of Mexicanness or Blackness with downward or upward mobility does not imply that there are fixed elements to unitary national or racial cultures, but rather that mobility was linked in their minds to those identities at that time. Moreover, the strong intergenerational upward mobility of U.S.-born Mexicans has promoted a Mexican culture of mobility in New York.

Carla and Emmanuel also accepted mentoring from a series of good mentors who opened up both doors and their ways of thinking about their future, promoting their mobility. This upward mobility brought them after high school into a series of academic and professional contexts in which the meaning of Mexicanness was neutral or positive, helping them. Eddie's blocked mobility, however, compelled him to work in the immigrant economy, where Mexicanness is often a stigmatized status associated with being undocumented and exploitable. Finally, Carla and Simone and Emmanuel were celebrated in their families for how well they kept the immigrant bargain, as was Eddie, until he dropped out of school.

Surprising Mexican Second-Generation Mobility

This study's findings echo patterns found in U.S. census data: U.S.-born second-generation Mexicans in New York City graduate from college at dramatically higher rates than their U.S.-born counterparts in other studies in other places. Over the last thirty-plus years, nearly all major studies have reported that 13 to 14 percent of U.S.-born second-generation Mexicans graduate from college (see table 1.1).[19]

The remarkable consistency of this rate for U.S.-born Mexicans in other studies and in census data nationally contrasts dramatically with the increasing and much higher rates for U.S.-born Mexican men and women in census data for New York City and in this study, especially

Table 1.1   **College Graduates among U.S.-Born and Foreign-Born Mexicans in the NYCOMP Study and in Other Studies**

College Graduates	NYCOMP	U.S. Census: New York City	U.S. Census: United States	Bean, Brown, and Bachmeier 2015
U.S.-born second- generation Mexicans	(c. 2009) Men: 42% Women: 46%	(2010) Men: 38% Women: 44% (2017) Men: 44% Women: 46%	(2010) Men: 13.5% Women: 15.2% (2020) Men: 16.3% Women: 20.2%	(2004) 13.5%
Other groups		(2010) Non-Hispanic White: 60% Non-Hispanic Black: 25% Asian: 40% Latino: 8% Puerto Rican: 15% Dominican: 15% Colombian: 25%		

Source: Author's compilation.

[a] Rendón (2019, 269–75) does not report rates of college graduation, so I calculated it from her appendix describing the cases. There were forty-two participants in the study, including ten in college and one in high school when interviewed, leaving thirty-one who had finished or stopped their schooling, of which 5 or 16 percent were college graduates. Then subtracting the five undocumented participants from those subtotals yielded thirty-seven U.S. citizen participants, of whom 4 or 14 percent were college graduates. I am reporting Rendón's percentages here not to compare Los Angeles and New York but rather to be able to better compare my set of participants with hers. Proportionally more of my participants graduated from college, and they generally got more education and earned more income than her participants. She had four U.S. citizen participants out of thirty-seven (11 percent) who earned $50,000 or more, while half of my participants (forty-eight of ninety-six) were College Graduates or High Fliers who earned an average of nearly $59,000 ($58,723) at time 2, average age twenty-eight, in roughly the same year, 2008–2009.

Telles and Ortiz 2008	NLSY97 (Duncan et al. 2017)	Rendón 2019	Portes and Rumbaut 2001	Kasinitz et al. 2008
(1980s) Second generation: 13% (c. 2000) Third generation: 14%	(2013–2014) 13.5%	(c. 2007–2013) 14%[a]	(1999–2000 and after) 13%	
				(c. 2000) Puerto Ricans: 16% Dominican: 26% South American: 26% Native Black: 15% West Indian: 28% Chinese: 64% Native White: 54%

Figure 1.1   College Attainment or Higher of Mexican and U.S.-Born Men and Women Ages Twenty-Five and Older, 1990–2020

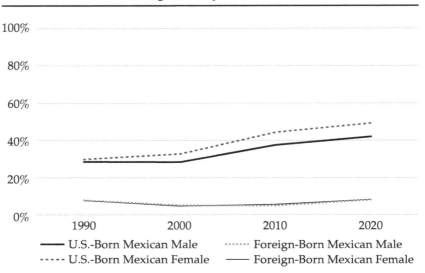

Source: Ruggles et al. 2023a, 2023b, 2023c, 2023d; U.S. Census Bureau 2000 (5 percent census sample). See table 1.2. Thank you to Dr. Mara Getz Sheftel.
Note: "5 percent" here describes how the sample is constructed. Every year the Census Bureau makes a random 1 percent of the ACS microdata available. The 5 percent estimates are period estimates that combine the microdata for the preceding five-year period (for example, the 2020 5 percent sample includes data from 2016 to 2020). According to the Census Bureau, the main advantage of the 5 percent estimates is their increased statistical reliability, especially for less-populated areas and small population subgroups.

compared to their foreign-born counterparts, as shown in figures 1.1, 1.2, and 1.3. The 2010 census showed that nationally 13.5 percent of males and 15.2 percent of females among U.S.-born Mexicans age twenty-five or older had a BA degree or better. The numbers improved some in 2020 to 16.3 percent of males and 20.2 percent of females. But looking at census data only for New York City shows that U.S.-born Mexicans have had higher educational attainment than that since the 1990s. Their educational attainment has only increased since then.

Figure 1.1 shows that 29 percent of U.S.-born Mexican men age twenty-five or older in New York City had a BA in 1990, a share that increased to 42 percent by 2020, while U.S.-born women's BA attainment increased from 30 percent to 49 percent over the same period (see table 1.2 in note).[20] This high educational attainment contrasts sharply with BA attainment for foreign-born Mexican men in New York City, which went from 8 percent in 1990 to 5 percent in 2010 to 8 percent in

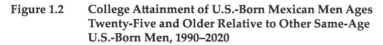

Figure 1.2   College Attainment of U.S.-Born Mexican Men Ages
Twenty-Five and Older Relative to Other Same-Age
U.S.-Born Men, 1990–2020

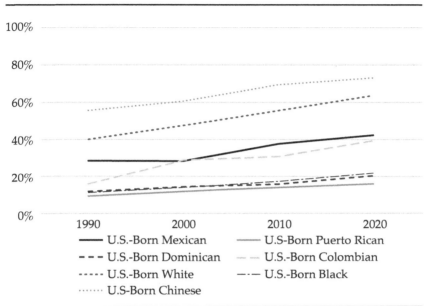

— U.S.-Born Mexican   — U.S-Born Puerto Rican
- - - U.S.-Born Dominican   — — U.S.-Born Colombian
- - - - - U.S.-Born White   —·— U.S.-Born Black
········· U.S-Born Chinese

Source: Ruggles et al. 2023a, 2023b, 2023c, 2023d; U.S. Census Bureau 2000 (5 percent census sample). Analysis by Dr. Mara Getz Sheftel.

2020, and for foreign-born Mexican women, whose BA attainment fluctuated from 8 percent in 1990 to 6 percent in 2010 to 8 percent in 2020.[21]

Although this study's research design cannot extrapolate to the larger population, I am heartened that the percentages of college attainment for U.S.-born NYCOMPers were close to those found in the census data: at time 2 (2005–2012), 44 percent of U.S.-born NYCOMP men (versus 38 percent in the census data in 2010, near time 2) and 51 percent of NYCOMP women (versus 44 percent in the 2010 census data) had a BA or better (N = 75).

U.S.-born Mexicans in New York had college graduation rates more similar to those of other non-Mexican groups in the 2010 census data and in other studies, as shown in table 1.1 and figures 1.2 and 1.3.[22] In *Inheriting the City*, whose representative sample of second-generation participants were all U.S.-born or lawful permanent residents interviewed between 1999 and 2001 (during this study's time 1), the sociologists Phil Kasinitz, Mary Waters, John Mollenkopf, and Jennifer Holdaway found that 16 percent of Puerto Ricans, 26 percent of Dominicans,

Figure 1.3   College Attainment of U.S.-Born Mexican Women Ages Twenty-Five and Older Relative to Other Same-Age U.S.-Born Women, 1990–2020

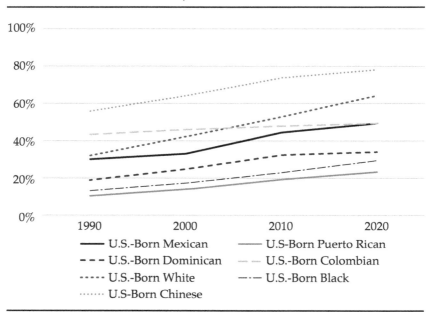

Source: Ruggles et al. 2023a, 2023b, 2023c, 2023d; U.S. Census Bureau 2000 (5 percent). Analysis by Dr. Mara Getz Sheftel.

26 percent of South Americans, 15 percent of native Blacks, 28 percent of West Indians, 64 percent of Chinese, and 54 percent of native Whites had BAs or higher. (They did not study Mexicans.)

The higher rates of college graduation among U.S.-born Mexicans in New York compared to their U.S.-born Mexican counterparts and counterparts of other national origins in other studies suggest that something is going well for U.S.-born Mexicans in New York City (and badly for foreign-born Mexicans) that we should try to understand.

These high college graduation rates are even more impressive when we consider that they represent a single-generation jump that is much larger than that found in most comparable studies. For example, the difference between the mean of seven years of schooling for NYCOMP participants' parents and their U.S.-born children's mean of fourteen years is close to the jump reported in the 2008 book by the sociologists Edward Telles and Vilma Ortiz, *Generations of Exclusion*: in their sample, immigrant parents had a mean 7.4 years of education compared to 13.1 years for their U.S.-born children. But the second-generation college graduation rates reported in *Generations of Exclusion* remained at 13 percent (14 percent for the third generation, and 6 percent for the fourth), while NYCOMP and the census (2020 American Community Survey) found the college graduation rates of U.S.-born second-generation Mexicans to be over 40 percent.[23]

Rates of graduation for U.S.-born Mexican men and women also increased more sharply than they did for other groups from 1990 to 2020. Figures 1.2 and 1.3 show that the percentage of U.S.-born Mexican men age twenty-five or older who graduated from college was higher than for U.S.-born Puerto Rican, Black, and Dominican men, and that this difference increased after 2010.[24] U.S.-born Mexican men's college graduation rates were closest to those of Colombian U.S.-born men, and closer to those of U.S.-born White men than to the rates among U.S.-born Puerto Rican, Black, and Dominican men. Their rates were lower, however, than those of U.S.-born Whites and Chinese.[25] Similarly, U.S.-born Mexican women age twenty-five or older had higher college attainment rates than U.S.-born Puerto Ricans, Blacks, and Dominicans, and their rates were closest to those of Colombians, though their rates, like men's, were also lower than those of U.S.-born Whites and Chinese.[26]

U.S.-born NYCOMP participants were as surprised as I was by their dramatic mobility. Many had told me, while in high school, that they did not expect to graduate from high school or go to college, that Mexicans "did not do that." Upwardly mobile participants told me when they were in high school or their early twenties that they were "the only Mexicans" they knew headed for college; others would end up in jail or become parents in their teens or early twenties. Their pessimism made some sociological sense. As a group, study participants presented individual, family, and structural conditions or actions that predicted against strong upward mobility for them. Only 55 percent of the participants did homework "always" or "regularly" in high school, and daytime drinking or gang activity often featured in the lives of the 37 percent who cut school "a lot" or "regularly." Some 53 percent of boys and 26 percent of girls had gang associations as teens. Moreover, census data also show that there were nearly three times as many Mexican-born students as U.S.-born students in their high schools in 2000, and that the former often left school without finishing.[27] Only 47 percent of Mexican-born sixteen- to nineteen-year-olds in New York City were enrolled in or had graduated from high school in 2000, versus nearly 90 percent of U.S.-born Mexicans.[28] In the minds of NYCOMPers—and in the minds of many teachers at that time—Mexicanness was linked with not pursuing higher education.[29]

Much has changed since 2000. The increasing rates of college attainment for U.S.-born Mexicans in New York City described in figures 1.1. and 1.2 corresponded to a dramatic reversal in the ratio of foreign- to U.S.-born Mexicans teenagers (thirteen- to nineteen-years old) from 2000 to 2020. There were 2.8 times as many foreign-born Mexican teens as U.S.-born Mexican teens in New York City in 2000 (time 1), but by about 2008 (time 2) there were twice as many U.S.-borns; by about 2019 (time 3), there were nearly ten times as many U.S.-born as foreign-born Mexican teenagers (see table 1.3 in note).[30] This change in the ratio of New York–born to Mexico-born Mexicans played a role in changing the meaning of being Mexican, especially in schools, as we discuss in chapter 3. By time 2, around 2008, Mexican teen migrants no longer predominated among the population of Mexican students in schools, and by 2019 they were a small minority of such students. This demographic change has also supported the emergence of a Mexican culture of mobility.

Mexican Second-Generation Mobility as a Strategic Case

I am happy that the study participants and I were impressively wrong about their futures! The surprisingly strong intergenerational mobility of U.S.-born second-generation youth in New York City, but not of their Mexican-born counterparts, makes studying them what the sociologist Robert Merton called a "strategic research site." Such a site shows the phenomenon under study "to such advantage and in such accessible form that they enable the fruitful investigation of previously stubborn problems and the discovery of new problems for further inquiry."[31] Here I analyze both the well-studied issue of immigrant intergenerational mobility and some less frequently and less well studied mechanisms promoting that mobility, such as integration into academically successful Black friendship groups in high school, models of masculinity, and intrafamily learning.

That U.S.-born Mexicans in New York would experience such a dramatic single-generation jump in mobility is even more impressive given how much harder upward mobility has become in America in the last half century. Indeed, the economist Raj Chetty and his colleagues find that while 90 percent of children born in 1940 could expect to have higher incomes than their parents, only 50 percent of those born in 1980 could expect this.[32] Chetty and his colleagues attribute this declining postwar intergenerational mobility to lower GDP growth and greater inequality in its distribution. Contrary to what most Americans believe, our country now offers less mobility than some European countries: only 8 percent of those born in the United States in the bottom 20 percent of income end up at age thirty in the top 20 percent, versus 13 percent in Canada, 12 percent in Denmark, and 9 percent in the United Kingdom. New York City's commuting area does better, at 10.5 percent.[33]

Deepening the puzzle of high Mexican intergenerational mobility among the U.S.-born second generation is that they live in a city lacking four of the five conditions that Chetty and his colleagues say promote mobility: less residential segregation, less income inequality, better primary schools, and greater social capital, such as education. The only Chetty-cited factor in upward mobility that these families had was greater family stability.[34] Given these facts, the grim racial exclusion story would be less surprising than the hopeful story describing how U.S.-born Mexicans in New York City have succeeded. In this light, U.S.-born Mexicans in New York look more like Jewish immigrants in New York one hundred years ago than like the bad assimilators depicted in problematic Mexicans theory.

To analyze mobility as NYCOMP participants moved through their teen and early adult years into full adulthood, I created four ideal type outcome categories. Ideal types are not the "best" example of the type, but rather a conceptual measuring stick with which to assess whether cases present the traits associated with the type. Ideal types are like syndromes—the clusters of symptoms (not all of which need be present) that doctors use to clinically diagnose disease based on what their patients tell them or their physical condition (not from a lab test).[35]

The outcome categories, from the least to the most upwardly mobile, are Stuck Muddlers, Shallow Slopers, College Graduates, and High Fliers. (We developed the categories from our narrative case analysis and tested it using a statistical measure, K-means cluster analysis; see the explanation and table 1.4 in note.[36]) The lives of Stuck Muddlers had been derailed by their undocumented status, by the demands of gang masculinity and linked consequences, or by other causes. Being "stuck," they had not typically graduated from high school and were only inter-mittently employed. Stuck Muddlers often abruptly lost jobs, either by quitting or because they were fired or laid off, and usually earned under $25,000 in their late twenties. For some, family dynamics were compli-cated. Shallow Slopers had typically graduated from high school, and some attended college, but had not gotten a degree. Their steadier jobs, usually paying $25,000 to $45,000 in their late twenties, supported lives more stable than those of Stuck Muddlers.

College Graduates had usually finished college and worked in jobs that paid middle-class incomes of between $45,000 and $65,000 by their late twenties and that offered career steps or pay increases, under-pinning fairly stable lives. (Some NYCOMPers who have not graduated college are categorized as College Graduates because their current and potential income and life chances were as strong or better than college graduate NYCOMPers. Police officers, for example, do not need to finish college, but earn very middle-class, college graduate incomes.) Nearly all High Fliers had finished college, many had gone to graduate or professional school, and all earned incomes over $65,000 in their late twenties that supported stable careers and family lives. Most College Graduates and High Fliers had married, and those with children had done so later in life. They were also more likely than Stuck Muddlers and Shallow Slopers to live at home with their parents in their twenties.

Early adulthood is the life-course phase (I also use the term middle adulthood, usually ages eighteen to twenty-five or thirty) when youth transition from their teen years to explore and gradually take on or settle into adult roles, including finishing schooling, working full-time, and, for many, marrying and starting to have children, after which they transition into established adulthood (ages twenty-five to thirty through about age forty-five; the loose time range reflects variation in when people take these steps). The mid-twentieth century saw American teenagers quickly transitioning to established adulthood by their early twenties, but the period of early adulthood has since grown longer for most. For those going to college or graduate school, established adulthood now may not begin until the late twenties or later. However, for those pursuing full-time work right after (or without finishing) high school and those who become young parents, the transition to established adulthood can still occur quickly, even in their late teens or early twenties.[37] In this study, participants were teens or early adults during time 1 (1997 to 2002) with an average age of nineteen, and most were established adults (by years and adult roles) by time 2 (2005 to 2012, average age of twenty-eight) and time 3 (2012–2018, average age of thirty-three).

How surprising NYCOMP participants' adult life outcomes were can be seen by comparing their predicted adult outcomes to their actual adult outcomes, as I do in table 1.5. Taking account of structural and family conditions (such as having an undocumented, deported, or absent parent) and individual practices in high school (for example, cutting school a lot, hanging with a gang, regularly drinking too much), we would have expected sixty-one of the ninety-six participants to end up Stuck Muddlers or Shallow Slopers, but only forty-nine did so. Similarly, we would have expected thirty-five to become College Graduates or High Fliers, but forty-seven did so.

This study's first contribution is analyzing the processes and conditions that promote the strong upward mobility of a population whose starting conditions would not have predicted such mobility, and doing so over a much longer period than do most studies. This long-term,

Table 1.5   Expected versus Actual Time 2 (Average Age of Twenty-Eight)
             Outcome Categories

Gender	Stuck Muddler Actual Outcome (Expected Outcome)	Shallow Sloper Actual Outcome (Expected Outcome)	College Graduate Actual Outcome (Expected Outcome)	High Flier Actual Outcome (Expected Outcome)
Men	30% (57%)	24% (10%)	28% (20%)	18% (6%)
Women	30% (42%)	17% (17%)	30% (34%)	23% (6%)
Total	$N = 31$ ($N = 48$)	$N = 18$ ($N = 13$)	$N = 27$ ($N = 26$)	$N = 20$ ($N = 9$)

Source: NYCOMP data set. Analysis by author.
Note: I retrospectively assigned participants to expected time 2 outcome categories based on the individual traits or behaviors they reported in high school that would stymy mobility (including cutting school, not doing homework, doing academically badly in school, regularly drinking too much, hanging with a gang, or saying they expected a grim future) and on family or contextual conditions (including then being undocumented or having an undocumented, deported, or absent parent; having gang member siblings; or living in great poverty). I started by assuming that everyone was a 4 (High Flier) and then bumping them down one overall outcome category (to College Graduate) for having two negative conditions or habits, down two categories (to Shallow Sloper) for three negative conditions or habits, and down three categories (to Stuck Muddler) for more than three conditions or habits. It's too simple a method to capture the complexity of the cases, but the divergence from expected to actual adult outcomes suggests that interesting processes were at work to produce these better-than-expected outcomes.

intensive engagement with participants enabled me to deeply develop their cases as I discerned and empirically traced processes that would probably be invisible or understudied in shorter-term studies.

Second, if the evidence of overall U.S.-born second-generation Mexican mobility in the census data had not been as strong, the study would advance scholarly knowledge by identifying and tracing processes promoting mobility for those who went against the overall trend and did better than most others. That census data and this study both document strong intergenerational mobility for U.S.-born Mexicans in New York increases the study's strategic importance, including its utility in informing policies that promote mobility.

Third, this study contributes by showing how mobility was blocked for long-term undocumented participants and their families who engaged in the *same* processes as their U.S. citizen and Category Changer counterparts. By tracing processes over many years within and across cases that varied by legal status, I can describe how legal status blocked upward mobility for long-term undocumented Americans, and how getting legal status unblocked mobility in those cases. Moreover, our ethnographic data describe how participants and their families thought about legal status and how their legal status affected their decisions affecting mobility. The study spends relatively less time analyzing some oft-cited causes of blocked mobility for U.S.-born second-generation youth—for example, underresourced schools as a systemic feature of Black or Brown neighborhoods—because we seek to explain variation in adult outcomes among these ninety-six cases, and recognizing differences in schools helps explain that variation.

This section has sought, in Robert Merton's words, to "establish the phenomenon" in a strategic research site by showing with data that the object of analysis exists—that "object" here being the surprising and greater mobility of U.S.-born NYCOMPers compared to their undocumented NYCOMP peers and to their counterparts in other places and studies.[38] The following section takes the next analytical step in Merton's framework—"specify[ing] ignorance." There I review prior research to assess how it can or cannot explain this strategic case. This review will help us explain why and how this study's findings are so different from the results of other studies, and how this study's design and questions can help us gain new insights into immigrant mobility in America today.

Why Is Mexican Second-Generation Mobility Greater in New York City?

Why do both this study and the census data for New York show such strong mobility for U.S.-born Mexicans in New York, especially given the lower educational attainment for second and later generations demonstrated in other studies and places? This impressive mobility is not well explained by most theories or studies on mobility or immigration, making it not only strategic but analytically "inconvenient," and thus useful, by presenting a puzzle to explain.[39]

U.S.-born NYCOMPers' strong mobility was not an artifact of "picking winners" in our initial interviews, or of reinterviewing only successful participants at time 2. Initial interviews were selected to ensure sizable numbers of cases that varied in key demographic and theoretical categories. Moreover, I drew on my ten years of prior ethnographic research in these Mexican migrant communities in New York and Puebla, Mexico, described in my first book, *Mexican New York: Transnational Lives of New Immigrants*.[40] Having known many of these youth and their parents for years before the NYCOMP project began in 1997, I had some insight into the social categories into which they might fit. The initial cases included roughly equal numbers of young men (forty-nine) and women (forty-seven); those who were doing well in school (forty) and those who were doing poorly or had dropped out (forty) or whose educational future seemed uncertain (sixteen); and those with U.S. citizenship (sixty-two) or other legal status, including temporary visas (six), and those who lacked legal status at birth or on arrival in the United States (twenty-eight). We identified and developed "inconvenient" cases whose processes or outcomes went against theoretical expectations. Some participants, for instance, avoided "Black" schools and students, believing that doing so would keep them safe, while others chose Black schools or made Black friends, believing that doing so would help them succeed in school.[41] Other inconvenient cases emerged from participants' varying relationships to gangs.

We retained 85 percent of cases from time 1 to time 2 and ended up with a data set of ninety-six fully developed cases.[42] Most analysis in this book assesses mobility from time 1 to time 2. We make selective use of twenty-nine time 3 follow-up interviews of potential DACA applicants and special cases such as Black Mexicans.[43]

All names in the book are pseudonyms. They are also unique identifiers across my publications. The Carla in this book is the same Carla in *Mexican New York* and other articles. Where I discuss families as cases (such as in chapter 6) or discuss actions or relations of several family members, I add fake surnames to make the argument and linked cases easier to follow.

The following two lists present selected statistics about NYCOMP participants and their parents, focusing on education, income, legal status, and processes that promoted intergenerational mobility for U.S.-borns but were blocked in promoting mobility by lack of legal status for undocumented Americans. All mechanisms or statistics listed are discussed in the following chapters.

Demographic and Mechanism Profile of NYCOMP Participants
  Full data set: 96 cases
  Mean year of birth: 1980 ($N = 96$)
  Gender: 47 women, 49 men
  Mean years of education at time 2 (average age 28): 13.7 years ($N = 96$)
  Median years of education at time 2: women: 14 ($N = 47$); men: 13
      ($N = 49$)
  Mean yearly income at time 2: \$36,686 ($N = 93$)[44]
  Marital status at last interview (time 2 or time 3): 33 percent married;
      6.4 percent living with a partner; 5.3 percent in a domestic
      partnership (*union libre*); 8.5 percent divorced or separated;
      46.8 percent single, never married ($N = 94$)
  Had a positive adult nonrelative mentor in high school or early
      adulthood: 47 percent ($N = 92$)
  Was planful as a teen or early adult: 64 percent ($N = 95$)
  Was a gang member or associator as a teen or early adult: 53 percent
      of men, 26 percent of women ($N = 96$)

Expressed feeling obliged to keep the immigrant bargain: 78.5 percent ($N = 93$)

Had substantive contact with Whites: in middle school: 26 percent ($N = 63$); in adulthood (ages 25 to 30): 75 percent ($N = 69$)

Sociodemographic and Legal Status Profile of Parents of NYCOMP Participants

Parents' mean years of education: 7.2; parents' median years of education: 7 ($N = 60$)

Mother's mean years of education: 6.7; mother's median years of education: 6.0 ($N = 60$)

Father's mean years of education: 8.0; father's median years of education: 8.0 ($N = 60$)

Mother's mean year of arrival: 1976; mother's median year of arrival: 1975 ($N = 93$)

Father's mean year of arrival: 1977; father's median year of arrival: 1975 ($N = 88$)

Was mother ever undocumented?: yes, 87 percent; no, 13 percent ($N = 84$)

Was father ever undocumented?: yes, 93 percent; no, 7 percent ($N = 82$)

Parents' IRCA legalization program eligibility: 74 percent of mothers (69 of 93) arrived before 1982 and were eligible; 26 percent of mothers (24 of 93) arrived after 1982 and were not IRCA eligible; 74 percent of fathers (61 of 82) arrived before 1982 and were eligible; 26 percent of fathers (21 of 82) arrived in 1982 or later and were not eligible.

How would current research explain the surprising second-generation mobility among U.S.-born Mexicans in New York City? Or the wide variation in adult outcomes among both U.S.-born and Mexican-born NYCOMP participants? I focus first on studies with all or nearly all participants who were U.S. citizens or lawful permanent residents, and then on those with undocumented participants.

Studies of Immigrant Intergenerational Mobility with All or Mostly U.S. Citizen Participants

Neither the strong mobility shown in census data nor the strong mobility or variation in adult outcomes in the NYCOMP cases results from hyperselected immigrant parents with high educational levels and human capital reproducing their prior status in the United States, as seen in research on the Chinese second generation by the sociologists

Jennifer Lee and Min Zhou and on Nigerians by the sociologists Onoso Imoagene or Karen Okigbo.[45] These scholars argue that second-generation high achievement is more often a lateral reproduction of socioeconomic status than a single-generation vertical jump in status. High educational achievement for the second generation follows their parents' similarly high achievement. In the sociologist Wei Ting Lu's lovely words, Mozart explains this mobility more than Confucius.[46]

Indeed, NYCOMPers' parents seem *hypo*-selected, averaging only 7.2 years of education (6.7 years for mothers and 8.0 years for fathers of all participants; 6.3 years for mothers and 7.6 years for fathers of U.S.-born participants only). These figures are consistent with several prior large surveys I did in the 1990s and with census data.[47] Only four mothers and five fathers had done any college (all in Mexico), and their children were not all high achievers. Most parents earned little money when their children were teens or early adults. At time 1, the mean family income was $49,816; these families had an average of two and a half earners, so each earned under $20,000. Perhaps most remarkably, nearly all parents—87 percent of mothers and 93 percent of fathers—had been undocumented at some point. These percentages are higher than found in other studies of intergenerational mobility, such as 34 percent of Mexican mothers and 33 percent of Mexican fathers in *Parents without Papers* by the sociologists Frank Bean, Susan Brown, and James Bachmeier and 10 percent of Mexican parents in *The Asian American Achievement Paradox* by Lee and Zhou.[48]

U.S.-born NYCOMP participants' mobility and variation among them is also not explained by the kinds of family structures and communal infrastructure that promote educational mobility and are cited in many studies, such as having a two-parent family, participating in ethnic after-school programs, having older relatives or friends who are college graduates, or experiencing teachers' positive expectations or stereotypes. These are elements of most theories, including second-generation advantage theory, segmented assimilation theory, two-way assimilation theory, and hyperselected mobility theory.[49] Mexicans in New York in the 1990s and early 2000s lacked this infrastructure. Indeed, it was at this time that I helped make the case for support for after-school programs to the archdiocese of New York and the Mexican consulate. I also cofounded an educational and organizing nonprofit to address this need (Masany.org). Moreover, NYCOMP family structure varied very little and would be a weak explanation for their children's greater or lesser adult mobility: only 3.1 percent of NYCOMP participants lived with a single parent in middle school, while 90.7 percent lived with two parents.[50] Finally, NYCOMP participants and Mexicans in New York mostly lived in neighborhoods with underfunded, badly performing schools, higher crime, and overcrowding, and thus they faced many of the same harsh structural conditions as most other low-income immigrant families in New York.

Many prior theories of immigration compare national and ethnic group-level differences, positing differing causes for these, and making their case in differing ways. Classic assimilation theory—which was preeminent from the 1920s to the 1980s and persists to this day—argues that inherent genetic, racial, cultural, or religious differences in immigrant groups make some individuals more "assimilable." This view mostly ignores structural exclusion and discrimination, although Milton Gordon's 1964 *Assimilation in American Life* noted discrimination against Blacks. The sociologist Herbert Gans warned that racial discrimination and a restructuring of the economy could lead to second-generation decline.[51]

But the strong intergenerational mobility in this study cannot be explained by theories that focus or rely on assimilation, on Mexican ethnic culture, or on inner-city culture. Culture of poverty theories, per Oscar Lewis's 1961 *Children of Sánchez*, argued that Hispanic culture had self-defeating traits that reproduced poverty. This view echoes the problematic Mexicans narrative that pervades American public life.[52] But if the problem was Mexican ethnic culture, why would there be variation within the NYCOMP sample, and why would U.S.-borns have such higher mobility in the census data?

Segmented assimilation theory as developed by the sociologists Alejandro Portes, Rubén Rumbaut, Min Zhou, and Patricia Fernández-Kelly argues that families with lower mobility are at higher risk of their second-generation youth assimilating into oppositional, often Black, inner-city culture and adopting a "reactive ethnicity" that does not embrace educational achievement and work as paths to a better life.[53] But very few NYCOMP participants evinced characteristics of segmented assimilation theory's oppositional, reactive ethnicity, and those few who did, via gang masculinity, either mostly grew out of it by their midtwenties or exhibited other behavior that contradicted it, such as working full-time. Moreover, NYCOMP participants associated Blackness with *upward* mobility, with being powerful and cool, rather than with oppositionality. Black Mexicans—study participants who identified as Black as teens but abandoned this identification as early adults—and other upwardly mobile youth in this study were helped by their Black friends, by "Black" programs (perceived as intended for Black students) or organizations, and by other associations with Blackness, contrary to the story of segmented assimilation theory.[54] Finally, segmented assimilation theory posits oppositionality as an enduring cultural trait, but most study participants had abandoned the oppositional elements of teen culture by their early to midtwenties.[55]

Racial exclusion theories reject cultural explanations and argue that discrimination and structural exclusion cause the lower mobility of U.S.-born second- or later-generation Mexicans, a position developed in the 1970 book by the sociologists Leo Grebler, Joan Moore, and Ralph Guzman, *The Mexican-American People*.[56] Thirty years later, the sociologists Edward Telles and Vilma Ortiz reinterviewed the same participants interviewed by Grebler, Moore, and Guzman to document very limited intergenerational mobility, which Telles and Ortiz argue was blocked by structural and racial inequality and discrimination, including under-funded schools. By the third generation, the stalling of educational mobility had led Mexican Americans to become a "permanent working class."[57] The sociologist María Rendón extends these arguments in her 2020 book *Stagnant Dreamers* by explaining limited mobility as rooted in exclusion and discrimination, bad schools and uncaring teachers, structural violence in neighborhoods, and social isolation and lack of the networks that serve as levers (*palancas*) for mobility. Rendón's participants were mostly U.S. citizens or lawful permanent residents, both academically high- and low-performing, whose fortunes had converged in working-class lives by their midtwenties.[58] (Rendón's title can be misconstrued as offering a deficit-oriented analysis, because *stagnant* is an adjective for Dreamers, but she analyzes how structures block and stagnate the Dreamers in her study.)

Theories focusing on racially driven discrimination and structural exclusion do not explain the strong mobility of the U.S.-born second generation in New York and of NYCOMPers. As we will show, while nearly all NYCOMP participants were zoned into low-performing schools, getting into better schools increased their mobility. Moreover, neighborhood violence, discrimination, social isolation and segregation, and a lack of networks were not widely reported in NYCOMPers' accounts. Although some NYCOMP participants, especially the upwardly mobile, reported discrimination—13.5 percent reported discrimination at work—they mostly noted that they had overcome it, even discrimination that was racially motivated.[59] Finally, while upwardly mobile youth in most other studies typically moved into "White" spaces (for example, colleges or workplaces where Whites predominated), upwardly mobile participants in this study moved into more diverse spaces—not just into White spaces but also into Black and Brown middle-class neighborhoods, schools, and workplaces, some of which had few Whites or none at all.[60]

The relatively small role that NYCOMP participants assigned to discrimination is not, I think, an artifact of being interviewed by a young (and later middle-aged) White male professor. Most time 1 first interviews were done by Latina and Latino student research assistants, and most participants did not give discrimination a big causal role. Moreover, in my current DACA and COVID research projects in New York State, nearly all participants tell me and the study's Mexican-, Chilean-, and Colombian-origin researchers a lot about discrimination (without our asking), especially by police, a key cause of the "traffic stop to deportation pipeline."[61] The NYCOMP research was mostly done in the late 1990s and early 2000s. Were it done now, after the Dreamer and Black Lives Matter movements and the societal talk of systemic racism in recent years, participants would likely discuss discrimination more.[62]

Research on mobility and discrimination should consider historical era and place. Grebler, Moore, and Guzman's study was done before the civil rights movement had opened many doors, and their older respondents had been in school during the Jim Crow era. Discrimination-based exclusion still exists, but not in the apartheid-like form it took before the implementation of civil rights laws and programs.[63] Moreover, research shows that discrimination, including by phenotype, varies by place. For example, darker-skinned Mexican immigrants in Texas experienced worse discrimination and lower socioeconomic attainment than their counterparts in California in the 1940s *and* in the 1980s.[64]

Finally, key factors in studies analyzing intragroup heterogeneity cannot explain variation in NYCOMPers' adult outcomes. The sociologists Richard Alba, Tomás Jiménez, and Helen Marrow reanalyzed Telles and Ortiz's data and found greater mobility among those whose parents had more education, those who had moved out of Mexican enclaves, and those who had a non-Mexican spouse.[65] The "origins and destinations" theory of the sociologists Renee Luthra, Roger Waldinger, and Thomas Soehl focuses on individual and family traits, experience in the United States, *and* impacts of the country of origin to explain variation not only in cross-group but also in intragroup outcomes.[66] By not "keeping their backs" to the border, that is, by considering home-country experience, these researchers argue that they are able to generate new analytical leverage. But there was very little educational variation among NYCOMPers' parents, and 98 percent of NYCOMPers who were married, partnered, or dating at age twenty-eight (which was most of them: eighty-four of ninety-six) were with a Mexican partner—61.9 percent of whom were U.S.-born Mexican Americans; 27.4 percent were Mexican-born documented or naturalized U.S. citizens, and 8.3 percent were Mexican-born and undocumented. Only one participant had a documented non-Mexican Hispanic partner (1.2 percent), and one had a Black U.S. citizen partner (1.2 percent). Census data show that 76 percent of Mexican-origin men and 71 percent of women were married or partnered with another Mexican-origin person in 2021, up from 51 and 54 percent in 1990, respectively.[67]

Finally, the large majority of NYCOMP participants' families came from the two small, contiguous villages of Ticuani and El Ganado, so variation in home-country contexts does not explain divergent second-generation adult outcomes. However, as we discuss later, the social cohesion without propinquity among immigrants from Ticuani and El Ganado in New York does contribute to intergenerational mobility.

Research on Minority Cultures of Mobility

The sociologists Kathy Neckerman, Jennifer Lee, and Prudence Carter argue that minority cultures of mobility recognize discrimination and offer tools to succeed anyway.[68] The sociologist Jody Agius Vallejo analyzes the operation of a Mexican culture of mobility among her study's middle-class participants in California and identifies key mechanisms promoting that mobility, such as ethnic professional associations and living at home as adults.[69] Similarly, the sociologist Vivian Louie identifies key mechanisms that promote mobility among Dominican and Colombian youth, including support from schools, teachers, and non-family mentors.[70]

I use and extend this work in several ways. First, prior research on minority cultures of mobility mostly starts with middle-class minorities and analyzes how they reproduce that status, while this study examines a large single-generation jump establishing such a culture and related practices. Second, nearly all upwardly mobile youth in this study went to public schools and local public universities. They were not plucked from their public schools and put on a mobility express train, for example in the Prep for Prep program.[71] They *created* roads to mobility that others are following. Third, this study both identifies new (to the research on migration) mechanisms promoting mobility—such as friendship strategies and the embracing of Blackness—and situates them within a context that increases their efficacy—the pro-mobility and immigrant-friendly environments of New York City and New York State.

Research on Intergenerational Mobility

Since the 1967 publication of Peter Blau and Otis Duncan's *The American Occupational Structure*, intergenerational mobility research has documented that more-educated, higher-income parents transmit advantages to their children, who do better partly because they can stay in school longer.[72] Subsequent research explaining how parental background affects children's later success has focused either on the social dynamics of education (for example, Annette Lareau's analysis of parental strategies of "concerted cultivation" or natural child-rearing) or on school structures (for example, tracking).[73] Alan Kerckhoff's

Diverging Pathways and Karl Alexander, Doris Entwisle, and Linda Olson's *The Long Shadow* use a life-course perspective to analyze intergenerational studies for what hurts or helps mobility, the latter tracking first-graders for twenty-five years.[74]

Recent research asks new questions or uses new data and methods to study intergenerational mobility. The sociologist David Grusky and the economist Timothy Smeeding and their colleagues note that prior work documents the cumulative advantage conferred by higher-SES parents on their children but does not explain "how that advantage is transmitted . . . [how it] varies across the life course, and . . . what structural arrangements mediate that transmission."[75] The sociologists Lisa Keister, Jody Agius Vallejo, and E. Paige Borelli gained analytical leverage on this issue by looking at longitudinal data (from the National Longitudinal Survey of Youth: 1979, NLSY79) rather than onetime studies (as most immigration research does) to find that Mexican Americans are experiencing greater than expected middle adult wealth accumulation in later generations, and that different adult outcomes are possible for those with "similar starting points," dependent on demographic, social, and other factors.[76] The sociologist Mara Getz Sheftel's work suggests that upward mobility among Mexican immigrants may be higher than it seems because some successful immigrants return to Mexico.[77] Other research on intergenerational mobility analyzes White men's income and career advantages, but also mentoring programs and other remedies promoting minority or women's mobility.[78]

I build on this research by identifying concrete mechanisms and conditions that promote or inhibit mobility and by following my participants for many years. This long-term case development enables me to show starting conditions of low parental education and income and then to trace mechanisms promoting upward mobility for U.S.-borns, but not for their undocumented peers.[79]

Research on the Impacts of Legal Status or the Inclusion of Undocumented Participants

Most research on legal status analyzes how lacking it harms immigrants and their families and how they address those harms. The analyses of the sociologist Veronica Terriquez and others have shown that Mexican intergenerational mobility is positive, but slowed by lack of legal status.[80] The sociologist Joanna Dreby documents the impact of a lack of legal status on intrafamily dynamics and children's relationships at school, while Angela Garcia describes how undocumented immigrants "pass" as documented while driving to avoid detection.[81] The sociologists Cecilia Menjívar, Laura Enriquez, Caitlin Patler, and others and the psychologists Hiro Yoshikawa and Carola Suárez-Orozco show that lack of legal status undermines immigrant health and child development—for example, by constraining their access to health care, by creating toxic stress that impedes brain development and learning, and even by affecting romantic relationships.[82] The sociologists Leisy Abrego and Kevin Escudero and others analyze how Dreamers organized to challenge their exclusion from public colleges.[83]

Most research on prior historical periods of immigration either ignored legal status or posited that the second generation's citizenship would eliminate intergenerational impacts. However, the sociologist Peter Catron found that children whose immigrant parents were already U.S. citizens in 1910 had more education and income as early adults in 1920 than those whose parents intended to become citizens in 1910, and also that gains were greater the longer the parents had been citizens and for groups, like Jews, that were facing more discrimination.[84]

This book contributes to an emerging theoretical perspective positing that having or lacking American citizenship or legal status strongly determines paths of immigrant intergenerational mobility and integration by including or excluding people from key institutions (the labor market, social insurance programs, universities) and formal politics (voting). Bean, Brown, and Bachmeier's *Parents without Papers* shows that lacking legal status creates basic membership exclusion for undocumented parents that harms mobility for their U.S. citizen children and later generations. The sociologist Laura Enriquez analyzes how lack of legal status imposes intergenerational punishment on the children of undocumented immigrants.[85] The sociologist Roberto Gonzales shows that the lives of undocumented youth who attend college converge with the lives of their high school dropout counterparts, making legal status a master status that follows a person across contexts and overwhelms other identities or statuses.[86]

Undocumented status has become more harmful since the 1990s for several reasons. Undocumented people stay undocumented longer: in 2019, the median duration was fifteen years for all undocumented persons, and 83 percent of undocumented Mexicans had lived in the United States for over a decade, most of that time with no chance to legalize.[87] Moreover, immigration law has been enforced since 2013 through the federal "Secure Communities" program, through which all fingerprints from local law enforcement are shared with U.S. Citizenship and Immigration Services (USCIS).[88] Such changes especially lead the children of immigrants, who are mostly U.S. citizens, to suffer stigma and toxic stress and to fear the police, who are supposed to protect them.[89] Finally, recent research argues that undocumented Mexican immigrants and their children (again, mostly U.S. citizens) are penalized by racialized illegality—the social reality that being Mexican or "looking Mexican" leads to greater discrimination, including by police, and harms longer-term life chances.[90]

This prior research helps explain why and how long-term undocumented NYCOMP participants were harmed, but it cannot explain variation in NYCOMP mobility. Research focusing on harms due to a lack of legal status usually does not also gather data on counterpart cases of those who have or who gain (Category Changers) legal status or U.S. citizenship; nor do they follow participants for years, as this study does. Moreover, larger-scale work, such as Bean, Brown, and Bachmeier's, documents the intergenerational impacts of parents' lack of legal status but does not empirically describe how those impacts happen, as this book does.

Gaining Different Analytical Leverage from Different Questions and Different Answers

Beyond studying a strategic case of surprising intergenerational mobility among U.S.-born Mexicans in New York, this study begins with a different question than most prior studies and gathers and analyzes data differently. Most prior studies of immigration compare how ethnic groups fare relative to each other—for example, by comparing average income for entire ethnic groups. They thus describe a statistical central tendency (for example, average or median income or education) that often becomes "the Mexican story" or "the Chinese story" when repeatedly cited. Because Mexicans as a group start with less education and income and lower rates of legal status than many groups, these comparative analyses tend to analyze why and how much Mexicans lag behind other groups. Such analyses have led, at least indirectly, to a great deal of deficit-oriented research and public discussion of correlations between, for example, educational levels or neighborhood poverty rates and specific groups' outcomes.[91] Most such research does not have data on the processes or mechanisms promoting better outcomes for some in those groups or neighborhoods.

Conversely, this book starts with a theoretically diverse set of ninety-six children of Mexican immigrants in New York City who were followed for over a decade. It seeks to explain intra-ethnic variation in the data set and strong U.S.-born second-generation mobility in the census data. Its case-oriented approach traces processes within and across the ninety-six cases that promoted or inhibited their mobility. This focus on comparing cases over time moves away from questions of how children of Mexican immigrants become culturally more "American," or how immigration changes American culture, and toward an examination of the inclusionary or exclusionary laws, policies, and structures, as well as individual and collective practices and habits, that promote or inhibit second-generation mobility.[92]

Explaining why and how some participants were more upwardly mobile than others focuses the analysis, first, on differences in their cases that emerged in participants' own accounts of their lives, across other cases, and in our observations of them over time. These included differences in the extent to which adult children kept the immigrant bargain, in individual habits of mind and conduct, and in having, lacking, or gaining legal status, which was easier for children of earlier-arriving NYCOMP parents than for those who came later, due to changes in immigration law. By moving the camera out with reference to comparable studies, such as María Rendón's *Stagnant Dreamers* (based on work in Los Angeles at the same time), I also posit that other factors promoted this impressive intergenerational mobility, including public supports in New York City and New York State for immigrants and low-income people greater than those found in other places, the different dynamics of settlement and integration, and different interactions with the built environment that led to different meanings of Mexicanness and different links to place and mobility in New York than seen in other studies.

NYCOMP Research Design, History, and Methods: Generating New Analytical Leverage

Several features of the NYCOMP research design increase its leverage to analyze second-generation upward mobility compared to other studies.

Recruiting Study Participants

First, we recruited study participants in ways that helped us capture variation and increase data quality. When NYCOMP's time 1 began in 1997, I had been in the field for a decade in New York and in Ticuani and El Ganado, the Mexican small towns from which 74 percent of respondents' parents originated (mostly Ticuani). I knew and had written about many NYCOMP parents and youth in my dissertation and in my 2006 book *Mexican New York*. I drew on these prior relationships to introduce three student research assistants—Sara Guerrero-Rippberger, Agustin Vecino, and Sandra Lara—to the community. I made sure we drew cases from different social networks, which varied by the section of Ticuani where they lived, their own or their family's legal status, when they migrated, where they lived in New York, how they did in school and work, and whether or not they were linked to the Comité (the Committee), which organized public transnational Ticuani life, or the Ticuani Youth Group, a sort of youth elite (some called its members *creida* [conceited]). We also interviewed youth whose parents were from other towns in Puebla and from neighboring states or Mexico City. A plurality of participants initially lived in Brooklyn, and all were in New York City. By time 2, participants were living in all five New York City boroughs as well as in New Jersey and New York suburbs and Long Island. A few had moved to Rhode Island or South Carolina.

We used ethnographically embedded snowball sampling in the United States and Mexico. In regular snowball sampling, interviewees are asked to refer the researcher to others to interview. Ethnographically embedded snowball sampling does this too, but leverages ethnographic immersion. My research assistants and I were often in the field in Mexico and New York during time 1 (1997 to 2002), and regularly but less often during times 2 and 3. We went to parties, movies, family dinners, and Mexican and Ticuani (or El Ganado) religious, public, or sports events. For two weeks each year, we were in Mexico for the feast of Ticuani's patron saint, a time when many from New York's Ticuani population return to celebrate. We asked Ticuanense (as people from Ticuani are called) youth I had known for years and others we came to know to introduce us to others. We discussed our theorizing with participants and asked them to introduce us to specific types of people, such as teen migrants or Black Mexicans. More "strong ties" than "weak ties," our snowball referrals came through family members or friends, even when we already knew the new person.[93] Many youth talked to us, and some even asked to be interviewed.[94] Doing interviews and ethnography in both New York and Mexico helped. Some people we knew from New York were too busy for interviews there, but they were glad to be interviewed in Mexico, when they were on vacation. Others, such as those who had fled gang problems in New York, said that they felt safer talking to us in Mexico.

Finally, we interviewed as many family members and friends of participants as possible because they were stronger referrals, and also because such interviews could triangulate interviewees' accounts and offer Rashomonic perspective via alternative accounts of the same events or relationships. (This recruitment practice runs counter to the practice in surveys of trying to "control for" social effects by not interviewing people in the same families or social groups, out of fear of their mutual influence.) We documented in our notes and case narratives how our participants and their friends and family members influenced each other.[95] Moreover, we gathered historical family data, including parents' year of arrival and changes in legal status. Often dating back over thirty years, these data enabled the analysis of intergenerational trends and correlations of outcomes with changes in immigration law.

Gathering Data over Several Life-Course Phases

The second element of the NYCOMP research design that increased its analytical leverage was its deep development, analysis, and triangulation of the cases over many years as participants moved through life-course phases. The cases draw on deep data and ongoing analysis generated via repeat interviews, direct observation, and triangulation with other cases through three research phases: time 1 (1997 to 2002, average age 19), time 2 (2005 to 2012, average age 28), and time 3 (2012 to 2018, average age 33). I followed up with some cases as I revised this book, including in 2023. At time 1, we wrote case narratives that we then updated at times 2 and 3 and whenever we met or spoke with study participants. The final case narratives averaged eight to nine single-spaced pages; narratives for some key participants were over twenty pages long.

We started following some participants at time 1 in their late teens or early twenties, when they were entering early adulthood (ages eighteen to twenty-five to thirty), and we tracked them through their mid to late twenties and early or midthirties, by which time most had entered established adulthood (ages twenty-five or thirty to about age forty-five) by finishing their schooling, starting full-time work, and marrying or becoming parents. We started with others in their early adulthood and tracked them well into or even mostly through their established adulthood, thus extending our capacity to analyze how teen and early adult processes or habits affected later adult outcomes.

We revisited the same participants at time 2 and used the project's deep archival infrastructure to strengthen our research and relationships with them. For example, in follow-up interviews we always asked about issues reported in the last one, and participants often remarked that they were glad we remembered those events. Moreover, repeatedly interviewing their friends and families enabled us to trace processes, knowledge, and actions across cases over time for individuals as well as for families and friend groups. Finally, long-term research enabled us to document, analyze, and learn from changes in how study participants understood their lives and relationships as they moved through the life course.[96]

If most one-off interview studies offer "snapshots," this study offers a flipbook—a series of actions one "sees" by flipping the pages—or a stop-action movie in which movement is "seen" as snapshots presented in quick sequence (think *Wallace and Gromit*). Keeping with these metaphors, if our interviews were like drawings to be flipped through, our periodic ethnographic observations were like videos of specific moments.

Gathering data repeatedly over years enabled us to avoid what the sociologist Dale Dannefer calls the "Time 1 Encapsulation Effect" seen in long-term studies that, for example, gather extensive data on children but then have only outcome data for them as adults. These studies have no data on what happened in the middle of their respondents' stories that could explain how their outcomes occurred.[97] This study traced decades of family history by collecting data on what happened in the time between time 1 and time 2 *and* in the past, before time 1, including data on parents' and participants' legal status on arrival and changes in it over time.[98] We did "maintenance" ethnography between and during times 1 and 2 by attending parties and events and talking to participants and their friends and family. With a few key cases, I stayed in touch right through the manuscript's final revision.

Analyzing Long-Term Ethnographic Data Using Ethnographic Narrative and Statistical Methods

The third part of the NYCOMP research design was to analyze the ninety-six cases using both case-oriented ethnographic methods and variable-oriented statistical analysis, seeking, first, to use the strengths of each to partly address weaknesses in each, and second, to leverage the powerful combination of intra- and cross-case process tracing to analyze deeply researched causal mechanisms using logical (not statistical) inference.

We created a case narrative database of our ninety-six cases and a variable-oriented database (VODB) that coded each case for 386 variables (over 700 Excel columns) for statistical analysis. (A third database, the set theoretical database, is used only in the appendixes; though we do not discuss it here, we invite readers to take a look at the set theoretical appendixes.) The sociologist Charles Ragin and his colleagues argue that if statistical research is predictive, in that it seeks to establish how much change in X correlates with change in Y across a population, holding the influence of other variables constant, case-oriented research is "retrodictive," that is, it seeks to explain how things came to be within one case or comparatively across several cases.[99] By assessing how much a key independent variable (the treatment) correlates to an outcome (the dependent variable) for a whole population (or data set), controlling for other variables, statistical analyses tell a probabilistic "central tendency" story for that group.[100] In contrast, case-oriented research like this project uses deep case knowledge to trace processes within and across cases, placed within context, to describe *how* processes or mechanisms promoted outcomes—including, in this book, how participants' understandings affected their actions. Case-oriented approaches better accommodate "equifinality" because they can trace the various causal pathways or sets of conditions that led different cases to the same outcome.[101]

We developed case narratives iteratively through time 2 and time 3 and used these case narratives to create a variable-oriented coding scheme, which we used to code all ninety-six cases.[102] We coded for commonplace variables, such as years of education, but also for processes emerging in our ethnographic work ("ethnographic variables"), such as a participant's model of masculinity or whether a participant had a mentor, and the strength of that mentoring relationship. In the interviews, we asked both guided narrative questions (for instance, how interviewees' lives were going on specific issues, including educational and legal status history) and questions seeking concrete data (years of education, years of living with or apart from their family, and so on; see online appendixes: https://www.russellsage.org/publications/dreams -achieved-and-denied).[103] Although we mostly used variables for which all or most cases were coded, for some variables we had fewer cases. If we realized that specific data were missing from a case, Sara Guerrero-Mustafa (formerly Guerrero-Rippberger) or I called the participant or their parents, most of whom we knew. In this book, we always report how many cases we used in a statistical run, which were mostly non-inferential means tables and cross tabs.

We do not statistically generalize to the larger population using the NYCOMP data set because it is not representative. Rather, we use statistical analysis of the full NYCOMP data set to partly address key limitations in ethnographic case analysis. Although ethnographic analysis can deeply describe very interesting cases, it can analyze only a few cases in narrative form in published material. It also has difficulty putting all cases into analysis simultaneously and in establishing how widespread the specific processes or mechanisms are, or how they correlate with outcomes for all cases in the study.[104] Case-oriented analysis can logically infer how common or significant a case is, but it is also useful to know whether your deeply researched case or cases are theoretically fascinating because they deviate from what theory predicts or if they represent larger trends among your cases.[105] (Set theoretical analysis excels at discerning this difference; see appendixes.)

We use case-oriented ethnographic analysis to address key weaknesses in statistical analysis, which can tell us how common a correlation is, and whether it is a real correlation or "noise" in the data, but cannot describe how the posited causal mechanism works (and in correlational studies usually cannot assert an "effect"). Statistical analysis can measure the net-effect of a treatment on an outcome (or on a correlation with an outcome), controlling for other variables. Conversely, case-oriented analysis can describe mechanisms that explain correlations with outcomes, and it can use intra- and cross-case process tracing to logically infer causality by describing how these mechanisms work, step by step, in each case. Case-oriented analysis can explain, for example, how the controlled-for factors work for different types of cases. In this way, it can analyze complex causality and equifinality by tracing how cases with different conditions reach the same outcome by different and sometimes theoretically deviant pathways.[106]

This study's validity does not depend on statistical generalization to a larger population. Rather, its research design is well suited to do *logical* inferential causal analysis by intra- and cross-case process tracing, buttressed by statistical analysis of our ninety-six cases.[107]

My research design joins those of a growing number of scholars who argue for the analytical value of studies that flip the approach that is put "in the driver's seat" in integrative, mixed-methods studies. In mixed-methods research, it is common to begin with a large random-sample survey and then to interview a subsample to find out what people say is going on.[108] This approach has strengths linked to the representativity of a random sample. But sociologists, such as James Mahoney and Charles Ragin, and political scientists, including Gary Goertz, Henry Brady, and David Collier, have made the scholarly case for also using case-oriented approaches and methods as the main drivers of mixed-methods research, using statistical or other methods to supplement insights gained from these methods.

I contribute to this work by showing how a case-oriented, long-term ethnographic study can use the insights gained by developing cases deeply over many years to both analyze how mechanisms work and, using statistical methods, establish how much the mechanisms seen in the cases correlate with outcomes—in this study, adult outcomes for all NYCOMPers.

A key strength of long-term ethnographic studies is their deep case development. While historical studies develop cases via knowledge from prior research or the opening of new archives, ethnographers develop cases by personally collecting data that would not otherwise exist and simultaneously developing frameworks to analyze these data. For this book, we developed the cases iteratively through repeated rounds of data gathering, theorizing, and writing case narratives, and then we analyzed them using ethnographic, case-oriented, statistical, and set theoretical methods.[109]

An example can illustrate how combining these approaches deepens the analysis. Many research participants, especially young men, offered detailed analyses of how their high school choice, experience, and adult outcomes were affected by their thinking about and reactions to "step-ups"—a youth stepping in front of another (in the street or a school hallway) and asking what gang he is with, to see if he is a rival. "Looking back" at the challenger in a step-up (making direct, sustained eye contact) can escalate the situation into conflict and a fight. "Looking down" (not making sustained eye contact) can deescalate the situation, reducing the likelihood of a fight and its subsequent impact on the challenged student's high school career. Our coding enabled us to show how many participants usually looked down or looked back to a step-up in high school and to measure their reaction's correlation with their adult outcomes. Looking back rather than looking down correlated (significantly) with three years less of education and over $17,000 less income at age twenty-eight. Using ethnographic data and informants' accounts, we trace why they looked back or down, what they anticipated would happen, and the short- and long-term impacts on their mobility.

Here we follow Clifford Geertz and Elijah Anderson in using "experience near" concepts—or the "folk" concepts of our participants, that is, concepts they would recognize, such as "looking back" or "looking down"—and "experience far" concepts, such as correlations or adult outcomes categories, like "Stuck Muddlers" in this study.[110] Showing that looking down is statistically correlated with more adult education and income for the whole NYCOMP data set strengthens the ethnographic narrative analysis of tracing the steps to adult outcomes for a few cases, by showing that larger trends among all cases fall out as our case analysis would expect.

To save space and improve readability, only some statistical operations are presented in the book and its notes. The statistical and set theoretical analyses are presented fully in the online appendixes, which both explain the additional leverage gained and the limits on the claims that can be made analyzing the NYCOMP data set with these methods. I hope the appendixes will be useful, especially to graduate students hoping to use mixed methods.

How American Immigration Policies Affected NYCOMP Participants' Intergenerational Mobility

Fourth, this research design enables us to empirically assess how changes in American immigration policies affected immigrant parents' access to legal status and their children's adult mobility in two ways. First, because we followed participants and family members for so long, our data straddle immigration policy changes, enabling us to trace their impacts within and across cases. We captured data on legal status through three important periods when changes in U.S. immigration policy affected the mobility of the NYCOMP second generation and long-term undocumented Americans. During the "up to-IRCA" period—that is, until IRCA's amnesty program ended in 1988—most immigrants in this study who overstayed a visa or came without one legalized their status through either IRCA's amnesty program or their U.S. citizen children. In the second period—the moratorium period from the 1990s to the present day, except for DACA recipients—Congress made it harder to obtain legal status and made lacking status increasingly harmful, so most undocumented immigrants still cannot legalize their status.[111] Finally, the DACA era, since its enactment in 2012, has helped more than 800,000 undocumented Americans brought here as children obtain renewable work permits and protection from deportation. DACA strongly boosts upward mobility and security, especially through "gate-keeper" identity documents (such as driver's licenses and Social Security numbers) that enable DACA recipients to participate legally in key institutions like the labor market and health insurance programs.[112] But for long-term undocumented Americans ineligible for DACA, the moratorium period never ended. Today it is harder to get legal status than in the past, and the impacts of being undocumented are worse. And finally, DACA, the deferred prosecution policy created by President Barack Obama in 2012, was revoked by President Donald Trump in September 2017, though the U.S. Supreme Court forced his administration to partly reverse itself. President Joe Biden reinstated DACA, but the Supreme Court ruling only preserved DACA for pre-2017 DACA holders. For the time being, it is no longer possible to file new DACA applications. Litigation continues, and DACA is still in danger.[113]

Second, having data that straddle policy periods creates further analytical leverage to track changes in the lives of Category Changers—study participants who were brought to the United States as children and who managed to become lawful permanent residents (not DACA)—after they gained legal status compared to the lives of both those who always had U.S. citizenship or legal status and those who remained undocumented. Table 1.6 shows that 65 percent of NYCOMP participants were U.S.-born, 6 percent came with a visa, and 29 percent were undocumented upon arrival in the United States. These Mexican-born participants averaged 7.9 years of age upon arrival, meaning that if they could get legal status, they were likely to grow up as 1.5-generation youths, fluent in English and with prospects higher than those of teen migrants. Analytical leverage stems from this 29 percent dropping to 15 percent by time 2, when the average age was twenty-eight.

Subsequent changes in Category Changers' lives can be attributed, with careful case contextualization and process tracing, to legal status

Table 1.6   The Legal Status of NYCOMP Participants over Time

Legal Status	On Arrival or at Birth (U.S.-Borns)	Time 1 (Average Age: Nineteen)	Time 2 (Average Age: Twenty-Eight)	Time 3 (Average Age: Thirty-Three)
Undocumented	29.2%	20.8%	14.6%	6.3%
Any visa (excludes DACA)	4.2	2.1	0	0
Permanent visa	2.1	11.5	7.3	12.6
U.S. citizen	64.6	65.6	78.1	81.1
N	96	96	96	95[a]

Source: NYCOMP data set. Analysis by author.
[a] Although we conducted fewer time 3 interviews, we recontacted nearly all non-U.S.-born informants to offer help in applying for DACA. Assuming that U.S.-borns were still citizens, we coded all but one case at time 3 on legal status.

change. Category Changers are living counterfactual cases, which are useful for logical causal inference: because the same persons were changing legal status category (moving from the control group of those lacking status to the treatment group of those with it), doubt was reduced over whether their better post-legalization lives could be due to an unnoted difference between legalizers and nonlegalizers. This inference is backed up by research—much of it on the effects of the 1986 IRCA legalization program—showing that life improves for parents and their children when they gain legal status.[114] Finally, while we categorize DACA recipients separately from Category Changers, getting even partial and temporary inclusion (via a work permit and social security number, which function like partial legal status) in DACA greatly improved the lives of those who were undocumented (see chapter 5).

Our deep and long-term individual and family case knowledge enables us to gauge how U.S. policies affected individual and intergenerational mobility and family dynamics. As noted earlier, nearly all of the participants' parents (86 percent of mothers and 93 percent of fathers) had been undocumented at one time, but most of them (78 percent of mothers and 82 percent of fathers) later gained legal status via IRCA's amnesty programs or their U.S. citizen children. Indeed, most parents had become lawful permanent residents or U.S. citizens by the late 1990s and were able to legalize their undocumented children. Legalization became much harder after the 1990s. Most participants who were the children of parents who legalized via IRCA told us that being undocumented as a child, teen, or even early adult did *not* harm their later adult life because they knew that they could and would legalize their status, that it was in process. Conversely, all children of the

20 percent of parents who could not legalize told us that lacking legal status had harmed them. Most of them had grown up knowing that they could not legalize, or they found out in high school and realized that working hard in school would not lead to better jobs. U.S. immigration policies thus created mixed-status families in which the younger U.S.-born siblings enjoyed benefits both big (having a Social Security number) and small (being allowed to go on class trips) that from which their undocumented older siblings were excluded.

Our data show that U.S. immigration policies directly affected which children would become long-term undocumented Americans. The parents of U.S.-born study participants tended to have arrived around 1973, most of the parents of Category Changers had come around 1981, and the parents of long-term undocumented participants had migrated to the United States in 1985 or afterwards, when they were ineligible to legalize via IRCA and thus unable to legalize their undocumented children. The link between later arrival and an immigrant's inability to legalize their own status or their children's status is documented in a 2019 book I coauthored with Don Waisanen and Guillermo Yrizar Barbosa.[115] Of over eight hundred Mexicans surveyed in 2012 (in the Mexican consulate and in public places, like parks), 93.7 percent of those who had been in the United States for five years or less, 92.3 percent of those in the country between six and ten years, and 89.7 percent of those who had been here between eleven and fifteen years were undocumented. The rate of undocumented status dropped steeply, to 46 percent, for those who had been in the United States more than twenty years—that is, for those who arrived in 1992 or earlier. Most of them had come in the pre-IRCA period (after 1988), after which time legalization became harder.

This analysis shows, first, that most of those who could legalize did so, contrary to the public narrative promoted by some that undocumented immigrants do not legalize because they do not respect U.S. laws. These data show, as do many studies on the impacts of the IRCA legalization, that parents who immigrated under prior, more humane laws were better able to help their children legalize and to have better adult lives.[116] This research shouts the clear implications of its results: legalizing undocumented parents and children quickly promotes better individual, family, and societal outcomes and integration.

New Takes on Well-Studied Processes and New Analysis of Less-Studied Processes

In the chapters that follow, we offer new takes on some well-studied processes and new analysis of less studied or not-studied processes in immigration research. Chapter 2, for instance, extends my own and Vivian Louie's work by analyzing the evolution of the immigrant bargain as families age. In families where everyone has legal status or citizenship and adult children live at home, older children who finish college quickly earn more than their parents, helping with the family budget and helping their younger siblings navigate school and college, thus keeping the immigrant bargain fully. Conversely, older children who lack legal status cannot earn much more than their parents, often do not attend college, and cannot help the family budget or their younger siblings as much, thus keeping the immigrant bargain less fully.[117] Chapter 3 on schools analyzes how the different beliefs in the Mexican community on how Blackness or Mexicanness promoted or derailed educational careers affected NYCOMP participants' high school choice and subsequent educational and life trajectories. This analysis of how various meanings of being Mexican affected high school choice in the late 1990s sets up the later analysis of how practices, such as going to college or not, acquire ethnic meaning. Chapter 4 analyzes how and why mentors could promote the mobility of U.S.-born and Category Changer study participants but not of their undocumented peers. This chapter begins to fill in a surprising lack of research on mentoring in much prior work on the children of immigrants.

Finally, our research design offers analytical leverage on the role of culture in mobility that central tendency analyses telling a single "Mexican" or "Chinese" story cannot, due to "slippages" in the sociological lives of theories that stem from several sources. Even where significant intra-ethnic group difference exists, scholars often do not extensively analyze the cases in the minority (such as lower-achieving Nigerian second-generation adult children), engage them in print, or look at their impact on the theoretical story.[118] Moreover, the elements of many theories can be recombined to predict different outcomes. And specific findings—for example, that Chinese, on average, get more education than Mexicans—tend through repetition in public debate to become meta-narratives taken to reflect ethnic or national cultures writ large. Assessments of each group's "assimilability" follow, even if the original theorists did not make such arguments.

The issue is not whether culture can affect adult mobility—it can—but rather what *type* of culture is posited to do so, and how that happens. Segmented assimilation theory does well in theorizing that the second generation's culture will emerge from material circumstances. But it also posits that a nearly uniform "mainstream" American culture exists outside the inner city, where an oppositional culture prevails, and causes downward mobility for children of immigrants integrating into it.[119] But adult NYCOMP participants showed not only almost no reactive ethnicity but rather its opposite. Their mobility was most often blocked by their legal status. Second-generation advantage theory reclaims a causal role for ethnic culture (often avoided after the 1973 Moynihan Report) and largely avoids this central tendency story problem by positing that children of immigrants take ethnic practices from both America culture and their parents' home-country culture to chart mostly upwardly mobile paths. This theory also notes the class basis of parental cultures, as in Chinese cram schools.[120] Similarly, two-way assimilation theory describes assimilation as a closing of social and cultural distance from the mainstream, measured in terms of proficiency in English, intermarriage (mostly with Whites), educational attainment, and geographic mobility.

Yet what is "mainstream" America, or "the mainstream" in the 2020s, especially in urban neighborhoods and schools where Whites are often a minority or nearly absent? The difficulty of answering this question raises the further question of whether the White popula-tion or White mainstream culture—whatever that might be—should be used as the default comparison for assessing newcomer progress. What does it mean that many NYCOMPers spoke native English, graduated from college, and got good jobs, but had nearly no White friends and lived and worked in upwardly mobile social worlds with few or no Whites? Or that some of the professional adult worlds other NYCOMPers had integrated into were not just "White" spaces, though some of them mostly were? If we assume that White social worlds are the mainstream, then we have to explain mobility outside the mainstream.

It is problematic to presume the existence of a reified "mainstream," whether White or non-White, in studying immigration and multi-generational mobility and lives. The sociologists Pierrette Hondagneu-Sotelo and Manuel Pastor are similarly skeptical of the utility of the "mainstream" concept in *South Central Dreams*, their analysis of how, over time, Latino/a and Black residents of South Central Los Angeles created a shared sense of "home" there, despite earlier ethnic conflicts.[121]

I join this theoretical conversation in several ways. First, I posit that various types of cultures (youth cultures, school cultures, workplace cultures) can affect mobility, and that these vary by context. Second, I explicate how the practices and processes that affect mobility *came to be seen as ethnic* by my study participants, thus contributing to research on when and how ethnicity matters. Gans, analyzing the experience of prior European migrants, argued that ethnicity became symbolic—for example, as linked to ethnic celebrations, but not affecting life chances—for the later generations of European immigrants who had moved out of enclaves and into the mainstream.[122] Edward Telles and

Christina Sue argue that later-generation Mexican Americans' ethnicity has been durable and can be experienced as both symbolic and consequential—that is, that one's life chances are affected by phenotype, gender, surname, intermarriage, and language.[123] Tomás Jiménez and Adam Horowitz wonder how White became "just alright" in Cupertino, California, and linked to slacker academic performance (compared to Asian high achievement).[124]

This book develops "conjunctural ethnicity" theory, offered as a loosely hinged, Blumerian sensitizing framework that argues that we can understand how ethnicity acquires meaning and becomes positively or negatively consequential for outcomes by focusing on three sets of contexts.[125] The first context is the individual's life-course phase. The meanings of ethnicity and their links to outcomes can change as a person moves through the life course, which we do in this study by following participants into and through early adulthood and into established adulthood.

The second context is the set of local racial and ethnic hierarchies, population compositions, and institutions, such as schools and police, including the place of newcomers in these hierarchies and institutions, which can change over time. We analyze this context by following participants in their schools, homes, and workplaces through their more or less upwardly mobile lives and trajectories.

The third context is created by an immigrant group's phase of settlement, which points to how it is internally organized in the new society and how it is "seen" (or not) in the new society.[126] Here we analyze, for example, how the meaning of being Mexican in schools changed over time and how Mexicans in New York City related to place differently from, for example, Rendón's participants in her book *Stagnant Dreamers*. The conjunctural ethnicity framework helped me analyze how and why striving, academically high-achieving, second-generation Mexican teens adopted Black identities but abandoned those identities and felt Mexican again in their midtwenties, after graduating from college.

A key question stemming from this book is why NYCOMPers and many teachers saw dropping out of high school as a "Mexican thing" in the early 2000s, but so many U.S.-born Mexican youth now go to college, and help their relatives go too, thus making college part of the emerging Mexican culture of mobility. Drawing on the sociologist Cecilia Ridgeway's research, we can partly answer this question by looking at whether participants saw being Mexican as an ethnic identity that affected neither how they were treated nor their life chances, or as a status that could help or hurt them.[127] Ethnic meaning becomes attached to particular practices when group members and powerful others view them as ethnic, and thus making ethnicity a status. Rather than analyze national or ethnic traits or practices to gauge "assimilation," this book analyzes how specific traits or practices took on ethnic meaning for these participants and for others in their lives and affected their lives and mobility. Chapter 8 argues that fewer upwardly mobile youth move sequentially through contexts that make being Mexican a negative status or a source of stigma, while more upwardly mobile youth move through contexts that make being Mexican a neutral ethnicity or a positive status that opens doors.

A Framework for Explaining U.S.-Born Mexican Second-Generation Mobility in New York City

This study analyzes the unusual mobility of U.S.-born second-generation Mexicans in New York City in the census data and the variation in middle-adult life outcomes among study participants, focusing on sets of conditions and factors promoting or inhibiting mobility. A first set of conditions affecting mobility is part of the national story of how lacking legal status harms immigrants and their children. A second set of conditions arises from the choices made by New York City and New York State, including their inclusive policies toward immigrants. CUNY (City University of New York), where I teach, has been an especially effective mobility promoter. Third, features of New York City's built environment—including the subway, which enables cheap movement to jobs, classes, and internships—also promote mobility, with no need for NYCOMPers to leave their families or supportive social relationships to take opportunities. A fourth set of conditions that affected mobility were the social locations of Mexicans and of NYCOMP families and their patterns of incorporation in New York City, which also affected the meaning of Mexicanness and relationship to place in New York different from what has been found in other studies. Finally, we analyze variations in individual and collective or family practices, meanings, and habits that promoted mobility, including keeping the immigrant bargain into established adulthood, having strong mentors, being planful, living at home, avoiding gangs, and skillfully navigating the ethnic meanings of education in the Mexican community in the late 1990s and early 2000s.[128]

Over time these conditions have promoted both strong upward mobility and an emerging Mexican culture of mobility in New York City for U.S.-borns. But when long-term undocumented Americans in this study and their families engaged in the same practices and habits that made U.S.-borns upwardly mobile, their individual and collective mobility was blocked by their lack of legal status.

These mobility-promoting conditions may seem to be specific to New York City, but many of them could be replicated elsewhere. The mobility provided by the subway could be approximated by transportation programs in other places. CUNY's mobility-promoting function could be replicated (and has been) by smart investment in public universities in other places. That New York offers several such mobility-promoting conditions makes it a Mertonian strategic site that we can use in studying mobility and the policies promoting it.

I do not anchor this book with the concept of a Mexican culture of mobility because it is not "Mexican culture" per se that promotes or inhibits mobility in New York or the United States. Everyone in this study was Mexican, so how could that ethnic culture explain their different adult lives? Rather, I seek to analyze how these factors affected mobility and how ethnic meaning became (or did not become) attached to upward or downward mobility. The challenge is not to analyze the elements of some unchanging "Mexican" cultural tool kit that affect mobility, but rather to ask how these conditions affect upward or downward mobility and how that mobility is then understood as being "Mexican" or not, changing the meaning of being Mexican. In the emerging Mexican culture of mobility in New York City, going to college is a "Mexican thing" that is widely expected, as it is among many other groups in New York.

The chapters that follow analyze mechanisms that promoted or inhibited upward mobility into established adulthood for NYCOMPers. They examine the impacts of structural and institutional inequalities, governmental policies, intrafamily processes, and individual habits on NYCOMPers' adult mobility. To prevent the overwhelming impact of lacking legal status on adult mobility from swamping the analysis, some chapters trace the processes that promoted the mobility of participants who were either U.S. citizens or permanent residents and the mobility of their families, and then trace how the same processes were blocked for their undocumented counterparts. I follow this strategy in chapter 2 on intrafamily dynamics, in chapter 3 on schools, in chapter 6 on second-chance mechanisms, and in chapter 7 on masculinities. In chapter 4 on mentoring and in chapter 8 on friendship strategies and contextual meanings of Mexicanness, I focus mostly or only on participants and their families who were U.S. citizens or permanent residents to trace how other processes promote or inhibit mobility, absent the impacts of legal status. Chapter 5 on DACA focuses only on long-term undocumented cases who either got DACA status or did not, tracing how processes like mentoring, keeping the immigrant bargain, and going to better high schools could not help undocumented participants until they got DACA, which then dramatically boosted their incomes, career advancement, and life quality.

A quick note on language and ethnicity: When discussing specific cases, I mostly use the terms that people used to describe themselves, so some study participants are described as either Latinas/os or Hispanics, the two main descriptors they used. I also use "Hispanic" and "Latin" or "Latine" and "Latino/a/e" as pan-ethnic descriptors. I follow the convention in sociology (and Russell Sage Foundation house style) of using the noun form to refer to groups of people by racial or ethnic category ("Blacks," "Whites," "Hispanics," and so on), but to use "Black" or "White" only as adjectives when describing individuals. I translate from Spanish depending on the original usage and meaning. So "*Hay morenos*" (in the words of Vicky's mother) is translated as "There are Blacks" rather than "There are Black people," retaining the pejorative original meaning.

The book is mostly narrative case analysis. I analytically tell the story of a case or cases to show how combinations of processes or mechanisms and conditions promoted or inhibited participants' mobility. For most chapters, I also did statistical analysis to show the correlations of specific processes, mechanisms, and conditions with outcomes for all NYCOMPers. Finally, I did set theoretical analysis (using qualitative comparative analysis [QCA]) to determine how many cases presenting different combinations of processes, mechanisms, and conditions ended up, for example, as College Graduates or High Fliers.[129] The three methods of data analysis are integrated within the study: the mechanisms described in the narrative case development are operationalized for statistical and set theoretical analyses, but the different methods can illuminate different dimensions of the social reality being studied. The result is an extended epistemic and methodological reflection—a second "shadow" book, really.

As mentioned earlier, key statistical tables are presented in the text or in the notes, while all of the set theoretical analysis and much of the statistical analysis appears in the online appendixes. I hope readers interested in the full step-by-step statistical and set theoretical analyses will read these appendixes, which are written to be more accessible than some treatments of integrated methods. The set theoretical appendixes discuss cases developed in the narrative analysis, so readers will be familiar with them and should be able to see the extra insight gained by also using this other method. Finally, the "Overall Online Book Appendixes: Strategy, Epistemology, and Methods in the Long-Term Ethnographic New York Children of Migrants Project (NYCOMP)" describes concretely how we combined these approaches and related methods of data collection and analysis in this book.

In conclusion, two brief notes on this research and my place in the world. The first is a brief word about positionality, which I believe is constructed, in long-term work such as I have done, through one's relationships, commitments, and social locations rather than mechanically or essentialistically from one's ascriptive characteristics. I have used my social locations and tenured place in a public university to teach and mentor and do cutting-edge research while also trying to use that work to help those I work with and to challenge injustices in our society. This work has enacted my belief—and that of the larger movement for publicly engaged sociology and scholarship—that professors and universities, in addition to teaching and scholarship, should be publicly engaged and work to increase access to education, reduce injustice and inequality, and make our society better. My efforts have included institutional, community organizational, legal, direct service, and analytical work, writing public pieces such as op-eds, and service as an expert witness. A brief summary can be found in this note and in other publications.[130]

Second, as a researcher—and as a dad raising children from birth into early adulthood at the same time my research participants were moving from their teens into early and then established adulthood—I felt like I was living in parallel versions of America as I watched the paths outlined here unfold. In the American dream version, most participants and their families who were U.S. citizens or Category Changers were rewarded for their hard work, and it made me happy to celebrate their successes with them. I admired the *ganas*, the strong desire to succeed, and the hard work of these parents and children of immigrants.

In the long-term undocumented version of America, however, I watched, mostly unable to help, as the lives and hopes of promising young people were quashed by the impossibility of getting legal status, and as their parents came to realize that they had unknowingly put their children in an impossible situation. The parents believed that if their children studied hard and were good people, America would give them a chance to obtain legal status and have better lives. In my thirty-five years of doing fieldwork, I have repeatedly had to explain to disbelieving, often desperate, parents that there seemed to be no current way to legalize their own or their children's status, despite their children's good character and grades. (I always referred them to lawyers for legal advice, though most had no way to legalize.) I know many people who were deported, some permanently separated from their young, U.S. citizen children, when their only infraction was entering the United

States a decade or more earlier without a visa. I have gone to court as an expert witness many times. Working with the family and their lawyers, we can sometimes stop a parent's deportation, but sometimes not. When such cases are lost, the conversations with the families left behind in the United States—especially with the children—are hard. The subsequent harms imposed on the families cannot be described here.

These conversations and friendships have made clear to me that American immigration policies constitute a form of structural legal violence that allows institutions and systems to operate normally, even without racist or malicious intent by officers or agents, and have disproportionate and devastating consequences, especially for Mexican and Central American immigrant families.[131]

═ Chapter 2 ═

Intergenerational Bequeathal of Dis/Advantage and the Immigrant Bargain: The Impact of Legal Status on the Intrafamily Mechanisms Promoting Upward Mobility

Since I was young, I always thought like . . . deep inside . . . that I have to be obedient to my parents because of . . . all the hard work they have gone through. . . . I have respect for them.

—Simone

I got them into [got the mortgage for] this house. I made sure that they were okay making the monthly payments. And my sister and I split all the bills, like gas, all the maintenance that the house needs. We pay for anything that Kyle needs. We arrange it, whether it be cabs, whatever. . . . Kyle has three mothers, you know?

—Carla

IN DESCRIBING how they went to college, lived at home after college, bought a house together, and took on parental roles for their little brother, Kyle, Carla and Simone showed how they recognized and respected their parents' hard work and sacrifice for them. The two sisters did work that parents who are middle-class U.S. citizens usually do, such as negotiating the mortgage on the house they bought together, communicating with Kyle's teachers and advising him which classes to take or avoid, and handling the logistics of his many (in their view, over-indulged) extracurricular activities. Carla was only partly joking in saying that Kyle had "three mothers"; she and Simone in fact did a lot of parenting work. Although they sometimes felt jealous that Kyle

49

https://doi.org/10.7758/drwz9626.9883

had more opportunities than they did, they were devoted big sisters and good daughters who were proud to help their family thrive. The immigrant family bargain imposed extra burdens on them, but it also conferred the honor and happiness that came from helping their parents and their brother and making the family upwardly mobile.

As recounted in chapter 1, Eddie, the A student who dropped out of school to help his mother, found it very difficult to tell her of his decision, and in fact it was not until his math teacher visited the family, with the intention of convincing Eddie's mother to try to stop him from dropping out, that she found out. Eddie's account of that visit on a sunny June day was heartbreaking to hear and clearly hard for him to tell, even ten years later. His mother's disbelieving anger stemmed partly from the tragedy that had driven their migration. They had come to New York seven days after Eddie's father died, because his mother saw immediately that they could not survive in Mexico. Now her oldest child—who excelled academically and was a "decent, good boy," in his words—was leaving school and giving up on the promise of a better life that had driven them to migrate. Moreover, Eddie knew that his sisters and cousins, who looked up to him, would be discouraged by his decision to drop out of school. He also knew that it was "not normal" for a teacher to visit a student's home and that his math teacher would not have done so if he did not believe in Eddie and want him to succeed.

Eddie was like so many who grew up from grade school into full adulthood without legal status and eventually saw their prospects as markedly grimmer than their parents did. Despite his mother's fervent belief that education would open doors for him in America and that his good grades and character would be recognized, Eddie had seen that she was wrong. Without a Social Security number and legal status, education would not help him in America. Moreover, Eddie's clear-eyed act of dropping out helped her pay the rent and buy clothes for his (also undocumented) sisters, even though doing so further limited his own future mobility. It was hard for his mother to see the first-generation-type sacrifice he had made for his sisters and for her because she wanted so fervently for him to have the better second-generation life she herself had sacrificed to give him.

Eddie, Carla, and Simone all had good grades and were well liked by their teachers, who were mostly good ones. All three had kept the immigrant family bargain through their first year of high school by avoiding habits or activities that would harm their educational future (cutting school, joining a gang) and developing habits that promoted their educational success (always doing homework, obeying their parents). Moreover, all three were planful and thought about how their current actions would affect not only their own future but their family's as well.

Finally, all three had come to the United States as undocumented school-children under age ten.

Eddie had tried to keep the immigrant bargain—the reciprocal moral understanding that the children of immigrants will redeem their parents' sacrifice by doing well in school, helping their parents and younger siblings, and becoming ethical, well-educated people—but found that he could not do so into early adulthood.[1] Eddie's mother was distraught. When she finally talked to him again, she tried to convince him to return to school. By contrast, Carla and Simone were a great source of pride to their parents for keeping the immigrant bargain so well. Their parents beamed as they told me of their daughters' school success and how much they helped Kyle, while Carla and Simone rolled their eyes, embarrassed at their parents' pride.

Why did the lives of these three youth, who were doing all they could to succeed in school and life, diverge so dramatically and lead to vastly different adult individual and family mobility?

Legal status explains much of the difference. Carla and Simone were Category Changers: like Eddie, they came to the United States as undocumented children, but their parents had been able to become lawful permanent residents through the legalization program of the 1986 Immigration Reform and Control Act (IRCA). Eddie's mother, driven north by her husband's death, lost the path to legal status she had planned on when Eddie's grandfather, a naturalized U.S. citizen who was sponsoring them, died before their applications for legal status were approved. They were left adrift during the moratorium period after the expiration of the IRCA legalization program, when it became much harder to gain legal status. His grandfather's death closed the door to Eddie's future, and his lack of legal status made him unable to keep the immigrant family bargain on which his mother had based their whole future. Eddie and his sisters were still undocumented Americans as I wrote this in 2019, while Carla and Simone were U.S. citizens who each owned their own home and who, with their family, had celebrated their brother Kyle's college graduation. Carla and Simone were part of a second generation of U.S.-born or Category Changer Mexicans who are creating a Mexican culture of mobility in New York.

Much prior research analyzes how a lack of legal status harms undocumented immigrants, especially Dreamers, and can even impose intergenerational harms and punishments on second and later generations.[2] This chapter extends this work by documenting such harms among undocumented or mixed-status families with older undocumented children and contrasts them with the mobility of all-documented and Category Changer families. We describe and trace the mechanisms by which this mobility was either achieved or blocked by legal status.

Differential Bequeathals: How the Life Course, the Immigrant Bargain, and Intrafamily Processes Promote or Inhibit Mobility

This chapter analyzes how individual and familial life courses and intra-family processes enacting the immigrant bargain interact with legal status to promote (or inhibit) individual and family mobility and con-tribute (or not) to a Mexican culture of mobility, noting a key role played by older siblings. Many all-documented NYCOMP families—those in which all members were lawful permanent residents or U.S. citizens—experienced a jump in mobility because their incomes increased dramat-ically as their older children became early adults and started working full-time and because having legal status made efficacious their intra-family strategies, dynamics, and learning. For example, what families learned from their older children's experience with New York City's schools helped their younger children. They could also benefit more from New York City's and New York State's pro-mobility policies and practices, whose efficacy was blocked for undocumented NYCOMPers and their families. In all-documented families, all parties usually felt good about keeping the immigrant bargain, but this was not the case for all-undocumented families.

Category Changer families—those in which the parents or older siblings had been undocumented but later gained permanent legal status—experienced similar increases in income and benefited from the same intrafamily strategies, dynamics, and learning, and from New York's pro-mobility policies and practices. This legal status change was often intergenerational in execution and impact: many parents had earlier legalized via IRCA and then reunited quickly with their children in New York and began waiting for their children's legal status to come through. These still undocumented older children knew that their papers were *en tramites* (in process), so the wait did not usually affect their effort in school or the likelihood that they would attend college. When it came through, legal status enabled them, as early adult college graduates, to get better jobs, contribute more to the family budget, and help their younger siblings more. Older siblings' mobility enabled younger siblings (who were overwhelmingly U.S.-born in this study and nationally) in all-documented and Category Changer families to grow up in higher-income, often middle-class families and to benefit from their older siblings' knowledge of American educational, health care, and other institutions.

The lack of legal status for older, early adult children in all-undocumented families (families with no documented members) and in mixed-status families with undocumented parents and undocumented older siblings but U.S.-born younger children derails these mobility-promoting intrafamily dynamics. (Not all mixed status families have this configuration.[3]) Because they lack legal status, the earnings of older undocumented siblings do not rise much when they become early adults, so they contribute less to the family budget. They are also less likely to finish high school or go to college, so they are less able to help their younger siblings navigate the schools and other institutions. Even if they do go to college and can help younger siblings navigate the educational system, undocumented older siblings cannot get jobs commensurate with their education, as their U.S.-born peers can, so they are unable to help as much financially. In this way, the lack of legal status undermines the efficacy of the same intrafamily strategies and practices that promoted mobility in all-documented and Category Changer families.[4] Moreover, poverty can increase if undocumented children become parents as early adults, especially if they form their own household.[5] All this made it harder for family members to keep or feel they had kept the immigrant bargain.

A bequeathal is an inheritance, usually understood as wealth, that one generation leaves to the next. Here it describes a kind of familial social capital in the family's strategies, habits, and collective knowledge and capacity, including the knowledge and capacities learned as older siblings become early adults and the family ages from a younger to an older family. In general, older undocumented siblings gain less knowledge and experience negotiating American institutions like schools and financial systems and thus are less able to help their younger siblings and parents as much as documented or U.S.-born older siblings.[6] These differential bequeathals directly reflect how American immigration policies that enable legalization promote mobility and a Mexican culture of mobility, while those preventing legalization block them. The emerging Mexican culture of mobility does not offer the type of glass floor against downward mobility that wealthier families can offer even their academically underperforming children.[7]

The "life course" is a social science concept describing the passage from infancy through childhood and adolescence, into early and established adulthood, then middle age, retirement, dotage, and death. "Early adulthood" as a life-course stage emerged recently as a way to describe a transition from adolescence to full adulthood that often now takes longer than it did fifty years ago, when a high school diploma could secure a job that would support a family (for many, but not all, Americans). Early adulthood usually runs from ages eighteen to twenty-five but can extend to age thirty or older for people in some careers. One moves through early adulthood into established adulthood by finishing school, starting full-time work, and perhaps marrying and having children. Most parents prefer that their children accomplish these steps in this order.[8] Established adulthood begins when these transitions have taken place and lasts until one's own children become teens or early adults, usually by one's midforties.

Families also have life courses, driven by children becoming adults and parents aging. Family life-course movement can involve a change in living arrangements, such as when children leave their parents' home. Individual and family life courses are structural features of social life — our responsibilities, perspectives, rights, and relationships with family members change as we move through the life course. I focus here on families with children because I analyze multigenerational effects of legal status.[9] Moreover, while the families in this study were primarily heterosexual couples with children (the sample included few single parents), I recognize that there are many types of families in America, including same-sex partner families and others, whose family bargains also prescribe mutual obligations and expectations. I hope the ideas presented in this chapter prove useful in analyzing those families too.

The Immigrant Family Bargain and Intrafamily Mechanisms through the Individual and Family Life Courses

The immigrant family bargain is kept (or not), enacted, or modified through specific family strategies, dynamics, and learning.[10] "Family strategies" are conscious choices or patterns of collective behavior affecting a family's overall well-being, including early adults living with their parents, pooling their income with the family's, buying a house together, and helping siblings in schoolwork and decisions. The term "intrafamily dynamics" refers to how family members relate to each other, including how much they support each other and the roles taken by older and younger siblings. "Familial learning" describes how parents and children learn from their experience with American institutions, like schools and financial institutions. Family learning includes how parents change strategies for younger children based on their experience with older ones and how older children's roles change as they become early adults and often take on more parental jobs, such as helping younger siblings with homework and navigating the school system.

Family bargains are made in non-immigrant families, but they are freighted with extra meaning in immigrant families because the parents' sacrifice is profound and usually permanent because most immigrant parents give up their former lives when they migrate. Moreover, the stakes are higher and the dynamics more complicated than for native-born families because of the imbalance in knowledge, earning capacity, and ability to negotiate American institutions between English-speaking, and sometimes college-educated, early adults and their often less-educated parents who are not fluent in English.[11]

My own and others' prior research on keeping the immigrant bargain analyzed it with study participants who were teens or were entering early adulthood, when keeping that bargain was partly an aspirational stance, because there was still time to keep it.[12] Here we follow the same study participants into their late twenties and thirties to see what happened — that is, to trace how the immigrant bargain guided their choices and how much adhering to it promoted individual and family mobility. This long-term analysis expands the immigrant bargain concept to recognize the reciprocity between parents and children as they move through individual and family life courses and to assess its role in promoting intergenerational mobility.

This analysis also expands the concept by describing the obligations that this bargain imposes not only on children but also on parents and how lacking legal status undermines their ability to keep the bargain fully, sometimes causing family conflict. To keep the immigrant bargain, children honor and redeem their parents' sacrifice in concrete ways, including by being a good person, finishing school (college, if possible), getting a good job, and helping their siblings and parents, both financially and in their advice on negotiating American life. Parents are obliged to love their children and work hard to raise them, as parents in this study did, and to give them the platform from which to launch themselves successfully into early adulthood.

The launch of older U.S. citizen children into early adulthood in all-documented and Category Changer families plays a key role in keeping a family's intergenerational bargain and promoting family mobility. By helping their parents and younger siblings negotiate complicated American institutions and contributing financially with incomes that are usually much higher than their parents', early adults make their family more economically secure and give their younger siblings the advantages of growing up in a wealthier family. Early adult older siblings can thus keep the immigrant bargain in two directions — upwardly with their parents and downwardly with their younger siblings.

Conversely, long-term undocumented status undermines the ability of older siblings *and* their parents to keep the immigrant bargain and promote family mobility. Undocumented older siblings cannot keep the immigrant bargain fully in either direction because they are more likely to end their schooling before finishing college and to earn less working in the immigrant economy rather than the mainstream economy, thus contributing less to the family income. Unmet expectations can lead to family conflict when older undocumented siblings keep one part of the bargain but not others—for example, by quitting high school to work full-time, thus helping the family financially, but not finishing high school or college, or finishing college but still earning very little money. For their part, undocumented parents often cannot give their undocumented older children a path to legal status to enable them to launch into a mainstream early adulthood, like their U.S.-born peers, but parents may still emotionally expect or demand that their children keep all parts of that bargain, especially parents who have lost or sacrificed a lot to help their children.[13] Parents and older children can do everything in their power to keep the immigrant family bargain, but legal status prevents them from doing so, thus inhibiting mobility and creating a familial legal status disadvantage that can persist across generations.[14]

It merits note that the relatively easier path to intergenerational mobility in all-documented or Category Changer families is not the "glass floor" by which wealthier families insulate their lower-achieving children from downward mobility.[15] The upwardly mobile path open to these families is fairly narrow, and it is easy to get knocked off it. Still, this path is better than undocumented older children's early transition to full or established adulthood, which shows legal status as a key mechanism by which intergenerational legal status disadvantage is transmitted.

Mexicans also face more challenges to mobility than other immigrant groups. As in many immigrant groups in New York, most Mexican and Chinese early adults continue to live with their family, owing to New York's real estate and rental prices and parental pressure to stay home until married.[16] However, Mexicans in New York have higher rates of undocumented status than Chinese do: 54 percent of Chinese immigrants were naturalized U.S. citizens in 2013, versus 6 percent of Mexican immigrants in 2009.[17] Mexicans have also had fewer community organizations promoting education and fewer high-income donors to such organizations.[18] Hence, mobility-promoting intrafamily dynamics are less often interrupted by a lack of legal status in Chinese than in Mexican families. Moreover, with access to the extensive Chinese social infrastructure promoting education (programs for homework help, classical music lessons, test prep courses), Chinese teens with poorly educated or undocumented parents face less disadvantage than their Mexican peers. Although a Chinese dishwasher will not know how to get his child into a good New York City high school, the director of that child's after-school program and other parents will know and they will help.[19] Middle-class and wealthier Chinese parents derive honor from contributing financially to such programs, while their Mexican counterparts (with some exceptions) do not, for the most part, support or even know about such institutions.[20] Because Mexicans have less organizational support, older

Mexican siblings are even more important to the mobility chances of their younger siblings. If older siblings are undocumented, younger U.S. citizen siblings lose that crucial support, and there are not as many after-school institutions available to them to provide mobility-promoting knowledge as there are for their Chinese counterparts.

The analysis in this chapter compares the intrafamily dynamics of U.S. citizen and lawful permanent resident participants who mostly kept the immigrant bargain with those of long-term undocumented Americans who kept the bargain up until their undocumented status derailed their mobility. While all members of all-documented and Category Changer families profiled here felt like both sides had kept the immigrant bargain and the family had benefited from it, those in all-undocumented and mixed-status families with older undocumented children experienced variations of an unkept family bargain, despite doing their best to keep it, and they did not concretely benefit as much as their documented counterparts. These variations include the "broken" family bargain, the "grim realist" family bargain, the "faith in America–magical thinking" family bargain, and the "honoring academic achievement" family bargain. Some 43 percent (nine of twenty-one) of the undocumented parents of undocumented NYCOMPers expressed faith in America as a land of opportunity for their undocumented children. Similarly, 35 percent (nine of twenty-six) revealed family conflict stemming from the inability of undocumented parents and adult children to keep the immigrant bargain fully, or from the latter's status as the undocumented child in a mixed-status family.[21]

A Kept Immigrant Bargain and Mobility in An All-Documented Family: Vicky and Her Family

Vicky Fuerte and her two sisters were born in Brooklyn. After her parents legalized via IRCA, legal status was removed as an obstacle to their family's mobility. The Fuertes were an all-documented family whose younger members—Vicky's youngest sister, Lily, and her niece, Susanna—had seen sharp rises in income as Vicky and her older sister, Leeta, became adults who worked and could pass along their understanding of American schools and institutions. After first interviewing and shadowing Vicky in school at age eighteen, I periodically reinterviewed her, including at age twenty-seven and again in her thirties. Throughout the study, I periodically made ethnographic visits (meeting to talk or at events).[22] We return to Vicky's case in other chapters to analyze other issues. Over the years, Vicky and I have become friends.

Vicky's father had three years of school in Mexico and her mother had six years. They worked in restaurants and factories in New York, never earning much. When Vicky and her sister were young, their mother often did not work, so her father's $15,000 per year was their only income. This yielded a $3,000 per person per year income, or $8.22 per person per day, to cover the cost of living in New York City. When Vicky's mother worked, the extra income helped, but she earned less than her husband. Vicky's sister Leeta was five years older than Vicky, and Lily was eight years younger. In her senior year of college, Leeta had a daughter, Susanna, bringing the household to six people.

In early adulthood, Vicky and Leeta were able to dramatically boost the family's fortunes and mobility and help Lily and Susanna. The two older sisters both graduated from college and then got middle-class jobs while living at home and paying family expenses. With their contributions, the household's finances scarcely resembled the want of the two older daughters' teenage years. Their father's income had risen to $30,000, while her mother made $19,000. Leeta earned $60,000 in sales, and Vicky earned $85,000 as a paralegal. The combined family household income of four workers for six people was $194,000 (over $88 per day per person nearly ten times higher than when they were in high school).

Vicky's guidance in helping them navigate New York's public school system was especially helpful to Lily and Susanna. The valedictorian of her elementary school, Vicky had fought her parents to go to the academically stronger "Black" middle school rather than the local middle school that Leeta had attended. Now, having witnessed Vicky's later success, their parents forced Lily to go to the same Black middle school, though she had wanted to go to Leeta's local middle school.

The family's huge increase in disposable income enabled their parents to give Lily and Susanna advantages that had been impossible for Vicky and Leeta, such as paying for the twenty-year-old college student Lily's credit cards and cell phone. They also helped pay for Susanna's tutoring for Advanced Placement (AP) classes, prompting Leeta to complain: "If I had tutoring when I was young . . . [I] would have done better." Her mother responded: "We really didn't know. We thought that you just going to school was okay." Their parents also started taking Lily to and from school to prevent her from cutting classes. Leeta had cut high school a lot, but her parents did not know because they were at work.

Keeping the immigrant bargain, in its main elements, had dramatically improved the Fuerte family's mobility, moving them in one generation from far below the poverty line to firmly middle-class. The older daughters graduated from college, lived at home, and enhanced the family's income and ability to negotiate American schools and institutions, helping the younger children. By legalizing via IRCA and having U.S.-born children, the Fuertes family was spared the obstacles facing all-undocumented and mixed-status families.

A Well-Kept Immigrant Bargain for Teenage Category Changers: Carla, Simone, and Their Family

Carla and her older sister Simone were Category Changers. After their parents migrated, Carla and Simone had lived in rural Puebla with their grandparents for several years before reuniting in New York, at ages six and eight, with their parents, whom they did not recognize. Because their parents had obtained lawful permanent residency through IRCA, Carla and Simone knew that they would get legal status too—as they did, at ages thirteen and fifteen.

Although it took seven years, the girls' certainty of getting legal status kept them working hard in school, confident that academic success would bring rewards in adult life. Their right to attend public schools through twelfth grade despite being undocumented was protected by the 1983 U.S. Supreme Court decision *Plyler v. Doe*, which held that American notions of fairness could not hold a child brought to the United States legally accountable for their later undocumented presence, and that the United States had an interest in protecting the future of all children. New York's public schools treated Carla and Simone like any other bright students. Finally, knowing that their parents could secure them legal status, thus keeping the immigrant bargain, helped the daughters overcome the challenges of suddenly living with parents they did not know. Because they got legal status, Carla's and Simone's lives were essentially akin to those of high-achieving U.S. citizen study participants.

In every interview over two decades, Carla and Simone expressed a strong desire to keep the immigrant bargain. Describing herself as "obedient" to their parents, Simone in her midtwenties felt that she had honored them by graduating from college and getting a good job. For teenage Carla, learning of her mother's harsh childhood made her feel that achieving success was her "job"—the role she could take on to make that sacrifice worth it.[23] The parents, whom I have known for two decades, repeatedly told me how happy they were at their children's opportunities and success in the United States. Carla and Simone both excelled in high school and got college scholarships. All sides kept the immigrant family bargain well, and the family gained from it. Moreover, Carla and Simone were counterfactual thinkers who made their school choices explicitly considering how their choice would honor their parents' sacrifice and keep the bargain with them. Such thinking reflected their internalization of their parents' voices in ways consistent with the Mexican concept of *educación* (being well educated and adopting one's parents values and customs) and creating their own coherent life narratives as upwardly mobile success stories.[24]

Their little brother Kyle (fourteen years younger than Carla) had benefited from his older sisters' capacity to navigate American institutions. When their landlord tripled their rent, Carla (then in college) took the landlord to court, stopped their eviction, and found another apartment; then she arranged a mortgage that enabled the family to buy a house in a more suburban area, where they all still lived together a decade later.[25] This move put Kyle in a more competitive public school district than the one in Brooklyn—as indicated, the sisters said, when Kyle, a straight A student in Brooklyn, needed extra help in his new, better-funded school, which was mostly White, "calmer," and more suburban and had a higher teacher-student ratio. Kyle went on to graduate from high school, become a recruited athlete in college, and land a well-paying job after college.

For Carla and Simone, helping Kyle was another way of keeping the immigrant bargain, despite the complex dynamics involved. Carla's mother, knowing that her daughters could deal with American institutions better than she could, welcomed their help with Kyle and with household logistics. But Carla felt that her mother often relied on them too much, blurring the lines of responsibility and authority between older siblings and parents. This feeling came through in the twenty-six-year-old's exasperated but humorous description (noted earlier) of Kyle as having "three mothers." She elaborated: "Kyle has three mothers. . . . Half the time he just has two mothers, because my mother just assumes that we are going to take care of it. . . . That kinda annoys [me]. . . . I'm always the one [to say]: 'He's not my kid at the end of the day, he's yours.'"

Carla also described the uneasy imbalance between their parents' authority and the reality that she and her sister knew the steps that Kyle needed to take to succeed and how to take them.

> For them, it's that conflict. . . . "I'm the parent" . . . which I understand—they're the authority figure. . . . [But] they know that we know more. . . . We have to tell them what has to be done—not because we are trying to be the authority figure, but because we know that in the long run that's going to be the best thing . . . for Kyle . . . going to different camps or applying early for scholarships and having her [their mother] . . . submit the paperwork. . . . [It] is a reversal of roles.

The financial fortunes of Carla's family rose dramatically when the sisters became adults. When they were in high school, their parents together made just under $27,000 annually—$5,400 per person, or just under $15 per person per day. After Simone started working part-time in high school—earning $12 an hour at her first job, she made more than her parents—their family income increased to over $38,000 ($7,600 per person, or just under $21 per day per person). At time 2, when Carla and Simone had graduated from college and were living at home, the family's income had jumped to $140,000 a year, or $28,000 per person ($77 per day per person per year). The family income fell when Simone married, had a child, and got her own house in the neighborhood, but she had waited to move out until her sister could help more financially. The family enacted a collective mobility strategy that supported a larger Mexican culture of mobility in New York.

Carla's family shows some processes by which Category Changer families who all keep the immigrant bargain experience rising income and mobility. As mentioned earlier, older children grow up in younger and usually poorer families, while their younger siblings grow up in older and often richer families. Carla and Simone grew up in a house living on under $15 per day per person, but Kyle, the youngest child, grew up in an older family living on $77 per day per person. Kyle's older sisters knew the supports that would help him succeed, helped the family buy a house in a stronger school district, and helped pay for it all. Carla and Simone continued to keep the immigrant bargain into established adulthood, even with families of their own, and the whole family has benefited. Despite a few rough edges, the family members really liked each other, and all felt that they had done their part and done it well.

Keeping the immigrant bargain practically guaranteed upward mobility for those with legal status in this study: all the NYCOMP all-documented and Category Changer families who kept the immigrant bargain were upwardly mobile. This positive story contrasts starkly with the story of undocumented families, to whose varying ways of managing their blocked immigrant bargain we now turn.

Disruption of the Immigrant Bargain in Undocumented Families: Eddie and His Family

Eddie's promising academic career and work future were derailed by his lack of legal status. This derailing was triply cruel, because it later disqualified him in 2012 for immediate eligibility for DACA, which required a high school diploma, and because his original road to legal status had ended when his U.S. citizen grandfather died before Eddie got his visa. At the time when I had nearly finished writing this book, Eddie was almost forty and still undocumented.

As noted earlier, Eddie described himself as "a decent, good boy" who made no trouble and always did his schoolwork. He laughingly described how he would stop playing stickball by enthusiastically saying, "Let's go do our homework!," exhorting his friends to join him. He did so well in middle school that his teachers guided him away from his zoned high school, which students called "Jungle High," and into the new "Mundo Studies High," which offered more opportunity. His mother feared the Mexican gangs at Jungle High and agreed to the change. She knew little of the schools and trusted Eddie to make good choices. He picked high-achieving friends at Mundo Studies High (mainly "Afro-Americans"), did well in his studies, and was liked by teachers. Middle school friends had invited him to join the New York Atzlan gang, but he declined, telling me he had wanted to "respect . . . my mom." The gang members knew Eddie and did not hassle him. His great grades made him an example in his own and his extended family, as his Brooklyn-born cousin George confirmed to me.

During his freshman year, Eddie realized that his mother needed help. Other students were teasing him and his sisters about their worn, nonbrand clothes and sneakers. They never had money for extras and could pay only for food, rent, and bills. They were very poor. When Eddie was in high school (time 1), his mother made $350 per week, working fourteen hours a day, six days a week, or about $18,000 a year, at $4.66 per hour—well below New York's then minimum wage of $5.15 per hour.[26] This $18,000 translated to $4,500 per year per person for the family to live on in New York City. To understand how hard this was, consider that her $350 per week income yielded $1,400 per month (less when her hours were cut); after paying $900 for rent, they had $500 per month, or $125 per week, for four people. In other words, each member of the family had $31 per week, or *$4.43 per person per day*, for everything else—transport, food, clothes, books, notebooks, telephone, bills—in New York City.

To help, Eddie started working twenty-eight hours a week in eighth grade, and he would continue working until dropping out of school. He made $100 a week, or $4.28 an hour, and his earnings strongly increased the family's disposable income. When he quit school at age fifteen to work seventy hours for $300 a week, Eddie nearly doubled their household income, which jumped to $33,000 a year for four people, or $8,250 per person (about average for undocumented study partici- pant families).

When I last spoke to Eddie, he was thirty years old and despondent about his prospects. He had given up plans to return to school. The longer-term increase in family income seen in Vicky Fuerte's all- documented family and in Carla and Simone's Category Changer family had not occurred in Eddie's family, despite his excellent aca- demic record before dropping out.

Eddie had experienced the existential crisis extensively analyzed by Roberto Gonzales in his book *Lives in Limbo*: he realized that his lack of status meant that there would be no later return on his educational effort.[27] He did not see how finishing high school and going to college made sense if he lacked legal status:

> I always used to . . . lay down on my bed and start thinking. If I continued school, I graduated and got my diploma. But what happens after? I mean, I'm not a resident in this country. . . . What is that diploma gonna achieve me? What is it gonna give back to me if I don't have the papers? If you don't have a green card in this country, you can't work, even [if] you're a professional . . . they still won't give you that spot. . . . That's why I leaned over more into working. It makes no sense for me to finish school . . . having a diploma, then after going to ask for a job, and for the man not to give it to me.

Eddie spoke like an economist outlining the opportunity cost of his education, which he could not justify because his undocumented status would limit the returns on his investment. He told me that he could not justify forgoing income he could earn as a sixteen-year-old because his mother needed help then. And he could not imagine spending money on college only to end up in the same kind of job he had as a high school dropout.

Eddie quit school, but did not tell his mother, fearing her anger, which only grew worse after she found out when his math teacher visited their house to talk to her and to beg Eddie to reconsider. His mother "was really disappointed. . . . She started crying. . . . 'Cause my mom didn't agree with me." Not only was dropping out heartbreaking for Eddie's mother, but it also damaged his position of social honor in the family and became an issue of discussion in their extended family. His cousin George told him: "Dropping out is not the right thing to do!" Eddie told me: "I disappointed . . . half my family, because my sisters used to look up at me like, 'Oh, this guy is really going to do it!' But I had to do it. . . . I started helping out with the rent . . . $200 [of $900], plus the bills."

I asked Eddie what his mother had said when she finally spoke to him a year after he dropped out. He described their reconciliation this way:

> She came over to me and she was like, "I got to talk to you." . . . I was thinking . . . she is going to tell me to go back to school. . . . She came over and patted my shoulder and she said, "I'm sorry for disagreeing with you." And I am like, "You don't have to say sorry to me. It's supposed to be the other way around—for me to tell you that I'm sorry that I disappointed you. . . . But let's keep on. . . . I am helping you out."

His mother responded: "Yeah, I know, but what about you? . . . Don't just think of me, think of yourself. What are you going to do? You keep on cleaning. . . . You don't want to keep on doing that. I know you like to work, you like to earn money. . . . But think about the school." She thanked him for helping her, but she remained worried about his future and saw school as his only way forward.

Eddie was twenty-four years old during this interview. He brought up the subject of college, telling me, "I have been thinking about it, and I really want to do it." I offered help finding a way, but he did not follow through. I got back in touch when Eddie was twenty-eight, after President Obama had created DACA. I then led a service and research project through which I tried to connect him to free New York City DACA services. As noted earlier, Eddie feared giving the government his information and never applied for DACA. His cousin George told me that, in his midthirties, Eddie was unmarried, lived with his mother, and worked in the same jobs, making only minor gains in income.

Keeping the immigrant bargain was a key driver of upward mobility for all-documented and Category Changer families, and it should have helped someone as smart, hardworking, and committed to the immigrant bargain as Eddie. But undocumented status undermined both sides of the immigrant bargain for Eddie's family. His mother was furious when he broke the immigrant bargain by dropping out of school, after years of being a good son and thriving academically. Her sacrifices — which loomed even larger with the loss of her husband — had not been redeemed through Eddie, despite his hard work.[28] But for Eddie, his lack of legal status had discredited his mother's internalized voice; in contrast, the same internalization of their parents' voices had helped in the mobility-promoting choices made by Carla and Simone. Although Eddie had previously kept one part of the bargain by declining the invitation to join a gang, he did not listen to her demand that he continue school into college because his sober assessment pointed away from her imagined future for him. Moreover, Eddie's mother did not see (or could not discuss) the fact that Eddie was trying to keep another element of the immigrant bargain by dropping out of school and by concretely helping her and his younger siblings through his income.

Cruelly, after dropping out, Eddie was no longer considered a role model by his extended family. His cousin George sometimes told me that Eddie's family "did not value education" as his did, not recognizing how his legal status and Eddie's lack of it had affected their lives and decisions.

Though Eddie never pointed this out, his mother's legal status also prevented her from keeping her side of the immigrant bargain. She had done everything she could to help her children, but she could not provide the legal status platform that would enable Eddie to ride his academic achievement into college and a better adult life. As she had rightly feared, dropping out of school harmed his long-term life chances and precluded the benefits that would have come to his sisters by growing up in a house with a higher-income, college-educated sibling, especially if they had had legal status.

Finally, their undocumented status denied to Eddie and his mother the pleasure and honor of fully keeping their respective sides of the immigrant bargain. Eddie, who had been a role model for his extended family, instead became a cautionary tale when he rationally dropped out of school to help his mother.

That Eddie's math teacher tried to help underlines that exclusionary projects in American life can trump inclusionary ones and points to legal status rather than racial discrimination or cultural traits as the key factor in the derailed mobility of students in Eddie's position. Moreover, though the teacher told Eddie that he was smart enough for college, he never mentioned that Eddie, despite being undocumented, could have attended CUNY at in-state tuition rates. Supporting the educational careers of undocumented students in this way had become law in New York State by that time.[29] (I supported this effort by picketing at CUNY's central administration building and giving an expert deposition in a lawsuit against CUNY.) It appears that this dedicated public school teacher did not know about CUNY's in-state tuition policy for undocumented graduates of New York high schools. When I asked Eddie if knowing he could go to CUNY at in-state rates would have mattered, he said: "Of course. . . . 'Cause at that point . . . I used to think twelfth grade was the end." I asked if his undocumented status was responsible for this assumption. "Yeah, my other friends used to be like, ' . . . After this I want to go off to college and study. . . . ' For me, no."

This case shows the inconsistency between American immigration policy and key American values. America proclaims not only that hard work in school should be rewarded with good jobs and the chance to offer a better life to one's children, but also that the family, as such, should be valued and strengthened. But current U.S. policies undermine the moral economy of the family and its internal bargain, disrupting the intrafamily mechanisms that promote family upward mobility. As all-documented and Category Changer families gain in income and knowledge of American institutions over time, they can offer their children more opportunities, while all-undocumented and mixed-status families with older undocumented children cannot.

Eddie's undocumented status became a "master status."[30] His excludability and deportability, owing to his legal status, trumped the inclusionary intentions of his good New York City public school teacher (and later of a CUNY professor, me), whose professional mission was to help all his students.[31]

Eddie's legal status created an impossible choice for him between helping his mother and sisters, on the one hand, and continuing in school, on the other. Over the last three decades, I have had many conversations like the ones I had with Eddie. What is most shameful is that undocumented youth are right to not believe that America will give them a chance to legalize. For them, it is logical to drop out of school, because lacking legal status will limit their life chances no matter how much they study. As a dad working with these young people, I have found it dizzying to see how families like Eddie's learn that America is a land of opportunity, but not for them, while also celebrating the confirmation of the American dream reflected in the upward mobility of families like Carla and Simone's.

Grim Realist Parents and an "Accidental" Bargain in an All-Undocumented Family: Xavier and His Family

Xavier's dogged pursuit of education was even more impressive given the "grim realist" immigrant bargain his parents seemed resigned to offer their children. Xavier had come to the United States as a five-year-old, the youngest of three undocumented boys living with their undocumented parents—an all-undocumented family. Xavier's brothers quickly went to full-time work as teens. One married, had a child, and moved out by age twenty. The other brother, Lorencio, stayed home.

In one interview, Xavier remembered that his family was too poor to buy new clothes, and they never ate at a restaurant. The day Lorencio got his first paycheck, he brought Xavier to the local bodega and told him to pick out candy.

He took only two small candies costing 25 cents.

His brother laughed, urging Xavier: "'Go pick more!' I could not believe it," Xavier said. Through long-term work in construction, Lorencio gradually earned a decent living. When he married, his new family lived with his parents, to keep them afloat economically.

The family budget and living conditions when Xavier was in grade school reflected their poverty. When Xavier's family first arrived in the United States, all of them lived in one room they rented for $400 per month. Xavier's father earned $4.25 an hour working twelve hours a day, six days a week, for a total of $350 per week. The family had about $1,000 after rent for all five of them, or $200 per person each month ($6.67 per day per person). They saved money and moved into an apartment with a bedroom for which they paid $700 per month—half the father's income. Then Lorencio started working, earning $3.75 an hour cleaning up construction sites; working fifty hours a week, he made $175 per week. Their combined incomes moved the family out of absolute poverty, but those incomes were still limited, due to their legal status.

Unfortunately, some of the family's disposable income was literally consumed by Xavier's father, who often drank too much. His mother began working, making about $250 per week, boosting the family income to almost $800 per week, or nearly $3,200 per month. (By then, Xavier's other brother was living elsewhere with his own family.) They paid a babysitter $100 per week to take care of Xavier before and after school, to accommodate his parents' early work hours. His father started work at 6:00 AM and commuted an hour each way; his mother started at 7:00 AM, commuting one and a half hours each way. After they found out that the babysitter was giving Xavier's food to her own children instead of Xavier, Lorencio started dropping Xavier off at school. In first grade, Xavier walked himself home and did his homework alone.

At age twenty-eight (time 2), Xavier still lived with his parents and Lorencio's family, whose fortunes had improved somewhat. Lorencio's pay had increased steadily. He went from earning $3.75 an hour to $12 an hour in four years because, he said proudly, "I did the work of two people." In 2017, he was a supervisor at the same construction company, making $22 an hour, or $40,000 per year. He was still undocumented.

Xavier, also still undocumented, had nevertheless earned both a bachelor's degree and a master's degree and was now making $28,000 per year as a consultant. Their father was sick, so both parents had gone to part-time work (their mother cared for their father when he was not working), decreasing their joint income to $19,000 per year. The total household income was $87,000, with four working adults and eight members (Lorencio had three children), or $10,875 per person per year (just under $30 per day per person). They shared the $1,500 monthly rent (Lorencio paying $600, Xavier $800, and their parents $100) on a four-bedroom apartment in an outer-borough neighborhood. This was a far cry from the $6.67 per day per person they lived on when they first arrived in New York, but it still was not enough to live on in the city. Xavier had kept the immigrant bargain as fully as he could, and he had certainly helped increase the family's income. But Xavier felt keenly that he could not help his family as much as he wanted to; he was especially concerned that he could not earn more income to express his gratitude to his family for their years of sacrifice for him and his education. How much lacking legal status had depressed Xavier's earnings became clear when his income jumped after he got DACA (as we will see in chapter 5).

Xavier described his enrollment in college as "unlikely" and himself as "an outlier" who went despite his parents' expectation that, like his brothers, he would work full-time after high school. His parents "had no illusions" about what the future offered their undocumented children. Xavier said of his mother: "Just as her parents prepared her to go work as a [live-in] nanny at age twelve in Puebla . . . she prepared my brothers to work." She hinted to Xavier when he was in high school that he should think about working, saying that "work is good." She liked "*mi trabajito*" (my little work), and asked him: Wouldn't it "be nice to have a job . . . to have your own bit of money (*su dinerito*)?" Xavier stayed silent, but in his head he repeated: "*I want to go to college*, . . . [though] I had no idea how it was possible." Despite not knowing how he would be able to go, Xavier applied to college through a special program at his "awful" high school, which, like others in this study, he called "Jungle High."

Xavier laughed when I asked about the immigrant bargain, saying that his was an "accidental bargain." Having three years of education each and being undocumented, his parents, thinking that college was impossible for him, encouraged him to work. When Xavier was accepted at a college, they also did not realize that he would *live* there: "They were in shock when they dropped me off. . . . My mom cried. They were like: 'What is going on?'" Xavier's brothers sent him money for books and food. He graduated with a record that earned him a scholarship in graduate school, where he studied public health and a medical specialization.

Xavier's parents had offered him a "grim realist" immigrant bargain: *Like us, you can work at your little job, and together we can make enough to survive.* Xavier escaped this grim realist bargain only with the help of his brothers and very supportive teachers and counselors at Jungle High. He was lucky to have teachers who strongly encouraged and helped him in concrete ways. It was their voices, rather than his parents' "grim bargain" voices, that he internalized as he made plans to leave his teenage life and go to college.

When Xavier, then in his midthirties, read this chapter, he said that it portrayed his story well, but he also offered a few caveats. First, he saw his mother's encouragement to work as her attempt to "protect me against disappointment." She always told her children to attend to their jobs (*cuiden su trabajo*) because "we are not from here," a fact that ruled out college, she thought. His mother believed that it was the same in the United States as in Mexico: either parents paid for college or you did not go. Second, as a grown man, Xavier had more sympathy for his father than he had had in his twenties. He realized that his dad had used drinking to cope. Things were "much harder than he had thought" they would be in America. His father drank less now, making the family happier. Xavier's reflections illustrate a strength of long-term research: here we were able to capture changes in intrafamily relationships and the meanings attached to prior events.

Xavier reiterated his admiration for his parents' hard work, despite their health problems and his constant worry about their legal status: "Both my parents have this incredibly hard work ethic. I admire this. . . . My dad is still working—he is seventy. . . . My fear about them has gotten worse since Trump."

A Magical Thinking Bargain Based on the
American Dream in a Mixed-Status Family:
Celenia and Her Family

Celenia's family lived by their belief in the American dream. In their mixed-status family, Celenia and her parents were undocumented, while her two younger siblings were U.S.-born. Celenia had always known that her family had overstayed their visas, but she had not realized that their lack of legal status would affect her until her senior year in high school, when she and other students were discussing their future plans. Her grim realization that her legal status would block her from working legally coexisted with her family's strong belief in America as a fair country and a place of opportunity.

I have heard this kind of magical thinking from many parents who told their children to be good students and good people, to avoid trouble and work hard, because they could get a scholarship to college and even legalize their status that way. They would point to other Mexican students who had visas, not knowing that these students had arrived in the country with visas. These parents echoed the broadly held American belief in hard work as the key to attaining better adult lives. I do not use the term "magical thinking" to connote delusional thinking (such as that of a grief-stricken person waiting for the return of a dead loved one).[32] Rather, magical thinking here refers to parents' belief that America will treat their child fairly if they keep their side of the bargain with America, despite evidence to the contrary. That the parents' beliefs end up conflicting with their children's early adult reality (hence making them "magical thinking") indicts America's immigration policies, not the parents.

Celenia told me about her family's magical thinking during her senior year of high school:

> *Celenia:* It wasn't until senior year that I realized that I was undocumented. I knew all my life we overstayed our visa. . . . We had . . . no status per se, but I didn't know how it would really affect me *en carne propia*[33] . . . [or] if my mom knew or not. She would just say: "Do good in school and go to college, don't worry." . . . It's the notion that there are lots of grants and fellowships . . . that they will give you citizenship and give you everything if you're a topnotch student. . . . My mom

was always convinced that some way, somehow, miraculously, that would happen.

Author: She thought that . . . you would get . . . legalized 'cause you were a smart student?

Celenia: Yeah, something like that.

Author: She didn't have a specific plan; she just had a general belief. Did you talk to her about that a lot?

Celenia: Not really, because I believed her. I thought it could happen. She said a lot of students would come [with visas] from Mexico and they get status here. But it's different . . . because they are coming from over there [Mexico]. . . . We're some other category. We were here already. We didn't talk about it that much. She was like, just, "Go to school" . . . no matter what.

Author: They thought that this would just fix all the problems. Did you believe that would happen?

Celenia: I did.

Celenia's belief in her mother's reassurances revealed a belief that America is a fair country that rewards effort by young people and their families. I have often heard parents express this belief over three decades. This thinking was borne out within New York's schools, which placed Celenia in a gifted-and-talented program in middle school and an honors program in high school. Teachers supported her, and she had strong, long-term mentors.

But while her high-achieving peers were applying to competitive colleges, Celenia applied only to CUNY community colleges because she feared that filling out federal financial aid forms (FAFSA)—then required by CUNY senior colleges—would expose her family's status. (The forms asks for Social Security numbers and visa status, which many college counselors feared could "out" people's legal status. CUNY did not require that these parts of the form be filled in, but since the instructions did not say that, her fear was rational. Many school guidance counselors also believed it would out a family.) The disjuncture between Celenia's grades and her community college plans led friends to ask questions. She told them, "'I don't have papers.' They . . . [were] like 'What does that mean?'" Finally, a teacher, learning of her plans to apply only to community college, helped her apply to a CUNY senior college, from which she graduated with honors, though still undocumented and unable to work legally.

The strong belief shared by Celenia and her mother in a fair America promoted her educational achievement. Most undocumented students who persist despite knowing their status stubbornly believe that things will get better. Celenia also benefited from the growing Dreamer movement, which she joined in college. Such hope not only enabled her to keep trying but also secured her a graduate school scholarship. But her lack of legal status meant that, like Eddie and his mother, neither she nor her parents could fully keep the immigrant bargain, which Celenia would have fully kept had she been a U.S. citizen who could earn more as an early adult college graduate. Thousands of undocumented parents and children, like Celenia and her mother, have believed in an America that is better than our national policies for decades.

Conflict and Honor in the Immigrant Bargain in a Mixed-Status Family: Clara and Her Family

"I wasn't even supposed to be born here!" Clara told me, upset, recounting how her mother had left New York for Mexico, so that Clara's grandmother could help her mother after she gave birth to Clara, the first of her five children. Returning to New York a year later, Clara and her parents became undocumented; Clara's younger siblings would all be born in New York. Clara and her family exemplified the painful immigrant bargain contradictions that undocumented status forces on mixed-status families. Clara was one of many "doubly undocumented children" who felt undocumented within their own family because their parents could give their U.S. citizen children more opportunities, creating an internal status hierarchy in the family reminiscent of Cinderella and her stepsisters.

Clara's family was very committed to education. Her father, who had been valedictorian in his Mexican grade school, purposely worked a job that started at 4:00 AM so that he could be home by 4:00 PM to supervise his children's homework. He spoke more English than their mother and attended every parent-teacher meeting, though he did not always understand everything. (He asked Clara after one parent-teacher meeting if "college" meant *universidad* in Spanish. He had been too embarrassed to ask in front of the teacher.) After their homework got too hard for him to help them with, he sat with his children to make sure they finished it.

Clara said that her father was always supportive. "My dad would see me struggling . . . he's like . . . 'You finished your homework? You having trouble?' I was like, 'Yeah.' He was like, 'I wish I could help.' I was like, 'I know.'" He urged her to ask her teachers or friends for help. Clara's father was very proud of her school record and wanted her to go to college. Moreover, he specifically told Clara that he did not want to spend money on a *quinceañera* (a "sweet fifteen" party) but would rather save it for her college, which was her preference too.

Her father framed his and his wife's relationship with their children using the immigrant bargain, which became complicated by legal status. "They would always tell me . . . stories," Clara said, "and how they struggled. . . . They tell me . . . 'You could do it, Clara! We came here for you . . . to offer you more than what our parents gave us.' And I was like, 'Okay!'" Clara wanted to keep her part of the bargain by succeeding in school.

Intrafamily tension arose the first time Clara was denied an earned opportunity because of her legal status. Clara had a supportive school competition with her best friend Jennifer: "She's Italian. . . . She was quiet, soft-spoken like me. We were both responsible, and disciplined." Jennifer brought Clara an application for city-sponsored summer internships that were open only to academically gifted students. They would commute together, Jennifer said. Clara happily brought the form home, but when she asked what a Social Security number was, which was required on the form, her parents went silent. Then they told her that she did not have a Social Security number, and without one she could not apply. She described the scene:

> My dad was like . . . "You can't apply to it." I was like, "Oh, because I don't have this number?" He was like, "Uh huh." And then I saw like this sad look on his face, like he didn't want to show it, but I could see. . . . I just [went] to my room, and I was just thinking: *Why can't I apply?*

When Jennifer asked why she was not applying, Clara lied and said that she had to take care of her siblings that summer, thus hiding her undocumented status. Her lack of status forced her to present a version of herself and her family that brought her shame, an emotion tied to stigma.[34] Rather than presenting herself as the "responsible, disciplined" young woman she was, from a family who prized education, she had to present an image of a girl whose family made her do domestic work even if it cost her well-earned opportunities. This shameful story covered her legal status but made her into a type of Cinderella, a doubly undocumented child whose legal status made her a "less than" member of her own family (though this was not her parents' intention).

Turning down the chance to apply for the city internship was only the first time Clara had to forgo an earned opportunity due to her lack of legal status. She later had to pass up youth summer employment opportunities for which she had been recommended. Instead, she referred her lower-achieving U.S. citizen younger sisters to these jobs. She felt undocumented within her own family because she could not apply for opportunities she had earned but her less-qualified U.S.-born sisters could. A high school teacher asked Clara to apply for a college scholarship, but she did not because doing so required a Social Security number. She told the teacher that she did not want to apply, a lie that protected the secret of her legal status. She investigated and discovered that she also could not apply to study abroad, as her friends did. And without a Social Security number, she could not get internships, and she would graduate from college without such training. When I reinterviewed her years after college, Clara was making $150 to $180 per week as a nanny.

Fully confident and committed to school before losing the chance to do the summer internship in high school, Clara afterwards repeatedly experienced the same existential crisis about education that Eddie did. Why pursue education, she asked herself, if it could not improve her adult life by earning her a good job? She survived several bouts of such despair throughout college to succeed in graduating with good grades. Then she kept working as a nanny for the same professional couple she had worked for since high school.

Angry at her parents for placing her in an impossible position, Clara fought with her mother, asking why she had left New York and why she had brought Clara back. Invoking the immigrant bargain, she said in exasperation, "I don't get it. I've done everything she wanted—we end up fighting. She said I will understand once I have a kid." This answer did not satisfy Clara. Her anger made sense; her mother *did* create the situation. Clara's conflicted account at age twenty shows both her recognition of her mother's good intent and her own anger:

> "Why? Why you brought me here?" . . . We always had this fight. . . . Sometimes I feel bad because I talk to her like that, but she has to understand, *she did it (starts crying)*. She wanted me to have opportunities. To see her sadness, I feel bad. I approached her and told her it's her fault, but it's not her fault. . . . Before, 'cause I was like a teenager, I didn't care. But now I understand her, and I value her. . . . She never gave up on me . . . I never failed her. I'm always on top of schoolwork, always responsible . . . *(crying again, emotionally)*. I'm here. . . . I have to accomplish what I want, which is just to have an education. . . . [I want to] work with other people, help kids—help them go to school.

When Clara's younger U.S. citizen sister became pregnant in high school, Clara felt a double-edged anger: first, that her sister had "wasted" (her word) the chance to finish college and get the kind of good jobs unjustly denied to Clara, and second, that her sister had broken the immigrant family bargain. She related an angry conversation with her sister: "Why follow the same footprints as your parents? . . . Your parents came here to work hard, to offer you a better life . . . to become somebody else . . . and you get pregnant!?" For Clara, her sister's pregnancy wasted not only the chances she herself had been denied but also her parents' sacrifices.

Clara's father was especially careful to modify the immigrant bargain to recognize the limits put on Clara's ability to earn money by her lack of legal status. He ensured that, while she was in college and after she graduated, Clara was honored as a good example — the first in her immediate and extended family to go to college. Her father said that both her worth as a person and the esteem of others would be greater because of her education, despite the limitations she experienced from her lack of legal status: "My father, he always tells me, 'When you have an education, they're going to respect you . . . you know how to defend yourself well, and be articulate. . . . You don't have the job, [but] you already have the education, and they'll respect you.' He sees respect in education, and I see the same thing as him."

Clara's family focused on her achievements in public school, an institution where legal status did not formally limit her, and kept a virtuous silence on her inability to contribute much to the family coffers after her father had paid for college. Such silences are a form of "careful inattention" whereby others ignore another person's stigma as an act of respect. In this case, Clara's family chose to focus on the honor she had earned as a college graduate.[35]

Her parents' emphasis on education (even without economic return) benefited Clara's younger siblings in ways that would have been familiar to all-documented families with educationally successful early adult children. Clara kept helping her younger siblings with homework and educational decisions. She was especially close to her academically successful little brother; then nine years old, he was, in her words, a "mini me." She proudly recounted that he had told her he was "gonna beat" her in school. "He's like, 'I'm going to be a doctor,' and I'm like, 'Yeah, do it.' I'm seeing that he is looking up to me, and I feel happy."

But legal status also intruded into her relationship with her brother, who became confused after hearing news reports on television describing undocumented people as "criminals" whom the country should deport. He turned to her and asked: "'You don't have papers, right?' I'm like, 'No.' . . . He's like, 'Because you are a good person, you are not a criminal. . . . Why do they think we're criminals?'" That a nine-year-old boy who wants to be a doctor and is inspired by his older sister's educational example should have to wrestle with others' view of her as a criminal for being brought to the United States as a baby underlines the antifamily nature of current American immigration policy.

Clara's academic success did not yield the economic boost enjoyed by all-documented and Category Changer families of having an early adult college graduate in the house. The family's finances were stark.

Clara's father made about $16,000 per year, or about $300 per week. Clara's mother did not work when Clara was younger because she cared for five children. Hence, at time 1 in our study, all seven of them lived on her father's earnings, which came to about $6.25 per person per day. At time 2, when Clara was in college, she earned $150 per week babysitting. Unable to work in a job commensurate with her college education, she earned a master's degree and hoped for immigration reform. She also married, but her husband also lacked status. They both worked and improved the family finances. By time 2, Clara's father had worked for twenty years at the same restaurant, becoming an assistant chef, and made $600 per week, or $31,000 per year. Clara's husband made $400 per week, and she still made $150. The family of eight had a total income of $1,150 per week, or about $60,000 per year, which amounted to $7,500 per person per year, or $20 per person per day.

In chapter 5, we will see how Clara's family was "reenabled" to keep the immigrant bargain as a driver of mobility after Clara got DACA. Even having only one person get a work permit through DACA—which functions as partial legal status—helped the immigrant bargain promote family mobility.

Divergent Adult Outcomes and Bequeathals across Generations: Statistical Analysis

The detailed case analyses provided here have described how intrafamily processes—including keeping the immigrant bargain and family learning—and having legal status can lead to greater adult mobility, while lacking legal status blocks such mobility. Here our statistical analyses measure how much the same intrafamily processes and legal status correlate with overall adult outcome categories (High Fliers, College Graduates, Shallow Slopers, and Stuck Muddlers), years of education, and individual and family income at time 2, when it had been nine years since the first interviews and participants were twenty-eight years old on average. To save space, we present only some of our tables and discuss only some correlations. A full explication of the statistical analyses in this chapter may be found in the chapter 2 online statistical appendix.

Table 2.1 (in note) presents direct average correlations (means) between outcome variables at age twenty-eight (time 2)—education and income, and proportion of College Graduate and High Flier cases versus Stuck Muddlers and Shallow Slopers—and the categories of legal status and intrafamily processes analyzed earlier.[36] Study participants who kept the immigrant bargain (by finishing school, starting full-time work, helping their family, and then perhaps marrying and starting a family) got more years of education than those who did not (14.6 years versus 11.3 years), earned more money ($45,543 versus $28,397), and were more likely to be College Graduates or High Fliers (79.6 percent versus 18.2 percent). Respondents who kept the immigrant bargain by living at home through their twenties rather than moving out at that time did better: they had 14.6 versus 11.3 years of school and earned $35,172 versus $22,160 per year; 48.9 percent were College Graduates or High Fliers versus only 4.8 percent who were not.

Study participants with citizenship or legal status at time 2 got 1.1 to 1.4 more years of education, made between $11,000 and $20,000 more annually, and were 44 percent and 53 percent more likely, respectively, to be College Graduates or High Fliers than those lacking status. Moreover, participants whose mothers were U.S. citizens or had visas at time 1 — when respondents were teens or early adults and life trajectories were being set[37] — got one to two more years of education, made $22,000 to $23,000 more per year, and were 39 percent and 60 percent more likely to be College Graduates or High Fliers, respectively, at age twenty-eight, compared to those whose mothers were undocumented at time 1.

Regression equations enable us to estimate how much a change in one variable affects the correlation with an outcome, adjusting or controlling for other variables across a population or data set. Control variables help isolate the net correlation of a key independent variable (the treatment) and an outcome (education). We ran three regressions to assess how keeping the immigrant bargain correlates with years of school, income, and the odds of being a High-Flier or College Graduate, controlling for the mother's time 1 legal status and the participant's time 2 legal status. (We report only key takeaways here. The tables appear in the notes, and we fully explain the analysis and provide statistical tables in this chapter's online statistical appendix.) A first key finding is that keeping the immigrant bargain correlated with 2.1 years more education at time 2, while being undocumented correlated with 1.87 fewer years of education ($p > .000$; see table 2.2 in note).[38] Second, keeping the immigrant bargain correlated with 57.4 percent higher income ($p > .047$) at time 2 without controls, and with 66.9 percent higher income when controlling for legal status ($p > .003$; see table 2.3 in note).[39] Third, keeping the immigrant bargain correlated with a participant being 1.884 times more likely to be a College Graduate or High Flier ($p > .000$) at time 2, which increased to 2.844 times at time 2 and 2.661 times at time 3 when controlling for legal status (see table 2.4 in note).[40] Similarly, controlling for legal status, those keeping the immigrant bargain were 36.4 percent more likely to be College Graduates and High Fliers at time 2 and 39.9 percent more at time 3 ($p > .000$).

Rising Income and Institutional Knowledge
across the Life Course, Diverging by Legal Status

Our data show that the incomes of all-documented and Category Changer families rise more as they age than do those of all-undocumented and mixed-status families with older undocumented siblings (combined into one "undocumented" category for tables in this chapter). All families' incomes should rise as parents gain more work experience. But these dramatic increases in All-Documented and Category Changer families' incomes were driven not by rising parental incomes, but by contributions to family income by their older U.S. citizen children as they entered early adulthood and began working full-time (see table 2.5 in note).[41] Conversely, the incomes of all-undocumented families (including also mixed-status families with undocumented older siblings) rose less over time because their teenage or early adult children who worked full-time were paid as badly as their parents. These families' lower incomes matter both immediately, because they live in poverty, and over the long term, because intergenerational mobility is stymied if younger siblings, nearly all U.S. citizens, benefit less from the movement of older siblings and families along their life courses. Table 2.5 shows overall family incomes, the number of earners and members per household, and income per earner and per member at time 1, time 2, and time 3 for all-undocumented (including mixed-status) families, all-documented families, and Category Changer families. (Here DACA recipients are not considered Category Changers. Most of our time 2 interviews were finished by mid-2012, when DACA began.[42] Incomes are not adjusted for inflation. The table shows changes in reported income across categories of participants within different study times.)

Figures 2.1, 2.2, and 2.3 show in graphic form three striking trends in table 2.5. The first trend is the divergence in growth in income over time for the families of undocumented, U.S.-born, and Category Changer participants. Mean family income at time 1 for families of those still undocumented at time 2 was $38,600 versus $54,515 for U.S.-born participants and $39,704 for Category Changers (including those who were undocumented at time 1 but then legalized their status).[43] At time 2, the family income of participants who were still undocumented was $58,727, compared to family incomes of $84,079 for U.S.-borns and $96,000 for Category Changers. At time 3, undocumented family incomes had risen to a mean of $82,000, while the family income of U.S.-borns rose to $116,144 and Category Changers' family income fell to $78,000. The anomalous fall in Category Changers' family income at time 3 actually reflects upward mobility, as some high-achieving early adult Category Changers had formed their own households by then (as reflected in the

Figure 2.1   Family Earnings from Time 1 to Time 2 to Time 3 for U.S.-Born, Category Changer, and Undocumented Participants

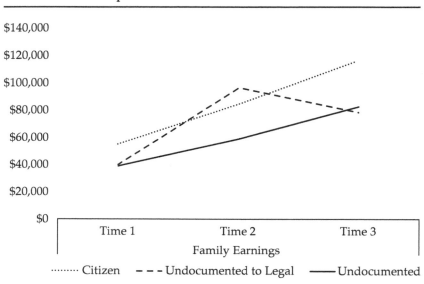

Source: NYCOMP data set. Figure created by Andrés Besserer Rayas.

table: Category Changer households had fewer members and earners at time 3 than households in the other categories).

These increases in average family income reflect larger increases in the average earnings per wage earner in the household from time 1 to time 2 for U.S.-born and Category Changer families compared to undocumented participants' families, as shown in figure 2.2 and table 2.5. These averages hide that most of the increase in income came from the much higher earnings of the adult children of immigrant parents.

Perhaps the most important statistic is the dramatic change in per-person income over time for undocumented households versus U.S.-born and Category Changer households in figure 2.3 and table 2.5. The time 1 per-person difference between undocumented families ($7,840 per household member) is under $4,000 less than for U.S.-borns ($11,446 per member) and only about $1,500 less than for Category Changers ($9,381 per household member).[44] But undocumented families earned $13,995 per member at time 2 versus $28,907 per person in the families of U.S.-born participants and $22,219 per person in Category Changers' families. Differences remained large at time 3, with $21,250 per member for undocumented participants, $31,736 per member for U.S.-borns, and

Figure 2.2   Income per Earner from Time 1 to Time 2 to Time 3 for U.S.-Born, Category Changer, and Undocumented Participants

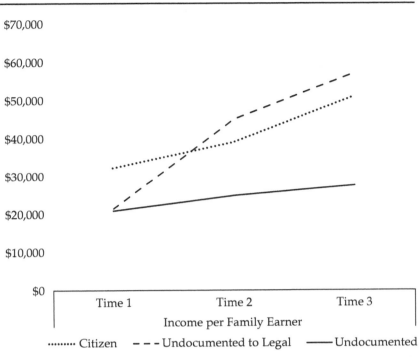

Source: NYCOMP data set. Figure created by Andrés Besserer Rayas.

a whopping $46,875 per member for Category Changers. Undocumented participants' families at time 2 and time 3 had more members (5.4 and 4.8, respectively), and by time 3 they also had more earners (3.0 versus 2.2 for Category Changers and U.S. citizens), but they made less overall and per member.

One curious statistic in table 2.5 merits note. At time 2, the number of earners had stayed about the same for U.S.-born and undocumented participants' families, but the latter had increased in number to 5.4 persons, while the former had fallen to 3.8 members. The increase in the number of undocumented participants' household members usually reflects the birth of a child to the mother or to an early adult child, while the drop in the number of household members for U.S.-borns mostly reflects the departure of early adults to form their own households. The former change would put more economic stress on a family than the latter.

**Figure 2.3   Per Person Income from Time 1 to Time 2 to Time 3
for U.S.-Born, Category Changer, and Undocumented
Participants**

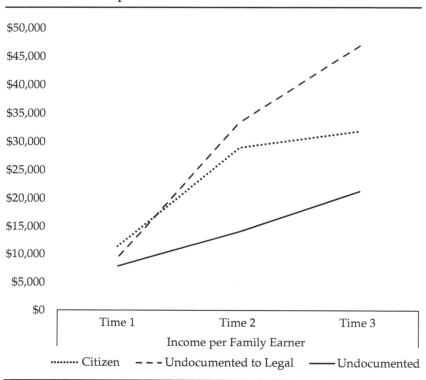

Source: NYCOMP data set. Figure created by Andrés Besserer Rayas.

These statistics show that current immigration policy derails the mobility-promoting mechanism of keeping the immigrant bargain and harms the life chances of both undocumented children and U.S. citizen children in undocumented and mixed-status families, limiting their future contributions to America. They also show concretely how the intergenerational transmission of disadvantage works in family budgets.

Although we cannot extrapolate from this small sample to the larger Mexican-origin population, it is reassuring that NYCOMP mean incomes are close to those in census data. Average NYCOMP family income (including all legal status categories) for time 1 (around 2000) was $49,816, slightly higher than the $44,188 for Mexican-origin persons in the 2000 census. This difference is probably attributable to there being more foreign-born (and likely undocumented) Mexican earners than U.S.-born

Mexican earners in the 2000 census, while the NYCOMP sample was 65 percent U.S.-born and 37 percent foreign-born. NYCOMP's average undocumented family income was $38,600—about $4,000 less than the census figure for the Mexican foreign-born (including documented and undocumented persons)—while Category Changers' income was $46,175, which was about $4,000 more than the census figure for the foreign-born. (Everyone in the undocumented and Category Changer categories was foreign-born.) The 2000 census figure for U.S.-borns of Mexican heritage, $56,250, was just under $2,000 more than the NYCOMP figure of $54,515. I do not seek to "scale up" and generalize to the larger population based on NYCOMP data, but rather to "scale down" by noting how close census data means are to NYCOMP data means.

Conclusion

Keeping the immigrant bargain greatly boosted single-generation upward mobility for U.S.-born and Category Changer NYCOMP participants. The adult study participants who finished college, lived at home, and kept—or even just wanted to keep—the immigrant bargain drove their family's upward income and mobility and made educational and other opportunities available to their younger siblings by sharing their knowledge of educational and other institutions in New York (even though they complained sometimes about having lacked such opportunities themselves when they were younger). Conversely, long-term undocumented participants who did these same "right" things could not enhance their family's well-being as much, nor could they keep key elements of the immigrant bargain. Lacking legal status, they earned less as adults, and because many of them dropped out of school, they could not advance family learning or help their younger siblings as much as their U.S.-born and Category Changer counterparts could for their families.

The success of U.S.-born and Category Changer NYCOMPers' families and the trends in the census data for New York City contrast starkly with the large body of research positing that upward mobility is mostly blocked by racial exclusion and discrimination, even for later-generation U.S. citizens. I seek here to explain these large differences in mobility by analyzing differences in historical eras, institutions, and built environment and how divergent meanings of Mexicanness emerge as upwardly and downwardly mobile youth move from their teens to early and then established adulthood.

Yet even in pro-mobility New York City, legal status is so determinative of life chances that undocumented immigrant children and U.S. citizen children of undocumented immigrants seem to come of age in a different historical era, even though of course they do not. The difference in their outcomes recalls the sociologist Glen Elder's description of the differences between those who became adults during the stagnant years of the Great Depression and those who became adults during World War II and the postwar economic and educational boom.[45] Undocumented youth seem to come of age in a legal status–based Jim Crow America, while their U.S. citizen counterparts live in a more open America that presents them with only the "usual" challenges of being Hispanic.

This reality conflicts with the story that America believes about itself and that immigrants believe about America. Despite progress on civil rights, a country that enacted several post–Civil War constitutional amendments to end invidious distinctions giving some people less human worth than others now has country-sized populations of 11 million undocumented persons and 5 million *children* with undocumented parents. These parents and children work as hard as their U.S.-born counterparts but do not enjoy the same rewards. Eddie's widowed mother worked fourteen-hour days, and their family lived on $4.43 per person per day.

Amazingly, many undocumented immigrant families believe in an America that is better than the one we have created. Many undocumented parents believe that if their children are good students and good people, America, a fair land of opportunity, will allow them to legalize. Perhaps most heartbreaking are the long-term undocumented Americans who know their chances to legalize are bad but who go to college anyway, betting on a better American future. America should honor such hard work and faith in the country by legalizing these Dreamers and their families. America needs upwardly mobile children of immigrants, for example, to care for aging Boomers and later to buy their houses as they downsize as empty-nesters. Allowing undocumented Americans to legalize would be a giant step toward a new intergenerational social contract between Boomers and immigrants.[46] It would also be the right thing to do.

= Chapter 3 =

How Did You Pick That School? Institutional Settings, Counterfactual Choices, Race, and Value Added (or Subtracted) in New York City High Schools

"SHE DOESN'T even use capital letters when she writes! . . . You want me to go to the 'dumb school'!"

Vicky Fuerte invoked her older sister's writing habits in angrily rejecting her parents' attempts to send her to the same local, zoned middle school that her sister and cousins attended rather than to Jackson Middle School, a competitive-entry school where she had been accepted. Her parents feared Jackson because, her mother said, *"hay morenos"* ("there are Blacks"). They wanted her to go to her sister's school, where there were more Mexicans, including her cousins, and where they believed she would be safer. In contrast, Vicky wanted to avoid what she and others in her community called the "Mexican schools" her cousins attended because so many of their students did not do well academically. In long conversations, she repeatedly told me that she feared becoming *"that Mexican girl"* — pausing to emphasize each word, challenging anyone expecting her too to drop out of school, get pregnant, forgo college, and work in a factory. Then an accomplished educational analyst in her thirties, Vicky's eyes still flared in recalling that time. Then she smiled, in recognition that she had not turned into that girl.

> If I would have chosen to be there (Presidents High), I know what would have happened: I wasn't going to be in high school. . . . I was lazy (about) doing work. . . . Once I did the switch . . . I was able to go to school. I had nobody to hang out with, nobody to call.

83

https://doi.org/10.7758/drwz9626.8052

Like Vicky, Chucho Bravo had changed schools as a strategy for educational success that he understood as changing the type of school he attended and his social context. Chucho graduated from a new high school where he had known no one upon entering after transferring out of his zoned high school, Presidents High, where his many gang-member friends had been. He shook his head disbelievingly as he told me how devoted he had been to cutting school with gang friends, and how a burst appendix had changed his life.

Chucho was one of many Mexican Americans raised in New York whose experience was as "the only Mexican," or one of only a few, in their elementary or middle schools in 1990s and early 2000s. Many Mexican parents in New York became lawful permanent residents through IRCA's legalization program and brought their children north. This reunification happened just as the first large cohort of New York–born children of Mexican immigrants were entering adolescence in the 1990s. For the first time, Mexican children were part of a visibly Mexican group in high schools. But new teen migrants faced the hardest challenges and often dropped out of school.

Reveling in this new comradeship, Chucho regularly cut classes with his teen migrant gang friends at Presidents High. But when he was hospitalized after emergency surgery for a burst appendix, his gang friends never visited, while his mother was there every day. Sounding like Saul on the road to Damascus, Chucho realized that his gang friends and habits were derailing his life. He switched schools, vowing to keep to himself, to choose his friends "very carefully" in the new school, and to graduate from high school "for my mom." Although his parents had given their blessing to Chucho's choice to be with his Mexican cousins and friends at his first high school, they later forced his younger sister, Linda, to pick a high school away from her Mexican friends, based on her brother's experience. Linda excelled in her "Black" high school and went on to college and a professional career.[1]

Starting this chapter by discussing what two teenage Mexican Americans *believed* about how their high schools helped or hurt their adult lives—rather than with analysis of structural discrimination or segregated schools, as many analyses would do—makes sense because their beliefs about the links between educational achievement and race (here, being Mexican or Black) guided them into stronger or weaker schools, promoting different adult outcomes.[2] Understanding how these NYCOMP teens chose and sometimes changed high schools matters because attending a zoned high school (versus a nonzoned school) correlated among all NYCOMP participants with earning $12,376 less at age twenty-eight.

This chapter explicates how and why NYCOMP students and parents picked their high schools and sometimes changed high schools, and how these choices sorted them into poorer-quality zoned schools or better-quality nonzoned schools with differential offerings by the school and learning by the students, leading to divergent adult lives. New York City in the late 1990s and early 2000s had geographical zone-based admissions for middle and high schools, as did other places that have been studied in prior research. But New York City's school choice system also enabled students to go outside their zone, often to better nonzoned schools. More planful students who used counterfactual analysis in picking their high school—often considering their older siblings' or friends' poor educational performance, sometimes including their parents in their decision, sometimes not including them—had better adult outcomes. Upwardly mobile study participants experienced much better high school (and sometimes middle school) contexts, and those school experiences led many into college and later into lives and careers that contributed to the emerging Mexican culture of mobility in New York City.

This chapter analyzes only U.S. citizen and Category Changer cases in depth so that legal status will not swamp the impacts of other factors. However, all cases are included in the statistical analyses at the chapter's end, in order to consider how variation in legal status and schools correlates with adult outcomes. Chapter 5 on DACA covers only undocumented cases.

Impacts on Long-Term Mobility of the Interaction of the School Choice System, Mexican Settlement Processes, Participants' Habits, and School Quality

The highly unequal institutional setting of New York City's public high school choice system of the late 1990s and early 2000s interacted with Mexican settlement processes and conjunctural ethnicity to impact adult mobility in three ways.

First, New York City's public school choice system sorted students into unequal schools in ways that contributed to divergent adult outcomes for NYCOMP participants. In their 2008 study, Kasinitz and his colleagues documented the sorting of different racial or ethnic groups into different types of New York City schools with corresponding outcomes, but here we analyze how members of the *same* ethnic group were sorted into and picked different types of schools, affecting their later outcomes.[3] There were three ways to get into New York's high schools in the 1990s and 2000s. The best-known way was testing into an elite public high school, such as Bronx Science. The Chinese second generation disproportionately test into elite schools, but only three NYCOMP participants did.[4] The second and most common way was to enroll at one's zoned school, which had to take all students in its geographic area. Finally, a student could apply to a non-elite but better school outside their zone, or they could enter an honors or other special program in a zoned school. Upwardly mobile NYCOMPers used this last strategy most often, to positive effect.

Wealthier catchment zones in New York City often had better zoned high schools, but our participants did not live in these neighborhoods, so we do not discuss them here. No NYCOMPers were in families or schools offering a glass floor against downward mobility. All zoned schools in our participants' catchment areas were categorized by the city's Board of Education as "marginally performing" or as a "school needing improvement." More than one was closed, reopened, and then closed again during the study; several had a series of principals who served for short periods, sometimes less than a school year.

Overall, attending their zoned high school hurt participants' learning, while attending a nonzoned school helped it. NYCOMPers said that by attending a nonzoned high school (and for some, a nonzoned middle school) or a special program in a zoned school, they learned more because they were studying with stronger students and teachers. Programs offered in these contexts, such as internships or mentoring, taught them how to navigate interviews and how to interact with adults in nonprofits, government agencies, and companies. At nonzoned schools, they could also avoid the difficult dynamics in their zoned schools.

The funneling effect, which concentrates weaker students in zoned schools, had only worsened these dynamics by high school. Stronger students were often advised by middle school teachers to avoid their zoned high school, while weaker students were either not so advised or were unable to get into a better high school. The advantages of better, nonzoned schools echo the positive impacts of magnet schools for María Rendón's "stagnant Dreamers" via similar mechanisms: students are moved out of dangerous schools and into better-resourced ones with more serious students (though magnet school graduates in Rendón's study did not do better as adults, as we discuss in the concluding chapter).[5]

Second, high school (and some middle school) choices were often driven by opposing beliefs regarding whether attending a "Black" school or a "Mexican" school posed more danger to educational achievement. Quite a few Mexican families believed that Black students—and for many, Puerto Rican students as well—posed threats to Mexican students and that going to high school with their Mexican friends would protect them from harassment and an underachieving Black school culture. In other words, they advocated the same "safety in numbers" strategy that guided Vicky's mother. Inaction reinforced this strategy: students who did not apply to other schools went to the zoned school.

What I call here the "reset button" strategy (see chapter 6) and the "avoid Mexicans" strategy were driven by the opposite fear—that moving en masse with Mexican cousins or friends to the local zoned high school would lead to cutting school and facing step-ups. Conversely, by going to a "Black" school where they "knew no one," students could hit the educational reset button, purposefully breaking with middle school friends to avoid being pressured to cut class with them in high school or having to face step-ups from other Mexicans, especially teen migrants. Many academically high-achieving U.S.-born participants chose their high school with not only the "avoid Mexicans" strategy in mind but also the strong link they perceived between Blackness and academic success in their schools, where most high-achievers were Black. (As mentioned in the last chapter, "Black" here refers to the dominant youth culture, which included African Americans, Puerto Ricans, and Dominicans.[6]) Contrary to most prior research, White students are not the key reference group in these calculations, because most New York City schools, and especially NYCOMPers' zoned high schools, have relatively few Whites and are institutional sites of commonplace diversity.[7]

Study participants' association of Mexicanness with low academic achievement reflected several social facts of settlement for, and the conjunctural ethnicity of, Mexicans in New York in the late 1990s and early 2000s. At the time, the city had nearly three times more Mexican teen migrants than U.S.-born Mexican teens, and these teen migrants had high dropout rates.[8] Simultaneously, the first large cohort of U.S.-born Mexican teens were entering New York's high schools, creating conflict over which group "represented" Mexicans.[9] Over the following twenty years, U.S.-born Mexican teens would come to number nearly ten times more than foreign-born Mexican teens in New York City, thus changing which group "represented" Mexicans in the city, creating a demographically different conjuncture that linked Mexicanness with going to college.[10]

Moreover, because Mexicans are more geographically dispersed in New York City than, for example, Dominicans, Mexican elementary and middle school students in the 1990s and early 2000s had often experienced being "the only Mexican," or one of only a few Mexican students, amid a Black and non-Mexican Hispanic majority.[11] For many, high school was the first school they attended with visible numbers of

Mexicans. Their greater numbers led some groups to target them, and Mexican gangs formed to defend themselves. For many, seeing so many Mexican-origin youth funneled into these zoned high schools changed what being Mexican meant in school: from being invisible, Mexicans were then linked to dropping out of school or being, as Vicky feared, "that Mexican girl." Interestingly, like the Irish 150 years earlier, learning anti-Black attitudes was part of the integration experience of many Mexican immigrant parents in New York, but most second-generation children, like Vicky, saw such attitudes as racist, and more often identified with the lives of Black students.[12]

Finally, students' habits of mind and conduct affected their adult lives and trajectories. Doing homework and not cutting school predictably improved later life outcomes but so did planfulness as a teenager. Having *any* counterfactual story about their high school choice (such as explaining why they avoided their zoned school) reflected planful thinking that promoted better outcomes in their adult lives, since they were using their stories as maps for their future.[13] Thus, counterfactual thinking about school choice has become part of a Mexican culture of mobility in New York.

In their counterfactual stories about school choice, U.S.-born participants often stressed that they had chosen the path that would best keep the immigrant bargain with their parents. They had internalized their parents' voices in making their choices and thus were able to construct biographical stories of themselves as good persons with *educación*.[14] However, lacking legal status discredited this inner parental voice. Many undocumented teens saw that their parents' belief that their hard work in school would be rewarded was not borne out: education helped their U.S. citizen peers, but not undocumented students.

Figure 3.1 depicts how study participants understood the interaction of New York City's school choice system with Mexicans' beliefs about race and academic success circa 2000, through processes that they believed affected them in school. The processes they posited as being more causal are shown in boldface. The processes start with the initial choice of a zoned or "Mexican" school versus a nonzoned "non-Mexican" school and then describes the social pressures that they posited could help or hurt their academic success. Counterfactually thinking students feared getting stepped up to or feeling pressured to cut school with Mexican friends in zoned "Mexican" schools, with harmful effects on their academic success, though some also discerned an academically successful path in these zoned schools through participation in honors or other special programs, which would partly insulate them from these pressures. Conversely, in the stronger nonzoned non-Mexican schools, NYCOMPers had some fear of getting stepped up to as the only Mexican

Figure 3.1   The New York City School Choice System and Educational Derailment Mechanisms in Students' Counterfactual Analyses

Factors affecting mobility: going to a zoned or nonzoned school; looking down or back (deescalating or escalating) when stepped up to; cutting or not cutting school (hookies). "Undocumented status" sits in the middle of the figure because it exerts influence in all schools, as undocumented students, having realized that educational hard work now will not be rewarded later with a higher income and better life, are more likely to cut school.

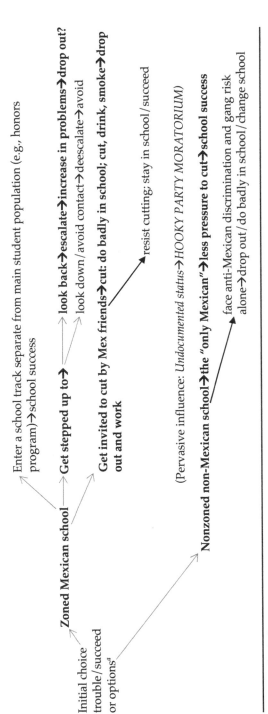

Enter a school track separate from main student population (e.g., honors program)→school success

Get stepped up to → **look back→escalate→increase in problems→drop out?**
look down / avoid contact→deescalate→avoid

Get invited to cut by Mex friends→cut: do badly in school; cut, drink, smoke→drop out and work

resist cutting; stay in school / succeed

(Pervasive influence: *Undocumented status*→*HOOKY PARTY MORATORIUM*)

Nonzoned non-Mexican school→the "only Mexican"→less pressure to cut→school success

face anti-Mexican discrimination and gang risk alone→drop out / do badly in school / change school

Zoned Mexican school

Initial choice trouble / succeed or options[a]

Source: Author's diagram.

Note: The pathways most frequently imagined as happening in zoned Mexican schools or in nonzoned non-Mexican schools are in bold. The figure considers only the effects of step-ups and cutting school, elements of most narratives. Even in zoned Mexican schools, there were two pathways that promoted school success, but these seemed to many participants to be less likely to occur.

[a] These were the most common initial options imagined in counterfactual assessments of which high school would foster or inhibit success.

(or as one of only a few), but they mainly described being free from the pressure to cut school or respond to step-ups by being away from their middle school friends and cousins and saw the benefits of being in school with stronger teachers and students, especially stronger Black students. The free-floating "Influence: Undocumented status → hooky party interregnum" describes undocumented students' disincentives to study hard because their legal status prevented them from converting more education as teens into more income as adults. High school thus became a time to have fun without fear of consequences for bad school performance, since their legal status had already imposed bad consequences by breaking the link between studying hard and better adult life outcomes. That teen migrants were mostly in zoned high schools strengthened the funneling effect and made counterfactually thinking NYCOMPers want to avoid those schools.

Figure 3.1 reflects the conjunctural ethnicity of Mexicans in New York City around this time. Conjunctural ethnicity is a sensitizing concept and framework that analyzes the meaning of ethnicity within local contexts, including local racial hierarchies, school cultures, and police cultures; historical contexts, including how settled and established a group is and how recognized it is by other groups; and the life course of the person or immigrant community.[15] Figure 3.1 shows how the meaning that being Mexican acquires can vary by school context.

Case-Based Counterfactual Analysis: How Beliefs about Race and Education, Habits of Mind and Conduct, and Value Added at School Affect Navigation through High School and Later Adult Outcomes

Counterfactual analysis is "what-if" analysis: What would have happened if a different choice had been made, or if an event had turned out differently? Statistical counterfactual analysis compares presumptively otherwise equal groups—for example, those who enter a drug treatment program and those who do not—and then argues that differences in subsequent drug use are due to the treatment program. The Achilles' heel of such analyses is the assumption that everyone was equal and the treatment program helped them all in the same way. But what if only people who want to stop using drugs go into such programs? Or if the treatment helped some more than others?[16] Statistical counterfactual analysis can tell us only how much a treatment helped; it cannot tell us how it helped.

Counterfactual analysis in historical, psychological, or ethnographic research that develops cases comes in several forms. First are thought experiments: imagining how history, or a life, would have been different had something in the past changed. Second is historically grounded counterfactual analysis: inserting alternative developments "into a real past," tracing that history to the point where it diverged from what was expected, and analyzing how that path then limited which alternative paths were feasible.[17] Although we cannot rerun the past, counterfactual analysis is useful for countries, organizations, and people making decisions with uncertain outcomes. A third type of counterfactual analysis traces sequences of events in comparable cases to discern how and why they diverged from what was expected and from each other. Very similar cases can be theoretical counterfactuals to each other, especially where analysts have deep case knowledge of the cases' contexts and sequences of events.[18] Here I offer three variations of such case-based counterfactual analysis: counterfactual matched proxy cases, intrafamily learning and decision reruns, and living counterfactuals.

To avoid confusion, please note the different uses of the word *counterfactual* to describe NYCOMPers' thinking and my own. First, I use *counterfactual* to describe whether NYCOMPers used what-if thinking in making high school choices (which corresponded with stronger adult outcomes). Second, the word *counterfactual* is used to describe the analytical leverage offered by Category Changer cases, including those here who went from a zoned school to a nonzoned school (and in other chapters, from lacking legal status to having legal status or DACA). Tracing how the lives of individual NYCOMPers changed as they changed categories removes the epistemic worry in other types of counterfactual analysis that unnoted differences between those who change categories and those who do not could have caused the improvement in the former's lives. Finally, I offer three concepts to describe the types of case-based counterfactual analysis done both by NYCOMP families and by me. Coining the "counterfactual matched proxy cases" concept, I traced processes within and across cases to infer what would have happened in one case based on what did happen in another. The "intrafamily learning and decision reruns" concept describes how I saw NYCOMP families rethinking their school choice decisions with their younger children or siblings, based on how the older ones had done. When they revised their thinking, I gave it this label. And last, the "living counterfactuals" is my concept to describe the analytical work that some cases can do, by enabling strong logical inference about how changing schools (or legal status) can affect the lives of Category Changers. However, these living counterfactual cases also thought counterfactually when deciding, for example, to change schools.

Counterfactual Matched Proxies with Parallel
Case Development: Proxies Avoiding or
Experiencing the Same Zoned-School Processes

Esteban and Valerio are counterfactual matched proxy cases. As New York–born Mexican students whose primary high school friends were non-Mexicans, they experienced step-ups by the Mexican teen migrants who policed the borders of Mexicanness and challenged U.S.-borns, whom they believed thought they were "better than" them.[19] I have known each of them for over fifteen years, done repeat interviews with them, and spent time with them. Such deep, long-term case development protects against what the counterfactual theorists Phillip Tetlock and Aaron Belkin call the "creeping determinism [of] outcome knowledge," which can lead one to see actual outcomes as inevitable.[20]

Valerio's counterfactual explanation for choosing Comercio High instead of his zoned school, Presidents High—to avoid the fights he would have gotten into there—resonates with Esteban's lived experience at Presidents High, his zoned school as well. Both believed that they would experience step-ups to for having mostly non-Mexican friends, but they differed in whether they would escalate or deescalate these challenges. As described earlier, step-ups occur when another youth steps into your path, gives you a "hard look" (sustained eye contact, conveying a challenge), and asks what gang you are with, to see if you are a rival. Responding by looking back could escalate the challenge into a fight, whereas looking down usually deescalates the situation and the chances of a fight.

As Valerio told me when he was a teen, he was a "Black" Mexican, a phenotypically "Mexican-looking" teen who had mainly Black and Puerto Rican friends.[21] He disassociated himself from Mexicans, especially Mexican teen migrants, believing that they enacted a compromised masculinity by mostly fighting other Mexicans and backing down from Puerto Ricans who picked on them. Valerio had considered attending Presidents High to be with his friends, but the death of a Mexican teen outside that school and the good experience at Comercio High of Valerio's older brother led his parents to rule out Presidents High. They told him he had to go to Comercio.

Valerio agreed with this choice, which also synced with the advice of his middle school adviser, who said that going to his zoned school would look bad on college and job applications and be a bad place to learn. Valerio summarized that conversation: "In your zone school, you're . . . with the bad kids . . . who behaved badly in school and didn't care about graduating and going to a better high school. . . . Those kids just make you do crazy things—sell drugs, smoke marijuana, make you

Figure 3.2   Counterfactual Proxy: Parallel Narrative Case Development for Esteban and Valerio

Esteban attends the treatment school (Presidents High) → is stepped up on → looks down → has no fights → achieves school success

knows people → does not cut class → achieves school success

Valerio attends the control school (Comercio High) → avoids step-ups (thus cannot look back) → avoids problems → achieves school success

knows no one → avoids invitations to cut class → achieves school success

Source: Author's diagram.

drop out of school." Valerio believed that Mexican youth usually either go to their zoned school, because they can only get in there, or "apply to where there's Mexicans. And then whatever one they get picked for, that's the one they go to." Valerio here was describing the same funneling process that Eddie experienced at Presidents High.

Valerio told me that if he had gone to Presidents High, he would have been stepped up to by Mexican teen migrants challenging him for having mainly Black friends, and he believed he would have looked back and gotten into fights, been distracted, and been expelled from school. As Valerio told me (and I witnessed when I shadowed him for several days), at Comercio High he walked through the hallways without encountering step-ups because few Mexican teen migrants went there and step-ups were uncommon at the school.

Valerio's counterfactual scenario was confirmed by Esteban when I interviewed him after having followed Valerio in school. (I did not use Valerio's name; they did not know each other.) Esteban had gone to Presidents High and hung out mainly with his high-achieving Chinese friends. He reported getting "hard looks" in step-ups by Mexican "immigrants [from] ESL classes . . . because they think I think I'm better than them, because I didn't have Mexican friends."[22] While Valerio always responded to hard looks by looking back, Esteban's "personal policy" was to deescalate by looking down. These dynamics are represented in figure 3.2.

That the perceptions of motive and the steps in the processes (step-ups, hard looks, and their likely impacts) were the same in Valerio's counterfactual thinking and in Esteban's lived experience makes them counterfactual proxy cases. Imagining what would happen at Presidents High (the "treatment" school, which is the factor posited to affect outcomes) led Valerio to choose Comercio High, where he did not face regular step-ups or hard looks from Mexican teen migrants (making it the "control" school, which puts impacts of the treatment school into relief by comparison). Esteban's experience suggests that Valerio was right. Because Valerio always looked back at hard looks, it was easy for him to imagine getting into fights in Esteban's high school but succeeding academically at Comercio.[23] Both Esteban and Valerio graduated from high school.

Collective Intrafamily and Friends Group Counterfactuals and Divergent Outcomes

Here we compare two cases where parents approached their younger children's high school choice decisions differently based on their older children's experience in the local zoned school, which they had chosen following the "safety in numbers" strategy. In the first case, the dismal educational performance of his older siblings made Emmanuel's mother more open to Emmanuel's desire to go to the nonzoned school. In the second case, the local zoned high school was eliminated as a possibility for Carmelita when her older sister dropped out, and her parents forced Carmelita to go to Catholic school. Some parents leaned toward the same high school for younger siblings if older siblings had done well there.

I have known Emmanuel for over twenty years and have interviewed him many times. As noted in the opening pages of this book, Emmanuel drew a clear causal line from his fourteen-year-old self choosing to avoid the zoned high school that his siblings had attended (where they had done poorly) to his successful adult life, including becoming a lawyer in his early thirties. He had dodged a bullet and chosen instead to go to a high school with mostly Black students because he hoped "not knowing anyone" would help him in school:

> I actually selected a high school that did not have any of my friends attending . . . because I knew what would happen if I went to a high school with all my buddies. . . . Everyone would . . . cut class and go to hooky jams or that park. It . . . helped me out that I was the youngest of the bunch, because it allowed me to see what they were doing with themselves and to try and avoid [that]. . . . When I was in eighth grade, everyone was in high school . . . so applying to a high school away from them, it helped me avoid that.

Emmanuel chose a high school that had mostly Black students and focused on health careers, Canady High, because he wanted to be a doctor. He showed planfulness in choosing a nonzoned high school to avoid bad outcomes, and also in finding one that was strong in his hoped-for field. He did not ask his siblings for advice. But he had to convince his mother, Lila, who had feared a school with too many Black students, and wanted him to go to the local zoned school that his siblings and cousins went to. Lila allowed herself to be moved from the "safety in numbers" strategy to the "avoid Mexicans" strategy based on Emmanuel's strong academic record and advice from his mentor, their parish priest, who convinced her that the "Black" school would be safe because it was mostly female and oriented toward medical careers.

Attending Canady High School changed Emmanuel's views on race and education. He had worried that attending a mostly Black high school "would be hell for me. . . . [I] was very closed-minded back in the day with regards to Blacks. . . . [I thought] they would rob you." He lived near public housing projects and had been robbed by Black youth. Emmanuel had no Black friends before high school. The school was a "culture shock. . . . I'm the only Mexican here! It was all Blacks. And then I got to know them and learned about their history." He made school friends, especially among West Indian students, and saw that they wanted the same future he did. He thrived at Canady. He also came to see his prior beliefs about Black people as "messed up."

Emmanuel still sometimes felt vulnerable as one of the only Mexicans in the school, but he adopted strategies to avoid conflict that could derail his plans. He maintained a "neutral operating identity" by not speaking in class too much, which would have risked ridicule for acting too smart. He avoided the lunchroom, doing homework in the library instead, and left right after school to avoid step-ups in settings or at times with less adult social control.[24] He did not cut class and was rarely invited to do so, because he knew no one. Emmanuel's strategies helped him benefit from his high school, which, in addition to having more AP classes, had health career internships and a mentorship program that opened doors. A key mentor in high school and college was Dr. Comer, a Black doctor who convinced Emmanuel that Elite University was a place for him. These dynamics are represented in figure 3.3.

I have known Carmelita's family for over twenty years, interviewed three of the four siblings and a parent, and seen them regularly at Mexican events in New York and Mexico. Her case started with the same facts as Emmanuel's: her older sister Jane had done badly in their zoned high school, Presidents High, so her parents forced Carmelita to go to Catholic school and did not entertain the idea of other public high schools. Jane had been a good student until high school, but she started cutting classes with her "street" friends (her father's word) at Presidents High. Jane said that she was "not a good girl in high school." She later got her GED and briefly attended college. When we last spoke, in 2018, she had a good job working for a union. But when her parents made their high school decision about Carmelita, all that was in the future.

**Figure 3.3   Family and Friendship Group Counterfactual Cases:
Emmanuel**

---

*Emmanuel's older siblings do badly in the zoned high school → Emmanuel
argues to his mother that he should go to the control school (the Black high school)
→ she accedes, rejecting the "safety in numbers" strategy → Emmanuel is successful
in high school → goes to Elite University → goes to law school*

Source: Author's diagram.

Jane's dropping out fundamentally changed how their parents chose
high schools for their three younger children, who had no choice but
to attend Catholic high schools.

Carmelita said:

> My sister went to public school. But my parents, since my sister did bad,
> they didn't want me to go to Presidents High. I cried because all my
> friends were going to public school, and I didn't want to go to Catholic
> school. But my parents wanted me to because they thought I was going to
> do the same. They told me that they didn't want it to happen again. And
> "if all your friends are going to public school, then they are going to be a
> bad influence." That's why they put me [in Catholic school]. I was upset.

Her parents especially wanted to separate her from her best friend,
who was "wild," Carmelita said. Her friend smoked, drank, and had
had sex before high school. Although Carmelita was a "good girl" in her
own and her parents' estimation, they feared a repeat of the bad impact
that public school had had on Jane, who had also been a "good girl" in
middle school.

Catholic school helped Carmelita avoid bad choices and develop
good habits. When I asked about cutting class, Carmelita laughed, saying
it was impossible in her Catholic school "because they would call my
house. But I think if I went to Presidents High and I could get away with
it, I probably would have." She knew of Mexican gangs at Presidents
High but chuckled when I asked about gangs at the Catholic school:
"I just can't picture it." She said that Catholic school instilled good work
habits in her, including doing her homework and studying a lot.

Carmelita's early adult assessment of her Catholic school's impact on
her was positive, especially when she juxtaposed it counterfactually with
what she thought would have happened had she gone to Presidents
High: "Honestly, I think about it and I'm thankful that I went there,
because my ex-best friend . . . she's pregnant. . . . Most of the people that
I went to junior high school with are . . . pregnant. . . . One . . . is in jail. . . .

Figure 3.4   Family and Friendship Group Counterfactual Cases: Carmelita

Carmelita's older sibling has a negative experience at the treatment school (Presidents High) → Carmelita's choice of school is restricted → she goes to the control school (a nonzoned Catholic school) → achieves school success for herself, her parents, and her siblings

Source: Author's diagram.

Everyone is not good." She saw a clear line from her high school choice to her better adult life (see figure 3.4).

In the Absence of a Counterfactual

Emmanuel, Valerio, Carmelita, and their parents chose nonzoned high schools as a counterfactual plan to avoid bad conditions in the zoned high school and to seek contexts with more opportunity. These choices all enacted the "avoid Mexicans" strategy and rejected the "safety in numbers" strategy. In contrast, Skinny chose to go to the functional equivalent of his zoned school in attending Vehicle High "to learn about cars" and be with his Mexican friends, who "all got accepted to that school." I have known Brooklyn-born Skinny since he was a teenager, having met him in Ticuani, and I have done several interviews with him. I have seen him regularly at Ticuani events in New York.

Skinny was excited about being with his group of Mexican friends at Vehicle High. He did not do the type of counterfactual thinking in picking a high school that Emmanuel and Valerio did in picking their schools. Skinny gave little thought to avoiding sites of step-ups that might cause conflict and endanger his chance to graduate from high school. He just went to the high school where he wanted to go. He also chose alone, not talking to his parents, who "didn't even know" about his choice because they got home from work at midnight. He described his first year in high school this way: half the year "I studied, and half the year, I cut class." Skinny was making more friends, including members of a gang he had helped found, the Mixtecos Locos.

Skinny's relationship to Black students was conflictual, in stark contrast to Emmanuel's and Valerio's reports that their relationships with stronger Black students helped them in school. Skinny described Vehicle High as "full of Black people. . . . We had so many problems between Mexicans and Blacks. . . . Everybody was scared to go [there]. And I met some other Mexican guys there." Skinny often fought with Black students he thought had given him hard looks.

Figure 3.5   The Absence of Counterfactuals in Framing School Choice: Skinny

---

Skinny goes to the zoned school (Vehicle High) to be with Mexican friends (some are in his gang) → cuts school a lot → encounters step-ups in school and fights with Blacks → is expelled → never gets a GED

Source: Author's diagram.

A fight pivoting on this Black-Mexican conflict ended his schooling. After Black youth had beaten a Mexican, Skinny and ten to fifteen of his "boys" fought Black students in a park near Vehicle High, swinging impromptu weapons they fashioned by taking off their shirts and wrapping their books inside them. "It was a bad fight. Some racial stuff. But they hurt people, and then we hurt them too." The police came. Skinny was expelled from school in tenth grade. He got work as a bike messenger in the same factory where his father worked, then another job in a production shop with other Mixtecos Locos. Starting at $6.75 an hour, he made $16 an hour by 2008 and earned over $40,000, with overtime, in 2007.

Skinny's description of his life at Vehicle High highlights several mechanisms that inhibited academic success and upward mobility among NYCOMPERs. Having chosen a school to be with his gang friends, Skinny began to cut classes. He always looked back when challenged and sought revenge for another Mexican in his last school fight. Enacting the "safety in numbers" strategy, he fought Black students and got expelled. His discussion of his high school choice was focused on being with his friends, recalling Valerio's comment that Mexican youth go where their friends go. Skinny also was positioned at the wrong end of intrafamily learning. The oldest child of parents who knew little about New York's schools and worked till late every evening, he made school choices alone. His father could not dissuade him from being in the gang and simply said, "Just take care of yourself." Skinny never got a GED (see figure 3.5.)

Looking back from established adulthood, Skinny seemed most proud of his children, who were doing well in school, but he also took pride in how his gang helped change the perception of Mexicans in New York. Blacks and Puerto Ricans had beaten up Mexicans without penalty when he was in middle school, he said, but now they knew not to "mess with the Mexicans. They're going to come hard." He seemed at peace with himself in his late thirties to early forties: he was making a reasonable living, was happily married, and had kids—whom he advised against joining gangs.

We did our last interview in the presence of a relative who lay terminally ill on a medical cot on the floor. The relative had no health insurance, so Skinny had taken him in, despite lacking space to do so. As we talked, Skinny's children and nieces and nephews repeatedly ran into the room to listen, thinking it would be exciting. It was not, so they left, after smiling and asking if the relative needed anything. Skinny's education story included getting expelled from school, but his home that lovely summer day was full of kind children who looked after their sick relative and spoke to Skinny with happiness and fondness. In his 1999 and 2007 interviews, Skinny showed nearly no regrets about his life.

Living Counterfactual Cases Who Changed the Type of School They Attended

Chucho Bravo and Vicky Fuerte were living counterfactual cases who changed between zoned and nonzoned high schools, in effect running do-overs of their own educational choices. Both were "inconvenient" cases who acted in unexpected ways, and more than once.[25] But by tracing their lives over a long period—especially after their negative experiences in zoned high schools—we can learn about how zoned and nonzoned schools and counterfactual thinking affected Chucho's and Vicky's adult life outcomes.

Chucho knew he could not get into a nonzoned school and was being socially promoted into high school despite low middle school grades. He avoided his zoned "Black" school, where he feared that Black and Puerto Rican gangs would see a solo Mexican as "an easy target." Following his guidance counselor's advice, he used his aunt's address to get into Presidents High, where he had Mexican friends. But Chucho had avoided one bad zoned school and gotten into another.

In 1999, he was pleased his first day at Presidents High to see Mexicans he knew, including some from his family's hometown, Ticuani. He made friends in Mexican gangs and began cutting school and doing badly. His account precisely describes zoned school funneling:

> The first day I met people that I grew up with, like, in elementary and that I used to know in the park. . . . I started to feel comfortable. We used to hang out together, take the same train. . . . I was shy. . . . But then I started hanging out. I changed a little. . . . Before I was very quiet. I wasn't allowed to go out. I started messing around with the crowd. In high school, Mexicans chilled with Mexicans, Chinese with Chinese. It's like a prison. . . . [I began] cutting class, going to hooky parties. It was just the friends that I had back then . . . all Mexicans.

I asked Chucho, in a neutral tone: "You said having all Mexicans in the school made it harder for you to do good?" He responded: "Yeah, especially being involved in gangs. For me it was because there was no other way . . . there was no cool Mexicans that does good. They were doing the same thing I was doing—cutting school, going for their GED, dropping out."

Chucho reported that there were many Mexican gang members at Presidents High who stepped up to others they thought were Mexican, either to recruit them or to threaten them.

> Some of them didn't even go to the school either. Some of them dropped out. They just came to the school to visit and start trouble. . . . They would be outside, or sometimes in the school. . . . It's easy to go in, they don't ask for IDs, metal detectors. Anybody could go in. . . . When I cut class, I'd go period four, five, six. Those were the lunch periods.

Chucho attended Presidents High before metal detectors were installed and security was tightened. His account resonated with other participants' accounts at the time: they also said that groups of young men would wait outside schools, or on routes from schools to subways, to step up to anyone who "looked Mexican." Chucho was never a formal gang member, but his risk of step-ups increased when people saw him hanging out with New York Atzlan, a gang that was then establishing its reputation, and assumed that he was a member. These gangs had U.S.-born members but also increasing numbers of Mexican-born youth whose prospects were blocked by their lack of legal status and English facility.[26]

By the end of his sophomore year, Chucho seemed to be on the verge of dropping out or formally joining a gang. He said: "I used to cut a lot. . . . I used to hate school. I was thinking about going to the GED." But then appendicitis nearly killed him and required emergency surgery. A doctor told him that there was "so much poison" from his burst appendix that they wore masks while vacuuming it out. In the hospital, Chucho had an epiphany: he realized that his gang friends were not really his friends, because they never visited. His mother said: "We are there for you because we are your family. But you were cutting school with those guys, and not doing your schoolwork, listening to them instead of us." Chucho decided to change schools and graduate.

Chucho first requested a transfer to Forrester High, a mixed, mostly Italian American school with some Chinese, Black, and Latino/a/e students. To keep the immigrant bargain, he wanted to get the diploma ("for my mom") rather than the "second-place prize, the GED." In 1999, as a nineteen-year-old, he said of Forrester High: "I was one of the few Mexicans there. Probably like five Mexicans, and I felt comfortable." In 2008 he told me: "I had to start all over . . . like I was a freshman. I did

Figure 3.6   A Category-Changing Counterfactual Case: Chucho

Chucho starts at the treatment school (Presidents High) → cuts class with gang members → fails → has a serious medical event → anticipating a bad outcome, has an epiphany

switches to a better school (the control school) → graduates "for my mom"

Source: Author's diagram.

not know anybody, the neighborhood was different, the school was different. I quickly made friends, but it was like a 'hi' and 'bye.' . . . It wasn't like, 'Hey, let's hang out.'" Chucho did not cut classes at Forrester High, attended night school to make up his lost credits, and got his diploma. His parents were proud, and he felt good.

His change from a zoned school to a nonzoned school enables us to trace how the context of school type affected Chucho's thinking, actions, and adult outcomes.[27] Chucho escaped the zoned school's negative effects by "exiting" and jumping to a better and nonzoned school, enacting the "reset button" and "avoid Mexicans" strategies.[28] As a nineteen-year-old, he had said that not knowing anyone at Forrester High helped him graduate. His beeper (this was before ubiquitous cell phones) went off constantly at Presidents High but almost never at Forrester High. Here, Chucho enacted the theory of the psychology and business professor Wendy Wood that changing habits is easier to achieve by avoiding contexts that promote the old habits rather than through willpower.[29] Chucho's change from a zoned to a nonzoned school created divergent trajectories and futures within a single life and case (see figure 3.6). Leaving Presidents High enabled him to start over, away from friends to cut with, and to focus on his schoolwork so that he could graduate.

Finally, Chucho's case also reinforces the social nature of understandings of race and school choice. His bad high school experience led his parents to block his younger sister Linda's later desire to go to Presidents High with her cousins. They supported her choice of Central Brooklyn High, which they saw as a "Black" school, and Linda thrived there.[30]

Chucho believed that his appendicitis epiphany saved him. In his thirties, he had gained seniority at his university administrative job and was valued for his skilled work. When I visited him there, I was happy to see that Chucho's teen expectations for himself (and my own) had been proved wrong.

Vicky Fuerte changed school categories twice, thus showing how the school choice system, Mexicans' beliefs about Blackness and Mexicanness and academic achievement, and the value added by the student and the school worked across school types and over time within one bio-graphical case.[31] Recall that Vicky was the High Flier who had to convince her parents to let her attend the academically stronger "Black" Jackson Middle School, where she thrived. But she chose her high school by herself, without counseling, and landed in the functional equivalent of her bad zoned school. Even her teachers there told her that she had to "get out," so she transferred to a better school in Manhattan, found a good mentor, and went on to Elite University and a well-paid paralegal job. In her thirties, Vicky earned a master's degree and now works in public education.

Vicky's High Flier trajectory conflicted with the childhood story about her told by her family, who she says treated her like "a dumb child" and "ugly duckling" because she did not speak until age four. She transferred from ESL into English-only classes in third grade and was her elementary school valedictorian. Vicky said that her teachers "loved" her and counseled against her zoned middle school, instead encouraging her to choose the academically stronger Jackson Middle School. Vicky visited and loved Jackson, especially the school uniforms.

However, Vicky's parents did not want her to go there. Jackson was far from their house and would require that she travel on the bus or subway. Her older sister, Leeta, would be unable to deliver her there en route to her high school, as she could if Vicky attended the local zoned middle school. School uniforms would cost extra, and Jackson was also in a "Black neighborhood. . . . My parents trust Hispanics. They distrust Blacks." She related, at age nineteen, that her mother had objected to Jackson because *"hay morenos"* [there are Blacks]. Vicky thought her parents feared she would get attacked at school. At age twenty-seven, Vicky spoke more about her parents' objection to Jackson:

> Well, my parents are racist. . . . I don't think that they know that they're racist. They just have these stereotypes of Black people as . . . being lazy and criminals. . . . They didn't want me to go to that school. . . . My mom says that, even now, every time she sees a Black man, she's really afraid—she tries to walk quicker (*laughing*). . . . Which really concerned me because my boyfriend is Black . . . (*laughs*). My dad doesn't know about the boyfriend yet.

Vicky's conflict with her parents pivoted on their embrace of the "safety in numbers" strategy, enacted when they sent her sister Leeta to the local school with Mexican cousins and youth they knew. But Vicky saw bleak prospects there. She argued that Leeta and their cousins had done what their parents wanted by going to the local zoned high school, but most of them did badly there. "Look how they turned out!" she yelled, objecting that her parents wanted her to go to the "dumb school" (as noted earlier). She saw Jackson as a school for smart students. Vicky disliked being Mexican then, associating it with cutting school and not speaking English. Her school friends were mainly Black and non-Mexican Hispanics, who she thought had more opportunity. She thought her parents feared that Jackson would make her "less Mexican." They teased her about her Black friends, saying, "Oh, you and your *moreno* [Black] friends," when she said things they did not agree with or understand.

Vicky saw social class differences between herself and her Jackson classmates, who lived in nicer neighborhoods ("in houses!") and whose professional-looking parents dropped them off at school in cars, while Vicky went to school alone by subway. Jackson's statistics (from the late 2000s, the oldest available) supported her perception: 97 percent of students in her zoned middle school, versus 53 percent at Jackson, qualified for free school lunch; over one-third of the students at her local zoned school were English Language Learners (ELLs), versus 1 percent at Jackson; and under 10 percent of students in the zoned school earned proficient scores on state math and English tests, versus over 80 percent at Jackson.

The social class distance made friendship difficult. Vicky could not imagine bringing friends to her tiny apartment, where her parents "do not speak English" and her overly controlling father regularly hit his daughters for any offense. For larger offenses, he had them put their hands over their heads and then he hit their bodies, through their clothes, to avoid leaving visible marks.

Her parents' worry that she would get harassed outside school was not baseless, but as it turned out, Vicky was not harassed, due to an ironic wrinkle in the meaning of race in context. Vicky told me that the school uniform signaled to neighborhood youth that the wearer was a Jackson student. Some Black youth robbed *Black* Jackson students outside school because, they said, Jackson students thought they were "better than" them. Vicky said that she was not robbed because she looked Mexican and so did not register on the local youths' "you think you are better" radar. Vicky was insulated from this Black-on-Black policing because she fell outside the socially relevant category of a Black student in a Jackson uniform.[32] This is the mirror image of Mexican teen migrant youth stepping up to Mexican American youth with non-Mexican friends at Presidents High.

Vicky loved Jackson Middle School but lacked her peers' parental guidance and class-based resources. In her first year at Jackson, she wanted to apply, like many other Jackson students, to Prep for Prep, a program that placed high-achieving minority students in private schools, but her parents refused. Then, lacking proper guidance from

Jackson staff in choosing a high school, she picked Future Professionals High School "by myself" after visiting it alone. Vicky thought that, because the students wore uniforms, the school would be academically strong like Jackson. The Future Professionals principal "basically BS'd" about the school being good, but she said, "It was horrible. Horrible."

Vicky had wanted to hit the social "reset button" and escape Jackson's uber-competitive social world, where "gossipers . . . used to talk about everybody and their mother. . . . I wanted to start fresh." Perhaps her biggest missed opportunity was Brooklyn Tech, one of the city's elite high schools. Vicky had gotten in, but no one told her it would a better choice than Future Professionals High School.

Vicky learned so little her first year at Future Professionals that "I felt like that year made me slower." A first ominous sign was that the school did not have math classes at her level. Having taken two years of high school math in seventh and eighth grades, she should have been in Math 5; instead, she was put with all freshmen in Math 1. School staff refused to believe that she belonged in more advanced classes, so she demanded that they give her a placement test and check her middle school transcripts, after which they found appropriate math classes for her at another school in the same building. Her science teacher assigned crossword puzzles in class. She avoided the lunchroom after seeing a student get "boxcut" when he "walked in a certain way." The school was so chaotic that she felt her time was better spent cutting class: "The teachers were always . . . reprimanding the bad kids . . . the disruptive kids, and I'd never been used to that. So . . . I started cutting class. . . . What's the point of me going?" When cutting, she stayed home to study or studied in the debate room.

What always impressed me in Vicky's accounts of her defiance was that she recognized the absurdity and injustice of these situations but did not let her anger overwhelm or paralyze her into staying in a "horrible" school or acting as others might have expected her to (in Vicky's words, being "that Mexican girl"). Even as a teenager, Vicky was exasperated and angry at what was wrong in her world, but she kept a planful perspective as she worked out her escape plan. She knew it was wrong that she learned more cutting class to study than by attending class, but her response was: *What is my plan to change things?*

The debate team saved her. Vicky credited the Future Professionals principal for "try[ing] to . . . make the school good" by creating "different programs . . . [and] the debate team." While her debate coach did not initially know how to coach them, he cared about the team and worked hard. Their team got soundly beaten in their first debate and wanted to quit, but they learned quickly. Vicky learned the evidence for both sides of all debates, to better refute her opponents' arguments:

"I knew *their* evidence, 'cause we all got the same evidence. . . . I used to learn the affirmative arguments, in case I was a negative, so that when they ran their argument, I would know exactly what arguments to run against them."

Though she was "the only Mexican kid on the debate team," she felt more socially at home at Future Professionals High than at Jackson. Vicky found short-term mentors at Future Professionals, three teachers who "told me that I had to get out of this school." When she transferred to Comercio High, the Future Professionals' principal said that she could not stay on its debate team because, he said, if all the smart kids left the school, how would they be able to make it better? She replied that she was not a "test tube experiment."

At Comercio High, Vicky thrived again, taking AP classes and being advised and mentored by Mr. Hibbert, who recommended next steps and opened doors for her. (Hibbert also shepherded Valerio to graduation.[33] Vicky was not friends with Valerio, but she knew who he was.) Hibbert and I became friendly, understanding that we both wanted to open doors for his students. Hibbert placed Vicky in an AP English class where other students had been handpicked by the teacher, who was skeptical of the new arrival. But Vicky rewrote papers several times in response to comments from her English teacher, who became a long-term mentor and friend—even setting her up as an adult with the person who became her life partner. Vicky subsequently got full scholarship offers at several competitive colleges.

Many High Fliers had a Mr. Hibbert. While most teachers I met in New York City public schools seemed dedicated to their students, some, like Hibbert, were amazing. He made it clear to me that my research mattered to him because he saw it as a way to help his students. If I helped them, he would be my advocate inside the school. Seeing this commitment in me, he was all in: he walked me through the school, introducing me to people so they would speak openly to me. Hibbert's devotion to his students (several of whom participated in this study) made them believe in themselves. He opened any door he could. All students should have a Mr. Hibbert.

Hibbert and I had a laugh on our first meeting. We had had several longish phone conversations before meeting. Given his laughter at my use of Yiddish words (for example, *fakakta*, meaning "useless" or "stupid"—literally, "for shit"), I had thought he was a middle-aged Jewish man. My desire to help his students led him to think I was a young Caribbean man. He turned out to be a middle-aged Caribbean man, and I was a non-Jewish White man in his thirties.

The debate team was Vicky's intellectual home at Comercio High too. Her team was in the top ten at a state-level competition hosted by a women's professional organization. By winning the individual competition, Vicky qualified for the nationals, but she could not go because the school could not fund her trip and her parents neither had the money nor understood the meaning of the debate competition for her future. Nevertheless, debate helped her develop argumentation skills that served her well in college and in her later career.

Vicky described fighting in her head with the competing images of the kind of Mexican and the kind of girl she would become. Her fear of becoming "that Mexican girl" increased when her college-age sister Leeta got pregnant when Vicky was in high school. (Leeta later graduated from college, despite her father's laments.) Vicky said: "I always tried not to be that Mexican girl. . . . I never even had Mexican friends up to that point. . . . All my friends have always been very diverse, mainly Black . . . school friends. I didn't wanna be the typical Mexican. . . . I was like the nerd Mexican with old clothes. So . . . I got picked on." But another image presented itself to her as well, one reinforced by her teachers' encouragement: "By fifth grade, it had become clear to me," she said, that she was understanding things faster than other students. "This was the thing that I had, and I was gonna hold on to— the smart girl."

Vicky's wary relationship with then-common meanings of being Mexican, and being a Mexican girl, can be understood when we consider Mexicans' conjunctural ethnicity in this period and its gendered meaning in her family. In her last semester of high school, Vicky earned an internship for high-achieving students that had her arriving home earlier than she did from regular school. Her father did not believe her explanation for coming home early and accused her of cutting school for a boyfriend, saying she would become pregnant like her sister and once again shame the family. When Vicky won a debate competition, her opponent congratulated her by saying she was "the only smart Mexican" she had ever known. Vicky only began to experience being Mexican as positive after she got a Mexican boyfriend in high school and he took her dancing at Mexican parties. She was also often the only Mexican, or one of only a few Mexicans, in her AP classes. She made friends with her mainly Black and Chinese AP classmates and thus linked being smart with being Black or Chinese. But, she said, these were "convenience friends" she could study with, or "IM [texting] friends." Her three main friends were Black. At Elite University, she made friends, but felt as out of place there as she had at Jackson.

Vicky's case illustrates the interaction of the school choice system in New York with Mexican parents' and students' beliefs about race and schooling and with student habits. Mexicans' conjunctural ethnicity was driven by the preponderance of teen migrants, reflected in an image of

Figure 3.7   A Category-Changing Counterfactual Case: Vicky

Vicky rejects bad zoned middle school (and parents' theories about race and school) → enrolls in better control school (Jackson Middle School) → without guidance, picks a bad zoned high school (Future Professionals High) → is advised by teachers to "get out" of Future Professionals High → switches to the better control school (Comercio High) → goes to Elite University → graduates from college and gets a commensurate job

Source: Author's diagram.

Mexicans as "ESLs," as participants put it, who dropped out to work or start families. But many Mexicans, including Vicky's parents, feared Black students. Vicky had to fight her parents' "safety in numbers" strategy to pursue a "Black achievement" strategy, also thus avoiding the negative dynamics of Mexican teen migrant life in her zoned middle school. Vicky succeeded so well in changing her parents' beliefs on race and schooling that when her younger sister, Zinia, wanted to go to the local "Mexican" middle school that Leeta had attended, her parents forced her to go to Jackson.

Determination is woven through Vicky's story, but so are descriptions of how emotionally difficult it was to navigate the controlling images and meanings of being Mexican, and her class identity in both strong and weak public schools as well as in mostly White private college and work settings.

Vicky's case shows profoundly unequal opportunity in different types of schools. Her middle school success had opened doors to an elite high school, but lacking proper advice, she picked a "horrible" zoned high school. By moving herself into a zoned school, she risked derailing what should have been a strong trajectory from middle school to a good high school and then to college. Future Professionals High could have been a disastrous educational endpoint, save for Vicky's student habits and keen intelligence. She cut classes to study in the debate room. She worked hard and excelled in those areas where she was challenged in school (the debate team). Finally, Vicky's teachers mentored her well by advising her to leave that school and helping her get into Comercio High, resetting her trajectory toward what her middle school performance had predicted (see figure 3.7.)

Vicky changed school categories twice, and thus her story offers us glimpses of what her alternative trajectories might have been. She became her own counterfactual proxy by jumping twice between a zoned school and a nonzoned school. She first defied her conditions by getting into Jackson, a selective middle school, but then fell through the advising cracks at Jackson and back into a zoned school, Future Professionals High. She kept working hard, and with the help of mentors, she jumped back into a stronger nonzoned school (Comercio High), which put her on a trajectory that led her to Elite University and then into well-paid legal work, graduate school, and finally professional work in public education.

Vicky ended up a High Flier, doing work she loved and living with a partner she loved. It has been a pleasure to see her as a grown-up during our periodic lunches or walks. Even the Christmas card she and her partner send each year makes me happy at her success and our friendship.

Statistical Analysis

The chapter so far has analyzed only U.S. citizen and Category Changer cases to avoid the overdetermining impact of legal status on adult outcomes. The statistical analyses here include all cases to assess how much legal status and school-related variables in this chapter correlate with adult outcomes. Some illustrative statistics are presented in this chapter's tables. A full presentation and explanation of all tables and the additive steps of analysis are in this chapter's online appendix.

Proportions and Means Tables: Assessing Single Relationships between Variables and Time 2 Outcomes

Table 3.1 (in note; see also the online statistical chapter appendix) shows simple correlations between three key outcomes at time 2 (age twenty-eight)—the overall outcome category (for example, High Flier), years of education, and income—and the processes analyzed in this chapter.[34] These variables operationalize institutional processes linked to school choice, students' habits of mind and conduct, and the beliefs of Mexican participants and their parents around the year 2000 on links between race and schooling. Overall, table 3.1 shows that having better habits of mind and conduct (including counterfactual thinking, doing homework, and not cutting school) and choosing a nonzoned school over a zoned school are linked to more mobility at age twenty-eight. That the proportion of College Graduates and High Fliers and the mean income and education are similar within each set of variables suggests that these categories tap into the same social reality.

Concrete examples clarify the point. The strongest correlations were for the habits of mind. Some 70.5 percent of planful teens became College Graduates or High Fliers, got a mean of 15.1 years of education, and made $48,800 per year at time 2, versus 6.6 percent of non-planful teens who became College Graduates (none became High Fliers) and a mean of 11.4 years of education and $25,037 per year of income among this latter group. Habits of conduct mattered too: 74 percent of those who always did homework were College Graduates or High Fliers at time 2, and they had received more education (15.4 versus 12.2 years) and had higher incomes ($49,204 versus $29,306) than those who did not always do homework. Choosing a high school based on beliefs about links between race and schooling correlated strongly with adult outcomes. No one (0 percent) who chose their high school mainly to be with Mexican friends became a College Graduate or a High Flier. They also got less education (11.4 versus 14.4 years) and earned less ($24,312 versus $40,315) than those who chose their high school for other reasons. By contrast, 76 percent of those who chose a high school to avoid Mexican friends were College Graduates or High Fliers and had more education (15.0 versus 13.5 years) and income ($60,608 versus $31,154) at age twenty-eight than those who had not chosen their high school for that reason.

Legal status had interesting correlations. Those with legal status had only 1.8 years more education at age twenty-eight (among the smallest correlations) but made over $26,000 per year more (among the largest differences in the table) than those who did not. This apparent contradiction reflects how educational institutions, especially in New York, seek to educate all students, while undocumented students are excluded by federal law from working legally.

Table 3.2 (in note; see also the online appendix) assesses correlations between adult outcomes and two "treatment" or independent variables: school quality, reworked into four categories described by study participants; and legal status, with a set of control variables.[35] The four categories are "exceptional value schools," which are nonzoned schools with extra offerings (such as AP classes, internships, and academically stronger students); "positive academic track schools," which are non-zoned schools that offer fewer extras and have a less selective student body than exceptional schools; "zoned schools," which have weaker academics and extras; and "no high school."[36] Legal status categories include U.S. citizens by birth; Category Changers who went from undocumented to lawful permanent residents or citizens by time 2; those with any visa upon arrival; and those who were undocumented at time 1 and time 2. We include "offspring" (having a child, and at what age) and gender variables, which are standard controls in analyzing educational attainment. We theorize that not having children or having them when older, doing homework and not cutting school, and being planful as a teen promote better adult outcomes.

The first column of table 3.2 shows the proportions of all NYCOMP participants in each variable subcategory. The next four columns show mean scores for each independent variable subcategory for time 2 outcome variables, including education, income, occupational ranking, and proportion in the top of four wealth categories.[37] The table shows that attending a better high school, being a U.S. citizen or having lawful permanent residency, not having children or having them later, doing homework and not cutting class, and being planful all promoted better adult outcomes.

We ran several regressions to separately assess how legal status (see table 3.3 in note) and high school quality (see table 3.4 in note) correlated with adult outcomes, controlling for variables that operationalize the processes studied in this chapter and for the standard control variables of gender and offspring.[38] (See online appendix tables 3.3a and 3.3b for regressions with no controls.) Table 3.3's key finding is that, adjusting for control variables, participants who were undocumented at both time 1 and time 2 got 1.7 years less education, earned $23,671 less per year, and were less likely to be in higher occupational or wealth rankings at time 2. Undocumented participants were 2,311 times less likely to be in the top wealth category. Being a woman was linked to earning $8,067 per year less income, while being planful was associated with 3.2 years more schooling and $26,123 per year more income. Table 3.4 also shows that attending a zoned school correlates with $12,376 per year less income and made participants over five times less likely to be in the top wealth category at time 2.

Taken together, these tables show that lacking legal status, even controlling for the effects of other variables, has statistically significant negative correlations with time 2 adult outcomes for all NYCOMPers. The size and direction of the correlations remain consistent even after adding controls, despite the relatively small number of cases.

Table 3.4 shows that, adjusting for controls, and compared to a high school with a positive academic track, going to a zoned high school was linked with 1.5 fewer years of education and $14,110 less in annual income at time 2. These participants were also 1.098 times less likely to be in the top occupational category and 126 times less likely to be in the highest wealth categories. Cutting school "sometimes" instead of "regularly" added two years of education at time 2. Finally, being planful was linked to $27,270 more income per year and made those participants significantly more likely to be in the top occupational and wealth status categories.

In sum, these statistics show that attending a better high school and having or getting legal status was linked to better lives at age twenty-eight. U.S. citizens and Category Changers earned more money, got more education, and were more likely to be in higher occupational and wealth categories than their undocumented counterparts. Statistical analysis assesses probabilistic trends in an entire database or population, and we use it here to confirm this chapter's analysis of the interaction of New York City's public school choice system with other sets of processes to promote or inhibit mobility for all cases in the NYCOMP data set.

Conclusion

In this chapter, we have analyzed how three sets of factors contributed to NYCOMP participants' adult life outcomes: New York City's unequal schools and school choice system; Mexican parents' and students' beliefs about the relationship between being Black or Mexican and schooling, reflecting their conjunctural ethnicity; and the differential offerings of unequal schools and the greater learning by students in stronger, nonzoned schools.

Racial exclusion theory, drawing on many strong empirical studies, posits that racial discrimination and the linked structural underfunding of schools have blocked the mobility of generations of Mexican Americans, writ large, mostly or nearly entirely. This chapter contributes to the analysis of the "inconvenient" case of dramatic U.S.-born second-generation Mexican mobility in New York City by tracing how and why school quality and related processes fostered greater or lesser adult mobility for NYCOMP participants. This variation in NYCOMPers' adult outcomes was strongly linked to the quality of their high school.

This finding offers a concrete point of comparison with a very similar fieldwork study done at the same time, María Rendón's *Stagnant Dreamers*. Why did nearly none of Rendón's study participants who went to magnet high schools that were designed to promote more achievement, and are functionally akin to nonzoned schools in this study, become upwardly mobile adults, while a majority of NYCOMP participants who went to nonzoned high schools or participated in special programs within zoned schools did become upwardly mobile? A fuller answer will be offered in the concluding chapter, but we can preview that explanation here. I argue that NYCOMP participants had greater mobility than Rendón's "stagnant Dreamers," for several reasons, including the greater benefit accruing to the former from New York City's pro-mobility policies, institutions, and built environment than was available to the latter in Los Angeles. (This is not to say that

Los Angeles does not support mobility, only that it did not seem to do so for Rendón's study participants.) This is also why NYCOMP participants had more mentors and benefited from them more than did Rendón's stagnant Dreamers, as we see in the next chapter. More generally, New York and some of its institutions and policies, including CUNY and its policies toward Mexican and undocumented students, effectively promote mobility. NYCOMPers benefited from these policies and institutions.

Two caveats are necessary to avoid misconstrual. First, this analysis rightly celebrates how much so many New York City public school teachers helped their students achieve better adult lives. Moreover, the students who knew to try to get into stronger schools, and were able to do so, were helped substantively by those schools to do better as adults. In these schools, students learned more, doors to college were opened, and networks were grown. But showing that those who skillfully navigated a deeply unequal school system did better does not let that deeply unequal school system off the analytical hook. All the schools should be good and should help all students succeed as adults. Studies like Rendón's or Telles and Ortiz's that fault underresourced and low-quality schools rightly point to systemic problems. My analysis could be useful to parents navigating the school choice process, but it does not belie the inequalities in New York City's educational system.

Second, the association between Mexicanness and doing badly in school was closely linked to social conditions in schools in the late 1990s and early 2000s. Mexicans' conjunctural ethnicity—including their degree of settlement, how they related to local racial and ethnic hierarchies in their schools and neighborhoods, and who was perceived as "Mexican"—was strongly influenced by there being three times as many teen migrants as U.S.-born Mexican teens in New York. The migrant Mexican youth, facing huge challenges to school success, either dropped out or, having only ever planned to work in the United States, never "dropped in" to school in New York. By 2020, however, there were nearly ten times more U.S.-born teens than Mexican-born teens, and the former had very high rates of high school completion, college attendance, and college completion.

Anyone who says that this analysis argues that Mexican culture blocks mobility is misusing it, distorting it, or misunderstanding it. In fact, the impressive single-generation jump in college attendance and completion documented in this study and in census data suggests that a Mexican culture of mobility is emerging in New York City, supported by the inclusionary practices and policies of New York City, New York State, and CUNY and other institutions. This increase was driven by the great *ganas* (desire) and strategizing of NYCOMP students and their families, who were able to identify the stronger public schools as levers of mobility (*palancas*, in Rendón's word) and then to use them, despite the challenges of settling in a new country in a city with a complicated and unequal educational system.

Finally, the social place and manner of Mexicans' settlement in New York has differed from that experienced by Rendón's stagnant Dreamers in Los Angeles. In New York City, U.S.-born second-generation Mexicans, unlike Rendón's LA participants, do not suffer as much from neighborhood stigma and an inability to take advantage of opportunities outside the neighborhood, a point we return to in the concluding chapter.

═ Chapter 4 ═

Mentors: Boosting Adult Outcomes and Offering Paths Out of a Hard Life

"WE HAD a tradition—we hang out every month. We used to go out to eat together . . . [in] an Italian restaurant. . . . We used to go chat for hours, until they shut down the place." Emmanuel, age thirty, had a sixteen-year mentoring relationship with his parish priest that lasted until the priest's death. Emmanuel's several mentors helped him thrive despite the hard teen life conditions he faced: an ill and undocumented mother, a brother who was in a gang (but who also financially supported him), and a constant financial struggle to cover necessities.

Thirty-two-year-old Vicky Fuerte told me that her grade school mentor "paid extra attention to me. She made me feel special." She also had a high school mentor, Mr. Hibbert, who "told me, 'Apply for this, apply for that.' So, I did." Her Women's Business Association (WBA) mentor shepherded her through the complicated college admissions process and even "bought me a sleeping bag, got me a ticket on the bus, and found me a student who could host me" at a prospective university before she decided where to go. Vicky said that her mentors helped her to avoid becoming "that Mexican girl" and to live away from a parent who used harsh corporal punishment and sometimes treated her as if she mattered only because she could bring shame to the family by getting pregnant.[1]

"If you feel very firmly about your decision, hold your ground, and I feel that they are going to come back and give you what you want," advised Suzie's work mentor as she was negotiating a higher salary for an internal promotion. Suzie's abrupt decisions not to go to college and to move in with her gang-member boyfriend after graduating from high school had endangered her chances for a better adult life. But by her midthirties, she had become middle-class without a college degree by taking smart advantage of each opportunity her long-term work mentor opened for her. By excelling in her work, Suzie had made them both look good.

114

https://doi.org/10.7758/drwz9626.3856

Speaking of her mentee's mother, Claudette told me, "The mom is changing; I see it. The first time I met her, she said, 'My daughter wants to go to school [college]. She keeps telling us, 'I want to go!'" This mother had been framing her daughter's insistence on college as a problem. But now, Claudette said, the daughter was "a step away from going. . . . I encourage[d] her to do it." In her role as a college student mentor to a high school student, Claudette had persuaded her mentee's parents to let their daughter go to college by revealing that, in spite of being undocumented herself, her father had encouraged her to go to college. Their U.S. citizen daughter, Claudette pointed out, would have even more opportunities.

In these vignettes, mentors helped study participants become upwardly mobile and live happier adult lives. The longer and deeper these mentor-mentee relationships were, the more helpful they were, especially for those youth facing hard teen or early adult conditions (such as an undocumented parent, a negative peer mentor, or living with domestic violence). Mentoring helped all U.S. citizen study participants who accepted it, but especially those facing hard conditions. For them, mentors were a guide through and out of their old lives. Indeed, as a main mechanism driving mobility among NYCOMPers, mentoring was one factor in helping participants become High Fliers and contributes strongly to the emerging Mexican culture of mobility in New York City.

Curiously, in most research on 1.5 or second-generation integration, social illegality, and mobility, including studies based in racial exclusion, legal exclusion, and assimilation theories, mentoring is mostly ignored, unnoted, or noted only for its absence.[2] (Vivian Louie's 2012 book *Keeping the Immigrant Bargain* is a notable exception.[3]) This is a missed opportunity, because such research regularly offers insight into processes and contexts in which mentoring could help promote mobility and well-being. For example, Richard Alba argues that the retirement of the baby boomers blurs lines between racial and ethnic groups and creates new opportunities for minority and second-generation advancement in traditionally White-dominated fields, such as finance.[4] Mentoring could be an important way to open up such opportunities. Moreover, my book builds on the pioneering work on mentoring of the psychologist Jeannie Rhodes and others.[5] Such research often focuses on children of immigrants, refugees, or minority or disadvantaged youth, but it seldom follows mentees into their adult lives, as this study does. This chapter contributes to both bodies of research by describing how being mentored as a teen affected study participants' teen and early adult lives and their adult outcomes.

This chapter analyzes the impact of mentoring on the established adult lives of four upwardly mobile U.S. citizen participants whose home lives and teenage decisions differed. The first case, Elmont, was a High Flier who stands in for the largest pattern in our study: most study participants with positive adult mentors also had other positive life conditions, including parents with legal status and good enough incomes. For them, mentorship was helpful but not necessary for their later success. I then explicate three cases presenting different challenging conditions.

Emmanuel's undocumented mother fought a serious illness during his teen years, his brother did not finish high school and was in a gang, and their family lived in what he described as a dangerous neighborhood. His mentors guided him out of his old life into Elite University and a career as a lawyer. Vicky escaped a harshly disciplinary father to get a graduate degree and work in education. Finally, Suzie started with good conditions—her parents had legal status and owned a house, and she had done well in school—but made decisions that derailed her academic career after high school. Her life was "re-railed" with the help of her work mentor and with her parents' and husband's support and commitment to their family relationship.

This chapter analyzes only U.S. citizen cases to avoid the over-determining impact of legal status, which blocked most of the help that mentors could offer undocumented mentees. The latter's experience is analyzed in chapter 5.

How and Why Mentoring Helps Children of Immigrants: The Scholarly and Best Practices Literatures

Mentors are nonfamily adults who help mentees in one or more of four ways. First, mentors can reframe how mentees imagine their possible futures—for example, by encouraging them to apply to more competitive colleges, or by explaining the concrete steps to take to achieve their goals. Most NYCOMP parents did not know these steps as well as most middle-class, college-educated parents did.[6] Second, mentors offer access to new experiences and opportunities that directly help mentees or prepare them to benefit from future experiences.[7] A summer internship in an office might or might not offer pay, but it does provide an intern the chance to learn the social rules of interviewing and office relationships. Third, mentors can help at any age, but they are especially important for teens and early adults, many of whom are unsure how to chart a successful course into the future as they make choices at turning points that can open up or close off later life opportunities.[8]

Finally, mentoring can be more helpful to youth whose parents face disadvantages, such as being undocumented, and youth who have vexed relationships with their parents. Mentoring gives them an opportunity to develop positive relationships with other adults who can help them rethink their future.[9] These dynamics can create virtuous circles of choices and actions that bring these youth into contexts that open still more doors. That most of the NYCOMPers' mentors were middle-class and college-educated was especially important for mentees applying to college or in professional settings.

As I use the term, "mentoring" relationships are reciprocal, and usually asymmetrical. They require both mentor and mentee to act. A mentoring relationship is not established if a potential mentor offers advice or opens doors but the mentee does not follow at least some of the advice or go through some of the doors. Mentors must also be able to offer good advice and/or access to resources, without which the relationship is more friendship than mentoring.[10] Mentoring relationships can vary in their length, intensity, and impact. In this study, the best mentoring relationships were long-term and multi-stranded, that is, they included informal social interaction, such as having lunch or talking about personal lives, and they offered concrete opportunity, such as introducing mentees to potential employers. Better mentoring establishes the type of authentic, caring relationships that make effective teaching possible, according to the education scholar Nell Noddings.[11] Mentors in this study helped at turning points (especially during the junior and senior years of high school), but they were also available over the years, whether mentees were asking for advice again or were being guided in later decisions by the mentor's internalized voice.[12]

Our study participants benefited both from formal mentoring in an established program and from natural mentoring through their daily life relationships.[13] High Fliers were especially likely to have both formal and natural mentors and to have a series of mentors. The most important natural mentors in this study were exceptional New York City public school teachers and staff: for twenty of the forty-five participants who had a main mentor in their last two years of high school, their mentor was a teacher. This largely unsung success of New York's public schools deserves analysis and celebration. Good bosses and religious leaders were other key mentors in this study.

Peer mentors' help can be similar to but also different from that of adult mentors. Peer mentors are usually successful relatives or friends who are about the same age as the mentee, who have had mentors themselves, and who pass on the lessons they learned from those mentors or from their own lives. Peer mentors are usually less able than adult mentors to open doors or offer resources, but they can help mentees reimagine possibilities and next steps—as when Elmont told his cousins to go to college outside New York City. Perhaps the most important difference between peer mentors and adult mentors is that the former are often embedded in the mentee's life, especially their family.

Mentors can be positive or negative. Negative mentors do the same things as positive ones, but their advice runs in the opposite direction, opening paths that harm their mentee's long-term prospects. A classic example is a younger relative being "apprenticed" into a gang. About one-third of our study participants reported having a positive peer mentor, while one-fifth reported negative ones. In contrast, just under half of them (47 percent) reported having a positive adult mentor, while only one (Federico) reported having a negative adult mentor (an uncle, whose advice contradicted his mother's).

How and how much mentors helped our study participants reflected Mexicans' phase of settlement in the late 1990s and early 2000s. Participants' parents had an average of seven years of education; few of these parents had access to professional networks that could lead to the professional and office jobs they wanted for their children. Moreover, U.S.-born Mexican teens and early adults at this time were outnumbered about three-to-one by Mexican-born teens, who often either dropped out or had never "dropped in" to school. Many academically successful Mexican American students thus felt like "the only ones" on track for college.

Mexicans' phase of settlement at the time also explains why most adult mentors to our study participants were not Mexican or Mexican American. There were fewer coethnic Mexicans established in professional fields, and those few Mexican professionals had mainly moved laterally from Mexico's elite world into New York's. They had little contact with people like my study participants. Only eight of forty-five positive adult mentors during the crucial last two years of high school were Mexican or Mexican American, while ten were non-Mexican Hispanics, eight were White, and three were Black. In the last two years of college, only six of thirty adult mentors were Mexican or Mexican American, while fifteen were non-Mexican Hispanics, seven were White, and three were Black. (Some study participants either were unclear about their mentor's ethnicity or did not report it.) The absence of adult Mexican mentors in professional fields probably reinforced some study participants' perception that Blackness or Whiteness, but not Mexicanness, was linked to upward mobility. This perception is changing as a Mexican culture of mobility emerges in New York.[14] The positive effects of these non-coethnic adult mentors underline a key finding in mentoring research: matching a mentor and mentee by ethnicity, race, or social class can help, but the duration, quality, and trust of a mentoring relationship strongly affects how much it helps.[15]

Elmont's Story: A High-Achieving Professional and Skilled Networker Supported through Mentoring

Elmont's story embodies the best-case scenario for the mechanisms that promote upward mobility, including mentoring. Here he stands in for the majority of upwardly mobile study participants who grew up in life conditions that supported mobility, who made good choices, and who were helped by mentors.

Elmont's father, who had a middle school education in Mexico, worked his way up from busboy to well-paid chef in a midtown restaurant in Manhattan. He earned enough to buy a building in a Brooklyn neighborhood that gentrified as Elmont and his cousins were growing up, providing what Elmont described as a refuge from the dangers that many young men faced because the family lived away from sites of regular conflict. Elmont's parents both got legal status via IRCA, after years of lacking it. Elmont and his siblings were born in Brooklyn, all went to college (earning two BAs and one associate's degree), and two went into finance. Elmont's zoned elementary school was good, as was his middle school, and he got into several good nonzoned high schools (including the elite Brooklyn Tech, which, not understanding its advantages, he declined because of its location).

Elmont admired his father, who supported him, including by taking the day off from work to go with him to the middle school to advocate that the academically very strong Elmont be placed in the gifted program, as he then was. Elmont's family members made choices to keep the immigrant family bargain, and they understood their success as fulfilment of that bargain. That understanding pervaded their accounts: the children kept their promise to their parents by doing well, and the parents, in talking to me, were proud of having given their children a strong platform from which to launch. That all were U.S. citizens or had legal status removed structural obstacles to keeping these promises.

I had known Elmont and his family since his late teens. Although I had not spent much time with Elmont himself, I had spent a lot of time with his father, a Ticuani *comité* (committee) member (see my book, *Mexican New York*), his mother, and his brother, whom I have also interviewed.[16] This account draws mainly on interviews conducted when Elmont was twenty-four (time 1) and thirty-two (time 2).

Elmont was planful and smart in negotiating his school and work careers, as well as in accepting and cultivating mentors. To avoid being identified as a "smart" kid who would get picked on in high school, he adopted a neutral operating identity and image by dressing, in his words, "baggy," shaving his head, and not speaking in class.[17] Elmont was friendly "in the hallways" with high-achieving strivers, but he mostly hung out with "other Latinos not in advanced classes." Elmont believed that his baggy appearance, social group, strong academic performance, and silence about his grades placed him in contradictory types of student categories.

For example, the principal, who taught one of his AP classes, had seemed surprised at Elmont's success. One day the principal stopped him in the hall to say: "'Elmont, you're excelling very well in high school. . . . Come to see me in my office.'" When the principal had first stopped him, Elmont thought there could be a problem. In his office, Elmont recalled, the principal "actually gave me suggestions on what to do. . . . And he said, 'Whenever you want, come by my office.' And I was just like, 'Okay, great.'" The principal recommended Elmont for OpenDoors, a mentoring program that helped underrepresented minorities move into finance, and encouraged his desire to develop new networks outside the city. Elmont did not get into OpenDoors in high school, but he tried again and got in as a sophomore in college.

We can describe the principal's apparent surprise at the juxtaposition of Elmont's baggy appearance and his high grades as a "cognitive dissonance resolution" rather than a microaggression or microinvalidation, which directly or indirectly convey a belief that another does not merit their position or has less worth.[18] The principal resolved this dissonance by basing his expectations on Elmont's performance and offering to mentor him.

The principal was not the only person confused by Elmont's appearance, friends, academic acuity, and modesty. When "other Latino guys" taking AP classes (including Colombians, who were seen as higher achieving as a group, and mostly all had legal status) would tell Elmont he should try to take AP classes too, he would say, "Yeah, maybe I should," without revealing that he was already in AP classes.

Elmont laughed in describing the cognitive dissonance he inspired in his future wife (a Latina) in college: "I was a math tutor, and she came to tutorial services. . . . She thought I was there to get tutoring. I was like, 'You need tutoring?' She said, 'Yes.' I was like . . . 'I'm actually one of the math tutors.' She said: 'No, you're not.' I said, 'I am.' . . . She didn't believe me." Elmont also told me what happened when he wore a sweatshirt from a top firm where he was interning junior year of college. His friends (Hispanic and Black) asked how he had gotten it, not registering that wearing the shirt during internship season meant that he had gotten a plum internship.

Elmont's handling of the meeting with the principal hints at how his social intelligence and confidence enabled him to thrive in mostly White and mostly Black social worlds. His smile as he recounted such events showed that he enjoyed having his academic acuity challenge others' cognitive categories that had been primed by his appearance, and that he appreciated when powerful others (Hispanic or non-Hispanic) saw his ability and helped him.[19]

Elmont's approach to doing interviews with me showed similar confidence. While he had known me during my many years in the Ticuani community and knew of the help I had given his father's *comité*, we were not friends in a way that would have given me the standing to ask for an interview as a favor; instead, we were friendly acquaintances. He agreed to an interview after being satisfied by my answers about what the interview would entail and how it would be used. The tone of our interview was professional and peer to peer—he was a financial professional who had deemed my social science project worth his time and trust. He showed up on time, dressed in a crisp suit and nice shoes. (I felt schlubby in my professor uniform of chinos and rumpled oxford shirt.) When the time he had promised for the interview was nearly up, he told me that he had to wrap up soon, and we did so. Most interviews ran longer than I had asked for, because the interviewee wanted to tell their story and be listened to. But Elmont did not need me to listen to his story. He saw value in telling it, but then he had work to do.

Elmont skillfully and purposefully had developed his professional networks and mentoring relationships in college. He liked his Black fraternity at White Upstate University, which he had joined for two reasons. First, Blacks had more "similar upbringings" to his own compared to White students at his university. But, he said, "I still hung out with the White friends." Second, joining a Black fraternity was a "prestige thing": membership gave him a ready set of friends and mentors who were more active, he thought, because Blacks were a minority: "Those guys, I saw their network. Because they were smaller, they had a lot stronger network, and not just there."

When Elmont met his new fraternity brothers, they were surprised: "Wow—a Mexican that speaks English. Are you from New York?" Their reaction showed that his success contradicted the dominant image of Mexicans at the time as either being from the West Coast and successful or being from New York and not as academically successful. Nevertheless, he felt welcome in his Black fraternity. Elmont's story echoes others' accounts of opting into Blackness, at least as an operating identity, in contexts where Blackness was associated with upward mobility and where Mexicanness was either associated with not going to college or not yet linked as a cognitive category to college. That Elmont's Black fraternity brothers were surprised that he spoke English natively suggests that they lacked an established cognitive category of college-going Mexicans who spoke English as a natal language.[20] This story again reflects Mexicans' stage of settlement in New York in the late 1990s and early 2000s. Given the positive educational and career trajectories of U.S.-born Mexicans in New York, this cognitive category should be changing dramatically.

Elmont converted his summer internships in finance through OpenDoor into a good job after college graduation. Shocked to discover that there were "only three or four Latinos" in a firm of over two thousand people, he started the Latino Financial Mentoring Network (a pseudonym) to give other recent Latino/a college graduates the kind of network that he "did not have coming out." But Elmont underscored that, "luckily, I had other folks, who were White, who helped me out and took me under their wing. And I felt very comfortable with them." He was also rightly proud when he told me that this mentoring program for Latinos/as in finance grew from its five founding members to over fifteen hundred members nationwide within five years. This dramatic growth illustrated Elmont's impressive capacity to excel simultaneously in several areas. While succeeding in a hard major, he (and others) had done the traveling and the face-time work to grow other chapters and create a working network. In founding the Latino Financial Mentoring Network, he was thrilled to meet older Hispanics in senior positions in finance from California and Texas. Being in New York, he had felt like the only Latino in finance, but he now realized, "I just happened to be in New York."

Elmont's mentor at work was a White Irish immigrant. Having an immigrant boss "relieved any stress I would have possibly at talking to someone, maybe because they were White." But Elmont still quietly analyzed his White colleagues' lives, trying to understand them. The idea of going on vacation someplace besides Mexico to visit relatives was new to him. His father had "taken us on, like, three vacations" in Elmont's whole life. After repeatedly hearing about Disneyland vacations from his work-mates, he went there alone, at age twenty-five, an anthropologist studying proxies for his White colleagues. He also learned how to talk about American football because that was the Monday morning conversation.

Elmont's several non-coethnic mentors, including older Black college students and his White Irish mentor, evoke Richard Alba's argument that Wall Street and related industries will increasingly recruit minorities as baby boomer retirements create a need for new elites for these jobs.[21] If Alba is right, there will be structural potential for more mentoring relationships that support greater mobility and a Mexican culture of mobility in New York City—like those that helped Elmont.

Elmont was a best-case scenario for mentoring and good life conditions. His parents had obtained legal status and U.S. citizenship, his family was close, and his father earned a good income that enabled them to buy a building whose value increased dramatically over time. Although Elmont succeeded more than most NYCOMPers, good life conditions and mentors helped him and others in similar ways. I heard Elmont discussed as someone to emulate in his extended family and the Ticuani community, both for his success and for fully keeping the immigrant bargain with his parents. In informal conversations and an interview with Elmont's parents, their calm optimism burst into celebration when talking about their son, their voices rising as they reported each new success of his. They tried but could not contain their pride in him or their joy that their American dream, in their words, had worked out even better than they had hoped. Given all their hard work and extensive service to the Ticuani community, they had come to a place of pride and joy that I found infectious. As a fellow parent, I was happy for them, and for Elmont.

Suzie's Story: Getting a Second Chance through a Work Mentor

Suzie's was a case of getting a second chance through mentoring, after her positive trajectory through her late teens took a sudden, dramatic turn that worried her parents and seemed to signal a harder future.

I have known Suzie, now over forty years old and a mother of two, since she was in her midteens. Her case draws on ethnographic observation in Brooklyn and Mexico and on repeat interviews with Suzie in her home and in her parents' home, as well as on interviews with her sister, her parents (whom I have known since the late 1980s), and her now-ex-husband. Suzie's parents were very helpful in opening initial doors for my research in Ticuani. I see them as friends and am seen as a family friend by them.

Suzie seemed destined to become a High Flier. A strong middle school student, she explicitly, counterfactually, chose not to go to Presidents High so as to avoid cutting school with her middle school friends going to "all those hooky parties," and to avoid the Mexican gangs she knew were in that school. She chose Mad Men High in Manhattan for its strong academic reputation and links to the marketing industry. She was also active in Ticuani cultural life and engaged in transnational practices that helped other children of Mexican immigrants become upwardly mobile by positively changing what being Mexican meant to them.[22] Suzie seemed set to attend college and work in marketing.

My research benefited from Suzie's social skill, confidence, and kindness. In my first fieldwork in Ticuani, just as people there were getting to know me, she introduced me to others by mentioning relationships I had with people in Brooklyn who were known to them, vouching for me, and giving us something to talk about. She did this with both older adult men who knew her father and her own teenage and early adult Ticuani friends. When Suzie vouched for me, people usually spoke openly when they next saw me, because they trusted her. Our friendship deepened as she went from teenager to young adult, then to grown woman with children, and our conversations broadened to include discussion of our children and our parents' health and news of mutual Ticuani friends, and my students who had worked on this project and become friends with her.

My own experience of Suzie makes it easy to understand why her mentor invested in her. She was clear-eyed in assessing how she had helped or harmed her prospects, and her keen social intelligence made her easy to talk to and trust. Talking about her divorce, she evinced no bitterness and emphasized that her ex-husband Peter was a good father.

Suzie's path had changed when she fell in love with Peter, who was twenty-two years old at the time. Peter had come to the United States at age fifteen, after having started working full-time in Mexico at age twelve. Ironically, he was an early member of the Brooklyn Rancheros gang that then "owned" Presidents High. Suzie and Peter dated while she was in high school and eloped right after her graduation. They lived in an apartment without furniture ("just a bed and a TV") and did not tell her parents where they lived so that they could not "steal" her back. In this they were following an old custom from rural Puebla: a suitor "robs" his girlfriend from her family, marries her, and then presents the family with the fait accompli. Some such elopements are driven by romantic love and enable couples to marry without waiting for their parents full consent and to avoid the great expenditures for fiestas that communally celebrate the new marriage, as described by Mexican anthropologist Federico Besserer.[23]

Suzie attended college for one semester but left to work full-time. Her parents, pioneer migrants from Ticuani who had legalized via IRCA, spoke English and had stable jobs with steady incomes and benefits. They had saved money and could pay to send their two daughters to college. Her parents were dismayed when Suzie eloped with Peter, the undocumented gang member who drank too much and had only six years of schooling.

Suzie's life was reset through her parents' stabilizing interventions, Peter's receptivity to them, and her work mentor. Despite their misgivings, Suzie's parents, determined to build trust with and help the new couple, started having regular weekend dinners with them. Suzie's father helped get Peter a better restaurant job. Moreover, the parents bought a (cheap) second house and gave it to the young couple, who made over $150,000 by selling it two years later; they were then able to buy another house that, in Suzie's words, was in a "non-Mexican neighborhood" in a suburb. There they hoped to avoid the problems they associated with Mexican neighborhoods in Brooklyn.

The young couple's deepening relationship with Suzie's parents helped Peter immensely. He stopped drinking and became, in Suzie's view, a conscientious father who did his fair share of housework, and sometimes more, especially the cooking, as she often worked long hours. By age thirty, Suzie was the second-highest-ranking person in her department at Financial Publishing, with discretionary authority to arrange the first layout of the main magazine they published.

That Suzie and Peter reconciled with her parents and deepened their relationship with them matters because negative family dynamics correlate with worse adult outcomes, as we saw in chapter 2. Indeed, moving out of their parents' house before they were settled as an adult was a key factor correlating with lower adult educational attainment and income among all NYCOMPers. Suzie never faltered, however, in expressing a strong desire to keep the immigrant bargain, not even early on when she and Peter eloped. Her parents' embrace of Peter led him to strongly invest in that commitment. (He felt he lacked such relationships with his birth family.) Moreover, Suzie's parents repeatedly told me that they had refused to see the couple's separation from them as permanent. They saw it not as a *robo* (theft) that might break their relationship with Suzie, but as a challenge they would learn to manage. They worried about her not going to college and about Peter's drinking, but they also believed that their best path toward helping her was to make Peter a full member of their family. Her parents' social intelligence here enacted the immigrant family bargain in unanticipated circumstances.

Suzie had begun working at Financial Publishing as a temp in yet another poorly paid low-level job. But she had impressed her bosses, including her future mentor, who told her to apply for the permanent job, which she got. As a U.S. citizen, Suzie was able to create and take an "earned opportunity" through her hard work.

Over the next decade, Suzie worked closely with her boss, an African American woman sixteen years her senior. They made each other look good. Her mentor helped Suzie by giving her more responsibility and discretion in their work. Suzie was a quick study and could easily learn their industry's regularly changing technology and explain it to her boss. She learned how her boss worked, got her own work done without supervision, and became irreplaceable in their small department. Her boss gave her the flexibility to maintain a good family-work balance. If Suzie had to leave early to pick up a sick child or attend a parent-teacher conference, her boss said, "Go." Similarly, Suzie worked nights and weekends as needed without being asked to ensure that the department's work was done well and on deadline.

Suzie's boss became her mentor and an inside advocate who advised her on negotiations and advocated for her behind closed doors—a clear expression that she considered Suzie her mentee. The company offered Suzie a promotion, but with only a $5,000 raise instead of the $10,000 she wanted. She believed that the company's attitude was, "She's young, she's been here so many years, and she's going to take it for the little bit of money that you're going to give her." She held out, fortified by her boss's advice:

> My boss says: "I think you can get it." . . . They will try to negotiate something, and then they come back and say, "No, I'm sorry, we can only give you this amount." When they went up to talk to Human Resources, they told me that they could only give me this amount, and I said, "Well, I'm not going to do it for that amount." So they said, "No," and I said, "Fine, then I won't take it." I left it at that.

Suzie's boss was right: the company returned to offer Suzie the $10,000 raise she wanted, and she took the promotion.

Suzie was grateful for how much she had learned from her mentor and how well they understood each other, but she also noted that her boss sometimes saw racial discrimination where she did not. Other study participants similarly believed that African Americans saw racial discrimination at work in situations where they did not. If Suzie's department was excluded from a meeting that included White male heads of other departments, her boss saw racial discrimination, while Suzie sometimes saw other reasons for their exclusion. When I asked Suzie if she saw discrimination in the company lowballing her in salary negotiations, she said that she suspected that her gender, age, and lack of a college education had more to do with it than her being Hispanic: "But I don't feel it's because I'm Hispanic. I feel that I'm too young, and I'm a girl, and they feel that they can save themselves that money." It merits note that Suzie associated discrimination only with race or ethnicity and did not see it as discriminatory to be lowballed because she was young or "a girl."

This point about how racial discrimination is seen or not seen raises questions on which I can only preliminarily reflect here. Suzie and other NYCOMPerswere not unique in this perception of discrimination. Other research shows that Caribbean and African immigrants and their second-generation children also believe that African Americans see racial animus in interactions when they do not.[24] How do we reconcile the well-documented history of anti-Black policies, structures, and institutional practices in America with reports that racial discrimination is "seen" more often by African Americans than by some Hispanics and by immigrant or later-generation Black people?

A first answer is that this project and much research was done before the murder of George Floyd in the spring of 2020 and before the emergence of the Black Lives Matter (BLM) movement. If such studies were conducted today, they would probably find higher perceptions of discrimination. Second, both perceptions can be true: African Americans like Suzie's boss may see discrimination more because they face it more than many Hispanics, and more than some Caribbean or African first and second generation persons, at least in some contexts. Discrimination against African Americans could also be prompted by the stigmatized traits associated in racist thinking with African Americans but not with Black immigrants. The two perceptions can also reinforce each other. Some Black immigrants seek to avoid anti–African American discrimination by emphasizing their accents or by displaying national symbols (such as a national flag on their clothing), as documented in Mary Waters's book *Black Identities*.[25]

I do not think Suzie and others in the second generation had different perceptions because they were using the dual frame of reference of their parents, who perceived less hardship in the new country compared with the greater hardship in their home country.[26] Rather, I suspect that their lived experience was different from that of their African American peers. Even within contexts of commonplace diversity in New York City, anti–African American discrimination, especially toward men, may persist alongside more affirming perceptions of first- or later-generation Hispanics and Asians as fellow immigrants, as descendants of immigrants, or as non-Black.

Finally, these differing perceptions of racial discrimination are contextual. Karen Okigbo documents how high-achieving second-generation Nigerian professional men in the United States who do not feel discriminated against in their universities or workplaces feel that their Blackness is the only thing seen by police who stop them.[27]

Vicky's Story: A High Flier and Mentor Magnet Escaping the Negative Image of "That Mexican Girl"

When asked how she would describe her mentoring history, Vicky Fuerte said: "Mentors have always found me, rather than the other way around." Vicky would be an Olympic champion mentee, if such a category existed: she had had ten adult and two peer mentors (and rejected a potentially negative peer mentor), including four at key turning points in high school. The mentoring had been varied, ranging from one mentor who helped her get into college to another who helped her overcome her father's *machista* low expectations of her as a girl. I have known Vicky for over fifteen years. Her case narrative draws on over ten hours of interviews and intermittent long conversations, meetings, walks, and phone calls. Over the years I have seen how Vicky's mentoring helped her overcome her fear of becoming (in her words) "that Mexican girl" to become a thriving adult.

Vicky's first mentor was a paraprofessional in elementary school who treated her like she "was special" by putting her in the advanced reading groups. That experience helped her transfer out of bilingual education into the gifted English-only class in third grade. Vicy's third-grade teacher was a "very loving, encouraging, and empowered Black woman" who made her feel that she belonged in the gifted class, despite being one of only three non-Black students and "the only Mexican." Vicky's grade school mentors also persuaded her parents to let her go to the "Black" school, the academically rigorous Jackson Middle School. Her Jackson mentor helped her "tough it out" when she struggled in math class, where, again, she was the only Mexican.

After her disastrous, uncounseled choice to go to Future Professionals High, Vicky transferred to Comercio High, where her high school mentor, Mr. Hibbert, helped reset her life chances. Hibbert was not Vicky's assigned guidance counselor, but he helped her when that counselor did not believe that she had taken the first two years of high school math while still in middle school at Jackson. (She had, as Hibbert confirmed.)

Vicky trusted Hibbert—"Whatever Hibbert told me to do, I did it." He opened doors for her, including with the Women Bankers' Association (WBA). Her WBA mentor guided her through college applications, and they become close. When her WBA mentor saw that Vicky was too shy to speak in group meetings, she took her to lunch to "just talk . . . on her own time." As a senior, Vicky was offered full-ride scholarships at competitive universities. Her parents wanted her to go to CUNY, so she could live at home, like her older sister. They saw no benefit to attending a more prestigious school ("They did not get it," she said) and feared that she would get pregnant at school. Living away also required that Vicky incur some college debt.

Her WBA mentor quickly laid out a plan to visit universities to help her decide ("I didn't even know you could do that") and arranged the visit logistics for her to visit a college in the far north of upstate New York. ("It was snowing, *in April*. No.") Her mentor helped her "decide to go to Elite University" and reassured her by breaking down her estimated debt into a monthly payment of about $50. "I was freaked out. . . . Even that $50 seemed like a lot to me," she recalled, smiling, at age thirty-two.

Vicky's WBA mentor also unwittingly, in helping her leave her family home to live away at college, removed her from exposure to her father's harsh treatment and words, driven by his fear that his daughters would get pregnant. When her older sister Leeta did get pregnant during Vicky's senior year, their father reacted harshly toward Vicky too, repeatedly telling her to "just go get pregnant, like your sister," and "get it over with." She wrote about this in her college application essay, which she shared with me at the time. As mentioned earlier, in her final semester of high school she came home earlier than normal because her competitive internship program ended before regular high school did. Her father accused her of cutting school to be with a boyfriend and threatened to lock her behind the *Puerta Negra* (Black Door), invoking a song in Spanish about young *novios* kept apart by the girl's jealous father. (Vicky *did* have a secret boyfriend, a Mexican, but she was not cutting, and she did not get pregnant.)

Her father's threats were not hollow. As an adult, Vicky told me that her father had regularly hit Vicky and Leeta, even when they were young adults, because "he didn't want us to mess up. And this was his way of keeping us in check," she said. He was more apt to use physical punishment when he drank, as he did regularly. Leeta had repeatedly threatened to run away. Once, Vicky's boyfriend waited outside for her after she returned home. They planned to run away together if her father hit her. She had had enough. But her father was asleep when she got home that night. Her father later came to regret his earlier conduct, changed his ways, and would treat their younger sister, Zinia, differently.

Vicky had the best grades of all WBA mentees and was picked to give the mentee speech at the association's end-of-year banquet. After the speech, WBA members congratulated her and offered help in her future job searches. The speech also helped persuade her parents to let her live away at Elite University. Living away gave her room to breathe, and with distance from her home life, she could see how unfairly her father had judged her. As a thirty-two-year-old, she told me that her father had said after the speech, "'Now I see that you mean something.' . . . I was *so pissed*. . . . He was proud of me—I see that as an adult. . . . I have kind of forgiven him." But even recounting the event as a grown woman, Vicky was clearly still angry. Her voice slowed down as she repeated his words "that . . . you . . . mean . . . something." The "p" in "pissed" was a hard plosive "p," expressing her fury that her father needed external proof of her worth and had beaten her rather than just value her as his daughter.

Vicky lamented later that her fears had led her to miss mentoring opportunities. At Elite University, she kept silent in class for fear of "saying something stupid" that might reveal that "I did not belong there." Places like Elite University value class participation highly, and high-performing students usually speak in class, sometimes to excess. Vicky reported that professors sought her out after reading her written work. "Are you Vicky?" they would ask, seeking to reconcile the insightful paper with this silent student and offering to mentor her. But she accepted none of these mentorship offers, still fearing that her professors would somehow discover that she did not belong there. She did accept help from her first-year roommate, a former Jackson classmate who had gone through Prep for Prep (as noted, the program that recruited top public school students into elite private and boarding schools) and hence knew what college professors would want. When Vicky got a bad first paper grade, her roommate went "line by line" through the paper with her to explain what the professor would be looking for.

As an adult in her late thirties with a graduate degree and working in education, Vicky actively recruited new mentors and had no fear that her peers would think she did not belong. When her public agency started a senior-junior staff mentoring program, she quickly signed up. Her senior mentor helped her formulate a plan to get into another division where Vicky saw more potential to grow at work. Having succeeded in making the move, she was now much happier.

Vicky's story shows how a series of good mentors helped a smart young woman overcome a series of obstacles to avoid the fate she feared (becoming "that Mexican girl") and create a thriving adult life for herself. Having many strong mentors in her life promoted Vicky's mobility despite hard home conditions.

Emmanuel's Story: Mentoring as an Escape Ladder and Door Opener to High Flier Status

Emmanuel used mentoring as a ladder out of hard circumstances and a path to becoming a High Flier.[28] His undocumented mother was gravely ill for several of his teen years, and his father had left the family years before. Emmanuel's two siblings did not finish high school, and his older brother, Thor, was in the X Street Boys gang. Mentoring played a key role in Emmanuel's unlikely road from growing up on X Street to becoming a lawyer. I have known Emmanuel for over fifteen years and interviewed him many times. I have interviewed his mother, brother, and some friends. He was in his late thirties when I drafted this chapter in 2018, and we have become friends.

Emmanuel had a series of mentors who helped create a virtuous cycle of opportunity for him. His first and longest-lasting mentor was his parish priest, Father X, who was, in his mother Lila's words, more "like his father to him" than his real father. Emmanuel would use the same words to describe Father X. (I chose the pseudonym "Father X" to reflect his ministry to and trust in the X Street Boys, whom many would have dismissed as bad kids.) Father X also mentored Emmanuel's mother Lila, guiding her in making key decisions. The priest advised Lila not to return to Mexico, a move she was considering to get Thor away from gangs. He argued that Emmanuel's potential would not get developed in Mexico, where he would have less opportunity. Following his counsel, she decided to stay in New York. Father X also advised Lila to let Emmanuel attend the "Black" high school rather than force him to go to the local zoned high school, and he later persuaded her to let her son live on campus at Elite University. In all these cases, Emmanuel's strong record and the trust Lila had in him and in Father X helped her choose the better path for her son.

Father X called himself a "parish priest," which he was, in the best meaning of that phrase. A New York Irishman (in his words) who spoke excellent Spanish with an awful "I learned this language as an adult" accent (about which I gently teased him), Father X was out in front working with and advocating for Mexican immigrants within the Catholic Church in the early 1990s. The Church had been slow to respond to the largest new ethnic group in its fold. Father X lived in a kind of time capsule in the years after Vatican II, when the Church had fought more directly for and alongside those in need. He was part of a group of older priests who believed that the Catholic Church's real mission was to help the poor and work to empower the poor, immigrants, and other vulnerable groups, rather than engage in culture war issues such as gay marriage. Father X helped his parishioners in deportation or eviction proceedings. I tried to help these priests by attending meetings with their Church superiors as an outside academic expert to argue that the Church needed to do more to help the Mexican community.

Perhaps the most important way Father X mentored Emmanuel was the one described at the opening of this chapter: he took the youth out to eat every month, to sit and talk, a practice they kept up while Emmanuel was at Elite University. Indeed, Emmanuel's interaction with Father X had been affirming since the first time he met the priest as a nine-year-old. Emmanuel was sitting in the parish hall after church and Father X asked if he could read and write in both Spanish and English. When he said yes, Father X exclaimed, "Wow!" This brief celebration of his bilingual ability made the boy feel like somebody ("He made me feel smart") and started a mentoring relationship that lasted sixteen years, until Father X's death. In the friendship created during these unhurried monthly meals, Emmanuel could ask Father X questions that could not emerge in other spaces, and Father X could help him because of their mutual trust.

Father X's mentorship helped change how Emmanuel thought about his future. After choosing to go to Canady High School, he was connected with Dr. Comer, his second main mentor.[29] Comer led a mentorship program at Canady High for minority students who were hoping to become doctors. If Emmanuel talked about Father X as his emotional father, he talked about Dr. Comer as his ambassador from a land of opportunity, a mentor who made him believe that he could join that world. Comer pushed Emmanuel to reimagine his future and made him feel that he could someday become "somebody" as his mentor had. Comer brought Emmanuel to see Elite University, where he had close links, and told the young man he could go there, given his record. "The fact that he believed in me, that I could make it in there [Elite University]—I was like, you know, maybe I have a chance. . . . I considered myself smart, but I didn't think I was that smart, that I could get into that school. When we went on the tour, he took me around to different departments." Emmanuel described Comer as "a father figure to me" and recalled how good it felt at age fifteen when "the old people" at a "high-end" restaurant asked Comer, "Is he your son? He's so handsome."

The college professor whose house Lila cleaned gladly helped Emmanuel write his college application essay. Comer advised him on what to write about in the essay. Rather than focus on his single mother's struggles (an old story for admissions committees), Comer told him to write about how he avoided gang life. That topic would make his essay stand out. Comer also reframed the entire gang issue for him. One night Emmanuel complained that Mexicans were fighting each other instead of fighting Blacks, who picked on them. Noting Comer's negative reaction, Emmanuel remembered he was African American and felt bad. But he took Comer's response to heart: "How about they just don't fight at all?"

Traveling the long social distance from X Street in Brooklyn to Elite University and law school, Emmanuel, like Vicky, was an unlikely High Flier. His story shows, first, that not all hard home life conditions are the same. Although she lacked legal status and was ill during his teen years, Lila, Emmanuel's single mother, effectively found and took counsel from mentors for herself and her son. She stayed in New York, got help for him with his college essay, and supported his decision to go to Canady High School for its mentoring program. Similarly, though he dropped out of high school and was in a gang, Emmanuel's brother Thor helped the family financially and supported his brother's academic pursuits, contributions that Emmanuel repeatedly and gratefully recognized as a teen and an adult.[30] Both Lila and Thor faced challenges themselves, but took exceptional steps to help Emmanuel.

By contrast, Vicky's hard home life conditions included a father who could not, in her view, see her value and had treated her like an "ugly duckling." Without knowing it, her mentor helped her escape from a home where corporal punishment was harshly administered and she did not feel valued.

Second, Emmanuel's mentors, both natural and formal, were long-term, caring, and effective. Natural mentoring came from his exceptional parish priest. The formal mentoring he received at his "Black" high school helped make a future like Dr. Comer's imaginable to Emmanuel. Comer spent time with Emmanuel and made him feel like he was somebody. The emotional bonds between Emmanuel and his mentors enabled him to accept and act on their advice. These were not one-off "how to go to college" sessions but rather old-school, long-term, one-on-one mentoring relationships that boosted Emmanuel's adult mobility and happiness.

Statistical Analysis of Long-Term Effects of Positive Mentoring

Vicky's and Emmanuel's stories show us *how* mentoring can help youth facing hard life conditions. The statistics reported here tell us *how much* having a mentor correlated with adult outcomes among all ninety-six NYCOMPers, even those with hard life conditions, such as having an undocumented mother. Some 67 percent of those who had any positive adult mentor as a teen ended up as a College Graduate or a High Flier at age twenty-eight, versus 31 percent who did not have a mentor. The former had nearly two years more schooling and made over $17,000 more per year than the latter (see table 4.1 in the note, explained fully in the online appendix).[31]

Having a positive adult mentor as a teen correlated with other relationships affecting adult mobility. As expected, having a positive adult mentor positively correlated with having a positive peer mentor as a teen: 44 percent with a positive adult mentor also had a positive peer mentor, versus only 9 percent of those who had no positive adult mentor (see table 4.2 in the note; see also the online appendix).[32] Having a positive adult mentor did not correlate negatively, however, with having a negative peer mentor, because negative peer mentors were often embedded in participants' lives—for example, Emmanuel's gang member brother. Moreover, fewer study participants with positive adult mentors escalated conflicts as teens (13 percent) or as early adults (11 percent) compared to those without adult mentors (64 percent and 60 percent, respectively). Such conflict escalations were often experienced with negative peer mentors and were linked to less adult income and education. Study participants said that their adult mentors helped them manage their relationships with embedded negative peer mentors to reduce risk to their own futures and help them make choices that would promote their adult mobility. I saw this dynamic repeatedly when I oversaw a mentoring program for several years during this period at the nonprofit I had cofounded.

Stronger mentoring over a longer period helped youth more than shallower mentoring relationships of shorter duration. To analyze this relationship, I recategorized all positive adult mentoring relationships to reflect their depth and duration, how much help was offered and accepted, and whether mentoring was offered before or during important decisions or at key turning points. In figure 4.1, "no mentoring" means that a participant had no positive adult mentor as a teen. "Minimal mentoring" indicates that the participant had help in an institutional setting such as school for a relatively short period, but not from anyone who fostered game-changing development or changes in their thinking. "Strong mentoring" was usually provided by individuals who started mentoring a participant in their teens and then usually continued mentoring them beyond their teen years by helping them develop or rethink things and gain access to contexts with more resources. Finally, "exceptional mentoring" came from those who improved participants' lives by mentoring them for many years beyond their teen years, advising them in their educational, career, and personal decisions, and opening doors into contexts with more opportunity and teaching them how to succeed there.

Figure 4.1 shows the overlap between having stronger mentors and becoming a College Graduate or High Flier: 73 percent of those without an adult mentor were Stuck Muddlers at age twenty-eight, while only 17 percent were High Fliers (see table 4.3 in the note).[33] Conversely, 33 percent who had exceptional mentoring were High Fliers, and only 3 percent were Stuck Muddlers. Similarly, those without mentors earned under $30,000 at age twenty-eight and had 12.2 years of education, while those with exceptional mentors earned over $70,000 and had 15.6 years of education. The online chapter statistical appendix presents more detailed findings.

Mentoring is especially important for those facing hard life circumstances. To avoid the overdetermining effect of legal status, we calculated the probability that participants who were U.S. citizens or lawful permanent residents would end up as Stuck Muddlers (versus any of the other three outcome categories), adjusting for (factoring out) three common hard home life conditions our informants faced: having an undocumented mother when the participant was an adult (time 2, at twenty-eight years old); living with domestic violence as a teen; or having a negative peer mentor.[34] Controlling for these hard home life

Figure 4.1 Mentor Quality and Time 2 Outcomes

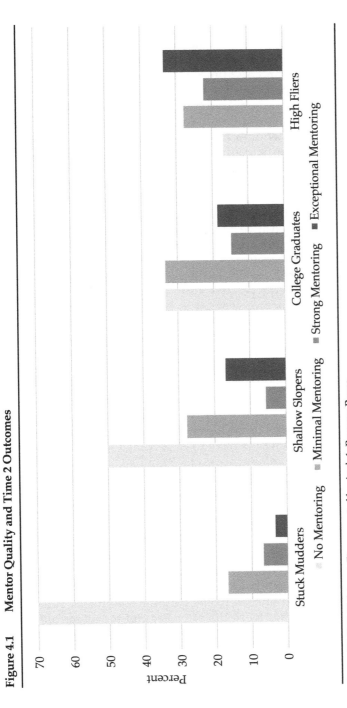

Source: NYCOMP data set. Figure created by Andrés Besserer Rayas.

conditions, having any positive adult peer mentor made a participant 12.6 times more likely to be a Shallow Sloper than a Stuck Muddler at age twenty-eight, 31.4 times more likely to be a College Graduate than a Stuck Muddler, and 37.2 times more likely to be a High Flier than a Stuck Muddler. (See table 4.4 in the note; see also the online chapter appendix.[35]) Mentoring helped these U.S. citizen NYCOMPers prosper despite the hard home life conditions they faced.

We also calculated how having a positive adult mentor affected the probability that participants who were U.S. citizens or lawful permanent residents and grew up in neutral versus negative conditions would become College Graduates or High Fliers. Of those who grew up with one or more of these negative conditions, 87 percent with positive adult mentors became College Graduates or High Fliers, versus only 7 percent who had no positive adult mentor.[36] (See table 4.5 in the note; see also the online chapter appendix.[37]) In contrast, of those in neutral home life conditions (no negative conditions present), 82 percent with a positive adult mentor were College Graduates or High Fliers, as were 48 percent of those who lacked a positive adult mentor. Hence, although having a positive adult mentor seemed to help those in positive or neutral home life conditions, it was nearly a prerequisite to becoming a College Graduate or High Flier for those facing hard home life conditions.

Finally, rerunning the same analyses to include undocumented cases confirmed that lacking legal status impeded mentors' efforts to help. The probability of becoming a College Graduate or High Flier for those with negative home life conditions and positive adult mentors fell, from 87 percent for U.S. citizens only to 61 percent of all cases; it also fell for those with neutral home life conditions and positive adult mentors, though by less, from 82 percent to 78 percent. (See table 4.6 in the note; see also the online chapter appendix.[38])

Lacking legal status stymied mentors' attempts to help their undocumented mentees, as we discuss in chapter 5.

Conclusion

Adult mentoring improved teens' upward mobility as adults. Elmont's case showed how mentoring helped a teen facing good conditions to build on them, while Emmanuel's and Vicky's cases showed how mentoring helped them overcome hard life conditions. Suzie's mentor helped her rerail her work life after her eighteen-year-old decisions nearly derailed it. Our data show that deeper and longer mentoring relationships helped more, especially for youth facing hard home life conditions, but also that legal status prevented some mentees from walking through the doors that mentors had opened for them.

Mentoring is nearly absent from most research on the children of immigrants, including from racial exclusion theory, assimilation theory, even legal exclusion theory. Many studies of long-term or intergenerational mobility do not discuss mentors.[39] In their work, the psychologist Carola Suárez-Orozco and her colleagues show that only 14 percent of youth, mostly girls, had mentors.[40] A key exception is Vivian Louie's innovative book, *Keeping the Immigrant Bargain*, in which upwardly mobile Colombian and Dominican second-generation youth said that supportive mentors and schools helped them succeed.[41]

María Rendón's *Stagnant Dreamers* offers perhaps the most apposite case here. Studying Mexican second-generation early adults who were mostly U.S. citizens, she found that the mobility of both those with a college education and those without was stymied. Only one of her forty-three participants had a cross-class mentor, while 47 percent in this study did, including 43 percent of boys and 51 percent of girls.

That most longer-term mentors in this study who were professionally employed were *not* Mexican in origin reflected Mexicans' stage of settlement in the late 1990s and early 2000s. At that time, there were fewer older Mexican professionals, and many of those few were elite lateral transfers from Mexico who had little contact with these children of migrants from rural Puebla. But that most participants were effectively mentored by Black, White, and non-Mexican Hispanics offers hope of more cross-ethnic mentorship arising as more and more professional and even elite economic and educational sectors open up with the retirement of aging baby boomers.[42] Moreover, while most mentors of NYCOMPers were non-Mexican, established professionals, dramatic Mexican mobility, and the emerging Mexican culture of mobility in New York City should support more such intra-ethnic, cross-class mentoring in the future.

Conversely, the absence of mentors in most studies in other places, or their inability to promote mobility even for the U.S.-born second generation, points to the need for more research on mentors, including studies that ask how pro-mobility contexts can make them more effective. Greater access to mentors is a key factor explaining why Mexican mobility has been greater in New York City than in other places that have been the focus of prior studies.

Small interactions within an established mentoring relationship can have big impacts.[43] Vicky had spent many miserable years in a legal job she disliked when I made the small observation that she sounded stuck and suggested that she go to therapy to get unstuck. That remark helped her reframe her thinking about therapists and about the real possibility of changing career paths, despite her high income as a paralegal. (Many higher-income second-generation adult children feel that they need to earn a lot of money to help their parents; moreover, switching to a lower-income job they like more may not make sense to their parents.) Vicky subsequently found a good therapist who helped her feel comfortable moving into education. Conversely, many participants' circumstances prevented them from accepting the help offered by my researchers and myself.[44]

Mentoring can help in two crucial ways analyzed in this chapter. First, it can change how young people imagine their futures. Second, mentors, who usually have higher social and cultural capital than their mentees can make transparent and legible processes that are opaque because they rely on tradition or a profession's unwritten rules. However, mentoring cannot overcome the structural limitations imposed by lack of legal status, because undocumented mentees cannot take the opportunities that mentors create for them. Nevertheless, undocumented mentees who got DACA (and its work permit) thrived with their mentors' help, as we discuss in chapter 5. Similarly, children whose parents legalized their status via IRCA similarly benefited from mentors' help. The policy fix is clear: legalizing undocumented young Americans would enable them to thrive and contribute more to American life.

Mentoring is an important part of an emerging Mexican culture of mobility in New York City. U.S. citizen and Category Changer Mexican NYCOMPers attended high school and college at high rates and found mentoring opportunities there. Moreover, the city's Mexican upward mobility infrastructure is more developed than it was twenty years ago. Since 2012, CUNY's Mexican Studies Institute has run a *becarios* (scholarship) program that places scholarship recipients in organizations for a year or more, helping them launch into professional careers. For twenty years, Masa has run after-school homework, mentoring, and empowerment programs for students and programs and organized support for parents. Other key parts of this infrastructure include the Qualitas of Life Foundation, which supports financial literacy; Mixteca, an organization that serves health and other community needs in Sunset Park; La Colmena, a workers' center on Staten Island; and New Immigrant Community Empowerment (NICE), an organization that empowers day laborers, especially women, by training them with new skills and to defend their rights and work safely. These organizations function like Chinese after-school programs in that they provide collective support to promote educational achievement and community empowerment. Although daunting challenges remain, these encouraging signs are part of the Mexican mobility story and reflect a Mexican culture of mobility emerging in New York City.

Chapter 5

DACA: A Revocable Program That Can Unblock Mobility and Make Private the Stigma of Undocumented Status

I<small>N HIGH</small> school and college, before DACA and before the Dreamer movement in 2006, Claudette "passed" as documented with her unaccented English, good grades, and careful concealment of her legal status. After the 2006 immigrants' rights marches, she criticized her Dominican, Puerto Rican, and Colombian classmates for making fun of Mexicans as "illegals" and always defended "them." But she never revealed that she was undocumented herself, or that she was Mexican. Claudette even withheld this information in a group counseling session, fearing other students would make fun of her for her lack of legal status.

Claudette also felt that some staff at her high school treated Mexicans differently. Her guidance counselor, who spent "more than half an hour" with her Colombian or other non-Mexican Hispanic students (who have higher rates of documented status and U.S. citizenship than Mexicans), spent "less than ten minutes" with her and her mother and told her just to go to CUNY. Claudette thought that the meeting was brief and the advice perfunctory because the counselor believed that Mexicans were all undocumented and that their only option was to go to CUNY. (Neither belief was true at the time.) Although she graduated from college, Claudette could not even get unpaid internships or a student teaching placement, because she lacked a Social Security number. She had wanted to become a teacher and inspire students, as her mentor Ms. T had inspired her. Claudette's undocumented status was a stigmatized master status that affected even her interactions with other Hispanic immigrant or U.S. citizen students and with her Colombian immigrant guidance counselor.

DACA made being undocumented less of a master status for Claudette and enabled her to hit the reset button. Though she had already graduated

https://doi.org/10.7758/drwz9626.5542

from college, after getting DACA she went back to an old professor who gladly helped her get an unpaid internship, which led to placements in human services jobs. She has excelled in this field ever since and been repeatedly promoted. Claudette said that having DACA converted her undocumented status from a social fact about her into a "private issue . . . an HR issue"—running in reverse C. Wright Mills's description of the work of sociology as making individual problems into social ones.[1] Mexicanness had signaled "illegality" in her high school, but DACA now limited the impact of her undocumented status on her life as a human services professional. In short, having DACA made Claudette less socially undocumented by giving her gatekeeper identity documents: a work permit, a Social Security number, and a driver's license.

Having DACA and these documents also opened up opportunities for Claudette—especially in employment commensurate with her educational level—that her undocumented status had previously blocked. DACA thus made being undocumented less a master status than a manageable private fact about herself. With DACA, she could navigate her work and social lives without the stigma of being undocumented, and she could engage in activities, like travel, that primed the "documented" category. To invoke a predominant theoretical trope, just as she had learned what it meant to be "illegal" through the many doors shut in her face, Claudette was now learning via DACA what it was like to "become functionally legal"—even if only in specific settings, and revocably—as DACA reopened many of those doors.[2] The long-term nature of this project enabled me to track how Claudette's life, jobs, and contexts changed over time, both before and after she got DACA.

Despite all of Claudette's post-DACA accomplishments and the decrease in her stress about her legal status, she remained grimly realistic about the future. She recognized that her DACA status was revokable and temporary. The chances of DACA continuing, along with the life she had built on it, were "always fifty-fifty," she said.

This chapter analyzes how DACA made being undocumented less of a master status for many in this study and opened up opportunities, especially for high-achievers, but could not "fix" key problems linked to undocumented status. Prior research shows that lacking legal status harms undocumented immigrants and their U.S. citizen children, and even grandchildren, causing what Menjívar and Abrego describe as legal violence. Roberto Gonzales and others have analyzed how being undocumented becomes a master status as youth move from the protection of school into the labor market and their adult lives, where their lack of legal status blocks their participation and advancement. Caitlin Patler, Carola Suárez-Orozco, and others have shown the harms to health of lacking legal status and the improvements in immigrants' health and their children's health when they get legal status or DACA. Other research shows that getting DACA strongly increases recipients' income as well as their ability to look for new jobs. The work of Laura Enriquez and Leisy Abrego and others shows that lacking legal status even interferes with intimate relationships: undocumented young people are fearful of marrying or starting families, knowing that they could be separated at any time for any reason—or for no reason.[3]

This chapter extends such research in two ways. First, it builds on prior chapters by analyzing how DACA unblocked some participants' earned opportunities and enabled their mentors to help them in ways they could not before DACA, when their mentees had lacked gatekeeper identity documents. (All DACA recipients get a work permit and Social Security number, but states control who can get a driver's license. New York State allowed DACA recipients to get a license.) Moreover, the chapter analyzes how having a work permit and Social Security number enabled DACA recipients to work legally, to look for jobs commensurate with their educational attainment, and to take advantage of earned opportunities, which had been difficult without a work permit. Having a work permit also moved the point at which they had to disclose their undocumented status further along in their relationship with an employer, to *after* an offer had been made and accepted, as part of the onboarding process. Pre-DACA, because they lacked a work permit, they were usually screened out immediately, well before an offer was made; in addition, their lack of a work permit often led them not to apply for a job, anticipating that they would be disqualified. With DACA, their undocumented status was converted into, in Claudette's phrase, "an HR issue" rather than a disqualifying and stigmatizing social fact. Taken together, these processes partly (if revocably) broke the link between Mexicanness and illegality in DACA recipients' interactions with the key American institution of the labor market, as well as in relationships with friends.

Second, this chapter extends prior research on racialized illegality, stigma, priming, and "passing" as documented. Stigma does harm by importing disqualifying traits of one category of person (for example, criminals) into perceptions of or interactions with members of another category (such as Mexicans).[4] Stigma is especially harmful when it affects interactions with institutions that should treat everyone equally, like schools and polling places.[5] Similarly, racialized illegality harms "Mexican-looking" people by silently priming negative traits often conveyed via specific images; these are "controlling images," in the words of Patricia Hill Collins, and Jessica Vasquez-Tokos and Kathryn Norton-Smith.[6] People "pass" by priming images seen as the opposite—here, images that prime the "documented person" cognitive category.

The sociologists René Flores and Ariela Schachter found that White Americans see Mexican-looking people as more likely to be undocumented or criminal, a perception that makes them want to call the police.[7] Not surprisingly, since NYCOMPers lived in an almost totally Black and Brown social world, they reported that the perception of racialized illegality linking Mexicans with being undocumented was mostly enacted by Puerto Ricans, Dominicans, and Colombians, who have lower levels of undocumented status. Even those who lived in neighborhoods with substantial White populations had few or no White friends, because many of those Whites were Orthodox Jews, who did not attend public schools, or Eastern European immigrants, with whom they were less likely to socialize. Moreover, because upwardly mobile study participants were less likely to attend their zoned high school, this important institution of integration and socialization was delinked from their neighborhood. Many study participants, both documented and undocumented, regularly spoke of their Puerto Rican, Dominican, and Colombian classmates as racializing and stigmatizing their Mexicanness by linking it to illegality.

This social fact—that non-Mexican Hispanic students, nearly all of them immigrants or children of immigrants, would associate Mexicanness with illegality and tease Mexican students about it—may be surprising, but it is consistent with research showing discrimination by "Mestizo" or "non-indigenous-looking" Hispanics against "indigenous-looking" Hispanic immigrants.[8] I put these descriptors in quotation marks to recognize that phenotype does not truly convey an individual's nationality or legal status. At the same time, I would invoke William I. Thomas and Dorothy Thomas's insight that if people believe that a situation or a phenomenon is real, "they are real in their consequences." Hence, if others believe that phenotype really does reveal a person's legal status, that belief constructs a social reality wherein phenotype is used for that purpose.[9]

Mexicanness is also linked to "illegality" in the minds of Asian immigrants. Enriquez and her colleagues analyzed the response of community organizations that were dismayed that undocumented Mexicans were getting California driver's licenses, which protect against deportation, but undocumented Asian immigrants were not. Asian immigrants did not apply for driver's licenses because they believed that licenses were not for them, but rather for undocumented people, like Mexicans. To promote applications for these driver's licenses, these community organizations mounted a campaign to "reracialize" driver's licenses as "Asian" also.[10] Similarly, the sociologist Jia-Lin Liu argues that undocumented Chinese immigrants see applying for asylum as the "Chinese" way to legalize, and that they regard being undocumented as a stigma that applies to Mexicans, but not to them. This belief persists even though it effectively leaves many permanently undocumented, since so many Chinese asylum applications fail.[11] This helps explain why Chinese undocumented youth applied for DACA at much lower rates than their Mexican counterparts. Indeed, only 740 immigrants from China (and Hong Kong) had obtained DACA as of 2017 (just under the 750 Canadian DACA recipients) versus 548,000 Mexicans.[12] Some 66 percent of immediately eligible Mexicans got DACA, versus 2.5 percent of eligible Chinese.[13]

Angela Garcia's insightful 2019 book, *Legal Passing*, recounts the belief of undocumented Mexican drivers in California—confirmed by the sociologist Amada Armenta's 2017 book *To Protect, Serve, and Deport*—that the police stop them because they see an "undocumented-looking" and "Mexican-looking" person driving and invent a pretext to stop them.[14] Garcia's respondents altered their presentation of self to avoid priming the image of "undocumented Mexican" and to prime "documented Hispanic" instead by changing out of work clothes into chinos and oxford shirts to drive home, driving newer cars, and even getting stylish haircuts. Priming dynamics differ in New York, where many believe that most Mexicans are undocumented and where most Hispanic people (Puerto Ricans, Dominicans, many South Americans) believe they appear phenotypically different from Mexicans and hence do not similarly prime an image of illegality. In some interactions in this study, Puerto Rican or Dominican students seemed to enact a dynamic that the psychologist Susan Fiske describes as "envy up, scorn down" toward Mexican students, whom they saw as having lesser status as persons, due to their presumed lack of legal status.[15] Over half of undocumented study participants, especially those who said that they "looked Mexican," reported that they had "passed" as documented.

High-achieving recipients were especially likely to mention no longer needing to pass as documented after they became DACA-holding adults. At that point, they were as documented as they needed to be in their relationship to a primary institution that determines life chances—the labor market. With their gatekeeper identity documents, they could participate more fully and safely in American life, whether doing internships or lowering their risk of deportation by being able to drive legally.[16] Some were able to gain lawful permanent residency after getting DACA.

Deferred Action: A Pragmatic but Revocable Band-Aid on America's Broken Immigration System

Deferred Action for Childhood Arrivals (DACA) was never intended to fix the problems linked to legal status for Dreamers. As a policy on enforcement of the law rather than a program created by a law, DACA was President Obama's attempt to use executive authority to at least partly ameliorate structural exclusions that could only be resolved by passage of an immigration reform law by Congress. (Obama's never-implemented Deferred Action for Parents of Americans and Lawful Permanent Residents, or DAPA, and a "DACA2" expansion were also executive actions.[17]) Such a reform law could include a pathway to legal status and citizenship for most of America's nearly 11 million undocumented people.

Facing decades of congressional inaction on immigration—during which the undocumented population had grown from about 3 million to over 12 million in the mid-2000s—Obama used executive branch authority to create programs of prosecutorial discretion, including DACA. DACA recipients are still deportable, but the DACA policy defers action on them—in the hope that Congress will reform immigration laws—and gives recipients work authorization, a Social Security number, and protection from deportation due to undocumented status. DACA does not prevent deportation for a crime, or even for minor infractions. In short, DACA tells long-term undocumented youth: We recognize that you are an undocumented adult through no fault of your own and that America has not offered you a permanent path forward. We recognize that you want the same chance to benefit from your hard work as your U.S.-born peers. All we can do without congressional action is offer temporary quasi-legal status and work permits so that you can go to college, work and drive legally, and start a family without the constant fear of deportation. With no other choice available, DACA was a good deal, especially for those who lived where ICE or police targeted and deported immigrants for minor offenses, such as getting a traffic ticket.[18]

DACA gave temporary and renewable status, work authorization, and protection from deportation to those who arrived in the United States before June 15, 2007; had resided here continuously ever since; had graduated from high school, gotten a GED, or were enrolled in adult education; and posed no threat to the United States. The Migration Policy Institute and the Pew Research Center estimated that 2.4 million people could have applied for DACA, though only about 830,000 applications were approved.[19]

President Donald Trump sought to end DACA by executive order in September 2017, but advocates sued. The Supreme Court ruled in 2020 that he had not followed the Administrative Procedure Act in ending DACA and ordered it reinstated for current DACA recipients. The Court did not, however, allow new DACA applications. Meanwhile, in another lawsuit by Texas and other states, a Texas district court ruled in 2018 that DACA must end (a ruling later upheld by the Fifth Circuit Court of Appeals) but permitted current holders to renew their work permits while advocates appealed the ruling. That case (for which I served as an expert witness for MALDEF, the Mexican American Legal Defense and Education Fund) is still in litigation and is likely to end up before the Supreme Court.[20]

DACA's Positive Impacts on NYCOMP Participants and Their Families

Study participants, especially higher-achieving ones, said that DACA dramatically advanced their careers and changed how they experienced themselves in relationship to key institutions as well as in their daily lives and presentation of self. Specifically, they said that DACA:

- Unblocked their educational and work careers and catalyzed "warp-drive" jumps in their success, enabling them to seek, take, and develop earned opportunities and new jobs and to walk through doors opened for them by their mentors that they had been unable to enter pre-DACA.

- Changed how they "passed" as documented by making their undocumented status less of a master status and more of a private status, thus decreasing the psychological work of passing and even opening a door to lawful permanent residency for some.

- Decreased the importance of being undocumented in intrafamily dynamics and intimate partner relationships, enabling recipients to better keep the immigrant bargain.

- Enabled them to move geographically and to explore their options in early adulthood rather than simply work all the time.

Starting with pre-DACA harms and detailing post-DACA benefits, we trace how DACA affected these processes in the cases presented here and extend the analysis to cases analyzed in prior chapters, recognizing that the program affected recipients differently, depending on their age and place in the life cycle. One caveat to this positive DACA story: huge numbers of people either did not qualify for DACA or feared giving their information to the federal government and hence did not apply, as we see in two cases discussed at the end of the chapter.

Carlotta's Story: DACA Resets an Educational Trajectory and Enables a Mentor to Help

Participating in the 2006 immigrants' rights marches changed how Carlotta thought about her legal status. After the marches and during

Obama's presidency, Dreamer organizations reframed undocumented status. Previously thought of as a dangerous personal secret, it became a sign of a broken system that denied these young Americans the same chances available to their U.S. citizen peers.[21] They thus converted their private problem of lacking status into a social problem, per C. Wright Mills.[22] Indeed, after she had worked in two Dreamer organizations, Carlotta's undocumented status had a different meaning for her than it had had for Xavier and Claudette at that age. Carlotta gathered signatures for the New York Dream Act (passed in 2019), which provides many undocumented New Yorkers with New York State funding for college. In seeking signatures, she was "out," directly telling people how she and many others struggled to go to college without funding, because they lacked legal status, owing to the nation's broken immigration system. She thus enacted Marshall Ganz's method of promoting change by telling stories of "self, us, and now."[23] Carlotta felt that this work helped her help others: "One day, hopefully, I will go to college and do something. . . . I'm going to work with my community. It's to unite us."

But redefining what her legal status meant to her did not blunt its impact on her early adult life. She still lost earned opportunities and could not walk through the doors opened for her by mentors. One regular customer who liked her good humor in managing the lunch rush at the deli where she worked offered her a job as a receptionist at his company. She thanked him, but when she disclosed that she did "not have papers," he apologetically withdrew the offer. She was later offered a job in a Dreamer organization and another job working for an elected official who had liked her volunteer work, but both retracted their offers after learning her status. Carlotta had never said that she had documents, but she had "behaviorally passed" as documented with her native English, college enrollment, and organizing acumen and energy. She did not prime the undocumented category.

In-state tuition at CUNY for undocumented students had been the law since 2002, but Carlotta's high school had not told her (or her brother, who graduated four years later) that she was eligible for in-state tuition rates when she graduated in the mid-2000s. Registering at CUNY, she was incorrectly charged international student rates (over double the in-state rates) and thus could afford to take only one class. She had to drop out. She did not learn of her right to in-state tuition until our first interview.

Carlotta worked as a nanny in college. Her boss, Esperanza, liked how much time she spent reading to her little son and wanted to help Carlotta. Esperanza was a non-Mexican Hispanic who directed a large nonprofit service organization, where she arranged an unpaid internship for Carlotta, who could not take it because she lacked a Social Security number. Esperanza was shocked: Carlotta had not primed the image of being undocumented, since she was in college, spoke unaccented English, and talked insightfully about that year's presidential election. Esperanza had asked Carlotta who she would vote for in the 2012 election, believing she was a citizen.

Such earned opportunities and mentoring were key mechanisms that promoted mobility for U.S. citizen NYCOMPers. The repeated blocking of earned opportunities and inability to take advantage of opportunities offered by her mentors due to her legal status cumulatively set a lower life trajectory for Carlotta.

Seeing Carlotta after she got DACA at age twenty-six was like meeting a different person. She brimmed with optimism, plans, and happiness. Her pre-DACA determination had felt grim as she dealt with not knowing what was possible or not as long as she was undocumented. After getting DACA, Carlotta was able to accept Esperanza's mentorship. She described her employer as "a great lady. One of the best people I have ever met." They mapped out a strategy that had Carlotta interning at a small nonprofit before moving on to internships at larger nonprofits or companies. For Carlotta, having DACA "will help to apply for internships." When we last saw each other in 2019, she was finishing her associate's degree and applying to bachelor's programs. Because Carlotta now knew about in-state tuition, she was taking three or four classes per semester. Getting DACA had hit the reset button for Carlotta's educational and work trajectories.

Getting DACA also enabled Carlotta to help her mother financially, help her younger U.S. citizen sisters navigate high school, and offer them advice on classes to take to be ready for college. She also felt able to marry her boyfriend, a U.S. citizen, with whom she rented a small apartment from her former teacher and mentor.

Carlotta explained that having several good mentors, as well as others who tried to help her pre-DACA and then were able to do so post-DACA, was "why I am not bitter." However, she recognized the reality that her DACA status was revocable and did not enable her to help her undocumented mother with legal status. She had avoided airports entirely before getting DACA, and she still feared travel. She noted that even on a post-DACA work trip, "I felt worried when we went through security." The TSA official "pushed it [her passport] with his finger to see if it was fake."

Xavier's Story: DACA Catalyzes Career and Income Jumps and Changes in Intimate Relationships in Established Adulthood after Years of "Passing"

Xavier passed so adeptly as "documented" that I had known him a decade before he disclosed his legal status to me. His revelation was especially surprising because other study participants had openly shared their status without my asking. Moreover, Xavier and I had become friends while I was doing research in his field of immigrant health. In disclosing his status to me, Xavier explained that, like gay men and lesbians coming out a generation earlier, "no one was out" in his pre-Dreamer generation of undocumented high school and college students. Indeed, listening to Xavier disclose his legal status felt like "coming out" conversations I had had with gay friends in the 1980s. Xavier worried that I would feel deceived by his not sharing this basic fact in ten years of friendship, but I did not. Rather, his explanation helped reorient my thinking by deepening my understanding of how undocumented status gets inside people's heads.

Like Xavier, most undocumented NYCOMPers came of age before the Dreamer movement, which strengthened from the time of the 2006 immigrants' rights marches through the 2016 presidential election. Only 19 percent of the undocumented study participants (five of twenty-six) actively engaged with the Dreamer movement, and only 30 percent (seven of twenty-three) were "out of the closet" as undocumented.

Legal status affected Xavier more as he transitioned from college to his working adult life than it had when he was a student. Being an undocumented student was not so hard because of his protected student status:

> In school you could claim being a student, right? You have a student ID. No one would ask any questions. But it gets more complicated to keep yourself "in the closet" after you get out of school. . . . A student ID . . . does not require a green card and works in the only situation in which you need an ID—to get into school. . . . But as a grown-up, you need an ID for many things—to get on a plane, a bus, into certain buildings, etc. Even your own kid's school. To find work, I had to lie to people—say I was a citizen. My whole life I was terrified to say anything publicly, because I'd be fired.

Xavier could work only at places that agreed to hire him as an independent contractor, which still required disclosing his status to them. They paid him less than others doing similar work. But working enabled him to help his family and to express his gratitude for their support while he was in college.

Passing was complicated for Xavier, but he wanted to get an adult job that would enable him to uphold another part of the immigrant bargain: "I had to help my parents financially." Noting that his parents had been working since they were fourteen, he said, "There's only so much time you can delay adulthood. . . . I have two older brothers who helped out my parents . . . I felt pressure." Xavier also believed that outing himself would have closed off future opportunities and forced him to work in the immigrant economy with his brothers, who would have felt, he feared, that their sacrifice for him had been wasted if he ended up working with them.

Passing requires not only that an individual police what they actually do (not disclosing their status) but also that they anticipate interpretations of their non-actions, such as regularly forgoing formal and informal earned opportunities. When Xavier was asked to apply for a better position at another organization, he declined because he feared asking them to hire him as an independent contractor. In informal professional conversations in which others were feeling out how poachable he might be, he felt vulnerable and either dissembled or expressed fealty to his employers.[24] He feared outing himself even in nonserious conversational inquiries, and felt that his reticence harmed his career: "You are not building the networks you need to get jobs. . . . They're not formal interviews . . . but an [informal] offer, awkward in this situation." He also feared that his reluctance to fly to conferences (because he lacked the ID to board a plane) would out him.

Xavier's fear was well placed. Because he had passed so well, he was included in conversations in which other undocumented professionals were discussed as candidates but dismissed because of their status. "They would say, 'No, don't hire him. He is undocumented. He cannot do it.'" Like Claudette, Xavier kept his secret because he wanted to be judged based on what he did, not on his stigmatized master status as undocumented. Xavier had had an implicit promise from his employer that he would not "out" Xavier by going public with his status, but then lost his job when some *bobo* (fool) in his field learned of his status and expressed surprise to others, outing him. Hearing this gossip, Xavier's boss quietly asked him to leave.

Getting DACA completely changed Xavier's work and career. He could now look for jobs with a work permit and hence could focus on his work of improving community health. He described DACA's huge impact:

> It's just a relief not to have to hide. I can focus now. . . . Before, my status was a distraction. . . . It's like hearing about a job opening—this is the big difference—and I can apply for it! . . . It sounds really simple—but my whole life it's been, I can't, I can't. . . . It's very emotional . . . [and] makes you a little sad sometimes that something so simple makes me so happy. . . . [With DACA,] there's some hope where there was none before!

Xavier experienced a warp-drive jump in his work life after getting DACA, building on ten years of excellent professional programming work. DACA enabled him to start having informal conversations about other jobs and apply for them without revealing his stigmatized undocumented status. He quickly got several offers, accepted one, and then created new programs at a medium-sized health care organization. He was soon poached away by a larger organization, which offered him a much higher salary and a bigger platform on which to innovate in delivering health care to immigrant families. In his midthirties, Xavier earned well over $100,000—quadruple what he had been paid in his first professional job in his early twenties.

Xavier worked seventy to eighty hours per week and was often exhausted, but he felt deeply satisfied in his work, especially because he had no need to worry about his legal status: "It's just a relief not to have to hide. I can focus now on my work. . . . Before, my status was a distraction. . . . I feel good doing this work. . . . This is my life."

Xavier had kept his legal status a secret from his college girlfriend until after they graduated. In college, his status had not mattered. But she did not understand why his status stopped him from flying to see her in another city, why he earned so little and could not apply for other jobs, or why he could not relocate to live with her. He lived with his family and had to help them financially. They broke up.

Xavier's next girlfriend, Maria, had been undocumented herself but had gotten status as a teen. He did not reveal his status to her either, fearing that, in those days before DACA, she might wonder if he was trying to get status through her. When he finally told her about his status, she just said, "Let's get married." But even after they had been together six years and were living together, he waited to marry her until he had DACA, to avoid any hint of attaching an ulterior motive to their union. This dynamic is analyzed well in Enriquez's 2020 book *Of Love and Papers: How Immigration Policy Affects Romance and Family*.[25]

Xavier and I had repeatedly discussed how he felt his status complicated his relationship with Maria, whom I had also come to know. I fondly remember Xavier's joy in talking about their future together after he got DACA: "Now you can visualize your future! Before you just couldn't do this [marry]. Now there is some stability."

Xavier's concealment of his status, even from the girlfriend he lived with, shows how legal status intrudes into the most intimate human relationships—a problem that DACA can only partly fix. At a time in their lives when this hardworking, public service–oriented couple should have been celebrating their love with families and friends, Xavier was hesitant about marrying. U.S. citizens living stable lives can start a life together simply by committing to each other. That was not enough with Xavier and Maria. Despite their love, Xavier refused to marry before getting DACA in order to protect their relationship from communal *chisme* (gossip)—the suspicion that he had married her to get status. But he also had an existential desire to insulate this most intimate part of his life from the stigmatization and exhaustion of lacking legal status, which he had been managing his entire life. Xavier wanted his love for his girlfriend to exist apart from his legal status. Such a wish is widespread among undocumented families.

Xavier's stress related to passing and being undocumented eased considerably after getting DACA. Yet Xavier still felt a slight terror when boarding a plane, because his undocumented status had made him fear identity document checkpoints. He had never been in trouble with the police, but he feared any interaction with them. Xavier still routinely did not disclose his prior status except on a need-to-know basis. He wanted to be known as a leader in health care in the Mexican community—without a "formerly undocumented" asterisk.

Finally, Xavier's joy as his life moved ahead was tempered by two of DACA's limitations. First, he knew that his DACA status and the better life he had built on it were revocable, for reasons he could not control: "You get your DACA letter [and it says,] 'We could revoke this at any time and deport you at any moment.'" Even during the Obama administration, Xavier feared, presciently, that another president could come in and cancel DACA.

Xavier's joy was also accompanied by the sadness of still being unable to help his family get legal status even after getting DACA for himself: "Then you realize your family won't benefit at all," he said. Not only did they remain ineligible for DACA, but he could not sponsor anyone, including his ailing, aging parents, as someone with permanent status could have done.

Claudette's Story: DACA Changes Undocumented Status from an Institutional and Social Issue to a Private Issue

Claudette believed that Mexicanness was linked to illegality in her high school, in meetings with her guidance counselor, and at work after she graduated from college. In her account, undocumented status intruded into her life both at anticipated, strategic moments (for instance, when applying for a job) and at unanticipated, everyday moments (such as in school). Her attempts to pass as a documented person were helped by her unaccented English, good grades, and social competence, but she still needed to constantly guard against revealing her deeply discrediting secret. She had revealed her status to only ten people in her life, including me. Getting DACA changed the salience of undocumented status in her life: once a master status she had to disclose up front when looking for jobs, being undocumented was now a private HR issue she could navigate and manage.

The stigma linking Mexicans and illegality was enacted daily in Claudette's "95 percent Latino" high school by Hispanic students from groups with lower rates of undocumented status (Colombians, Dominicans) and higher rates of U.S. citizenship (Puerto Ricans are all U.S. citizens by birth).[26] The stigma was particularly vivid when specific immigration topics were under discussion. Days after the 2006 immigrants' rights marches, some of Claudette's classmates made fun of Mexicans for being "illegals," or for "not having papers. . . . We took an immigration class. Everyone, most of the students, are like, 'Oh, Mexicans.' . . . They thought 'Mexicans' equals 'undocumented.' I see it everywhere: Mexicans are undocumented."

Classmates regularly asked Claudette about her legal status because she was Mexican. Fearing their ridicule, she always lied, saying she had documents. Claudette challenged derogatory comments about Mexicans and illegals but always hid her own status—as she recalled, with shame, in a pre-DACA interview when she was still in college:

Claudette: Students, not Mexican, would say, "So do you have papers?" I would say, "Of course I do." . . . I remember one guy, he would say, "You Mexicans come across the borders, you're wetbacks." I was like, "Why are you making fun of them?" Like *them*, not making fun of *me*. "They have to do it because they have families." . . . He was like, "Yeah, I understand, but there is too many of them." I was just trying to make him understand, there's nothing wrong with what we are doing, we are doing it for a better life. . . . I never told him, "Why are you making fun of *us*?" I always tell him, "Why are you making fun of *them*?"

Author: You had to pretend to be a citizen, or a legal resident, but you still defended undocumented people. Do you guys call them "illegals" in your school?

Claudette: No, I call them "undocumented."

Author: What did other kids say?

Claudette: "Illegals."

Author: What did you say to them when they would say "illegals"?

Claudette: "They're not 'illegals.' They just don't have papers, so that makes them undocumented." They were like, "They are 'illegal' because they are here illegal." I tried to cover my butt, even now in my job, there is this stigma—[a belief that,] because some Mexicans don't have papers, all Mexicans don't have papers. This guy just asked me yesterday—he is from Germany—he said: "Do you have papers?" I'm like, "Of course I do." I always put [on] this angry face, like, "What are you talking about?" . . . I get along with all the customers in my job. There is this guy . . . he is a professor . . . he asked me, "When are you graduating?" I told him, "Two years." . . . He said, "What are you gonna do?" . . . Now he is always asking me, "Do you have papers?" I'm like, "Yes." I think people do not know that undocumented people can go to CUNY. So I'm like, "I wouldn't go to school if I did not have papers, right?" He is like, "That is true."

These examples show that Claudette's everyday life in high school and college and at work was pervaded by her legal status. She had to constantly hide this key part of her story for fear of being discovered. The debate with her schoolmates—including the children of non-Mexican Hispanic immigrants condemning Mexicans for being "too many" and "illegal"—resonated with national debates on immigration. Other students rejected Claudette's explanations for how and why Mexicans migrate without a visa.

It merits note that other students, coworkers, and even customers felt free to ask Claudette about her legal status, as though the stigma of being "illegal" suspended the respect for privacy that most people would extend to others.[27] Claudette passed as documented so that her peers would treat her with the same simple respect they expected from others, but doing so generated shame that lingered even as she told her story years later.

Stigma even affected Claudette's participation in a student counseling group. She liked the group and the counselor, but she never revealed her status to them because "I was afraid she [the counselor] would tell everyone in the group. If they make fun of Mexicans, now they are going to make fun of me." That Claudette kept her legal status secret even in a counseling group shows how powerful the stigma linking Mexicanness and illegality was for her. The pain of these stories showed in Claudette's face: she would wince when talking about passing as documented or lying about her status.

Even public school staff equated Mexicanness with illegality, worsening the harm Claudette felt. School, after all, is an institution where all students should be treated equally.[28] As noted earlier, Claudette, her mother, and her friends believed that her Colombian guidance counselor treated Mexican students as "less than" because she presumed them to be undocumented. Claudette saw "through the glass" into the guidance counselor's office that with non-Mexican Hispanic students, she "was so friendly, she was so nice, and with us she was like, 'Don't come back. Don't bother . . . don't go to school,' because maybe she was thinking, 'You might start, but you might not finish college.'" The counselor assumed, Claudette thought, that Mexican students were "going to start working and like money better than books or helping their family. [She] had the real wrong impression about Mexicans there, I guess."

The guidance counselor told Claudette and her mother that she could apply to any CUNY school, but she did not discuss SUNY, which interested Claudette and which also had in-state tuition for undocumented students at that time; nor did the counselor mention other schools. Indeed, the counselor was so abrupt that Claudette's usually reticent mother said later that she did "not like that woman." Claudette saw the counselor's behavior as "discriminatory" and "racist" because "she knew . . . we didn't have papers. She was not interested . . . in helping us. . . . You would go to see her, and she would just ignore you." Claudette believed that the guidance counselor thought Mexicans would not help the counselor "build her career" as someone who could get students into prestigious "colleges, like Stony Brook and other places, Columbia—not CUNY."

In my view, the guidance counselor should also have told Claudette that she could attend a SUNY school at in-state tuition rates:

Author: You could have also applied to any SUNY school. She didn't tell you that?

Claudette: No. . . . Even though, like, I don't have papers?

Author: It's a state law, 'cause you graduated from a [New York] high school.

Claudette: She didn't say.

We cannot know from Claudia's account if the guidance counselor knew she could apply to SUNY. What we do know is that her guidance counselor, seeming to link Mexicanness with illegality, made a strong student feel less worthy of her attention and did not tell her of other options she had for college.

Claudette was angry in college at how much her lack of legal status limited her chance for a better job and a better life after college. She spoke about how unfair it was that her high-achieving U.S. citizen peers had opportunities that she did not: "Everybody [all U.S. citizens] can go out and get a job. But because I have this [undocumented] status, I can't. [I'm] going to be not like, a high school but like, a *college* graduate with no permission to work! It is like . . . 'Good, you did it [graduated]. *Now you stay there*'" (emphasis in original). Claudette's words here evoke the fairy-tale figure Cinderella, who, like Claudia, is treated as "less than" because of a status (stepsister) that she has not caused and cannot control. Like Cinderella, Claudia is prevented by her status from working in jobs commensurate with her educational achievements. Like Cinderella,

Claudia worked harder than others but was denied later rewards of that hard work. Indeed, after graduating from college, Claudette, unable to get a formal-sector job, returned to work in the same dry cleaners she had worked at in high school.

Claudette had wanted to be a teacher, like her mentor, Ms. T, but with no Social Security number, she could not do an internship in childcare or in the schools, which rightly require background checks. What makes her situation crueler is that Claudette's parents finally got legal status when she was twenty-four years old—too late to petition for legal status for her as a dependent child because she had aged out of eligibility. Between her newly documented parents and her U.S. citizen younger siblings, Claudette was alone as the only undocumented member of her family.

Getting DACA at age twenty-seven hit the reset button for Claudette, fostering a warp-drive jump at work, enabling her to benefit from mentoring, and changing how she passed as documented at work and in her social life. She would marvel at how much DACA had unblocked her life: "Before, you couldn't work at all. Only volunteer . . . and not in a hospital—you needed that nine-digit number. Or buy a car—no credit [without a Social Security number] . . . you *know* why you can't do it. Now you can do all those things."

After getting DACA, Claudette could finally accept the mentorship offered by her college professor when she had been a student but was unable to accept it because she had no Social Security number. After she recontacted him, his calls helped get her an unpaid internship, which she saw as an investment: "You're gonna see the profits of that work later." Her college degree, internship, and work permit enabled her to leave her job at the dry cleaners, and she quickly get a job in human services: "I can actually work at something I learned!" she reported, happy to be using her education. When we last spoke in 2023, Claudette had become a well-paid regional manager making nearly four times her pre-DACA income, with paid vacation, a 401(k), and good health insurance. She had recently turned down a promotion to become a director at her agency to preserve time for the family she would like to have.

Getting DACA also changed, in two important ways, how Claudette passed as documented in her social life as well as in her professional life: first, she no longer primed the undocumented category in social and work settings; second, having gatekeeper documents like a work permit decreased how much she was excluded due to her lack of legal status.

I call a work permit a "gatekeeper identity document" because it eliminates legal status as a bar to seeking and getting better jobs, especially for those with more education. DACA not only enables recipients to work legally but also changes the timing and impact of their legal status. Whereas, before having DACA, being undocumented was always the first thing that mattered and categorically eliminated most good jobs, having DACA—that is, still being undocumented but having a work permit—enables DACA recipients to seek and get much better jobs. Moreover, with DACA, a person's legal status is not a social or public stigmatizing fact that disqualifies them for jobs, but rather a private HR issue that is disclosed after an offer has been extended.

Claudette said that being undocumented and having DACA now felt like "part of my private life. . . . Now I feel it's a private thing." Indeed, Claudette said, her immediate supervisor did not know she was a DACA recipient for many years, because it was treated as confidential HR information, like health data. Even when she had a problem renewing her work permit because USCIS was slow in responding to her DACA renewal (submitted well in advance), the HR staffer worked with Claudette to lessen any impact on her. The issue was that her agency could not employ her in the interregnum between the end of her prior two-year work permit and the start of her renewal. Claudette and the HR staffer decided that if the new permit had not come through in time, she would take a long vacation right after the current permit ended and wait to see if it came through then. Moreover, as had happened with another DACA recipient at her agency whose work permit had lagged, the HR staffer told her that she would be placed on leave and her job would be preserved until she got her renewal. It was only when she was close to having to go on leave that Claudette shared her DACA status with her direct supervisor, who was very supportive.

Claudette also felt that several elements of her post-DACA life no longer signaled to others that she was undocumented. As she pointed out, "my accomplishments"—finishing college and working at a professional job—now suggested that she was documented. Moreover, while she felt that being a young Mexican woman with a bachelor's degree working at a dry cleaner primed the "undocumented" category—why else would a college graduate work there?—being a young, college-educated Mexican woman advancing steadily into supervisory roles at a social service agency primed the documented category.

Having DACA and related identity documents also enabled Claudette to take actions that primed the documented category in her social life, an arena that is even harder for undocumented people to navigate without disclosing their status. She qualified for a first-time homebuyer program, which required a Social Security number, and she traveled to Mexico and returned two weeks later. "Who goes to Mexico and comes back in two weeks?" Claudette asked. "Only documented people." Normally, undocumented people who return to Mexico spend more time there because of the high risks and costs of returning to the United States. Now she is asked about her status only to confirm that she has papers: "One of my friends' mother asked me, 'Tú tienes papeles, ¿verdad?' ('You have papers, right?') Yeah, I do." Claudette believed that telling her friends about her work and travel to Mexico reinforced their perception of her as documented. With DACA and related identity documents, she did not feel that she had to disclose that she was technically undocumented.

Visiting her grandmother in Mexico and returning not only signaled that Claudette was documented but made actually becoming a citizen or lawful permanent resident more concretely possible. DACA recipients are not allowed to leave the United States without permission, but they can do so for humanitarian or educational reasons through a process called advance parole (AP), which permits them to travel for a specified period and then legally reenter the United States. Because her grandmother had been quite ill, Claudette applied for and got advanced parole. She also discussed with her immediate supervisor her reason for leaving suddenly within the tight time frame approved for her travel, that is, for not putting in for time off well in advance. After a lovely visit with her *abuelita* (grandma), she returned to New York without incident.

Returning to the United States also opened a door for her: by legally reentering the United States with advance parole, the obstacle to legalizing her status after her prior undocumented entry, as a child, was eliminated. She said that having her path to legalization cleared "gives me a sense of security, knowing that I can *arreglar papeles* [arrange my papers], instead of waiting for Congress" (to pass immigration reform). She could meet someone, marry, and legalize her status without fear of being separated from any children she might have, which is a constant fear for many who lack legal status.

Claudette also said that DACA had helped her keep the immigrant bargain with her parents by redeeming their sacrifice with her accomplishments. She summarized DACA's impact:

> DACA really changed my life. It has given me opportunities I never thought I would have. Like going back to Mexico. When people asked, "What do you do?" I would tell them, and it made me feel proud of myself and my parents. All of this is paying back why my parents came in the first place, to give me a better life. It's me honoring all those efforts that my parents did, when they decided to come [to New York]. It's a way of giving back to my parents. I feel proud. DACA has changed a lot.

Getting DACA reduces some of the ways in which being undocumented becomes a master status and partly ameliorates some of the harms of lacking legal status. DACA gives people work permits and gatekeeper identity documents that enable them to move through many settings in the world as if they are documented or have become U.S. citizens. They can work legally and change jobs when they like; before DACA, many who were undocumented felt that they could not leave a job. The incomes of DACA recipients with more education can dramatically increase in a short time, revealing how much their lack of legal status had depressed their earnings. Being able to get driver's licenses makes driving less terrifying by disrupting the traffic stop to deportation pipeline. They are more likely to be able to continue in college and to be in a position to help their families financially. DACA recipients receive Social Security numbers and some benefits for which that number is required. DACA recipients can also imagine falling in love, marrying, and starting a family because they no longer fear being permanently separated by deportation from a partner or children. In short, by unblocking opportunities to participate in American institutions, like the labor market, DACA helps recipients boost their social mobility. DACA is especially helpful to higher-achieving recipients: in passing more easily as documented persons or citizens, they are able to avoid the harms due to lack of legal status, and their well-being improves.

Bruce's Story: An Exploited Mertonian Innovator Pre-DACA Becomes a Better-Paid Jack Kerouacian Explorer Post-DACA

Bruce came to the United States as an undocumented baby, was enrolled as a boy in dual-language programs in New York's public schools, and later talked his way into a good nonzoned high school. There he did well, began his own computer business, and was the "only Mexican goth skateboarder" in the student body. After graduating, he also started college. His family lived in a single-room occupancy hotel, often in one room, with one shared bathroom per floor.

Bruce was a Mertonian innovator: blocked from normal channels of advancement, he tried to advance outside the limits that his lack of legal status imposed on him.[29] He had started a computer business in high school because he could not legally work as an employee of a company. He got his first computer from a dedicated high school teacher who garbage-picked some computers and gave them to students by lottery. In his business, Bruce helped people set up or troubleshoot their home computers. He advertised by posting flyers on wealthy streets, being careful to avoid police, and the possibility of deportation, as he put them up. Bruce also took Microsoft certification courses, which he used as credentials to acquire clients.

Bruce later used his client list and experience to get hired by small tech companies, which paid him dramatically less than his peer employees who were U.S. citizens. (As freelancers, they openly discussed pay.) Even after a decade of doing highly skilled IT work, he made $750 every two weeks, working sixty to eighty hours per week. That was the equivalent of $6.25 an hour for sixty hours, $5.37 an hour for seventy hours, and $4.69 an hour for eighty hours—at a time when New York's minimum wage was $7.25 an hour. In another job, Bruce made $500 per week ($10 an hour) while his U.S. citizen peers in the same job made $1,300 per week ($16 to $17 an hour). Bruce paid income taxes using his ITIN (individual tax ID number) to be ready for a future legalization program.

Bruce left college when his boss said that he needed him to work full-time. His legal status drove that decision in two ways. Unsure whether he could get hired again as an independent contractor, he felt that he had to keep his boss happy by agreeing to work full-time. He also felt that, because he was undocumented, college would not lead to better jobs and hence would not be worth the money he would spend.

Bruce's legal status constrained his ability to grow his business. Without a Social Security number, he could not open a PayPal account, get credit cards, or register his business with the city. Hence, his business stayed in the informal economy, and he was able to get only small or one-off clients who were willing to "hire Joe Schmo with a flyer off the street. . . . I didn't build my own identity as a business because there was nothing to identify. . . . I used to lose customers . . . I didn't look like a legitimate business. I couldn't register [with the city] as an LLC or a small business." Customers could never be "confident who they were hiring." Bruce also realized that his business's growth—especially if he were to contract with large corporations—would be limited by his inability to get building permits in order to break through walls to run fiber-optic cables or rewire networks. He had good experience doing such work as a subcontractor, but he knew that he would never get his own permits without a Social Security number and a registered business.

Bruce's story has the elements of the "self-made man" story that America loves: a scrappy young entrepreneur drops out of college and runs his own business. But a lack of legal status prevented him from establishing a legal business identity and benefiting from the opportunities he had earned.

Bruce told me that just before DACA was announced, he was "in a rough spot . . . depressed . . . surviving, not really living." DACA freed him from the cramped geographic and mental "loop" of his undocumented life. He and his undocumented friends "used to be afraid of leaving the city of New York. But not now. . . . Before, I was limited, because if we got close to any border it created a paranoia, a fear—any cop, trooper, border patrol [agent] could approach you and ID you and deport you . . .

built-in insecurity." He contrasted this constant fear with his sense of inclusion and security after getting DACA: "I could rent a car and just drive to New Mexico. No fear. I could also move. I no longer have to defend my status, and not having a Social Security number. . . . I'm feeling like an American. I felt like I should be treated like an American before, because I grew up here. . . . [Getting DACA] was like being accepted into a club that I belonged to already, but they finally let me in."

Bruce described other concrete changes brought about by DACA. After getting a driver's license, he could use a car to do his IT work and rent a better apartment. He traveled for the first time. Being undocumented had "made me feel I couldn't go anywhere," he said. "You need a car, you need papers. I had to take public transportation. . . . Taking servers [computers] on the subway—not good. . . . And outside New York, you needed a car. Or trying to find an apartment—I (had) no credit score, so they would require cash up front, and you'd be living in a bad apartment. . . . It felt like starting over where my parents started, in tenements."

Before getting DACA, Bruce had to "take whatever housing would take me without a background check and a credit check," because he could not have passed either one. He lived in "not very good places" that were very far from his work. He spent four hours on the subway every day commuting. Like many undocumented people, he had had to pay two months' security deposit when moving into an apartment, then never got it back after moving. He did not even try to get it back, fearing any conflict could get him deported. With DACA, Bruce had a credit history, earned more money, and rented a nicer place closer to his work.

After getting DACA, Bruce rented his first car and drove to New Mexico, laughingly comparing himself to the protagonist of Jack Kerouac's classic book, *On the Road*. In New Mexico, which he had always wanted to visit, Bruce quickly got a restaurant job making nearly twice his pay in New York. When we last spoke, he was interviewing for IT jobs paying $17 to $25 an hour in New Mexico, much more than he had earned in New York, despite now being in a much cheaper city.

Having DACA increased Bruce's confidence that he could walk away from any job he did not like and that he was "worth more" on the labor market, which his New Mexico earnings confirmed. In his IT work in New York, he had been paid less than others but was "on call 24/7." In addition to being on call until 3:00 AM every day, he had to manage emergencies. "I would just go to bed at three o'clock, and . . . get a call to go to Boston," by bus or driving, if a client's servers went out during the night. In New York he had worked sixty to eighty hours per week for $750 every two weeks, but could not leave that job for fear that no one else would hire him without legal status. In New Mexico, he worked in a restaurant for the same pay, but on a regular schedule of forty or fewer hours.

Like other study participants, Bruce never told his long-term girl-friend about his status, fearing that knowing he was undocumented would damage her image of him, but he also believed that keeping his status secret from her hurt their relationship, since she felt he was hiding something. Even though the stability of his New Mexico job left him "happier at the end of the night"—after the havoc that his unpredictable IT work schedule had wreaked on his personal life in New York—they broke up.

Bruce's IT job had nearly prevented him from applying for DACA. His boss would not give him the time off to gather the documents to apply for DACA. For months, Bruce snuck away for a few minutes now and then to visit schools, health clinics, and the police (to get a statement from them showing he had no police record as evidence that he posed no danger to the United States). But eventually he needed a full day to work on the application, and his boss refused. Faced with the choice of staying undocumented at this IT firm, making less than his coworkers, or applying for DACA, Bruce chose DACA and quit his job.

Bruce smiled as he summarized the change in his life: "Getting DACA has been liberating." He no longer lived in fear of deportation or being treated as lesser than, and like others who got DACA, he felt that he could now "[get] my future back. . . . My peers could plan out their lives, but I could never really realize those plans." With a Social Security number and a driver's license, he could finally make plans, act on them, and seek out and take earned opportunities.

Clara's Story: DACA Decreases Intrafamily Conflict and Opens Up Work Opportunities

Clara's life improved dramatically after she got DACA by lessening the intrafamily conflict fostered by her long-term undocumented status, as we saw in chapter 2. Clara's undocumented status had blocked opportunities, and her predicament had made her angry at both her parents and her younger siblings, who, she felt, were wasting many opportunities they had as U.S. citizens. DACA helped resolve these conflicts.

First, DACA enabled Clara to go from working as a part-time, off-the-books babysitter to a full-time job with a nonprofit. Starting at $13 an hour, she made $18 an hour a year later—more than her parents. Second, DACA helped Clara's undocumented husband (she noted the irony of not falling in love with a U.S. citizen), who, upon learning that he was paid less than other workers with documents, asked his boss for a raise. When the boss refused, he quit. He became "depressed" when he could not find another job, and they were financially strapped. After getting DACA, the couple started their own tailoring business and earned much more. When I saw them in 2018, they were celebrating having just "landed the E Corporation account!" They were also giving or loaning clothes to students applying for summer internships to wear for interviews or work. Her husband was happy to give students "help he felt he never had."

Getting DACA strongly improved Clara's relationship with her mother. As an undocumented college student, as noted earlier, she had been angry at her mother for her role in her daughter's undocumented status. Now, Clara said, "I don't think about it [her legal status] no more because of DACA. I don't hold nothing against her—like a grudge, like before. I see the decisions she had to make—right or wrong—and take a risk, like we did with the store." With DACA, she said, "I see life differently now." Clara also became close to her U.S. citizen sister again. Her sister had gotten pregnant in high school, but now Clara said that she was a good mother and was glad that her sister was getting a master's degree in education. Clara believed that her sister was keeping the immigrant bargain. She felt less jealous of her after DACA removed obstacles in her own path, and she was close to her niece. Clara's mellowing was partly due to age (she was nineteen in the first interview and twenty-seven in the last one), but DACA had helped by unblocking her life.

Ironically, DACA led Clara to leave the master's degree program she had entered when she was undocumented because, without DACA, she could excel in school but not at work. After getting her work permit, she could earn more money to "help take care of her parents," who were getting older and struggling in their physically demanding jobs. She could keep the immigrant family bargain by staying in school as an undocumented student, but after getting DACA she could keep it by helping her parents financially.

Finally, Clara said, DACA had changed how she and her husband experienced their lives by making it less stressful to just walk around: "I'm not afraid like before. My husband—he can't believe it, not being afraid." Former president Trump's attempts to end DACA terrified Clara and her husband, reminding them that their new and better lives, along with their DACA work permit and protections, were revokable.

DACA Did Not Help All Undocumented Americans

DACA did not help four kinds of long-term undocumented Americans: those, like Eddie, who qualified for DACA but did not apply because they mistrusted the government; those, like Lorencio, who did not qualify; those, like Lobo, who qualified but could not document their lives enough to apply; and others who did not know they qualified. Many eligible people we met via the DACA Access Project believed that DACA was a kind of Dreamer program and required either being in or having graduated from college, so they did not apply.[30]

Lobo's Story: Eligible but Unable to Document His Presence

I worked with Lobo, a young father in his early twenties, through the DACA Access Project, which promoted DACA applications and did research on the impacts of having, lacking, or gaining legal status or DACA. Lobo qualified for DACA but could not gather the types of institutional proof—documentation of each six-month period since arrival—that DACA required. Lobo had mostly lived with his father, so most of the years he had lived in the United States his name was not on a lease. While he was then in adult education classes, he had not gone to school in the United States, so there were no school records documenting his continuous presence. And because he was rarely sick, he had no medical records. His employer was willing to write him a letter attesting to his many years of presence in the United States working for him, but the DACA Access Project lawyer, believing that one letter would not be enough proof, discouraged Lobo's application. He was still undocumented when we last spoke, when he was in his late twenties.

Eddie's Story: Eligible for DACA but Unwilling to Apply

After President Obama announced the DACA policy in June 2012, I contacted all undocumented study participants and offered help in applying for DACA and referral to free legal help through New York City's DACA program or the DACA Access Project. Most eligible study participants applied, but not Eddie. When we spoke, his tone conveyed that even discussing DACA made him sad about the life he had already lost. He feared giving the government his information, especially if a Republican became president.

Eddie and other undocumented Americans who had dropped out of high school to work from the 1980s to the present and who did not believe that America would reward their educational hard work with better adult lives were right. For the more than 800,000 who got DACA between 2012 and 2017, their work in school was partly recognized. But for Eddie and millions like him, America did not keep that promise. Eddie was nearly thirty years old before he could apply for DACA—too late to change his life, he felt. Cruelly, his rational choice to leave high school to work to help his family (when gaining legal status had seemed impossible) prevented him from immediate DACA eligibility, because he had not finished high school. He could have enrolled in continuing education and become DACA eligible.

Lorencio's Story: A Taxpaying Undocumented Immigrant Teaching His Children Moral and Civic Lessons

Even though Lorencio, Xavier's older brother, did not qualify for DACA because he was in his late thirties when DACA began, he clearly deserved the chance to legalize. Lorencio's school career had been truncated by his desire to help his family. Although their mother told them, "You are going to study, even if we can only eat beans," fourteen-year-old Lorencio felt guilty about studying when the family had to live in one room, both his older brother and father worked, and his father returned home exhausted after working twelve-hour days, six days a week. To help his parents, "I decided not to study." The $4.35 per hour he earned as a fourteen-year-old (he got work by lying about his age) helped his family and made him proud. As an adult, Xavier was extremely grateful for Lorencio's sacrifice, which had enabled him to study, and was very close to his brother.

Lorencio's philosophy as a parent of three children was based on the same commitment to family that had led him to quit high school to work. Indeed, in his midthirties, he felt even more responsibility as his parents aged and his father's health declined. "I feel that I have to be the hub of the family . . . that I am the head of house to follow. Because my father is old now. . . . My younger brother has his projects [school]. . . . I have not studied. I don't have a lot of schooling. But I try to be an example to follow."

Lorencio was rightly proud of having been a good son, brother, father, and provider. He began at his construction job as a laborer but within a year had become "the one in charge." For nine years before our interview, he had been the manager: "I now earn $22 per hour. It's not that bad. . . . It is not what one would hope, but the salary fits with what one knows how to do."[31] He liked his boss, who had offered steady work and increasing pay for a decade. (I believe Lorencio was underpaid. On PayScale in 2020, New York City construction site foremen were paid a median of $34 per hour, with median earnings of $80,000 per year; earnings ranged from $52,000 to $119,000.)[32] Lorencio had some sense that he might be underpaid, but he also did not know anyone doing his job who was a U.S. citizen. Moreover, he appreciated being recognized as valuable by his boss and given increasing responsibilities and higher pay, which had moved his family out of poverty and into a better life.[33]

Lorencio's children asked him once why their family could not visit relatives in Mexico, as their friends did. He explained that he would not be able to come back from Mexico because "I don't have the document." He was moved when his ten-year-old said, "I will just loan you mine," referring to his birth certificate.

Lorencio loved America. Speaking of his brothers, he said, "We were raised here. I have more than half my life here. I am a Yankees fan. I also like the Giants. I go for the Jets, with Mark Sanchez." With a conviction resonant with the optimistic findings of the political scientists James McCann and Michael Jones Correa—whose book *Holding Fast* documents that immigrants respond to increasing anti-immigrant sentiment by investing themselves in American institutions—Lorencio said that, though he felt that America had denied him some opportunities and many Americans were hostile to immigrants, he was grateful for the opportunities the country had given him and his children: "Although you do not have documents, you still have the opportunity to work, and to enjoy life here. I respect America first because it gave me the opportunity to come and establish myself and have a family."[34] He was proud that his three children were doing well in school, spoke English well, and were American citizens.

Lorencio expressed his gratitude to America by teaching his children to be good citizens and by paying taxes "for the past fifteen years" with the ITIN he had obtained expressly for that purpose, so that he would be ready for a legalization program. He said that he did not mind paying taxes because he wanted to support the schools and police in the city where he was raising his children.

> I pay my taxes every year. . . . It does not matter to me that they don't give me my refund. . . . Not that it [the tax money he paid] doesn't matter to me, rather that . . . it's a way to be good with the government. . . . I am not good with it in one way [being undocumented], but I try to be a good person . . . another contributor.

He used paying taxes as a lesson for his children in civic responsibility, telling them that his taxes helped pay for their schools. "My children are the ones I am teaching, how things are here. . . . What I give them [paying taxes to the government], that is what they [schools] can give you." Paying taxes, he taught them, was one of the ways a responsible grown-up and father took care of his own children and other people's children, because schools were funded by taxes.

At the same time, Lorencio told his children to study hard so they would have a better life than his. When "I come home tired at night," he told them, they were seeing how immigrants lived in this country.

He wanted his children to get professional jobs in offices and the better lives those jobs would bring them.

Conclusion

This chapter has analyzed the ways in which getting DACA helped recipients, made being undocumented less of a master status, and had a positive impact on their relationships not only with American institutions but also with their families, friends, and themselves. DACA unblocked the earned educational and work opportunities that recipients had not been able to take advantage of pre-DACA, and it helped many thrive and earn dramatically more income in their post-DACA professional lives. Having DACA and related identity documents allowed them to participate in key American institutions, like the labor market and the financial system. DACA also enabled mentors to help their DACAmented mentees in ways they had not been able to help them before DACA; their mentees could now walk through the doors they opened for them. In a sense, DACA enabled recipients to learn to be functionally documented, just as many had learned as teens or early adults pre-DACA how to be "illegal."[35]

DACA was also emotionally good for recipients and their families. Getting DACA helped heal disruptions in intimate and family relationships caused by lack of legal status, including by lessening undocumented adult children's anger at their parents for their lack of status and enabling them to gain the honor of keeping the immigrant bargain more fully. Having DACA also decreased the existential fear that too many undocumented American adults feel all the time. I was particularly struck by Clara's statement that her husband "can't believe it, not being afraid" all the time. Having DACA made it possible to imagine marrying and having children, without the constant fear of permanent separation.

Getting DACA changed the social meaning of being undocumented. Recipients no longer had to work so hard to pass as documented, because they were in fact documented in the labor market. For Claudette, getting a work permit and gatekeeper identity documents, qualifying for a mortgage, and taking a brief trip to Mexico all made her interactionally documented with American institutions and primed the "documented" category to her friends and work colleagues in ways that had been impossible pre-DACA. DACA converted recipients' previously public and social undocumented master status into a private status at work—one disclosed not in the first conversation (leading to another lost earned opportunity) but only after a job offer had been made, when the information would be protected by HR rules.

This chapter has highlighted DACA recipients as living counterfactual cases who demonstrate how the lack of legal status harms lives and how lives improve after even a partial, revokable version of it, like DACA, is obtained. By following people for many years, this study documented both the hardships in people's pre-DACA lives and the improvements in their post-DACA lives, including better jobs, happier family relationships, and greater peace and well-being in their day-to-day lives.

Finally, because DACA is not a program based in a law but a policy based in prosecutorial discretion, the positive outcomes from obtaining DACA — better jobs and higher incomes, the ability to dare to marry and have children, the astonishment of not feeling constantly afraid — are all revokable. Although the better lives DACA recipients have built are real, they are not based on an enforceable right, like rights of citizenship, but rather can be revoked by executive order, as the forty-fifth president tried to do. We must do better by these Americans. The theoretical and policy implications are clear: offer a clear route to permanent legal status for the millions of undocumented Americans who were brought as children to the United States, the only home they have known.

Chapter 6

Second-Chance Mechanisms: Hitting the Reset Button for U.S. Citizens and the Derailment Button for Undocumented Americans

"IT's A SECOND chance. . . . It helps you, if you take advantage of it. I got it on two felony charges. If I still had those charges, I wouldn't be speaking to you from where I am right now."

For thirty-something Ernesto Vaquero, youthful offender status had kept the door open for him to get a good law enforcement job as an adult, despite having been imprisoned for a violent crime as a teen. As a U.S. citizen, Ernesto could take full advantage of second-chance mechanisms, and he used his jail time to change his thinking in his early twenties and go on to live a productive adult life. Policies creating second chances worked as intended for Ernesto and other U.S. citizen NYCOMPers.

"Listen, what's the whole point of you trying to talk to me. . . . I know I got no papers. . . . What's the point to paying for school [college]? And your mom or parents working their asses off just for you to go to school? And at the end you're not eligible for better jobs?"

High school student Saul Pacheco explained to after-school staff that he appreciated their efforts to help him, but he believed those efforts were futile, because his legal status would prevent him from getting better jobs later. Saul was talking to the same after-school counselors who had helped his undocumented older sister, Anita, turn her academic life around. He tried to explain to them how his belief that they and the Woods Explorers program could help him had been undermined because he had watched Anita succeed in high school with their help, only to then be unable to go to college or get a good job because she lacked legal status.

Ernesto's and Saul's stories illustrate that, for U.S. citizen youth, second-chance programs can help change their thinking and actions, promoting

168

https://doi.org/10.7758/drwz9626.3042

upward mobility, but that undocumented American youth who also change their thinking and actions are still blocked from upward mobility by their lack of legal status. Second-chance mechanisms enable U.S. citizen teens and early adults to start over after making mistakes, large or small, by changing their thinking and actions. Conversely, second-chance programs such as Woods Explorers could help undocumented Americans change their thinking and actions but could not change their legal status. Even if they graduated from college, they would not get a commensurate job as an adult. Nearly all U.S.-born NYCOMPers who used second-chance programs had become strongly upwardly mobile by their late twenties or early thirties, College Graduates or High Fliers, while their undocumented peers were all Stuck Muddlers or Shallow Slopers.

This chapter describes how three second-chance mechanisms worked in the lives of NYCOMPers: (1) academic second chances, such as summer school and night school; (2) extracurricular and organizational second chances, such as after-school programs helping students think differently about school and their futures; and (3) criminal justice second chances, especially youthful offender status and prosecutorial discretion. These mechanisms allowed U.S. citizen teens and early adults to hit the "reset button" so that their early mistakes did not preemptively close doors for their whole lives. But for their undocumented counterparts, lack of legal status blocked the logic of these mechanisms in academic settings and escalated the impacts of any mistake in legal settings.

This chapter's insights on how second-chance mechanisms affected NYCOMPers' adult outcomes and understanding of their lives are possible because our long-term fieldwork study followed the same people for many years. We were able to see adult outcomes and to use study participants' understandings, as well as our own, of the conditions or causes that led to their adult outcomes and places.

Second-chance mechanisms are wise public policy whose logic runs counter to the increasingly punitive narratives underpinning many American criminal justice and school policies in the last forty years.[1] The American penal system has veered away from an early orientation toward reform and education toward an increasingly punitive approach to youthful infractions and crimes that treats teens as adults, removes judicial sentencing discretion, and imposes racially disparate penalties for similar crimes. Felony convictions eliminate many or even most future job and other prospects for young people.[2] In education, small infractions that would in the past have been handled as in-school disciplinary matters are increasingly turned into criminal matters by police in schools.[3] These officers often see students as potential criminals who must be controlled, not as students who need guidance. Students discern these negative perceptions and respond to meet expectations.[4] These perspectives feed the school-to-prison pipeline and its logical result—the prison-industrial complex.[5]

This chapter analyzes second chances in the cases of youth who have made mistakes, sometimes serious ones, and raises larger questions: What should be the consequences of youthful mistakes for the young person and for society? What are society's goals? Punishment? Deterrence? Rehabilitation? Nurturance? At their best, second chances promote a virtuous circle: a young person taking a second chance can be led into contexts and routines (steady work, career, marriage) that promote desistance from bad conduct and persistence of good conduct.[6]

In this chapter, I trace how second-chance mechanisms helped U.S. citizen study participants and promoted intergenerational mobility but also document the blocking of these same mechanisms by a lack of legal status and how low the trigger for harm or deportation was for undocumented youth.[7] While U.S.-borns could make stupid or serious mistakes and still have good adult lives, undocumented youths' lives could be derailed by very small mistakes, such as drinking a beer in public or getting in an argument. I only analyze second-chance mechanisms seen in this study.

New York City and New York State are more inclusive of immigrants than many places in America, offering better contexts for upward mobility. For the most part, both the city and state governments do not "see" legal status in dealing with undocumented people.[8] New York City police are not supposed to ask about legal status except when investigating a crime or when asking might help an undocumented victim of violence. New York City created a municipal ID in 2014 partly to remove the stigma of being undocumented in interactions where an ID was needed, such as when entering one's child's school. New York State passed in 2019 both a Dream Act, which gives some undocumented college students access to New York State funding, and a Greenlight Law, which enables established undocumented residents to get a standard driver's license. Driving without a license has been a main driver of deportation and family separation in New York State.[9]

New York City's and New York State's new legal and institutional inclusions should provide some second chances that were unavailable to Anita and Saul in the early 2000s. Today undocumented students can graduate from high school and attend college with New York State Dreamer funding, and they can drive to their college campus with their New York State driver's license. But their exclusion from the labor market and their deportability are federal issues that are beyond the power of New York City or New York State to remedy (even if they do not cooperate with ICE's attempts to deport people for minor offenses).

Although it is uncommon in academic analysis, I use the word *stupid* to describe many (not all) of the youthful mistakes that prompted NYCOMPers' need for a second chance. The cases analyzed here suggest that, rather than respond to stupid teen actions with condemnatory, life course–altering punishment, there is virtue in treating them as mistakes from which youth should be allowed to recover.

Second-Chance Research

Most research on immigration and the second generation does not discuss institutional second-chance mechanisms or their impacts on intergenerational mobility. Immigration itself is seen as a restart in American history, and research shows that affirmative action has especially helped children of immigrants, but few studies analyze second-chance programs to help youth.[10] One exception, Kasinitz, Mollenkopf, Waters, and Holdaway's *Inheriting the City*, notes that New York's educational system offers second chances, but these authors do not analyze how they work, differences in how they work for U.S. citizen youth versus undocumented youth, or how they work in legal settings.[11] Later segmented assimilation theory analyzes cases of "extraordinary" achievement, but not institutional policies offering errant youth another chance.[12] Roberto Gonzales's *Lives in Limbo* analyzes how legal status blocks upward mobility for both those who quit high school and those who go to college, but he does not compare them with their U.S. citizen peers.[13] I draw on and extend these insights in comparing how second chances work for U.S. citizens and undocumented Americans.

Most research using racial exclusion, legal exclusion, or assimilation theory does not consider second-chance mechanisms; nor does it compare the different effects of these mechanisms on U.S. citizen youth and undocumented youth.

Most research on second chances does not consider legal status, but it does offer tools to analyze how legal status affects the lives of those who need a second chance. Research in psychology and sociology focuses on how "generativity" narratives help those facing challenges or failures by motivating them to take steps toward a better life. Young parents may "turn their life around" for a new baby. Those leaving jail may say that its deterrent effect will cause them to reorient their lives. Such stories matter because they become theories of action for future behavior.[14] Such narratives guide a person to better choices and retrospectively assign redemptive meaning to past challenges.[15] Here, transformation happens when a person narratively reframes the meaning that they give their history, with subsequent effects on their future choices and outcomes. Such retrospective reframing echoes the prospective framing of teen counterfactual thinkers whose choice of better schools—partly to keep the immigrant bargain after internalizing their parents' voices—led to stronger adult outcomes.

Second-chance educational research asks whether second-chance programs are equitably distributed, under what conditions students accept or reject second chances, and whether these programs offer real second chances or just put a new gloss on the system's failures.[16] Some debate whether community colleges are a pragmatic second chance or a dead end that amounts to a broken promise to students.[17] The major benefits from CUNY's open access policy—a kind of second-chance policy in creating paths into college for students who did poorly in high school—include higher adult income and more educationally focused parenting strategies, as documented by the sociologists Paul Attewell and David Lavin in a longitudinal study.[18]

The 2007 Second Chance Act sought to change punitive policies and advance a redemptive criminal justice approach to the young, echoing eighteenth- and nineteenth-century American Protestant and Quaker philosophies.[19] New York City and New York State never fully abandoned these redemptive options, though the state's Rockefeller-era drug laws are quite punitive. Research on persistence in or desistance from crime emphasizes that second chances can promote better longer-term outcomes for both offenders and society.[20]

Second-Chance Policies in Youthful Criminal Justice and Education in New York City and New York State

New York State's Criminal Procedure Law (article 720) provides that, for most crimes, youthful offender (YO) status is mandatory for those who were sixteen to eighteen years old at the time they committed the crime. YO status may not be mandatory for more serious crimes and is left to the discretion of the judge, who considers whether the youth acted in a group or was the primary agent in the crime. For youth convicted of a serious crime, a presentence investigation assesses whether YO status is appropriate. If granted, YO status provides for confinement in a juvenile facility and shorter sentences than those for adults. If the conviction is set aside, a "youth adjudication" is imposed; if YO recipients avoid legal trouble while on probation, they will not have a criminal record.[21] With YO status, their lives will not be ruined by a stupid or even a serious teenage mistake as long as they avoid future trouble.

This approach fits with emerging science showing that the brain does not fully develop until about age twenty-five, especially those areas of the brain that assess risks and future implications of current action, which develop later than cognitive capacity.[22] These findings have reassured many of us who have parented teenagers.

New York City's schools are profoundly contradictory on second chances. They have brought armed "peace officers" into schools, but these school police too often treat disciplinary issues, formerly dealt with by deans, as crimes, ensnaring youth in inescapable legal complications.[23] But New York City schools vary a lot. Even schools in low-income neighborhoods can boost educational attainment, and the city also offers several kinds of second-chance programs, even to youth who have been violent.[24]

Our study participants used several second-chance programs, including summer school, night school, and weekend school, to make up failed or missed classes; they also used "safety transfers" out of schools made unsafe by, for example, gang conflict. The city offers so-called "transfer schools" and youth adult borough centers (YABCs) (which have low faculty-student ratios) to students who have attended at least one year of high school and need more credits to advance, those who have dropped out, and those who will age out before graduating.[25] Research shows that YABCs and transfer schools help students finish high school, with graduation rates 12 percent higher than those of their peers in other schools. [26] These programs help students reset their lives and go on to work, other training, or college.[27]

After-school and extracurricular programs offer second chances—or "preemptive first chances"—by helping students develop in supervised settings outside school hours. The abundance of such programs in Chinese and upper-middle-class communities contrasted with their scarcity in Mexican communities in New York in the late 1990s and early 2000s and contributed to different educational outcomes.[28] After-school programs can guide errant youth away from friends and contexts that foster missteps and toward imagining a different future in which their actions are guided by second-chance activities, different peers, and mentors. This is how narrative work helps convert near-thinking U.S. citizen youth (who do not consider how current actions could affect their future lives) into counterfactual thinkers (who do consider such possible future impacts). Undocumented status undermines such narrative work, insinuating itself into individual and family stories.

Tales within Families: Second Chances Taken, Derailed, or Denied

Deeper insight into how second-chance mechanisms work to promote U.S. citizens' upward mobility but not the mobility of the undocumented can be gained by examining how these mechanisms functioned in three families with youth who needed second chances: the undocumented Pachecos and the U.S. citizen Maestro and Vaquero families. Tracing processes within family biographies covering many years illuminates how older children's experiences and family learning affect the actions and choices of younger siblings.

The Pacheco children faced horrible circumstances (which they disclosed to us as adults): poverty, physical abuse, and long-term undocumented status for the three older children, whose father had died. The younger children were U.S. citizens with an undocumented father; two other children had died. Nevertheless, Anita Pacheco, the second-oldest child, benefited enough from an educational second-chance program to graduate from high school. Her changed trajectory was derailed by her undocumented status, however, when she tried to go to college and enter the workforce. For her little brother Saul, her derailing was a negative example.

We interviewed Anita and Saul several times and interacted with them and other family members at home and in public spaces over the course of more than fifteen years. Anita's case traces how a second-chance program works well but is derailed by legal status, while Saul's case shows the example of derailment delegitimizing the same program for younger siblings. Another younger sibling, Darrell, was deported—in effect, for drinking a beer in public, an infraction that would have had only minor consequences for a U.S. citizen youth.

The Pachecos' experience contrasts with that of Ernesto Vaquero and his cousin Valerio, both of whom used second-chance mechanisms to overcome substantial educational failings and serious legal charges that would have derailed their lives if they had not been U.S. citizens.[29] The derailing of the Pacheco children's aspirations also contrasts with Agustin Maestro's experience: he was caught for pulling a stupid college prank, but the incident was "quarantined" by the second-chance mechanism of prosecutorial discretion, leaving his future intact. The long-term outcomes for these youth, who started in this project as teens and were last interviewed in their early to midthirties, were starkly different. The U.S. citizen youth who committed violent crimes all prospered as adults, while all three Pachecos struggled and two still lacked legal status, with little hope of getting it. One of the siblings faced years in jail if he returned to the United States after getting deported. Tracing how second-chance mechanisms either worked or did not within families, whether for small infractions or for serious crimes, shows both how second-chance programs promote mobility for U.S. citizen youth and the role of legal status in fostering or squashing life chances.[30]

Ernesto and I have known each other since he was sixteen. I kept in touch into his late thirties and have done over ten hours of interviews with him. I knew and repeatedly talked to Valerio and Agustin Maestro from their teens to their midthirties. Agustin was a member of the Maestro family, as described in my book *Mexican New York*.[31] He shared his dumb mistake with me soon after making it as a college student, and then discussed it more as a working adult professional. Later, in his thirties, he became a high-ranking public school administrator.

The Pacheco Family: Second-Chance Mechanisms Derailed and Denied by Undocumented Status

Anita Pacheco's Story: Generative Thinking Promoted by Second-Chance Mechanisms, but Still Excluded Due to Undocumented Status

Anita was the second-oldest of six Pacheco children whose undocumented parents had little schooling and earned very little. The three older Pacheco children had lived apart from their parents for years. They felt that they came to know their mother only after they arrived in the United States, undocumented, at the ages of five, seven, and nine. Anita, Saul, and Darrell had a different father (who had died before I met them) than their three younger siblings, who were U.S.-born.

The Pachecos disciplined their children abusively, including by hitting in places on their bodies where bruises would not show, as Anita and Saul recounted in interviews as adults. The parents controlled their children's contact with others, forbidding them to visit friends' homes, bring their friends home, or share their phone number. All three older Pacheco children described getting beatings until they left home at age eighteen. Anita felt the burden of being the oldest girl. Her mother, who had her first child at age fourteen, made Anita do the housework and childcare while she worked. When her mother returned to Mexico for three months when her brother died, Anita said she was put in charge of the family's domestic work: "I was left alone. As being the oldest, I had to take the kids to school, pick them up, cook for them, and do laundry. Pretty much what a mother had to do, I did it. My dad would give me money for the week to go do shopping."

Anita and Saul reported that their parents also strongly encouraged their learning. Their stepfather would give them extra summer homework and review it. Their parents expected them to go to college but did not know what this required. Like many undocumented parents, Anita said her parents thought that American colleges would give their children scholarships and a chance to legalize.

Anita did well in grade school but joined a gang in middle school; compared to her home life, the gang felt nurturing. She began cutting school, drinking, and not doing homework. Then, during her second year of high school, Anita joined the Woods Explorers. Her mother agreed to it, seeing the program as a way to get Anita away from her gang friends. A Woods Explorers teacher became for Anita "more like a counselor. . . . I could talk to her about everything, and she tried to help me. She really did." The teacher helped Anita reframe her view of school, from a dead end to a chance for a better life, and fashion a generative, second-chance narrative. Anita stopped cutting school with gang friends and stopped drinking and using drugs. Instead, she hung out with others who participated in Woods Explorers, did wilderness trips, and learned leadership skills. The effects were dramatic: "My grades started going up, I started to attend school more." She also attended classes to learn how to become a peer mediator, and her grades jumped from failing to Bs. Anita graduated from high school.

The Woods Explorers made Anita a Woods Explorers mentor after graduation. Her monthly mentor stipend was $400 per week—her highest-ever earnings. Woods Explorers also awarded Anita a small college scholarship and offered her a job if she could not attend college right away. But Anita's undocumented status would combine with her unstable home life to derail her second-chance life.

Anita had created a generative narrative that reoriented her choices, actions, friends, and time allocation. When asked if Woods Explorers offered her "a second chance," she said: "That is actually how I felt about it." She was given a pin to symbolize her act of choosing "challenges I want to accomplish." She had thrived by taking the second chance that Woods Explorers offered. But the agency she exercised in making better choices could not prevent structural conditions from derailing her life.

First, her mother changed her mind on Woods Explorers and grew to resent Anita's unavailability to do the chores and childcare she had done in the past. She also feared that Anita would get pregnant on a Woods Explorers camping trip. When Anita and her mother fought over Woods Explorers, Anita argued that she was unfairly burdened with family work while her brothers, both older and younger, did nothing. Anita forged her mother's signature to go on a camping trip. Her mother had refused to sign the form because she did not believe that Anita was going camping with Woods Explorers but rather "staying in the city . . . to hang out with friends," and most likely a boyfriend. Her parents saw little value in Woods Explorers. When Anita turned eighteen, her mother threw her out of the house, with two weeks' notice. Her mother explained that she "couldn't take care of another person . . . and that I was too old," even though Anita's older brother still lived there. Having nowhere else to go, she moved in with her boyfriend's parents for two months before getting a job and renting a single room.

Second, Woods Explorers' good intentions to help Anita were stymied by her undocumented status. Had Anita been a U.S. citizen, she could have taken the job that the program offered and used the scholarship for college. Sadly, neither Woods Explorers nor her high school's staff told Anita that a 2002 New York State law had made it possible for undocumented youth like her to go to public college at in-state tuition rates, which the scholarship would have mostly covered. Like many New York high schools at the time, they most likely did not know about the law. As a result, many high schools continued not to encourage undocumented students to go to college. Anita learned about her right to in-state tuition rates at public colleges from me in an interview in 2008, when she was a twenty-six-year-old mother.[32] Anita also made it harder for teachers and Woods Explorers staff to help her by keeping her undocumented status a secret in an effort to avoid the shame it made her feel.

Anita's horrible epiphany that her undocumented status had not stopped her in high school but was blocking opportunities she had earned through Woods Explorers occurred when she met with an admissions counselor at a local private college targeting low-income students:

> When you're in elementary through high school, it wasn't really that hard, because it's public school and you can go to it. You don't have to really pay anything. Once you're out there and it's like, "Okay, now you have to pay for college," then reality hit me. . . . I went to Woods Explorers trips . . . and everything was paid for me. . . . It didn't hit me until I graduated from high school. It's not like I thought it would be. Maybe being also naive, I went to For Profit College. I told them my whole situation. I actually left there crying, that's how bad he [the For Profit admissions counselor] made me feel. . . . Because I tell him my situation, and the guy was like, "We don't have any special programs for people like you." My interview was like . . . a minute and a half, after waiting an hour and a half! I just started crying when I left.

Anita's next five years were dark. Her rented room "wasn't far from my parents, but I just felt too lonely. . . . I've always been with a big family, so maybe it's affecting me because I'm by myself now." She started drinking more with "the wrong friends" from work and sometimes got falling down drunk. This pattern continued until she met Juan, who asked her to stop drinking and stay in at night with him. U.S.-born Juan worked as a manager, made more money, and lived a calm life. She had been struggling after her mother kicked her out, and Juan helped her get out of that life. After they married and had two children, Anita lived in her husband's relatively peaceful New Jersey city, far from her old life. She qualified for DACA, got lawful permanent residency through Juan, and made plans to become a U.S. citizen.

The course of Anita's life was a series of chances missed, recovered, and taken, but also chances and dreams denied. I met Anita when she was sixteen and reinterviewed her several times into her thirties. Her work life hinted at what might have been. As mentioned, she showed such skill as a peer mediator that Woods Explorers offered her an internship with a $400 per week stipend (for thirty-five hours) and tried to hire her. Her income fell below minimum wage after she was kicked out by her mother, to $250 per week (for sixty hours). When I interviewed her in 2009 (pre-DACA), she was managing a deli and translating orders from Black and White customers for her undocumented Mexican and Central American coworkers. Her pay had risen in three years from $6 an hour to $9 an hour. She liked the job because she could leave and walk to pick her kids up from day care on time. But her $270 per week take-home pay in her early thirties was $130 per week less than the stipend she had been offered at age eighteen.

Anita had thought a lot about how her life would have been different had she been a U.S. citizen. "I would have gone to school. . . . I've always wanted to study . . . and be working for Woods Explorers. Right now, I would have been an instructor. I would be working with the students." Asked what she would be doing with them, she replied, "I would try to help them, like they [Woods Explorers] helped me," adding, "I would want to show them that there is more." She told me how proud she had been of traveling to North Carolina with Woods Explorers, when most kids in her Bronx neighborhood had not "even gone to Staten Island."

Having spent some time with Anita, I could easily imagine her effectively helping Woods Explorers students see their mistakes and potential and encouraging them to make good choices going forward. In this way, her missed opportunities were not just her own. They were also the opportunities missed by all the kids she did not get to help, making them America's missed opportunities. The country needs more smart young people who want to devote their lives to helping others thrive.

Despite so many chances lost to her undocumented status, Anita was not a bitter adult. She had finally obtained legal status at the time of our last interview, in her late thirties, but she could not go to college then, she said, because her two children were her priority. We spent part of a beautiful September day chasing her kids around the playground before our interview, an activity that I reassured her I did not mind. By then, my kids were teenagers and I missed chasing little guys around. Her kids were surprised that I knew the "Monster" game: the grown-up growls like a monster and chases the kids, but slowly, and haplessly, so that the kids always escape and feel clever and powerful. I played this game endlessly with my own kids, and we rarely tired of it.

Anita seemed happy in her life, in her marriage to a good man, in her neighborhood with its good schools and day care, and in a job that fit her schedule. She had settled contentedly into the endless logistics of young parenthood: school drop-off and pickup, dinner, bath time, shopping, laundry, and so on. As a grown woman in her late twenties, she had confronted and forgiven her mother for the abuse, for which her mother had apologized. Anita's generous act helped her and her mother find a peace they had not had before. Anita's is not a story of failure but rather one of creating a meaningful life, with dignity, in hard circumstances.

Despite its happy ending, Anita's story makes me angry at a society that could not help a girl and then a young woman who overcame so much and wanted to help others. Her dream to become a teacher and help other kids develop their lives successfully was a simple, decent, and worthy one, which should not have been denied. We as a country should not waste such dreams, nor should we squash the dreams of the millions of children who have grown up in America but been formally excluded from key American institutions in the only country they know as home.

Anita showed maturity, grace, and resilience in telling her story. She was clear-eyed in identifying her own missteps and also in seeing how her legal status and abusive parents stacked the deck against her. She showed anger when she described having to do all the housework growing up because she "was a girl" in her parents' house, but later she took in her brothers when they needed a place to stay.

I recalled Anita's generosity when I felt myself getting angry at her parents when I sought her out in 2012 to make sure she knew about DACA. I wanted to offer help in applying, as I did with all undocumented study participants. Not having a working phone number or email for Anita, I sent two letters to her old address and went three times to her apartment in the Bronx. The first two times, no one answered the door after I announced myself in Spanish and referred to the letters, though I heard adult voices. The third time, a young man (a cousin, I think) answered, and I explained that I knew Anita through my research and could help her apply for DACA if she wanted. He said that they had gotten the letters but had not given them to Anita. He took my card and cell phone number and promised to give the letters to her, but he did not know if she would call me. An older woman I took to be Anita's mother hovered behind him but made no eye contact with me. I thanked them and left. Anita did call later. We had a nice reunion and discussed the possibility that she would apply for DACA.

Saul Pacheco's Story: Intrafamily Learning and the Stripping of a Second-Chance Mechanism

The narrative of Anita's little brother Saul shows how insidiously undocumented status undermines second-chance mechanisms within a family. Because Saul was younger than Anita, he saw how her changed course and raised hopes in adolescence came to naught when her undocumented status imposed its limits in early adulthood. Seeing the game as rigged in ways that his sister had not seen, having no prior example to learn from, he refused to reorient himself to the redemptive or generative narrative that Woods Explorers promoted. Woods Explorers helped young people change how they thought and acted about their future, but it could not change how legal status limited undocumented Americans' futures.

Saul's and Anita's stories have most of the same biographical elements of poverty, parental abuse, lack of parental support beyond high school, early gang activity, drinking, and drug use. As siblings helping each other in an abusive household, their stories are tightly interwoven. Both left their parents' house at age eighteen, and they had lived together off and on as adults. Both felt shame at being undocumented, but how they handled it, and its social meaning, differed for them. Anita found being undocumented "embarrassing" and rarely disclosed it, especially "not [to] people who had papers." Indeed, she told classmates and workmates that she had legal status because that fit better with the image of a hardworking kid who had turned herself around: "At that point . . . I tried to be more outgoing, trying to do better."

Saul also felt shame and frustration that undocumented status held him back and separated him from his U.S. citizen peers: "To see that they're accomplishing something that you wish you could accomplish . . . [but] you simply can't because you're undocumented . . . it's embarrassing. . . . [It makes you] stay away from those kind of people [U.S. citizens]." Saul's high school friends were mostly other undocumented young men who formed a gang and discussed the limits imposed by their status. He dropped out of school because "I started hanging out with different people and also knowing the fact that . . . I was illegal . . . that I would . . . never . . . really achieve anything." As a boy in his family, Saul did not have to care for his siblings (unlike Anita), so he had more time to hang out with the gang. With these friends, he started drinking, using drugs, and even robbing or "hurting people," as he put it, with shame. Being with the gang "felt better" than being at home for Saul, as it had for Anita.

Saul had seen Anita and other undocumented youth making huge efforts to go to college but still ending up in the same kind of bad jobs he anticipated getting. Saul did not want his parents to work hard and spend their money helping him get ahead when his legal status would leave him "not eligible for better jobs. . . . Good jobs. . . . And it's something that is still happening. I still see it with . . . people . . . going to college . . . that they are not going anywhere. . . . They still are stuck in the same hole."

The negative lesson that Saul learned — that such efforts were futile — made it hard for Woods Explorers to reach him. He had entered the program because his sister pushed him to do so, hoping it would help him as it had helped her. But even though Saul recognized the good intentions of the Woods Explorers staff, he also clearly saw that, even if their interventions could help him change one problem—how he looked at his life—the program could not solve the bigger problem that limited how much his changed behavior could help him—his lack of legal status. In spite of the programs' good intentions, Saul felt that Woods Explorers' confidence- and team-building exercises made false promises to the undocumented. He tried to explain his situation to the Woods Explorers staff.

> I remember telling one of the instructors from Woods Explorers, "Listen, what's the whole point of you trying to talk to me . . . and I know I got no papers." . . . I always had that in my mind, and it's sad, I think about it a lot, and I know that back then I had a chance to do it better. . . . [In one exercise] we had to climb a tower, and he told me, you know, "Conquer all your fears." Which I did all of that. . . . But now my fear is that . . . I was different from everybody else. I know I was an illegal. . . . I knew that this guy [a U.S. citizen student] was coming out of high school going to a good college. . . . So then it was something I had most of the time in my head.

Here the voices of significant others trying to help Saul imagine and create a better life story for himself were undermined by his knowledge of how legal status blocked him from achieving that better life. He rejected the story that Woods Explorer tried to get him to adopt as his own story—that if he conquered his fears and developed himself, he could succeed. His answer was: *No, it won't matter. You don't get it that I am undocumented.*

Saul left Woods Explorers and dropped out of school, actions that only increased the distance between what he had hoped for and what his life was becoming: "As I'm getting older, you know . . . I was twenty . . . I started thinking, 'I wanna have what you call the American dream,' . . . bigger house, family, and a good job." But being undocumented put the American dream out of reach: "I feel like I can't do nothing about it. Hopeless, and sometimes frustrated." His story recalls the British sociologist Paul Willis's "lads," who resisted school because they saw the educational system as rigged to get them to behave but not to get ahead.[33] While the lads' working-class lives and schools blocked their upward mobility, their insight into the system sealed their fate by discouraging them from seeking the academic credentials that could have helped them.

Years later, Saul was arrested, at age twenty-five, and did six months in jail for assault during a robbery. Where Woods Explorers had not been able to reorient his thinking, because it could not fix his legal status problem, his stint in jail did change his thinking. His girlfriend left him while he was imprisoned. He had not told her he was in a gang, and when he was convicted, she said she "had better plans for her life." Jail scared Saul, and he never wanted to go back. He said that jail made him realize that his gang friends were leading him down a bad path. Talking to him two years later, I learned that Saul was living with Anita and working with his brother in a deli. His daily routine was intentionally boring: go to work in the morning, go back home, and stay in, every night. He contrasted his high school thinking with his post-jail thinking: "Before I just used to get twisted and I didn't put any mind into my future, and right now I want to start a future." His plan was to stay away from his old friends and seek alternative routes forward, despite his legal status.

A talented artist, Saul had hoped to study art in college. After telling him he could attend college despite being undocumented, I called the local community college to set him up with an admissions interview, but he never followed up because he felt that his status would prevent him from ever getting a "real job" as an artist. Instead, he planned to become a tattoo artist—"not really a good profession," he said, but it "could be a professional thing." Saul thought that he could open a tattoo parlor, charting what Robert Merton would call an innovator's path.

Saul's undocumented story had an ironic twist. A felony conviction usually leads to deportation, but Saul was released on probation. He thought that his case was simply missed and not reported to immigration authorities, though it may not have met New York City's standard for delivering released prisoners to the immigration authorities when they leave prison. Saul met with his probation officer regularly, was working, and hoped for a better future. Save for his criminal conviction, he would have qualified for DACA and gotten a renewable work permit.

Saul's story is especially sad to write about in light of the optimism he exuded in his first interview as a teenager. He had said that he wanted to go to college and become a Marine or a lawyer. His older brother (in college, paid for by his parents), sister (Anita), and stepfather were helping him in school, so he felt supported. At fourteen, he had already worked three years delivering Mexican food, and he reported no gang activity. He knew he was undocumented but hoped anyway for college and a career. He had said he was a "positive thinker" who wanted "to study a lot and become somebody when I'm grown up." This interview was conducted just before Anita's legal status derailed her life, a development that made Saul stop believing that he could do better.

In our last interview, when he was two years out of jail, Saul was different. He looked down when he spoke and seemed unsure what to say next. While I looked up information on the local community college during our interview, I remember having a feeling that he would not follow through. He had been excited when telling me he wanted to be an artist, but then seemed to panic when I offered to help him register for an art class. He did not return my follow-up calls.

Saul's confidence increased when Anita joined that interview. She helped him remember things and encouraged him. It was helpful when Saul sometimes was talking with Anita and seemed to forget me. The way Saul and Anita supported each other was clear. He gratefully recounted how much his sister had helped him get his life back on track. Anita was as frank about Saul's mistakes as she had been about her own, but without judgment. She knew the hard road he had traveled but loved him and wanted to help him. Emerging from such hard circumstances, the two siblings showed a care for each other that was impressive and redemptive.

Darrell Pacheco's Story: Undocumented Status, Beer Drinking, and Legal Escalation

Saul and Anita's older brother Darrell got deported, in effect, for drinking beer outside his house. Darrell was issued what Anita described as "open container tickets" for public drinking. Such "desk appearance" tickets require a court appearance, but fearing deportation, Darrell took the bad advice of his friends and did not go to court. Had he appeared in court, Darrell would probably have been ordered to pay a fine, and the case would have been closed. For many years, New York City authorities have referred to ICE only undocumented immigrants convicted of serious crimes, and then only with a warrant signed by a judge (and not just a request from ICE, the so-called ICE detainer). They do not refer anyone to ICE for drinking a beer outside. But Darrell's failure to show up in court triggered a warrant for his arrest, which happened when he was stopped in a random subway bag check. When Anita tried to post bail for Darrell, the officer told her that ICE would deport him upon his release.

Darrell was deported to Mexico, but he returned a few months later; ever since, he had lived under the threat of prison time if caught. In Darrell's case, undocumented status once again derailed a second-chance mechanism. Had he been a U.S. citizen, he would not have feared deportation if he simply went to court to pay the ticket for drinking a beer in public. But the warrant made his deportability the only fact about him that the court system "saw." Darrell's deportation also made him ineligible for DACA, for which he was otherwise qualified.

The Vaquero and Maestro Families: Second-Chance Mechanisms Offered, Taken, and Now Supporting Better Established Adulthoods

Ernesto Vaquero's Story: Second Chances in School and the Legal System

Ernesto Vaquero was a teen for whom second chances were made. He smiled in recounting that he had been so difficult as a teenager that his mother and grandmother asked a court for help controlling him. "My mother said I was so bad that [she] 'just couldn't handle it.'" He was sometimes violent and disruptive, and he yelled at teachers. He shot a random woman with a slingshot, fought often, and ran with his cousin Valerio in the Los Catorce gang. His martial arts teacher told him that fighting was a last resort, but Ernesto *liked* fighting, which for him, he said, was sometimes "about hurting." The fight that landed him in jail was with the "illegal" who had stabbed Valerio. Nevertheless, second-chance mechanisms helped U.S. citizen Ernesto become a law enforcement agent in his thirties and a father with three children.

I first interviewed Ernesto in 1999 when he was sixteen years old, having met him in New York and then done a Ticuani overnight run in Mexico with him and about one hundred other youths and adults from Ticuani.[34] We did follow-up interviews in 2006, 2007, and 2015 and have kept in touch. Ernesto is a friend. When he has sought my advice or help, I have gladly offered it.

Ernesto felt ignored by his father, who abandoned his mother, and then by his mother, who left him with his grandmother and aunt and returned to Mexico. He loved this aunt, who stuck with him through good times and bad times. He reconciled with his mother during this study.

Ernesto's interviews all showed a desire to "dominate" others, in his words. In his teens and early twenties, he wanted to be a "street elite," a good, feared, and respected fighter, and eventually a Navy Seal or air marshal.[35] He said, with some irony, that being "macho," a trait of men in his family, had been taught to him by the women who raised him: "I was told that Vaqueros are not governed by women, they *govern* the women. They're not *told* what to do, they *tell* what to do. . . . That mentality was always in my head, even when I was little. . . . I was brought up like that" (emphasis in original).

Ernesto's early work career was punctuated by sudden departures from jobs that bored him. "Nothing can challenge me," he said. Ernesto landed jobs easily because he was friendly and articulate, and he excelled at the work before getting bored. He hated the deference inherent in service economy jobs. His story about himself and his actions changed after he worked in law enforcement. Settling into a professional career with good pay and prospects helped Ernesto turn away from gang life, fighting, and job-jumping and focus instead on his career and the better life it enabled.[36]

The chaotic pattern of Ernesto's life persisted until his mid to late twenties, when his life changed catalytically over a span of five years into his early thirties. At age twenty-six, Ernesto's personal life perplexed him: "My life [was] complicated." By his mid to late twenties, he had had three children by two women, the first while he was a teen. He consistently saw only his first child, his son Boydan. But by his early to midthirties, he regularly saw his two sons and paid child support. (The grandparents of his daughter had asked not to have contact with him.) Ernesto requested transfer back to the New York area (after living away for several years) to be closer to his children. Ernesto was able to become a happier and more responsible father and citizen because of second-chance mechanisms.

Second-Chance Mechanisms in School   Ernesto used second-chance mechanisms to restart a topsy-turvy school career. He had started high school in an honors program, of which he seemed proud as a sixteen-year-old. He did seem to me to belong in an honors program: agile in conversation, Ernesto asked good questions and challenged the arguments of others. But he soon fell off the honors track and was dropped from the debate team for absences. He needed second-chance educational programs to graduate from high school.

When I asked Ernesto how he started high school as an honors student but nearly did not graduate, he located the fault both inside and outside himself: "I mixed with the wrong crowd. . . . I followed the girls. . . . That's why . . . I started cutting." In his midtwenties, he happily recalled his social status in high school: "Graves High was mine. . . . I owned that school." He said everyone loved him. He had "Vaquero's Crew" — a mixed boy-girl friendship group with whom he cut school. Shaking his head, he told me that he had cut part or all of 160 of 180 school days! He had started high school well, but "I just dropped off the work."

When Graves High transferred Ernesto to Midland High because of his bad attendance record, he realized that he was failing out of high school, a notion inconsistent with his sense of himself as smart. He used New York City's educational second-chance mechanisms to make up missing credits. Not knowing anyone at Midland High, he had no one to cut with. Ernesto began listening to his teachers, who had always said he could do better, and he even accepted a teacher's mentorship. He said he had gone to "night school, summer school. I went to evening school.

I was in school 24/7. I slept in school." I asked him: Did he really make up two or three years of schoolwork in just six to eight months?

> *Ernesto*: I had to. . . . I even did extra homework for the teachers, and they gave me a credit. . . .
>
> *Author:* So they were really on your side. They wanted you to graduate.
>
> *Ernesto:* They see potential. They said I'm just throwing everything away. So many teachers have said it to me.
>
> *Author:* Were there any teachers you were really close to?
>
> *Ernesto:* I was close to a lot of teachers. I never looked at teachers like enemies, like other kids do. There was one teacher in particular, his name is Mr. F, he was my history teacher . . .
>
> *Author:* So what did he say to you?
>
> *Ernesto:* . . . What am I doing with my life? Where do I see myself going? And I told him, "I don't really know yet."

Ernesto earned the needed credits and graduated from high school at age nineteen. Midland High counselors helped him apply to and get into CUNY, where he earned an associate's degree. He enrolled in a four-year college but stopped going after getting his law enforcement job, which required only some college.

The prerequisite for this dramatic redemption story was being a U.S. citizen and thus being able to legally work after school. Ernesto's transfer to Midland High jolted him into seeing that he could no longer sustain the fantasy of being both the popular head of Vaquero's Crew who cut school and a smart student with a bright future. He realized that he had to work toward just one of these roles, not both. He even accepted mentoring from Mr. F, as he had not done with prior teachers. Being a U.S. citizen, Ernesto could benefit from rethinking his life and working via educational second-chance programs toward the elite law enforcement future he wanted. However, he still nearly pulled defeat from the jaws of victory at age eighteen when he got in the fight that landed him in jail, triggering a legal second-chance mechanism.

Youthful Offender Status as a Legal Second-Chance Mechanism   Ernesto's life pivoted, for the worse and then for the better, around fights defending and avenging his cousin Valerio. When Ernesto was eighteen, Valerio was stabbed by an older "illegal" (his word) immigrant youth.[37] Ernesto went to find the attacker—to fight him "one on one"—and beat him badly. He did not hide his face: "I was like, 'Look at me,' 'cause everybody else had headbands, bandannas, hoods . . . 'I want you to look at me and remember who did this to you.'" He was proud of the beatdown he gave his cousin's attacker, which conveyed the message that attacks on the Vaquero family would be promptly avenged.

The problem was that the guy did remember him. Months later, he (with fifteen of his friends) cornered Ernesto in a McDonald's: "He lifted up his shirt and he showed me that he had a gun. I'm like, 'Okay, cool. We could do this any way you want,' I told him. . . . And he starts laughing. . . . And my friend that works at McDonald's . . . I asked him if there was a back exit? And he was like, 'No.'" A police officer walked into this standoff and intervened. The youth Ernesto had beaten had reported the attack to the police, which Ernesto did not know. When the youth pointed Ernesto out as the attacker, the officer arrested him.

Ernesto was jailed for nearly a year. But because he was still only eighteen years old, he was given youthful offender (YO) status. He saw the cop's arrival as a divine intervention that saved him and taught him to change his ways: "I guess God does things for a reason then. I never question Him. . . . I guess to teach me a lesson. . . . [It] taught me good. . . . How do you explain the cop just coming out of nowhere?" He said jail scared him and made him think differently. "I didn't wanna spend the rest of my life behind bars . . . not doing nothing with my life." The days in jail were long, and Ernesto was scared by the other inmates facing long prison terms. He realized that violence could rob him of his future. His change in thinking embodies the kind of generative and redemptive second-chance story that is central to desisting from a criminal career.[38]

In 2015, Ernesto reflected on how, at thirty-two, his life was different because of YO status, which he credited with saving his future. Distrusting his public defender, his family spent $10,000 on a private lawyer, who Ernesto believed ensured that he got YO status, preserving his future. "I was left on youthful offender status, meaning I had no record. . . . There is no conviction. I just did my probation and that was it. . . . I have it sealed, so that's why I could hold any government position." YO status enabled Ernesto to hold federal jobs. Being hardworking, smart, and fluent in Spanish, he had earned regular promotions at his law enforcement job.

In our 2015 interview, I reminded Ernesto of how he had summed up his life at twenty-three: "My life is complicated." How would he describe his life, I asked, at age thirty-two? He replied: "My life is almost complete. . . . I have my family, I have support, some education. . . . I have a different kind of friends—all law enforcement usually. Mostly Asians." After starting at about $45,000 nine years earlier, he now earned over $90,000 per year, from raises driven by performance-based promotions and deployments to different agencies that wanted his bilingual skills. He had taken placement tests for New York law enforcement jobs to try to return permanently, which he later did.

Ernesto had changed a lot in the seventeen years I had known him when I first drafted this chapter. He still had edgy energy, but seemed happier. He still wanted to be more of an elite, but he also felt that he had become somebody. In his midthirties, he earned more money at a good government job and had a "more peaceful" relationship with his ex-wife than he had earlier. He had seen his sons only infrequently before his transfer back to New York enabled him to see them three or four times a week. He proudly told me that one of his sons wants to follow him into law enforcement. He and his ex-wife were talking about the children moving in with him: "I will be happy as a single dad."

When I asked Ernesto how YO status had affected his life, he responded, "It's a second chance . . . if you take advantage of it." He further reflected that, without YO status, "maybe I woulda been on the opposite side of where I am now [in law enforcement]. . . . It's like, you did something, but you didn't do it. It's like a lesson learned. Now move on with your life. . . . I learned a valuable lesson. . . . It opened my eyes." Ernesto also said that, compared to his younger self, he was now better able to imagine the implications of his actions *before* acting: "I learned that if you do the crime, consequences follow. I didn't get that then [as a teenager], not in the heat of the moment. I was more in tune with my emotions than rational thinking." Jail scared Ernesto, but getting a second chance with YO status gave him time to become a counterfactual thinker and make better decisions.

Ernesto's life shows how YO status fosters hope and better choices and actions. But this happy outcome would have been nearly impossible if Ernesto had lacked legal status. Although the school transfer would have been possible, Ernesto would most likely have been deported after being convicted of assault. His undocumented status would have prevented YO status from kicking in. After being deported, he most likely would have returned to New York to be near his children while only eking out a living. His life and his children's lives would be completely different, and worse.

Valerio's Story: Second-Chance Mechanisms Keeping Doors Open and Creating Space for Maturation

Valerio benefited from legal second-chance mechanisms in different ways than Ernesto did.[39] Valerio and two siblings were enmeshed in gang life. They all deliberately broke away from the Los Catorce gang in the same year in their twenties, in birth order, as if a family alarm clock of socially expected durations had gone off. Valerio and his siblings were all regularly stopped by police, but only Valerio was ever charged with a crime and so needed a legal second-chance mechanism. The factual and empirical wrinkle here is that Valerio's attempt to use YO status before he was eligible gives us a counterfactual glimpse into what would have happened if he had not gotten it. The events described here happened several years after his stabbing, for which his cousin Ernesto had retaliated.

After dropping out of college, Valerio had tried to join the Army but was turned down because he had criminal charges pending from fights. To make himself eligible for military service, he tried to use YO status before it had cleared his record.

> Once I got out of [high] school, my life went down again. . . . I got locked up six or seven times. . . . I was actually going to go into the Army. But the Army didn't accept me because I still had too many court dates. . . . I had one for assault and battery, and assault and battery on a cop, which was a felony. . . . [The Army] told me . . . "You have to go back to court, and when you're done you can come to us, and we'll talk to you about enrolling in the Army." I was like, "I thought you guys would help me." They completely turned their back to me. I went back to court.

Valerio was facing five to seven years in prison for a fight with a Puerto Rican police officer in his neighborhood. Ethnicity mattered here: Valerio's lawyer used disparaging statements the police officer made about Mexicans to bargain down penalties and dismiss charges.[40] Valerio nearly scuttled the deal by laughing at the judge for believing the fanciful gang name the officer said Valerio used. After getting YO status, Valerio still could not join the Army, because he was on probation. He was then recruited to work undercover security in his low-paid port security job, but his uncleared charges caused issues again.

> The feds [asked] me, why didn't I sign up [saying] that I had prior misdemeanor charges? I told them, "Because they were supposed to be erased." . . . The judge told me [at age] eighteen I was still . . . a youthful offender, so they were supposed to [seal the records]. So the feds were like, "We need somebody with a clean record." And I told them . . . "You guys can do it for me." And they was like, "We'll see what we can do." And they needed me 'cause . . . I look like a simple guy, but I have like this thug mentality, they told me.[41]

After Valerio got off probation, YO status sealed his record and the feds hired him for the undercover work. Later, in his midtwenties, he used his work with the feds as a selling point in reapplying to the Army, which quickly accepted him. Valerio had used a deliberate strategy to leave a bad context and move into a new one to "become somebody." In an interview after joining the military, he said he intended to permanently change and "might stay in the military more than twenty years." His parents were quietly proud that he had chosen to "do something" with his life. When he was interviewed in his thirties, Valerio had no criminal record and was thriving in his military career.

Valerio's family offers a counterpoint to the Pachecos. In both families, siblings were deeply involved in gangs in their teens and early twenties, and parental discipline was harsh or abusive. Valerio's parents, with more education and income than the Pacheco parents, were able to hire a lawyer for his felony case. As U.S. citizens, Valerio and his siblings could change their futures by changing their thoughts and actions, but the Pacheco siblings' undocumented status blocked the effect of redemptive thinking or action. The collective exit of Valerio and his siblings from their gang shows a virtuous spreading of redemptive thinking and action for U.S. citizens. Anita Pacheco's redemptive thinking but blocked story only disheartened her younger siblings.

Valerio benefited from YO status. Like Ernesto, he had endangered his future with his bad choices. YO status promoted better long-term outcomes for Valerio, his future family, and the United States by making his military service possible. YO status preserved a feasible pathway to responsible adulthood for Valerio. How many places to be socially productive are there for a guy who likes to fight? The military gave Valerio a stable job that had career steps, that he liked, and that supported his marriage and family—all conditions that promote desistance from crime.[42] Had he lacked legal status, Valerio would most likely have been deported for the fight with the police officer.

An ironic closing note: Valerio's wife came to New York as a small child and was still undocumented after they had children. Valerio's repeated deployments delayed their marriage. Here, long-term undocumented status affected the most intimate fabric of American life by leaving the wife of an active-duty serviceman and the mother of his U.S. citizen children at risk of deportation by the country he was deployed to a combat zone to defend. They have since married and adjusted her status, but had she been detained by ICE before that—perhaps after being stopped while driving their children to the doctor, as has happened to others in my studies—she could easily have been deported. Her marriage to an active-duty military husband or her being the mother of his U.S. citizen children would not have prevented it.

Agustin Maestro: A Stupid College Prank and Prosecutorial Discretion

Agustin Maestro is now a senior staff member in an excellent New York public school, married with three children, and owns a house in a suburban place near others in the extended Maestro family. When we last spoke, he made more than $100,000 per year after being rapidly recruited to better schools and promoted within them. But all this success came after a youthful mistake from which he was saved by the second-chance mechanism of YO status and by certain life conditions.

Agustin was a student at Presidents High during the great influx of Mexican teen migrants in the late 1990s and early 2000s. As a college-bound, U.S.-born Mexican American, he rarely had classes with "ESLs" (his term)—English as a Second Language students who regularly stepped up to him in school, on the street, or at Mexican parties.[43] He and his Buendia and Maestro cousins had been Wannabes: they acted like gang members (for example, by writing their street names on walls) but stopped doing that after a violent conflict with what he called "real" gang members. Like other cousins, Agustin said that living in the gentri-fying Hillock Gardens neighborhood helped him escape gang entangle-ments. He further distanced himself from Brooklyn by attending college upstate. Agustin's change of heart was able to reset his life path because he was a U.S. citizen, unlike the undocumented Pachecos.

Agustin's successful college career was nearly derailed by "being stupid . . . a college prank." While waiting to go to a campus party, his friends realized that the campus store's metal grating was unlocked. They were helping themselves to chips and soda when a campus police officer arrived. They apologized and offered to pay, but instead they were arrested and held in the county's juvenile corrections facility for a week until making bail. Agustin felt humiliated when he was stripped down to his underwear and given an orange jumpsuit to wear. He feared that he had ruined his life: "I can't believe this is happening to me. . . . I got locked up in a cell. . . . Everything's electrical. Damn, man, I don't belong here! . . . What the fuck did I get myself into!?" He knew a felony conviction would stop him from being a teacher, his life goal.

The university provided a lawyer to advise him, and Agustin's family hired the lawyer, who knew the judge and bargained "in the back room" for no conviction and the dropping of the charges after community service. Agustin thought this was a "great" solution. The lawyer had appealed to prosecutorial discretion, saying that his client was a good kid who did something stupid but merited a second chance. Agustin vowed not to make "the same mistake again."

Agustin was too ashamed to call his father to pick him up, though his father came to the jail anyway. Agustin called a friend instead after posting bail. Furthering his shame, the jail had lost his clothes, so he returned to the dorm in his orange "Corrections" jumpsuit. His friend gave him a coat to cover himself. His stupid stunt did not fit with the life story he had told himself up to that point and made his commitment to keeping the immigrant bargain look uncertain.

While Agustin did not mention this, it seems wildly disproportionate to jail college students for eating filched chips and soda. It is hard to imagine a White college student with wealthy parents being so harshly treated for so small an infraction. Indeed, it makes no sense for a university to criminally prosecute any student for such a stupid stunt. The narrowness of Agustin's upward mobile path can be seen here. He was not living a life with a glass floor, whereby his parents' wealth and institutional connections would have prevented him from downward mobility, even if he was an academic underperformer. He was strong academically, but when he made a stupid mistake, he was subjected to severely disproportionate penalties that required significant financial sacrifice from his parents to resolve. What if he had come before a judge who denied him YO status? What if his parents had not had the funds to pay for a private lawyer? With a felony on his record, Agustin would have been barred from teaching.

Although Agustin's college prank threatened his dream of becoming a teacher, his status as a college student got him access to a locally connected lawyer. His parents, now U.S. citizens, could pay for the lawyer who helped clear his record. Agustin's U.S. citizenship protected him, whereas Darrell was deported for a smaller infraction (drinking beer in public) than Agustin's (potato chip and soda theft), though neither mistake should be one that changes the course of a young person's life. Once revealed, Darrell's previously hidden undocumented status became the only salient fact about him, while Agustin's U.S. citizenship lowered the stakes.[44] When Agustin later became a teacher of New York City schoolchildren, the wisdom of having given him a second chance became apparent.[45]

Conclusion

This chapter has analyzed how second-chance mechanisms help U.S. citizen youth who make mistakes become productive, upwardly mobile adults, while legal status prevents such mechanisms from helping undocumented American youth. U.S. citizen youth in the study were able to benefit from after-school programs, special school programs, and practices fostering redemptive thinking that helped them imagine how better decisions and actions could lead to better outcomes in the future. Thinking more "generatively" helped Ernesto reorient his life. Conversely, Anita Pacheco's redemptive thinking and actions changed how she thought and acted, but she could not walk through the doors for work or college that her high school graduation and the Woods Explorers had opened because she was undocumented. Anita's sad story dissuaded her brother Saul from trying harder in school. Why go to college, he asked reasonably, if he was going to end up in the same kind of job held by high school dropouts because he lacked legal status? He saw that redemptive thinking could work for his U.S. citizen peers, but not for undocumented students like him.

Legal system second chances hit the reset button for U.S. citizen teens who made a mistake. Ernesto's stint in prison moved him away from fighting and gang life. He saw the gift that YO status offered him and redeemed this second chance by going on to a successful adult life in law enforcement, which a criminal record would have blocked. Valerio's bad actions did not permanently bar him from his military career. YO status held that door open for him. Agustin Maestro's stupid chips and soda raid was remedied by prosecutorial discretion, leaving open his road to becoming a teacher. Ernesto, Valerio, and Agustin's U.S. citizenship and the YO mechanism prevented their youthful mistakes from becoming negative turning points.[46]

Undocumented status was all that was bureaucratically "seen" in Darrell Pacheco's minor encounter with the police, so he was deported after not showing up for court—ironically, for fear of deportation. The second chances given to Ernesto and Valerio despite their committing serious violence contrast dramatically with Darrell's deportation for drinking a beer.

Our long-term research enabled us to document how second chances gave U.S. citizen teens and early adults who had made bad choices the time to change their thinking and actions in order to reset their lives. Second chances allowed them to become counterfactual thinkers after they made mistakes. This occurred much later in their lives than it did for those who counterfactually picked their high school, but in time to salvage a good future. The logic behind YO status syncs with emerging brain science in that it keeps societal doors open until a teen or early adult is old enough for their brain to have matured. But YO status did not help undocumented youth because their legal status quickly became their only legally visible feature.

Providing second-chance mechanisms is good public policy for youth who need them, for their current and future families, and for society. Youth who go into early adulthood with criminal records face tremendous odds, especially because that record blocks them from applying for public-sector jobs—a key path to mobility for U.S. citizen study participants.[47] As is made clear when we juxtapose Ernesto's and Valerio's lives with Anita's, Saul's, and Darrell's, the children and spouses of the U.S. citizen youth who benefited from second-chance mechanisms had better lives than would have been possible without those mechanisms and without legal status.

═ Chapter 7 ═

Masculinities and Long-Term Outcomes: How Mexican Mobility Masculinity Promotes and Gang Masculinity Inhibits Mobility

"**I**N THE school, they duck their head to me now . . . because I looked at them hard. I stopped caring [about school] . . . I wanted to be cool, instead of, like, [doing] good in school."

Federico, a U.S. citizen, told me that, after he joined a gang, other students lowered their eyes ("duck[ed] their head") when he gave them a "hard look" (sustained eye contact conveying a challenge), but also how joining the gang led him from being an honors student to being a dropout. Adopting "gang masculinity" and habits derailed Federico's academically successful life, even though he left the gang about two years later. Even in his early thirties, his life had not gotten back onto its pre-gang track.

"I didn't want to stare back. I managed to get this far because I *didn't* stare back."

By contrast, Xavier explained how not responding to hard looks helped him succeed. His undocumented status made him fear that any conflict could escalate into deportation for himself and his family. Living strictly by "Mexican mobility masculinity" helped him avoid problems, thrive in school, and attract door-opening mentors. By his midthirties, he had legalized his status and thrived working in health care.

These vignettes illustrate how differing masculinity models enacted in high school promoted or harmed adult outcomes and life chances. Federico and Xavier had both loved and done well in middle school. But undocumented Xavier went to Jungle High, while U.S. citizen Federico was in the honors program at Graves High, a stronger school. These factors should have helped Federico and hurt Xavier, but fifteen years later

https://doi.org/10.7758/drwz9626.4733

Xavier was thriving while Federico struggled. In this chapter, I explicate these unexpected outcomes by tracing how Federico's enactments of gang masculinity (such as "looking back" when challenged with a hard look) closed doors for him, while Xavier's enactments of Mexican mobility masculinity (such as "looking down" when challenged with a hard look) opened doors. These differing masculinities affect adult mobility by encouraging different school and life habits, changing relationships to the immigrant family bargain, prioritizing different conceptions of social time, and prescribing different responses to challenge, all of which led Xavier and Federico into contexts offering different opportunities.

My 2006 book *Mexican New York: Transnational Worlds of New Immigrants* analyzed the ways in which the lives of study participants challenged the predominant theories that immigrant women experience gendered liberation in the United States, while men lose power, privilege, and honor, especially if undocumented.[1] That book traced the maintenance of some Mexican traditions by both first-generation women migrants and their U.S.-born and/or -raised daughters alongside their acceptance of some (but not all) elements of "American" femininity. Moreover, first-generation migrant fathers did not simply lose power or honor in the United States, but in fact generated some power and honor, both through their civic work and their economic success here, while second-generation men sought to claim male privileges they imagined they would have had (and imagined their fathers had or would have had) in Mexico.

This chapter similarly challenges common theories and public narratives about Latino masculinity, which posit that Latinos, including Mexicans, respond to marginalization and discrimination as a group by adopting hypermasculinities like gang masculinity or "perilous masculinity." These masculinities require that a man respond to challenges or violence from other men by escalating and defeating them, to avoid losing face in front of their peers. NYCOMP participants told a different story. While twenty of the forty-nine male teenagers enacted some element of gang masculinity (such as looking back when challenged), few *mainly* enacted that masculinity, and when they did they were always challenged by other men and women in their lives, who worried for their welfare. Moreover, most study participants *ran away* when faced with violence or a weapon. By their mid to late twenties, nearly all of the men in the study enacted Mexican mobility masculinity almost exclusively. This movement away from conflict, fighting, and gang habits by NYCOMPers in their midtwenties comports with decades of research on gang desistance.[2] Timing matters because earlier desistance helps one's future more.

Theoretical Conversations and Framework: Mexican Mobility Masculinities and Gang Masculinity

Gang and Mexican mobility masculinities are analytical ideal types that I developed after tracking how cases evolved over many years. As with any analytical type, not all gang members enact all elements of gang masculinity, and not everyone enacting such elements is a gang member. Like most analytical types, it draws on prior research. Unlike much research, however, I focus not on gang membership itself as the outcome but on how habitual enactments of gang masculinity or Mexican mobility masculinity affect or correlate with adult outcomes.

Gang masculinity is a form of hypermasculinity that stresses dominance over others.[3] It emphasizes fearlessness in facing challenge and the right to respond with violence. Gang masculinity prizes guarding one's honor against challenge and keeps account of both acts of honor and insults from rivals. It requires that a young man spend time occupying and defending symbolic spaces, be they permanent (a street corner) or temporary and constituted (a *sonido* party).[4] Many gang members find that fighting ("having each other's back") bonds them; some also take pleasure in dominating others through fighting. Many Mexican teen migrants used gang masculinity to guard against perceived insult by second-generation Mexican American youth, who they believed thought they were better than them because of their U.S. birth and English fluency.

Gang masculinity also prizes loyalty to the gang. Gang life is often compartmentalized from a member's life outside of the gang, and alcohol or drug use, which is common, intensifies feelings of belonging among members and lowers inhibitions.[5] Gang masculinity posits that men govern relations with women and rationalizes the right of men to treat women violently.

Gang masculinity often conflicts with the immigrant family bargain.[6] As previously noted, this reciprocal bargain obligates children to redeem their parents' sacrifice by finishing school, getting a good job, living at home as an adult to help their parents and younger siblings, and being good persons.[7] NYCOMPers who adopted gang masculinity often declared their respect for their elders, but their actions regularly violated the immigrant bargain and distressed their parents, as they told me. Parents worried when their adult children did not finish high school or college, set a bad example for their siblings, did not help enough economically, or moved out. In parents' eyes, the immigrant bargain was not kept, or not kept well, when adult children missed key steps in the bargain or did not uphold it for as long as socially expected. Similarly, some adult children felt intense pressure to succeed in ways they either could not do or did not want to do, leading them to resent or discredit their parents' expectations.[8]

Mexican mobility masculinity has first- and second-generation versions. Second-generation Mexican mobility masculinity prescribes first that men should keep the immigrant bargain by completing all its steps, thus promoting their own and their younger siblings' upward mobility. Second, they should treat their wives or girlfriends as equal partners and support their children if they become parents. Third, second-generation mobility masculinity bestows honor through longer-term success in school, work, and family and through avoidance or management of the honor conflicts that drive gang masculinity. Some siblings, especially older, undocumented brothers, adopt first-generation Mexican mobility masculinity, which resembles the parental side of the immigrant bargain. They forgo more education to start full-time work earlier in their lives to help their parents and younger siblings. They often gain honor in their family's eyes, though some parents criticize them for not enacting the second-generation version of mobility masculinity.[9]

While gang masculinity echoes the sociologist Eli Anderson's folk category of being "street," mobility masculinity resonates with "decent." Mobility masculinity echoes Shaun Harper's research showing that high-achieving African American men understand masculinity to be generated by leadership, achievement, and preparation for the future.[10] I describe this mobility masculinity as "Mexican" to reflect the reality that gender, ethnicity, and family relations are experienced jointly or intersectionally. Mexican mobility masculinity was the predominant model for NYCOMP families, contrary to the negative images of Mexicans and masculinity in American life.[11] Labeling mobility masculinities as "Mexican" does not mean that they are *only* Mexican or Mexican American, nor are the traits of mobility masculinity named above exhaustive. "Mainstream" masculinity also prescribes similar steps of going to college, finding well-paid employment, marrying, and having children. Similarly, the prescribed steps in gang masculinity recur in elements of "hegemonic" masculinity, such as requiring a hostile response to challenge or asserting dominance over women, though enactors of hegemonic masculinity often benefit from institutional, racial, and economic positions of power.[12] The masculinities contrasted here are heterosexual and cisgendered because nearly all study participants were publicly heterosexual and cis.

Studies of Masculinity, Mobility,
Immigration, and the Second Generation

This chapter brings into conversation research literatures on gender and masculinity, mobility, and the second generation that mostly do not talk to each other. Almost no research on second-generation mobility analyzes how masculinity affects it, but many would offer strategic sites to do so.[13] How, for example, are models of masculinity changing on Wall Street as jobs previously hoarded by White men open up to non-White newcomers?[14] Or to women? Sociology analyzes White men's earnings and career advantages as well as systemic discrimination and the barriers confronting women and minorities.[15] Most research does not empirically explain how advantages accrue, though some propose remedies such as mentoring women or minorities.[16] Most such work does not analyze the types of masculinity organizing life in these sites.

Most research on masculinity, including pioneering work by R. Connell, Michael Kimmel, James Messerschmidt, Michael Messner, and Todd Reeser, takes masculinity itself as the object of inquiry and describes how varying masculinities emerge and function.[17] This research often posits hegemonic and marginalized or subordinated masculinities, created by institutional and societal, class, sexual, and racial hierarchical positions. Often, this work posits that hypermasculinized men become Mertonian innovators who find alternative routes (such as crime) to status and power.[18] Much of it posits hegemonic masculinity as a partial cause of the hypermasculinity of marginalized minority men.[19] Some research points to schools as the site where young Black boys can be taught that their future selves are hypermasculine and criminal.[20] Other work argues that hegemonic masculinity is driven partly by globalization and the undermining of working-class masculinity.[21] Still other scholars point to how non-gender-conforming boys navigate their identities in high school;[22] how hybrid masculinities emerge from changing societal navigations of gender;[23] and how manhood acts elicit deference from others,[24] perpetuating gender inequality.[25]

Little research empirically links types of masculinity with concrete outcomes. One exception is the "Daddy Bonus" demonstrated by the sociologists Melissa Hodges and Michelle Budig: higher income accrues to managerially employed, college-educated, heterosexual, married men with children, but not to their female counterparts.[26] Another is the innovative work of the sociologist Ed Flores, who analyzes how church-based programs help former gang members change their lives by changing their model of masculinity.[27] The sociologist Victor Rios argues that interaction with police and the criminal justice system reinforces and teaches "detrimental forms of masculinity," hyper-masculinizing Black and Latino masculinity and harming Black and Latino youth.[28] The sociologist Diedre Royster offers an agile analysis of the evolution of Black and White young men's masculinity through a series of potential-denying encounters for the former but not for the latter.[29] A fascinating *American Journal of Public Health* review analyzes how much men of color's adherence to hegemonic mainstream masculinity affects their health.[30] Here we analyze how enacting different teen or early adult masculinities led to divergent outcomes as established adults.

Perilous Masculinity, Wannabe Moments, and Avoiding Trouble for Future Gain

Accepting that structural exclusion drives hypermasculinity, the sociologist Alberto Lobo de la Tierra argues that overfocus on hyper-masculinity has made perilous masculinity a hegemonic framing of Black and Latino men.[31] For Lobo de la Tierra, perilous masculinity is a "one-dimensional" hypermasculinity premised on Blacks and Latinos learning to be men by showing fearlessness in violent confrontations and by controlling women. He argues that this framing leads us to miss other masculinities, such as that shown by older Dominican men playing dominos on summer nights on the same streets posited to promote hypermasculinity.[32] The perilous masculinity framing would also have difficulty understanding African American men who define their masculinity by their achievements and leadership, or the trust that others place in them.[33]

Perilous masculinity has other issues. First, it often analyzes enactments of hypermasculinity and their consequences, and their meaning within relationships with like-situated friends, to yield a "moment of truth" trope. Many deeply researched studies intimately describe situations wherein a Black or Brown youth acts violently because he fears losing face in front of his peers if he does not.[34] This research can explain why some youth choose violence, but not why so many do not, or why some youth purposefully avoid such contexts.

The second problem with this frame is attentional: Which research participants, interactions, and relationships do we analyze? Rios focuses on thirty boys who had been in detention (twenty-seven for nonviolent offenses) and ten who were seen as "at risk," so it makes sense that most of his research participants saw the world this way—as a place where violence had to be enacted to save face.[35] Rios's research participants, however, are the mirror image of mine: only eight of the ninety-six participants in my study had gone to jail, and only sixteen had ever been detained, even briefly, by police. Most of them ran away from "moments of truth" and thereafter avoided the sites where such moments took place, including Mexican *sonido* (DJ) parties.[36] These study participants made fun of themselves as Wannabes who acted like gang members until confronted with a knife or gun. Then, realizing that acting like gang members was putting their safety and imagined futures at risk, they ran from these "come to Jesus" moments.

Moreover, both study participants' accounts and my fieldwork over two decades underline that pushback from family and friends promoted their desistance from both real gang activities and Wannabe gang activities.[37] Parents, siblings, wives, and friends exhorted these young men to stop hanging out, drinking, and fighting. Not a single parent in this study encouraged gang activities, and pressure to avoid or desist from gang involvement increased as young men entered their early twenties, married, or had children. Parents used carrots and sticks, offering to pay for college or help them get jobs; some even did psychotherapy with their sons. Other parents threatened to kick their sons out of the house or send them to Mexico, and a few followed through. Fathers modeled mobility masculinity in their words and deeds and exhorted their sons and other relatives to live "tranquil" lives. Older siblings and cousins offered concrete advice on avoiding gang life or charting a course out of it by joining the military or "getting out of Brooklyn" to live away at college.

Finally, as established adults, former gang members spoke of friends serving long prison sentences, not with pride but with sadness at their friends' lost lives. They expressed relief that it was not them serving those sentences. Manuel, whose case we profile in this chapter, told me that he was now the only visitor to an old gangmate who was serving over forty years. He went once a year, to play checkers. His friend's story made Manuel fear jail, and he retired from gang life.

The concept of perilous masculinity as the single, unitary, and hyper form of Black and Latino masculinity seems potentially dangerous to me. Given that police culture and other cultures in America already seem to lead police not to "see" the actual Black person, especially a Black man, before them but to only see a threat, scholars should work hard to describe various masculinities. Hopefully, our work can help change our institutions and police training and culture to promote a more just America.[38]

Curiously, much research on perilous masculinity does not engage Mitchell Duneier's 1994 book *Slim's Table*.[39] Challenging the predominant framing of Black men as pathologically hypermasculine during the underclass debate of the 1980s and 1990s, Duneier analyzed how a group of Black men who met regularly in a cafeteria enacted masculinity practices that conveyed and created respectability and honor for themselves as men. He spent months in the cafeteria with the men and extended his research by following them into other contexts and relationships. Duneier's study was a model of empirical research contradicting predominant, controlling images of masculinity.[40]

Conceptions of Social Time and Prescribed Use in Mobility Masculinity and Gang Masculinity

Gang and mobility masculinity are premised on different conceptions of social time, with different socially expected durations, habits, and life steps, which sync differently with the immigrant family bargain, and can help or harm mobility.[41] Their different prescribed habits to enact masculinity create different allocations of real time and experiences of social time. Mobility masculinity prescribes a series of steps and time frames for achieving socially desirable goals that help one's family, deepen family trust, and confer honor.

Conversely, gang masculinity, with fewer social steps and less varied social time frames, prescribes habits with worse outcomes, harming the immigrant bargain and eroding family trust. A young man joins a gang and hangs out, perhaps fighting or robbing or becoming a leader. But then what? In my study participants' accounts, gang life offers few new social steps with career-type rewards, unless the gang moves into high-risk business in drugs or brothels. Study participants described long-term gang life, with its constant need to stay vigilant to offense and willing to fight in response, as an emotionally exhausting Groundhog Day of hanging out, partying, and defending one's honor. Moreover, the potential costs of these habits increased with age as teenage gang members became adults before the law and some of them had children; unlike in their teens, they now feared what they might lose. As described to me, gang masculinity's goal was to uphold itself, but it hurt mobility and compromised the keeping of the immigrant bargain.

Gang habits may harm life prospects via the "popular kid" dynamic, wherein younger teens precociously engage in "adult" behaviors, such as drinking, thus limiting the development of their "soft" skills to negotiate the difficulties of adolescence and adulthood. Lacking soft skills may contribute to gang habits like continuing to have life-altering conflicts into one's late twenties and early thirties.[42]

A practical reason why gang masculinity harms adult life outcomes is its requirement that so many hours be spent hanging out, thus "eating up" time that could be devoted to study or work. Most active gang members among the study participants spent Friday to Sunday nights hanging out—that is, walking on their streets, defending their turf, staying vigilant to challenge, going to parties, and venturing into places where they would be challenged by another gang. Many hung out on weekday afternoons and nights and regularly attended hooky parties. Conversely, youth enacting first- or second-generation mobility masculinity mostly avoided hanging out in these public places, thus avoiding step-ups.

Table 7.1 presents the models of masculinity that predominated or coexisted for the cases profiled here at time 1 (average age nineteen) and at time 2 or time 3 (average age twenty-eight and thirty-three, respectively), corresponding time use, and relationship to gangs. Many participants enacted elements of both masculinities as teens but increasingly enacted only mobility masculinity in their mid to late twenties. They did better than those whose time was governed by gang masculinity habits at that age and later.

Book bags provide a clear illustration of contradictions between mobility masculinity and gang masculinity. Manuel described a gang member's "typical day—we would be sent to . . . a certain school . . . and we had to come back with stuff . . . like a gold chain, beeper, book bags. That's the most you could get out of a school (*laughs*)."

Conversely, Juan (who did not know Manuel) had his backpacks stolen. He had enacted Mexican mobility masculinity by getting good grades and being "a good kid." His mother rewarded him with a JanSport backpack—"the coolest" brand then—and he carried *all* his books home in it every night to study. Juan answered lots of questions in class and looked down when confronted with bigger kids' hard looks and insults: "I would just . . . keep walking and ignore them. . . . Big kids would . . . smack me in the back of the head . . . and I would just be like, 'Ow!' I wouldn't do anything. I was just a calm kid." After bigger kids stole his JanSport backpack, his mother got him a cheaper one and told him to carry plastic grocery bags to carry his stuff home if that one got stolen. But Juan was tired of the abuse. He started hanging out with his cousins' gang and changed from wearing chinos and shoes to very baggy pants and sneakers. After Juan fought a backpack stealer, backed by his cousins, the abuse stopped.

Xavier's and Federico's Counterfactual Cases

Federico's and Xavier's starting conditions predicted very different outcomes, making them counterfactual cases to each other. How did Federico, a U.S. citizen in an honors program in a better high school who lived in a safer neighborhood, end up as a Stuck Muddler at age thirty? And how did Xavier, an undocumented student in a tough high school

Table 7.1 Masculinity Types and Time Use at Time 1 and Time 2 or Time 3

Name	Dominant Masculinity Type at Time 1	Time 1: How Free Time Was Spent, Including Creating It by Holding Hooky Parties	Dominant Masculinity Type at Time 2 or Time 3 (Last Contact)	Time 2 or Time 3: How Time Was Spent and Whether Involved in Any Street Conflicts
Xavier (never associated with a gang)— Time 1: age twenty-three Time 2: age thirty-six	Governed by Mexican mobility masculinity (head-down masculinity).	Spent no time hanging out on street. Mainly studied and relaxed indoors with friends.	Governed by high-achieving mobility masculinity.	Worked sixty to eighty hours per week. Career was thriving. No street conflict involvement.
Federico (gang member)— Time 1: age sixteen Time 2: age twenty-nine	Gang masculinity increasingly governed habits and time use to the point where it became fully governing.	Cut school and went to hooky parties. Dropped out and hung out with his gang. Left jobs in conflict, for example, for drinking.	Gang masculinity was barely edged out by mobility masculinity as he became a responsible and religious father and husband.	Spent no time hanging out on the street. Went to church three nights a week and one full weekend day. Still got into street conflicts.
Manuel (gang leader)— Time 1: age twenty-one Time 2: age thirty-three	Governed by gang masculinity. Worked, but mobility masculinity was not a key source of identity.	Went to parties Friday to Sunday and hooky parties during the week. Hung out on the street on weekends and some weeknights.	Trying to abandon gang masculinity to become something different.	Spent no time hanging out. Spent nine hours working, two hours providing childcare, four hours watching TV, and five hours sleeping. Avoided street conflicts.
Gordo (gang member)— Time 1: age thirty-two (had known him for ten years) Time 2: age forty-three	Governed by gang masculinity, hanging out a lot, but also by mobility masculinity, always working.	Hung out on the street every day. Went to parties or drank with friends Friday to Sunday.	Governed by mobility masculinity as a responsible father.	Spent no time hanging out on the street. Was the primary caregiver to kids. Still got into some street conflicts. *(Table continues on p. 204)*

Table 7.1 (Continued)

Name	Dominant Masculinity Type at Time 1	Time 1: How Free Time Was Spent, Including Creating It by Holding Hooky Parties	Dominant Masculinity Type at Time 2 or Time 3 (Last Contact)	Time 2 or Time 3: How Time Was Spent and Whether Involved in Any Street Conflicts
Valerio (gang member)—Time 1: age fifteen Time 2: age twenty-seven	Gang masculinity was dominant, but also worked, so mobility masculinity was present.	Hung out "every day" after school. Partied every weekend.	Governed by mobility masculinity as a responsible father.	Spent no time hanging out on the street. Worked long hours, including abroad. Still got into some street conflicts.
Donal (gang leader)—Time 1: age nineteen Time 2: age thirty-one	Governed by gang masculinity. Worked, but lost jobs or quit. Always in conflict.	As an eighteen-year-old recent high school dropout, watched TV six hours a day, hung out outside the schools two to three hours a day, worked six hours in the evenings, and hung out after 11:00 PM and on weekends.	Gang masculinity was still active. Conflict had led to loss of most jobs, but hung out much less.	Worked eight to nine hours a day. Hung out at home after work and late into the night, playing music. Hung out with the gang when they asked him to. Still got into street conflicts.
Emmanuel (negotiated associator)—Time 1: age nineteen Time 2: age twenty-eight	Mobility masculinity increasingly dominated gang masculinity in role as negotiated associator.	Hung out on the street as an early teen. Hung out less, then nearly none at all, as an early adult. Did not hang out as a middle adult.	Governed by mobility masculinity and young professional masculinity.	Spent no time hanging out on the street. Worked fifty hours per week. Got into no street conflicts.

Source: NYCOMP dataset. Analysis by author.

who lived in a tough neighborhood, who got stepped up to regularly, end up as a High Flier in his midthirties? Here we trace how Federico's and Xavier's enactments of gang masculinity and mobility masculinity, respectively, led them into contexts that closed or opened doors and reinforced habits that harmed or hurt their established adult mobility and lives.[43]

Xavier's Story: Mobility Masculinity as a Guide through and beyond Jungle High

After reading this chapter in draft, Xavier said: "I feel survivor's guilt . . . [as] one of the few . . . who went through all this and [did] not end up messed up. . . . I escaped." His survivor's guilt was primed daily even as he helped immigrant families at the clinic where he worked as an adult.

Xavier faced challenges that pushed others toward gang masculinity, fueling the growth of Mexican gangs in the late 1990s and mid-2000s. First, as noted earlier, Xavier and his family were undocumented, and his parents imagined only a low-wage future for him. Second, Xavier's father drank alcoholically, causing financial problems and worry. Third, Xavier's family lived in Vista Heights, where hard looks and street step-ups regularly occurred. Fourth, despite being an excellent student, Xavier received no advice to apply to better high schools, so he ended up in his zoned high school, Jungle High, a "bad" high school in Brooklyn that was "a very violent experience," in Xavier's words. (Jungle High was closed, reorganized, and reopened over the course of this study.) Finally, Xavier was a U.S.-raised undocumented Mexican with mostly non-Mexican friends in a zoned high school: he was the perfect target for step-ups. He faced the kind of challenges that led some to have only Mexican friends, hang with a gang, cut school, or drop out for full-time work.[44]

I first met Xavier when he was an undergraduate at Competitive Liberal Arts College. Here I draw on over ten hours of interviews with him from his twenties to his midthirties, ethnographic conversations over nearly twenty years, and an interview and conversations with his brother Lorencio.

The undocumented status of Xavier's family informed their life choices, habits, and imagined futures. As mentioned earlier, his brother, who was nine years older, left high school and home by his late teens to form his own family. Another brother, Lorencio, who was eight years older than Xavier, left high school to work full-time, giving Xavier a better chance. Lorencio increased his income to $40,000 by his late thirties. Xavier's mother constantly cautioned Xavier to avoid problems, fearing deportation. No one in the family knew what rights undocumented people had or what might cause deportation, but they knew that deportations could happen after minor police interactions. The family's caution was justified. USCIS data available via Syracuse University's TRAC system show that 69 percent of about 100,000 people deported over a fifteen-year period ending in 2017 in New York State had no criminal convictions at all or had only minor traffic or other violations.[45] This uncertainty made dread a backdrop emotion to Xavier's daily life.

Xavier's family offered conflicting models of masculinity. His father was an "alcoholic and gambler . . . an urban drinker . . . who everybody knows." He was popular on the street with other drinking men who played dominos and gambled (and became indebted) in bodega bookie operations. Adopting this "urban drinker" masculinity model could have derailed Xavier's academic and career plans. But he also had the example of Lorencio, who enacted first-generation mobility masculinity by working full-time as a teen to stabilize the family. His brothers gently teased Xavier for always looking down at hard looks, but they did too. Their financial support of him through college showed admiration for their studious *hermanito* (younger brother).

Xavier described Jungle High as the perfect site for hard stares and step-ups by Mexicans because it was then becoming "gang central" (his words), for three reasons. First, Mexican teens who "just came from Mexico" were "pass-through" students, who went to school mainly to learn English "for two years, or two months, then drop out. Few made it out." Second, Mexicans—who were highly visible, study participants said, because of their lack of English, their presumed lack of legal status, their heavy presence in ESL classes, and sometimes even their clothing—were at the "bottom of the status hierarchy. . . . If you're a Mexican . . . you've already lost." This made them easy targets for African Americans, Dominicans, and Puerto Ricans. Xavier said:

> Newer immigrants that grew up . . . in Puebla . . . had a problem speaking English . . . they didn't really speak in class. . . . They had their own cliques, which were recent immigrants that spoke mainly Spanish. I think that was very important on how these smaller Mexican gangs were formed, because they were pushed to the side . . . isolated from everyone else. So then they start . . . in high school . . . taking this identity of *Mexicano*, whether you watched *American Me* or a gang movie. . . . You start wanting to be in a group too.

Mexicans formed gangs for protection, sometimes modeling themselves on movies like *American Me*, and they looked hard at Mexican Americans in particular, to prove themselves.[46] Finally, Jungle High had become "gang central," Xavier said, because its zoning placed it "at the center of [Mexican] gangs." Located in a middle-class neighborhood that students had to travel to, Jungle High was a school that no gang had a geographical claim to "own." That caused conflict: "Cops [were] everywhere from 3:00 to 6:00 PM . . . [because of] fights after school." Xavier said that, by the early 2000s, Jungle High "had ten gangs of *Mexicanos*."

Xavier's description echoes that of Donal, a Mexican teen migrant who dropped out of Jungle High at the same time Xavier was there. He described Jungle High as being "like in jail. . . . You can't really smile at nobody in jail. . . . [At Jungle High] I had to be tough all the time, I had a serious look in the classroom, I had a serious look in lunchtime, I had a serious look when I got out of my house. . . . I had to be *cara dura* (hard face)." Donal reported that Black and Puerto Rican youth would say "you fucking Mexicans" while passing in the halls and would beat them up in the bathrooms. Donal formed a gang. After dropping out, he waited near Jungle High at 2:30, when school let out, to meet girls and step up to possible Mexican rivals before work at 5:00. Xavier always looked down at Jungle High; Donal always looked back.

If Jungle High was the perfect site for step-ups, Xavier was the "perfect guy to step up to," he said. Especially when he was in ninth and tenth grades, Mexican teen migrants stepped up to him for representing an integration they felt was denied them. "I was one of maybe very few *Mexicanos* who had grown up here and understood the codes. What to do, and how to talk, and what kind of friends to have." As a Mexican who spoke native English, had grown up in Brooklyn, and had three high-achieving best friends who were Chinese, Puerto Rican–Italian, and African American, Xavier was a bad fit for the newcomer teen migrants' mental categories of and prescriptions for being "Mexican." He thought that they challenged him for thinking he was "better than" them:

> When more Mexicans started coming into the Jungle . . . they saw me already . . . established. . . . I knew a lot of people . . . the stares came . . . out of curiosity . . . jealousy. . . . [They] wanted to know what clique [gang] I was in. . . . The stares were like a challenge. And I was like a stranger to them. . . . That was the weirdest part, 'cause I wasn't a stranger. . . . I grew up in Brooklyn.

Xavier was an easy step-up because his student leader friends were unable to "have my back" in a fight, and he had to ride the bus back to Vista Heights with students who had stepped up to him. He faced constant hard looks and got punched a lot by Mexican teens policing his nonconformity to their notion of being Mexican and enacting gang masculinity.[47]

How Mobility Masculinity Helped Xavier Negotiate Adolescence and Early Adulthood Successfully   Xavier used mobility masculinity to successfully negotiate these dynamics and create opportunities. His mobility masculinity was based in sober appreciation of and aversion to the unknowable costs of confrontation: "If you grow up in Vista Heights . . . you know if you engage [by looking back] you could end up getting beaten up really badly. . . . You just wanna avoid fights. . . . I understood that being stared down can quickly escalate into something else—pretty bad. . . . I would just keep walking."

Xavier's aversion to conflict had also grown from seeing violence. When Xavier was in high school, his oldest brother went with friends to buy beer for a party celebrating his first child's birth and returned hours later from the hospital, swollen and stitched up, after a Mexican gang mistook them for rivals. Xavier also saw a student kicked in the head "so hard you could hear . . . the thump" on the ground, which he thought had caused permanent disability. Xavier described always walking away to avoid confrontation as "almost like muscle memory."

Xavier's mobility masculinity made looking down virtuous and not shameful: "I didn't feel degraded or ashamed to walk away," he said, nor did he feel like a *puto* (a derogatory term akin to "faggot") for avoiding a fight, as Federico and others did. Rather, Xavier knew that lacking legal status made him vulnerable to unforeseeable, escalating consequences. When his U.S.-born cousins asked why he always walked away, he said: "You guys have the privilege to be short-fused . . . because [you] are born here." Looking down helped him get to college: "I didn't want to stare back. I managed to get this far because I *didn't* stare back." Xavier also knew that other roads to mobility, such as the military, were closed to him because of his legal status. Similarly, Xavier rejected his father's "urban drinker" masculinity: "To this day, I refuse to drink in front of them," he told me, though he sometimes had a beer with friends. Not drinking helped him be academically successful.

The hard looks and step-ups declined markedly in the eleventh and twelfth grades as Xavier became known as a student leader who publicly opposed replacing security guards with armed police officers, presciently predicting that the move would criminalize disciplinary infractions.[48] Teen migrants went from stepping up to him to being proud of him: "He's one of us, and he's made it."

Xavier's academic achievement and conflict avoidance in a low-performing school marked him as one of the students in whom teachers invested more instructional, developmental, and emotional effort. Xavier found excellent mentors at Jungle High: "If you're teaching at Jungle High, you want to help." He was never penalized for cutting class because teachers, who struggled to keep classroom order, knew that he would learn more studying on his own. At his biology teacher's direction, he cut class to study for a Regents exam from a Barnes & Noble prep book. He would be the only one of thirty students to pass it. She "thanked him for trying" and congratulated him with a $10 bookstore gift card. Caught once by a truant officer and placed "in the holding cell" classroom at school, the principal pulled him out, saying, "What are *you* doing here? . . . ridiculous."

Jungle High staff channeled Xavier into the Program for Leadership and College (PLC), and the PLC social worker opened doors for him. Xavier became a volunteer teaching chess to elementary school students in the surrounding upscale neighborhood, work for which he was given a Civic Service Award. He met other student leaders and adults with strong networks who helped him make an educational plan. The social worker printed out a list of colleges for him and helped him apply. In his midthirties, Xavier smiled when he told me, "I kept that paper. . . . It was sacred to me." The list was proof that others saw promise in him. Xavier would get a full scholarship to college.

Xavier's legal status limited the adult opportunities that his mobility masculinity would have opened for him had he been a U.S. citizen. One reason he became a "super volunteer" in high school was to hide his inability to work legally. As noted earlier, he worked intermittently as an underpaid consultant until getting DACA at age thirty, after which his career and income soared and he became a High Flyer.

Federico's Story: Gang Masculinity Derails a Positive Life Trajectory

As a twenty-nine-year-old, Federico looked back and explained how his life had gone off track when he was a high school sophomore: he failed out of "the honors classes with all Chinese kids . . . 'cause I stopped caring. I wanted to be cool." Being cool for Federico meant cutting school for hooky parties and drinking, joining a gang, looking back at hard stares, and dropping out of school. What had been an upwardly mobile life was derailed in part by the practices and habits of gang masculinity.

Juxtaposing Federico's life with Xavier's shows how enacting different models of masculinity led them to develop different habits and channeled them as teens into different contexts that created different long-term life chances and trajectories. I draw here on close, contemporaneous study of sixteen-year-old Federico's life, including shadowing him in school and at home for several days and interviewing him, alone and with his mother; on talks and interviews with his mother over the next decade; on interviews with him at ages twenty-eight and twenty-nine, both alone and with his wife; and on phone conversations with him and with his mother in 2017–2018, when he was in his early thirties and I was drafting this chapter. When we reconnected in 2016, Federico had gone two years without a drink and was a married father and churchgoer.

Federico made a lot of what I call "adult Thanksgiving table" disclosures, whereby adult children tell their parents about teenage transgressions they had hidden from them at the time. I interviewed and shadowed Federico in his sophomore year of high school, during the time he was joining the gang, which he sought to conceal from me and his mother. He sometimes let slip things about the gang in our conversations, but he deflected questions, abetting his mother's belief that he was safe because his new friends' parents, like her, were from Ticuani. I suspected at the time that he was getting involved in a gang, which Federico confirmed when he shared the full story at ages twenty-eight and twenty-nine.

Federico played compartmentalizing cat-and-mouse games in managing what he was doing sophomore year. He compartmentalized in his presentation of self to his mother by swearing that he did not drink and that his friends from Ticuani were "safe" and not in a gang. He carefully monitored what he told his mother (and me) to avoid disclosing indications that he was in or was joining a gang.

Federico also played a cat-and-mouse game of selective memory with himself. When it was clear that he had to attend summer school, Federico asked me how many cuts you needed in summer school to get kicked out, as he seemed intent on doing. Months after he got kicked out of summer school for missing too many days, he told me he was a victim of bad school regulations: they had kicked him out as he was trying to catch up! So he had no choice but to drop out altogether, he reasoned, and then did so. When I recounted to him his earlier plan to cut just enough to get kicked out, he denied it. Having reframed his dropping out as the result of an uncaring system, his selective memory had let him off the hook. My sense was that he truly disbelieved my account of our earlier conversation.

Comparing Federico's and Xavier's Counterfactual Cases   Federico's advantages over Xavier as high school started were negated by his enactment of gang masculinity. Counselors steered Federico into Graves High's honors program, which had helped other study participants, who also saw Graves as much better than Jungle High. Xavier's undocumented status closed doors that his educational record should have opened, while Federico's status as a U.S. citizen meant no doors were closed to him due to his status. He started with all doors open to him, but Federico's gang habits and, later, his drinking, would close those doors. Moreover, Federico's neighborhood was not a symbolic center of gang life, as Xavier's was. Gang masculinity undermined Federico's promising life trajectory via the cumulative effect of his teen and early adult choices. Where Xavier avoided conflict, Federico sought it. Xavier did his homework; Federico did not. Xavier never drank or hung out on the street, while drinking and hanging out became daily activities in Federico's gang life. Both students had alcoholic fathers, but only Federico began a social habit of drinking regularly as a teen.[49]

Cutting school with the gang had already harmed Federico's chances when I shadowed him in school. Indeed, when I asked his mother's permission to follow him, she asked me to follow him *every day*, to stop him from cutting. His math teacher told me that Federico had cut class only sometimes at first; in the second semester, however, he was in school only fifty of ninety days and almost never in May and June. This math teacher asked me to help him engage Federico and others in class, which I tried to do. The teacher seemed dedicated, running the math club, for instance, for years after funding for it was cut. He liked Federico, whom he described as "relatively bright." Federico "always promised to do better" when encouraged, but he never followed through: "I never had a start with him. Ever," said the teacher. This teacher's reports show once again that gang masculinity habits harmed Federico's schooling and adult mobility.

My experience of Federico was similar. He seemed conflicted, reporting that his English teacher "would always be on my case" about his homework—because, "you know, she cared"—but that he would yell at her like "an idiot." He said he never did homework because he worked or "was out" with gang friends. Even in class, "I would get a paper and write . . . new rhymes and stuff," glorifying his gang and denigrating rivals. I remember Federico's English teacher trying to discuss how one killer manipulated the other in Truman Capote's *In Cold Blood*. Her teaching was interesting, and she sought to draw students out, including Federico directly. But Federico and others were checked out. I remember thinking, during the long silences after she posed questions, that Federico would not graduate. Yet I also saw Federico and his classmates discussing with interest their history teacher and the fall of the Roman empire to the Goths. Federico cut school even on days when we had agreed I would shadow him. He could not sit in some parts of the cafeteria and had to walk the long way to some classes to avoid places where rival gangs congregated.[50]

Federico's worsening school attendance in his sophomore year went lockstep with his deeper involvement with the New York Atzlan and other gang-linked changes that harmed his adult mobility. He dropped out at age sixteen. He got a GED in his twenties while in rehab. I arranged and brought him (then age twenty-nine) to meet the head of a community college counseling program he liked, but he never applied.

Federico doubled down at turning points when Wannabes would have stepped away from gang life. For example, Federico was hanging out so much with gang friends that others saw him as a gang member, and since he was getting stepped up to as if he were already a gang member, he decided to join and get the benefits of being one: "I just wanted to be a New York Atzlan . . . 'cause every time they stop me, they ask me if I'm a New York Atzlan." This turning point at which Federico escalated his gang involvement was exactly when many gang desisters in the study stopped hanging out with gang members. Similarly, upon joining the gang, Federico changed his friendship group from multi-ethnic friends to almost all Mexican gang members, including many teen migrants, an association that was linked for NYCOMPers with lower adult outcomes (per the funneling effect in school and related processes, discussed in chapter 3).[51]

Federico described three big immediate benefits of being an Aztlanista: the respect and fear of others, hooky parties, and girls. After he joined the gang, people stopped making eye contact with him. "People at school don't, like, start with you. They don't even look at you . . . 'cause they're scared." Generating fear and dread in others was a benefit of gang masculinity for Federico.[52] The summer after Federico dropped out of school, he told me that he had hung out with the Atzlan "two or three times a week" during the school year, usually at hooky parties where "you drink, you dance, and you smoke," and "there are girls." Drinking alcohol was new to him because his mother, with whom he lived (but not his father), did not allow it. And "as soon as everybody knew I was with somebody [a gang]," he said, " . . . girls are attracted to you more. You get more girls." But the status of being in a gang brought a new problem: "Everybody wants to be your friend . . . [but] you get more enemies . . . they tag you. He's down with them."

Federico's gang career derailed his life. Over the next year Federico worked but also spent more time with the gang, sometimes robbing people in the street or subway. He was repeatedly stopped (but not formally arrested) by police, who showed him pictures of himself in their "gang book" in the police station. Federico's hyper-aggressive stances and hard looks created frictions with both rival and allied gangs, and even within the Atzlan, because he "acted stupid" when drunk, as others who knew him told me. His father, wearing Federico's coat, was once stopped by the Aztlan at gunpoint. Escalating threats led his mother to move them out of New York eighteen months after he had joined the gang. Federico gave hard looks at his new suburban high school until "preppies" told him to stop. Alone, he backed down.

In his early twenties, Federico moved back to New York to live with his father. He began drinking with his father's Mexican friends and gradually adopted their *yo mando* masculinity (*yo mando* means "I am in charge; I give the orders"): "I started hanging out with so many Mexicans . . . seeing things . . . the macho way. . . . In Mexico, there's a lot of *machismo*. . . . It's different than here in New York." He liked the camaraderie of hanging out, especially the *albures* — the skilled wordplay among Mexican men that reinforces friendship.[53] Federico's Spanish as an adult was much better than it was when he was sixteen and unable to converse with his mother and me in Spanish. Now he was proud and felt more Mexican for learning *callejero* (street) Spanish from hanging out with his father's friends:

Federico: That's where I started learning my . . . fluent Spanish. . . . A lot of people don't know I'm born here because I'm fluent in Spanish.

Author: But your Spanish wasn't that good when you were in high school, right?

Federico: No.

Author: You didn't like talking in Spanish with me.

Federico: No. But now you see me . . . what the streets got me . . . being in the street with all those Mexican guys drinking.

Hanging out with these men, he decided he would not marry a "girl from Brooklyn" (too "independent") and instead would marry a deferential girl from rural Puebla. But looking back at age twenty-nine, Federico did not like some things that these drinking men had taught him about women: "I'm more stuck on the way I was taught by these Mexicans, which is not good . . . [they said,] 'Your fuckin' woman, she has to do what you say.'" And if she does not, "'You have to hit her.'"

Federico's enactments of gang and *yo mando* masculinity harmed his adult life. Both masculinity types valorize habits that lead to conflict and disruption — giving and responding to hard looks, regular drinking, responding violently to challenge, and spending too much time hanging out. These habits are reflected in Federico's estimate, at age thirty, that he had held fifty different restaurant jobs in thirteen years. Each time, he walked off the job in conflict with his boss, or he was fired for drinking, or he left after getting bored. His truncated education qualified him only for entry-level jobs, mostly in the immigrant economy. His undocumented coworkers would ask him: "Why are you working with us when you speak English and were born here?"

Overall Trends among All Study Participants

While we traced how the processes of gang masculinity or mobility masculinity affected adult outcomes for Xavier and Federico, statistical analysis can show us how much these processes and habits correlated with adult outcomes among all NYCOMPers at time 2 (age twenty-eight). The overall news is good. Although many participants (thirty-eight of ninety-six) associated with gangs in their teens or early twenties, only nine were still doing so by their late twenties, and seven of these nine were "retired" and telling others to avoid gangs.[54] Only one participant was still an active gang leader.

We focus on gang masculinity because twenty-six of forty-nine men had gang associations versus twelve of forty-seven women. All eight of the participants who reported being gang leaders were men, as were nine of the thirteen fully inducted members. Gang habits persisted into adulthood for more men than women.

We discerned several types of relationships to gangs: (1) gang leader, (2) inducted gang member, (3) never associated (with a gang), (4) negotiated associators, and (5) did not mention. These types correlated strongly with adult outcomes. Being a gang leader or inducted member (having been formally "jumped in") harmed adult life outcomes. Nineteen of twenty-one gang leaders and members were Stuck Muddlers or Shallow Slopers as adults, and sixteen had only a high school diploma or less at age twenty-eight (five started but left further schooling). Those who never associated with gang members did better: eleven of twenty were College Graduates or High Fliers, and fourteen of twenty-two had some post–high school education. Those who did not mention gangs to us also did well: eight of twelve were College Graduates or High Fliers, and all had some post–high school education.[55]

Perhaps most interesting were those with a negotiated association with gang members. This group had the highest adult outcomes: fourteen of seventeen had postsecondary schooling, and twelve of eighteen were College Graduates or High Fliers. Negotiated associators skillfully managed their relationships with the gang members in their lives, including family members and childhood friends who later joined gangs. Some hung out with gang members as teens but never became gang members themselves, and they had usually stopped hanging out by their early twenties, using strategies (such as leaving parties before they ended to avoid the subsequent fights) to make sure they were not involved in events that would endanger their future.[56]

Several specific events and habits linked to gang masculinity correlated with adult outcomes at time 2. Interestingly, being stopped and frisked by the police did *not* correlate with adult life outcomes: eleven of twenty-four who reported being stopped and frisked became College Graduates or High Fliers, while thirteen became Stuck Muddlers or Shallow Slopers. Conversely, being arrested or detained by the police was associated with adult outcomes: of sixteen arrested or detained, twelve had become Stuck Muddlers by age twenty-eight.[57] Of eight male participants who had spent time in jail (awaiting trial or post-conviction), five were Stuck Muddlers by age twenty-eight; three got the legal reset button of youthful offender status and became College Graduates or High Fliers.

Four habits enacting gang masculinity correlated strongly with worse adult outcomes. First, most participants who looked back when given a hard look (fourteen of twenty-three) became Stuck Muddlers or Shallow Slopers by age twenty-eight, while most of those who looked down (thirteen of twenty-two) became College Graduates or High Fliers.[58] Second, only nine participants (eight men and one woman) continued any gang affiliation at age twenty-eight or afterwards. All had reported looking back as teens, and all but one were Stuck Muddlers at age twenty-eight. (The one who was not had gotten YO status and was a College Graduate by age twenty-eight.) Third, seventeen participants continued to have frequent or life-altering conflicts (such as walking off jobs and getting in fights) in their late twenties and early thirties; sixteen of them had looked back as teens. For example, when Thor's immediate boss insulted him, he walked off a well-paying job that he liked and that had room for him to advance. He did not seek help from the restaurant owners, who liked him. When they fired him, the owners asked why he had not come to them when he had the problem with his immediate boss.[59] They would have helped him, they said, but now it was too late. He had not thought to talk to them.

Fourth, eleven participants kept hanging out on the street or partying with gang members (a habit signaling that the gang was the primary relationship) through their late twenties, even after marriage or having a child. At that age, most others had desisted in response to the demands of their wives or partners or out of a desire to reduce risk after becoming a parent. Ten of the eleven who kept hanging out with gang members had become Stuck Muddlers by age twenty-eight; the eleventh got YO status and became a College Graduate.

The overall links between enacting gang masculinity and adult life outcomes can be seen in two other statistical measures. Table 7.2 (in the note) shows that gang leaders and inducted members got an average (or mean) of three fewer years of school and earned nearly $21,000 per year less; it also shows that only 9.5 percent became College Graduates or High Fliers, versus 61.6 percent in all other categories.[60] The online chapter appendix presents a fuller set of statistical operations, including means excluding undocumented cases (to remove the influence of legal status) and a regression (with controls) correlating gang membership with adult correlations. Results fit our expectations: those enacting gang masculinity had lower adult outcomes at time 2 than their counterparts enacting Mexican mobility masculinity.

Timing for Declining or Desisting from Gang Involvement: Earlier Is Better

Over half the men in this study enacted some element of gang masculinity as teens, but most had desisted by their midtwenties, in line with much prior research.[61] Most such research explains that specific factors promote desistance, such as having a good job or good marriage, or networks that lead to opportunity, and moving through the life course. This chapter contributes to an innovative angle of research that is well represented by Ed Flores's *God's Gangs*, which analyzes how changing one's model of masculinity can contribute to gang desistance.[62] Here we extend that work by also analyzing how one's model of masculinity contributes to the decision to decline or accept invitations to join a gang in the first place, and how desistance affects later adult outcomes. Declining invitations or desisting earlier in life is better.

I observed four types and timings of declination or desistance from gang habits. First were the Never Beens, like Xavier. They avoided gangs, enacted Mexican mobility masculinity, and had strong adult outcomes. Because we have already profiled several Never Beens, we do not discuss them further here. Next were the Wannabes and Early Desisters: they engaged in some gang habits as teens but fully switched to mobility masculinity in their teens or very early twenties to avoid danger and achieve their larger goals. The third type, the Just in Times, left gang habits behind in their midtwenties, often by conscious decision, to avoid what they increasingly saw as life-altering risks. Finally, the Late in the Days maintained gang masculinity habits into their late twenties or thirties but then abandoned them, having come to believe that those habits had held them back. While the movement away from gang habits and masculinity of the Just in Times and Late in the Days seemed driven by their movement into established adulthood (when they were working full-time, marrying, having children, and so on) and led them to base their masculinity in other sources of identity and honor (such as taking care of their families), the declination of or near-immediate desistance from gang activity of the Never Beens, the Wannabes, and the Early Desisters stemmed from clearly seeing the threat posed by gang habits to the long-term goals that would gain them such honor and keep the immigrant bargain.

Wannabes and Early Desisters: The Buendia Cousins

Wannabes and Early Desisters engaged in gang habits and identity practices as teens but more often enacted mobility masculinity. They abandoned gang habits or performances early, soon after their first encounters with gang conflict, especially violence that they thought endangered their long-term goals. As teens and early adults, the male Buendia cousins began going (without their parents) to Mexican parties, especially *sonidos* (DJ parties), where Mexican teen migrants and men would step up and ask what gang they were with.[63] They were often asked if they were with the Brooklyn Rancheros. The cousins would explain that they were not a gang, but others did not believe them. "My cousins were in it [the Rancheros]," said one member of the family, "but . . . we're just a big group and . . . they thought we were a gang. They got misled." At first, the Buendia cousins liked being perceived as a gang and adopted a clique name from the 1990s movie *American Me*, which they often watched. But then the Brooklyn Rancheros, which had grown because of an influx of teen migrants, started getting into fights with them.

The turning point came when the violence escalated. A fight outside a Manhattan club left several Buendia cousins bloodied and one arrested (but later released without charge). In another incident, the Rancheros waited outside a club and fired a shotgun at the Buendias, wounding one cousin. (During that period, I had earlier seen the Rancheros waiting outside that club late at night, staring hard at the people leaving. I looked down.)

Elmont Buendia, home from college, saw these incidents as a terrifying "reality check." Admitting that he had been "naive" about the dangers at *sonidos*, he stopped going to them—"not worth it," he concluded. Elmont gladly returned to college. He had purposefully lived away at college, and he counseled his younger cousins to also "get out of Brooklyn" for college. Rick Buendia, still living in Brooklyn, said that these incidents made him realize that he was less invested in gang life than friends who kept hanging out. "I wanted to graduate," he said, and to go to college. Rick could not cut high school with his friends to go to hooky parties because he "would have been thrown off the team [his sports team]." Rick took Elmont's advice and stopped hanging out, and he also left Brooklyn for college.

The Buendia cousins did not feel shame for no longer attending Mexican parties, because staying away protected their dreams of the future. Rick and three cousins actually met with the Brooklyn Rancheros in Prospect Park to "peace it out," telling them that they were not a gang, did not want problems, and would stop going to Mexican parties. When the Rancheros asked if they wanted to join them, they declined. Retreating from this field enacted Mexican mobility masculinity by removing them from contexts of conflict and putting them in contexts that promoted their educational progress.

The Buendia cousins were perhaps better able to desist from gang habits because they lived in or near middle-income neighborhoods or in places that were gentrifying. This was especially helpful as they moved into their teen and early adult years. When they were at home, they could get away from gang conflicts, unlike young men who lived in structurally violent Los Angeles neighborhoods that blocked mobility, as described by María Rendón.[64] Their parents were also lawful permanent residents and had well-paid jobs in restaurants and private clubs or worked as mechanics or in other relatively well-paying blue-collar jobs. The only Buendia cousin at the shotgun incident who persisted with gang habits was Tono, who finally stopped after his father issued an ultimatum: leave the gang or leave the house.

Just in Times: Valerio and His Siblings

Just in Times were actively involved in gang life and habits but desisted by their midtwenties and purposefully changed their lives. As teens, three Vaquero siblings—Valerio, Jaime, and Maria Teresa—and one cousin, Ernesto (see chapter 6), formed Los Catorce (The Fourteen) and hung out into their midtwenties. All stopped gang activity within eighteen months in a group epiphany for which their parents had prayed. Quitting reset their life trajectories, which I followed for another ten years. Their neighborhood had more street crime and hard looks than the Buendias' neighborhood, but they were helped in desisting by the fact that their building was physically closed off from the neighborhood and thus more secure.

The Vaquero siblings loved fighting and were good at it. Valerio and Jaime were big men, and separately they told me that they fought "like animals"—fearlessly, knocking their opponents out. After a Mexican gang beat his little brother, Valerio went to fight them alone; he got stabbed in the collarbone, inches from blood vessels in his neck. Maria Teresa was their designated female fighter.[65] Jaime described fighting as a weekend habit. When I noted that they seemed to like fighting, Jaime responded wistfully:

Jaime: Yeah. . . . It was an every-weekend thing. We used to enjoy it every weekend. It was an every-weekend thing.

Author: Instead of like, going to the movies?

Jaime: We'd go to parties . . . every weekend . . . we got into fights.

(In writing this chapter, I remembered Jaime's comment and searched for "every weekend" in the transcription: it came up twelve times in a document of over seventy pages, always in reference to fighting.) Like most in this study, the Vaqueros mainly fought other Mexicans.

The Vaquero brothers looked for offense in their daily lives. Once, after shadowing Valerio in school, I went with him and his girlfriend (a good student who calmed him) on the subway, where Valerio kept throwing hard looks at another Latino youth, who sometimes looked back but who also seemed afraid, trying to avoid eye contact.[66] Valerio said he "did not like that kid . . . he thinks he's tough." I feared he would fight the other youth right there, but his girlfriend's stop came and we got off.

What changed? In their midtwenties, the Vaquero siblings, seeing that their lives were headed in directions they feared, changed their habits—including their response to perceived challenges—and how they spent time. Jaime and his wife had argued over his fighting with the gang, but he did not change his view until their first son was born. Describing that change to me while caring for his two-year-old, he said that his wife

> was like, "You got to stop doing this," when she was pregnant. . . . "You have a son on the way." . . . But I wouldn't listen. I was hardheaded. . . . After he was born, I quit everything. . . . I just told my brother I wasn't going to hang out with them anymore. . . . They was like, "Okay, you got a family now."

Jaime stopped fighting, but he missed it: "We used to have a lot of fun. Yeah, it was definitely hard giving that one up. . . . I still sometimes . . . be wanting to go back. My brother be coming home with stories . . . we saw this guy; we fucked him up. . . . I was like, damn, I wish I could have been there."

Maria Teresa's epiphany happened during her last fight. Her opponent kept stabbing a safety pin into her face. Maria Teresa had just smashed her opponent's "head into the pole . . . and she was bleeding. . . . She already stopped fighting," when Maria Teresa suddenly "got up off her," realizing she could hurt or kill the girl, go to jail, or lose her eye. She said she felt "too old" to be fighting. Maria Teresa stopped going out and moved to New Jersey to live "away from the problems." She stopped fighting after that.

At age twenty-four, Valerio joined the military in an effort to decisively change his life's direction. "I'm trying to better my life. . . . If you do really well, you can . . . become an officer. . . . [If I stay here in Brooklyn] all I'm going to do . . . is keep beating people up, and I'm tired of beating people up already." When Valerio was a teenager, fighting excited him, but he now feared its consequences:

> I did expect to be a gang banger for life. . . . When you're a kid, you think differently than when you grow old, you start thinking. . . . You don't really want to do this anymore. . . . [You're] tired of looking over your shoulder. . . . When you have kids and somebody approaches you . . . and shoots you right in front of your kids."

Valerio now saw his gang habits as blocking his ability to become the kind of man he wanted to be, so he redirected his life into the military. Nearly forty when I drafted this in 2019, Valerio was thriving, had two children, and had been promoted in rank several times.

All three Vaquero siblings realized that their gang habits, especially fighting, were leading them toward jail, injury, or death and away from the adult lives they wanted. They enacted what the social psychologist Wendy Wood calls "friction" — changing bad habits by avoiding the contexts of their enactment and entering new contexts that fostered better habits (rather than relying on willpower).[67] Their stories also confirm research finding that strong marriages, careers, and institutions foster desistance from crime and promote happier lives in the long term.[68]

Late in the Days: Manuel and Gordo

Late in the Days did not abandon gang habits until, as established adults (late twenties and thirties or later), they saw how these habits had already harmed their lives. Their transition away from gang life was slower and harder than it was for Wannabes, Early Desisters, and Just in Times.

"Ever since I left the gang, my teenage years is over." That was how Manuel explained his life to me when he was a thirty-two-year-old married father of two. (He was twenty-one at his first interview.) A leader of New York Atzlan for twelve years, he disclosed that he had been "in two years of detox" since he stopped hanging out at age thirty. This metaphor of gang life as an addiction that had shaped him and his thinking had been clear in our last interview. When I pointed out that whatever I asked him about, he always returned to the gang, he agreed, saying: "I feel I get caught up in it [discussing the gang] 'cause that's like the only life I've chosen for myself, you know? That's the only real thing I've done." That this young father felt he had not done anything else and that his teen years ended when he was thirty led me to rethink social time and steps in gang mobility. Although he seemed to be trying to assess his life using the socially expected steps and durations of mobility masculinity, he kept defaulting to his gang life's steps and durations.

The parameters of Manuel's adult life were set in his teens by bad luck, and his embrace of gang masculinity and the contexts into which it led him. Manuel's father died when he was thirteen. His mother then worked more hours, coming home very late, and he was left on his own after school. At fourteen, during his "American phase" (his words), he joined an African American, mixed-ethnicity gang that robbed Mexicans. But as a high school junior, he saw Mexican gangs fighting—"getting at it, you know, hard"—and his "mind turned" to joining. His friendship group changed from one with no Mexican friends in middle school to only Mexican friends in high school. When Manuel retired from gang life at age thirty, he was called an OG (Original Gangster), an honor recognizing him as a founder and leader.

Gang habits derailed Manuel's education. He cut school "a lot" because the New York Atzlan were "all about [hooky] parties." He never did homework and often hung out Monday through Thursday. He always hung out partying and drinking on weekends, from Friday to Sunday night. He switched high schools several times over "beef" (gang problems that got him safety transfers to another high school), before dropping out. Manuel never got a GED.

He decided to leave gang life after three developments in his late twenties. First, a close gang friend was sentenced to over forty years in jail for violent crimes. While visiting, Manuel realized that his friend would be seventy years old upon release, when "his life is already over." Second, he grew bored with a life of gang habits. The routine of hanging out, drinking, fighting, and hating now drained him:

> What made me change my mind . . . I gotta be honest, I just got tired. . . . You just like, put your mind into so much like, I guess, *hate*, you know? . . . Like, think about who you're gonna hit next? Or what party we're gonna go to next? It's mostly . . . partying and hanging out. . . . It's not much to it [gang life] . . . you just, do it so much . . . [it] takes a toll on you. . . . I've done *enough* partying (*laughing*).

Manuel said that it was the same routine at a Mexican party, at a hooky party, or hanging out: "The same thing—just get drunk . . . girls . . . [if] we get into a fight in the street . . . that's the whole gang thing (*laughs*) . . . tagging up the walls."

Finally, Manuel felt that gang habits prevented him growing as an adult and earning more money, and that they also fostered harmful traits, like enjoying hurting others. His change in perspective made me think of new research that judgment centers in the brain do not fully mature until one's midtwenties, and sometimes not until age thirty.[69]

Manuel: Ever since I left like, the gang, I feel like . . . my teen years is over. . . . I've been acting like a kid all this time. . . . Now I feel like . . . I'm just starting to grow up . . . to realize things.

Author: What kinda things?

Manuel: Like how I am and how I, like, how I talk. . . . I would like to improve my vocabulary. . . . Somebody told me, like, read a little bit more. . . . I would like to get into other things . . . just to keep away from, thinking about hurting somebody . . .

Author: So, you think, so being in the gang makes you think about hurting people?

Manuel: Yeah.

Author (prompted by Manuel's prior statement): It's like, fun, hurting people?

Manuel: Yeah . . .

Author: Huh, wow . . . it sounds like you're really looking. . . . Do you regret the time you spent . . . in the gang?

Manuel: I regret maybe like, putting too much time into it and not enough time . . . to improve myself . . . like with my money, that's my main thing.

Manuel's mother and he had a "don't ask, don't tell" policy on his gang life. She never asked if he was in a gang, even when he came home bloodied, and he "never put it [gang activities] in front of her." But by age thirty-two, he was feeling pressure to earn more money. He made $29,000 per year working at a retail store, where he felt he was not seen as a prospect for promotion because sales jobs went to "[college] girls from Jersey."

Manuel's gang masculinity harmed his adult life. Gang habits led him to drop out of high school and never get a GED or postsecondary training, dimming his job prospects. The exhaustion of twelve years of gang habits had driven Manuel's retirement from gang life. Looking back at age thirty-two, he had some regrets about his gang life and habits and was unsure how to move forward. But by no longer spending his time hanging out with the gang, he created the friction that helped him change his habits and leave behind the daily practices of gang life.

Gordo's life was centered on gangs from his late teens to about age thirty, when health problems, gang dynamics, and family protests pulled him away. Unlike the presumption that only one form of Latino masculinity was available, per perilous masculinity theory, gang masculinity never went unchallenged in his life. His family had always demanded that he enact mobility masculinity, and he did so more and more as he got older. By his late thirties, Gordo was refocused on his family and health and doing well, though he still got into some small street conflicts.

Gordo's entry into gang life had followed a pattern common in the late 1990s and mid-2000s. His early high school friendship group, which had included Italian teens from his neighborhood, changed to nearly all Mexicans after he started playing basketball in the Mexican League with his newly arrived cousin, Mousy. Gordo's gang life conflicted with keeping the immigrant bargain via mobility masculinity. He always worked full-time, but he spent most of his free time hanging out and drinking with the gang, the Lejoneros, even after marrying and having a child. He finished high school but dropped out of college in his first semester.

Gordo's relationship with gang life was conflicted. He knew that others feared him for "hanging out with the Lejoneros. . . . Sometimes I liked it and sometimes I didn't. Most of the time I didn't, because they didn't know the real me. . . . I missed out on nice friends because of that." He said he was "lucky" that he was never stabbed, shot, or arrested in his many fights.

Gordo was sometimes dragged into conflicts that he had tried to avoid. Once, some gang members were "talking shit" to him and sitting on his car after a Mexican party. Knowing his non-gang cousins wanted to avoid fighting, Gordo was talking it out when the Lejoneros leader, Johnny, came out and escalated things: "I wanted to talk my way out of it. . . . I didn't want to look bad in front of the girls too. . . . But . . . when my friend Johnny says, 'Listen, let's just go at it,' I had no choice. . . . I couldn't back out because then I would look like . . . a punk . . . a *puto*. . . . My rep to them was I hanged out with the Lejoneros, so I had to be tough." Gordo fought to avoid losing face, despite wanting to enact mobility masculinity by talking it out. Years later, Johnny went to a party the night his first child was born and was killed in a case of mistaken identity by members of a gang that had no conflict with the Lejoneros.

Gordo's dedication to the gang caused family friction as his gang masculinity came into open conflict with his father's mobility masculinity. Gordo's father had gone from being a dishwasher to working as a chef in an upscale restaurant, and he had also purchased two small buildings in Brooklyn that brought him rental income. Gordo's father worked a lot, and he had once gotten Gordo a job at his restaurant. He often told his son to live a "tranquil life." In contrast, Gordo was committed to the gang, even going out with them *on his wedding night*. He responded to his angry wife the next day the same way other gang members said they had done: telling his wife that, when they got married, "she knew who I was." After his son's birth, Gordo's father told him to "slow down" and stop going out, for the sake of his family.

Gordo's family tried several tactics to deal with his drinking and gang activities. For example, they sought to moderate his gang habits by emphasizing his family obligations. In his late twenties, his mother Bonita would have him watch his little sister (nearly twenty years younger) when he hung out, knowing he would not endanger her. He had to bring her home early, ensuring a mid-evening check-in. His sister confirmed that she and her mother secretly colluded to keep her "good big brother" safe. His parents ignored clear evidence of Gordo's gang habits. Even when his father found weapons in his car, he ignored them, only saying, "Be careful."

Sometimes the "elephant in the room" became visible—for instance, when a gang would crash a Mexican party or baptism.[70] "My parents would [say,] 'Wow, look at that gang coming in.' . . . When they [the gang] come to say, 'What's up?' with me. They're like, 'Do you know them?,' and I'm like, 'Yeah.'" Such encounters made the reality temporarily visible, but his family continued to hope he would outgrow gang life and drinking.

In Gordo's early thirties, his father raised the stakes about his drinking and hanging out after finding him passed out in the morning in the hallway of their building. His father hit him with a broom to get him up. Of this period, Gordo said: "My father was always on me about that. . . . He would grab me and my wife and talk to me *in front of my wife* so she would know that he was on her side." Asked what his father said, Gordo replied, "That I have to change. . . . If I don't change, he was going to throw us out." This threat was not empty because Gordo's father owned the building and charged them reduced rent. That Gordo admired his father made it harder for him to resist his demands to be more responsible.

The tipping point came when Gordo's health failed in his midthirties, partly from his drinking, and he had to stop working. Gordo became indignant when the gang began excluding him. Their treatment was especially hurtful to him when he compared it to his devotion to the gang, with whom he had spent his wedding night. The steadfast support of his family and his wife during his recovery—compared to the gang's continued exclusion—made him realize what he had missed.

He recovered and reoriented his life toward being a good father, husband, and son. He apologized to his wife and stopped hanging out. He was healthy again when we did our last interview in his early forties, and he was coaching his son's sports team, picking up his kids at school, and working part-time. Gordo's mother (whom I have known since the 1980s) cried in telling me how much better he was doing.

Conclusion

This chapter has shown that gang masculinity harms adult outcomes and lives, whereas Mexican mobility masculinity helps them. Gang masculinity prescribes and develops habits of mind and conduct that derail individual and family mobility. Gang habits take up so much time that they crowd out the prescribed steps and expected durations of mobility masculinity that keep the immigrant bargain and promote mobility, like going to college and helping younger siblings with their schooling. Gang masculinity prescribes harsh responses to challenges and puts youth in contexts where they experience frequent challenges that could become negative turning points. By contrast, mobility masculinity prescribes de-escalation and puts youth in safer contexts, like school and work, that also promote mobility.[71]

This analysis contributes to research on gender and masculinity, immigration, and mobility by engaging theories from each field in its analysis of unusual and perhaps unique data that link teen models of masculinity with adult outcomes among all NYCOMPers and trace the mechanisms by which models of masculinity produced those outcomes for specific NYCOMPers as they became adults, giving their stories empirical beginnings, middles, and (established adult) ends.[72]

This chapter challenges the problematic Mexicans theory and perilous masculinity theory as expressions of "Mexican" culture. Although most male NYCOMP participants enacted some gang masculinity behaviors as teens, their gang habits were continuously challenged by their families, especially their fathers, who nearly all enacted only Mexican mobility masculinity.[73] Mexican mobility masculinity was the predominant model even for teen NYCOMP participants, and it had become the nearly exclusive model by established adulthood. When I asked adult study participants who had been in gangs about the need they had felt as teenagers to respond to challenges with violence to avoid feeling like a "punk" (or a *puto*), they laughed and said that they were glad such thinking had not led to grave injury or prison.

These findings diverge from the theoretical story in racial exclusion theory. NYCOMP study participants did not report being broadly blocked by racial discrimination or harmed by structurally violent neighborhoods, as María Rendón's stagnant Dreamers did in Los Angeles. Rather, their adult mobility was lower at least partly because they enacted gang masculinity for longer than their peers who declined, desisted from, or were never involved in gangs.

This chapter supports research showing the utility of programs, like those studied by Ed Flores in *God's Gangs*, that teach young men to anchor their masculinity in taking care of their family, achieving in school or at work, avoiding conflicts, and asking for help and fellowship with others in doing so, thereby also reinforcing the immigrant family bargain.[74] Moreover, schools and institutions should think about what they teach young men about masculinity when they interact with them. If teachers believe that misbehaving Black and Hispanic boys have a "jail cell with their name on it," as the education scholar Ann Ferguson writes in *Bad Boys: Public Schools in the Making of Black Masculinity*, many will respond with hypermasculinity.[75] If our institutions treat all young men as if they are our own sons, worthy of love and investment, they will learn and enact a model of masculinity that seeks to redeem that trust and to realize their promise.

= Chapter 8 =

Friendship Strategies, White Contact, and Mexicanness as an Identity or a Status: Sequentially Constructing the Meaning of Mexicanness in Upwardly or Downwardly Mobile Contexts and Trajectories

BROOKLYN-BORN Bartolo described how White, Orthodox Jewish students often insulted his undocumented coworkers at the deli near their school by yelling at them: "'Hey, you freaking wetback!'" One time Bartolo responded to a student who spoke to him this way, presuming he was undocumented: "I confronted the guy. I started to speak English, and he looked surprised. . . . I took it very offensive. . . . I am not a wetback."

Jonathan, also born in Brooklyn, reported his boss saying to him: "'You'll go as far as you wanna go in this company.' He feels I am one of the go-to guys. . . . There is tons of room for me to grow." His boss, a "basic White guy," had rapidly promoted him from support staff to department manager. Jonathan felt that being Mexican gave him "a slight advantage" at work because he spoke Spanish and could expand the business into Spanish-speaking markets.

These interactions illustrate the difference between ethnicity as a status and ethnicity as an identity. When some students saw Bartolo's "Mexican" appearance and job and presumed that he was undocumented, they felt justified in speaking abusively to him and the other deli workers, making Mexicanness into a negative status. Conversely, Jonathan believed that his ethnicity helped him a bit in his job by providing an extra advantage on top of the opportunities he created by his

227

https://doi.org/10.7758/drwz9626.2080

innovative work. For him, Mexicanness became a neutral ethnicity, or even a slightly positive status.

This chapter analyzes how ethnicity acquires different meanings and can prescribe different ways of interacting in a sequence of varying contexts that offer more or less opportunity. It asks related questions: Why did having Black friends in high school predict better adult life outcomes for NYCOMPers? How did some Mexican youth become strongly upwardly mobile while having no substantive relationships with Whites in a city whose population was then 35 percent White and in which Whites were overrepresented in higher-paying jobs and institutions? Bartolo's and Jonathan's different experiences generate questions about how the meaning of Mexicanness varied across the life course for upwardly or downwardly mobile Mexican youth. And how do these different meanings relate to a Mexican culture of mobility in New York City?

Tracing how different life trajectories led study participants into contexts where being Mexican had such different meanings illuminates the apparently contradictory images they used as social compasses to guide their lives and as heuristic tools to explain them. Looking at these images as "map[s] of and for the world," in the words of the anthropologist Clifford Geertz, we can see that they laid out expectations of what the world would offer and prescribed the strategies and practices they would use in making their way in it.[1]

Heuristics are simple tools that prior experience suggests will work; they can be used to make predictions or decisions and to understand the world when confronting uncertainty. The "gaze heuristic" helps pilots assess whether they can get their crippled plane back to the airport or whether they must make an emergency landing.[2] Résumés are heuristics that help the hirer efficiently assess applicants for a job, despite knowing they have incomplete information. NYCOMP participants used these images to explain their lives contemporaneously and retrospectively. Vicky Fuerte used her desire to avoid becoming "that Mexican girl" as a social compass and heuristic in charting an upwardly mobile path through a "Black" school and a "White" college and in her professional adult life.

These youth had to navigate several dominant images of Mexicans in the late 1990s and mid-2000s. The first and perhaps most common image in the schools was the "teen migrant dropout"—the recently arrived, undocumented teen who often left school to work. This image was commonly linked to gang membership for men. Young undocumented women migrants had to confront the image of "that Mexican girl" who, it was presumed, would drop out of school, not go to college, and probably become a young mother. The countervailing image of upwardly mobile, U.S.-born teens and early adults was that of being "the only one" in their social group going to college rather than ending up "dead, in jail, or pregnant." A third prevailing image of Mexicans was that of the *familia unida* (close, strong family). Finally, because few study participants identified with the image of the "hardworking Mexican immigrant man" (not a teenager), we discuss it less.

These images were key heuristics and social compasses in NYCOMPers' decisions that affected their upward mobility, including who to pick as friends, a key focus in this chapter. Even though these images were not usually accurate descriptions of the person or the population, study participants used them to make decisions and understand their lives.[3] Images can contradict reality but still affect adult outcomes. Most U.S.-born participants who said that they were "the only one" of their friends and family members to attend college or to avoid jail or pregnancy were *not* the only ones to so succeed, as shown by census and NYCOMP data, as well as by their own lives. I believe that these youth knew and feared the dominant images of teen migrant dropouts, gang members, and "that Mexican girl," and so they defined themselves in contradistinction to those images. Without a widely held cognitive category of "Mexicans who go to college" (which would make college a "Mexican thing" to do, just as it was widely seen as an Asian or White middle-class thing to do), they felt alone in that category. (To avoid misconstrual: here I describe situations circa 2000. Since then, the emergence of a Mexican culture of mobility in New York has made going to college "a Mexican thing," as I discuss in the concluding chapter).

The image of being "the only one" was nevertheless a key premise of counterfactual teen thinking (for example, in choosing a high school) that promoted greater upward mobility when they became adults. Similarly, the strong family image underlay the desire of parents and adult children to keep the immigrant bargain, which promoted mobility and fostered a Mexican culture of mobility in New York. Scholars should challenge the use of images as lazy shorthands for entire social groups—see, for example, Charles Murray's effective, nefarious, data-free "thought experiment" attack on 1980s social welfare programs that featured "welfare queens."[4] But the empirical analysis here of the impact of controlling images on study participants' decisions and mobility can deepen understanding.[5]

I tell two empirical stories. First, I analyze how NYCOMPers' friendship patterns and strategies reflected Mexicans' conjunctural ethnicity in New York in the late 1990s and mid-2000s by showing how and why having Black, White, and pan-Latino friendships, while also having Mexican friends, was linked to upward mobility, but having *only* Mexican friends at home *and* at school correlated with downward mobility.

Second, I track the evolution of study participants' substantive relationships and contact (or lack thereof) with Whites and explain the variations in such contact with mobility and across contexts. "Substantive relationship" denotes less intimacy than friendship (though such a relationship could be a friendship) but more than acquaintance or routine relationship with coworkers, teammates, bosses, teachers, or religious leaders. Tracking relationships with Whites engages a domain assumption and practice in American sociology: taking integration into a White "mainstream" and comparison to the "White reference group" (as the sociologists Jennifer Lee, Min Zhou, Tomás Jiménez, and Adam Horowitz call it) as a correlate and measure of upward mobility.[6] But some very upwardly mobile NYCOMPers had never had any substantive relationships with Whites, not even in their professional workplaces as adults, and some with lower mobility trajectories developed substantive White relationships through an early transition to full-time work right after (or even before) finishing high school. I get additional leverage on this issue because, unlike most studies, my data can track friendships and substantive relationships with Whites from middle school through early and into established adulthood, correlate them with adult outcomes, and explain how those outcomes happened.

My prior work analyzed the construction of the meaning of ethnicity within three different contexts—the local context, the individual life course, and the communal settlement phase—to explain how and why some upwardly mobile U.S.-born Mexicans identified when they were teens as Black to become upwardly mobile, but then identified again as Mexicans as successful early adults.[7] Here we analyze the increasingly positive, negative, or neutral meaning of Mexicanness as study participants moved from middle school to established adulthood. As noted before, one factor driving positive change in meaning was that U.S.-born Mexican teens had stronger educational outcomes and greatly outnumbered Mexican-born teens by around 2010 (just after time 2 of the study, 2008–2009). Earlier, around 2000 at time 1, there had been nearly three times more Mexican-born teens than U.S.-born teens in New York.[8] Moreover, psychologists from Erik Erikson onward argue that ethnicity becomes less urgent in adulthood, and especially in established adulthood, when it becomes a more "achieved identity" or stable platform on which to navigate adult choices, though how this works with children of immigrants is less studied.[9]

Finally, I argue that the meaning assigned to being Mexican varies with the different contexts into which upwardly and downwardly mobile youth move. The upwardly mobile often move into contexts where their Mexicanness is either an ethnicity that does not affect their work prospects or a positive status that improves their prospects, while the downwardly mobile often move into contexts where Mexicanness is a negative status signaling powerlessness and exploitability. To concretize: Did the participants like Bartolo feel that being Mexican signaled to others that they were socially "illegal" (regardless of legal status), and hence could be treated badly, or did it signal that they and their family were "immigrants like us," as the owner of Jonathan's company put it to his High Flier, U.S.-born Mexican protégé?

This analysis does not fit neatly with either problematic Mexicans theory or racial exclusion theory because it analyzes disparate *intra*-ethnic outcomes.[10] It traces the specific processes — school contexts and friendship strategies — that set different participants on paths that moved them sequentially into upwardly or downwardly mobile contexts that conferred different meanings on Mexicanness. Had there been few positive contexts into which NYCOMPers could pass in New York, we would see a negative story of racial exclusion like those of the "stagnant Dreamers" in Los Angeles. Similarly, this analysis does not align with some research on intra-ethnic heterogeneity because upward mobility here did not stem from variation in parental education; nor was it the result of a non-Mexican or non-Hispanic partnership or marriage, as 98 percent of partnered adult study participants had a Mexican-origin partner.[11]

Theoretical Conversations

Friendship and Adult Lives and Outcomes

Friendships feature in much prior research on discrimination and adult mobility. Since Gordon Allport's 1954 book, *The Nature of Prejudice*, social psychologists have argued that more contact between members of different groups decreases prejudice between them, especially where groups have equal status, pursue common goals, and do not compete, and where sanctions exist against discrimination.[12] Sociologists studying immigration often use intergroup friendship as an indicator (or cause) of group integration (or exclusion) and mobility.[13] Research shows that having strong, supportive friendships with pro-social friends in adolescence is linked to better later teen or adult outcomes, including in emotional well-being and the achievement of adult tasks such as finding steady, satisfying work; having antisocial friends, on the other hand, is linked with worse outcomes.[14] Belief that adolescent friendships would affect their children's later life outcomes led parents in this study to ask their children if they had met a friend "on the street" or at school. The same belief led many NYCOMPers, especially the upwardly mobile, to pick friends and high schools — thus, picking social contexts — with explicit thought as to how those choices could affect their future. Here we advance such research—and empirically assess the beliefs of NYCOMPers and their parents—in two ways: first, by analyzing the correlation of friendship strategies to upwardly or downwardly adult trajectories and outcomes; and second, by describing how the differing contexts into which upwardly and downwardly mobile youth in the study moved over the years affected the meaning of Mexicanness.[15]

Culture: Its Place and Role in Research on Assimilation, Integration, and Mobility

Culture has a tortured history in analyses of integration and mobility. One pernicious concept of culture posited that an ethnic group's culture mainly promoted or inhibited integration and mobility. Hence, some argued in the 1960s and 1970s that Mexican Americans did not value education and were oriented toward immediate rewards, citing high dropout rates as indicators of cultural deficiency rather than structural conditions pushing students to work.[16] The anthropologists Signithia Fordham and John Ogbu argue that Black students resist doing well in school out of fear that their Black peers will ostracize them for "acting White."[17]

Alejandro Portes and Rubén Rumbaut consider structural conditions as central parts of segmented assimilation theory, but they also argue that Mexicans embrace an oppositional "reactive ethnicity" due to their integration into a "rainbow underclass" culture.[18] These theories presume a unitary or predominant ethnic culture that either promotes or inhibits achievement. The impulse to talk about "Mexican," "Black," or "White" culture as either a cause of or an obstacle to mobility is reinforced by the primacy of group-level statistical analysis in sociology, which tells a central tendency story about ethnic groups. But "Mexican culture" does not explain variation in NYCOMPers' adult outcomes, or why being Mexican acquired different meanings in different settings.

Other research sidesteps the culture argument, even in analyzing upwardly mobile integration or assimilation. Richard Alba, Tomás Jiménez, and Helen Marrow analyze the decrease in the "the social and cultural distance to the mainstream," focusing on concrete actions like intermarrying, mostly with Whites, or moving into Whiter places.[19] But what is the "mainstream" here? Is it mainstream "culture" or mainstream "institutions"? And how would a theory of assimilation like this deal with a context with nearly no White students, like the one in which most NYCOMPers went to school? How would it account for the mostly ethnically mixed contexts into which they moved in their adult jobs, including more than a few contexts in which few or no Whites were present? How do contexts in which upwardly mobile, middle-class college graduates live in a mostly Black and Brown world fit with this concept of a "mainstream"? At the very least, these conditions delink the concept of "mainstream" from Whiteness.

That such central tendency stories about ethnic culture cannot explain the complicated and divergent meanings of Mexicanness for NYCOMP participants underscores the need to analyze in context the meaning of ethnicity and its working links to achievement. Some scholars have done this. The education scholars Karoline Tyson, William Darity, and Domini Castellino found that only one of eight North Carolina middle and high schools showed the "burden of acting White" dynamic, and in that one school there were big income differences between Blacks and Whites and few Blacks in advanced classes.[20] In all other schools, they found what I call the "burden of being nerdy": working-class students, both Black and White, felt pressure not to excel more than other working-class students, who would "think that I think I am better than them," to echo the words of NYCOMPers. Similarly, Jiménez and Horowitz found that the numerical predominance of high-achieving Asian students in Cupertino, California, had "flipped" Whites' position in the social hierarchy: Whiteness had become linked to slacking underachievement.[21] Lee and Zhou argue that, given the hyperselectivity among Asian immigrants, not just an Asian culture but also a professional *class* culture is imported, one that is expressed in ethnic Chinese institutions that promote high achievement. These institutions teach skills and take steps like those taken by that upper-middle-class parents, including preparing their children to take standardized tests and to present the "right" set of skills and extracurricular activities.[22] Karen Okigbo analyzes a similar hyperselectivity and expectation of high achievement among Nigerians.[23] Finally, my earlier research showed that some Mexican youth adopted Black identities as teens to facilitate their academic success and upward mobility.[24] We extend that work here by arguing that the meaning of Mexicanness differs for the upwardly and downwardly mobile, due to the different contexts into which their trajectories bring them.

Status: A Causal Mechanism for Inequality

This analysis of the changing meaning of Mexicanness as youth move along different mobility trajectories from middle school into and through early adulthood and into established adulthood converses with three key analyses of status: Max Weber's early-twentieth-century work on the sources of inequality, the work of Roberto Gonzales and others on the harm to early adult lives inflicted by a lack of legal status, and Cecilia Ridgeway's work on how treating gender as a status can promote inequality.[25]

Gonzales argues that legal status becomes a master status that constrains the lives of undocumented youth as they move from adolescence into early adulthood by excluding them from early adult rituals and institutions, especially the labor market. The trajectories of educationally high-achieving undocumented youth converge in the same grim adulthood as those of high school dropouts. My data tell a story of divergence driven by legal status and by friendship strategy, which brings an individual into contexts that make Mexican ethnicity either a neutral identity or a positive or negative status.

The meaning of Mexicanness matters. Amada Armenta has shown that "looking Mexican" can be made into a negative status leading to racially profiled traffic stops and deportation, while Angela Garcia has shown that undocumented Mexican immigrant drivers, understanding how police see them, seek to pass as "legals" by changing how they dress or the car they drive.[26] Laura Enriquez, Cecilia Menjívar, Caitlin Patler, and others have analyzed the intergenerational punishments imposed on the children of "Mexican-looking" or "undocumented-looking" parents and drivers. Mexicanness thus becomes an intergenerational negative status.[27]

Weber posited that differences in resources, power, and status cause inequality. The powerful hoard resources to perpetuate their power and pass the benefits of inequality to their children. Status categories justify inequality by painting some types of persons as "better" than others, or more deserving of power or wealth. Ridgeway argues that American sociology focuses too much on the privileged classes' retention and hoarding of power and resources and on macro structures, while not paying enough attention to the creation of status distinctions to justify and perpetuate inequality.[28] Ridgeway analyzes the creation in interaction of status categories, which become independently causal once they are embodied in organizational structures and habits. Hence, status creates inequality when the social context "makes status beliefs implicitly salient to participants and relevant to their concerns in that setting."[29]

Ridgeway's analysis illuminates the evolving meanings of Mexicanness as a status marker or as an ethnic identity for participants as they move from their teens into established adulthood. Whether upwardly or downwardly mobile, youth enter sequentially into different contexts that confer meaning on Mexicanness in positive or negative images. Ethnic identity that is not a status can signify cultural or religious difference while not signaling to others that the person with that identity can be treated as lesser than, as a status can do.[30] In contexts where Mexicanness signals legal status, it also signals exploitability and powerlessness, becoming a negative status. Such contexts can situationally override an individual's actual legal status in assigning meaning to being Mexican. For example, U.S. citizens working in "immigrant" jobs are sometimes treated like "illegals."

Here I focus primarily on how Mexicanness became an identity or status at work, also the main site of White contact. Different mobility trajectories bring people into contexts that make being Mexican more or less salient or relevant to the activity at hand and link being Mexican more or less closely with negative or positive traits and images (such as "illegal" versus "good role model to his students"). In this way, being Mexican becomes a status versus an identity.

Friendship Strategies, White Contact, Legality, and Mobility

This section comparatively analyzes the evolving meanings of Mexicanness for more or less upwardly mobile cases. I begin by explaining the statistical association of different friendship strategies in sequential time periods with life outcomes at time 2 (average participant age around twenty-eight). We call these friendship "strategies" because teen participants often prospectively chose friends with an eye to their possible impact on their own future, and then, as adults, they retrospectively attributed their life outcomes partly to their teenage choice of friends. My analysis of only U.S.-born citizens and Category Changers, to avoid the overdetermining effects of legal status, ironically highlights the close link between Mexicanness and illegality in contexts where U.S. citizens feel that they are treated like "illegals."

I next analyze the patterns of study participants' substantive relationships with Whites as they moved through the life course from middle school into established adulthood. Prior research in American sociology links an increase in substantive relationships with Whites with greater mobility. This was indeed the most prominent pattern: as NYCOMPers got older or became more upwardly mobile, their substantive contact with Whites increased, usually because they were moving out of very segregated school settings into more integrated or Whiter spaces in college and the workplace. But NYCOMPers also presented other patterns, including increased White contact via downward or stalled mobility in early adulthood, and the fascinating cases of upwardly mobile youth with no or nearly no substantive contact with Whites into early and even established adulthood.

American sociology's habit of taking substantive contact with Whites as a signal of integration or upward mobility is less useful in understanding New York. Because the city's geography and public institutions, especially its schools, are very segregated, most non-White children have little contact with White children in school.[31] New York is also hyper-diverse. As a result, Mexicans live as a minority among other minorities who constitute a majority (ironies of language abound) in their neighborhoods.[32] Indeed, New York City's 320,000-plus Mexicans counted in the American Community Survey in 2020 were only about 3.6 percent of its population, but in 2020 that population was bigger than the total population of major American cities like Newark, New Jersey; Orlando, Florida; and Pittsburgh, Pennsylvania.[33] Moreover, Mexicans, unlike Dominicans in New York, are not concentrated in a few neighborhoods; thus, Mexican children do not grow up, for the most part, in "Mexican" neighborhoods, as they do in Los Angeles.

Friendship Patterns: Contexts and Strategies

Figure 8.1 shows NYCOMPers' history of friendship strategies of College Graduates and High Fliers at time 2.[34] It shows trends in the chances of having specific types of friends in each time period for those who became adult College Graduates or High Fliers rather than Shallow Slopers or Stuck Muddlers at time 2. If friendships and adult outcomes were unrelated, all lines would be straight and converge on zero. Lines above zero indicate that people who ended up as College Graduates or High Fliers as adults more often had friends in each such group in the designated time period (middle school, high school 1, the first two years of high school, and so on). Lines below zero mean that people with friends in those groups in that period were less likely to end up as College Graduates or High Fliers as adults and more likely to have become Stuck Muddlers and Shallow Slopers. Friendships resulted from choice (of friends and of nonzoned school) and context (who lived in their neighborhood or attended their zoned school). I focus most on friendship patterns in high school and college; the gaps are largest at these times, showing that choice of friends mattered more when participants were teens and early adults than it did in their late twenties and early thirties. The movement away from zero in the figure's overall trends starting in middle school and high school and toward it again in established adulthood (age thirty) shows that a participant's friendship group and strategy were less related to adult outcomes in those periods. At the greatest distance from zero in high school and college, these friendship choices and strategies were strongly linked to different trajectories and had their greatest impacts.

The light gray line showing that a participant had Black friends surprised me, even though I had analyzed this issue before.[35] Those with Black friends in their first two years of high school were 36 percent

Figure 8.1   Friendship Strategies across Time and Adult Outcome Groups: Stuck Muddlers and Shallow Slopers versus College Graduates and High Fliers

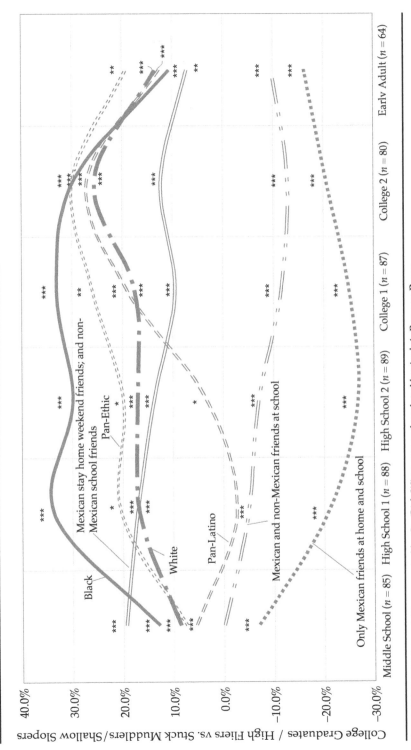

Source: NYCOMP data set. Figure created by Dr. Dirk Witteveen and updated by Andrés Besserer Rayas.

* $p \leq 0.05$; ** $p \leq 0.01$; *** $p \leq 0.001$

more likely to become College Graduates or High Fliers at time 2. This percentage stays over 30 percent through college. This pattern graphically reinforces my prior finding that Blackness was linked in participants' minds with higher academic achievement. The continued large gap through college reflects how comfortable many participants felt with Black students in college, including in Black fraternities, on sports teams, and in preprofessional associations. Being non-White marked an in-group boundary.[36] Blacks, Mexicans, and other Hispanics supported each other at mostly White colleges, thus promoting the success of all. The cases of Elmont, Vicky Fuerte, Emmanuel, and others showed these processes at work (see chapter 4). There were no participants in this study for whom having Black friends was linked to lower adult outcomes.[37]

When shown a draft of figure 8.1, Carla, a mother in her midthirties when we spoke in 2020, was surprised, but she quickly understood it. (Carla was featured in my earlier research.[38]) Noting the dramatic correlation between having Black friends in high school and being an adult College Graduate or High Flier, Carla observed that this finding reflected "the bubble I lived in and knew. . . . The people doing well were Black, so those were the ones I emulated." She knew in 2020 that these findings were not reflected in the larger society, not even in New York, but they accurately captured the "bubble" in which she had grown up: most successful students were Black, and there were few White or Asian students.[39]

The second overall trend is that College Graduates and High Fliers were more likely to have had White or pan-Latino friends than Shallow Slopers and Stuck Muddlers. This trend converged with having Black friends in the later college years. These trends reflect the movement of College Graduates and High Fliers into college and the contexts it opened up, with some differences. The gap in having White friends widened significantly from high school to college because most participants attended high schools with few White students and then met more in college. Similarly, nearly everyone had pan-Latino friends in high school, and Pan-Latino friends became more linked to mobility in college—especially at mostly White colleges—as fellow members of social and professional networks.[40]

The figure dramatically shows a third overall trend that was described to us by study participants—the use of three types of Mexican friendship strategies. The first strategy—having only Mexican friends at home *and* at school—is strongly correlated to worse adult outcomes. They were nearly 30 percent less likely to be College Graduates or High Fliers at age twenty-eight. This line shows the friendship strategy of those who went through elementary and middle school as one of only a few

Mexicans and then were funneled into their zoned high schools, which had many teen migrants in ESL classes. Seen as Mexicans in these schools, some formed Mexican gangs for defense. This friendship strategy, which reflected the reality in the late 1990s and early 2000s, was used by only fourteen of ninety-six cases. It reflected not "Mexican" culture but rather a teen migrant or gang-masculinity-inflected subculture; many of these fourteen cases were gang members. Most NYCOMPers' friendship strategies included White, Black, and pan-Latin friends.

The other two types of Mexican friendship strategies describe other meanings that Mexicanness came to have at this time. A second strategy in the figure shows a small negative gap for those who had both Mexican friends (including teen migrant or gang affiliated friends) and also non-Mexican friends at school. The smaller size of the gap probably reflects the incomplete enactment of gang masculinity of those who cut school with their gang-affiliated friends (harming their adult outcomes) but also had other friends. This group never comprised more than 15 percent of participants.

Finally, the most common strategy (over 60 percent in high school and college) of future High Fliers and College Graduates was to hang out at home with Mexican cousins and friends on weekends, while mostly avoiding large public events and Mexican parties, and also to have non-Mexican friends at school ("Mexican friends who stay home on weekends; and non-Mexican school friends"). This strategy promoted upward mobility because these teens avoided trouble by staying home on weekends, and because their non-coethnic friends often helped them in school, such as by forming study groups with them. With the emergence of a Mexican Culture of Mobility in New York, we would expect to see the relative size of these lines change so that having Mexican friends will be linked to higher percentages ending up as College Graduates or High Fliers.

Figure 8.1 illustrates a two-part argument. First, it confirms that friendship strategies matter, especially during high school, a key turning point that sets a life trajectory, even if trajectories can change.[41] It shows that some Mexican youth in this study became upwardly mobile partly through friendships with non-Mexican students they met in stronger academic programs. Being in such programs separated them from the negative academic dynamics in weaker schools or programs and among Mexican teen migrants, who faced the hardest obstacles in school and often dropped out. Second, it shows that their friendships changed as they moved from middle school to their later twenties to age thirty. Their school friendship choices helped them because, in choosing Black, White, and pan-Latin friendships, they were choosing academically stronger contexts, as my conversations then lead me to believe

NYCOMPers understood when they made those choices. That all lines trend toward zero (no gap) in their later twenties and up to age thirty confirms that the type of friends chosen had less effect on their success in later early adulthood and established adulthood, when their life trajectories were more set.

Substantive Relationships with Whites

Table 8.1 documents whether a participant reported "regular, meaningful contact/relationship with Whites" during six discrete time periods—elementary school, middle school, high school, college age (eighteen to twenty-five), ages twenty-five to thirty, and over age thirty—and in what context: at school, in their neighborhood, at work, in sports or extracurricular activities, or in friendship. A "substantive" relationship is defined as a peer friendship or an asymmetrical but reciprocal relationship, such as good mentoring from a coach, teacher, or boss.[42] Having a White teacher or boss was not coded as substantive unless the relationship deepened to promote mobility and development. Prior research shows that having substantive relationships with Whites is linked with higher educational achievement among Hispanics and African Americans.[43] However, the absence of White friendships need not predict lower outcomes—an implicit domain assumption in much American sociology—as we saw in the range of outcomes for the many NYCOMP participants who grew up in contexts without Whites or who had no substantive relationships with Whites in contexts that had them.

Most research documenting correlations between White or multiethnic friendships and minority student achievement assesses these correlations across entire populations but does not have the data to describe *how* these friendships helped. The subsequent usage or reporting of such studies often asserts that problems in Black (or other minority) culture (presumed as unitary) cause lower achievement and that contact with White "mainstream" culture raises it. But racial cultures are not unitary.[44] For example, the markedly different beliefs on carrying guns (as a sacred right versus a regulatable privilege), immigration, race, and women's rights of Whites who voted for Hillary Clinton or Joe Biden and those who voted for Donald Trump reflect dramatically different "White" cultures.

To preempt misconstrual, I preview one finding. That those with more substantive White relationships had stronger outcomes does not reflect some influence of "White" culture but rather the privileged positions held by Whites in New York. Upwardly mobile participants' academic and work success did not result from increased contact with Whites; instead, their success brought them increasingly into contact

Table 8.1 Frequency of and Contexts for Substantive White Relationships over Time

	Middle School	High School 1 (First and Second Years)	High School 2 (Third and Fourth Years)	College (Ages Eighteen to Twenty-Five)	Early Adult (Ages Twenty-Five to Thirty)	Middle Adult (Ages Thirty and Older)
Had a substantive White relationship	26%	36%	45%	64%	75%	71%
Context	70% at school; 8% at school and in neighborhood; 4% in neighborhood; 4% in sports; 4% socially	65% at school; 19% at school and elsewhere; 3% in neighborhood	50% at school; 18% at school and elsewhere; 14% at work and elsewhere	31% at school; 22% at school and elsewhere; 33% at work; 10% at work and elsewhere	6% at school; 67% at work; 22% at work and elsewhere	0% at school; 88% at work and elsewhere
N	63	71	74	73	69	39

Source: NYCOMP data set.

with Whites. Some participants said that learning to "talk White" (in their words) to customers helped them at work. But this adaptation reflected Whites' institutional position in New York rather than something magical in "White" culture. Similarly, that those who had Black friends in high school did better as adults did not reflect the influence of a unitary "Black" culture but rather the association for NYCOMP participants between AP classes and Black students.

Overall Patterns over Time in Substantive White Contact   Table 8.1 tells a story of childhood and teenage geographic and institutional segregation from Whites and increasing contact via college and work through early and established adulthood. It shows the deep segregation in New York City's neighborhoods and schools underpinning most participants' lack of substantive relationships with Whites in their early lives. Only 26 percent reported having substantive White relationships in middle school, while some 74 percent reported having had no such relationships. This is remarkable in a city where non-Hispanic Whites were still the largest major demographic group—in 2000, 35 percent of the New York City population was White, 27 percent was Hispanic, 25 percent was Black, and 10 percent was Asian. (The 2010 census figures were 33 percent non-Hispanic White, 29 percent Hispanic, 23 percent Black, and 13 percent Asian.[45]) The number of those with no substantive relationships with Whites fell to 64 percent (36 percent yes) in the first two years of high school, 55 percent in the second two years of high school, 36 percent during the college-age years, 25 percent in early to established adulthood, 29 percent after age thirty, and 22 percent at last contact of any kind. The biggest drop occurred in the transition from high school to college, and then to early established adulthood; during these periods, 64 percent and 75 percent, respectively, had substantive White relationships.

The context of substantive relationships changed over time. Some 70 percent of the minority who had substantive relationships with Whites in middle school had them at school, and 8 percent had them both in school and in their neighborhood; thus, 78 percent of such relationships were linked to school. About 4 percent of participants' substantive relationships with Whites were in their neighborhood, 4 percent were in sports, and 4 percent were in a social venue. The numbers are similar in the first two years of high school: 65 percent of those who had substantive White relationships had them in school, 19 percent had them in school as well as elsewhere, and only 3 percent had them in their neighborhood. By the third and fourth years of high school, 68 percent of such relationships were school-based—18 percent had them both in school and in other arenas of life—while the 14 percent who had these relationships at work included the 2 percent who had them both at work and at school. By college age, 31 percent of substantive White relationships were just from school and 22 percent were from school and another arena; the 43 percent that were from work alone included 10 percent from work and other areas. By early middle or early established adulthood, only 6 percent of substantive White contacts were from school, while 67 percent were just from work and another 22 percent were from work and other arenas, for a total of 89 percent from work. By full adulthood (age thirty and older), 88 percent of such relationships were from work or from work and other arenas.

Relationships with Whites and Mexicanness as an Identity or Status

This story of increases in substantive relationships with Whites over the life course masks key differences in the timing, context, and content of those relationships that affected whether being Mexican became an identity or a status. Given that most substantive contact happened at work, we mostly analyze how meanings of Mexicanness were constructed in the workplace, though we also discuss how Mexicanness worked as a negative status in school and other sites in ways that undercut future mobility.

Four patterns emerge. Twelve participants had no substantive White relationships into early or established adulthood. Eight were Stuck Muddlers (six) or Shallow Slopers (two) at time 2 (the first pattern), but four were College Graduates or High Fliers (the second pattern). The second pattern contradicts over fifty years of research taking White contact as a sign of integration and mobility. In the third pattern, eight participants had no prior substantive White relationships but developed them as early adults in college or later in their work life as College Graduates, or (in the fourth pattern for all other cases) when they left school to work as Stuck Muddlers or Shallow Slopers, making a quick transition to established adulthood.

Table 8.2's eight cases present different dynamics for the links between substantive White relationships and later upward mobility. Many cases cannot be explained by the predominant theory positing that more White contact promotes greater mobility and integration and that less such contact results in less mobility and integration. Hence, while some College Graduates and High Fliers had always had substantive White contact (Marianne) or had it continually from high school onward (Jonathan), others with no White contact were nevertheless upwardly mobile (Rosalyn). Moreover, many whose substantive White relationships emerged in early adulthood did so by becoming Stuck Muddlers

Table 8.2   Type of White Contact, Mobility, Work Setting, and Meaning of Mexicanness

Case	Type of White Contact	Mexicanness as (Negative or Positive) Status or Identity?	Mobility	Work Setting
Rosalyn	No White contact	Identity	High Flier	Private, professional
Angelica	No White contact	Negative status	Stuck Muddler	Immigrant economy; ethnic enclave; service sector
Bartolo	White contact via teenage early transition to adulthood	Negative status	Stuck Muddler	Immigrant economy; service sector (with White boss and clients)
Galen	White contact via profession during early and middle adult transition	Positive Status	High Flier	Public school
Lucia	White contact via profession during middle adult transition	Positive Status	High Flier	Public school
Jonathan	White contact constant since high school	Identity	High Flier	Private firm
Marianne	Constant White contact	Identity	High Flier	Private firm
Linda	White contact before high school; none in high school as part of upward mobility strategy of choosing a "Black" school and Black friends; White contact again in early adulthood	Identity	College Graduate	Private firm

Source: NYCOMP data set.

or Shallow Slopers early on, as teenagers, and then transitioning early into established adulthood of full-time, low-paid work (Bartolo). That everyone in table 8.2 was a U.S. citizen underlines the strong influence of context in creating the meanings of Mexicanness.

Moreover, we see in table 8.2 that whether Mexicanness became a neutral identity or a negative status did not track with substantive White relationships. Ethnicity serves as an identity in providing practices and a sense of belonging, but it does not signal to others that they can be treated differently based on group identity. Ethnicity as an identity is not salient in the allotment of rewards at work, while ethnicity as a status works exactly that way.[46] In the table, "negative status" refers to working in a context where one is often discriminated against or disregarded by members of a dominant group (customers, clients, or coworkers, for example, or Whites, non-Mexican Hispanics, or Blacks) without fear of penalty. By contrast, "positive status" refers to the greater meaning that a person's ethnicity is given by their colleagues and institutions at work. In the table, Mexicanness was a negative status in two cases—one participant who had substantive contact with Whites, and one who did not. The work setting in both cases was the (Dominican) immigrant economy, where Mexicanness is tightly linked to illegality, making it a status. Conversely, Mexicanness was a positive status for two professionals who worked in New York's public schools and came to be regarded by their professional peers and students as role models. Their Mexicanness caused others to offer more help and to see their success as vital to the school's mission. Ironically, the negative-status cases and the positive-status cases are the obverse of each other, reflecting the dangerously close link in public understanding between being Mexican and being undocumented.

Perhaps the most interesting contrast is between the upwardly mobile College Graduates who did not "feel Mexican" at work (that is, they did not feel that being Mexican harmed their work life) and those who felt stigmatized at work for being Mexican. An upwardly mobile trajectory moves one into contexts where being Mexican usually does not signal being "illegal," while a blocked trajectory often brings one into contexts, including the immigrant economy, where it does, even for U.S. citizens. The alignment of Mexicanness with "illegality" is socially dangerous and fostered by American policies and politics.

No Substantive Relationships with Whites

As noted, twelve study participants (six Stuck Muddlers, two Shallow Slopers, and four College Graduates or High Fliers) reported having never had a substantive relationship with a White person. The trajectories of Stuck Muddlers and Shallow Slopers led into contexts with no or few Whites: not attending college, working full-time after high school, or hanging out with gangs (male Stuck Muddlers). These cases fit the predominant theory.

The four College Graduates with no substantive contact with Whites were theoretically more interesting. Either they were in contexts with Whites but had no substantive relationships with them, or they were in contexts with no Whites. In New York City, it is quite possible to go through public schools and universities and into a middle-class job and never have substantive contact with Whites. We discuss two such cases here: one in the mainstream economy and one in the immigrant economy.

Rosalyn: No Substantive White Relationships and Mexicanness as Both an Identity and a Status   Rosalyn Buendia, a Category Changer who had become a U.S. citizen, went through all her public schools and public university and became a middle-class homeowner never having had a substantive White relationship. When asked about friendships with different ethnic groups, Rosalyn, then in her late twenties, wryly pointed to me as her only White friend, though she said I was "not really White" because "You know so much about Ticuani." I have known Rosalyn since she was about ten years old and have spent time with her family in Mexico and Brooklyn over the course of many years. I have been very happy to see Rosalyn and her siblings thrive. I draw here on this long relationship, at least four recorded interviews, and a long case narrative.

Rosalyn insightfully described the racial dynamics in two different White worlds: in one her Mexicanness was an identity, and in the other it was a status. The first was the world of "the Italians" who owned the meat market where she worked in high school. She rarely interacted with her employers but was friendly with her mostly Mexican immigrant coworkers. She did not feel that her identity affected how others treated her at work. The second world was her high school internship as a receptionist for Big Wealth Management, which trained her to speak more formally on the phone. Rosalyn learned to manage relationships with "White American men . . . in suits," who expected her to follow them when they came in to deliver their messages (in a time before cell phones).

> Yeah, if I had to pick up the phone and take a message down, I had to say, "Good afternoon, Big Wealth Management Company, Rosalyn Buendia speaking. How can I help you?" And . . . write down the number, who's it for, "Sure, sir, he'll call you back," or "I'll let him know as soon as he gets back into his office." I would see the financial analyst coming in. I had

to follow him and make sure it was a good time to come into his office, knock, and be like, "Sir, you got a phone call."

Rosalyn liked the position because she got paid more than other interns, and "I learned interpersonal skills. . . . I learned how to talk, how to greet people. . . . I had to act older, to be somebody I wasn't [at the time]. . . . I can't just come into an office and be like, 'Hey, you got a phone call.' I had to be more formal." Rosalyn did well and was offered a permanent position after graduating from high school, but she declined it to attend college.

Rosalyn saw a pigmented, gendered hierarchy at Big Wealth Management that made being a Mexican woman feel like a negative status. The people at the top were all "White Americans" and "all men" who interacted little with her. Support staff were lighter-skinned Hispanics. "The majority were Dominicans, but not the Dominicans that *look* Dominican. . . . They were light-skinned . . . the guys were very clean-cut, very formal, you know. . . . If you were to meet them, you would be like . . . 'You're Puerto Rican.'" For her, looking Dominican meant being darker-skinned, looking more "Black" than "Puerto Rican." (Rosalyn understood that she was describing stereotypical images, but she also knew that her peers would understand what she meant to convey with these descriptions.) Rosalyn's Mexicanness was an object of curiosity for these Dominican men, who tried to chat her up with lines like, "Oh my God, such a pretty Mexican," oblivious to how this pitch racialized her and disqualified them with her.

Rosalyn recounted another episode in which her Mexicanness ran counter to expectations and could have become a negative status, illustrating the complexities of racial and ethnic meaning in a hyperdiverse New York. When asked if she ever felt that she had been discriminated against, she said no, but added that, if she was, she would work extra hard to prove herself, being "pretty sure I can handle it." She then recounted what a nurse had said in a hospital practicum when she told her that she was Mexican: "Oh, you know, I didn't know Mexicans could go to school like that" (that is, get a four-year degree). When I asked about the nurse's race or ethnicity, Rosalyn whispered that she had been Black. Whispering back, I asked why she was whispering.

Rosalyn (laughing, still whispering): I don't like to say "Black" and "White." . . . I feel like I'm discriminating myself . . . 'cause I have a lot of Black friends, and it's not that just 'cause of one comment that I'm gonna hate all of them.

Author: It's a really weird thing, right? I understand; that's what I thought you were thinking . . . like someone would think you were anti-Black because you were telling us that this Black lady said, "I didn't know Mexicans could do that."

Rosalyn: And I told my friends that, and they're all Black, and I'm like, "You know, she said that." And they were like, "Who the hell does she think she is?" . . . They defended me.

Rosalyn also believed that the nurse, who was older than her, had a nursing certification but not a nursing degree (which would have brought her higher pay) and so was "jealous or envious . . . of the young people coming in" with nursing degrees.

Rosalyn's response resonated with her friendship strategy during high school and after, a strategy that fostered her upward mobility. Although she did not say that she was Black—as Black Mexicans did—Rosalyn said "I felt like I fit in" with Black people because "we liked the same music, we did talk the same way." Her siblings and cousins teasingly called her "Afro-Mex." She mostly avoided Mexican parties as a teen but returned regularly to Ticuani, her family's hometown. Rosalyn attributed her academic success partly to having Black friends. In high school, her Black best friend was valedictorian, and she made her other close friends "in AP classes."

Rosalyn later quit nursing, earned a master's degree in accounting, and got well-paid work with her sister at Beautiful People Management. In that job in 2017, she handled clients' logistics but rarely saw them. She was then in her late twenties and engaged to a kind and hardworking Mexican man who was in college. She lived with her family in a middle-class New York suburb where Italians, though the biggest group, were a minority and where increasing numbers of Hispanics and Asians also lived. The neighbors were nice to the Buendia family, but they had not made real neighborhood friends after several years of living there.

Rosalyn's Mexican identity did not become a status that limited her established adult life, though some moments in her story suggest the possibility that it might have. In sometimes being seen as "the pretty Mexican" or "the Mexican who could go to college," she fell outside others' cognitive category of "Mexican," making her Mexicanness salient where it should not have been, per Ridgeway's analysis of how statuses form and have impact. Nevertheless, Rosalyn was able to finish a master's degree and change jobs and contexts to enter well-paid work using her professional training. She could comfortably identify with her Black student peers in the master's program and had mostly Black friends, but she also worked well with Beautiful People Management's mostly White clients. Being Mexican was not a master status for Rosalyn, as it is for long-term undocumented Mexican immigrants and for U.S. citizens working with them, as we can see in two other cases.

Angelica: Mexicanness as a Negative Status in the Immigrant Enclave Economy
Even though New York–born Angelica had almost never had any contact with Whites, her Mexicanness became a status signaling illegality and exploitability at her job in a Dominican bakery in a Dominican enclave. She made less than any U.S. citizen in the study—$300 cash for fifty-six hours per week, or $5.36 per hour (at a time when New York State's minimum wage was $7.15 per hour). She lived with her Mexican husband, another underpaid U.S. citizen, and their three children in a one-bedroom apartment they shared with another family—twelve people in all. Angelica paid $500 per month (42 percent of her income) for day care for her youngest child. Her life was hard for the whole decade I knew her in this study. She was insightful and funny, but grimly realistic about her life. She laughed dryly when she said that she had gotten pregnant at fourteen "on purpose . . . to get out of my house," because her naturalized U.S. citizen father beat her for fear she would get pregnant and leave, as her older sister had done.

Angelica's Mexicanness became a negative status at the Dominican bakery in the Dominican neighborhood she grew up in. She code-switched to a Dominican accent so easily that her friends teased her for being a "DominiMexican." Her Dominican boss liked her. But Angelica believed that her boss and the bakery's Dominican clients equated Mexicanness with illegality, and they treated badly and spoke harshly to recently immigrated Mexican employees. (Relatively fewer Dominicans than Mexicans and Central Americans are undocumented.[47]) She said that "Dominicans . . . think they are owners of the world . . . and have the right to anything here. . . . Some of them are racist. They're like, 'Oh, Mexicanos, que son inmigrantes' (Mexicans, they are immigrants). . . . And I'd be like, 'You didn't come here as an immigrant?'"

Author: What do you think it means—*son inmigrantes*?

Angelica: Like they don't have papers. They don't have a right. We are invading the U.S.

Discussing two Mexican men recently hired at the bakery, Angelica said, "I've seen how they take advantage of them. They give them all those hours of work and little pay." I asked whether she knew how much they were paid.

Actually, I tried asking them . . . when . . . I started working there. [They told her that the boss had told them:] "We're going to pay you this, but don't tell your coworkers what it is you're getting paid." . . . The recent one . . . is twenty-three years old. When they come from Mexico, they don't know English, they don't know nothing. They don't even know

how to defend themselves. I've noticed how many hours he was working.
I think even more hours than me.

Angelica learned that her coworker worked sixty-five hours a week
and made $250 to $275 weekly, which worked out to between $3.85 and
$4.23 per hour versus the $7.15 per hour minimum wage at the time.

In Angelica's account, her Dominican employer felt that she could
pay Mexicans less than others, and the bakery's Dominican clients felt
that they could speak badly to and about Mexicans. In this context,
Mexicanness became a status signaling illegality and exploitability. (It
bears note that even though Angelica was paid well under minimum wage
herself, she mostly worried that her newly arrived Mexican coworkers
were more exploited than she was.) That meaning of Mexicanness also
harmed Angelica and her children, who were growing up in an over-
crowded household whose income was much lower than it would have
been if there had been no "Mexicans are illegals" stigma legitimizing the
lower wage paid to her by her Dominican boss.

White Contact through Early Transition to Adulthood

Those in a smaller but important group developed their first substantive White relationships at work while in and after leaving high school,
when they made an early transition into established adulthood by moving
into full-time work instead of going to college and, in many cases, having
children.[48] Unlike Rosalyn's nonsubstantive relationships with her White
bosses at Big Wealth, Bartolo's close bond with his White boss of over
ten years made his Mexicanness an identity in that relationship, but it
became a negative status in interactions with student customers and
undocumented coworkers.

*Bartolo: Mexicanness as a Status for a U.S.-Born Mexican American with
a White Work Relationship in an Early Transition to Adulthood*   Bartolo
spoke so quietly in interviews that I had to lean forward to hear him. His
startlingly open regrets about school made me feel slightly awkward,
even though we had known each other for years through his close friend
Emmanuel. The changes in the meaning of Bartolo's Mexican identity
over time as he moved from his teens into established adulthood were
driven by his own choices, by context, and by structural conditions.

Bartolo's ethnic identity trajectory followed one pattern for Mexican
youth who became early adults in the late 1990s and early 2000s in that
he and two cousins were the "only Mexicans" in their elementary and
middle schools and had Black and Hispanic friends, but not White

friends. He met more Mexicans in high school and began cutting school with them for hooky parties; in high school he had only Mexican friends at school and at home. Bartolo became an X Street Boy, got tattoos, and embraced gang masculinity, including fighting. His high school grades dipped from 88 percent his freshman year to 64 percent his senior year, and he dropped out of high school to work when his girlfriend said she was pregnant (he later learned she was not). He never got a GED. Police detained Bartolo several times, though they never criminally charged him.

Bartolo openly showed both quiet pride in his work and regret at not finishing high school. His sober, thoughtful, thirty-something self seemed incongruent with his fighting past. In his adult life, Bartolo's Mexicanness had become an identity or a status depending on who he interacted with.[49] He said that deli customers—mostly older Jews and students at the local yeshiva (religious school)—often mistreated the Mexican and Central American men working there, using Spanish curses learned from their "maid" or "gardener." As noted earlier, a student once called him a "freaking wetback!" as he took out the garbage. Bartolo corrected the student, firmly, and often used Yiddish words to challenge the students, saying he would "kick [their] *tuchus* (backside)" if they said offensive things. He felt bad working in an "immigrant job . . . working in a restaurant, instead of coming home nice and clean. . . . White-collar . . . I shoulda stayed in school instead of working in a restaurant . . . like blue-collar—below blue-collar." Even his undocumented coworkers teased him for working there, because he spoke English, had gone to high school, and was born in Brooklyn. For Bartolo, Mexicanness became a negative status through his interactions with the deli's customers, who treated its workers badly, and his coworkers' teasing him for being a U.S.-born person working in an "undocumented" job.

Bartolo's Mexicanness could also be an ethnic identity linked to his good work. He was proud of doing his job well and felt valued by his White boss, who had increased his pay (from $6.25 to $14 per hour) and responsibilities over the eleven years he had worked at the deli. He had gone from "dishwasher to counterman," could do "the work of three people," and translated between his boss and coworkers. He took and filled orders and set up on-site catering for events. Bartolo's description of his skill at managing the deli, the work of others, and the mostly White customers revealed the soft skills that many employers believe minority men lack.[50]

Bartolo liked working with customers and was good at it. Responding to my question in response to his *tuchus* story, he reported not feeling humiliated by being nice. He talked to customers with "respect . . . like a sophisticated person," but he code-switched to "talk ghetto" with his coworkers. When he moved out of state for a girlfriend, his boss teased him: "I can't believe you are doing this to me!" The boss and his coworkers gave Bartolo a $300 going-away present.

White Contact through Upwardly Mobile Transition to Adulthood

Galen Maestro: A High Flier's Social Isolation and No White Substantive Contact until Early Adulthood, with Mexican Identity as a Positive Status Galen Maestro was a High Flier and bilingual New York City public school teacher with a master's degree. He earned over $80,000 annually by his midthirties, when he was also married, with two children. The changes in the meanings of Galen's Mexicanness over his life course and across contexts were dramatically different from Bartolo's and Angelica's experiences.

I had known Galen since he was a teenager, interviewed him at ages eighteen and twenty-six, and saw him regularly at Ticuani events. A likable young man with a huge laugh, Galen generously shared his friends with me and my research team in Mexico and Brooklyn and helped us by enthusiastically telling others of our research. Even as a teen, he spoke to me as a fellow educator.

Galen said that his 1990s neighborhood was 90 percent Black and Puerto Rican. As the "only Mexican," he was lonely in his elementary and middle schools. "[I would] mind my own business," he said. "If somebody talked to me, I would talk back, but I wouldn't really go the extra mile to [join] a certain group. . . . I just felt like an outcast." As an adult, he called it a time when "I didn't have an identity—I didn't identify myself with other people." The other Mexican in his high school transferred to a Catholic school after two weeks.

Galen believed that this social isolation helped him succeed. Describing it as "for the best," he reflected that "maybe if I had grown up in a bigger, stronger Mexican population, I may have associated myself with that group, and maybe I wouldn't have, you know, been as careful about school, as I was. I would've wanted to hang out with those people instead of studying. . . . It's not a stereotype, I just feel that." Mexican teen immigrants, he said, assumed "that being an immigrant meant that working was imminent, thus it could . . . cause one to drop out." By later in high school, more Mexicans had enrolled, and they invited Galen to Mexican weekend parties. Seeing the danger to his long-term goals, he declined, but he always greeted the new Mexican teen migrants in school and "[did] not ignore [them]." His social isolation protected his teen self from the lure of cutting and going to teen migrant hooky parties.

Although he avoided Mexican parties, Galen did not dissociate himself from being Mexican, as some High Fliers did. Galen regularly returned with his family to Ticuani, even in his twenties and thirties. Galen and his brother were well respected among Ticuanenses as successful school nerds who did not party. Galen rejected gang masculinity and enacted Mexican mobility masculinity by avoiding Mexican parties in New York, finishing college, working professionally, and living at home with his parents.

In his thirties, his Mexicanness became a positive status for Galen at work. An older White public school teacher who mentored him through his hard first years of teaching told Galen that being the only Mexican teacher in a school full of Mexican and Central American students made his success matter more: "He would remind me that I'm important to that school. . . . He would never want to see me leave because 'as the lone Mexican teacher' in there, he says to me, a lot of people look up to me. Those are his words . . . 'a lot of kids look up to me.' . . . He feels that I can help them, even though I may not know it." His mentor encouraged Galen to endure because he was proof to students that they could make it too. Galen's role as a Mexican teacher brought him a positive status that invested his actions with extra meaning for students, for whom he served as a model, and brought him strong mentor support.

Milana: No Substantive Relations with Whites until Established in a Professional Career   Milana came to the United States as an eleven-year-old undocumented girl and did not get permanent legal status until her midtwenties. She said that lacking status did not harm her, however, because she always knew that she would become legal through her lawful permanent resident parents, who had legalized via IRCA in the 1980s. Still, she knew not to discuss her legal status outside her family.

Milana attended mostly "White "schools but was in ESL classes until her senior year, so she never made White friends. Whites in her high school were "nice," but Milana was too "shy" to speak English to them. Her public school and college friends were mostly Latinas. After college, Milana worked in New York's public schools as support staff, until she earned two master's degrees, at which time she became a professional staff member. I had known Milana for over two decades. She was serious, but laughed at surprising moments. Milana appreciated the larger meaning of this project and told her story hoping that it would help others.

Milana's first substantive relationship with a White person, her first boss in her first professional job, came in her early thirties, just as being Mexican was taking on deep, positive personal and professional meaning for her. "That woman embraced me," was how she described this first boss. Now a guidance counselor, Milana believed that being a Mexican, a woman, and a Latina deepened her work's meaning because she was able to connect with students through these identities. She would tell them that she had been undocumented, and she made and hung in her office a sign declaring that undocumented students can go to college. Milana felt that she was a symbol to students, especially Mexican immigrant students:

> *Milana:* I am more Mexican, if there is a Mexican [student] with me. . . . I can relate with them . . . maybe I can help them.
>
> *Author:* Do you feel like a symbol . . . someone who was able to make it as a Mexican?
>
> *Milana:* As a Mexican, and as an immigrant . . . and as a Latina, as a woman, I feel like I can tell the girls, "Okay, you could do this. . . . There are options." . . . I do use myself as a role model. I say, "I was an immigrant. I was undocumented."

Milana's Mexicanness never harmed her life chances, in her account, because knowing that she had a path to legal status via her parents prevented Mexicanness from becoming linked to illegality for her, an association that might have hurt her school effort. Moreover, her lack of substantive White relationships did not reflect stymied mobility, but rather New York's segregated schools. Mexicanness became a positive status for Milana in her professional job by making her an important example to her Mexican immigrant and undocumented and young women students and by inspiring her first White boss to make an extra investment in her.

Substantive White Contact from Childhood or High School

Jonathan: Substantive White Contact Starting in High School and After for a High Flier   Comparing Jonathan's case with Galen Maestro's illuminates the impact of context on the meaning of Mexicanness. Both came of age in the late 1990s to mid-2000s, and both went to mostly Black and Hispanic elementary and middle schools and nonzoned high schools. But there had been more White people in Jonathan's school, work, and social life since he was in high school. I have known Jonathan since he was ten years old and am friends with his father. I interviewed him in high school, in his early twenties, and finally at age twenty-nine. I have also seen him and talked with him regularly at Mexican events. When we last spoke, he was in his thirties, had two children, and made over $100,000 per year.

Even as a teen, Jonathan's tone in interviews was authoritative: he was explaining things to me, not asking if he had answered my questions (as some seemed to worry). Jonathan was likable, and he organized events for a Mexican sports club of which his father Leo (with whom he was close) and I were founding members in the early 1990s. Jonathan would regularly make fun of Leo and me as old guys in the club. (I was in my early thirties!) He was socially skilled, worked hard, and was a happy, if tired, working father when we last spoke.

The change in substantive White contact for Jonathan stemmed from his father's strategy to get his sons into stronger schools in a safer neighborhood. Leo used the address of Jonathan's aunt to get him into the academically stronger Federalist High School, which had more White and Asian students than most other Brooklyn schools. It offered bilingual classes, native language instruction in Chinese and Spanish, and language classes in Greek, Arabic, French, and Italian. The school population had traditionally been about one-third Asian, one-third White, and one-third Hispanic, with few Blacks. Jonathan's father told me that they bought a house and moved to the wealthier Winston neighborhood—in the Federalist High school zone—to give their children better and safer schools and streets.

Jonathan and Galen navigated Mexicanness in the late 1990s differently, but the fact that both ended up as High Fliers shows that different paths can lead to the same outcome, thus showing equifinality.[51] While Galen withdrew socially to succeed, sports opened opportunities for Jonathan: after running with his father's club, he ran track in high school with mostly White and some Latino teammates. In an interview in high school, Jonathan had laughed at how diverse his friends were: "An Italian, a Russian, a Mexican, and an Irishman—sounds like a joke."

Galen's withdrawal strategy made sense in a harsh social world, including one I saw with my own teenage children. Middle-class American parenting culture often urges teens to be more socially engaged, but middle school and high school friendships can lead to bad decisions and stupid actions, and they can be toxic. Some High Fliers in this study withdrew in school to avoid negative social dynamics and studied instead. This strategy partly explains why study participants who mainly hung out at home with cousins on weekends did better than many others.

Jonathan felt that, at Federalist High, being Mexican meant being "an ESL" (his words). As the number of Mexican teen migrants in the student body grew in his junior and senior years, his social location changed: "I was an outsider to the Spanish groups in high school because [being] in the Spanish groups meant ESL. . . . And in high school I was . . . in . . . [AP] classes. . . . There were not many Spanish kids in those classes." He notably used the old-school adjective "Spanish" to describe Spanish speakers, echoing older 1990s administrators in these schools in their identification of Spanish speakers by their language, rather than as "Latinos/as" or "Hispanics" or by their country of origin. Teen migrants invited Jonathan to join a gang, but he declined. After that, they would stare hard at him when he socialized with White or non-Mexican friends. He would look away, enacting Mexican mobility masculinity. He also dressed a "little baggy" (loose pants), but not "too baggy," to avoid signaling either that he was an easy step-up or that he was in a gang.

Jonathan became close to his White boss at a sporting goods store where he worked while in high school. Unlike Bartolo's service-sector job, which made his Mexican identity a negative status to clients, Jonathan's part-time job gave him experience with demanding White customers in a context where his boss introduced him to customers as an accomplished runner, which he was. His Mexicanness was not his most salient identity at his job, where he ably explained the pros and cons of various running shoes, earning customers' loyalty and his boss's respect. He saw their demandingness not as racial entitlement but as a high-end customer trait, and he managed it well, drawing on his status as an elite runner and running shoe expert.

The meanings of Mexicanness in Jonathan's early adult life ran on parallel tracks. For many, being Mexican in high school was a negative status, one linked to stymied mobility. But Jonathan avoided contexts where Mexicanness could have this meaning. His early adult life also proceeded sequentially through contexts in which Mexicanness was linked with upward mobility, including his rapid rise as an adult in his marketing company, which was staffed mostly by Whites; his growing leadership role in the Mexican sports club; and his embrace of Ticuani events, to which he even brought his U.S.-born, South American college girlfriend (and now wife).

At work, Jonathan felt that his Mexicanness was "a slight advantage," because he spoke Spanish and dealt effectively with clients in Spanish-speaking countries. The company's owner advanced him quickly from support staff to project manager to department manager, one tier below senior management. When I asked about racial and ethnic divisions of labor at the company, he confessed to not thinking that way, but he recognized that top management was all Jewish, Greek, or Italian. Jews had founded the company. But ethnicity did not determine roles at work, he said, and the company had a "pretty good mix" of ethnicities, including Hispanics. When I asked about his boss's ethnicity, he said: "I don't really know what the hell he is. For all I know, a basic White guy. I never actually asked him. I get along with him. It's more who he likes, who he picks. . . . He has his 'chosen ones,' I call them." Jonathan's boss liked him and invited him to join the fantasy baseball league soon after joining the company. He also explicitly discussed Jonathan's future at the company, telling him (as noted in this chapter's epigraph) that there was "tons of room" for him to grow there. Jonathan explained that his boss's high opinion of him and his value to the company were driven largely by his acumen in developing new analytic programs to assess where and to whom to sell company services, including in new markets in Latin America.

The meaning of Jonathan's Mexicanness varied across time and across contexts. He deescalated hard looks in high school and later was comfortable inhabiting a White-Hispanic world built on college, sports, and upward mobility. He embraced Mexican mobility masculinity, helped build a youth-serving institution (the sports club), and advanced rapidly in a company, run by "a basic White guy," where being bilingual helped him. From middle school into his midthirties, Jonathan did not experience his Mexicanness as a negative status, as Bartolo and Angelica did, because he moved sequentially into upwardly mobile contexts.

Like other NYCOMPers, Jonathan was sometimes asked to declare his ethnicity or nationality. For example, at college parties in his mostly White college (in New York City), he was asked: "What are you? . . . Italian, Arab, or what?" Other NYCOMPers were asked the same question by other immigrants or U.S.-borns. These questions were driven partly by a common understanding in New York that since people from the same country can differ phenotypically, appearance is an unreliable indicator of nationality or languages spoken. People sometimes spoke to Suzie (see chapter 4) in Chinese, and to others in the study in Hindi or Arabic.

Substantive Relationships with Whites throughout Their Lives

Marianne: Becoming an Ethnic Entrepreneur   Marianne's interviews felt like Jonathan's: she explained things to me, rather than seeking to answer my questions correctly. She was justly proud of her multiple successes — as a Latina who made it despite long odds, as a woman who succeeded in the corporate world, and as an adult daughter who had saved and grown her family's business. Marianne clearly felt comfortable in authority, but worried that she might not find a good life partner. Our last interview was conducted in her family's restaurant in a gentrifying neighborhood to which she had adapted their business plan. She periodically interrupted the interview to instruct workers.

Marianne went to elementary and middle schools with mostly Black and Puerto Rican students, some students with Eastern European immigrant parents, and "very few Mexicans." She had one Russian friend, but most of her friends were Black, Puerto Rican, or Dominican. Her Puerto Rican and Dominican friends teased her for being Mexican. She chose Marketing High School to work in that field, avoiding her zoned high school because it was "dangerous . . . and full of drugs." Marketing High had mostly Latina/o/e and Black students, with some Whites. Through a Marketing High program, Marianne developed a strong relationship with a middle-aged White woman in marketing who mentored her through college and her first corporate job. She smiled in recounting her mentor's advice on courses to take and internships to apply for, as well as on navigating corporate life.

At her mentor's urging, Marianne applied for and got scholarships to private colleges in upstate New York. She persuaded her parents that she would do better if she could live at college and just study, rather than work weekends in their restaurant. At her primarily White college, she mostly hung out with "Asians, Indians, and Latinas." After college, she landed a job in a big insurance company with mostly White employees. She was "one of two" Latinas. In both institutions, she felt that "I represent Latinos. . . . I was the only one. . . . I had to adapt to that [White corporate] culture." She felt that her White classmates were more prepared for such a culture. They "had after-school stuff like ballet or baseball . . . were tutored or . . . [took] advanced classes." She believed that most of her classmates had a car (which I confirmed for her college via *U.S. News & World Report*) and that their parents "were already in their professions, as opposed to if you are from a low-income background. . . . [As] a Mexican . . . another Latino . . . or Black, your dreams are not as high. You do dream, but you're like: 'How the hell do I get there?'"

Marianne loved marketing but did not enjoy working for others, having grown up working in her family's restaurant: "I wanted to do the whole corporate thing. . . . And I could have moved up more . . . as a woman. . . . I was young and ambitious, so I *was* moving up. But I wanted to be my own boss, and it just happens that my family had a restaurant." Laid off in a downturn, she brought her business skills to her family's struggling Mexican restaurant.

Gentrification-driven rent increases for the restaurant and its main clients—local Mexican immigrants—had led to fewer clients and higher expenses, creating a crisis her parents could not resolve. Marianne reoriented their restaurant from serving mainly Mexican immigrant men toward serving the White and other hipsters and young professionals who greatly outnumbered Mexicans in the neighborhood: "We are giving them the real [Mexican] food, and they want the whole experience of Mexico." She raised prices, volume, and profits. At age thirty, she said: "I basically saved the business." She easily chatted with White customers and arranged write-ups for the restaurant in local blogs, creating a buzz in the hipster community. Marianne's pride in her work for the family restaurant was well deserved.

One insightful reader of this book in draft asked if Marianne felt like she was "selling out" by pivoting from a mostly Mexican to a mostly White clientele. But Marianne showed no regrets: their Mexican clientele was decreasing and could not support the business, while the White hipster clientele was increasing and could pay more. Moreover, she was proud to have saved the business when her parents could not. Marianne seemed to love being a Mexican culinary ambassador, reveling in getting "a lot of publicity . . . and going mainstream . . . that is what this restaurant is bringing to the public. . . . We are proud of being Mexican, we are proud of our food."

The meaning of Mexicanness for Marianne varied by context and over the life course. In grade school, she was teased for being Mexican. Through high school and college and in her corporate life, she felt like a lone "other" representing Mexicans and Latinas. She had to adapt to Black youth high school culture, then White and Black college culture, and then White corporate culture. Her ability to move capably in and between many cultural worlds fostered success in each. In her thirties, her pride in her business success was also pride in being Mexican and in keeping the immigrant bargain and saving her family's restaurant: "I am not doing an immigrant job. I am doing the American dream. . . . I am not working for somebody. . . . I am working for myself." She did, however, feel that being an educated Mexican woman boss posed challenges. The Mexican immigrant men she employed teased her for getting into restaurant work the "easy way" (via college and her parents' restaurant). And it was hard, she said, to date or find a life partner: most men who were interested in her were Mexican immigrants who felt intimidated by her education and career success.

Conclusion

This chapter has tracked how participants' friendship strategies from middle school to established adulthood correlated with their adult outcomes, and how substantive White relationships were or were not linked to upward mobility. We have described Mexicanness working as a neutral identity or positive status for upwardly mobile study participants, but mostly as a negative status for their downwardly mobile counterparts.

This analysis interrogates an enduring domain assumption in American sociology that more White contact signals upward mobility, integration, or "assimilation."[52] Our data tell a more interesting story.

First, the minority of NYCOMP participants who had always had substantive contact with Whites attended academically stronger schools, which enhanced their chances of becoming College Graduates or High Fliers. But timing and contexts show two other patterns of increased White contact in early adulthood: in one, higher-achieving youth met Whites in college or at work after college; in the other, many met Whites during or just after they left high school, in an early transition to full-time work and toward established adulthood as Stuck Muddlers or Shallow Slopers.

Finally, an important minority were upwardly mobile without substantive White contact. In most sociological theories, lack of White contact implies segregation and lack of opportunity, but here it showed segregation accompanied by movement into middle-class lives that featured either no Whites in college, at work, and in the neighborhood, or first contact with Whites only in these later work or professional contexts. Continued demographic change and racial segregation in America suggest that this pattern will grow.

These findings also do not fit with the problematic Mexicans theory or racial exclusion theory because they stem from an analysis of varying intra-ethnic mobility. They describe Mexicanness becoming a status that affects one's life chances or an ethnic identity that does not affect life chances, depending on context. For NYCOMPers, Mexicanness became a negative status linked to illegality in immigrant economy jobs, even for U.S. citizens, while the upwardly mobile experienced Mexicanness as either a neutral ethnic identity or a positive status that helped them in their work.

To reiterate a caveat: I here analyze meanings of Mexicanness during a specific conjuncture in the 1990s and 2000s. Since then, a Mexican culture of mobility has been emerging among U.S.-borns, a movement that includes impressive one-generation upward mobility in families whose members are all documented. This movement is also supported by a new historical conjuncture at which U.S.-born Mexican youth greatly outnumber foreign-born youth and U.S.-born Mexicans as a group have impressively high college completion rates.

This study differs from prior studies in that it analyzes the *emergence* of a minority culture of mobility rather than the workings of an established minority culture of mobility. Place plays a key role here: this Mexican culture of mobility would not be emerging as strongly had there not been the kind of pro-mobility supports and contexts present in New York City into which U.S.-born, second-generation NYCOMP participants could move and work.

═ Chapter 9 ═

Conclusion: Empirical, Theoretical, and Policy Stories and Recommendations

I︢T SEEMS quixotic and dicey to write conclusions and recommend policy in these times, for two reasons. First, America is split today not just on how to address issues but on what is real and what is fake—the country is in an epistemic crisis. Even the Covid-19 virus, which has killed over a million Americans, is seen as fake by millions of Americans. Similarly, millions of Americans believe that former president Trump won reelection in 2020 and was robbed by massive voter fraud. Those in the mob that attacked the U.S. Capitol on January 6, 2021, to try to stop the 2020 election results from being certified, have since been described as "tourists" or "patriots" by some members of Congress who were captured on video fleeing that same mob. Psychologists tell us that we resist new arguments and data that conflict with our entrenched beliefs; more often we dismiss such arguments and data rather than perceive them as reasons to rethink our beliefs.[1] Yet even if I am yelling into the wind, I make specific policy recommendations in this concluding chapter in the hope that they will strengthen the positions of those who seek to make America fairer and better.

Second, America's current reckoning with systemic racial injustice rightly calls for structural change, and many are understandably impatient with incremental change or smaller goals. Driven dramatically by videos of White police officers killing Black people, the Black Lives Matter (BLM) movement has galvanized a cross-racial movement demanding justice and changes in policing. The MeToo movement has similarly promoted a reckoning on gender and sex discrimination and abuse by powerful men. These are necessary and positive steps. In a similar vein, this book has documented the impact on the lives of undocumented immigrants of a structural and historical civil rights challenge in America— systemic inequality in access to legal status. Lack of legal status has derailed the mobility of undocumented Americans, even when they do

261

https://doi.org/10.7758/drwz9626.7908

the same "right" things as their U.S. citizen peers. To meet this civil rights challenge, we recommend here the structural change of legalizing millions of undocumented Americans and their families.

In analyzing the dramatic upward mobility of the U.S.-born Mexican second generation in New York City, this book has also necessarily analyzed what *is* working. NYCOMPers' success stands in contradistinction to the predictions of problematic Mexicans theory, which portrays Mexicans as poster children of negative assimilation, and to the expectations of racial exclusion theory, which is based on a different empirical story. New York City and New York State offer pro-mobility and immigrant-friendly contexts and policies that promote more intergenerational mobility than was shown in studies done in other places. This context offers concrete supports that drive mobility, protect immigrant families, and make immigrants' own mobility-promoting practices more efficacious than has been the case elsewhere.

Moreover, Mexicans' more recent arrival in New York City and their patterns and settlement practices in the city have created a different relationship to place (and between place and ethnicity) than in other places that have been studied. Although specific practices can harm mobility, such as enacting gang masculinity into adulthood, these dynamics, taken together, have supported a strong Mexican culture of mobility in New York and redefined Mexicanness in a new historical conjuncture.

In this concluding chapter, I first offer empirical and theoretical summations and then suggest specific policy steps. In the first section, I ask why adult mobility outcomes are different in New York and in this study than outcomes in other studies. Is this is a New York story? I then analyze the different empirical and theoretical stories, including racial exclusion theory, and the extra leverage made possible by NYCOMP's research design. Then I consider the emerging Mexican culture of mobility in New York, including suggestions for pragmatic programs and policies, such as mentoring, that can promote mobility, especially among the U.S.-born second and later generations. In the last two sections, I discuss the dangers of making policy proposals in the context of America's epistemic crisis—with Americans unable to agree on what is true or real and what is a lie—before diving in anyway to make larger proposals for policy and structural change.

A central question orients this conclusion: How and why is intergenerational mobility among U.S.-born second-generation Mexicans in New York City so much greater—both among participants in this study and in census data—than it is for their counterparts in prior studies mostly done in California and Texas?

Three Types of New York Stories

A regular response to presentations of these findings has been to say that they tell "a New York story." But there are three types of New York stories, and this book does *not* tell one of them: the dismissive declaration that these study findings, though interesting, emerge *sui generis* from New York's contexts and hence cannot help us understand other places in America.

This book does tell a second type of New York story that emerges from the pro-mobility, immigrant-friendly context created by New York City and New York State. This context is neither wholly unique to New York nor somehow magical, and most of its elements could be adopted elsewhere to promote mobility (save for the subway and a few other elements, though good public transit programs exist or could exist in other cities). Pressure to adopt such policies may increase as more of America becomes more diverse and as children of immigrants come of age and begin voting.[2]

Finally, this book tells a third New York story of how the efforts by the city and state to include and protect immigrant families are being stymied by federal immigration policies. In this third New York story, America has frustrated the efforts of the city and the state and chosen to punish rather than embrace immigrant families.

New York City and New York State have promoted mobility for immigrant families by protecting them and by taking institutional and programmatic action. Many city and state institutions and policies signal both symbolic and real institutional inclusion of all immigrant families and promote intergenerational mobility. As noted earlier, New York State now permits established undocumented New Yorkers to get a standard driver's license (reducing deportations) and has made them eligible for scholarships at public New York universities, funded with New York State tax dollars. The state created and funded the $2.1 billion Excluded Workers Fund to help families who were purposefully left out of federal safety net programs during the Covid-19 pandemic. Since 1989, CUNY has offered in-state tuition for undocumented graduates of the city's high schools, and health care has long been offered to all New Yorkers, regardless of legal status. The city similarly honors ICE requests to turn over undocumented people only if they have committed serious crimes and if ICE has an order signed by a judge. These measures have supported the intergenerational mobility of immigrant families, including mixed-status families, because undocumented parents of U.S. citizen children are less likely to bring their children for doctor and dentist visits, or to use other supports that their children need and are entitled to, if they fear exposing their own legal status.[3] That fear is greater in places that do not treat all immigrants as full and equal members of the community, as New York seeks to do.

Despite the steps taken in New York City and New York State to treat all New Yorkers like members of the community, neither the city nor the state can grant undocumented Americans legal status or remedy the exclusion from the labor market that breaks the link between teen and early adult educational work and their hopes for better adult jobs. Moreover, federal policies intrude into the workings of local institutions and authorities to convert them into agents of deportation, even in a relatively liberal "blue" state like New York. Since 2013, every person fingerprinted and booked into a local jail in the United States is searched for in both the FBI databases (to catch wanted criminals) and the USCIS databases (to find undocumented people). Despite repeated claims by three administrations that these searches mainly lead to the deportation of criminals, some 69 percent of over 100,000 people deported from 2002 to 2017 in New York State had no conviction, not even a traffic violation.[4] Traffic offenses were a top cause of deportation, and not only in "red" upstate counties but also in New York City and "bluer" counties. These data point to what my coauthors and I call New York's "traffic stop to deportation pipeline."[5]

Context Matters: Why Do Rendón's *Stagnant Dreamers* and Telles and Ortiz's *Generations of Exclusion* Tell Different Empirical and Theoretical Stories than This Study?

We can address questions of why NYCOMPers and U.S.-born Mexicans in New York City census data empirically show more mobility by engaging theoretical stories in other studies to identify elements that vary across them.[6] Empirical stories are what data directly tell us (such as graduation rates). Theoretical stories are the posited causal processes and sequences of steps that explain the empirical story; here that includes tracing processes over time to explain divergent outcomes among different NYCOMP cases.

María Rendón's *Stagnant Dreamers* and Edward Telles and Vilma Ortiz's four-generation study *Generations of Exclusion* are analogues for this study. They offer dramatically different empirical stories of nearly no second-generation mobility, in contrast to the wide variation in mobility documented in this study. Limited or blocked mobility is the dominant empirical story in these and other well-done studies. This empirical difference reasonably led the authors to seek to explain what blocked mobility, and structural racial exclusion seemed a good theory. Second, like this study, Rendón's *Stagnant Dreamers* intimately analyzes participants' accounts and other data to posit what blocked or boosted mobility. Third, Rendón's study was done in Los Angeles at about the same time NYCOMP was done in New York. I recognize that comparing Rendón's study and this one is not a comparison of "Los Angeles" and "New York" (or San Antonio, Los Angeles, and New York, to include Telles and Ortiz's study), but rather a comparison of the social worlds described by participants and other data and rendered by the authors into an account—a point to which we return.

Generations of Exclusion argues that first- and second-generation (and later generation) Mexicans experience academic and economic progress (compared to their parents), but that this progress is blocked by underfunded schools and discrimination, leaving the third and later generations stranded in a "permanent working class." Rendón's *Stagnant Dreamers* tells a similarly grim empirical story of the convergence of high- and low-achieving U.S. citizen second-generation men who nearly all ended up struggling and earning about $15 per hour at ages twenty-four to twenty-eight from 2007 to 2013. Rendón posits that second-generation mobility was blocked by structural factors, including dangerous and segregated neighborhoods, underfunded schools and uncaring teachers, and social isolation. Drawing on the work of the sociologists Ricardo Stanton-Salazar, Vivian Louie, and others, Rendón explains that even academically high-achieving second-generation youth lack the networks and social leverage capital—or *palancas* (levers), in her words—to advance in school or their careers, but also that immigrant communities develop social bonding capital that prevents the second-generation decline that some theorists predict.[7]

The different empirical stories told in *Stagnant Dreamers, Generations of Exclusion*, and this book underpin different theoretical stories. For example, Rendón's participants told an overwhelmingly negative story of pervasive discrimination and indifferent, gate-closing public school staff, an unforgiving criminal justice system, and only one cross-class ethnic mentor (a public school teacher) among forty-two study participants. Telles and Ortiz similarly cite racial discrimination and underfunding in public schools as key causes of immobility; they do not mention upward-mobility-promoting mechanisms like mentors and second-chance programs.

Contrast these grim facts with the 47 percent of NYCOMP participants who had nonfamily adult mentors—mostly non-Mexican and disproportionately New York City public school teachers, nearly all of whom were middle-class—who coached them into better schools and opened other doors to opportunity. Their story is more like those told in Vivian Louie's *Keeping the Immigrant Bargain*, where mentors were key supports boosting mobility. Many U.S.-born NYCOMPers who had made mistakes benefited from second-chance mechanisms that made middle-class futures possible for them. Rendón and Telles and Ortiz do not discuss such mechanisms. Moreover, the ability of NYCOMPers to avoid zoned schools was partly determined by their prior school performance (stronger students were often told to avoid zoned schools) and their habits of mind and conduct, such as counterfactual thinking in choosing their high school. Rendón's and Telles and Ortiz's uniformly grim empirical outcomes understandably led them to tell a theoretical story of racially driven structural exclusion. My more varied outcomes led me to analyze, among other things, how some NYCOMPers navigated unequal schools differently—sometimes with help from public school teachers, sometimes through counterfactual thinking—in order to succeed. That examination then led me to tell a more process-based than structural story of mobility.

The different empirical and theoretical stories in this study and in Rendón's and Telles and Ortiz's studies can help us infer what factors promoted greater mobility for second-generation Mexicans in New York. NYCOMPers described a New York City with different physical, institutional, and social infrastructure than was found in the neighborhoods described in *Stagnant Dreamers* and *Generations of Exclusion*. Those studies describe participants living in profoundly segregated neighborhoods that offered limited opportunities and seem to have constituted their whole world. Moreover, the stigma of coming from those neighborhoods harmed their prospects in interactions outside them—for example, in job searches. In *Stagnant Dreamers* and *Generations of Exclusion*, neither schools nor mentors helped open doors to better college or work opportunities beyond the neighborhood. Indeed, Rendón's book leaves the reader with the impression that the study participants could have been born, lived, and died on the same block, never having had any real chance to seek opportunities beyond the neighborhood.

Conversely, U.S.-born NYCOMPers, even some of those who lived in segregated neighborhoods they saw as dangerous, described lives with more opportunity. I believe that New York's context differs from those in California or Texas described in other studies in ways that promote intergenerational mobility and support an emerging Mexican culture of mobility in New York. Two sets of factors promoted mobility for NYCOMPers, whereas their absence or opposite stymied mobility in *Stagnant Dreamers*, *Generations of Exclusion*, and other racial exclusion studies. The first set of factors stems from New York City's more pro-immigrant mobility context (compared to those described in these other studies), which recalls an era when Americans believed that the government could help solve common problems. The second set of factors involves settlement and incorporation processes for Mexicans in New York City, and for NYCOMP families especially. These processes have enabled many, especially the upwardly mobile, not only to escape the harms of living in "bad" neighborhoods but also to leverage community-level social capital and strategies (the *palancas*) in ways that uphold the immigrant family bargain and promote intergenerational mobility. Among those ways are the previously unanalyzed dynamics of how NYCOMPers related to place, which reflect Mexicans' evolving conjunctural ethnicity in New York City. These factors led to or helped create the supportive contexts into which upwardly mobile NYCOMPers sequentially moved.

New York City's Pro-Mobility Context

New York's pro-immigrant mobility context is premised on the belief that government can help solve problems. Despite its dizzying inequality and segregation, New York City has been better able than most places in America to preserve or extend the mobility-promoting protections and benefits of public institutions and policies. This pro-mobility context includes: (1) the city's strongly pro-immigrant political class and ethos; (2) strong public institutions—including hospitals, many good schools, and, especially, public transportation—and a commitment to treating all immigrants as New Yorkers, regardless of status; (3) a more diversified and apparently more open economy (compared to those described in other studies) with a labor market comprising large, strong public and nonprofit sectors that offer good jobs—with pay influenced by unions—and a private sector that makes higher-paid jobs available to newcomers; and (4) strong mobility-generating institutions—especially CUNY and nonprofits that help newcomers—that support collaborative efforts on behalf of immigrants, such as those between CUNY and the Mexican consulate.[8]

I recount New York City's and New York State's many pro-immigrant mobility institutions and measures here, but because pro-immigrant mobility measures are not discussed in Rendón's and Telles and Ortiz's studies, I do not similarly profile Los Angeles and San Antonio. This makes sense, because their worse empirical outcomes led these authors to analyze why there had not been more progress. But the fact that these other places also have pro-immigrant policies makes me wonder whether such policies were unknown, not noted, or not as effective in the places those studies were done.

New York City's political class and institutions are generally pro-immigrant, and the city and state have been leaders in protecting immigrants. As impossible as it seems today, in the 1990s Republican mayor

Rudy Giuliani sued the federal government (more than once) to protect the rights of undocumented New Yorkers.[9] New York City's term limits have increased turnover and immigrant representation on the city council. Ever since Mayor Ed Koch signed an executive order in 1989, New York City has limited how its police share information about the legal status of victims or suspects with outside agencies, and the city does not honor ICE detainers—requests by ICE to detain a person held in custody for deportation—except for those who have committed a serious or violent crime, and the request is made with a judicial warrant.[10] The city has long had the Office of Immigrant Affairs, whose commissioner is a city cabinet member who reports directly to the mayor. New York State has the Office for New Americans, which serves "new New Yorkers." We noted earlier that New York State now uses state tax dollars to offer undocumented New Yorkers in-state tuition at public universities, allows them to get a standard driver's license, and created the Excluded Workers Fund to help those who lost jobs but were excluded from federal pandemic relief measures.

New York City's public institutions have mostly sought to treat immigrants as fellow New Yorkers, regardless of legal status. Before New York City school board reforms twenty years ago, noncitizen immigrant parents could vote in board elections.[11] The city's schools have worked, for example, with nonprofit advocates and the Mexican consulate to create a version of the Mexican *matricula consular* (consular registration ID, with a hologrammatic photo) that the public schools could accept as ID so that parents can enter their own children's schools. The city also created IDNYC so that all New Yorkers, regardless of legal status, can get a government-issued ID. The IDNYC card also offers incentives, like museum discounts, to encourage wide uptake by New Yorkers, to prevent it from becoming stigmatized and linked to a lack of status. New York City's health insurance programs are open to everyone, including undocumented immigrants, and offer care on a sliding scale. The city also created a fund to pay for DACA applications and offered free legal services and grants to help applicants pay the $465 application fee. New York has an unusually strong nonprofit sector that both helps immigrants and employs them. Indeed, nonprofits employ 18 percent of all workers in New York, and 34 percent of nonprofit workers are foreign-born (64 percent are women, and 56 percent are people of color).[12]

New York's economy, in NYCOMPers' accounts, is more integrated and draws in more U.S.-born second-generation Mexicans than is the case in Rendón's Los Angeles or Telles and Ortiz's Los Angeles and San Antonio. In Rendón's world, there were few networks reaching out of the neighborhood and into colleges or into jobs paying more than $15 per hour, and little chance to move into middle-class neighborhoods—a key sign of mobility for Rendón. NYCOMPers encountered more economic opportunity than did "stagnant Dreamers." Average annual pay for NYCOMPers at age twenty-eight was $37,090, and 36 percent of them made $50,000 or more at that age (around 2010). And even though 34 percent of NYCOMPers worked in immigrant economy jobs, some of these jobs, like forklift operator or waiter, paid well and offered pay step increases. Similarly, some low-paying entry-level sales jobs for men employed in the "oxford shirt and chinos" economy had potential for growth and increased income. Sixty-seven percent of adult NYCOMPers worked in upward-mobility-promoting jobs: 30 percent were employed in the pink-collar economy—for example, as secretaries—or held other jobs with pay steps and benefits; 13 percent were teachers or police or were in the military; and 24 percent had highly skilled jobs in fields like accounting, IT, and law. Finally, in contrast to "stagnant Dreamers," most upwardly mobile NYCOMP participants encountered little to no anti-Mexican discrimination on the job, and in fact most of them saw being Mexican as nonconsequential or even as helpful in their jobs. Meanwhile, their downwardly mobile counterparts, including U.S. citizens, felt that being Mexican was linked to illegality and exploitation.

CUNY as an institution is a driver of bottom-to-top mobility. Indeed, CUNY's websites have prominently bragged about findings by *Harvard* economists like Raj Chetty and analysts from the Brookings Institution that CUNY colleges push more students who started off in the bottom fifth of the income distribution into the top fifth by middle adulthood than any other colleges. Six CUNY four-year colleges and six CUNY two-year colleges have ranked nationally in the top ten institutions that promote bottom-to-top mobility in their categories.[13] Baruch College, where I teach, was ranked first among four-year colleges in 2018 in the *Chronicle of Higher Education* for promoting student mobility.[14]

CUNY has collaborated extensively in the last fifteen years with the Mexican consulate in New York to promote the well-being and mobility of Mexicans and their children. Led by former CUNY vice chancellor Jay Hershenson, CUNY created a commission in the late 1990s and then a Mexican Studies Institute in 2012. CUNY also developed effective outreach campaigns to Mexicans. These efforts were driven both by demands from community leaders and by research and data (including mine) showing that in the early 2000s Mexicans in New York believed that undocumented people could not go to college, that a student had to go full-time, and that it cost over $10,000 per year, none of which was true.[15] The Mexican consulate in New York worked with CUNY's Mexican Studies Institute to develop the "Windows of Educational Opportunity" program and has advertised it in its waiting room, through which over five hundred people pass daily. Baruch College's Marxe School has hosted over two hundred community and organization leaders in capacity build-ing via the Baruch College–Mexican Consulate Leadership Program, which offered workshops and classes on issues such as fundraising and one-on-one consulting. CUNY collaborated with the consulate to pro-mote DACA applications through the DACA Access Project (aka the Mexican Initiative on Deferred Action, or MIDA). CUNY's "Citizenship Now" offers free immigration-related legal assistance to the CUNY com-munity, the largest such university-based program in the country. The CUNY Mexican Studies Institute created a *becarios* (students with scholar-ships) program that has thus far funded and placed over two hundred students in career-building internships.[16] The Mexican consulate in New York has been a strong driver of Mexican integration and upward mobility in other ways, including collaborating with health care and other public institutions in New York and other places.[17]

The Dynamics of Settlement and Incorporation and the Emerging Culture of Mobility for NYCOMP Families

The second set of mobility-promoting factors involves the processes of settlement and incorporation documented among NYCOMP families, including the previously unanalyzed dynamics of how they relate to neighborhoods. In his 2012 book *Great American City*, the sociologist Robert Sampson convincingly demonstrates the lasting impact of place on adult lives. People who grew up in mobility-blocking neighborhoods or cities have lower average adult mobility than those who grew up in mobility-promoting neighborhoods.[18] The effects of neighborhood or place are not uniform but rather vary by race and gender; in some studies, White men have more mobility than Black men, and women have more mobility than men.[19]

Studies of intragroup heterogeneity similarly emphasize the impor-tance of geographic mobility in promoting social mobility.[20] But place exerts effects in other ways. The sociologist Van Tran describes how and why Black West Indian youth have stronger adult outcomes than their African American neighborhood counterparts: the former spend less time on the street or in public places, thus avoiding the police and the gang entanglements that Rendón says make violence a structural fea-ture of the neighborhoods of "stagnant Dreamers." I build on Sampson's and Tran's research by identifying several mobility-promoting ways in which NYCOMP families related to their neighborhoods and the meaning that their ethnicity acquired (or did not acquire) in relation to place.

First, NYCOMP participants did not live in "Mexican" neighbor-hoods; nor did they have the same attachment to, or feel as limited by, their neighborhoods as participants in Rendón's study did. Rendón's participants came from "two of the most poverty-stricken neighborhoods in Los Angeles." One was 78 percent Mexican in origin and 92 percent Latino/a/e, and the other was 36 percent Mexican in origin, 61 percent Latino/a/e, and 37 percent African American.[21] There were no "Mexican" neighborhoods like these in New York in the early to mid-2000s, when these youth were coming of age, and there are probably none today. Moreover, New York embodies the anthropologist Steven Vertovec's concept of superdiversity and the urban analyst Susanne Wessendorf's concept of commonplace diversity. As cities become more diverse, such diversity becomes the normal lived experience of their residents.[22]

I believe that such commonplace diversity can change the meanings of ethnicity and how it becomes tied to place. Reflecting New York's brand of commonplace diversity, even in the emerging "Mexican" neighborhood of Sunset Park, Mexicans constituted only 13 percent of the total population and 20 percent of the Hispanic population in 2000 in its main zip code, while Puerto Ricans made up 22 percent and 32 percent, respectively.[23] NYCOMP participants did not bear the stigma of being from a "Mexican" neighborhood in school or in job searches, as *Stagnant Dreamers* reports for Los Angeles residents. Although NYCOMPers did not face this stigma, some, especially the less upwardly mobile, did say that being Mexican signaled illegality in school and in the immigrant economy in the late 1990s to mid-2000s. For the most part, however, this stigma did not follow the upwardly mobile into their (stronger) high schools, into college, or into their professional jobs, where being Mexican was sometimes a positive status.

The empirical differences in mobility between this study and the many other studies offering a racial exclusion story cannot be explained solely as the result of recruitment of participants from very poor neighborhoods. Other studies telling a racial exclusion story drew on representative samples for cities or regions (for example, *Generations of Exclusion* and *Parents without Papers*) or on nonrepresentative but large school-based samples in two cities (*Legacies*), but their findings align with Rendón's, not with mine.

Second and relatedly, the meaning of "being Mexican" is different in New York than in Rendón's Los Angeles neighborhoods, and its meaning varied widely for participants, both over time and by institutional context. Mexicans are relatively new immigrants in New York, and their place in the city's racial hierarchies was not "set" during this study, unlike the ethnic and place stigma experienced by Rendón's "stagnant Dreamers." Mexicans and their second-generation children in New York inhabit an "in-between" space in terms of stigma or status. Seen as not Black, not Puerto Rican, and not Dominican, Mexican immigrants in New York avoid the harshest stigmas directed at "Black" persons, and Black men, especially.[24] Moreover, the common perception of Mexicans in New York City by later-generation descendants of immigrants— whether White, Black, or Hispanic—as fellow immigrants is part of New York's story about itself. Mexican gangs may have worried police greatly around 2000, but they did not displace the image of "hardworking Mexicans" in the public imagination.[25] With their impressive academic attainment, U.S.-born Mexicans seem more like Koreans and Colombians than groups with lower rates of college graduation, such as Puerto Ricans and Dominicans.

Such optimism does not describe the exclusion and challenges confronting undocumented parents and their mostly U.S. citizen children, as reported in this book, or the undocumented Americans who grew up in the United States but continue to be excluded because of legal status, or those living in places like Rendón's Los Angeles or Telles and Ortiz's Los Angeles and San Antonio.

Third, NYCOMP participants and their parents belonged to communities in mobility-promoting ways that were different from those described in *Stagnant Dreamers* or not described at all in other studies. Most NYCOMP families were from Ticuani or El Ganado, the two socially coherent, long-term migrant-sending communities analyzed in depth in my book *Mexican New York*. Immigrants from these communities went from being mostly undocumented to mostly documented under the 1986–1988 legalization program or under prior immigration laws that made it easier to legalize through one's U.S. citizen child.[26] If the parents of Rendón's "stagnant Dreamers" migrated after 1986, which seems likely, they would have been less able to gain legal status, and the challenges to mobility for their U.S.-born children would have increased. Moreover, the continuing support and sense of belonging offered by the coherent Ticuanense and Ganadense communities helped insulate NYCOMPers from possible negative neighborhood effects and helped generate the *palancas* (levers) that "stagnant Dreamers" lacked.[27] Even Ticuanense and Ganadense families who lived in different and even distant places in New York City could still spend social time with family and friends on weekends and holidays and participate in Mexican community convening events like sports leagues and national celebrations, which created large public spaces where most people present were Mexican. Hence, NYCOMPers partly grew up in nongeographical Ticuanense or Ganadense communities that insulated them from some dangers of place.

Fourth, NYCOMP families' settlement patterns and strategies combined with New York's rent laws and evolving real estate market to help reduce the negative impacts of place and generate mobility. Ticuanense and Ganadense immigrants did not "transplant" their rural communities to one or two New York neighborhoods, exposing immigrants uniformly to one neighborhood's conditions, as happened with Rendón's "stagnant Dreamers" in two poor Los Angeles neighborhoods. (Similarly, Dominicans in New York have settled in high population concentrations in Washington Heights and Jackson Heights.)

The ninety-six NYCOMP participants lived in thirty-four neighborhoods and places at time 1 and time 2, including nineteen neighborhoods where only a single study participant lived and twelve where only two or three lived. NYCOMP families' dispersion reflected Mexicans' larger pattern in New York through the early 2000s, as documented in *Mexican New York*.[28] Moreover, while many NYCOMP families first lived in underresourced, marginalized neighborhoods, others started off in economically more mixed neighborhoods, and many purposefully sought out what Sampson calls "mobility by neighborhood" by moving as their children grew older.[29]

We can see such place mobility in the movement between three neighborhoods with the largest numbers of NYCOMP participants over the course of the study. Some twelve NYCOMPers lived in Vista Heights—widely described by them as a "dangerous" or "bad" place—at time 1, when they were teens, but only two lived there at time 2 (average age twenty-eight). Similarly, no participants lived in Middle-Class Island Suburb at time 1, but nine had moved there, via Ticuani networks, at time 2, some from Vista Heights. Moreover, seven places that participants called "better" places to live and that were not listed at time 1 showed up in the place data at time 2, including four places in other states. Some NYCOMPers moved from good places to better places: the thirteen participants living in the middle-class Boro Terrace neighborhood at time 1 were down to eight at time 2, five having moved to places like Middle-Class Island Suburb. NYCOMP teen and early adult men told me that being able to "escape" street troubles in places like Vista Heights by returning to their nicer Boro Terrace neighborhood helped them become successful adults.

Fifth, the lives of NYCOMP participants, especially the upwardly mobile, were not based in their neighborhoods in the ways described by "stagnant Dreamers." NYCOMPers often lived in neighborhoods with multiple ethnic, national-origin, racial, or religious communities of neighbors whose youth lived together in a friendly enough way, even if they did not become friends. This was especially true for those who lived in places that were mainly Black or had large numbers of Hasidic, Eastern European, or non-Spanish-speaking immigrant families. Upwardly mobile NYCOMPers also spent less time hanging out in public as teens and early adults, echoing Van Tran's finding for West Indian youth.[30]

Finally, because many NYCOMP participants generated their primary friendship groups in high school, those who attended stronger schools had potential friends who were stronger students, including many Black teens who took AP classes and went on to college. Upwardly mobile NYCOMPers' friendships and ties with similarly mobile Black peers contrast strongly with Rendón's picture of the lack of interaction between Mexicans and African Americans, even in one of her study's neighborhoods that was 37 percent African American. Making friends with high-achieving Black students in non-neighborhood high schools helped U.S.-born second-generation NYCOMPers keep the immigrant bargain and promoted mobility and a Mexican culture of mobility.[31]

Mobility was helped by three other dynamics of place: New York's real estate market, the city's regulation of that market, and NYCOMP families themselves. Some Ticuanenses leaving places like middle-class Boro Terrace for places like Middle-Class Island Suburb kept their Boro Terrace apartments and sublet them to Ticuanense friends who were either leaving neighborhoods like Vista Heights or moving from a more expensive apartment in Boro Terrace to their friend's bigger but usually cheaper one (due to long-term residency and limited yearly rent increases). They stayed in their good neighborhood but paid less rent, freeing money up for expenses like college. NYCOMP family mobility tweaks Robert Sampson's insight that "neighborhood trajectories matter" for life chances.[32] Many NYCOMP families lived in marginalized neighborhoods that gentrified over the twenty years of this study. Because New York's rent laws restrict yearly increases, many families were not priced out of gentrifying neighborhoods and even benefited from the gentrification. A few had purchased small buildings in these "bad" neighborhoods, whose value increased tremendously over the two decades of this study.

Finally, the art scholar and museum director (and former researcher on this project) Sara Guerrero-Mustafa (formerly Guerrero-Rippberger) has insightfully noted a building-level effect. Although Mexicans are usually minorities within neighborhood populations, many Mexican extended families stay together for years in the same buildings where they rent apartments, thus creating a Mexican community of support within their Mexican/extended family building. These NYCOMP families experienced mobility by neighborhood by staying in the same relatively affordable building while their neighborhood gentrified around them. These dynamics helped families keep the immigrant bargain, become upwardly mobile, and create a Mexican culture of mobility by linking them to resources, such as cheaper rents in places with stronger schools.

Subways and Schools: How Two Key New York City Public Institutions Promoted Mobility for Second-Generation NYCOMP Adults

Two final public institutions, New York City's public schools and its subway system, help explain not only NYCOMPers' overall stronger mobility than is shown in studies of other places, but also differences in outcome among NYCOMPers. While most NYCOMP families lived in the catchment areas of weaker public schools, New York's school choice system enabled some to unlink their school options from their neighborhood. Upwardly mobile study participants, especially, got into better-performing schools by using relatives' addresses in stronger catchment zones, by moving briefly into such a zone, by applying directly for admission to those stronger schools, or by requesting a "safety transfer." (Citing gang threats, they could change schools.) NYCOMP participants had moved an average of 2.75 times by age twenty-eight to seek opportunity or avoid problems, and 28 percent had moved to get a family member—usually a young man—away from danger. This practice is not discussed in *Stagnant Dreamers* or *Generations of Exclusion*.

NYCOMP participants also used school strategies akin to those of the Chinese second generation documented in Kasinitz, Mollenkopf, Waters, and Holdaway's book *Inheriting the City* (2008).[33] Unlike the Chinese in New York, who had gained disproportionate shares of seats in New York's four elite high schools, upwardly mobile NYCOMPers developed and shared knowledge of how to get into better schools or avoid worse (especially zoned) schools. Because they were not focused only on the four elite schools and were also helped by teacher mentors in finding good schools that would accept them—including newly formed high schools looking for good students, which offered new students a fresh start—these NYCOMPers often had several better options beyond their zoned school. While NYCOMPers lacked institutions that disseminated such knowledge throughout the immigrant community—like Chinese after-school programs and cram schools—they shared such knowledge widely within the Ticuanense and Ganadense communities in New York. Older college-attending NYCOMPers told younger relatives and friends to "get out of" their problematic neighborhoods for high school, leaving behind their problematic friends. These older NYCOMPers also helped others apply to CUNY (the main college NYCOMPers attended) and advised them throughout their educational careers (and in related work, such as internships), thus driving intergenerational mobility. The widening gap between the academic and career trajectories of less and more upwardly mobile NYCOMPers looks less like the structurally overdetermined bad outcomes in *Stagnant Dreamers* and *Generations of Exclusion* and more like what the sociologist Alan Kerckhoff describes as "deflections" from mobility at each point of inclusion or exclusion in the British school system.

Finally, the subway made it possible for many upwardly mobile NYCOMP participants to escape the long shadow of their underresourced schools or neighborhoods, and to do so without having to leave their families or other sustaining social ties. NYCOMPers' social mobility did not require geographic mobility, nor did place so strongly set their life chances.[34] As described in chapter 3, many upwardly mobile NYCOMPers applied to better middle and high schools away from their friends and neighborhoods. If they got into a better school, the subway made it possible to get there, and they could still live with their parents and within other nurturing or supporting relationships. (These rides were usually free, because New York City gives its students free MetroCards that cover rides to and from school, and to an after-school activity.) Moreover, living with parents through early and into established adulthood did not make NYCOMPers feel stagnant or fully block their opportunities, as it did for Rendón's "stagnant Dreamers." Living together, especially in upwardly mobile NYCOMP families, helped all family members keep the immigrant bargain, and it also saved on rent, boosted family income, and enabled younger siblings to benefit from intrafamily learning about the schools. Family members who bought a house together were building wealth together.

Moreover, the subway democratized access to out-of-neighborhood opportunities in ways that car dependence could not in California and Texas. The subway made it possible for upwardly mobile NYCOMPers to benefit from demographic and other changes that were creating openings in coveted high-income jobs and professions.[35] Emmanuel took the subway from his family's apartment on X Street (a "dangerous" place, he said) first to a strong nonzoned high school that provided him with mentors, and then, with his mentor's help, to Elite University, internships, law school, and work as a lawyer in Manhattan. He traveled his upwardly mobile path on the subway while living on X Street.

Counterfactual Conversation with Rendón's Stagnant Dreamers *and Telles and Ortiz's* Generations of Exclusion

This New York context helped make the mobility-promoting mechanisms analyzed in this book efficacious in ways that the same or similar mechanisms were not in Rendón's Los Angeles and Telles and Ortiz's Los Angeles and San Antonio. For example, Rendón analyzes how the social bonding capital generated over time by immigrant parents and families reduced the influence of gangs and criminal justice system entanglement and helped in job searches to prevent second-generation decline, but it *did not* promote mobility. The social bonding capital observed by Rendón emerges, in my framing, partly from the prescriptions of the immigrant family bargain (go to college, go to work) and also its proscriptions (avoid trouble, do not hang out on the street). But the immigrant family bargain was more efficacious in this study than in Rendón's because New York's context supported immigrant families in ways that Rendón's two Los Angeles neighborhoods seem not to have done for her study participants, and in ways that are not mentioned in Telles and Ortiz's book or in most other studies.

Rendón's study also differs from this one epistemically in where the theoretical story starts. For example, where Rendón sees violence as a structural feature of her two neighborhoods, this study analyzes how young men enacting Mexican mobility masculinity kept the immigrant bargain more fully and moved into mobility-promoting contexts like better schools and professional jobs. Most of those enacting gang masculinity—which includes responding violently to attacks on other members—kept the immigrant bargain less well and moved into contexts that limited their own and their family's mobility. Treating violence as a structural part of a neighborhood makes sense when studying very violent neighborhoods, but NYCOMP participants did not widely describe neighborhood violence as endemic to the places they lived in the long-term, or as a condition from which they could not extract themselves, or which had harmed their long-term well-being or mobility. Hence, my study focused on how different masculinities help explain diverging trajectories. NYCOMPers' reports sync with research showing that immigrant youth have less exposure to violence and lower rates of crime than their U.S.-born peers.[36]

To reiterate, comparing Rendón's analysis and this one does not compare "Los Angeles" and "New York," but rather the social worlds described by study participants and other data and written into our accounts. If Rendón had followed participants drawn from geographically dispersed, longtime sending communities whose first-generation parents had mostly obtained legal status and who lived in many different Los Angeles neighborhoods, her empirical and theoretical stories might have been more like mine. Similarly, in reading *Stagnant Dreamers*, I wondered about the absence of mobility-promoting mechanisms in her participants' lives. Where were the good teachers, guidance counselors, or mentors? Where were Mexican sports leagues or second-chance mechanisms? Where was UCLA and, especially, where was the California State University system? This system, which research has shown to have among the best mobility-promoting colleges in America, is the CUNY of California (I say boosterishly).[37] I do not here imply that these supports were present and Rendón missed them. Rather, given the quality of Rendón's data and analysis, I believe that her study participants would likely have talked about such supports had they been present in their lives and been efficacious.

Similarly, if I had recruited participants from two of the most impoverished neighborhoods in New York and most of them went to neighborhood schools where they experienced nearly no Black-Mexican interaction, and had no mentoring links beyond the neighborhood, my empirical and theoretical story might be more like Rendón's. Recognizing these possibilities does not invalidate the logical inferences that Rendón and I draw but rather highlights the need to make the case for the cases we theorize from and to establish the contextual and other bases for our logical inferences.[38] NYCOMP participants' adult mobility was boosted by their contexts and conditions, which were much more supportive than those reported in *Stagnant Dreamers*, *Generations of Exclusion*, and other racial exclusion studies.

Analytical Leverage from the NYCOMP Research Design

This study's unusual research design enables it to ask and answer different types of questions than those driving many other studies. Rather than comparing central tendencies of attainment across groups over time in what David Fitzgerald metaphorizes as an "ethnoracial Olympics," this study is case-driven, in that it follows the processes that boosted or inhibited mobility among study participants as they grew up.[39] It draws on participants' accounts and other data and on triangulation among accounts from linked participants to describe how specific mechanisms promoted or inhibited mobility from their teen and early adult years into their established adulthood. With its deep, extensive family history data, the study is also able to trace how changes in American immigration policy—especially permitting or denying legal status to immigrant parents—helped or harmed the adult outcomes of their children. Its use of case-oriented, statistical, and set theoretical analysis enables it not only to describe how mechanisms promoted or blocked mobility but also to document the correlation of specific ethnographic variables with adult outcomes like years of education or income at age twenty-eight. Finally, because it comparatively traces the trajectories of long-term undocumented American participants, U.S. citizen participants, and Category Changer participants, it gains extra leverage in assessing how and how much lacking or gaining legal status affected or correlated with NYCOMPers' adult lives. Longer versions of the statistical and set theoretical analyses and an analysis of the epistemic, methodological, and analytical underpinnings of this book are found in its online appendixes.

NYCOMP families are also Mertonian strategic cases because they experienced so much mobility despite lacking key factors usually theorized to promote upward mobility. Given not only that the average NYCOMP parent had seven years of education but also that NYCOMP parental and adult child-years of education did not correlate significantly, other mechanisms identified, such as keeping the immigrant bargain and embracing Mexican mobility masculinity, better explain more of their empirical story.[40]

This book explains the dramatic mobility of Mexicans in New York City using structural inequality and exclusion; institutional and programmatic contexts; and group-level, family-level, and individual strategies, practices, and processes. Some may see the focus on individual practices as supporting the "moral failure" argument that, if, for example, youth just did their homework or accepted mentoring, they would do better as adults. While these practices certainly help mobility, such an assertion misses the book's larger points.

My analysis shows the structural and institutional causes of poverty or stymied mobility—especially lack of legal status—and brings different values to the discussion of policymaking. Rather than assign individual blame and allot punishment, the book seeks to identify how we can promote better lives for America's young people, including undocumented Americans. Others may criticize the book for analyzing the relationship of individual or family practices to adult outcomes rather than focusing only on the structural exclusion that seems to overdetermine outcomes in other studies. But I also focus on individual and family strategies and practices because these findings can help us design policies and support practices that could promote mobility for more American families, including immigrant families. Having more mentoring programs or teaching planfulness will not fix structural exclusion, but taking such steps could help many young Americans and their current or future families to thrive.

The Emerging Mexican Culture of Mobility

This book has documented an emerging Mexican culture of mobility in New York City. The "minority culture of mobility" concept coined by Neckerman, Lee, and Carter in 1999 described the cultural tools created by already middle-class African Americans to navigate relationships with Whites in public spaces and with their poorer African American relations.[41] Agius Vallejo significantly expands the concept's reach by analyzing how established and newly middle-class Mexican Americans navigate that status and by identifying some mechanisms that moved them into the middle class. Her conclusions coincide broadly with my own. Agius Vallejo argues that educational tracking, coethnic or White middle-class mentors, "giving back" to their families (part of the immigrant bargain, in my framing), ethnic professional associations, and parents with legal status promoted their mobility into the middle class, and helped them manage their relationships with Whites in middle-class spaces and with poorer coethnics.[42] Similarly, Vivian Louie describes how institutional support and mentors promote mobility among Colombian and Dominican youth.[43]

This book further develops the minority culture of mobility concept in three ways. First, it describes the *emergence* of a Mexican culture of mobility among NYCOMP families, whose average of seven years of parental education would have predicted against dramatic upward mobility. These families thus presented a strategic case, because prior research on minority cultures of mobility analyzed people already in the middle class. Second, the book develops the minority culture of mobility concept by showing how and how much other mechanisms promoted or correlated with intergenerational mobility over many years for our ethnographically large data set of ninety-six study participants and their families. Finally, by situating these practices and policies within New York City's and New York State's pro-mobility and immigrant-friendly institutional and social contexts, the book demonstrates how a different conjunctural ethnicity for Mexicans can be supported. Specific practices that promoted mobility were not "Mexican," but they came to be seen as Mexican over time as Mexicans told each other that this was "how we do this"—for example, "We Mexicans go to college." Although this culture of mobility promotes mobility, it is not a condition that can insulate against downward mobility the way wealthy families' glass floors keep their less academically successful children in high-income adult lives.

The sociologist Ann Swidler's notion of a culture as a set of tools for addressing issues facing a group helps us identify mechanisms that promoted mobility among NYCOMP families.[44] U.S. citizen NYCOMP participants and their families who kept or sought to keep the immigrant bargain did better in the long run than their undocumented peers who also kept or tried to keep the immigrant bargain. These "all-documented" families benefited from intrafamily learning and higher incomes as their older children became early adults and started working. Similarly, youth who sought out better schools (and used counterfactual thinking to pick them) and who picked friends and types of friends who they thought would help them do well in school, did better in school and experienced greater adult mobility. Given the high drop-out rates for Mexican teen migrants in the late 1990s and early 2000s, many academically successful Mexican youth picked Black friends from their academically stronger classes and were more likely to become adult College Graduates or High Fliers. Similarly, boys enacting Mexican mobility masculinity as teens, and especially as early adults, did better as adults than those enacting gang masculinity.

These practices and tools do not reflect "Mexican" culture but rather describe how these Mexican families successfully navigated the structural, institutional, and social contexts that their youth encountered. However, families who kept the immigrant bargain understood practices such as enrolling their children in after-school programs as embodying Mexican immigrant culture and its keel of *ganas* (desire), or being "hungry" to succeed. Similarly, the meaning of being Mexican varied over time and across the different contexts into which upwardly and downwardly mobile NYCOMPers sequentially moved from their teen years into established adulthood. The upwardly mobile were more likely to move into contexts where being Mexican was an ethnicity that did not affect their mobility or a positive status that they believed helped their careers. Downwardly or less mobile NYCOMPers were more likely to work in places where being Mexican was a negative status that signaled illegality and exploitability, even for U.S. citizen NYCOMPers in the same workplaces. This study contributes to our understanding of how specific practices come to be understood as having ethnic cultural meanings in their context, which can change as individuals move through a series of contexts and their life course.

The elements of a Mexican culture of mobility have strengthened in New York as the contexts or conjunctures for such practices have changed. First, demographic change has changed the meaning of being Mexican in school. The ratio of Mexican teen migrants to U.S.-born teens in New York City has changed from nearly three times more foreign-born Mexican teens in the late 1990s to nearly ten times more U.S.-born Mexican teens around 2020. This demographic change created a social context in which Mexican academic performance is not so linked to Mexican teen migrants' hard school experiences and high rates of dropout, pushout, and never-dropped-in, but rather to the much higher academic achievement of U.S.-born teens and early adults. Similarly, Mexican gangs do not feature as prominently in the stories that second-generation youth told us in 2020s compared to the late 1990s and early 2000s.

Second, there is now greater knowledge and more community social capital in the Mexican community in New York about the educational system and other systems that promote mobility. The extensive sharing of information among NYCOMP families about how to navigate the educational system and the commitment to college as a way of keeping the immigrant family bargain have propelled college attendance and overall mobility. Moreover, the glaring absence of after-school and other institutions supporting Mexican youth academic achievement in the late 1990s and early 2000s contrasts sharply with the increase in the number and capacity of Mexican-led and Mexican-serving non-profit organizations that promote educational achievement and other forms of advancement (including one on whose board I served for two decades).[45] More non-Mexican after-school organizations have been reaching out to the Mexican community in the last decade as well.

Moreover, CUNY, a key institution driving mobility for those from the bottom fifth of income as teens into the top fifth as adults, has become a main institutional support for U.S.-born Mexicans in New York City. Indeed, while slightly more Mexican seventeen- to twenty-four-year-olds were in public than private colleges in 2000 (1,372 to 1,184, respectively; 53.7 percent versus 46.3 percent), twice as many attended public colleges in 2010 (4,878 in public college versus 2,230 in private colleges; 68.6 percent versus 31.4 percent), and 5.6 times as many in 2021 (16,730 in public colleges [84.3 percent] versus 2,880 in private colleges [14.7 percent]).[46] I believe most of these public college students are CUNY students. In addition, the CUNY Mexican Studies Institute, with financial support from organizations like APEM and from the Mexican government, has awarded hundreds of scholarships to Mexican students—including career-building internships, thus offering them a key American middle-class mechanism promoting mobility.

Third, and consistent with Jody Agius Vallejo's and Vivian Louie's research, Mexican youth and their families continue to use New York's public schools to promote mobility by enrolling in honors programs and attending academically stronger schools, where cross-ethnic mentors can help them.[47] While the few elite New York high schools still mostly educate Asian and White students, many younger siblings in this study were guided by upwardly mobile older siblings or caring teachers into strong middle and high schools and then into college, as reflected in the increasing percentage of Mexican youth attending and graduating from college. NYCOMPers also benefited from nonfamily adult mentoring: 47 percent had mentors, who were Mexican, non-Mexican Latino/a/e, White, and Black. Going forward, the number of U.S.-born Mexican college graduates in professional jobs who can mentor the younger generation should only increase.

Fourth, the meaning of undocumented status has changed, and more so over time in New York State and New York City. This study began before the Dreamer movement was established; at that time, undocumented status was mostly experienced as an individual problem. Today the Dreamer movement has successfully reframed undocumented status as an indication of America's broken immigration system, and it has portrayed long-term undocumented youth as worthy pursuers of the American dream. New York City and New York State have given this changed understanding structural and institutional expression. While the federal government continues to mostly define these undocumented Americans by their deportability, New York City and New York State have increasingly included them in institutions that define them as full members of our community—as "us"—and given them benefits, like college scholarships, funded with state tax dollars, into which these undocumented Americans also pay. Such inclusion can only help promote individual and family mobility.

The minority culture of mobility theory posits that already middle-class Black families developed cultural tools to achieve such mobility despite racially discriminatory institutions and contexts.[48] Agius Vallejo argues that middle-class Mexican Americans from a working-class background are more likely to see themselves, and to be seen by others, as minorities, while those from a middle-class background who remain in the middle class are likely to see themselves and to be seen as "closer to Whites." Although no study participants in this book started in the American middle class (as did some of Agius Vallejo's participants, all of whom were middle-class during her study), most of those who became middle-class did not see themselves as "White," even after moving to the suburbs and living amid many White neighbors. They more often saw themselves as Latino/a/e or Hispanic, or they felt an affinity with Black Americans. This difference reflects the different contexts of our studies: Agius Vallejo's participants lived in mostly Brown-White worlds in Southern California, where race and ethnicity tracked, while my participants lived as children in a mostly Black-Brown world with ethnic hyperdiversity, then encountered more Whites and Asians when they entered college or the workplace as teens and young adults.

Most NYCOMP participants did not feel that their upward mobility separated them from the Black and Brown people with whom they grew up. Indeed, a theoretically key minority of participants became middle-class without *any* substantive relationships with White people: they went from New York's public schools and colleges into middle-class jobs where they interacted almost exclusively with Black and Brown people. Others moved into more integrated neighborhoods or suburbs with more (but not a majority of) White people. NYCOMPers who lived in the small Ticuanense enclaves emerging in New York suburbs got along well with their White neighbors, but also with their Asian, Indian, non-Mexican Latino/a/e, and Italian neighbors.

The differences between Agius Vallejo's upwardly mobile participants and mine were driven partly by differing contexts. Although New York is profoundly segregated by race, with population concentrations in "Black," "Hispanic," and "White" neighborhoods, no ethnic group is a majority in most New York City neighborhoods, and especially not Mexicans. This commonplace hyperdiversity has increased in recent years. Returning again to the example of a "Mexican" neighborhood like Sunset Park/Windsor Terrace in Brooklyn, in 2017–2018, at 45 percent of the Hispanic population, Mexicans had become the largest group among Hispanics (next were Puerto Ricans at 25 percent), but they were still a minority in overall population: foreign-born Mexicans made up 26 percent of the neighborhood's population, compared to 42 percent for foreign-born Chinese.[49] This hyperdiverse context contrasts with the descriptions of mostly Brown and White social worlds by participants in Agius Vallejo's and the sociologist Cynthia Duarte's research.[50] But many places in America seem likely to become increasingly diverse as the Black, Asian, and Hispanic populations grow and become more upwardly mobile. Moreover, America's overall demographic profile is likely to become more mixed as many cities, suburbs, and rural areas become more diverse and many White areas become more segregated, especially in the growing number of states that have become migration destinations over the last thirty years.[51] With such demographic change, the mobility-promoting dynamics described in this book should become more common.

I call this a Mexican culture of mobility because elements of it are organized or experienced as ethnic Mexican practices and programs. But these elements do not describe all Mexicans and are not unique to Mexicans. Mexican and Chinese after-school programs do much the same work, from helping with homework and test prep to guiding families in applying to high school or college. Similarly, Chinese and Mexican (as well as White, Black, and other) families in New York City—including my family—have sought to identify and get into better public schools in the city, get their teen or early adult children into career-building internships, and find good mentoring. Although Chinese (and wealthier White and Black) communities have built a great deal more capacity to do such things, Mexicans in New York have been upwardly mobile in many of the same ways.[52] These differences in mobility-promoting community capacity stem in large part from the impact of relatively wealthier Chinese immigrants, who gain honor from their established practice of contributing to Chinese educational and other institutions that support their less-affluent compatriots. By contrast, wealthy Mexican immigrants are mostly disengaged from their less-well-off compatriots.[53]

I do not argue here that the mechanisms and conditions promoting the mobility of participants in this study and in New York City do so inexorably. Indeed, this research finds that, (1) contrary to most prior work and public discourse, U.S.-born Mexicans in New York experience strong intergenerational mobility, but (2) legal status derails mobility for undocumented Americans, as demonstrated by the rerailed mobility of Category Changers and DACA recipients. These findings offer reason for both optimism and grim exasperation. The optimism stems from this study's documentation of strong intergenerational mobility for a group whose starting conditions would not have predicted it. The American dream is not only still alive but thriving in the Mexican community in New York. But grim exasperation is a fair response to watching over the twenty-plus years of this study as hardworking undocumented Americans had their lives derailed by their lack of legal status, and to knowing that they still have no way to gain such status.

We Could Make Things Better: Doable Fixes to Promote Mobility and Improve Well-being

As this book documents, undocumented youth and their families engaged in the same mobility-promoting practices as their counterparts with legal status, but did not enjoy the same mobility. The structural change of legalization is the main proper fix to that problem. In other respects, however, my recommendations partly diverge from those of the academics who correctly diagnose the underlying structural issues causing inequality but argue that only major structural change can help.

This book also gives us a glimpse of what *is* working, even without structural change, to promote mobility for the U.S.-born second generation. Intergenerational mobility within these Mexican immigrant families was impressive and occurred via mechanisms consistent with America's story of itself as a place where hard work is rewarded with a better life for oneself and one's children. Families and individuals who kept the immigrant family bargain experienced more long-term mobility, and the incomes and educational levels of their adult children were dramatically higher. Teens who listened to their parents by doing their homework, not cutting class, picking good friends, and avoiding gangs did better as adults than those who did not make these choices. Teens who were more planful and who counterfactually assessed decisions for their likely future consequences did better than their less planful peers. And second-chance mechanisms helped U.S. citizen participants who had made mistakes recover and go on to live better adult lives. Good mentoring also helped U.S. citizen participants, especially those facing hard home conditions.

These findings suggest some concrete ways to promote more mobility, whether through changes in law or better immigrant integration policies. Our current immigration policies control who gets in, but then leave them on their own to integrate successfully into American society. This laissez-faire approach is bad for America because it harms immigrant families and fails to promote upwardly mobile integration that would help create what the urban planner Dowell Myers calls a new intergenerational bargain between immigrants and baby boomers and other Americans.[54] The postwar American economic boom was driven by policies that could be adapted to our own era to promote the common good. College attendance and later incomes jumped in the decades following World War II, driven by the millions of veterans who, after going to college on the GI Bill, could then buy houses with subsidized mortgages, while relying on strong federal spending on public schools and infrastructure. (I recognize that racial discrimination affected which groups enjoyed or were excluded from these benefits.) Americans should want immigrant families to succeed because the country's future increasingly depends on them doing so. As boomers and the following generations retire and age, they will need families with good incomes to buy the houses they want to sell as well as professionals to take care of them in their dotage. Self-interest is not a noble motivation, but it is a valid one. The Covid-19 pandemic highlighted the urgent need to craft a stronger intergenerational bargain that more tightly knits together older American families with younger American families, including immigrants, into a shared and hopefully better common future.

This book shows the longer-term benefits of second-chance and mentoring programs. Second-chance programs gave all U.S. citizen teens in this study the chance to change and move on from their serious or stupid youthful mistakes into productive adult lives. This rehabilitative policy focus evokes an American tradition of seeing wayward youth as needing correction, not unending incarceration. Mentoring, both natural (teachers) and formal (programs), effectively helped many teens and early adults move into better adult lives, especially those facing hard home conditions. Such programs should be expanded. Similarly, being planful helped many study participants think their way through decisions that opened better futures. Planfulness is taught in some successful programs, such as Geoffrey Canada's Harlem Children's Zone and the Washington Heights Expeditionary Learning Academy.[55] Even more teens could be helped if planfulness were taught more widely. Similarly, this book shows that specific intrafamily processes and the immigrant bargain helped teens grow into better adult lives. America could support such intrafamily mechanisms not only by legalizing parents but also by changing the tax code to support these mechanisms— for example, by providing tax breaks for young adults who buy a home with their parents.

To anticipate critiques, I know that creating and funding more mentoring programs, for example, will not fix systemic racial injustice or inequality, but they are still worth doing because they open doors that help young people like NYCOMPers to succeed and create better lives for themselves and their families. It is a false choice to say we must choose between advocating for systemic change or developing programs that provide immediate concrete help. Moreover, evidence suggests that America is changing in ways that could reinforce such mobility-promoting mechanisms. Finance and related industries, for example, increasingly need to recruit non-White professionals to fill vacancies left by retiring White baby boomers.[56] As more American cities become more diverse and populated mostly by people of color, White monopolies on good jobs may decrease, opening up more opportunity for second-generation youth.

None of these recommendations are meant to suggest that racial discrimination and its manifestations are problems of the past, especially given the police violence against so many Black and Brown Americans and the increased activity of White supremacist groups, such as those that seditiously stormed the U.S. Capitol on January 6, 2021. The reinforcement of such views by political leaders is a threat to American democracy. But these larger trends do not negate the real progress that is being made for many in the second and later generations of many groups, including Mexicans in New York City. These contradictory realities not only reflect some of America's challenges but also suggest some ways forward.

America's Epistemic and Moral Crises: What Is Real and What Is Fake? What Is Right and What Is Wrong?

Senator Daniel Patrick Moynihan famously quipped, "You are entitled to your opinion. But you are not entitled to your own facts." Moynihan's point seems quaint in an age when powerful actors use institutions to promote lies and disseminate them to algorithmically targeted voters through omnipresent social media or news platforms. While mainstream media mostly report factual news, many platforms mislead or lie, and misinformation is reproduced at a massive scale in social media. These Orwellian echo chambers pose dangers to societal cohesion and democratic institutions because they create two Americas, which believe in different versions of reality, one of which is unlinked to fact.

The beliefs behind these parallel universes are also driven partly by America's perennial moral arguments and policy narratives about poverty, inequality, threat, and race. Policy narratives are stories that political leaders tell about problems.[57] How they define a problem then justifies what they propose as the right policy to address it. Two linked policy narratives are relevant here. In stark general terms, Republicans believe that poverty results from moral failure: the poor are poor because welfare programs sap their will to work. Republican senator Orrin Hatch stated this position clearly when he responded to Democratic senator Sherrod Brown's question in 2017 about why Republicans were passing huge tax cuts for the wealthiest American corporations and investors when funding for the Children's Health Insurance Program (CHIP) had not been extended. Hatch reportedly responded "with fury," saying that he had "invented" CHIP and that "the reason CHIP's having trouble is we don't have any money anymore."[58] He explained away the apparent contradiction between forgoing revenues by giving the wealthy tax cuts but then lacking the funds for children's health insurance this way:

> I have a rough time wanting to spend billions and billions and trillions [and] trillions of dollars to help people who won't help themselves, won't lift a finger, and expect the federal government to do everything. . . . Unfortunately, the liberal philosophy has created millions of people that way, who believe everything they are or ever hope to be depend[s] on the federal government rather than the opportunities that this great country grants them.[59]

The policy narrative here is clear: public social programs create lazy, undeserving poor people, most of whom are believed to be Black, so cutting social programs and giving money back to hardworking (White) Americans makes sense. But research shows that most poor people do work but are paid badly, and that a disproportionate share of the nearly $2 trillion tax cut passed in 2017 went to large corporations and the wealthy.[60] These facts support a different policy narrative, such as raising the minimum wage so that work will lift people out of poverty, or spending needed funds so that poor children have enough to eat or can go to the doctor when sick.

Dangerous White nationalist narratives are amplified by social media, which algorithmically target people to increase hate, anger, and social division and promote "replacement theory" (the belief that Jews and immigrants seek to replace White Americans). The sociologists Jessica Dawson and Dana Weinberg argue that the January 6, 2021, attacks can be partly explained by algorithmic targeting, which has amplified and supported the redefinition of patriotism from defending America against foreign enemies to defending America against Democrats, the Justice

Department, and the FBI.[61] I think that the protesters chanting, "Protect your Constitution," while violently attacking the Capitol and obstructing Congress from performing its constitutional duties believed they were doing the right thing.

These parallel epistemic realities help explain the contradiction between Americans' long-term strong support for opening a road to legal status and citizenship for Dreamers—some 74 percent supported this measure in a 2020 poll—and the perpetual deadlock that prevents the passage of such reform in Congress.[62] Although most Americans see the unfairness of keeping children who grew up in the United States in undocumented status forever and support legalizing them, many Americans, and especially Republican primary voters, believe that "illegal" immigrants are a threat to their America and their American way of life, and have taken their jobs, drained American coffers, and made America more dangerous.

One of the clearest analyses of why and how some Americans blame immigrants for their troubles comes from the sociologist Arlie Hochschild, who came to know people in a Louisiana parish (county) that had experienced job loss and grave illness due to environmental pollution by the petrochemicals industry after environmental regulations were ended, defanged, or underfunded.[63] Hochschild's participants were bitter that after working so hard for so many years, they still did not have stable jobs, could not buy houses, and could not send their children to college. They could not even safely eat the fish they pulled from the bayous. Hochschild distilled their complaints into a central metaphor: we are all standing in line, waiting to achieve the American dream, but the line does not move because the federal government keeps letting undeserving women and Black people and illegal immigrants cut into the line ahead of us. They are getting all the things we worked so hard for, paid for with our tax dollars. One of her participants said: "I live in your metaphor."

How do we address these parallel epistemic universes and the policies they promote? I can only make a few suggestions here. The first place to start would be to follow Dawson's and Weinberg's recommendations that the algorithms used by social media platforms should be open to public scrutiny and require review by a panel of experts. Given how profoundly they have affected all dimensions of American life—and political life worldwide—this proposal seems appropriate. Social media companies should also be prohibited from capturing data on or targeting active-duty military, minors, or other specified vulnerable groups or groups central to national security and public safety.

We should try to fix America's pressing problems through universal approaches (such as Social Security) where possible. Family-strengthening changes to the tax code, investments in public health and infrastructure, and mentoring programs could all have broad support. A universal approach is less intuitively possible with immigration, however, because the fundamental story that opponents of immigration tell—and that underpins Hochschild's metaphor—is that immigrants are *them*, and they are hurting *us*, the "real" Americans. I recommend several alternative approaches.

First, advocates for legalizing America's 11 million undocumented people and helping over 5 million children with undocumented parents should continue with the policy narrative that successfully anchored the Dreamer movement: Dreamers are Americans who want the same things that other American children want, and they only need a fair chance to go to college and work legally. This narrative could be reinforced by the argument long made by the religious left: that like all Americans and all people, immigrants are, in the words of former president Obama, "children of God."

Second, I think the "Undocumented and Unafraid" campaign of immigrant youth has worked. Its resonance with the successful campaigns for gay rights and marriage equality points to perhaps another road to increased political leverage. If everyone knows someone who is undocumented, there may be less resistance to legalization, which would be understood as helping a friend. There are overlaps between immigration and universalistic approaches; for example, pro-family policies would help all families, including immigrant families, and could be promoted by describing the harms to all families of current policies. The anti-family orientation of current American immigrant policies must go.

Finally, I think advocates for legalizing undocumented Americans should organize politically and fight in other peaceful ways. Organizing means building alliances, getting out the vote, and engaging in other shoe-leather activities, which, as recent elections have shown, can have big impacts. I also think that using the courts to support policies and programs that protect Dreamers (such as DACA) is a smart strategy.

Policy Proposals

With this sobering assessment of the hard road that any policy changes will face, I offer this book's main policy proposal: America must create paths to legalization and citizenship for most of its 11 million undocumented persons, especially those who came as children and grew up as undocumented Americans. There are (at least) five reasons for doing so.

First, legalizing undocumented Americans would bring America's actions more into line with its image of itself as a just nation that rewards hard work and values its children. Policies that exclude undocumented Americans, especially parents, have downstream spillover effects that harm their U.S. citizen children and other family members. As the National Academies of Sciences, Engineering, and Medicine's Committee on Population reported in 2015:

> Policies designed to block the integration of undocumented immigrants or individuals with a temporary status can have the unintended effect of halting or hindering the integration of U.S. citizens and lawful permanent residents in mixed status families. Laws are often designed to apply to individuals, but their effects ripple through households, families, and communities, with measurable long-term, negative impacts on children who are lawful U.S. citizens.[64]

America's long-standing anti-legalization policies have had harsh and long-term impacts on the health, well-being, and even brain development of U.S. citizen children and other relatives in mixed-status families. Ignoring these harms, despite so much evidence that they exist, is inconsistent with America's best values.

Second, and relatedly, America believes itself to be a nation that values family and rewards hard work. But this book and other research show that long-term undocumented status disrupts the intrafamily processes that promote upward mobility in families where everyone has legal status. Chapter 2 described the benefits for all-documented families as the older children became young adults and could help their younger siblings in school and earn more than their parents. In contrast, the older siblings in undocumented families, derailed into work, were more likely to drop out of school and were less likely to help their younger siblings in school; nor could their earnings augment the family budget enough to help move their family out of poverty.

America believes itself to be a country that cherishes family, but its policy of maintaining a large population of long-term undocumented Americans undermines the intrafamily bargain by which parents sacrifice for their children and children redeem that sacrifice by finishing school, working hard, and helping their families, including their younger siblings. Long-term undocumented status prevents parents from giving their kids the ability to launch because they cannot give them legal status, so in early adulthood their children cannot earn more money and help their families as much as their educated peers. In its hostility to these families, U.S. immigration policy is anti-family and un-American.

Third, America's policy of maintaining a huge population of long-term, perhaps permanently, undocumented persons creates an insidious societal division of a kind that the Fourteenth and Fifteenth Amendments sought to end. The disastrous consequences of America's prior experiment in maintaining two or more categories of person—citizen and slave—should make us recoil at the state of our country today: within our borders, a country-sized population lives without the protections of fundamental human and constitutional rights. Although undocumented persons are, in theory, protected equally by American law, in practice their rights are easy to trample because the central fact of their existence in American society is their deportability.[65] In their minds, and the minds of those who exploit them, the same police to whom they would appeal for help are the ones who could deliver them to ICE for deportation. The lack of knowledge among many immigrants, institutional agents (police, teachers, health workers, and so on), and the general public that immigrants have rights makes it easier to exploit their vulnerability. Hence, factory workers or day laborers are often not paid, despite having a right to be paid for their work, because bad employers know that they are unlikely to take legal action.[66] Corrupt police officers give undocumented immigrants extra tickets—for example, for not wearing a seat belt when they are in fact wearing one—because they know that immigrants, fearing deportation, will pay the tickets, without complaint.[67]

The extreme vulnerability of undocumented immigrants and their families stems not only from their exploitation by bad actors but also from the ontological fact of their illegality as a master status. Let's revisit the case of Juana, who was told by the police officer who pulled her over that he did so because "you're Mexican." He gambled that she didn't have a driver's license and would pay the fine, fearing deportation, rather than contest the ticket as unjust. Juana's ability to resist this corrupt behavior was blocked by her deportability and her fear. In another case, Syra and her husband, who did not have a car, did not call an ambulance in two medical emergencies—she had a miscarriage late at night and was bleeding heavily, and another time their U.S. citizen son was in respiratory distress—because they feared that the police (who always come with an ambulance, they told me) would ask about their legal status and deport them. They feared that their children would be put in foster care, and that they might never see them again. America should not be a country where parents are afraid to ask for help in medical emergencies.

Fourth, maintaining a large population of undocumented Americans is not only unjust but economically stupid for America in the long run. A bitter irony in the current political moment is that undocumented persons subsidize our Social Security system.[68] About one-third of those identifying as Tea Party members—who demonized undocumented immigrants as a key cause of America's problems during the Obama administration—were retired and drawing Social Security benefits. Yet our Social Security system is propped up by undocumented immigrants, who pay into the system but cannot draw benefits from it. Indeed, Michael Goss, the Social Security Administration's chief actuary, finds that some 8 percent of the contributions to the Social Security Earnings Suspense Fund, which helps keep the system solvent, come from undocumented workers. In 2010, this contribution amounted to $12 billion. Goss also found that legalizing immigrants would make Social Security more solvent in the long term.[69] Maintaining immigrants' undocumented status over the long term makes little tax sense, because doing so depresses school attainment and lifetime earnings, shrinking tax revenues and perhaps overall economic output.[70] Similarly, Trump voters support the denial of public benefits to immigrants and their children, even children born in the United States, but rely themselves on those benefits more, on average, than do Democratic voters.[71]

Finally, legalizing long-term undocumented Americans is a just action that would improve our democracy. America has a crisis of low voter turnout, especially among Hispanics and younger Americans. Turnout in 2018 among voters over age sixty-five was about 30 percent higher than among eighteen- to twenty-four-year-olds, and White voters turned out at 17 percent higher rates than Hispanics (though this gap is narrowing), according to the U.S. Census Bureau and Michael McDonald's United States Election Project.[72] There is a huge generation gap in participation between baby boomers and younger groups; Gen Xers and millennials seem to lack faith in American institutions and the central ideas they embody.[73] Although legalizing long-term undocumented people alone will not fix problems like low voter turnout and lack of trust in U.S. institutions, it will remove a fundamental and systemic fault line running through American society. Having a country-sized population of people and their children who cannot vote or fully participate in civic and political life can only harm American democracy. Fixing this crisis is urgent because most of these 11 million undocumented persons have or will have U.S.-born children who grow up experiencing America as a place that denies simple human dignity to their parents.

Guide to Online Appendixes

T HIS APPENDIX differs from most in being a guide to the book's online appendixes (https://www.russellsage.org/publications /dreams-achieved-and-denied) that reflects the larger project's dual goals. The book's primary goal is to explain why and how so many children of Mexican immigrants in this study became upwardly mobile while others did not. The book's secondary goal is to report on a nearly book-length epistemic and methodological exercise in combining case-oriented and net-effects methods within this long-term ethnographic project. Banishing most such analysis to online appendixes keeps the book to a readable length. The Russell Sage Foundation is generously making those appendixes available as free downloads. Interested readers, especially graduate students, can think of the online appendixes as a free extra book. I hope readers find these contributions interesting, including the "code all cases and all processes" approach, the analysis of the epistemology of accounts in ethnography and ethnographic interviewing, and the concrete applications of set theoretical and statistical methods in a long-term ethnographic project.

This book has three types of appendixes. The first is a set of overall strategy, epistemology, and methods appendixes (appendixes A to J) that describe the thinking underpinning the project and the concrete steps we took to combine case-oriented and net-effects (statistical) approaches and methods, including how we developed our ethnographic case narratives and how we created databases for statistical and set theoretical analysis.

The second and third types are statistical and set theoretical chapter appendixes that analyze the same causal processes posited in each chapter's narrative case analysis, but operationalized as variables for statistical analysis and as conditions for set theoretical analysis. For example, the statistical appendix for chapter 4 assesses how much having a mentor or having better mentors correlates with adult outcomes, controlling for hard life conditions (such as having an undocumented parent) that the case narratives showed made the mentoring more important for later adult mobility. The appendix fully defines the variables, relates the

https://doi.org/10.7758/drwz9626.1588

hypotheses, and progresses from descriptive statistics (cross tabs) to inferential statistics (regression with control variables), estimating correlations between a key independent variable (or treatment—in chapter 4, mentors) and dependent variable (or outcome, that is, income or education). Similarly, chapter 4's set theoretical appendix does qualitative comparative analysis (usually described as "QCA" using "truth table" and "prime implicant" analyses) for conditions (social processes) examined in the chapter's case narratives by measuring the overlap between cases with certain sets of conditions and cases with specific outcomes (here, being College Graduates or High Fliers). For clarity, the NYCOMPers whose cases are developed in the book chapter are named in the QCA truth tables, and their stories are told using the QCA results.

Taken together, these appendixes make the case for the legitimacy of (and offer a practical guide for) several new or adapted ways of combining statistical and case-oriented data-gathering methods and data-analyzing techniques within long-term, case-oriented ethnographic research.

I wrote the manuscript for this more than twenty-year-long project, as well as all related proposals and articles. I conducted about one-third of the initial interviews and two-thirds of the time 2 and time 3 interviews and case narratives. I did all the initial statistical runs, and I rethought and recoded the variables after writing the case narratives, drawing on deeper understandings that emerged through writing and reflecting on results from earlier statistical runs. I benefited greatly from (now Dr.) Dirk Witteveen's epistemic capacity and concrete help in rerunning and rethinking these statistics to their final versions presented here. Similarly, while I introduced set theoretical analysis to my research team, I also greatly appreciated (now Dr.) Nico Legewie's collaborative work in designing the first longitudinal multidimensional analytical protocol (LMAP) database, taking the lead in learning the technique, and running our first QCA analyses.[1] After Nico had moved on and could no longer work on the project, I realized that the initial design and the thinking behind it could not do the analytical work we were asking it to do, because they did not sufficiently channel the case-oriented theorizing in each specific chapter. To fix this problem, I created a new QCA dataset, by creating and calibrating new conditions corresponding very closely to the processes analyzed in each chapter, and by recalibrating some extant conditions from the first QCA database. I then reran the set theoretical analyses, which are presented in those appendixes.

Although I wrote all these appendixes myself, I list former students and research assistants as coauthors of specific appendixes to recognize their contributions in thinking through, adapting, and applying these techniques. In particular, I note that the insights of (now Dr.) Sara

Guerrero-Mustafa (formerly Guerrero-Rippberger) into the cases and our conversations about them were essential in creating the variable-oriented database (VODB), which captures as ethnographic variables the social realities that she and I understood from our interviews and relationships with study participants over many years. Her insightful case narratives also helped develop the book's insights. Although the book mostly uses cases I developed, Sara's insights and cases have informed my thinking. Similarly, the statistical analysis in this book would not have been possible without the VODB Excel architecture built by (now Dr.) Guillermo Yrizar Barbosa that enabled it. Blanca Ibanez supported this project and others for several well-organized years with keen intelligence and valued friendship. Thank you, Guille, Blanca, and Sara, as well as Dr. Stephen Ruszczyk, Dr. Nico Legewie, and others.

Appendix A: Introduction: The Intellectual Joys of Being Wrong, and How Following the Data for Many Years Helped Me Get Things Right

Appendix A offers a brief history of the project, describing how study participants' better-than-expected (by me and by them) life trajectories required that I rethink my initial hypotheses—which relied on segmented assimilation theory and my time 1 interviews—that girls would be ethnicized into better futures, while boys would be racialized into worse ones. When this did not happen, I iteratively revised both the questions I asked participants and my theorizing. I also developed the four overall outcome categories—Stuck Muddlers, Shallow Slopers, College Graduates, and High Fliers, described in detail in appendix A— to better explain unanticipated mobility. Iteratively revising the research questions, data gathering, and theoretical explanation is part of the emergent theme approach in this project. To further interrogate the initial question, I briefly discuss why gender did not seem to have the expected big impacts on adult income and educational levels, and why discrimination did not feature as prominently in the case narratives as I had anticipated.

Appendix A also describes the sources of analytical leverage stemming from the long-term nature of this project and its combination of methods. In short, following some cases for nearly two decades and getting data on the history of everyone in each family enabled this project to gain insight into how different American immigration policies affected the adult mobility of the children of Mexican immigrants in New York. The ability to analyze intergenerational mobility through original case data is uncommon and, in my view, cool. This appendix also presents selected findings that reinforce the larger argument, such as that ever having had undocumented parents has no impact on one's adult outcomes, because nearly all study participants' parents had been undocumented at some point. It was only parents and adult children who remained undocumented over the long run whose adult mobility was harmed.

Appendix B: Pragmatically Combining Net-Effects and Case-Oriented Approaches in Long-Term Ethnographic Research: The Emergent Theme Approach

Appendix B describes the pragmatic philosophy underpinning this long-term ethnographic research project. It first compares the epistemology as well as the strengths and weaknesses of statistical or net-effects versus case-oriented research. It describes the dangers, first, of believing in what the sociologist Andrew Abbott calls general linear reality (GLR)—the notion that social actors behave like variables and hence regression fully captures and describes social reality—and second, the limits of much case-oriented ethnography that theorizes off the most interesting cases but cannot usually assess how common a social process is or how related it is to later outcomes within the same data set.[2] The appendix differentiates between the research designs required for statistical inference rather than logical inference, and it suggests biology rather than physics as the better analogue for thinking about social science. It then makes the case for the analytical legitimacy of using statistical methods within a nonrandom, case-oriented data set picked to enable us to observe theoretically significant variation and then follow the cases over many years and get adult outcome data.[3] It analyzes how this case-oriented approach differs from the typical ways of combining large surveys and interviewing in which a "nested" subsample of interviews are done to get data on what participants think is happening then.

Appendix C: Methods of Analysis and Commensuration in a Long-Term Ethnographic Project

Appendix C describes concretely how I sought to use the leverage, and address the limitations, of statistical or net-effects and case-oriented approaches by adopting, adapting, or creating methods to include all NYCOMP cases in the analysis. My epistemic and methodological goals were to develop ways to trace the whole arc of each case, including processes within cases, and to compare cases and assess patterns in the whole data set. I use biographical and comparative narrative case analysis to anchor each chapter, but I also adapt or develop new techniques for quantitative and set-theoretical analyses. We created three linked databases to use the two kinds of case-oriented analysis and methods (narrative case analysis and set theoretical analysis) and one kind of net-effects (statistical) analysis and methods. We first created the case narrative database—composed of ninety-six full biographical case narratives, most between eight and twenty single-spaced pages long—for use in our biographical and comparative narrative case analysis. Next, we created the variable-oriented database to use the "code all cases and all processes" approach. This approach codes for the "usual suspect" variables, such as income, and for "ethnographic" variables, such as whether a study participant responded to step-ups in high school by looking back or looking down. Finally, we developed two databases for set theoretical analysis using qualitative comparative analysis, a quantitative but case-oriented method to gauge the overlap of sets of conditions and outcomes. I refer to these data sets together as the New York Children of Migrants Project, or NYCOMP.

Appendix D: Long-Term Narrative Case Development

Appendix D describes the concrete steps and methods we used in doing long-term case development for all ninety-six cases over two decades. We developed the cases as internally coherent biographies that enabled us to identify social processes to compare across cases. Appendix D details how we wrote case narratives and did other work at time 1 and how we further developed these cases in later interviews and fieldwork through times 2 and 3.

Appendix E: Ethnographic Thickness and Thinness in Long-Term Research

Appendix E uses a framework of embeddedness and intimacy to discuss natural variation in the often changing relationships between ethnographers and different informants over time. Thicker cases and closer relationships can yield more insights, though some thinner relationships offer special insights, as can happen in an expert-to-expert interview. This appendix also analyzes examples of ethnographic fraying in this long-term research, including the ending of a key long-term research relationship in the project.

Appendix F: Doing Biographical and Comparative Case Analysis

Appendix F is a how-to appendix that describes how we wrote the biographical case narratives and used them in biographical and comparative case analysis so we could fully describe each case while also putting all cases into the analysis. The epistemic goal is to compare cases not as variables but as cases, putting as many of their functional elements as possible into play in the comparison without being overwhelmed by complexity.

Appendix G: Set Theoretical Analysis: Comparative Qualitative Analysis and the Longitudinal Multidimensional Analytical Protocol

Appendix G describes how we did another kind of case-oriented analysis: qualitative comparative analysis.[4] QCA is a set theoretical analysis that first identifies discrete elements in different types of cases and outcomes and then does a numerical Venn diagram analysis to measure the overlap between a set of cases showing a specific set of conditions, and the set of cases showing specific outcomes—the typical outcome here being College Graduates or High Fliers (versus Shallow Slopers and Stuck Muddlers).

This approach is often used in Europe and mostly ignored or misunderstood in the United States. It can address a weakness in ethnography, its case-oriented cousin, by putting all cases into play in analysis, as well as the weaknesses in statistical analysis by assessing overlap between cases that fit combinations or sets of conditions and cases showing a specific outcome. As such, it is more agile than statistics in analyzing "equifinality"—the concept that several causal pathways can lead to the same outcome—especially in small-N studies like this one. QCA enables us to discern the overlap of cases showing the outcome of interest (being a College Graduate or a High Flier) and its negation (being a Stuck Muddler or a Shallow Sloper). There are often more sets of conditions overlapping lower- than high-outcome sets of cases, which I describe as being able to "unstir the milk in the coffee." When used with deep case knowledge and data, QCA can help us analyze how various pathways lead to higher or lower outcomes. My hope is that its usage here will encourage broader adoption. To make the somewhat oblique logic of this method more accessible, the chapter appendixes include tables with the names of the cases analyzed in the chapter.

Appendix H: The "Code All Cases and All Processes" Approach: Net-Effects Data Management, Organizing and Coding Techniques, and the Variable-Oriented Database

Appendix H describes an approach I hope will become more widely adopted: the "code all cases and all processes" approach.[5] This approach follows a case-oriented ethnographic logic in identifying the key processes to code, but codes and analyzes them as variables for statistical analysis. Because it codes "usual suspect" variables, such as adult income, as well as social processes, such as the immigrant bargain, I can analyze, for example, how much keeping the immigrant bargain correlated with adult income or with the overall outcome category. This approach overcomes a limit of ethnographic analysis, which usually analyzes the most interesting cases, while also overcoming a weakness in statistical analysis: having only data on variables or questions that were asked because they were known to the researcher before the project was fielded, or because they were part of preexisting data sets.

Appendix I: Ethnography, Interviews, and the Epistemology of Accounts

Appendix I analyzes the epistemology of accounts in interviews set within ethnographic fieldwork research. A great strength of ethnography is that it gives researchers the chance to get around the problem of people not always doing what they say they do, or often not telling researchers about things they want to hide or think unworthy of discussion, by allowing researchers to directly observe what people actually do. I also use interviews in my ethnographic work because we need our participants' understandings of events to make sense of them. Recall Geertz's question regarding how we know whether the "wink" of an informant indicates a wink, a blink, or having something in their eye.[6]

Moreover, we may want to understand social processes and mechanisms that we cannot observe directly—for example, mental processes, such as the counterfactual analyses that higher achievers used in picking their high school—or participants' insights that may only become clear to them retrospectively, such as how their high school choice affected their later opportunities. Every interview is an account offered by the participant and generated dialogically (to varying degrees) with the researcher.[7] The analytical work that such accounts can do varies with the type of relationship the researcher has with the participant, how much of a formed story the participant has, what stage of research the researcher is in, which of several types of interview is being conducted, and who the ethnographer is. The appendix lists seven different types of interviews, including standard guided narrative interviews, account-deepening interviews, and expert-to-expert interviews.

Appendix J: The NYCOMP Data Set as a Sample: Epistemology, Methodology, Representativeness, and Process in Social Science Research

In analyzing the use of the NYCOMP data set for specified purposes but also as a sample, appendix J assesses how representative (or unrepresentative) the data set is and lays out the argument for making logical (not statistical) inferences from the book's findings. The appendix discusses the NYCOMP project's recruitment strategies and practices, which sought to capture theoretically important variation, and the project's high retention rate. It also looks at the theoretical leverage gained by having long-term data for individuals and families; by combining narrative case analysis, set theoretical analysis, and statistical analysis; and by considering larger social facts such as institutional or census data. The appendix proposes an approach to assessing the relative merits of studies based on the representativity to a population, the thickness of the cases, and the relationships with participants.

= Notes =

Chapter 1: Introduction: Dreams Achieved and Denied

1. All personal, neighborhood, organization, and business names are pseudonyms.

2. For more explanation, see Smith 2014. See Jennifer Jones's (2022) insightful analysis of race as a shared status that can include more than one racial group.

3. Jessica Vasquez (2010) offers insightful analysis of variation in processes of racialization and phenotype; see also Murguia and Telles 1996.

4. For impressive long-term ethnographic research, see Black 2009 and Gonzales 2016.

5. Clausen 1991, 1993; Sewell 1992; Smith 2014.

6. McKnight 2015; Reeves 2017. I thank Andrés Besserer Rayas for raising this question.

7. Krugman 2020; see also Chavez 2013; Lewis 1961; Longazel 2013.

8. Chavez 2013; Menjívar and Abrego 2012; see also Hajer and Laws 2008; McBeth and Lybecker 2018.

9. Feagin and Eckberg 1980; Rendón 2019; Telles and Ortiz 2008; see also FitzGerald 2014.

10. Kasinitz et al. 2008.

11. Alba, Jiménez, and Marrow 2014.

12. Portes and Rumbaut 2001; Portes and Zhou 1993.

13. Keister, Agius Vallejo, and Borelli 2015, 1015; see also Agius Vallejo 2012a, 2012b; Agius Vallejo and Keister 2020.

14. Luthra, Waldinger, and Soehl 2018.

15. Jiménez 2009; Jiménez and Fitzgerald 2007.

16. Abrego and Gonzales 2010; Bean, Brown, and Bachmeier 2015; Brabeck, Sibley, and Lykes 2015; Castañeda et al. 2015; Duncan et al. 2020; Friedman and Venkataramani 2021; Gonzales 2016; Hamilton, Patler, and Savinar

2021; Menjívar and Abrego 2012; Menjívar and Kanstroom 2014; Patler, Hamilton, and Savinar 2020; Patler and Pirtle 2018; Patler et al. 2019; Smith et al. 2021; Vaquera et al. 2014; Watson 2014.

17. Smith 2006, 2014.

18. Alba, Jiménez, and Marrow 2014; Jiménez and Horowitz 2013; Lee and Zhou 2015; Smith 2014.

19. Bean, Brown, and Bachmeier 2015; Kasinitz et al. 2008; Lee and Zhou 2015; Portes and Rumbaut 2001; Rendón 2019; Telles and Ortiz 2008.

20.

Table 1.2   Years of Education for U.S.- and Foreign-Born Mexican Men and Women, 1990–2020

	U.S.-Born Mexican Men in New York City				Foreign-Born Mexican Men in New York City			
	1990	2000	2010	2020	1990	2000	2010	2020
Less than high school	28%	25%	14%	11%	66%	65%	56%	47%
High school/GED	18	19	21	22	18	30	30	35
Some college	26	28	28	25	8	7	9	10
College or more	29	29	38	42	8	5	5	8
	U.S.-Born Mexican Women in New York City				Foreign-Born Mexican Women in New York City			
	1990	2000	2010	2020	1990	2000	2010	2020
Less than high school	16	23	12	11	67	67	60	52
High school/GED	23	19	17	18	19	21	26	31
Some college	31	23	26	22	7	6	8	8
College or more	30	33	44	49	8	5	6	8

Source: Ruggles et al. 2023a, 2023b, 2023c, 2023d; U.S. Census Bureau 2000. Analysis by Dr. Mara Getz Sheftel.

21. This study found higher percentages of college graduates for foreign-born participants (both documented and undocumented) than are seen in the census: 18 percent of men and 25 percent of women at time 2.

22. Thank you to Dr. Mara Getz Sheftel for running these census data analyses.

23. Census calculations by Dr. Mara Sheftel; Bergad 2011.

24. Adjusted Wald tests show that a higher estimated percentage of U.S.-born Mexican men had a BA degree or higher compared to U.S.-born Puerto Rican, Black, and Dominican men in the same sample year at a level of $p < 0.05$. Thank you to Dr. Mara Getz Sheftel, who ran these analyses.

25. Adjusted Wald tests show that U.S.-born White and Chinese men had a higher estimated percentage with a BA degree or higher compared to U.S.-born Mexican men in the same sample year at a level of $p < 0.05$. Thank you to Dr. Mara Getz Sheftel.

26. The percentages from figures 1.1 and 1.2 are as follows: Starting in 1990 at 29 percent, U.S.-born Mexican men's rate of college graduation had increased by 2020 to 42 percent, compared to 16 percent for U.S.-born Puerto Rican men, 20 percent for U.S.-born Dominican men, 40 percent for U.S.-born Colombian men, 64 percent for U.S.-born White men, 22 percent for U.S.-born Black men, and 73 percent for U.S.-born Chinese men. Similarly, after starting in 1990 at 30 percent, rates of college graduation for U.S.-born Mexican women by 2020 were 49 percent versus 23 percent for U.S.-born Puerto Rican women, 34 percent for U.S.-born Dominican women, 49 percent for U.S.-born Colombian women, 64 percent for U.S.-born born White women, 29 percent for U.S.-born Black women, and 78 percent for U.S.-born Chinese women.

27. Smith 2006, 2014. Thank you to Professor Andy Beveridge for running this statistic.

28. I thank Professor Andy Beveridge for running the census numbers on the relative numbers of these subgroups in 2000. The statistics on the schooling of Mexican-descent students come from Bergad 2011.

29. Smith 2006, 2014.

30. I say "about" 2008 and 2019 because those years sit in the middle of the five-year American Community Survey (ACS) 5 percent files used in these calculations (2006–2010 ACS and 2017–2021, respectively). The 2000 statistics are from the 2000 Decennial Census. I thank Dr. Andy Beveridge (Emeritus, Queens College, CUNY) and Dr. Susan Weber-Stoger, both of Social Explorer, for running these numbers.

Table 1.3   Number and Ratio of U.S.-Born and Foreign-Born Mexican Youth Ages Thirteen to Nineteen, 2000–2021

Mexican Youth Living in New York City	Total Mexican Youths Living in New York City	U.S.-Born Mexican Youths	Foreign-Born Mexican Youths	Ratio of Foreign-Born to U.S.-Born Youths	Ratio of U.S.-Born to Foreign-Born Youths
2000	20,725	5,491	15,234	2.8	0.36
2006–2010	30,342	20,373	9,969	0.5	2.04
2017–2021	39,290	35,545	3,745	0.1	9.49

Source: U.S. Census Bureau 2000, 2010, 2021. Thank you to Dr. Andy Beveridge and Dr. Susan Weber-Stoger of Social Explorer for running these statistics.

31. Merton 1987, 1.

32. Chetty, Grusky, et al. 2017; Chetty et al. 2014.

33. Chetty, Grusky, et al. 2017.

34. Chetty, Grusky, et al. 2017; Chetty et al. 2014.

35. George and Bennett 2005; Weber 1946, 1949.

36. The four outcome categories were based on four factors at age twenty-eight (time 2): educational level; individual income; occupational prestige, stability, and potential; and individual and family wealth and security. Dr. Dirk Witteveen ran a K-means cluster classification, which tests how the categories we derived from our narrative case analysis fared when subjected to a K-means cluster algorithm. That algorithm forces the cases into groups—here four groups based on four dependent variables: education, income, occupational ranking, and overall wealth group.

   The first two dependent variables are years of education and income at time 2. The third variable, occupational ranking, is based on a nine-category ranking we developed from the universe of jobs held by our participants and from what they and we believed were the pay, conditions, and prospects offered by such jobs: illicit work in the underground economy (0); no job/not working after school completion (1); work in the immigrant economy with little advancement potential—for example, as a garment factory worker (2); work in the immigrant economy in work offering career steps, such as construction (3); a position in the mainstream, lower-rung service and manufacturing economy with few career steps such as low-level retail (4); a solid blue-collar or white-collar job with decent income and benefits, such as delivering mail or working in construction (5); skilled work in the mainstream pink-collar economy offering career steps and benefits, such as an executive assistant position (6); a solidly middle-class semiprofessional or professional position with career steps—for example, police work, military service, or a teaching position (7); a professional job, for example, as a lawyer or accountant (8).

   We believe that this ranking is better than standard sociological occupational prestige rankings because the latter are externally established measures of prestige, whereas ours are empirically derived categories linked to our thick case data on the pay, conditions, and prospects offered to participants over time by different types of jobs and on assessments of the types of jobs held by participants and their families.

   The wealth group ranking is similarly generated from our data. We categorized participants based on how much they earned and saved; on whether they rented or owned a home; on their overall security, including whether they lived paycheck to paycheck; and on whether they had more earners in the household, including any with a stable job offering career steps. For more explanation and use of these operations, see the chapter 3 online appendix.

   Table 1.4 shows that the K-means cluster algorithm groups just over 80 percent of the cases in the same way as our narrative grouping. Moreover, the main difference in classification occurred among those who were classified by our grouping as College Graduates but were grouped by the K-means cluster algorithm as High Fliers. This 80 percent coincidence is a very strong score and should give readers confidence in the overall outcome categories.

Table 1.4   Comparison of Clustering Algorithms Based on Dependent Variables and Qualitative Typologies

| | K-Means Clusters Classification | | | | | |
| | Outcome Variables: Education, Income, Occupation, and Wealth | | | | | |
Qualitative Typology	Category 1: Stuck Muddlers	Category 2: Shallow Slopers	Category 3: College Graduates	Category 4: High Fliers	Total	Percent Agreement
Stuck Muddlers	**31**	0	0	0	31	100.0
Shallow Slopers	2	**14**	1	1	18	77.8
College Graduates	0	5	**16**	6	27	59.3
High Fliers	0	0	4	**16**	20	80.0
Total	33	23	14	26	96	80.2

Source: NYCOMP data set.
Note: K-means cluster algorithm—forced to cluster four groups—was applied based on the four dependent variables (education, income, occupational ranking, and overall wealth group). Dissimilarity measure = L1 (Manhattan distance). Random start. Analysis by Dr. Dirk Witteveen.

37. Arnett 2006; Dannefer 2003, 2008, 2013, 2020; Danziger and Rouse 2008; Eliason, Mortimer, and Vuolo 2015; Oesterle 2013; Rumbaut and Komaie 2010; Settersten, Furstenberg, and Rumbaut 2005. I mostly use the term "established adulthood" to describe study participants' life-course stage at time 2 or time 3, when they were in their late twenties to late thirties or even early to mid-forties. I also use the term "middle adulthood"—which is usually used in reference to those in their thirties and forties—which highlights the move from the exploration of one's twenties into the full-time adult roles and routines of careers, child-rearing, and so on. When citing others who use the term "middle adulthood," I also use that term (see Reifman and Niehuis 2022; Mehta et al. 2020). I recognize that other types of transitions into adulthood and paths through the life course may not be described by these concepts (see Fredrickson Goldsen, Jen, and Muraco 2019), but I use these because they describe most of my study participants' life trajectories.

38. Merton 1987.

39. Duneier 2011; George and Bennett 2005; Smith 2014.

40. Smith 2006.

41. Duneier 2011; George and Bennett 2005; Smith 2014.

42. We added eight long-term undocumented cases in the late 2000s to bring the total to ninety-six cases. We retrospectively gathered the same time 1 data for these cases and followed them for a decade or more, including times before and after DACA began. I am still in touch with six of the

eight. A fuller description of the data set and its development can be found in the "Overall Online Book Appendixes: Strategy, Epistemology, and Methods in the Long-Term Ethnographic New York Children of Migrants Project (NYCOMP)" (https://www.russellsage.org/publications/dreams -achieved-and-denied). Nearly all initial time 1 interviews were done by a team of one graduate student, two undergraduates (now Dr. Sandra Lara-Cinisomo, Dr. Sara Guerrero-Rippberger, and Agustin Vecino, now a school principal in California), and me. I did 25 to 30 percent of the interviews, either solo or with a student. Nearly all time 2 interviews were done by Sara Guerrero-Rippberger (about 30 percent) and me (about 70 percent). All time 3 interviews were done by Sara and me.

43. After DACA was announced in 2012, I called all undocumented participants and offered to help them apply for its benefits. Sara Guerrero-Rippberger and I did the follow-up interviews that she and I had conducted with them and with some other participants showing emergent processes of interest, yielding twenty-nine cases at time 3 that we mostly used to describe how mobility processes work over the course of many years.

44. $N = 93$, excluding one participant who earned over $300,000.

45. Imoagene 2017; Lee and Zhou 2015; Okigbo 2021.

46. Lu 2013.

47. Smith 2006; Smith, Waisanen, and Yrizar Barbosa 2019.

48. Bean, Brown, and Bachmeier 2015; Lee and Zhou 2015.

49. Alba and Nee 2003; Imoagene 2017; Kasinitz et al. 2008; Lee and Zhou 2015; Lu 2013; Okigbo 2021; Portes and Rumbaut 2001; Tran 2015.

50. Some 83.5 percent lived with two parents and siblings only, and another 7.2 percent lived with two parents, siblings, and other adults, mostly relatives, who contributed to the household budget. The rest of the participants lived in other extended family household forms, with nonparent relatives, or with friends.

51. Gans 1992; Gordon 1964.

52. Chavez 2013; Lewis 1961; Newton 2008.

53. Portes and Fernández-Kelly 2008; Portes and Rumbaut 2001; Portes and Zhou 1993.

54. Smith 2014.

55. Perlmann and Waldinger 1997; Waldinger and Feliciano 2004.

56. Grebler, Moore, and Guzman 1970; Moore and Cuéllar 1970.

57. Telles and Ortiz 2008.

58. Rendón 2019.

59. Only ten of seventy-four cases we could code on discrimination at work reported it.

60. Agius Vallejo 2012a, 99; see also Anderson 2011; Hochschild, Weaver, and Burch 2012; Kasinitz et al. 2008; Vickerman 1999.

61. Smith et al. 2021.

62. I use "Dreamer" to refer to the broader social movement demanding a path to legal status for undocumented Americans. I don't use the term "DREAMer," which I understand to refer to those whose status could have been changed by more than ten bills introduced in Congress, none of which passed both the House and Senate.

63. Alba, Jiménez, and Marrow 2014.

64. Catron, Loria, and Farr 2023; Murguia and Telles 1996; Roth 2012; Roth and Martin 2021; Telles 2014.

65. Alba, Jiménez, and Marrow 2014.

66. Luthra, Waldinger, and Soehl 2018.

67. Bergad 2023.

68. Neckerman, Carter, and Lee 1999.

69. Agius Vallejo 2012a, 2012b.

70. Louie 2012.

71. For information on this program, visit Prep for Prep's website: https://www.prepforprep.org.

72. Blau and Duncan 1967.

73. Lareau 2011; see also Crosnoe 2006.

74. Alexander, Entwisle, and Olson 2014; Kerckhoff 1993.

75. Ermisch, Jäntti, and Smeeding 2012, 7–8; see also Abramitzky et al. 2021; Grusky, Smeeding, and Snipp 2015; Morgan, Grusky, and Fields 2006; Smeeding, Erikson, and Jäntti 2011.

76. Keister, Agius Vallejo, and Borelli 2015; see also Alba, Jiménez, and Marrow 2014; Keister 2011.

77. Sheftel 2023.

78. Dondero 1997; Hodges and Budig 2010; Kram 1988; Kram and Isabella 1985; Stanton-Salazar 2001.

79. Brady and Collier 2010; Burawoy 1998, 2003, 2005; Duneier 1994, 1999, 2011; George and Bennett 2005; Katz 1997, 2001b, 2002; Mitchell 1983; Ragin 2008; Smith 2006, 2014; Timmermans and Tavory 2012.

80. Perlmann 2007; Terriquez 2014.

81. Dreby 2010, 2015; Garcia 2019; see also Knowles, Persico, and Todd 2001; Menjívar and Kanstroom 2014; Menjívar, Abrego, and Schmalzbauer 2016; Toomey et al. 2014.

82. Abrego 2008; Abrego and Gonzales 2010; Castañeda et al. 2015; De Maio and Rodriguez 2022; Escudero 2020; Gonzales 2016; Hamilton, Hale, and Savinar 2019; Hamilton, Patler, and Hale 2019; Menjívar and Abrego 2012; Nichols 2013; Winham and Florian 2015.

83. Abrego 2008; Abrego and Gonzales 2010; Castañeda et al. 2015; De Maio and Rodriguez 2022; Escudero 2020; Gonzales 2016; Hamilton, Hale, and Savinar 2019; Hamilton, Patler, and Hale 2019; Menjívar and Abrego 2012; Nichols 2013; Winham and Florian 2015.

84. Catron (2019) probably underestimates how much citizenship increased income and education because many parents intending to become U.S. citizens in 1910 were likely to have done so by 1920, boosting their children's prospects. In contrast, most long-term undocumented parents cannot apply for citizenship.

85. Bean, Brown, and Bachmeier 2015; Enriquez 2015, 2020; Gonzales 2016.

86. Gonzales 2011, 2016; see also Cebulko 2014; Goffman 1961, 1963.

87. Gonzalez-Barrera and Krogstad 2019; Krogstad, Passel, and Cohn 2019.

88. Formally, the Secure Communities program is section 287(g) ("Delegation of Immigration Authority") of the Immigration and Nationality Act. For more information, see, for example, Criminal Justice Coordinating Council (n.d.).

89. Armenta 2017a, 2017b; Garcia 2019; Menjívar 2014; Menjívar and Gómez Cervantes 2016; Smith et al. 2021.

90. Armenta 2017a, 2017b; Enriquez 2017a, 2017b; Flores and Schachter 2018; Garcia 2019; Herrera 2016; Menjívar 2021; Smith et al. 2021; Smith and Besserer Rayas 2022; Watson 2014.

91. Valencia 1997; Valenzuela 1999.

92. Foner and Frederickson 2004; Golash-Boza 2021; Kasinitz et al. 2008; Nsangou and Dundes 2018; Okigbo 2021; Waters 1999a, 1999b. Nolan Kline (2019) looks at immigration policing's harmful effects on immigrants' health.

93. Granovetter 1973.

94. The $25 honorarium at time 1, when many were teens, was a strong incentive.

95. Brady and Collier 2010; Burawoy 1998, 2003; Duneier 1999; Ewick and Silbey 1995; Feagin, Orum, and Sjoberg 1991; George and Bennett 2005; Katz 1997, 2001b, 2002; Polkinghorne 1988; Polletta 1998; Polletta et al. 2011; Ragin 2008; Smith 2006, 2014; Somers 1994. Kathleen Gerson and Sarah Damaske (2020) offer methodological, theoretical, and practical advice on interviewing.

96. Black 2009; Burawoy 2003; Katz 1997; Smith 2014.

97. Dannefer 2013, 2020.

98. Clausen 1993; Dannefer 2013; Elder 1974; Laub and Sampson 2003, 2020.

99. Ragin has made this point writing solo and with others (Berg-Schlosser et al. 2008; Ragin 2008; Rihoux and Ragin 2008), and in two National Science Foundation–sponsored workshops on the scientific bases of quali-tative research (Ragin, Nagel, and White 2004; see also Small 2009a, 2009b,

2011). For the perspective of political scientists, see Brady and Collier 2010; Clarke and Primo 2012a, 2012b; George and Bennett 2005; Katz 2001a, 2001b.

100. Observational studies estimate associations between treatment and outcome variables, controlling for other variables; propensity score matching strengthens the method by matching treatment and control groups on key attributes. Experimental research design is posited to strengthen claims of causal inference by eliminating other variation between cases and controlling the treatment and who gets it. All use regression, but different sampling or research designs, or types of regression, support different claims to causal authority. See Dunning 2012; Gangl 2010; Morgan 2013; Morgan and Winship 2007; Winship and Morgan 1999.

101. George and Bennett 2005; Duneier 2011; Fine 1993; Katz 2001b, 2002; Ragin 2008; Small 2009a, 2009b, 2011; Smith 2014. Garry King, Robert Keohane, and Sidney Verba (1994) are often held up as a foil in discussions warning against inflexibly using the conditions needed for statistical inference in assessing case-oriented work, including their belief that there is one logic (the statistical one) of interference in social science.

102. The coding template—the Variable-Oriented Data Base (VODB) template—is available in the online statistical appendixes. The team included Sara Guerrero-Rippberger; Guillermo "Guille" Yrizar Barbosa, who created the variable-oriented Excel spreadsheet into which we coded; Stephen Ruszczyk; Blanca Ibanez; and Nico Legewie. Guille's building of the Excel architecture enabled later statistical analysis.

103. Kathleen Gerson and Sarah Damaske's 2020 book on interviewing was useful here.

104. Brady 2010; Brady and Collier 2010; Burawoy 1998, 2003; Duneier 2011; Feagin, Orum, and Sjoberg 1991; George and Bennett 2005; Hammersley 1990; Ragin 2008; Smith 2014.

105. See Katz 1997 on ethnography's warrants.

106. Bennett and Checkel 2015; Brady and Collier 2010; George and Bennett 2005; Goertz 2017; Goertz and Mahoney 2012; Mahoney 2000, 2001, 2004; Mahoney and Barrenechea 2019; Mahoney and Goertz 2004; Ragin 2008; Smith 2014.

107. Brady and Collier 2010; George and Bennett 2005; Hammersley 1990; LeCompte and Goetz 1982; Ragin 2008; Smith 2014.

108. The memorable phrase "in the driver's seat" is from James Mahoney's cover-blurb endorsement of Gary Goertz's 2017 book *Multimethod Research, Causal Mechanisms, and Case Studies*. Others making this case include Bennett and Checkel 2015; Brady and Collier 2010; George and Bennett 2005; Mahoney 2000, 2001, 2004; Mahoney and Barrenechea 2019; Mahoney and Goertz 2004, 2012; Ragin 2008; Smith 2014. See Mario Luis Small's 2011 review of mixed-methods approaches and methods.

109. Small (2011) underlines the difference between approaches and methods of data collection and data analysis; see also Jerolmack and Khan 2017; Ragin 2008.

110. Geertz 1973, 1974; Anderson 1990, 2000, 2015.

111. For example, in this period Congress imposed a ten-year ban on visas for anyone who was undocumented for over a year. Thus, undocumented mothers risk ten or more years of separation from their children if they seek legal status through them. Similar risks face the undocumented person who marries a U.S. citizen. For an insightful analysis of the process of becoming a citizen, see Bloemraad 2006.

112. On DACA's effects, see Amuedo-Dorantes and Antman 2017; Castañeda et al. 2015; Friedman and Venkataramani 2021; Gonzales and Burciaga 2018; Gonzales, Terriquez, and Ruszczyk 2014; Hamilton, Patler, and Savinar 2021; Kuka et al. 2020; Patler et al. 2019; Patler and Pirtle 2018; Pope 2016; Ruszczyk 2015; Smith, Patler, et al. 2019; Vaquera, Aranda, and Gonzales 2014.

113. See Smith 2023b.

114. A great deal of work analyzes the effects of undocumented status on children, parents, and families, including how a change of legal status improves lives; see Aranda, Menjívar, and Donato 2014; Enriquez 2015, 2016, 2017a, 2017b, 2020; Gleeson and Gonzales 2012; Gonzales 2011, 2016; Gonzales, Terriquez, and Ruszczyk 2014; Guzmán and Jara 2012; Hainmueller et al. 2017; Holmes 2012, 2013; Kerani and Kwakwa 2018; Marrow 2009; Menjívar and Abrego 2009, 2012; Menjívar, Abrego, and Schmalzbauer 2016; Menjívar and Gómez Cervantes 2016; Patler, Cabrera, and Dream Team Los Angeles 2015; Patler et al. 2019; Patler and Pirtle 2018; Philbin et al. 2018; Pope 2016; Rojas-Flores et al. 2017; Ruszczyk 2015; Smith et al. 2021; Suárez-Orozco and Yoshikawa 2013; Yoshikawa 2011; Yoshikawa, Suárez-Orozco, and Gonzales 2016.

115. Smith, Waisanen, and Yrizar Barbosa 2019.

116. Amuedo-Dorantes and Bansak 2011; Amuedo-Dorantes, Bansak, and Raphael 2007; Bean, Brown, and Bachmeier 2015; Brabeck, Sibley, and Lykes 2015; Kossoudji and Cobb 2002; Rivera-Batiz 1999; Valentín-Cortés et al. 2020.

117. Louie 2012.

118. Alejandro Portes and Patricia Fernández-Kelly (2008) describe cases that contradict segmented assimilation theory as "exceptional," arguing that they are due to stern parental figures fighting reactive ethnicity, or to non-family mentors opening doors. In their analysis, these cases remain exceptions rather than grounds for revisiting the theory. Jennifer Lee and Min Zhou (2015) examine the adaptations of some nonsuccessful Chinese and Vietnamese adult children, many of whom grow up outside their ethnic communities; to see themselves as successful, they adopt different frames

of reference and do not identify mainly as Chinese or Vietnamese. Osono Imoagene's (2017) insightful study of Nigerian high achievement notes but does not analyze its minority of lower-achieving cases.

119. Portes and Rumbaut 2001.

120. Kasinitz et al. 2008; Lee and Zhou 2015; Lu 2013.

121. Hondagneu-Sotelo and Pastor 2021.

122. Gans 1979.

123. Telles and Sue 2019.

124. Jiménez and Horowitz 2013; see also Smith 2014.

125. Blumer 1958.

126. Smith 2014. Such work focuses on the longer-term meanings and impact of ethnicity and hence differs from, for example, Eli Anderson's 2011 book, *The Cosmopolitan Canopy*, which analyzes how racial and other differences are pushed into the interactional background in specific kinds of public space to create a cosmopolitan canopy.

127. Reskin 2003; Ridgeway 2011, 2014; Ridgeway et al. 2009; but see Okamoto 2003.

128. On planfulness, see Clausen 1991; Sewell 1992.

129. See Berg-Schlosser et al. 2008; Rihoux and Ragin 2008.

130. NYCOMP began in the 1990s as basic research to study, among other things, why so many second-generation Mexican youth were telling me that Mexicans did not go to college and to explore how we might promote more college attendance and completion. It was not conceived of as participant action research (PAR), in which community members are part of the research team that decides on the questions to pursue and methods to use. But NYCOMP, drawing on over ten years in the field already when it began in 1997, has always been an immersive and reflexive ethnographic project. I developed long-term relationships, including close friendships, from this project. Long conversations with these friends over a meal or a beer or while walking to or from some community meeting helped my thinking, enabling me to test out my hypotheses and incorporate new insights gleaned from my friends' thoughts. Several study participants offered comments on this manuscript, and I revised in response. I have sought to help anyone in the study who asked as they dealt with problems ranging from deportation to college applications, finding affordable health care or counseling, or needing a job reference. I also referred them to admissions counselors, lawyers, social workers, or others as needed. Hence, while this project did not start as a PAR study, it has some elements of that approach and reflects my long-term relationships, commitments, and locations.

Here I offer a short summary of my publicly engaged work that highlights its role in or relationship with my research. (Other discussions can be found in Smith 2022, 2023a, 2024). It was not always clear to me as I did this research and related work how it would be helpful, or what would or would not lead to publications, as I pursued my scholarly day job. This life combining research, service, and strategy was not accidental. I recall thinking, as a young graduate student and while walking home from teaching an adult English as a Second Language class, that if I got my doctorate and was awarded tenure, I would be insulated from constant money worries and could focus on my research and my work, including service work, with immigrant communities.

My publicly engaged scholarship really started in the research for my senior thesis at the University of Delaware, where I taught English in labor camps to Mexican mushroom pickers in Kennett Square, Pennsylvania, during my senior year and wrote my senior thesis on migration and labor relations in that industry. I later went to these workers' sending communities in Moroleon, Guanajato, and lived with their families for a summer. In my twenties, in graduate school, I helped many people apply for the 1986 legalization program (which ended in the fall of 1988) under the 1986 Immigration Reform and Control Act (IRCA) and taught English to flower vendors in the basement of the building where they lived in Upper Manhattan. Working with others, I also tried to help them negotiate with police, who would detain them for days for selling flowers without a permit, which they could not get for various reasons. Because this was before cell phones, the flower vendors detained by police had no way to notify their families.

The research for this book started officially in 1997, in a project seeking to understand why and how second-generation Mexicans in New York were going into full-time work or to college after high school. Based on insights from that work, and with the prior example of an organization promoting college applications created earlier in Los Angeles by graduate student Sandra Lara-Cinisomo (now Dr. Lara-Cinisomo), several of us cofounded the Mexican Educational Foundation of New York, which later merged with Masa and which had been created by Angelo Cabrera and others. I served on the MexEd and Masa boards for twenty years, the last eight as the chair of Masa, this educational and organizing nonprofit for Mexican families in the South Bronx. I was content in late 2020 to step down, knowing that the staff and board members were already running things well. After two decades, it felt a bit like sending a child to college.

My efforts with and at CUNY—always collaborating with colleagues and community members—have included work to push CUNY to recruit and retain more Mexican students; to offer nonprofit organizational and individual training to Mexican and immigrant communities in my role as leader of the Mexican Consulate–Baruch College CUNY leadership program for a decade; and to help several hundred people apply for DACA or permanent residency through the DACA Access Project. I also served as an elected member of the advisory board of CUNY's Mexican Institute (and on the board of its predecessor commission). I have raised funds to offer scholarships to community leaders enabling them to earn master's degrees, recruited them, and then applauded their continued community work after attaining that degree. I am immensely proud of my many former students who have gone through this informal pipeline, made possible by the commitment to this work of the Marxe School and its former dean, Dr. David Birdsell. Alumnae of this program include two cofounders of United We Dream (Walter Barrientos and Cristina Jimenez), one of whom won a MacArthur Foundation grant (Jimenez); Angelo Cabrera, who cofounded Masa and is a founding board member of the American Dream Charter School; and New York City's current commissioner of the Mayor's Office of Immigrant Affairs, Manuel Castro, who wrote the foreword for this book. In general, it has been an immense pleasure and honor to teach and mentor so many students, especially those who have worked to help the community or have contributed in so many other ways.

These CUNY efforts included one-off events as well as sustained work like that with the commission and the Mexican Studies Institute and leading the Baruch College–Mexican Consulate Leadership Program for its ten-year history. That program brought hundreds of leaders from many Mexican community organizations into Baruch for trainings in fundraising, applying for nonprofit status, developing a board, and other nonprofit issues. It also offered hands-on capacity-building work for these community organizations and nonprofits.

I built off these relationships from the leadership program and those from my informal pipeline and other work in designing the DACA Access Project in 2014 with former Marxe master's degree students who now worked at or led immigrant organizations. We had formed a working group to study why so many fewer Mexicans had applied for DACA in New York than anticipated and to explore what could be done to boost applications. The answer was the DACA Access Project, which combined nonprofit capacity building, research, and direct service in helping several hundred undocumented youth apply for DACA and permanent legal status. The DACA Access Project asked the research question: What are the impacts of having, lacking, or gaining legal status or DACA? The project has continued that research through academic grants. Its findings are partly reported in chapter 5 of this book and will also be published elsewhere. In its service component, the DACA Access Project screened over 1,700 persons for DACA and other legal status remedies and helped over 300 get DACA and more than 50 get permanent legal status.

The data and analysis from the DACA Access Project have been used in publicly engaged and useful ways. For instance, I wrote a data brief for the New York State Greenlight Campaign, which successfully sought to pass a law enabling established undocumented immigrants to get New York State standard driver's licenses. Lack of a license was a key driver of deportation and family separation (Smith et al. 2021). Using DACA Access Project data, I wrote an op-ed that was published two days before the lower chamber of the New York Assembly passed the Greenlight Law, which was later signed into law by Governor Andrew Cuomo. I also used these data and analysis in drafting and recruiting other scholars to sign an amicus brief defending DACA from cancelation in 2019 (our argument, also made by others, was used in upholding DACA), as well as in a case alleging discrimination against DACA recipients by Wells Fargo. That case settled for $20 million.

Drawing on my research in Mexico and with immigrants, I have also worked as a pro bono expert or "low bono" expert (charging a nominal fee) in cases fighting deportation, including removal cases, convention against torture cases, asylum cases, and others.

My current publicly engaged research studies the impacts of the pandemic on immigrants and on how, and how much, the 2021 New York State Excluded Workers Fund ($2.1 billion) helped recipients' health and well-being. This project also draws on my long-term relationships with community leaders.

131. On legal violence, see Menjívar and Abrego 2012; on the deportation pipeline, see Armenta 2017a, 2017b; Garcia 2019; Philbin et al. 2018; Smith et al. 2021; on waiting as a form of domination, see Auyero 2012.

Chapter 2: Intergenerational Bequeathal of Dis/Advantage and the Immigrant Bargain: The Impact of Legal Status on the Intrafamily Mechanisms Promoting Upward Mobility

1. Espino 2016; Valdés 1996; Valenzuela 1999. Joana Dreby's 2010 *Divided by Borders* analyzes how transnational families similarly cannot keep the immigrant bargain, as the children left behind often did not go to college in Mexico—the goal for which their parents sacrificed—but instead either migrated north themselves or went to work without college as adults.

2. Bean, Brown, and Bachmeier 2015; Enriquez 2016, 2017a, 2017b, 2020.

3. I talk about "mixed-status families with undocumented parents and older siblings," rather than "mixed-status families," because this is the dominant pattern, and it affects family and younger sibling mobility. Many more older children than younger children are undocumented. Most younger ones tend to be U.S.-born, even to undocumented parents, given that 83 percent of undocumented Mexican immigrants, and 66 percent of all-undocumented immigrants, have been in the United States for ten years or more. In one large field study, over 90 percent of the oldest children of undocumented parents were U.S.-born (Lopez, Passell, and Cohn 2021; Smith et al. 2021).

4. Enriquez 2015; Hainmueller et al. 2017; Menjívar and Gómez Cervantes 2016; Philbin et al. 2018; see also Smith, Patler, et al. 2019.

5. Treschan 2010; Treschan and Mehrotra 2013.

6. Younger U.S. citizen children may bring resources to the family that their undocumented siblings cannot, such as public benefits for which noncitizens are ineligible. We do not have full data on such benefits, so I do not discuss them. I doubt that the impact of having some U.S. citizen children would change the overall findings here very much, given the dramatic differences across types of families.

7. McKnight 2015; Reeves 2017.

8. Arnett 2006; Dannefer 2003, 2008; Elder 1974; Feliciano and Rumbaut 2019; Powell et al. 2016; Roberts 1995; Settersten, Furstenberg, and Rumbaut 2005.

9. I use family theory to help explain how different types of immigrant family strategies emerge over time and affect the long-term mobility of children, but I recognize that different types of families, including post-divorce or blended families, childless families, minority families, and nonheterosexual or nontraditional families, have correspondingly different life courses (see Heaphy 2018; Kille and Tse 2015; Puszyk 2016; Rosenfeld 2010).

10. Smith 2006; for insightful development of the concept, see Louie 2012 and Agius Vallejo 2012a, 2012b; see also Handel and Whitchurch 1994.

11. For an analysis of family bargain dynamics between older immigrants and their U.S.-raised Chinese children, see Sun 2021.

12. Agius Vallejo 2012a, 2012b; Louie 2012; Smith 2006.

13. Dreby's 2020 and 2015 analyses of the unmet expectations of parents and children in transnational families is especially apposite here.

14. Bean, Brown and Bachmeier 2015; Enriquez 2015.

15. McKnight 2015; Reeves 2017.

16. Kasinitz et al. 2008.

17. Shih and Xu 2013; Bergad 2011; Chen et al. 2018.

18. Chin 2001; Cordero-Guzman 2005; Kwong 1987.

19. Lee and Zhou 2015; Lu 2013.

20. Louie 2012; Lu 2013. Similarly, the sociologist Karen Okigbo analyzes the pressure that Nigerian immigrant parents put on their U.S.-born second-generation children to keep a hyperselective, high-achieving immigrant family bargain that requires their children to attend a prestigious college and usually graduate school as well, embark on a lucrative career, and marry another Nigerian in the same ethnic group and religion. Nigerians rely on high family income and social capital and on affirmative action programs more than on ethnic institutions like Chinese after-school programs. Although success is calibrated differently for Nigerian, Chinese, and Mexican

immigrants, the same logic of parent-child reciprocity underpins their immigrant bargains (see Imoagene 2017; Kasinitz et al. 2008; Okigbo 2021).

21. The number of cases can vary across different variables, because we coded only where we had concrete evidence in the case file.

22. "Shadowing" is following a study participant around during their day. Like all ethnographic practices, it is negotiated with the person you follow and varies by context and by person. For this study, we had come to know the participant before asking and later got their parents' permission to shadow them. The practice is built on established trust, which is deepened as the study participant and the researcher get to know each other. In our research, no study participant was shadowed when we first met them (see McDonald 2005; Trouille 2021; Trouille and Tavory 2019).

23. Smith 2014.

24. Pratt, Arnold, and Mackey 2001, drawing on Bakhtin 1982 and Vygotsky 1978; see also Espino 2016; Valdés 1996; Valenzuela 1999.

25. Smith 2014.

26. This yearly income calculation assumes that when Eddie's mother was sick and could not work, or when the factory had less work, her income could have been lower. She earned $350 per week and was gone fourteen to fifteen hours a day, including her time spent commuting to and from work, so she probably worked about twelve and a half hours. Eddie's mother was working a lot and making very little.

27. Gonzales 2016.

28. Dreby 2010, 2015.

29. Bozick and Miller 2014. Enacted in 2000, the law remains in place to this day.

30. Gonzales 2016; Hughes 1945; Ridgeway et al. 2009.

31. Marrow 2009.

32. Didion 2005.

33. As Celenia used the term *en carne propia*, which can be translated as "in my own body/person," it means she did not realize that she would be personally affected.

34. Goffman 1963.

35. Ibid.

36.

Table 2.1 **Associations between the Immigrant Bargain and Family History and Outcomes at Time 2**

	Education (Years)	Yearly Income (Dollars)	College Graduate or High Flier (versus Stuck Muddler or Shallow Sloper)
	Mean	Mean	Percentage
Felt obliged to keep the immigrant bargain			
No	11.3	18,360	10.0
Yes	14.6	42,435	61.6
Unknown ($N = 3$)	9.7	24,388	—
Felt an urge to keep the immigrant bargain with a younger sibling			
No	13.4	35,841	46.3
Yes	14.7	45,000	65.2
Unknown, not applicable ($N = 6$)	13.0	17,394	16.7
Kept the immigrant bargain			
No	11.3	28,397	18.2
Yes	14.6	45,543	79.6
Unknown ($N = 3$)	9.7	20,054	—
Reported their family was ever mixed-status			
No	14.3	44,118	66.7
Yes	13.6	36,022	44.3
Unknown ($N = 8$)	13.3	28,020	50.0
Living at home in early adulthood			
Moved out	11.0	—	4.8
Lived at home through twenties	14.0	35,712	48.9
Lived at home until moving to own household in later twenties	15.8	57,442	92.3
Lived at home until middle adulthood	14.9	43,176	70.6
Bought a house with family			
No	13.4	36,026	42.2
Yes	14.4	39,000	65.5
Unknown ($N = 3$)	13.7	32,667	33.3
Reported domestic violence in the household			
No	14.3	37,346	54.1
Yes	11.8	36,273	35.0
Unknown ($N = 2$)	11.5	22,000	—

(Table continues on p. 320)

Table 2.1 *(Continued)*

	Education (Years)	Yearly Income (Dollars)	College Graduate or High Flier (versus Stuck Muddler or Shallow Sloper)
	Mean	Mean	Percentage
Mother's legal status at time 1			
Citizen	14.1	44,233	55.0
Visa holder	15.1	43,508	76.2
Undocumented	13.2	21,433	16.7
Unknown ($N = 43$)	13.0	34,290	41.9
Participant's legal status history at time 2			
Citizen	14.0	41,710	59.1
Undocumented to legal	13.7	32,026	50.0
Undocumented	12.6	21,013	6.3
Sample mean	13.7	36,797	49.0

Source: NYCOMP data set. Analysis by Dr. Dirk Witteveen.

37. Gonzales 2016; Arnett 2006.

38.

Table 2.2   Correlations between Keeping the Immigrant Bargain and Years of Education at Time 2

	Baseline	Controlling for Legal Status
	β	β
Kept immigrant bargain (yes)	2.031***	2.105***
Mother's legal status at time 1 (reference = citizen)		
Visa holder		0.628
Undocumented		0.612
Unknown		−1.069
Participant's legal status history at time 2 (reference = citizen)		
Undocumented to legal status		−0.962
Remained undocumented		−1.870*
Summary statistics		
N	96	96
R^2	0.172	0.294
F	19.54	6.19
Prob. > F	.000	.000

Source: NYCOMP data set. Analysis by Dr. Dirk Witteveen.
* $p \leq 0.05$; ** $p \leq 0.01$; *** $p \leq 0.001$

39.

Table 2.3   Correlations between Keeping the Immigrant Bargain
and Income at Time 2

	Baseline		Controlling for Legal Status	
	β	Percent Δ	β	Percent Δ
Kept immigrant bargain (yes)	0.454*	57.4	0.512*	66.9
Mother's legal status at time 1 (reference = citizen)				
Visa holder			−0.070	
Undocumented			−0.223	
Unknown			−0.600	
Participant's legal status history at time 2 (reference = citizen)				
Undocumented to legal status			−1.167**	−68.9
Remained undocumented			−0.676	
Summary statistics				
N	95		95	
R²	0.042		0.201	
F	4.06		3.69	
Prob. > F	.047		.003	

Source: NYCOMP data set. Analysis by Dr. Dirk Witteveen.
* $p \leq 0.05$; ** $p \leq 0.01$; *** $p \leq 0.001$

40.

Table 2.4   Correlations between Keeping the Immigrant Bargain and Being a College Graduate or High Flier at Time 2 and Time 3

	Time 2				Time 3			
	Baseline		Controlling for Legal Status		Baseline		Controlling for Legal Status	
	β	Margin	β	Margin	β	Margin	β	Margin
Kept immigrant bargain (yes)	1.884***	37.2%	2.844***	36.4%	2.056***	38.1%	2.661***	39.9%
Mother's legal status at time 1 (reference = citizen)								
Visa holder			1.691				0.641	
Undocumented			1.859				1.614	
Unknown			−0.46				−1.098	
Participant's legal status history at time 2 (reference = citizen)								
Undocumented to legal status			−1.365				−1.002	
Undocumented			−5.737*	−60.3%			−3.966*	−54.8%
Summary statistics								
N	96		96		80		80	
Pseudo R²	0.16		0.415		0.178		0.314	
Chi²	21.22		55.18		19.11		33.81	
Prob. > Chi²	0		0		0		0	

Source: NYCOMP data set. Analysis by Dr. Dirk Witteveen.
* $p \leq 0.05$; ** $p \leq 0.01$; *** $p \leq 0.001$

41

Table 2.5   Family Earnings, Overall and per Earner and Member at Time 1, Time 2, and Time 3

	Family Earnings			Number of Family Members			Number of Family Earners			Income per Family Earner			Income per Family Member		
	Time 1	Time 2	Time 3	Time 1	Time 2	Time 3	Time 1	Time 2	Time 3	Time 1	Time 2	Time 3	Time 1	Time 2	Time 3
Status from arrival to time 2															
Citizen	$54,515	$84,079	$116,144	5	3.8	3.8	2.5	2.4	2.2	32,651	39,484	51,398	11,446	28,907	31,736
Undocumented to legal status	39,704	96,000	78,000	4.8	4.2	3	2.7	2.8	2.2	21,606	45,333	57,250	9,381	33,319	46,875
Remained undocumented	38,600	58,727	82,000	4.8	5.4	4.8	2	2.4	3	21,067	25,106	27,833	7,840	13,995	21,250
Overall/constant	49,816	80,309	106,264	5	4.1	3.8	2.5	2.5	2.3	29,092	37,162	46,784	10,568	26,262	30,813
N	39	55	25	63	78	37	65	78	36	38	53	23	37	52	24

Source: NYCOMP data set. Analysis by Dr. Dirk Witteveen.

42. Time 1 covers participants' lives up to the time of the first interview, when their average age was nineteen. Time 2 covers their lives through the second interview, around age twenty-eight. We did time 3 interviews after President Obama created DACA in 2012. We reinterviewed long-term undocumented youth who were DACA-eligible to offer help in applying and to learn how DACA had changed their lives. We also reinterviewed some U.S.-borns and Category Changers who we knew had experienced interesting life developments. Because many teenage participants did not know their parents' income, our time 1 family income data are incomplete. At time 2, our early adult participants mostly knew their family's income. We have fewer family income data from time 3 because we did not try to reinterview everyone in the data set. We have family income data for thirty-nine of ninety-seven participants at time 1, for fifty-five of ninety-seven at time 2, and for twenty-five of ninety-seven at time 3. Although incomplete data are never good, our deep case knowledge, often confirmed across cases, and our participants' narrative explanations of how their legal status and keeping of the immigrant bargain affected their lives strengthen our bases for taking these statistics seriously, which have reasonable significance levels for small-N studies.

43. An outlier who made over $360,000 a year was excluded from the analysis so as not to skew the results.

44. Gee, Gardner, and Wiehe 2016; Goss et al. 2013; Greenstein et al. 2018. The real impact would be larger because U.S. citizens and legal permanent residents would qualify for public programs like the earned income tax credit (EITC) and effectively have their income boosted.

45. Bengtson et al. 2005; Clausen 1993; Elder 1977; Gonzales 2016; Smith 2006.

46. Myers 2007.

Chapter 3: How Did You Pick That School? Institutional Settings, Counterfactual Choices, Race, and Value Added (or Subtracted) in New York City High Schools

1. See Smith 2014.

2. For other research on the dynamics of schools and long-term mobility, see Alexander, Entwisle, and Olson 2014; Bertraux and Thompson 2017; Blau and Duncan 1967; Elder 1974; Ermisch, Jäntti, and Smeeding 2012; Grusky, Smeeding, and Snipp 2015; Kerckhoff 1993; MacLeon 2008; Morgan, Grusky, and Fields 2006; Willis 1977.

3. Kasinitz et al. 2008.

4. Ibid.

5. Rendón 2019, 115–16.

6. Smith 2014.

7. Jiménez and Horowitz 2013; Lee and Zhou 2015; Vertovec 2007, 2022; Wessendorf 2013, 2014.

8. Smith 2014, 2016.

9. Smith 2006, 2014.

10. Thank you to Dr. Andrew Beveridge and Dr. Susan Weber-Stoger of Social Explorer for running these statistics.

11. Bergad 2020; Smith 2006.

12. Roediger 1991; Smith 2006, 2014.

13. Clausen 1991; Dannefer, Kelley-Moore, and Huang 2016; Fussell 2014; Sewell 1992.

14. Bakhtin 1982; Mackey, Arnold, and Pratt 2001; McAdams 1993; McAdams et al. 1997; Valdés 1996.

15. Elsewhere (Smith 2014) I develop this concept fully.

16. Gangl 2010; Kuhn, Everett, and Silvey 2011; McNulty, Dowling, and Ariotti 2009; Robinson, McNulty, and Krasno 2009; Winship and Morgan 1999; Smith 2014.

17. Elster 1987; Knight and Winship 2013; Robinson, McNulty, and Krasno 2009; Tetlock and Belkin 1996; Mahoney 2000; Mahoney and Barrenechea 2019.

18. Burawoy 2005; Feagin, Orum, and Sjoberg 1991; George and Bennett 2005; Katz 2001; Lamont 2009; Lamont and White 2009; Mahoney 2000; Mahoney and Barrenechea 2019; Ragin and Becker 1992; Ragin, Nagel, and White 2004; Smith 2006, 2014.

19. Buckley and Carter 2005; Morrill and Musheno 2018; Smith 2014; Waters 1999a.

20. Tetlock and Belkin 1996. I extend the analysis in Smith 2014.

21. Smith 2014.

22. Ibid.

23. Here we adapt Jon Elster's (1978) argument that counterfactuals are stronger when inserted into a real past by inserting Valerio into Esteban's description of Presidents High. Quantitative work discussing "counterfactual accounts of causality" includes Gangl 2010; McNulty, Dowling, and Ariotti 2009; Robinson, McNulty, and Krasno 2009; Winship and Morgan 1999.

24. Smith 2008.

25. Duneier 2011; George and Bennett 2005.

26. Smith 2006.

27. Trouille 2021; Trouille and Tavory 2019.

28. Hirschman 1970.

29. Wood 2019.

30. Smith 2014.

31. George and Bennett 2005; Ragin and Becker 1992; Ragin, Nagel, and White 2004.

32. Neckerman, Lee, and Carter 1999; Smith 2014.

33. Smith 2014.

34.

Table 3.1 The Correlations of Institutional, Habitual, Legal, and Conjunctural Variables with Time 2 Outcomes: Proportion of College Graduates or High Fliers, Mean Years of Education, and Yearly Income

Variable Number	Variable (Trait, Habit, or Institutional Setting)	College Graduate or High Flier at Time 2	$p >$	N	Eta	Mean Time 2 Years of Education	$p >$	N	Eta Squared	Mean Time 2 Yearly Income	$p >$	N	Eta Squared
1	Went to zoned high school	Yes: 30% No: 63%	.016	80	0.321	Yes: 13.1 years (went to zoned school) No: 14.6 years	.006	80	0.093	Yes: $29,473 No: $48,539	.059	77	0.047
2	Went to nonzoned high school	Yes: 66% No: 30%	.003	76	0.392	Yes: 14.6 years (went to nonzoned school) No: 12.9 years	.002	76	0.118	Yes: $49,336 No: $28,970	.056	73	0.051
3	Was in special program in high school	Yes: 85% No: 44%	.014	86	0.292	Yes: 15.5 years No: 13.7 years	.011	86	0.074	Yes: $54,638 No: $38,141	.190	83	0.021
4	Reported benefit to going to better high school?	Yes: 76% No: 34%	.000	75	0.416	Yes: 15.1 years No: 13.1 years	.000	75	0.170	Yes: $54,391 No: $30,362	.019	72	0.076
5	Told exceptional story about self?	Yes: 69% No: 17%	.000	93	0.502	Yes: 15.1 years No: 11.8 years	.000	92	0.378	Yes: $49,214 No: $26,294	.008	91	0.077

#	Question	%	p	N	val	Years	p	N	val	$	p	N	val
6	Planful as teen or early adult?	Yes: 70% No: 6.6%	.000	95	0.563	Yes: 15.1 years No: 11.5	.000	94	0.448	Yes: $48,800 No: $25,037	.006	92	0.081
7	Planful through early adulthood?	Yes: 70% No: 6.7%	.000	94	0.560	Yes: 15.0 No: 11.6 years	.000	94	0.401	Yes: $49,000 No: $24,475	.005	91	0.086
8	Had a counterfactual story?	Yes: 65% No: 42%	.048	75	0.228	Yes: 14.8 years No: 13.1 years	.006	75	0.099	Yes: $43,027 No: $34,027	.088	73	0.040
9	Counterfactual recoded as positive story, not as negative story or no story	Yes: 82% No: 18%	.022	36	0.563	Positive story: 15.0 years Negative or no story: 12.0 years	.060	34	0.103	Positive story: $45,696 Negative or no story: $27,000	.260	35	0.038
10	Always did homework?	Yes: 74% No: 11.5% (did homework rarely or never)	.000	76	0.580	Yes: 15.4 years No: 12.2 years	.000	76	0.424	Yes: $4.9204 No: $29,306	.050	73	0.053
11	Played hooky or cut school regularly?	Yes: 16% No: % (cut school a few times or never)	.000	83	0.516	Yes: 11.9 years No: 15.2 years	.000	83	0.444	Yes: $28,665 No: $46,350	.067	80	0.042

(Table continues on p. 328)

Table 3.1 *(Continued)*

Variable Number	Variable (Trait, Habit, or Institutional Setting)	College Graduate or High Flier at Time 2	$p >$	N	Eta	Mean Time 2 Years of Education	$p >$	N	Eta Squared	Mean Time 2 Yearly Income	$p >$	N	Eta Squared
12	Had legal status? (U.S. citizen or legal permanent resident = yes; undocumented = no)	Yes: 57% No: 0%	.000	96	0.413	Yes: 14.0 years No: 12.2 years	.000	95	0.053	Yes: $44,126 No: $17,800	.022	92	0.057
13	Had only Mexican friends in high school?	Yes: 9% No: 71%	.000	82	0.563	Yes: 12.0 years No: 15.0 years	.000	74	0.274	Positive: $48,760 Negative: $28,413	—	—	—
	Had non-Mexican friends in high school?	Yes: 68% No: 11%	.000	80	0.475	Yes: 15.0 years No: 11.8 years	.000	75	0.285	Yes: $24,973 No: $49,476	.033	73	0.062
14	Had Black friends or institutions that promoted upward mobility?	Yes: 82% No: 0%	.000	83	0.454	Yes: 15.3 years No: 13.2 years	.002	75	0.121	Yes: $48,801 No: $24,117	.038	73	0.058
15	Avoided Mexican friends in choosing a high school?	Yes: 76% No: 42%	.016	64	0.313	Yes: 15.0 years No: 13.5 years	.021	61	0.086	Yes: $60,608 No: $31,154	.005	74	0.105
16	Chose to go to a Mexican high school?	Yes: 0% No: 61%	.001	73	0.386	Yes: 1.4 years No: 14.4 years	.002	67	0.133	Yes: $24,312 No: $40,315	.055	72	0.052

Source: NYCOMP data set. Analysis by author.

Table 3.2   Descriptive Statistics of Independent and Dependent Variables

	Proportion of Cases by Category	Education in Years (Mean)	Yearly Income in Dollars (Mean)	Occupation Ranking (1–8) (Mean)	Wealth Group (1–4) (Percentage in Top Four)
Treatment variables					
High school quality					
Exceptional value school	0.188	15.8	69,778	6.5	33.30
Positive academic track	0.438	14.7	41,258	5.2	33.30
Zoned school	0.333	12	24,652	3.6	3.10
No high school attendance	0.042	7.3	19,500	3	0.00
Legal status history: From arrival to time 2					
Citizenship by birth	0.646	14	46,438	5	37.10
Went from undocumented to lawful permanent status	0.146	13.7	32,026	5.3	14.30
Undocumented at both times	0.146	12.2	17,800	2.8	7.10
Had a visa upon arrival	0.063	15	46,500	5.7	50.00
Control variables					
Legal status at time 1 (about age nineteen)					
Citizen	0.656	13.9	45,986	5.1	36.50
Undocumented	0.208	12.4	23,468	3.2	5.00
Temporary visa	0.021	17	27,000	5	0.00
Permanent visa or green card	0.115	14.4	39,564	6	45.50
Gender					
Male	0.51	13.4	45,068	4.6	26.50
Female	0.49	14	35,050	5	34.00

(Table continues on p. 330)

Table 3.2 (*Continued*)

	Proportion of Cases by Category	Education in Years (Mean)	Yearly Income in Dollars (Mean)	Occupation Ranking (1–8) (Mean)	Wealth Group (1–4) (Percentage in Top Four)
Offspring					
No children	0.552	14.2	44,723	4.6	32.10
Parent as teenager (under twenty)	0.104	12.4	22,236	4.6	0.00
Parent in college (age twenty to twenty-three)	0.104	12.4	38,100	4.7	20.00
Parent at age twenty-four or older	0.24	13.8	38,348	5.3	43.50
Homework					
Never did/rarely did	0.292	11.7	28,262	3.5	0.00
Did often/always did	0.208	12.8	39,000	4.3	30.00
Not enough information	0.5	15.3	47,591	5.7	47.90
Cutting school					
Cut regularly	0.323	11.9	29,407	3.8	6.50
Cut sometimes	0.052	15.2	40,100	5.4	20.00
Cut almost never	0.427	15.4	49,375	5.3	43.90
Did not cut	0.063	14.2	29,867	6.3	33.30
Unclear	0.135	12.1	41,538	4.8	46.20
Planful					
No	0.365	11.3	25,358	3.7	5.70
Yes	0.635	15.1	48,658	5.4	44.30
Sample	1.000	13.7	40,163	4.8	30.20

Source: NYCOMP data set.

Note: $N = 96$. Occupational status is an ordinal variable whereby $1 = \ldots$, $2 = \ldots$, $3 = \ldots$ Wealth status summarizes several factors ($\ldots$) and is classified as: 1 (top) $= \ldots$, $2 = \ldots$, $3 = \ldots$, and 4 (bottom) $= \ldots$ Analysis by Dr. Dirk Witteveen.

36. The zoned school variable does double duty here by operationalizing the impact of both New York's school choice system and the student's friendship and high school choice strategy. The processes are so closely related (collinear) that we can use only one of them in the statistical analysis.

37. The occupational ranking has nine categories derived from our participants' jobs and assessed by participants and us by the pay, conditions, and future prospects. Category 0 was unemployed, so we use a 1–8 scale here. Wealth group ranking is a composite drawn from case data. See the chapter appendix for details.

Table 3.3   Adjusted Coefficients of Legal Status History Predicting Correlations with Time 2 Outcomes (All Controls Added)

	Education (Years)	Income (Dollars)	Occupational Status (Ranked 1–8)		Wealth Status (Reference = Bottom Category vs. Top Category)	
	β	β	β	OR	β	OR
Legal status history (reference = citizen consistent)						
Undocumented to legal	-0.222	-5,816	0.228		0.743	
	(0.600)	(5,336)	(0.668)		(2.663)	
Undocumented in both	-1.673**	-23,671***	-2.556***	0.078	7.746**	2,311.967
	(0.560)	(5,291)	0(.709)		(2.919)	
Any visa upon arrival	1.635*	5,780	1.480		-18.478	
	(.777)	(6,959)	(0.839)		(7.824)	
Gender (female)	-0.782	-8,067**	-0.555		1.446	
	(0.418)	(3,776)	(0.446)		(1.412)	
Offspring (reference = no children)						
Parent as teenager (younger than twenty)	0.177	-3,262	0.954		17.627	
	(0.703)	(6,227)	(0.712)		(3.601)	
Parent in college (ages twenty to twenty-three)	-1.143	1,395	-0.426		3.089	
	(0.662)	(6,191)	(0.775)		(2.693)	
Parent at twenty-four or older	-0.691	-5,929	0.167		4.914	
	(0.477)	(4,620)	(0.521)		(2.502)	
Homework (reference = never/rarely)						
Often/always	-0.154	55	0.181		-16.1750	
	(.860)	(7,736)	(0.864)		(2.760)	
Not enough information	1.295	-1,036	1.994*		-19.580	
	(.785)	(7,210)	(0.781)		(2.023)	

Cutting school (reference = regularly)				
Sometimes	1.857	−1,897	0.997	−1.640
	(1.057)	(9,381)	(0.999)	(9.672)
Almost never	0.409	−11,456	−0.981	0.696
	(0.859)	(7,747)	(0.845)	(3.558)
Not	0.217	−17,214	0.022	−0.741
	(1.108)	(9,875)	(1.081)	(4.175)
Not enough information	0.399	7,134	1.128	−6.846
	(0.901)	(8,459)	(0.967)	(4.220)
Planful (yes)	3.170***	26,123***	1.282	−4.015
	(0.648)	(6,425)	(0.726)	(3.848)
High school quality (reference = positive academic track)				
Zoned school		−12,376**	−0.955	5.425*
		(4,196)	(0.502)	(2.123)
Exceptional value school		6,266	0.669	−16.908
		(5,154)	(0.603)	(4.975)
Did not go to high school		−695	0.319	21.316
		(12,061)	(1.548)	(1.318)
Constant	11.584***	38,514***		15.022
	(0.419)	(4,717)		(2.760)
Summary statistics				
N	96	95	96	96
F	10.29	5.71	61.52	140.11
Prob. > F	.000	.001	.000	.000
R^2	0.578	0.460	0.166	0.539

Source: NYCOMP data set. Analysis by Dr. Dirk Witteveen.

Note: Models applied: ordinary least squares regression (education, income), ordinal logistic regression (occupational status), and multinomial logistic regression (wealth status). One outlier was dropped from the model predicting income. Although a full multinomial logistic regression was fitted on the data, the table displays only the significant contrast between the bottom category and the top category (wealthiest). OR = (proportional) odds ratio.
$* p \leq 0.05;\ ** p \leq 0.01;\ *** p \leq 0.001$

Table 3.4 **Adjusted Coefficients of High School Quality Predicting Correlations with Time 2 Outcomes (All Controls Added)**

	Education (Years) β	Yearly Income (Dollars) β	Occupational Status (Ranked 1–8) β	OR	Wealth Status (Reference = Bottom Category versus Top Category) β	OR
High school quality (reference = positive academic track)						
Zoned school	-1.504***	-14,110**	-1.098*	0.334	4.842**	126.742
	-0.411	-4,325	-0.507		-1.849	
Exceptional-value school	0.211	5,212	0.657		-16.946	
	-0.504	-5,399	-0.609		-4.336	
No high school attendance	-5.009***	812	0.597		13.631	
	-1.239	-13,062	-1.455		-1.143	
Gender (female)	-0.586	-7,906	-0.543		1.14	
	-0.377	-3,982	-0.449		-1.243	
Offspring (reference = no children)						
Parent as teenager (under twenty)	-0.196	-8,697	0.446		19.935	
	-0.607	-6,388	-0.696		-3.47	
Parent in college (ages twenty to twenty-three)	-0.701	-1,621	-0.692		3.513	
	-0.606	-3,418	-0.746		-2.307	
Parent at twenty-four or older	-0.057	-5,484	0.182		3.161	
	-0.451	-4,783	-0.515		-1.652	
Homework (reference = never/rarely did homework)						
Did homework often/always	0.217	-981	0.273		-16.193	
	-0.762	-8,011	-0.841		-2.451	
Not enough information	0.988	-3,287	1.745		-18.401	
	-0.712	7,494	-0.775		-2.148	

	(1)	(2)	(3)	(4)
Cutting school (reference = cut regularly)				
Cut sometimes	2.002*	−1,903	1.264	−0.088
	−0.927	−9,748	−0.99	−3.641
Almost never cut	0.498	−12,309	−1.105	2.823
	−0.765	−8,053	−0.843	−3.015
Did not cut	−0.17	−18,106	0.005	−0.717
	−0.96	−10,107	−1.119	−4.427
Not enough information	0.718	3,050	0.616*	−1.434
	−0.848	−8,916	−0.953	−3.43
Planful (yes)	1.913**	27,270***	1.293	−4.598
	−0.644	6,781	−0.733	−2.958
Legal status at time 1 (reference = citizen)				
Undocumented	−0.666	−16,771**	−2.147**	5.311**
	−0.462	−4,868	−0.63	−1.665
Temporary visa	1.525	−17,664	0.231	4.227
	−1.17	−12,309	−2.924	−4.195
Permanent visa or green card	0.698	4,605	1.154	−3.5
	−0.573	−6,031	−0.66	−2.442
Constant	12.662***	40,896***		14.738
	−0.456	−4,795		−2.451
Summary statistics				
N	96	95	96	96
F	12.92	4.98	60.14	129.99
Prob. > F	0	0	0	0
R^2	0.681	0.419	0.162	0.5

Source: NYCOMP data set.

Note: The models applied are ordinary least squares regression (education, income), ordinal logistic regression (occupational status), and multi-nomial logistic regression (wealth status). One outlier was dropped from the model predicting income. Although a full multinomial logistic regression was fitted on the data, the table displays only the significant contrast between the bottom category and the top category (wealthiest). OR = (proportional) odds ratio. Analysis by Dr. Dirk Witteveen.

$* p \leq 0.05; ** p \leq 0.01; *** p \leq 0.001$

Chapter 4: Mentors: Boosting Adult Outcomes and Offering Paths Out of a Hard Life

1. Vicky and I talked through how to describe her father's physical punishments. I did not directly describe his punishments because they were not central to Vicky's story about how mentors helped her. But Vicky had one hesitation after reading an earlier version of the chapter in which I had called her father's actions "abusive." She explained in an April 2020 email: "It was so nice catching up with you. Thank you for sharing the chapters; just finished up. It's weird reading about myself; I had forgotten some of those things happened. Overall, I think my story is accurate. The only part that doesn't feel quite right to me is seeing my dad as 'abusive.' Yes, he did discipline us; I just don't see it as domestic violence or abuse. I think that's the norm among Mexicans and other immigrant groups (at least the ones I know). Everyone got beat. I don't think my dad saw it as abuse either because that's how he was raised, and he didn't know anything different. But I can see how other people might see it that way." Respecting the trust Vicky had placed in me to tell her story, the chapter now refers to "physical" or "corporal punishment." I understand her sentiment.

2. The 1.5 generation is children who migrate to the United States and arrive at about age ten or under so that their experience growing up is closer to that of their U.S.-born counterparts than that of older, teen migrants. Research that does not explicitly analyze mentoring includes Alba and Nee 2003; Bean, Brown, and Bachmeier 2015; Jiménez 2009, 2017; Kasinitz et al. 2008; Lee and Zhou 2015; Portes and Rumbaut 2001; Telles and Ortiz 2008. Research lamenting the dearth of mentoring includes Fernández-Kelly 2015; Gonzales 2016; Suárez-Orozco, Suárez-Orozco, and Todorova 2010.

3. Louie 2012.

4. Alba 2012. On how globalization and demographic and economic restructuring created openings as Whites fled New York and ethnic networks filled vacant jobs, see Sassen 2001 and Waldinger 1999. Scholarship analyzing how mentoring helps women and minorities includes Dondero 1997; Kram 1988; Kram and Isabella 1985; Louie 2012; Stanton-Salazar 2001.

5. Rhodes 2004; see also the journal edited by Rhodes, the *Chronicle of Evidence-Based Mentoring*, and Herrera, DuBois, and Grossman 2013.

6. Rhodes 2004.

7. Fernández-Kelly 2015; Hernandez-Wolfe and McDowell 2012.

8. Elder 1974, 1998; Elder and Rockwell 1979; Laub and Sampson 2003; Rumbaut 2008.

9. DuBois and Karcher 2013; Grossman et al. 2012; Rhodes 2004.

10. A related form of relationship here is that with a broker—someone who offers you helpful advice, information, or opportunity, but not as part of a larger, ongoing relationship. A broker might give a student information on how to get a GED or apply to college but would not be a longer-term guide in life. In short, the difference between a broker and a mentor is one of degree of relationship and type of help offered.

11. Noddings 1999, 2002.

12. Rumbaut 2008; Elder 1974.

13. Rhodes 2004.

14. Neckerman, Carter, and Lee 1999; Smith 2005, 2008, 2014.

15. DiMaggio and Markus 2010; Fernández-Kelly 2015; Gaddis 2012; Portes 2016.

16. Smith 2006.

17. Smith 2008, 2014.

18. Much research on microaggressions, microassaults, and microinvalidations understandably focuses on how such interactions between White people and people of color harm the latter. Elmont's interactions engage this research. First, his case documents that his appearance caused cognitive dissonance not only for his White high school principal but for other Latino/a/e students he knew in high school and college, including his future wife. Second, rather than just focus on this as a microaggressive interaction, Elmont's case history shows that this dissonance stemmed partly from his strategic adoption of a neutral operating identity in high school and a baggy look, which he maintained in college. Although this neutral operating identity was intended to help him navigate between contradictory cognitive categories, Elmont also enjoyed confusing and overcoming appearance-based expectations. His case engages areas that Derald Wing Sue and his colleagues (2007) have identified as key research issues on interactions between persons of color and coping mechanisms and adds the issue of how others (Whites or people of color) can resolve cognitive dissonance without microaggression.

    Elmont's case also resonates with anthropological, psychological, and cognitive research showing that such cognitive categories develop early in life and inhere in everyday life (Brubaker 2002, 2009; Brubaker, Loveman, and Stamatov 2004; Cerulo, Leschziner, and Shepherd 2002; DiMaggio 1997; Gil-White 2001; Heimer 2001; Jerolmack 2007; Lamont and Molnár 2002; Smith 2014; Swidler and Arditi 1994). Recognizing that such social categories inhere in psychological and social life is not to say their meanings and content are naturally occurring or unproblematic. Rather, disparaging social categories and images of racial, ethnic, sexual, or other minorities should be pointed out and resisted. David Embrick, Silvia Domínguez, and Baran Karsak's (2017) work summarizes the predominant research on microaggressions in psychology and education and proposes some contributions that sociological analyses could make. Sue et al. (2007) is the most widely cited article; see also Collins 2008; Kendi 2019. Other research describes microaggressions: against sexual minorities (Nadal 2014; Nadal et al. 2011; Platt and Lenzen 2013; Weber et al. 2018); as experienced by African American faculty (Hunn et al. 2015; Pittman 2011; Solórzano, Ceja, and Yosso 2000); as they affect African American health (Hall and Fields 2015); as used in voter suppression (Parker et al. 2018; Solórzano, Allen, and Carroll 2002); toward White people living in Appalachia by underlining the stigmatized meaning of "Appalachian" in some usages (Cummings and Forrest-Bank 2019); as experienced differently by Black, Latino/a/e, Asian, and White people (Forrest-Bank and Jenson 2015); and as experienced by undocumented parents (Jiménez-Castellanos and Gonzales 2012).

19. Elmont did not discuss the mental energy required to challenge such categories, about which I hope to ask him someday.

20. Alba and Nee 2003; Brubaker, Loveman, and Stamatov 2004; Giddens 1984; Gil-White 2001; Swidler 1986.

21. Alba 2012.

22. Smith 2006.

23. Besserer 2009. There is an uglier side to this *se la robo* custom: some girls were kidnapped and forced into marriage because the family feared the shame of having their daughter suspected of being sexually active or raped outside of marriage (see Guerrero-Rippberger 1999). Either way, the girl's life was altered by force: if she had been "stolen" and raped, marriage was supposed to fix it by retroactively sanctifying the relationship. If she had run off with her boyfriend, marriage would retroactively bless that relationship. This awful custom in Mexico has corollaries in the United States, enabled by the fact that, as of 2018, twenty U.S. states did not have a minimum legal age for marriage (Kristof 2018).

24. Kasinitz et al. 2008; Markert 2010; Okigbo 2021; Waters 1999a.

25. Waters 2001; see also Markert 2010; Okigbo 2021.

26. Suárez-Orozco and Suárez-Orozco 2001.

27. Okigbo 2021.

28. Smith 2008.

29. The school was named after Alexa Irene Canady, who was the first Black neurosurgeon in the United States. She had nearly dropped out of college owing to a crisis of self-confidence. For more information, see Wikipedia, "Alexa Canady," https://en.wikipedia.org/wiki/Alexa_Canady.

30. Smith 2008.

31.

Table 4.1   Dichotomous Measure of Positive Adult Mentorship: Correlations with Overall Outcomes, Years of Education, and Income

Outcome of Having or Not Having a Positive Adult Mentor	Time 2 Outcome: College Graduates and High Fliers	Time 3 Outcome: College Graduates and High Fliers	Time 2: Education in Years	Time 3: Education in Years	Time 2: Annual Income (Dollars)	Time 3: Annual Income (Dollars)
Did not have a positive adult mentor	31% (15 of 48 cases)	53% (8 of 15 cases)	12.5 ($n = 48$)	13.2 ($n = 17$)	32,485 ($n = 46$)	61,222 ($n = 9$)
Had a positive adult mentor	67% (29 of 43 cases)	90% (9 of 10 cases)	15.3 ($n = 43$)	16.8 ($n = 12$)	49,950 ($n = 42$)	81,775 ($n = 12$)
N	91	25	91	29	88	21

Source: NYCOMP data set.

32.

Table 4.2   Correlations between Having or Not Having a Positive Adult Mentor and Having or Not Having Positive Peer Mentors, Negative Peer Mentors, Escalating Conflict, and Continuing Conflict in the Teens and in Early and Middle Adulthood

Mentorship Status	Reported Having a Positive Peer Mentor	Reported Having a Negative Peer Mentor	Experienced Escalating Conflict as a Teen or Early Adult	Experienced Continuing Escalation of Conflict as an Adult
Had a positive adult mentor	14 of 32 (44%)	8 of 33 (24%)	4 of 30 (13%)	4 of 32 (11%)
Did not have a positive adult mentor	9 of 40 (22%)	25 of 64 (39%)	39 of 61 (64%)	18 of 30 (60%)
Total ($p >$)	23 of 72 ($p > .013$)	33 of 82 ($p > .682$)	43 of 91 ($p > .000$)	22 of 62 ($p > .013$)

Source: NYCOMP data set.

33.

Table 4.3   Mentor Quality and Time 2 Outcomes: Distributions

Positive Adult Mentor Score	Stuck Muddlers	Shallow Slopers	College Graduates	High Fliers
No mentor	73.3%	50.0%	33.3%	16.7%
Minimal mentor	16.7	27.8	33.3	27.8
Strong mentor	6.7	5.6	14.8	22.2
Exceptional mentor	3.3	16.7	18.5	33.3

Source: NYCOMP data set.
Note: N = 93.

34. We use undocumented mother rather than father or parents because we have slightly more mothers than fathers in the data set and more data on mothers' legal status than fathers'. The statistical relationship works in the same direction for father's legal status.

35.

Table 4.4   Mentor Quality and Time 2 Outcomes: Predictive Models among U.S. Citizen Participants Only

	Base = Stuck Muddlers					
	Shallow Slopers versus Stuck Muddlers		College Graduates versus Stuck Muddlers		High Fliers versus Stuck Muddlers	
	Coefficient	RRR	Coefficient	RRR	Coefficient	RRR
Mentor score (reference = none/negative)						
Positive	2.536*	12.6	3.447**	31.4	3.616*	37.2
Domestic violence in the family (reference = no)						
Yes	−0.03		−0.896		−0.598	
Unclear	1.466		−17.415		−17.305	
Mother's status at time 2 (reference = citizen)						
Had a visa	−18.145		0.417		0.082	
Undocumented	−21.24		−19.439		−19.598	
Unclear	−1.819		−1.258		−1.23	
Negative peer mentor (reference = no)						
Yes	−0.176		−1.417		−0.155	
Unclear	16.91		18.073		17.29	
Constant	0.353		0.037		−0.365	

Source: NYCOMP data set. Analysis by Dr. Dirk Witteveen.
Notes: N = 68. R^2 = 0.239. RRR = relative risk reduction.
Significance levels of key variable indicated **$p < .01$; *$p < .05$

36. In this run, we also considered the father's legal status.

37.

Table 4.5   Positive Adult Mentor Quality and Time 2 Outcome Distributions: U.S. Citizens and Legal Permanent Residents

Youth Conditions	Adult Mentor	Probability of Becoming a College Graduate or High Flier at Time 2
Negative (29)	Positive (15)	.867
	Negative or absent (14)	.071
Neutral (51)	Positive (22)	.818
	Negative or absent (39)	.483

Source: NYCOMP data set. Analysis by Dr. Dirk Witteveen.
Note: N = 80. A "negative" youth situation refers to an undocumented mother or undocumented father at time 2, a negative peer mentor as a teen or early adult, or domestic violence at any time.

38.

Table 4.6   Positive Adult Mentor Quality and Time 2 Outcome Distributions

Youth Conditions	Adult Mentor	Probability of Becoming a College Graduate or High Flier at Time 2
Negative (39)	Positive (23)	.609
	Negative/absent (16)	.063
Neutral (54)	Positive (23)	.783
	Negative/absent (32)	.438

Source: NYCOMP data set. Analysis by Dr. Dirk Witteveen.
Note: N = 94. A "negative" youth situation refers to an undocumented mother or undocumented father at time 2, a negative peer mentor as a teen or early adult, or domestic violence at any time.

39. Telles and Ortiz 2008.

40. Suárez-Orozco, Suárez-Orozco, and Todorova 2010, 86.

41. Louie 2012.

42. Alba 2012.

43. Small 2009a, 2009b, 2017.

44. I actually analyzed whether my interactions with study participants over time seemed to affect their outcomes or be correlated with those outcomes.

Given that ethnographers interact extensively with participants, we would anticipate some impact—what I call "Hawthorne effects," after the famous Hawthorne experiments. I found that my interactions and help seemed to positively affect outcomes for some undocumented participants and some young men moving from gang to mobility masculinity (see Smith 2022 for a brief exposition; see Smith 2019 for a fuller one; see also Smith 2023a).

Chapter 5: DACA: A Revocable Program That Can Unblock Mobility and Make Private the Stigma of Undocumented Status

1. Mills 1959.

2. Roberto Gonzales's 2011 article and, especially, his 2016 book established this phrase in the research literature, but he was not alone. Work by Cecilia Menjívar, Leisy Abrego, Joana Dreby, and others also empirically analyzed undocumented life.

3. For research on DACA's effects, see Amuedo-Dorantes and Antman 2017; Castañeda et al. 2015; Friedman and Venkataramani 2021; Gonzales and Burciaga 2018; Gonzales and Ruszczyk 2021; Gonzales, Terriquez, and Ruszczyk 2014; Hamilton, Patler, and Savinar 2021; Kuka et al. 2020; Patler et al. 2019; Patler and Pirtle 2018; Pope 2016; Smith, Patler, et al. 2019; Smith et al. 2021. For work on the effects of legal status, see Aranda, Menjívar, and Donato 2014; Enriquez 2015, 2016, 2017a, 2017b, 2020; Gleeson and Gonzales 2012; Gonzales 2011, 2016; Gonzales, Terriquez, and Ruszczyk 2014; Hainmueller et al. 2017; Holmes 2012, 2013; Landale et al. 2015; Marrow 2009; Menjívar and Abrego 2009; Menjívar, Abrego, and Schmalzbauer 2016; Patler, Cabrera, and Dream Team Los Angeles 2015; Patler and Pirtle 2018; Patler et al. 2019; Philbin et al. 2018; Pope 2016; Rojas-Flores et al. 2017; Smith et al. 2021; Suárez-Orozco and Yoshikawa 2013; Yoshikawa 2011; Yoshikawa, Suárez-Orozco, and Gonzales 2016.

4. Fiske 2011; Goffman 1963.

5. Smith 2017; see also Minnite 2010.

6. Chavez 2013; de Genova 2012; Menjívar and Kanstroom 2014; Smith 2017. Patricia Hill Collins (2000) says that "controlling images" objectify, for example, Black women as matriarchs or welfare recipients. Jessica Vasquez-Tokos and Kathryn Norton-Smith (2017) insightfully analyze how Latina/a/e youth navigate these controlling images. See also Vasquez-Tokos's earlier work on the impact of gender and phenotype on how flexible one is allowed (by others) to be in self-identifying (Vasquez 2010; see also Roth 2012; Roth and Martin 2021; Telles 2014).

7. Flores and Schachter 2018; see also Armenta 2017b; Gómez Cervantes 2021; McDermott, Knowles, and Richeson 2019; Menjívar 2021.

8. Armenta 2017b; Gómez Cervantes 2021; Herrera, DuBois, and Grossman 2013; Menjívar 2021.

9. Thomas and Thomas 1928, 571.

10. Enriquez 2017a, 2017b.

11. Liu 2022.

12. U.S. Citizenship and Immigration Services 2017.

13. Migration Policy Institute, n.d.

14. Garcia 2019; Armenta 2017a.

15. Fiske 2011.

16. Smith et al. 2021.

17. More information about the two DACAs and DAPA can be found at National Immigration Law Center, n.d.

18. Smith et al. 2021; Smith and Besserer Rayas 2022.

19. Why so many fewer people applied for DACA than demographers had estimated were eligible is an important question, and one answered in a paper I coauthored with DACA Access team members (Smith, Yrizar Barbosa, et al. 2019; Smith et al. 2022). Focusing on the best-case scenario for New York City, which had its own publicly funded DACA program, we analyze the drop-off from early applications to later ones, as documented in Krogstad and Gonzalez-Barrera (2014). DACA's benefits, and the likely costs of canceling the policy, are extensively analyzed in Smith, Patler, et al. (2019). For other research on DACA and the undocumented population, see Capps, Fix, and Zong 2016; Capps et al. 2016; Gonzales, Terriquez, and Ruszczyk 2014; Gonzales and Ruszczyk 2021; López and Krogstad 2017; Mathema 2017; Noe-Bustamante, Flores, and Shad 2019; Passel and Cohn 2009; Pastor, Sanchez, and Carter 2015; Singer, Svajlenka, and Wilson 2015; Warren and Kerwin 2015; Zong et al. 2017.

20. See Smith 2023b.

21. See Abrego 2008.

22. Mills 1959.

23. Ganz 2009.

24. Xavier's insight that "illegality" leads undocumented people to be excluded, or to self-exclude, from such earned opportunities to guard their secret echoes the sociologist Mario Small's (2009b) analysis of how institutions create or limit opportunities for interaction that can increase networks and access to resources and affect social inequality.

25. Enriquez 2020.

26. Babich and Batalova 2021; Connor and Budiman 2019; Hamilton, Patler, and Savinar 2021; Hamilton and Hagos 2020; Lopez, Gonzalez-Barrera, and Krogstad 2018.

27. Goffman 1963.

28. Matsuda et al. 1993/2018.

29. Merton 1938. Criminal youth are often used as examples of innovators because they become successful in crime rather than legitimate work. By contrast, Bruce, despite being fully excluded from the labor market, sought alternative, legitimate means to advance.

30. Smith et al. 2022.

31. Ahora gano veintidos pesos la hora. No está tan mal . . . no es como uno quisiera, pero el salario viene conforme a lo que sabes hace.

32. PayScale 2024.

33. Bailey and Waldinger 1991; Hagan, Hernández-León, and Demonsant 2015; Yrizar Barbosa 2020.

34. McCann and Jones-Correa 2020.

35. Gonzales 2011, 2016.

Chapter 6: Second-Chance Mechanisms: Hitting the Reset Button for U.S. Citizens and the Derailment Button for Undocumented Americans

1. Alexander 2010; Green 2013; Schoenfeld 2016.

2. Alexander 2010; Cavico, Mujtaba, and Muffler 2014; Goffman 2014; Pager 2003.

3. Nolan 2011.

4. Goodman 2010.

5. Heitzeg 2016; Lewis and Solórzano 2006; McGrew 2016; Meiners and Winn 2010.

6. Berger et al. 2017; Laub and Sampson 1993, 2003, 2020; Pallmeyer and McAdams 2018; Rocque 2015; Rocque, Posick, and White 2015; Schneider 1999.

7. Abrego and Gonzales 2010; Cuevas and Cheung 2015.

8. De Graauw, Bloemraad, and Gleeson 2013; Délano and Nienass 2014; Enyioha 2019; Smith et al. 2021; Winders 2013.

9. Smith, Yrizar Barbosa, and MIDA Team 2019; Smith et al. 2021. See also Caitlin Dickerson's 2022 piece in the *Atlantic*, documenting how the Trump administration's family separation policy circumvented safeguards meant to avoid separating children and parents.

10. Alba and Nee 2003; Bok, Bowen, and Shulman 1998; Massey et al. 2003.

11. Kasinitz et al. 2008.

12. Portes and Fernández-Kelly 2008.

13. Gonzales 2016.

14. Smith 2014.

15. Bruner 2002; Hill, Turiano, and Burrow 2018; McAdams, Josselson, and Lieblich 2006; Pratt, Arnold, and Mackey 2001; Roy and McAdams 2006; Smilde 2007.

16. McFadden 1995, 1996; McFadden and Walker 1997; Munns and McFadden 2000; Pallmeyer and McAdams 2018; Schudde and Goldrick-Rab 2015; Townsend 2000.

17. Dennison and Gallagher 1986; Grubb 2002; Grubb, Badway, and Bell 2003; Levinson 2005; Pincus 1980; Prince and Jenkins 2005; Rose 2012; Weis 1985/2019.

18. Attewell and Lavin 2007.

19. Green 2013; Schoenfeld 2016.

20. Berger et al. 2017; Laub and Sampson 1993, 2003, 2020; Rocque 2015; Rocque, Posick, and White 2015; Schneider 1999.

21. Section 720.35 of the law states: "Youthful offender adjudication; effect thereof; records. 1. A youthful offender adjudication is not a judgment of conviction for a crime or any other offense, and does not operate as a disqualification of any person so adjudged to hold public office or public employment or to receive any license granted by public authority, but shall be deemed a conviction only for the purposes of transfer of supervision and custody pursuant to section two hundred fifty-nine-m of the executive law."

22. Eisenberg et al. 2005; Pujol et al. 1993.

23. Goffman 2014; Morrill and Musheno 2018; Nolan 2011.

24. Davis and Warner 2018; Rose 2012; Smith 2014.

25. See New York City Department of Education 2018. For more information on YABCs, see New York City Public Schools, n.d.

26. New York City Department of Education 2006; Metis Associates, n.d.

27. Bailey and Merritt 1999; Light 1999.

28. Lu 2013; Lee and Zhou 2015.

29. Smith 2014.

30. Bennett and Checkel 2015; Brady and Collier 2010; George and Bennett 2005; Mahoney 2000, 2001, 2004; Mahoney and Barrenechea 2019; Mahoney and Goertz 2004, 2012; Ragin 2008; Smith 2014.

31. Smith 2006, 2014.

32. I am sure that Anita did not remember being told in 1998 in her first interview that she was eligible for in-state tuition rates. It was our standard

practice to share this information, though we put off doing so until after the interview to avoid affecting what interviewees said. Besides telling them about their right to in-state tuition in New York State, we always referred them to appropriate supports for other issues. My field notes from the first interview do not mention this, but I noted telling her and her brothers in follow-up interviews.

33. Willis 1977.

34. Smith 2006, 135.

35. Katz 1988.

36. Laub and Sampson 2003.

37. Smith 2014.

38. Laub and Sampson 2003; McAdams 1993, 2006; McAdams, Josselson, and Lieblich 2006.

39. I analyze Valerio's use of a legal second chance here; see Smith (2014) for my analysis of his educational second chances.

40. Smith 2014.

41. Ibid.

42. Laub and Sampson 2003.

43. Smith 2006, 2014.

44. Délano 2018; Winders 2013.

45. Statistical and set theoretical analyses for this chapter can be found in its online chapter appendixes.

46. Elder 1974, 1987, 1998; Rumbaut 2005.

47. Cavico, Mujtaba, and Muffler 2014; Jacobs 2015; Pager 2003; Westrope 2018.

Chapter 7: Masculinities and Long-Term Outcomes: How Mexican Mobility Masculinity Promotes and Gang Masculinity Inhibits Mobility

1. Curran et al. 2006; Guerrero-Rippberger 1999; Hagan 1998; Hondagneu-Sotelo 1994; Mahler 1995; Massey 1995; Massey and Espinosa 1997; Menjívar and Salcido 2006; Nobles and McKelvey 2015; Pessar and Mahler 2003; Smith 2006.

2. Flores 2012; Gormally 2015; Schneider 1999.

3. Connell 1995; Kimmel, Hearn, and Connell 2004; Luyt and Foster 2001; Messerschmidt 1997.

4. Smith 2006, 227.

5. Bergen-Cico et al. 2014; Griffin et al. 2009; Hunt, Joe-Laidler, and MacKenzie 2005; Mackenzie, Hunt, and Joe-Laidler 2008.

6. Louie 2012; Smith 2006; Agius Vallejo 2012a, 2012b.

7. Living at home as an adult is the norm in immigrant families in New York City; Kasinitz et al. 2008.

8. Abrego 2014; Dreby 2010, 2015; Gonzales and Ruszczyk 2021; Menjívar, Abrego, and Schmalzbauer 2016; Ruszczyk 2015.

9. Smith 2008.

10. Anderson 1990, 2000; Harper 2004; Matsuda et al. 2012.

11. Archer and Yamashita 2010; Connell and Messerschmidt 2005; Messerschmidt and Messner 2018; Pease 2002.

12. Connell 1995; Kimmel, Hearn, and Connell 2004; Luyt and Foster 2001; Messerschmidt 1997.

13. One such site is affirmative action; see Alba 2012; Alba and Nee 2003; Bean, Brown, and Bachmeier 2015; Gonzales 2016; Kasinitz et al. 2008; Louie 2012; Mollenkopf 2013; Neckerman, Lee, and Carter 1999; Portes and Rumbaut 2001.

14. Alba 2012.

15. Barnum, Liden, and Ditomaso 2017.

16. Bilimoria, Joy, and Liang 2008; Johns 2013.

17. Connell (1995), especially, opened a way to look at these issues for many of us, myself among them, and Messner (2011) offers a useful way to teach about them. See Connell and Messerschmidt 2005; Kimmel 2010; Kimmel, Hearn, and Connell 2004; Messerschmidt et al. 2018; Messner 1997; Messerschmidt and Messner 2018; Reeser 2011.

18. Connell 1995; Connell and Messerschmidt 2005; Edwards 2004; Gutmann 1996; Kimmel, Hearn, and Connell 2004; Messerschmidt 1997; Rios 2009, 2011. But see Shaun Harper's (2004) research on African American men's understanding of masculinity.

19. Cheng 1999; Jensen 2010.

20. Ferguson 2001.

21. Beasley 2008.

22. Pascoe 2007.

23. Bridges and Pascoe 2014.

24. Schrock and Schwalbe 2009.

25. Anderson 2009; Bridges and Pascoe 2014; Elliott 2020; Martin 1998; Messerschmidt 2019; Messerschmidt et al. 2018; Schippers 2007.

26. Hodges and Budig 2010.

27. Flores 2012.

28. Rios 2009, 151; Rios 2011.

29. Royster 2007.

30. Griffith, Gunter, and Watkins 2012.

31. Lobo de la Tierra 2016.

32. Contreras 2013.

33. Duneier 1994; Harper 2004.

34. Among these deeply researched ethnographies are Phillippe Bourgois's *In Search of Respect* (2002) and Patricia Fernández-Kelly's *The Hero's Fight* (2015).

35. Rios 2009, 151.

36. Smith 2006.

37. Berger et al. 2017; Laub and Sampson 1993, 2003, 2020; Rocque 2015; Rocque, Posick, and White 2015; Schneider 1999.

38. Rod Brunson (2007) analyzes how Black men's experiences teach them that police do not like Black people. Frank Baumgartner, Derek Epp, and Kelsey Shoub's (2018) study of 20 million traffic stops documents that Latinos and especially Blacks are stopped more often and punished more harshly than Whites (see also Brown and Frank 2006; Brunson and Miller 2006; English et al. 2017; Gelman, Fagan, and Kiss 2007; Knowles, Persico, and Todd 2001; Lawson 2015; Lundman and Kaufman 2003; Nix et al. 2017).

39. Duneier 1994. Neither Rios (2009) nor Lobo de la Tierra (2016) cite *Slim's Table*, which directly analyzes masculinity, but both cite Duneier's 1999 book *Sidewalks*.

40. Collins 1998; Katz 1997; Vasquez-Tokos and Norton-Smith 2017.

41. Abrego 2014; Dreby 2010; McAdams 1985, 1993; Merton 1984; Merton and Sorokin 1937; Roberts 1995.

42. Guyll et al. 2014.

43. One of these habits was drinking, a core gang activity. It developed into an addiction for Federico, but not for Xavier. Both men had alcoholic fathers who drank to excess daily. While we cannot know if Federico or Xavier had a greater predisposition to alcoholism, we can trace how Federico's gang masculinity made drinking a daily activity for him as a teen and led him into contexts and relationships that harmed his mobility, while Xavier's mobility masculinity did the opposite (see Hingson et al. 2000; O'Neill and Sher 2000).

44. Smith 2006, 2014.

45. Romero 2006; Smith et al. 2021.

46. Smith 2006, 2014.

47. Smith 2014.

48. Morrill and Musheno 2018; Nolan 2011.

49. My epistemic stance here is that I do not presume that having an alcoholic parent affected Xavier's and Federico's lives equally, or that they
had equal propensities for alcoholism. But we can trace causal steps:
Federico's embrace of gang masculinity made drinking part of his daily
life, promoting more drinking and a drinking career, which is strongly
linked to alcoholism, while Xavier rejected drinking almost entirely as
a teen and mostly still did as an adult (see Ellickson, Tucker, and Klein
2003; Zucker 2008).

50. Smith 2014.

51. See also Smith 2014.

52. Katz 1988; Smith 2006, 2014.

53. *Albures* commonly use innuendo and double meaning and can often be
misogynistic and homophobic.

54. Schneider 1999.

55. Active avoidance of gangs (the third group) had neutral correlations
with adult outcomes (nine each in the higher and lower overall outcome
groups), but eleven of eighteen had some postsecondary education.

56. Bovenkerk 2011; Pyrooz and Sweeten 2015; Smith 2008; Wagner-Pacifici
2010.

57. Rumbaut 2008; Rumbaut and Komaie 2010.

58. These numbers are likely to underreport the correlation given that many
higher-achieving participants, mostly women, mentioned neither looking
back nor looking down and so were not coded for it.

59. Smith 2008.

60.

Table 7.2   Gang Membership and Time 2 Overall Life Outcomes,
Education, and Income

Ever in Gang?	Proportion of College Graduates or High Fliers at Time 2	Mean Education at Time 2 (in Years)	Mean Yearly Income (Dollars) at Time 2
Gang leaders and inducted members	9.5%	11.5	26,000
No association with a gang, negotiated associators, or did not mention	61.1%	14.5	46,995
N	96	93	91
	$p > .000$	$p > .000$	$p > .063$

Source: NYCOMP data set.

61. Berger et al. 2017; Laub and Sampson 1993, 2003, 2020; Rocque 2015; Rocque, Posick, and White 2015; Schneider 1999.

62. Flores 2012.

63. Ragland 2003.

64. Rendón 2019. As an undergraduate, Sara Guerrero-Rippberger worked on the original research and had this insight about gentrifying neighborhoods. Sara returned to do interviews and case narratives as a PhD student. She is now Dr. Guerrero-Mustafa.

65. Belknap and Bowers 2016.

66. Valerio was so confident that he did not mind if I walked with him, sat with him, and talked with his friends, who accepted me and thought the project was cool. I sometimes interacted with them and sometimes just stayed quiet and tried to disappear. There was also little social distancing in my shadowing of Federico when he was with his friends, except where I felt my presence might crowd him or when he asked me to "hang back" for a minute. Other participants were different. Carla (see chapters 2 and 3) asked me to keep more distance. I was introduced to her teachers and friends, but she did not want me in her conversations; she also asked me to follow her at a distance in the hallways and to not sit right next to her in class. She did not ask for that degree of social distance in her neighborhood, in Mexico (her family was from Ticuani), or in other contexts.

67. Wood 2019.

68. Laub and Sampson 2003.

69. Brodwin and Gould 2017; Johnson and Johnson 2009.

70. Zerubavel 2006.

71. Elder 1974, 1998; Rumbaut 2008.

72. Roger Waldinger and Cynthia Feliciano (2004) argue against predicting adult outcomes based on teens' apparent trajectories (see also Schneider 1999). Dale Dannefer (2003, 2020) critiques studies that follow up with teen study participants as adults and get only their adult outcomes but do not get the middle parts of their stories, which are crucial to explaining how those outcomes happened.

73. The few fathers who did not strongly enact Mexican mobility masculinity either drank alcoholically or had abandoned the family. No fathers in this study promoted gang masculinity.

74. See Deuchar and Weide 2018 and Flores 2012; see also Berger et al. 2017; Laub and Sampson 1993, 2003, 2020; Rocque 2016; Rocque, Posick, and White 2015; Schneider 1999.

75. Ferguson 2001.

Chapter 8: Friendship Strategies, White Contact, and Mexicanness as an Identity or a Status: Sequentially Constructing the Meaning of Mexicanness in Upwardly or Downwardly Mobile Contexts and Trajectories

1. Geertz 1973.

2. In psychology, heuristics are "efficient cognitive processes, conscious or unconscious, that ignore part of the information" when a person is making decisions (Gigerenzer and Gaissmaier 2011; Hamlin 2017).

3. For research on the role of cognitive categories and images as structuring or causal forces in social and mental life, see Brubaker 2002, 2009; Brubaker, Loveman, and Stamatov 2004; Cerulo, Leschziner, and Shepherd 2002; Collins 1998; DiMaggio 1997; Gil-White 2001; Heimer 2001; Jerolmack 2007; Lamont and Molnár 2002; Okigbo 2021; Smith 2014; Swidler and Arditi 1994.

4. Murray 1984.

5. See Hill Collins 2000; Roth 2012; Roth and Martin 2021; Telles 2014; Vasquez 2010; Vasquez-Tokos and Norton-Smith 2017.

6. Jiménez and Horowitz 2013; Lee and Zhou 2015; March 1982; see also Alba, Jiménez, and Marrow 2014.

7. Smith 2014.

8. Smith 2006; census data analysis by Andrew Beveridge and Susan Weber-Stoger of Social Explorer.

9. Erikson 1963; Mahler 1995; Marcia 1980; Moss and Tilly 1996; Oboler 1995; Phinney 1989, 2006; Suárez-Orozco, Abo-Zena, and Marks 2015; Suárez-Orozco, Suárez-Orozco, and Todorova 2010; Umaña-Taylor et al. 2014.

10. Agius Vallejo 2012a, 2012b; Agius Vallejo and Keister 2020; Keister, Agius Vallejo, and Borelli 2015.

11. Alba, Jiménez, and Marrow 2014; Keister, Agius Vallejo, and Borelli 2015.

12. Allport 1954; Pettigrew and Tropp 2008; Pettigrew et al. 2011.

13. Alba and Nee 2003; Gordon 1964; National Academies of Sciences, Engineering, and Medicine 2015; Portes and Rumbaut 2001.

14. Allen et al. 2019; Comer and Poussaint 1992; Csikszentmihalyi 1990; Csikszentmihalyi and Schneider 2000; Kansky, Allen, and Diener 2016.

15. Robert Crosnoe's 2000 paper was helpful in my thinking here, especially about the sequential contexts into which upwardly or downwardly mobile contexts can bring teens moving into and through early adulthood.

16. Lewis 1961; Telles and Ortiz 2012.

17. Fordham and Ogbu 1986.

18. Portes and Rumbaut 2001.

19. Alba, Jiménez, and Marrow 2014.

20. Tyson, Darity, and Castellino 2005.

21. Jiménez and Horowitz 2013; see also Blumer 1958; Bobo and Hutchings 1996.

22. Lee and Zhou 2015; Lu 2013; Okamoto 2003.

23. Okigbo 2021.

24. Smith 2014.

25. Gonzales 2016; Reskin 2003; Ridgeway 2011, 2014, 2019; Ridgeway et al. 2009; Weber 1946.

26. Armenta 2017a; Garcia 2019; see also Smith 2008 (on manipulating the meaning of ethnicity in context) and Smith et al. 2021.

27. Enriquez 2015; Menjívar and Salcido 2002, 2006; Sigona 2012; Smith et al. 2021.

28. See Fiske 1993; Higley 1995; Lenski 2013; Tilly 1997.

29. Ridgeway 2014, 79.

30. Brubaker, Loveman, and Stamatov 2004; Jones 2022; Ridgeway 2014.

31. Mader, Hemphill, and Abbas 2018.

32. Chen, Kasinitz, and Zukin 2015; Foner, Duyvendak, and Kasinitz 2019; Vertovec 2006, 2007; Wessendorf 2014.

33. Using 2020 ACS data files, Laird Bergad estimated that there were over 321,000 Mexican-origin persons in New York City. The census numbers no doubt undercount the actual population, and because they live in irregular housing, want to avoid immigration authorities, and often do not appear on the housing or other lists employed by the census, Mexican immigrants are especially likely to be undercounted.

34. Thanks to Dr. Dirk Witteveen, formerly a CUNY doctoral student and now of Oxford University, for constructing this table, and to Andrés Besserer Rayas, who updated the labels.

35. Methodologically, figure 8.1 offers a better measure of the correlation of Blackness with mobility than my 2014 *American Sociological Review* article (Smith 2014), which coded whole cases for participants being helped or harmed by links with Black friends or "Black" institutions. Coding for having or not having Black friends over six sequential time periods allows figure 8.1 to assess correlations between long-term trends and adult outcomes.

36. Jones 2022.

37. Smith 2014. Such cases surely exist, but their absence here is notable.

38. Smith 2006, 2014.

39. Ibid.

40. We do not discuss the line for pan-ethnic friends from figure 8.1 because it had few cases and lacked statistical significance. I believe that, with more cases, it would be significant. Those with pan-ethnic friends had two or more types of non-coethnic friends. Those with only one type of non-coethnic friends (Blacks) were not coded as having pan-ethnic friends.

41. Comer and Poussaint 1992; Csikszentmihalyi 1990; Csikszentmihalyi and Schneider 2000; Dannefer 2013, 2020; Elder 1974, 1998; Laub and Sampson 1993, 2003, 2020; Rumbaut 2008.

42. When participants described Whites as "immigrants," such as Polish immigrants, we did not code them as White but mainly as immigrants; however, we coded those identified as "Jews" or "Italians" as White, per common New York usage. These coding decisions affected only one or two cases.

43. Hamm 2000; Way and Chen 2000.

44. We could make a better case for a predominant Chinese culture than for others (Hsin and Xie 2014; Kasinitz et al. 2008).

45. City of New York Department of City Planning 2013.

46. Brubaker 2002; Brubaker, Loveman, and Stamatov 2004; Ridgeway 2014.

47. Durand, Telles, and Flashman 2006; Israel and Batalova 2020; Riosmena and Massey 2012.

48. Collins 2000; Danziger and Ratner 2010; Danziger and Rouse 2008; Osgood, Foster, and Courtney 2010.

49. For analyses of such situational ethnicity, see Gluckman 1940; Okamura 1981.

50. Holzer 1999; Moss and Tilly 1996.

51. George and Bennett 2005; Ragin 2008.

52. Alba, Jiménez, and Marrow 2014; Jiménez and Horowitz 2013; Lee and Zhou 2015; March 1982; D. Smith 1987.

Chapter 9: Conclusion: Empirical, Theoretical, and Policy Stories and Recommendations

1. Fiske 2011; Levine 2021.

2. Ramakrishnan and Bloemraad 2008.

3. Aranda, Menjívar, and Donato 2014; Enriquez 2015, 2016, 2017a, 2017b, 2020; Gleeson and Gonzales 2012; Gonzales 2011, 2016; Gonzales,

Terriquez, and Ruszczyk 2014; Hainmueller et al. 2017; Holmes 2012, 2013; Marrow 2009; Menjívar and Abrego 2009, 2012; Menjívar, Abrego, and Schmalzbauer 2016; Patler, Cabrera, and Dream Team Los Angeles 2015; Patler and Pirtle 2018; Patler et al. 2019; Philbin et al. 2018; Pope 2016; Rojas-Flores et al. 2017; Ruszczyk 2015; Smith et al. 2021; Suárez-Orozco and Yoshikawa 2013; Yoshikawa 2011.

4. Smith et al. 2021; see Syracuse University's TransActional Records Clearinghouse (TRAC), which makes USCIS data publicly available to researchers, free of charge.

5. Smith et al. 2021; see also Bean, Brown, and Bachmeier 2015; Gonzales 2016; Menjívar and Gómez Cervantes 2016; Suárez-Orozco 2017; Suárez-Orozco, Abo-Zena, and Marks 2015; Suárez-Orozco and Yoshikawa 2013; Varsanyi 2010; Varsanyi et al. 2012; Yoshikawa 2011.

6. Two main interlocutors draw on large-scale random samples, which should enable extrapolation to the larger population. *Generations of Exclusion* (Telles and Ortiz 2008) draws on large random samples in San Antonio and Los Angeles surveyed thirty-five years apart; nearly 60 percent of the original respondents were surveyed at the later date, as well as many of their then-adult children. *Parents without Papers* (Bean, Brown, and Bachmeier 2015) draws on a representative random sample of 1.5- and second-generation twenty- to forty-year-olds in five counties in metropolitan Los Angeles.

7. Gans 1992; Louie 2012; Stanton-Salazar 2001. See Joel Perlmann and Roger Waldinger's (1997) critique of second-generation-decline thinking.

8. Alejandra Délano's 2018 book *From Here and There: Diaspora Policies, Integration, and Social Rights beyond Borders* ably analyzes how the diasporic policies of the Mexican consulate and other consulates can promote stronger destination-country integration for the first and second generations.

9. For an account of one such suit (there were several), see Firestone 1996.

10. For New York City's administrative code on detainers, see: https://www.nyc.gov/assets/immigrants/downloads/pdf/nyc-detainer-laws.pdf.

11. Varsanyi 2005.

12. New York City Comptroller 2020.

13. Chetty, Friedman, et al. 2017; Reber and Sinclair 2020.

14. *Chronicle of Higher Education* 2018.

15. With "Undocumented Immigrants and CUNY," a 2006 CUNY diversity grant for which I served as principal investigator, we did over seven hundred surveys via the Mexican consulate and used these findings to advise CUNY. In the overall efforts described here, I must recognize the work of my CUNY colleagues, including Jesus Perez; Alan Wernick; Angelo Cabrera; Richard Alvarez, then CUNY's overall director of admissions; Alyshia Gálvez and Jose Higuera, the first and second directors of the Mexican Studies Institute; and members of the business community,

including Barbara Fernandez, Jorge Suarez, Jaime Lucero, members of the Association of Mexican Entrepreneurs and Professionals (APEM), and members of the Mexican Studies Institute's advisory board, especially Mariana Sanchez de Ovando. I have been proud and lucky to participate in many of these efforts, including serving as a member of the commission and the Mexican Studies Institute's advisory board and leading the Mexican Initiative on Deferred Action and the Baruch-Consulate Leadership Program. Apologies to anyone not mentioned here. I am glad to be among such excellent colleagues.

16. The program has been partly funded by the Mexican government, by Mexican immigrant business owners, and increasingly by the APEM.

17. Délano 2018; Gálvez 2011.

18. Alexander, Entwisle, and Olson 2014; Rendón 2019; Sampson 2012.

19. Chetty and Hendren 2018a, 2018b. Chetty and his colleagues direct the Opportunity Insights project at Harvard, which presents papers and makes data sets available for analyzing upward mobility and other issues. Their findings echo those of Karl Alexander, Doris Entwisle, and Linda Olson in their 2014 book *The Long Shadow*.

20. Alba, Jiménez, and Marrow 2014; Keister, Agius Vallejo, and Borelli 2015.

21. Rendón 2019, 26.

22. Vertovec 2007; Wessendorf 2013, 2014. On new destinations of Mexican migration, see Marrow 2011; Massey 2020; Zúñiga and Hernández-León 2005.

23. Smith 2006, 30.

24. Bonilla-Silva 2006; Lee and Bean 2007; Marrow 2011; Massey 2007; Murguia and Saenz 2002; Smith 2006.

25. Savelli 2005.

26. Smith 2006. Some 72 percent of fathers and 73 percent of mothers were from Ticuani, 9 percent and 8 percent were from El Ganado, and 6 percent and 9 percent were from Mexico City (though these immigrants from Mexico City had earlier left Ticuani or El Ganado for Mexico City with their own parents). We have town-of-birth data for sixty-eight fathers and sixty-six mothers, and more for state of birth. Forty-eight mothers came from Ticuani, five from El Ganado, six from Mexico City, and the rest from other places in the Mixteca. Forty-nine fathers came from Ticuani, six from El Ganado, four from Mexico City, two from Ciudad Nezahuacoyotl, and others from other places in the Mixteca region. The parents for whom we do not have town-of-birth data were all from the Mixteca region, mostly Puebla, with a few from the bordering states of Oaxaca and Guerrero.

27. As noted earlier, I borrow the term *palancas* from Rendón, who draws on Stanton-Salazar (2001) to analyze how immigrant parents generate social capital that helps the second generation avoid downward mobility but does not help them climb up the social ladder and out of their neighborhoods.

28. Smith 2006; see also Bergad 2020.

29. Sampson 2012; see also Chetty and Hendren 2018a, 2018b.

30. Tran 2015. Running statistics, I found that upwardly mobile NYCOMPers either hung out on the street less in their teens and early twenties or reduced the amount of time they hung out in their twenties. Less mobile NYCOMPers hung out more and kept doing so through their twenties. Analyses available from the author upon request.

31. It would be interesting to see if the emergence of a shared Latino/a-Black sense of home in South Central Los Angeles, per Hondagneu-Sotelo and Pastor (2021), will change mobility patterns, or if the mobility of both communities will be blocked.

32. Sampson 2012.

33. Kasinitz et al. 2008.

34. The lives of this study's participants presented a pointed contrast to the lives of those discussed in Alexander, Entwisle, and Olson 2014. I thank Andrés Besserer Rayas for pointing out that the subway enabled these youth to move in geographic and social space while continuing to live with their families.

35. Alba, Jiménez, and Marrow 2014; Alba 2012.

36. MacDonald and Saunders 2012; Rumbaut and Ewing 2007; Sampson 2008.

37. Chetty, Friedman, et al. 2017; Chetty, Grusky, et al. 2017; Reber and Sinclair 2020.

38. See especially Brady 2010; Brady and Collier 2010; see also Cho and Trent 2006; Remler and Van Ryzin 2014; Ziliak and McCloskey 2007.

39. FitzGerald 2014.

40. Merton 1987. Cross tabs of mother's and father's education with study participant education at age twenty-eight were not significant. Parents with six years of school were as likely to have college-educated children as those with nine or sixteen years of education.

41. Neckerman, Carter, and Lee 1999.

42. Agius Vallejo 2012a, 2012b.

43. Louie 2012.

44. Swidler 1986.

45. Many nonprofits, including Masa, have long been supported by first-generation immigrant and businessman Jaime Lucero.

46. Data are from the 2000 U.S. decennial census and the 2010 and 2021 single-year American Community Survey. Thank you to Professor Andrew Beverage (Emeritus, Queens College CUNY) and Dr. Susan Weber-Stoger, both of Social Explorer, for running these numbers.

47. Agius Vallejo 2012a, 2012b; Louie 2012.

48. Neckerman, Carter, and Lee 1999.

49. Virgin and Warren 2021; Yim 2021.

50. Agius Vallejo 2012a, 2012b; Duarte 2008, 2020.

51. Marrow 2011; Massey 2020; Zúñiga and Hernández-León 2005.

52. Some culturally driven differences are likely to affect mobility, such as the practice of sending U.S.-born Chinese children to live with relatives in China until they are old enough to return to New York for middle school or high school. Among other mobility-promoting effects, this practice enables parents to save more money. Chinese families also spend more of their disposable income on education, including on after-school programs. Finally, Chinese students study for more hours than other students.

53. APEM is one of several key exceptions in the Mexican community. Some in the Mexican elite have been very active and sought to recruit others to do philanthropic work.

54. Myers 2007.

55. Warner 2014.

56. Alba 2012; on possibilities for change, see Hochschild, Weaver, and Burch 2012; Hochschild et al. 2013.

57. Hajer 1995; Hajer and Laws 2008.

58. Scott 2017.

59. Ibid.

60. Danziger and Haveman 2002; DeLuca, Clampet-Lundquist, and Edin 2016; Edin and Lein 1997; Edin and Shaefer 2015; Huang and Taylor 2019.

61. Dawson 2023; Weinberg and Dawson 2021.

62. Krogstad 2020.

63. Hochschild 2018.

64. National Academies of Sciences, Engineering, and Medicine 2015.

65. De Genova 2002, 2005; Gonzales 2016.

66. Chin 2012; Cleveland, Lyon, and Smith 2003; Cunningham-Parmeter 2008; Fisk and Wishnie 2005; Gleeson 2010; Gomberg-Munoz and Nussbaum-Barberena 2011; Núñez 2010.

67. Bustamante and Gamino 2018; Menjívar 2014; Smith et al. 2021.

68. Campbell 2016; Goss et al. 2013; Sakuma 2014.

69. Campbell 2016; Goss et al. 2013; National Committee to Preserve Social Security and Medicare 2017; Sakuma 2014. Goss estimates the immigrant contribution to the Social Security Earnings Suspense Fund at 5 to 11 percent, so I am rounding to 8 percent.

70. Guzmán and Jara 2012.

71. Brownstein 2017.

72. Misra 2019; U.S. Elections Project, n.d. Professor McDonald, an expert on election issues, is the co–principal investigator on the Public Mapping Project (http://www.publicmapping.org/), which seeks to make the process of drawing electoral districts more transparent and fair by enabling the public to participate in them.

73. Gramlich 2019; but see Cilluffo and Fry 2019.

Guide to Online Appendixes

1. Legewie 2013.

2. Abbott 2001.

3. Bernstein et al. 2000; Clarke and Primo 2012a, 2012b; Knorr Cetina 1999; Latour and Woolgar 1986; Lieberson and Lynn 2002.

4. I wrote this appendix but in doing so drew on Nico Legewie's guide on QCA (Legewie 2013), on conversations over the course of this project, and on Sara Guerrero-Rippberger's insights into cases.

5. I wrote this appendix, but it summarizes the collective work of my team in creating the variables to code for in the VODB. Sara Guerrero-Rippberger and Guillermo Yrizar Barbosa are listed as second authors, the former because of her substantive insights into the variables in the cases and the latter for creating a database to capture all of these many variables. Nico Legewie and Stephen Ruszczyk participated in the VODB development.

6. Geertz 1973.

7. Portelli 2018.

References

Abbott, Andrew. 2001. *Time Matters: On Theory and Method*. Chicago: University of Chicago Press.

Abramitzky, Ran, Leah Boustan, Elisa Jacome, and Santiago Perez. 2021. "Intergenerational Mobility of Immigrants in the United States over Two Centuries." *American Economic Review* 111(2, February): 580–608. https://doi.org/10.1257/aer.20191586.

Abrego, Leisy. 2008. "Legitimacy, Social Identity, and the Mobilization of Law: The Effects of Assembly Bill 540 on Undocumented Students in California." *Law and Social Inquiry* 33(3, Summer): 709–34. https://doi.org/10.1111/j.1747-4469.2008.00119.x.

———. 2014. *Sacrificing Families: Navigating Laws, Labor, and Love across Borders*. Palo Alto, Calif.: Stanford University Press.

Abrego, Leisy, and Roberto Gonzales. 2010. "Blocked Paths, Uncertain Futures: Postsecondary Education and Labor Market Prospects of Undocumented Latino Youth." *Journal of Education for Students Placed at Risk* 15(1/2): 144–57. https://doi.org/10.1080/10824661003635168.

Agius Vallejo, Jody. 2012a. *Barrios to Burbs: The Making of the Mexican American Middle Class*. Palo Alto, Calif.: Stanford University Press.

———. 2012b. "Socially Mobile Mexican Americans and the Minority Culture of Mobility." *American Behavioral Scientist* 56(5, May): 666–81. https://doi.org/10.1177/0002764211433807.

Agius Vallejo, Jody, and Lisa Keister. 2020. "Immigrants and Wealth Attainment: Migration, Inequality, and Integration." *Journal of Ethnic and Migration Studies* 46(18): 3745–376. https://doi.org/10.1080/1369183X.2019.1592872.

Alba, Richard. 2012. *Blurring the Color Line: The New Chance for a More Integrated America*. Cambridge, Mass.: Harvard University Press.

Alba, Richard, Tomás R. Jiménez, and Helen B. Marrow. 2014. "Mexican Americans as a Paradigm for Contemporary Intra-Group Heterogeneity." *Ethnic and Racial Studies* 37(3): 446–66. https://doi.org/10.1080/01419870.2013.786111.

Alba, Richard, and Victor Nee. 2003. *Remaking the American Mainstream: Assimilation and Contemporary Immigration*. Cambridge, Mass.: Harvard University Press.

Alexander, Karl L., Doris Entwisle, and Linda Olson. 2014. *The Long Shadow: Family Background, Disadvantaged Urban Youth, and the Transition to Adulthood*. New York: Russell Sage Foundation.

Alexander, Michelle. 2010. *The New Jim Crow: Mass Incarceration in an Age of Colorblindness*. New York: New Press.

Allen, Joseph, Rachel Narr, Emily Loeb, and Alida Davis. 2019. "Beyond Deviancy-Training: Deviant Adolescent Friendships and Long-Term Social Development." *Development and Psychopathology* 31(5): 1609–18.

Allport, Gordon. 1954. *The Nature of Prejudice*. Boston: Addison-Wesley.

Amuedo-Dorantes, Catalina, and Francisa Antman. 2017. "Schooling and Labor Market Effects of Temporary Authorization: Evidence from DACA." *Journal of Population Economics* 30(1): 339–73. https://doi.org/10.1007/s00148-016-0606-z.

Amuedo-Dorantes, Catalina, and Cynthia Bansak. 2011. "The Impact of Amnesty on Labor Market Outcomes: A Panel Study Using the Legalized Population Survey." *Industrial Relations: A Journal of Economy and Society* 50(3): 443–71. https://doi.org/10.1111/j.1468-232X.2011.00642.x.

Amuedo-Dorantes, Catalina, Cynthia Bansak, and Steven Raphael. 2007. "Gender Differences in the Labor Market: Impact of IRCA." *American Economic Review* 97(2): 412–16.

Anderson, Elijah. 1990. *Streetwise: Race, Class, and Change in an Urban Community*. New Haven, Conn.: Yale University Press.

———. 2000. *Code of the Street: Decency, Violence, and the Moral Life of the Inner City*. New York: W. W. Norton.

———. 2009. *Against the Wall: Poor, Young, Black, and Male*. Philadelphia: University of Pennsylvania Press.

———. 2011. *The Cosmopolitan Canopy: Race and Civility in Everyday Life*. New York: W. W. Norton.

———. 2015. "The White Space." *Sociology of Race and Ethnicity* 1(1, January): 10–21. https://doi.org/10.1177/2332649214561306.

Aranda, Elizabeth, Cecilia Menjívar, and Katharine M. Donato. 2014. "The Spillover Consequences of an Enforcement-First U.S. Immigration Regime." *American Behavioral Scientist* 58(13, November): 1687–95. https://doi.org/10.1177/0002764214537264.

Archer, Louise, and Hiromi Yamashita. 2010. "Theorising Inner-City Masculinities: 'Race,' Class, Gender, and Education." *Gender and Education* 15(2): 115–32. https://doi.org/10.1080/09540250303856.

Armenta, Amada. 2017a. *Protect, Serve, and Deport: The Rise of Policing as Immigration Enforcement*. Berkeley: University of California Press.

———. 2017b. "Racializing Crimmigration." *Sociology of Race and Ethnicity* 3(1, January): 82–95. https://doi.org/10.1177/2332649216648714.

Arnett, Jeffrey Jensen. 2006. *Emerging Adulthood: The Winding Road from the Late Teens through the Twenties*. New York: Oxford University Press.

Attewell, Paul, and Michael Lavin. 2007. *Passing the Torch: Does Higher Education for the Disadvantaged Pay Off across the Generations?* New York: Russell Sage Foundation.

Auyero, Javier. 2012. *Patients of the State: The Politics of Waiting in Argentina*. Durham, N.C.: Duke University Press.

Babich, Erin, and Jeanne Batalova. 2021. "Immigrants from the Dominican Republic in the United States." Washington, D.C.: Migration Policy Institute,

April 15. https://www.migrationpolicy.org/article/dominican-immigrants-united-states-2019.

Bailey, Thomas, and Donna Merritt. 1999. *School-to-Work for the College Bound: Strategies for Maximizing the Educational Opportunities of School-to-Work Students*. MDS-1198. Berkeley: University of California, Graduate School of Education, National Center for Research in Vocational Education, October. https://www.sreb.org/sites/main/files/file-attachments/school-to-work_college-bound.pdf?1632071109.

Bailey, Thomas, and Roger Waldinger. 1991. "Primary, Secondary, and Enclave Labor Markets: A Training Systems Approach." *American Sociological Review* 56(4, August): 432–45. https://doi.org/10.2307/2096266.

Bakhtin, Mikhail. 1982. *The Dialogic Imagination: Four Essays*. Austin: University of Texas Press.

Barnum, Phyllis, Robert Liden, and Nancy Ditomaso. 2017. "Double Jeopardy for Women and Minorities: Pay Differences with Age." *Academy of Management Journal* 38(3, November): 863–80. https://doi.org/10.5465/256749.

Baumgartner, Frank R., Derek A. Epp, and Kelsey Shoub. 2018. *Suspect Citizens: What 20 Million Traffic Stops Tell Us about Policing and Race*. Cambridge: Cambridge University Press.

Bean, Frank D., Susan K. Brown, and James D. Bachmeier. 2015. *Parents without Papers: The Progress and Pitfalls of Mexican American Integration*. New York: Russell Sage Foundation.

Beasley, Christine. 2008. "Rethinking Hegemonic Masculinity in a Globalizing World." *Men and Masculinities* 11(1, October): 86–103. https://doi.org/10.1177/1097184X08315102.

Belknap, Joanne, and Molly Bowers. 2016. "Girls and Women in Gangs." In *The Wiley Handbook on the Psychology of Violence*, edited by Carlos Cuevas and Callie Marie Rennison. New York: Wiley-Blackwell.

Bengtson, Vern L., Alan C. Acock, Katherine R. Allen, Peggye Dilworth-Anderson, and David M. Klein. 2005. "Theory and Theorizing in Family Research: Puzzle Building and Puzzle Solving." In *Sourcebook of Family Theory and Research*, edited by Vern L. Bengtson, Alan C. Acock, Katherine R. Allen, Peggye Dilworth-Anderson, and David M. Klein. Thousand Oaks, Calif.: SAGE Publications.

Bennett, Andrew, and Jeffrey T. Checkel, eds. 2015. *Process Training: From Metaphor to Analytic Tool*. Cambridge: Cambridge University Press.

Bergad, Laird W. 2011. "The Latino Population of New York City, 1990–2010." Latino Data Project Report 44. New York: CUNY Graduate Center, Center for Latin American, Caribbean, and Latino Studies, November. https://opencuny.org/nlerap4ne/files/2011/11/The-Latino-Population-of-New-York-City-1990-2010.pdf.

———. 2020. "The Geographical Distribution of the Latino Population of the New York City Metropolitan Area, 2018: A Statistical and Map Data Base." New York: CUNY Graduate Center, Center for Latin American, Caribbean, and Latino Studies, March. https://academicworks.cuny.edu/cgi/viewcontent.cgi?article=1087&context=clacls_pubs.

———. 2023. "Spouse and Unmarried Partner Choices among Largest Latino Nationalities in the New York Metropolitan Region 1980–2021." Latino Data Project Report 112. New York: CUNY Graduate Center, Center for Latin American, Caribbean, and Latino Studies, May. https://clacls.commons.gc .cuny.edu/wp-content/blogs.dir/7199/files/2023/05/BERGAD-Spouse-and -Unmarried-Partner-Choices-Among-Largest-Latino-Nationalities-in-the -New-York-Metropolitan-Region-1980-2021.pdf.

Bergen-Cico, Dessa Kristen, Arnett Haygood-El, Timothy Noble Jennings-Bey, and Sandra D. Lane. 2014. "Street Addiction: A Proposed Theoretical Model for Understanding the Draw of Street Life and Gang Activity." *Addiction Research and Theory* 22(1): 15–26. https://doi.org/10.3109/16066359 .2012.759942.

Berger, Rony, Hisham Abu-Raiya, Yotam Heineberg, and Philip Zimbardo. 2017. "The Process of Desistance among Core Ex-Gang Members." *American Journal of Orthopsychiatry* 87(4): 487–502.

Berg-Schlosser, Dirk, Gisèle Meur, Benoît Rihoux, and Charles C. Ragin. 2008. "Qualitative Comparative Analysis (QCA) as an Approach." In *Configurational Comparative Methods: Qualitative Comparative Analysis (QCA) and Related Techniques,* edited by Benoît Rihoux and Charles C. Ragin. Thousand Oaks, Calif.: SAGE Publications.

Bernstein, Steven, Richard Ned Lebow, Janice Gross Stein, and Steven Weber. 2000. "God Gave Physics the Easy Problems: Adapting Social Science to an Unpredictable World." *European Journal of International Relations* 6(1, March): 43–76. https://doi.org/10.1177/1354066100006001003.

Bertraux, Daniel, and Paul Thompson. 2017. *Pathways to Social Class: A Qualitative Approach to Social Mobility.* New York: Routledge.

Besserer, Federico. 2009. "Inappropriate/Appropriated Feelings: The Gendered Construction of Transnational Citizenship." In *Gendered Citizenships: Transnational Perspectives on Knowledge Production, Political Activism, and Culture,* edited by Kia Lilly Caldwell, Kathleen Coll, Tracy Fisher, Renya K. Ramirez, and Lok Siu. New York: Palgrave Macmillan.

Bilimoria, Diana, Simy Joy, and Xiangfen Liang. 2008. "Breaking Barriers and Creating Inclusiveness: Lessons of Organizational Transformation to Advance Women Faculty in Academic Science and Engineering." *Human Resource Management* 47(3, Autumn): 423–41. https://doi.org/10.1002/hrm.20225.

Black, Timothy. 2009. *When a Heart Turns Rock Solid: The Lives of Three Puerto Rican Brothers On and Off the Streets.* New York: Vintage.

Blau, Peter Michael, and Otis Dudley Duncan. 1967. *The American Occupational Structure.* Glencoe, N.Y.: Free Press.

Bloemraad, Irene. 2006. *Becoming a Citizen: Incorporating Immigrants and Refugees in the United States and Canada.* Berkeley: University of California Press.

Blumer, Herbert. 1958. "Race Prejudice as a Sense of Group Position." *Pacific Sociological Review* 1(1, March): 3–7. https://doi.org/10.2307/1388607.

Bobo, Lawrence, and Vincent L. Hutchings. 1996. "Perceptions of Racial Group Competition: Extending Blumer's Theory of Group Position to a Multiracial Context." *American Sociological Review* 61(6, December): 951–72. https://doi.org /10.2307/2096302.

Bok, Derek, William G. Bowen, and James L. Shulman. 1998. *The Shape of the River: Long-Term Consequences of Considering Race in College and University Admissions*. Princeton, N.J.: Princeton University Press.

Bonilla-Silva, Eduardo. 2006. *Racism without Racists*. Lanham, Md.: Rowman and Littlefield.

Bourgois, Philippe I. 2002. *In Search of Respect: Selling Crack in El Barrio*. Cambridge: Cambridge University Press.

Bovenkerk, Frank. 2011. "On Leaving Criminal Organizations." *Crime, Law, and Social Change* 55(4, May): 261–76. https://doi.org/10.1007/S10611-011-9281-X.

Bozick, Robert, and Trey Miller. 2014. "In-State College Tuition Policies for Undocumented Immigrants: Implications for High School Enrollment among Non-Citizen Mexican Youth." *Population Research and Policy Review* 33(1, February): 13–30. https://doi.org/10.1007/s11113-013-9307-4.

Brabeck, Karina M., Erin Sibley, and M. Brinton Lykes. 2015. "Authorized and Unauthorized Immigrant Parents: The Impact of Legal Vulnerability on Family Contexts." *Hispanic Journal of Behavioral Sciences* 38(1): 3–30. https://doi.org/10.1177/0739986315621741.

Brady, Henry. 2010. "Data-Set Observations versus Causal-Process Observations: The 2000 U.S. Presidential Election." In *Rethinking Social Inquiry: Diverse Tools, Shared Standards*, 2nd ed., edited by Henry E. Brady and David Collier. Lanham, Md.: Rowman & Littlefield.

Brady, Henry E., and David Collier, eds. 2010. *Rethinking Social Inquiry: Diverse Tools, Shared Standards*, 2nd ed. Lanham, Md.: Rowman & Littlefield.

Bridges, Tristan, and C. J. Pascoe. 2014. "Hybrid Masculinities: New Directions in the Sociology of Men and Masculinities." *Sociology Compass* 8(3, March): 246–58. https://doi.org/10.1111/soc4.12134.

Brodwin, Erin, and Skye Gould. 2017. "The Age Your Brain Matures at Everything— It Isn't Even Fully Developed until Age 25." *Business Insider*, November 8. www.businessinsider.com/age-brain-matures-at-everything-2017-11.

Brown, Robert, and James Frank. 2006. "Race and Officer Decision Making: Examining Differences in Arrest Outcomes between Black and White Officers." *Justice Quarterly* 23(1): 96–126. https://doi.org/10.1080/07418820600552527.

Brownstein, Ronald. 2017. "Federal Anti-Poverty Programs Primarily Help the GOP's Base." *Atlantic*, February 6. https://www.theatlantic.com/politics/archive/2017/02/gop-base-poverty-snap-social-security/516861/.

Brubaker, Rogers. 2002. "Ethnicity without Groups." *European Journal of Sociology* 43(2): 163–89. https://doi.org/10.1017/S0003975602001066.

———. 2009. "Ethnicity, Race, and Nationalism." *Annual Review of Sociology* 35(August 11): 21–42. https://doi.org/10.1146/annurev-soc-070308-115916.

Brubaker, Rogers, Mara Loveman, and Peter Stamatov. 2004. "Ethnicity as Cognition." *Theory and Society* 33(1, February): 31–64. https://doi.org/10.1023/B:RYSO.0000021405.18890.63.

Bruner, Jerome. 2002. *Making Stories: Law, Literature, Life*. New York: Farrar, Straus and Giroux.

Brunson, Rod K. 2007. "'Police Don't Like Black People': African-American Young Men's Accumulated Police Experiences." *Criminology and Public Policy* 6(1, February): 71–101. https://doi.org/10.1111/j.1745-9133.2007.00423.x.

Brunson, Rod K., and Jody Miller. 2006. "Gender, Race, and Urban Policing: The Experience of African American Youths." *Gender and Society* 20(4, August): 531–52. https://doi.org/10.1177/0891243206287727.

Buckley, Tamara R., and Robert T. Carter. 2005. "Black Adolescent Girls: Do Gender Role and Racial Identity Impact Their Self-Esteem?" *Sex Roles* 53(November): 647–61. https://doi.org/10.1007/s11199-005-7731-6.

Burawoy, Michael. 1998. "The Extended Case Method." *Sociological Theory* 16(1, March): 4–33. https://doi.org/10.1111/0735-2751.00040.

———. 2003. "Revisits: An Outline of a Theory of Reflexive Ethnography." *American Sociological Review* 68(5, October): 645–79. https://doi.org/10.2307/1519757.

———. 2005. "For Public Sociology." *American Sociological Review* 70(1, February): 4–28. https://doi.org/10.1177/000312240507000102.

Bustamante, Juan José, and Eric Gamino. 2018. "'La Polimigra': A Social Construct behind the Deportation Regime in the Greater Northwest Arkansas Region." *Humanity and Society* 42(3, August): 344–66. https://doi.org/10.1177/0160597617748165.

Campbell, Alexia Fernández. 2016. "The Truth about Undocumented Immigrants and Taxes." *Atlantic*, March 25. https://www.theatlantic.com/business/archive/2016/09/undocumented-immigrants-and-taxes/499604.

Capps, Randy, Michael Fix, and Jie Zong. 2016. "A Profile of U.S. Children with Unauthorized Immigrant Parents." Washington, D.C.: Migration Policy Institute, January. https://www.migrationpolicy.org/research/profile-us-children-unauthorized-immigrant-parents.

Capps, Randy, Heather Koball, James D. Bachmeier, Ariel G. Ruiz Soto, Jie Zong, and Julia Gelatt. 2016. "Deferred Action for Unauthorized Immigrant Parents: Analysis of DAPA's Potential Effects on Families and Children." Washington, D.C.: Migration Policy Institute, February. https://www.migrationpolicy.org/research/deferred-action-unauthorized-immigrant-parents-analysis-dapas-potential-effects-families.

Castañeda, Heide, Seth M. Holmes, Daniel S. Madrigal, Maria-Elena DeTrinidad Young, Naomi Beyeler, and James Quesada. 2015. "Immigration as a Social Determinant of Health." *Annual Review of Public Health* 36(1): 375–92. https://doi.org/10.1146/annurev-publhealth-032013-182419.

Catron, Peter. 2019. "The Citizenship Advantage: Immigrant Socioeconomic Attainment in the Age of Mass Migration." *American Journal of Sociology* 124(4, January): 999–1042. https://doi.org/10.1086/701297.

Catron, Peter, Maria V. Loria, and Sarah E. Farr. 2023. "Contextual Boundaries: Skin Tone Stratification and Skill Transferability among Mexicans in the Age of Mass Migration." *SocArXiv*, March 2. https://doi.org/10.31235/osf.io/5ckv6.

Cavico, Frank J., Bahaudin G. Mujtaba, and Stephen C. Muffler. 2014. "Criminal Background Checks in Employment: An Unfolding Legal Quandary for Employers." *Journal of Law and Criminal Justice* 2(1, March): 41–103. http://jlcjnet.com/journals/jlcj/Vol_2_No_1_March_2014/4.pdf.

Cebulko, Kara. 2014. "Documented, Undocumented, and Liminally Legal: Legal Status during the Transition to Adulthood for 1.5-Generation Brazilian Immigrants." *Sociological Quarterly* 55(1, Winter): 143–67. https://doi.org/10.1111/tsq.12045.

Cerulo, Karen A., Vanina Leschziner, and Hana Shepherd. 2002. *Culture in Mind: Toward a Sociology of Culture and Cognition*. New York: Routledge.

Chavez, Leo R. 2013. *The Latino Threat: Constructing Immigrants, Citizens, and the Nation*, 2nd ed. Stanford, Calif.: Stanford University Press.

Chen, Kuo-Su, Lynn Monrouxe, Yi-Hsuan Lu, Chang-Chyi Jenq, Yeu-Jhy Chang, and Pony Yee-Chee Chai. 2018. "Academic Outcomes of Flipped Classroom Learning: A Meta-analysis." *Medical Education* 52(9, June 25): 910–24. https://doi.org/10.1111/medu.13616.

Chen, Xiangming, Philip Kasinitz, and Sharon Zukin. 2015. *Global Cities, Local Streets: Everyday Diversity from New York to Shanghai*. New York: Routledge.

Cheng, Cliff. 1999. "Marginalized Masculinities and Hegemonic Masculinity: An Introduction." *Journal of Men's Studies* 7(3, June): 295–315. https://doi.org/10.3149/jms.0703.295.

Chetty, Raj, John N. Friedman, Emmanuel Saez, Nicholas Turner, and Danny Yagan. 2017. "Mobility Report Cards: The Role of Colleges in Intergenerational Mobility." Working Paper 23618. Cambridge, Mass.: National Bureau of Economic Research, July. https://doi.org/10.3386/w23618.

Chetty, Raj, David Grusky, Maximilian Hell, Nathaniel Hendren, Robert Manduca, and Jimmy Narang. 2017. "The Fading American Dream: Trends in Absolute Income Mobility since 1940." *Science* 356(6336, April 28): 398–406. https://doi.org/10.1126/science.aal4617.

Chetty, Raj, and Nathaniel Hendren. 2018a. "The Impacts of Neighborhoods on Intergenerational Mobility I: Childhood Exposure Effects." *Quarterly Journal of Economics* 133(3, August): 1107–62. https://doi.org/10.1093/qje/qjy007.

———. 2018b. "The Impacts of Neighborhoods on Intergenerational Mobility II: County-Level Estimates." *Quarterly Journal of Economics* 133(3, August): 1163–1228. https://doi.org/10.1093/qje/qjy006.

Chetty, Raj, Nathaniel Hendren, Patrick Kline, and Emmanuel Saez. 2014. "Where Is the Land of Opportunity? The Geography of Intergenerational Mobility in the United States." *Quarterly Journal of Economics* 129(4, November): 1553–1623. https://doi.org/10.1093/qje/qju022.

Chin, Margaret. 2001. *When Coethnic Assets Become Liabilities: Mexican, Ecuadorian, and Chinese Garment Workers in New York City*. Philadelphia: Temple University Press.

———. 2012. *Sewing Women: Immigrants and the New York City Garment Industry*. New York: Columbia University Press.

Cho, Jeasik, and Allen Trent. 2006. "Validity in Qualitative Research Revisited." *Qualitative Research* 6(3, August): 319–40. https://doi.org/10.1177/1468794106065006.

Chronicle of Higher Education. 2018. "Colleges with the Highest Student-Mobility Rates, 2014." *Chronicle of Higher Education* 64(41, August 24).

Cilluffo, Anthony, and Richard Fry. 2019. "Gen Z, Millennials, and Gen X Outvoted Older Generations in 2018 Midterms." Washington, D.C.: Pew Research Center, May 29. https://www.pewresearch.org/fact-tank/2019/05/29/gen-z-millennials-and-gen-x-outvoted-older-generations-in-2018-midterm.

City of New York Department of City Planning (CNY DCP). 2013. *The Newest New Yorkers: Characteristics of the City's Foreign-Born Population.* NYC DCP 13-10. New York: CNY DCP, December. https://www1.nyc.gov/assets/planning /download/pdf/data-maps/nyc-population/nny2013/nny_2013.pdf.

Clarke, Kevin A., and David M. Primo. 2012a. "Overcoming 'Physics Envy.'" *New York Times*, March 30.

———. 2012b. *A Model Discipline: Political Science and the Logic of Representations.* New York: Oxford University Press.

Clausen, John. 1991. "Adolescent Competence and the Shaping of the Life Course." *American Journal of Sociology* 96(4, January): 805–42. https://doi.org /10.1086/229609.

———. 1993. *American Lives: Looking Back at the Children of the Great Depression.* New York: Free Press.

Cleveland, Sarah, Beth Lyon, and Lynn Smith. 2003. "Inter-American Court of Human Rights Amicus Curiae Brief: The United States Violates International Law When Labor Law Remedies Are Restricted Based on Workers' Migrant Status." *Seattle Journal of Social Justice* 795. https://scholarship.law.columbia .edu/faculty_scholarship/3444.

Collins, Patricia Hill. 1998. *Fighting Words: Black Women and the Search for Justice.* Minneapolis: University of Minnesota Press.

Collins, Randall. 2008. *Violence: A Micro-Sociological Theory.* Princeton, N.J.: Princeton University Press.

Comer, James P., and Alvin F. Poussaint. 1992. *Raising Black Children: Two Leading Psychiatrists Confront the Educational, Social, and Emotional Problems Facing Black Children.* New York: Penguin Books.

Connell, R. W. 1995. *Masculinities.* Cambridge: Polity Press.

Connell, Robert W., and James W. Messerschmidt. 2005. "Hegemonic Masculinity: Rethinking the Concept." *Gender and Society* 19(6, December): 829–59. https:// doi.org/10.1177/0891243205278639.

Connor, Philip, and Abby Budiman. 2019. "Immigrants Share in U.S. Nears Record High but Remains below That of Many Other Countries." Washington, D.C.: Pew Research Center, January 30. https://www.pewresearch.org /short-reads/2019/01/30/immigrant-share-in-u-s-nears-record-high-but-remains -below-that-of-many-other-countries/.

Contreras, Randol. 2013. *The Stickup Kids: Race, Drugs, Violence, and the American Dream.* Berkeley: University of California Press.

Cordero-Guzman, Héctor R. 2005. "Community-Based Organisations and Migration in New York City." *Journal of Ethnic and Migration Studies* 31(5): 889–909. https://doi.org/10.1080/13691830500177743.

Criminal Justice Coordinating Council. n.d. "Secure Communities and 287(g)." https://cjcc.georgia.gov/secure-communities-and-287g.

Crosnoe, Robert. 2000. "Friendships in Childhood and Adolescence: The Life Course and New Directions." *Social Psychology Quarterly* 63(4): 377–91. https:// doi.org/10.2307/2695847.

———. 2006. *Mexican Roots, American Schools: Helping Mexican Immigrant Children Succeed.* Palo Alto, Calif.: Stanford University Press.

Csikszentmihalyi, Mihaly. 1990. *Flow: The Psychology of Optimal Experience*. New York: Harper & Row.

Csikszentmihalyi, Mihaly, and Barbara Schneider. 2000. *Becoming Adult: How Teenagers Prepare for the World of Work*. New York: Basic Books.

Cuevas, Stephany, and Amy Cheung. 2015. "Dissolving Boundaries: Understanding Undocumented Students' Educational Experiences." *Harvard Educational Review* 85(3): 310–17. https://doi.org/10.17763/0017-8055.85.3.310.

Cummings, Karen, and Shandra Forrest-Bank. 2019. "Understanding Appalachian Microaggression from the Perspective of Community College Students in Southern West Virginia." *Journal of Sociology and Social Welfare* 46(2, June): article 5. https://doi.org/10.15453/0191-5096.4097.

Cunningham-Parmeter, Keith. 2008. "Fear of Discovery: Immigrant Workers and the Fifth Amendment." *Cornell International Law Journal* 41(1): article 2. https://scholarship.law.cornell.edu/cilj/vol41/iss1/2.

Curran, Sara R., Steven Shafer, Katharine M. Donato, and Filiz Garip. 2006. "Mapping Gender and Migration in Sociological Scholarship: Is It Segregation or Integration?" *International Migration Review* 40(1, February): 199–223. https://doi.org/10.1111/j.1747-7379.2006.00008.x.

Dannefer, Dale. 2003. "Cumulative Advantage/Disadvantage and the Life Course: Cross-Fertilizing Age and Social Science Theory." *Journals of Gerontology Series B: Psychological Sciences and Social Sciences* 58(6, November): S327–37. https://doi.org/10.1093/geronb/58.6.S327.

———. 2008. "The Waters We Swim: Everyday Social Processes, Macrostructural Realities, and Human Aging." In *Social Structures and Aging Individuals: Continuing Challenges*, edited by K. Warner Schaie and Ronald P. Abeles. New York: Springer Publishing Co.

———. 2013. "Age and Sociological Explanation: Expanding Horizons in the Study of Aging and the Life Course." *Contemporary Sociology* 42(6, November): 793–800. https://doi.org/10.1177/0094306113506870.

———. 2020. "Systemic and Reflexive: Foundations of Cumulative Dis/Advantage and Life-Course Processes." *Journals of Gerontology: Series B: Psychological Sciences and Social Sciences* 75(6, June): 1249–63. https://doi.org/10.1093/geronb/gby118.

Dannefer, Dale, Jessica Kelley-Moore, and Wenxuan Huang. 2016. "Opening the Social: Sociological Imagination in Life Course Studies." In *Handbook of the Life Course*, vol. 2, edited by Michael J. Shanahan, Jeylan T. Mortimer, and Monica Kirkpatrick Johnson. Cham, Switzerland: Springer.

Danziger, Sheldon H., and Robert H. Haveman, eds. 2002. *Understanding Poverty*. Cambridge, Mass.: Harvard University Press.

Danziger, Sheldon, and David Ratner. 2010. "Labor Market Outcomes and the Transition to Adulthood." *The Future of Children* 20(1, Spring): 133–58. https://doi.org/10.1353/foc.0.0041.

Danziger, Sheldon, and Cecilia Elena Rouse. 2008. *The Price of Independence: The Economics of Early Adulthood*. New York: Russell Sage Foundation.

Davis, Jonathan Ryan, and Nathan Warner. 2018. "Schools Matter: The Positive Relationship between New York City High Schools' Student Academic

Progress and School Climate." *Urban Education* 53(8, October): 959–80. https://doi.org/10.1177/0042085915613544.

Dawson, Jessica. 2023. "Who Controls the Code, Controls the System: Algorithmically Amplified Bullshit, Social Inequality, and the Ubiquitous Surveillance of Everyday Life." *Sociological Forum* 38(S1, September): 1082–1105. https://doi.org/10.1111/socf.12907.

De Genova, Nicholas P. 2002. "Migrant 'Illegality' and Deportability in Everyday Life." *Annual Review of Anthropology* 31(October): 419–47. https://doi.org/10.1146/annurev.anthro.31.040402.085432.

———. 2005. *Working the Boundaries: Race, Space, and "Illegality" in Mexican Chicago.* Durham, N.C.: Duke University Press.

———. 2012. "Border Scene and Obscene." In *A Companion to Border Studies,* edited by Thomas M. Wilson and Hastings Donnan. Oxford: Wiley-Blackwell.

De Graauw, Els, Irene Bloemraad, and Shannon Gleeson. 2013. "Funding Immigrant Organizations; Suburban Free Riding and Local Civil Presence." *American Journal of Sociology* 119(10, July): 75–130. https://doi.org/10.1086/671168.

Délano, Alejandra. 2018. *From Here and There: Diaspora Policies, Integration, and Social Rights beyond Borders.* Oxford: Oxford University Press.

Délano, Alejandra, and Benjamin Nienass. 2014. "Invisible Victims: Undocumented Migrants and the Aftermath of September 11th." *Politics and Society* 42(3, September): 399–421. https://doi.org/10.1177/0032329214543259.

DeLuca, Stefanie, Susan Clampet-Lundquist, and Kathryn Edin. 2016. *Coming of Age in the Other America.* New York: Russell Sage Foundation.

De Maio, Mariana, and Nathian Shae Rodriguez. 2022. "The Use of Twitter to #Defend DACA & DREAMers." *Journal of Ethnic and Cultural Studies* 9(2, May): 49–65. https://doi.org/10.29333/ejecs/968.

Dennison, John D., and Paul Gallagher. 1986. "Canada's Community College Systems: A Study of Diversity." *Community College Journal of Research and Practice* 19(5): 381–93. https://doi.org/10.1080/1066892950190502.

Deuchar, Ross, and Robert D. Weide. 2018. "Journeys in Gang Masculinity: Insights from International Case Studies of Interventions." *Deviant Behavior* 40(2):1–15. https://doi.org/10.1080/01639625.2018.1443761.

Dickerson, Caitlin. 2022. "'We Need to Take Away Children': The Secret History of the U.S. Government's Family-Separation Policy." *Atlantic,* August 7. https://www.theatlantic.com/magazine/archive/2022/09/trump-administration-family-separation-policy-immigration/670604/.

Didion, Joan. 2005. *The Year of Magical Thinking.* New York: Alfred A. Knopf.

DiMaggio, Paul. 1997. "Culture and Cognition." *Annual Review of Sociology* 23(1, July): 263–87. https://doi.org/10.1146/annurev.soc.23.1.263.

DiMaggio, Paul, and Hazel Rose Markus. 2010. "Culture and Social Psychology: Converging Perspectives." *Social Psychology Quarterly* 73(4, December): 347–52. https://doi.org/10.1177/0190272510389010.

Dondero, Grace M. 1997. "Mentors: Beacons of Hope." *Adolescence* 32(128, Winter): 881–86.

Dreby, Joana. 2010. *Divided by Borders: Mexican Migrants and Their Children.* Berkeley: University of California Press.

———. 2015. *Everyday Illegal: When Policies Undermine Families.* Berkeley: University of California Press.

Duarte, Cynthia. 2008. "The Negotiation of 3rd+ Generation Mexican American Ethnicity in Los Angeles." PhD diss., Department of Sociology, Columbia University.

———. 2020. "Beyond Symbolic Ethnicity: Strategic Ethnicity and the Negotiation of Identity among Third-Plus Generation Mexican Americans in Los Angeles, CA." *Journal of Interdisciplinary Humanities: Latinx Identities* 37(2): 100–118.

DuBois, David L., and Michael J. Karcher. 2013. "Youth Mentoring in Contemporary Perspective." In *Handbook of Youth Mentoring,* 2nd ed., edited by David L. DuBois and Michael J. Karcher. Thousand Oaks, Calif.: SAGE Publications.

Duncan, Brian, Jeffrey Groger, Ana Sofia Leon, and Stephen Trejo. 2020. "New Evidence of Generational Progress for Mexican Americans." *Labour Economics* 62(January): 1017771. https://doi.org/10.1016/j.labeco.2019.101771.

Duneier, Mitchell. 1994. *Slim's Table: Race, Respectability, and Masculinity.* Chicago: University of Chicago Press.

———. 1999. *Sidewalks.* New York: Farrar, Straus and Giroux.

———. 2011. "How Not to Lie with Ethnography." *Sociological Methodology* 41(1, August): 1–11. https://doi.org/10.1111/j.1467-9531.2011.01249.x.

Dunning, Thad. 2012. *Natural Experiments in Social Sciences: A Design-Based Approach.* New York: Cambridge University Press.

Durand, Jorge, Edward Telles, and Jennifer Flashman. 2006. "The Demographic Foundations of the Latino Population." Appendix C in *Multiple Origins, Uncertain Destinies: Hispanics and the American Future: Panel on Hispanics in the United States,* edited by Marta Tienda and Faith Mitchell. Washington, D.C.: National Academies Press.

Edin, Kathryn, and Laura Lein. 1997. *Making Ends Meet: How Single Mothers Survive Welfare and Low-Wage Work.* New York: Russell Sage Foundation.

Edin, Kathryn, and H. Luke Shaefer. 2015. *$2 a Day: Living on Nothing in America.* Boston: Houghton Mifflin Harcourt.

Edwards, Lisa M. 2004. "Measuring Perceived Social Support in Mexican American Youth: Psychometric Properties of the Multidimensional Scale of Perceived Social Support." *Hispanic Journal of Behavioral Sciences* 26(2, May): 187–94. https://doi.org/10.1177/0739986304264374.

Eisenberg, Nancy, Amanda Cumberland, Ivanna K. Guthrie, and Bridget C. Murphy. 2005. "Age Changes in Prosocial Responding and Moral Reasoning in Adolescence and Early Adulthood." *Journal of Research in Adolescence* 15(3): 235–60. https://doi.org/10.1111/j.1532-7795.2005.00095.x.

Elder, Glen H. 1974. *Children of the Great Depression: Social Change in Life Experiences.* Chicago: University of Chicago Press.

———. 1977. "Family History and the Life Course." *Journal of Family History* 2(4, December): 279–304. https://doi.org/10.1177/036319907700200402.

———. 1987. "Families and Lives: Some Developments in Life-Course Studies." *Journal of Family History* 12(1–3): 179–99.

————. 1998. "The Life Course and Human Development." In *Handbook of Child Psychology*, vol. 1, *Theoretical Models of Human Development*, edited by William Damon and Richard M. Lerner. New York: Wiley.

Elder, Glen H., and Richard C. Rockwell. 1979. "The Life-Course and Human Development: An Ecological Perspective." *International Journal of Behavioral Development* 2(1, March): 1–21. https://doi.org/10.1177/016502547900200101.

Eliason, Scott R., Jeylan T. Mortimer, and Mike Vuolo. 2015. "The Transition to Adulthood: Life Course Structures and Subjective Perceptions." *Social Psychology Quarterly* 78(3, September): 205–27. https://doi.org/10.1177/0190272515582002.

Ellickson, Phyllis, Joan S. Tucker, and David J. Klein. 2003. "Ten-Year Prospective Study of Public Health Problems Associated with Early Drinking." *Pediatrics* 111(5, part 1, May): 949–55. https://doi.org/10.1542/peds.111.5.949.

Elliott, Karla. 2020. *Young Men Navigating Contemporary Masculinities*. Cham, Switzerland: Springer.

Elster, Jon. 1978. *Logic and Society: Contradictions and Possible Worlds*. Chichester, U.K.: Wiley.

————. 1987. "Solomonic Judgments: Against the Best Interest of the Child." *University of Chicago Law Review* 54(1, Winter): 1–45. https://doi.org/10.2307/1599714.

Embrick, David, Silvia Domínguez, and Baran Karsak. 2017. "More than Just Insults: Rethinking Sociology's Contribution to Scholarship on Racial Microaggressions." *Sociological Inquiry* 87(2, May, special issue): 193–206. https://doi.org/10.1111/soin.12184.

English, Devin, Lisa Bowleg, Ana Maria del Rio-Gonzalez, Jeanne Tschann, Robert Agans, and David Malebranche. 2017. "Measuring Black Men's Police-Based Discrimination Experiences: Development and Validation of the Police and Law Enforcement (PLE) Scale." *Cultural Diversity and Ethnic Minority Psychology* 23(2, April): 185–99. https://doi.org/10.1037/cdp0000137.

Enriquez, Laura E. 2015. "Multigenerational Punishment: Shared Experience of Undocumented Immigration Status within Mixed-Status Families." *Journal of Marriage and Family* 77(4, August): 939–53. https://doi.org/10.1111/jomf.12196.

————. 2016. "'Nomas Cásate'/'Just Get Married': How Legalization Pathways Shape Mixed-Status Relationships." In *Beyond Black and White: A Reader on Contemporary Race Relations*, edited by Zulema Valdez. Thousand Oaks, Calif.: SAGE Publications.

————. 2017a. "Gendering Illegality: Undocumented Young Adults' Negotiation of the Family Formation Process." *American Behavioral Scientist* 61(10, September):1153–71. https://doi.org/10.1177/0002764217732103.

————. 2017b. "'A Master Status' or 'The Final Straw'? Assessing the Role of Immigration Status in Latino Undocumented Youths' Pathways Out of School." *Journal of Ethnic and Migration Studies* 43(9): 1526–43.

————. 2020. *Of Love and Papers: How Immigration Policy Affects Romance and Family*. Berkeley: University of California Press.

Enyioha, Jessica C. 2019. "College Access for Undocumented Students and Law." *Educational Considerations* 45(1): article 7. https://doi.org/10.4148/0146-9282.2168.

Erikson, Erik H. 1963. *Youth: Change and Challenge*. New York: Basic Books.

Ermisch, John, Markus Jäntti, and Timothy M. Smeeding. 2012. *From Parents to Children: The Intergenerational Transmission of Advantage*. New York: Russell Sage Foundation.

Escudero, Kevin. 2020. *Organizing while Undocumented: Immigrant Youth's Political Activism under the Law*. New York: New York University Press.

Espino, Michelle M. 2016. "The Value of Education and Educación: Nurturing Mexican American Children's Educational Aspirations to the Doctorate." *Journal of Latinos and Education* 15(2): 73–90. https://doi.org/10.1080/15348431.2015.1066250.

Ewick, Patricia, and Susan Silbey. 1995. "Subversive Stories and Hegemonic Tales: Toward a Sociology of Narrative." *Law and Society Review* 29(2): 197–226. https://doi.org/10.2307/3054010.

Feagin, Joe R., and Douglas Lee Eckberg. 1980. "Discrimination: Motivation, Action, Effects, and Context." *Annual Review of Sociology* 6: 1–20.

Feagin, Joe, Anthony Orum, and Gideon Sjoberg, eds. 1991. *A Case for the Case Study*. Chapel Hill: University of North Carolina Press.

Feliciano, Cynthia, and Rubén G. Rumbaut. 2019. "The Evolution of Ethnic Identity from Adolescence to Middle Adulthood: The Case of the Immigrant Second Generation." *Emerging Adulthood* 7(2, April): 85–96. https://doi.org/10.1177/2167696818805342.

Ferguson, Ann Arnett. 2001. *Bad Boys: Public Schools in the Making of Black Masculinity*. Ann Arbor: University of Michigan Press.

Fernández-Kelly, Patricia. 2015. *The Hero's Fight: African Americans in West Baltimore and the Shadow of the State*. Princeton, N.J.: Princeton University Press.

Fine, Gary Alan. 1993. "Ten Lies of Ethnography: Moral Dilemmas of Fieldwork." *Journal of Contemporary Ethnography* 22(3, October): 267–94. https://doi.org/10.1177/0891241193022003001.

Firestone, David. 1996. "Giuliani to Sue over Provision on Welfare." *New York Times*, September 12.

Fisk, Catherine, and Michael J. Wishnie. 2005. "The Story of 'Hoffman Plastic Compounds v. NLRB': Labor Rights without Remedies for Undocumented Immigrants." In *Labor Law Stories: An In-Depth Look at Leading Labor Law Cases*, edited by Laura J. Cooper and Catherine L. Fisk. New York: Foundation Press.

Fiske, Susan. 1993. "Controlling Other People: The Impact of Power on Stereotyping." *The American Psychologist* 48(6, May/June): 621–28. https://doi.org/10.1037//0003-066X.48.6.621.

———. 2011. *Envy Up, Scorn Down: How Status Divides Us*. New York: Russell Sage Foundation.

FitzGerald, David. 2014. "The Sociology of International Migration." In *Migration Theory: Talking across Disciplines*, edited by Caroline Brettell and James Hollifield. New York: Routledge.

Flores, Edward Orozco. 2012. *God's Gangs: Barrio Ministry, Masculinity, and Gang Recovery*. New York: New York University Press.

Flores, René D., and Ariela Schachter. 2018. "Who Are the 'Illegals'? The Social Construction of Illegality in the United States." *American Sociological Review* 83(5, October): 839–68. https://doi.org/10.1177/0003122418794635.

Foner, Nancy, Jan Willem Duyvendak, and Philip Kasinitz. 2019. "Introduction: Super-Diversity in Everyday Life." *Ethnic and Racial Studies* 42(1): 1–16. https://doi.org/10.1080/01419870.2017.1406969.

Foner, Nancy, and George Frederickson. 2004. *Not Just Black and White: Historical and Contemporary Perspectives on Immigration, Race, and Ethnicity in the United States.* New York: Russell Sage Foundation.

Fordham, Signithia, and John Ogbu. 1986. "Black Students' School Success: Coping with the Burden of 'Acting White.'" *Urban Review* 18(3): 176–206. https://doi.org/10.1007/BF01112192.

Forrest-Bank, Shandra S., and Jeffrey M. Jenson. 2015. "The Relationship among Childhood Risk and Protective Factors, Racial Microaggression and Ethnic Identity, and Academic Self-Efficacy and Antisocial Behavior in Young Adulthood." *Children and Youth Services Review* 50 (March): 64–74. https://doi.org/10.1016/j.childyouth.2015.01.005.

Fredriksen Goldsen, Karen I., Sarah Jen, and Anna Muraco. 2019. "Iridescent Life Course: LGBTQ Aging Research and Blueprint for the Future: A Systematic Review." *Gerontology* 65(3): 253–74.

Friedman, Abigail, and Atheendar S. Venkataramani. 2021. "Chilling Effects: U.S. Immigration Enforcement and Health Care Seeking Among Hispanic Adults." *Health Affairs* 40(7, July): 1056–65. https://doi.org/10.1377/hlthaff.2020.02356.

Fussell, Elizabeth. 2014. "Warmth of the Welcome: Attitudes toward Immigrants and Immigration Policy in the United States." *Annual Review of Sociology* 40(July): 479–98. https://doi.org/10.1146/annurev-soc-071913-043325.

Gaddis, S. Michael. 2012. "What's in a Relationship? An Examination of Social Capital, Race, and Class in Mentoring Relationships." *Social Forces* 90(4, June): 1237–69. https://doi.org/10.1093/sf/sos003.

Gálvez, Alyshia. 2011. *Patient Citizens, Immigrant Mothers: Mexican Women, Public Prenatal Care, and the Birth Weight Paradox.* New Brunswick, N.J.: Rutgers University Press.

Gangl, Markus. 2010. "Causal Inference in Sociological Research." *Annual Review of Sociology* 36(August 11): 21–47. https://doi.org/10.1146/annurev.soc.012809.102702.

Gans, Herbert J. 1979. "Symbolic Ethnicity: The Future of Ethnic Groups and Cultures in America." *Ethnic and Racial Studies* 2(1): 1–20. https://doi.org/10.1080/01419870.1979.9993248.

———. 1992. "Second-Generation Decline: Scenarios for the Economic and Ethnic Futures of the Post-1965 American Immigrants." *Ethnic and Racial Studies* 15(2): 173–92. https://doi.org/10.1080/01419870.1992.9993740.

Ganz, Marshall. 2009. "What Is Public Narrative: Self, Us, & Now." Working paper, Harvard University. http://nrs.harvard.edu/urn-3:HUL.InstRepos:30760283.

Garcia, Angela. 2019. *Legal Passing: Navigating Undocumented Life and Local Immigration.* Berkeley: University of California Press.

Gee, Lisa Christensen, Matthew Gardner, and Misha E. Wiehe. 2016. "Undocumented Immigrants' State and Local Tax Contributions." Washington, D.C.: Institute on Taxation and Economic Policy, March. https://itep.org/undocumented-immigrants-state-local-tax-contributions-2017/.

Geertz, Clifford. 1973. *The Interpretation of Cultures: Selected Essays*. New York: Basic Books.

———. 1974. "'From the Native's Point of View': On the Nature of Anthropological Understanding." *Bulletin of the American Academy of Arts and Sciences* 28(1, October): 26–45. https://doi.org/10.2307/3822971.

Gelman, Andrew, Jeffery Fagan, and Alex Kiss. 2007. "An Analysis of the NYPD's Stop-and-Frisk Policy in the Context of Claims of Racial Bias." *Journal of the American Statistical Association* 102(479, September): 813–23. https://doi.org/10.1198/016214506000001040.

George, Alexander L., and Alexander Bennett. 2005. *Case Studies and Theory Construction in the Social Sciences*. Cambridge, Mass.: Belknap Press of Harvard University Press.

Gerson, Kathleen, and Sarah Damaske. 2020. *The Science and Art of Interviewing*. New York: Oxford University Press.

Giddens, Anthony. 1984. *The Constitution of Society: Outline of the Theory of Structuration*. Oxford: Polity Press.

Gigerenzer, Gerd, and Wolfgang Gaissmaier. 2011. "Heuristic Decision Making." *Annual Review of Psychology* 62: 451–82. https://doi.org/10.1146/annurev-psych-120709-145346.

Gil-White, Francisco J. 2001. "Are Ethnic Groups Biological 'Species' to the Human Brain? Essentialism in Our Cognition of Some Social Categories." *Current Anthropology* 42(4, August–October): 515–54. https://doi.org/10.1086/321802.

Gleeson, Shannon. 2010. "Labor Rights for All? The Role of Undocumented Immigrant Status for Worker Claims Making." *Law and Social Inquiry* 35(3): 561–602.

Gleeson, Shannon, and Roberto G. Gonzales. 2012. "When Do Papers Matter? Institutional Analysis of Undocumented Life in the U.S." *International Migration* 50(4, August): 1–19. https://doi.org/10.1111/j.1468-2435.2011.00726.x.

Gluckman, Max. 1940. "Analysis of a Social Situation in Modern Zululand." *Bantu Studies* 14(1): 1–30, 147–74.

Goertz, Gary. 2017. *Multimethod Research, Causal Mechanisms, and Case Studies*. Princeton, N.J.: Princeton University Press.

Goertz, Gary, and James Mahoney. 2012. *A Tale of Two Cultures: Qualitative and Quantitative Research in the Social Sciences*. Princeton, N.J.: Princeton University Press.

Goffman, Alice. 2014. *On the Run: Life in an American City*. Chicago: University of Chicago Press.

Goffman, Erving. 1961. *Asylums: Essays on the Social Situation of Mental Patients and Other Inmates*. New York: Anchor Books.

———. 1963. *Stigma: Notes on the Management of Spoiled Identity*. New York: J. Aronson.

Golash-Boza, Tanya. 2021. *Race and Racisms: A Critical Approach*. Oxford: Oxford University Press.

Gomberg-Munoz, Ruth, and Laura Nussbaum-Barberena. 2011. "Is Immigration Policy Labor Policy? Immigration Enforcement, Undocumented Workers, and the State." *Human Organization* 70(4, Winter): 366–75. https://doi.org/10.17730/humo.70.4.n253284457h28312.

Gomez Cervantes, Andrea. 2021. "'Looking Mexican': Indigenous and Non-Indigenous Latina/o Immigrants and the Racialization of Illegality in the Midwest." *Social Problems* 68(1): 100–117.

Gonzales, Roberto G. 2011. "Learning to Be Illegal." *American Sociological Review* 76(4, August): 602–19. https://doi.org/10.1177/0003122411411901.

———. 2016. *Lives in Limbo: Undocumented and Coming of Age in America.* Oakland: University of California Press.

Gonzales, Roberto G., and Edelina Burciaga. 2018. "Segmented Pathways of Illegality: Reconciling the Co-existence of Master and Auxiliary Statuses in the Experiences of 1.5 Generation Undocumented Young Adults." *Ethnicities* 18(2, April): 178–91. https://doi.org/10.1177/1468796818767176.

Gonzales, Roberto G., and Stephen P. Ruszczyk. 2021. "The Legal Status Divide among the Children of Immigrants." *Daedalus* 150(2, Spring): 135–49. https://doi.org/10.1162/daed_a_01851.

Gonzales, Roberto G., Veronica Terriquez, and Stephen P. Ruszczyk. 2014. "Becoming DACAmented: Assessing the Short-Term Benefits of Deferred Action for Childhood Arrivals (DACA)." *American Behavioral Scientist* 58(14, December): 1852–72. https://doi.org/10.1177/0002764214550288.

Gonzalez-Barrera, Ana, and Jens Manuel Krogstad. 2019. "What We Know about Illegal Immigration from Mexico." Washington, D.C.: Pew Research Center, June 28. https://www.pewresearch.org/short-reads/2019/06/28/what-we-know-about-illegal-immigration-from-mexico/.

Goodman, Joan F. 2010. "Student Authority: Antidote to Alienation." *Theory and Research in Education* 8(3, November): 227–47. https://doi.org/10.1177/1477878510381626.

Gordon, Milton. 1964. *Assimilation in American Life: The Role of Race, Religion, and National Origins.* New York: Free Press.

Gormally, Sinead. 2015. "'I've Been There, Done That . . .': A Study of Youth Gang Desistance." *Youth Justice* 15(2, August): 148–65. https://doi.org/10.1177/1473225414549679.

Goss, Stephen, Alice Wade, J. Patrick Skirvin, Michael Morris, K. Mark Bye, and Danielle Huston. 2013. "Effects of Unauthorized Immigration on the Actuarial Status of the Social Security Trust Funds." Actuarial Note 151. Washington, D.C.: Social Security Administration, April. https://www.ssa.gov/oact/NOTES/pdf_notes/note151.pdf.

Gramlich, John. 2019. "Young Americans Are Less Trusting of Other People—and Key Institutions—than Their Elders." Washington, D.C.: Pew Research Center, August 6. https://www.pewresearch.org/short-reads/2019/08/06/young-americans-are-less-trusting-of-other-people-and-key-institutions-than-their-elders/.

Granovetter, Mark S. 1973. "The Strength of Weak Ties." *American Journal of Sociology* 78(6, May): 1360–80. https://doi.org/10.1086/225469.

Grebler, Leo, Joan W. Moore, and Ralph C. Guzman. 1970. *The Mexican-American People: The Nation's Second Largest Minority.* New York: Free Press.

Green, David A. 2013. "Penal Optimism and Second Chances: The Legacies of American Protestantism and the Prospects for Penal Reform." *Punishment and Society* 15(2, April): 123–46. https://doi.org/10.1177/1462474513477789.

Greenstein, Robert, Elaine Maag, Chye-Ching Huang, Emily Horton, and Chloe Cho. 2018. "Improving the Child Tax Credit for Very Low-Income Families." Washington, D.C.: Urban Institute, U.S. Partnership on Mobility from Poverty, April. https://www.cbpp.org/sites/default/files/atoms/files/urban_ctc_paper.pdf.

Griffin, Christine, Andrew Bengry-Howell, Chris Hackley, Willm Mistral, and Isabelle Szmigin. 2009. "'Every Time I Do It I Absolutely Annihilate Myself': Loss of (Self-)Consciousness and Loss of Memory in Young People's Drinking Narratives." *Sociology* 43(3, June): 457–76. https://doi.org/10.1177/0038038509103201.

Griffith, Derek M., Katie Gunter, and Daphne C. Watkins. 2012. "Measuring Masculinity in Research on Men of Color: Findings and Future Directions." *American Journal of Public Health* 102(suppl., 2, May): S187–94. https://doi.org/10.2105/AJPH.2012.300715.

Grossman, Jean, Christian S. Chan, Sarah E. O. Schwartz, and Jean E. Rhodes. 2012. "The Test of Time in School-Based Mentoring: The Role of Relationship Duration and Re-Matching on Academic Outcomes." *American Journal of Community Psychology* 49(1, March): 43–54. https://doi.org/10.1007/s10464-011-9435-0.

Grubb, W. Norton. 2002. "Learning and Earning in the Middle, Part I, National Studies of Pre-Baccalaureate Education." *Economics of Education Review* 21(4, August): 299–321. https://doi.org/10.1016/S0272-7757(01)00042-5.

Grubb, W. Norton, Norena Badway, and Denise Bell. 2003. "Community Colleges and the Equity Agenda: The Potential of Noncredit Education." *Annals of the American Academy of Political and Social Science* 586(1, March): 218–40. https://doi.org/10.1177/0002716202250226.

Grusky, David, Timothy M. Smeeding, and C. Matthew Snipp. 2015. "A New Infrastructure for Monitoring Social Mobility in the 21st Century." *Annals of the American Academy of Political and Social Science* 657(1, January): 63–82. https://doi.org/10.1177/0002716214549941.

Guerrero-Rippberger, Sara. 1999. "But for the Day of Tomorrow: Negotiating Femininity in a New York Mexican Identity." Senior thesis, Sociology Department, Barnard College.

Gutmann, Matthew C. 1996. *The Meanings of Macho: Being a Man in Mexico City.* Berkeley: University of California Press.

Guyll, Max, Madon Stephanie, Spoth Richard, and Lannin Daniel. 2014. "Popularity as a Predictor of Early Alcohol Use and Moderator of Other Risk Processes." *Journal of the Study of Alcohol and Drugs* 75(6): 919–28. https://www.doi.org/10.15288/jsad.2014.75.919.

Guzmán, Juan Carlos, and Raúl C. Jara. 2012. "The Economic Benefits of Passing the DREAM Act." Washington, D.C.: Center for American Progress, October. https://www.immigrationresearch.org/system/files/economic-benefits-dream.pdf/.

Hagan, Jacqueline Maria. 1998. "Social Networks, Gender, and Immigrant Incorporation: Resources and Constraints." *American Sociological Review* 63(1, February): 55–67. https://doi.org/10.2307/2657477.

Hagan, Jacqueline, Rubén Hernández-León, and Jean-Luc Demonsant. 2015. *Skills of the Unskilled: Work and Mobility among Mexican Migrants.* Berkeley: University of California Press.

Hainmueller, Jens, Duncan Lawrence, Linna Martén, Bernard Black, Lucila Figueroa, Michael Hotard, Tomás R. Jiménez, Fernando Mendoza, Maria I. Rodriguez, Jonas J. Swartz, and David D. Laitin. 2017. "Protecting Unauthorized Immigrant Mothers Improves Their Children's Mental Health." *Science* 357(6355, September 8): 1041–44. https://doi.org/10.1126/science.aan5893.

Hajer, Maarten A. 1995. *The Politics of Environmental Discourse: Ecological Modernization and the Policy Process.* Oxford: Oxford University Press.

Hajer, Maarten A., and David Laws. 2008. "Ordering through Discourse." In *The Oxford Handbook of Public Policy Laws*, edited by Robert Goodin, Michael Moran, and Martin Rein. New York: Oxford University Press.

Hall, Joanne M., and Becky Fields. 2015. "'It's Killing Us!' Narratives of Black Adults about Microaggression Experiences and Related Health Stress." *Global Qualitative Nursing Research* 9(2, July): 1–14. https://doi.org/10.1177/2333393615591569.

Hamilton, Erin R., Jo Mhairi Hale, and Robin Savinar. 2019. "Immigrant Legal Status and Health: Legal Status Disparities in Chronic Conditions and Musculoskeletal Pain among Mexican-Born Farm Workers in the U.S." *Demography* 56(1, February): 1–24. https://doi.org/10.1007/s13524-018-0746-8.

Hamilton, Erin R., Caitlin C. Patler, and Jo Mhairi Hale. 2019. "Growing Up without Status: The Integration of Children in Mixed-Status Families." *Sociology Compass* 13(6, June): e12695. https://doi.org/10.1111/soc4.12695.

Hamilton, Erin R., Caitlin Patler, and Robin Savinar. 2021. "Transition into Liminal Legality: DACA's Mixed Impacts on Educational and Employment among Young Adult Immigrants in California." *Social Problems* 68(3, August): 675–95. https://doi.org/10.1093/socpro/spaa016.

Hamilton, Tod G., and Rama Hagos. 2020. "Race and the Healthy Immigrant Effect." *Public Policy and Aging Report* 31(1, December 28):14–18. https://doi.org/10.1093/ppar/praa042.

Hamlin, Robert. 2017. "'The Gaze Heuristic': Biography of an Adaptively Rational Decision Making Process." *Topics in Cognitive Science* 9(2, April): 264–88. https://doi.org/10.1111/tops.12253.

Hamm, Jill. 2000. "Do Birds of a Feather Flock Together? The Variable Bases for African American, Asian American, and European American Adolescents' Selection of Similar Friends." *Developmental Psychology* 36(2): 209–19. https://doi.org/10.1037//0012-1649.36.2.209.

Hammersley, Martyn. 1990. "What's Wrong with Ethnography? The Myth of Theoretical Description." *Sociology* 24(4, November): 597–615. https://doi.org/10.1177/0038038590024004003.

Handel, Gerald, and Gail Whitchurch. 1994. *The Psychosocial Interior of the Family.* New York: Aldine de Gruyter.

Harper, Shaun R. 2004. "The Measure of a Man: Conceptualizations of Masculinity among High-Achieving African American Male College Students." *Berkeley Journal of Sociology* 48: 89–107.

Heaphy, Brian. 2018. "Troubling Traditional and Conventional Families? Formalised Same-Sex Couples and 'The Ordinary.'" *Sociological Research Online* 23(1, March): 160–76. https://doi.org/10.1177/1360780418754779.

Heimer, Carol. 2001. "Cases and Biographies: An Essay on Routinization and the Nature of Comparison." *Annual Review of Sociology* 27(1, August): 47–76. https://doi.org/10.1146/annurev.soc.27.1.47.

Heitzeg, Nancy A. 2016. *The School-to-Prison Pipeline: Education, Discipline, and Racialized Double Standards.* Santa Barbara, Calif.: Praeger.

Hernandez-Wolfe, Pilar, and Teresa McDowell. 2012. "Speaking of Privilege: Family Therapy Educators' Journeys toward Awareness and Compassionate Action." *Family Process* 51(2, June): 163–78. https://doi.org/10.1111/j.1545-5300.2012.01394.

Herrera, Juan. 2016. "Racialized Illegality: The Regulation of Informal Labor and Space." *Latino Studies* 14: 320–43. https://doi.org/10.1057/s41276-016-0007-1.

Herrera, Carla, David DuBois, and Jean Baldwin Grossman. 2013. *The Role of Risk: Mentoring Experiences for Youth with Varying Risk Profiles.* New York: MDRC.

Higley, Stephen. 1995. *Privilege, Power, and Place: The Geography of the American Upper Class.* Lanham, Md.: Rowman & Littlefield Publishers.

Hill, Patrick L., Nicholas A. Turiano, and Anthony L. Burrow. 2018. "Early Life Adversity as a Predictor of Sense of Purpose during Adulthood." *International Journal of Behavioral Development* 42(1, January 1): 143–47. https://doi.org/10.1177/0165025416681537.

Hill Collins, Patricia. 2000. "Gender, Black Feminism, and Black Political Economy." *Annals of the American Academy of Political and Social Science* 568(1, March): 41–53. https://doi.org/10.1177/000271620056800105.

Hingson, Ralph W., Timothy Heeren, Amber Jamanka, and Jonathan Howland. 2000. "Age of Drinking Onset and Unintentional Injury Involvement after Drinking." *Journal of the American Medical Association* 284(September 27): 1527–33. https://doi.org/10.1001/jama.284.12.1527.

Hirschman, Albert O. 1970. "The Search for Paradigms as a Hindrance to Understanding." *World Politics* 22(3): 329–43. https://doi.org/10.2307/2009600.

Hochschild, Arlie Russell. 2018. *Strangers in Their Own Land: Anger and Mourning on the American Right.* New York: New Press.

Hochschild, Jennifer, Jacqueline Chattooadhyay, Claudine Gay, and Michael Jones Correa. 2013. "Introduction." In *Outsiders No More? Models of Immigrant Incorporation,* edited by Jennifer Hochschild, Jacqueline Chattooadhyay, Claudine Gay, and Michael Jones Correa. Oxford: Oxford University Press.

Hochschild, Jennifer, Velsa Weaver, and Traci Burch. 2012. *Creating a New Racial Order: How Immigration, Multiracialism, Genomics, and the Young Can Remake Race in America.* Princeton, N.J.: Princeton University Press.

Hodges, Melissa J., and Michelle J. Budig. 2010. "Who Gets the Daddy Bonus? Organizational Hegemonic Masculinity and the Impact of Fatherhood on Earnings." *Gender and Society* 24(6, December): 717–45. https://doi.org/10.1177/0891243210386729.

Holmes, Seth M. 2012. "The Clinical Gaze in the Practice of Migrant Health: Mexican Migrants in the United States." *Social Science and Medicine* 74(6, March): 873–81. https://doi.org/10.1016/j.socscimed.2011.06.06.

——. 2013. *Fresh Fruit, Broken Bodies: Migrant Farmworkers in the United States.* Berkeley: University of California Press.

Holzer, Harry J. 1999. *What Employers Want: Job Prospects for Less-Educated Workers*. New York: Russell Sage Foundation.

Hondagneu-Sotelo, Pierette. 1994. *Gendered Transitions: Mexican Experiences of Immigration*. Berkeley: University of California Press.

Hondagneu-Sotelo, Pierrette, and Manuel Pastor. 2021. *South Central Dreams: Finding Home and Building Community in South L.A.* New York: New York University Press.

Hsin, Amy, and Yu Xie. 2014. "Explaining Asian Americans' Academic Advantage over Whites." *Proceedings of the National Academy of Sciences of the United States* 111(23, May 5): 8416–21. https://doi.org/10.1073/pnas.1406402111.

Huang, Chye-Ching, and Roderick Taylor. 2019. "How the Federal Tax Code Can Better Advance Racial Equity: 2017 Tax Law Took Step Backward." July 25. Washington, D.C.: Center on Budget and Policy Priorities. https://www.cbpp.org/sites/default/files/atoms/files/7-25-19tax.pdf.

Hughes, Everett Cherrington. 1945. "Dilemmas and Contradictions of Status." *American Journal of Sociology* 50(5, March): 353–59. https://doi.org/10.1086/219652.

Hunn, Vanessa, Dana Harley, Willie Elliot, and James P. Canfield. 2015. "Microaggression and the Mitigation of Psychological Harm: Four Social Workers' Exposition for Care of Clients, Students, and Faculty Who Suffer 'A Thousand Little Cuts.'" *Journal of Pan African Studies* 7(9, April): 41–54. http://www.jpanafrican.org/docs/vol7no9/7.9-6-Jackson-Hunn.pdf.

Hunt, Geoffrey, Karen Joe-Laidler, and Kathleen MacKenzie. 2005. "Moving into Motherhood: Gang Girls and Controlled Risk." *Youth and Society* 36(3, March): 333–73. https://doi.org/10.1177/0044118X04266530.

Imoagene, Onoso. 2017. *Beyond Expectations: Second-Generation Nigerians in the United States and Britain*. Berkeley: University of California Press.

Israel, Emma, and Jeanne Batalova. 2020. "Mexican Immigrants in the United States." Washington, D.C.: Migration Policy Institute, November 5. https://www.migrationpolicy.org/article/mexican-immigrants-united-states-2019.

Jacobs, James B. 2015. *The Eternal Criminal Record*. Cambridge, Mass.: Harvard University Press.

Jensen, Sune Qvotrup. 2010. "Masculinity at the Margins: Othering, Marginality, and Resistance among Young Marginalized Ethnic Minority Men." *International Journal for Masculinity Studies* 5(1): 6–26. https://doi.org/10.18261/ISSN1890-2146-2010-01-02.

Jerolmack, Colin. 2007. "Animal Practices, Ethnicity, and Community: The Turkish Pigeon Handlers of Berlin." *American Sociological Review* 72(6, December): 874–94. https://doi.org/10.1177/000312240707200602.

Jerolmack, Colin, and Shamus Khan. 2017. "The Analytic Lenses of Ethnography." *Socius: Sociological Research for a Dynamic World Volume* 3(October 5): 1–11. https://doi.org/10.1177/2378023117735256.

Jiménez, Tomás. 2009. *Replenished Ethnicity: Mexican Americans, Immigration, and Identity*. Berkeley: University of California Press.

———. 2017. *The Other Side of Assimilation: How Immigrants Are Changing American Life*. Berkeley: University of California Press.

Jiménez, Tomás R., and David Fitzgerald. 2007. "Mexican Assimilation: A Temporal and Spatial Reorientation." *Du Bois Review* 4(2, Fall): 337–354. https://doi.org/10.1017/S1742058X07070191.

Jiménez, Tomás R., and Adam L. Horowitz. 2013. "When White Is Just Alright: How Immigrants Redefine Achievement and Reconfigure the Ethnoracial Hierarchy." *American Sociological Review* 78(5, October): 849–71. https://doi.org/10.1177/0003122413497012.

Jiménez-Castellanos, Oscar, and Gustavo Gonzales. 2012. "Understanding the Impact of Micro-Aggressions on the Engagement of Undocumented Latino Immigrant Fathers: Debunking Deficit Thinking." *Journal of Latinos and Education* 11(4): 204–17. https://doi.org/10.1080/15348431.2012.715492.

Johns, Merida L. 2013. "Breaking the Glass Ceiling: Structural, Cultural, and Organizational Barriers Preventing Women from Achieving Senior and Executive Positions." *Perspectives in Health Information Management* 10(Winter): 1e.

Johnson, David W., and Roger T. Johnson. 2009. "An Educational Psychology Success Story: Social Interdependence Theory and Cooperative Learning." *Educational Researcher* 38(5, June): 365–79. https://doi.org/10.3102/0013189X09339057.

Jones, Jennifer A. 2022. "'They Are There with Us': Theorizing Racial Status and Intergroup Relations." *American Journal of Sociology* 128(2): 411–61.

Kansky, Jessica, Joseph P. Allen, and Ed Diener. 2016. "Early Adolescent Affect Predicts Later Life Outcomes." *Health and Well Being* 8(2): 192–212.

Kasinitz, Philip, John Mollenkopf, Mary Waters, and Sarah Holdaway. 2008. *Inheriting the City: The Second Generation Comes of Age.* New York: Russell Sage Foundation.

Katz, Jack. 1988. *Seductions of Crime: Moral and Sensual Attractions in Doing Evil.* New York: Basic Books.

———. 1997. "Ethnography's Warrants." *Sociological Methods and Research* 25(4, May): 391–423. https://doi.org/10.1177/0049124197025004002.

———. 2001a. "From How to Why: On Luminous Description and Causal Inference in Ethnography: Part 1." *Ethnography* 2(4, December): 443–73. https://doi.org/10.1177/146613801002004001.

———. 2001b. "Analytic Induction." In *International Encyclopedia of the Social and Behavioral Sciences,* edited by Neil J. Smelser and Paul B. Baltes. Amsterdam: Elsevier.

———. 2002. "From How to Why: On Luminous Description and Causal Inference in Ethnography: Part 2." *Ethnography* 3(1, March): 63–90. https://doi.org/10.1177/1466138102003001003.

Keister, Lisa A. 2011. *Faith and Money: How Religious Belief Contributes to Wealth and Poverty.* Cambridge: Cambridge University Press.

Keister, Lisa, Jody Agius Vallejo, and Paige E. Borelli. 2015. "Mexican American Mobility: Early Life Processes and Adult Wealth Ownership." *Social Forces* 93(3, March): 1015–46. https://doi.org/10.1093/sf/sou102.

Kendi, Ibram X. 2019. *How to Be an Anti-Racist.* London: One World Publishing.

Kerani, Roxanne P., and Helena A. Kwakwa. 2018. "Scaring Undocumented Immigrants Is Detrimental to Public Health." *American Journal of Public Health* 108(9, September): 1165–66. https://doi.org/10.2105/AJPH.2018.304596.

Kerckhoff, Alan C. 1993. *Diverging Pathways: Social Structure and Career Deflections.* New York: Cambridge University Press.

Kille, David R., and Crystal T. Tse. 2017. "Whose Family Fits? Categorization and Evaluation of Same-Sex and Cross-Race-Parent Families." *Group Processes and Intergroup Relations* 20(1, January): 109–24. https://doi.org/10.1177/1368430215595106.

Kimmel, Michael. 2010. *Misframing Men: The Politics of Contemporary Masculinities.* New Brunswick, N.J.: Rutgers University Press.

Kimmel, Michael, Jeff Hearn, and Robert W. Connell. 2004. *Handbook of Studies on Men and Masculinities.* Thousand Oaks, Calif.: SAGE Publications.

King, Garry, Robert Keohane, and Sidney Verba. 1994. *Designing Social Inquiry: Scientific Inference in Qualitative Research.* Princeton, N.J.: Princeton University Press.

Kline, Nolan. 2019. *Pathogenic Policing: Immigration Enforcement and Health in the U.S. South.* New Brunswick, N.J.: Rutgers University Press.

Knight, Carly R., and Christopher Winship. 2013. "The Causal Implications of Mechanistic Thinking: Identification Using Directed Acyclic Graphs (DAGs)." In *Handbook of Causal Analysis for Social Research,* edited by Stephen L. Morgan. New York: Springer.

Knorr Cetina, Karin. 1999. *Epistemic Cultures: How the Sciences Make Knowledge.* Cambridge, Mass.: Harvard University Press.

Knowles, John, Nicola Persico, and Petra Todd. 2001. "Racial Bias in Motor Vehicle Searches: Theory and Evidence." *Journal of Political Economy* 109(1, June): 203–32. https://doi.org/10.1086/318603.

Kossoudji, Sherrie A., and Deborah Cobb-Clark. 2002. "Coming Out of the Shadows: Learning about Legal Status and Wages from the Legalized Population." *Journal of Labor Economics* 20(3): 598–628. https://doi.org/10.1086/339611.

Kram, Kathy E. 1988. *Mentoring at Work: Developmental Relationships in Organizational Life.* Lanham, Md.: University Press of America.

Kram, Kathy E., and Lynn A. Isabella. 1985. "Mentoring Alternatives: The Role of Peer Relationships in Career Development." *Academy of Management Journal* 28(1, November 30): 110–32. https://doi.org/10.5465/256064.

Kristof, Nicholas. 2018. "An American 13-Year Old, Pregnant, and Married to Her Rapist." *New York Times,* June 1. https://www.nytimes.com/2018/06/01/opinion/sunday/child-marriage-delaware.html.

Krogstad, Jens Manuel. 2020. "Americans Broadly Support Legal Status for Immigrants Brought to the U.S. Illegally as Children." June 17. Pew Research Center. https://www.pewresearch.org/short-reads/2020/06/17/americans-broadly-support-legal-status-for-immigrants-brought-to-the-u-s-illegally-as-children/.

Krogstad, Jens Manuel, and Ana Gonzalez-Barrera. 2014. "If Original DACA Program Is a Guide, Many Eligible Immigrants Will Apply for Deportation Relief." Washington, D.C.: Pew Research Center, December 6. https://www.pewresearch.org/short-reads/2014/12/05/if-original-daca-program-is-a-guide-many-eligible-immigrants-will-apply-for-deportation-relief/.

Krogstad, Jens Manuel, Jeffrey Passel, and D'Vera Cohn. 2019. "5 Facts about Illegal Immigration in the U.S." Washington, D.C.: Pew Research Center, June 12. https://www.pewresearch.org/short-reads/2019/06/12/5-facts-about -illegal-immigration-in-the-u-s/.

Krugman, Paul. 2020. *Arguing with Zombies: Economics, Politics, and the Fight for a Better Future.* New York: W. W. Norton.

Kuhn, Randall, Bethany Everett, and Rachel Silvey. 2011. "The Effects of Children's Migration on Elderly Kin's Health: A Counterfactual Approach." *Demography* 48(1, February): 183–209. https://doi.org/10.1007/s13524-010 -0002-3.

Kuka, Elira, Na'ama Shenhav, and Kevin Shih. 2020. "Do Human Capital Decisions Respond to the Returns to Education? Evidence from DACA." *American Economic Journal: Economic Policy* 12(1): 293–324. https://doi.org /10.1257/pol.20180352.

Kwong, Peter. 1987. *The New Chinatown.* New York: Hill and Wang.

Lamont, Michèle. 2009. *How Professors Think: Inside the Curious World of Academic Judgment.* Cambridge, Mass.: Harvard University Press.

Lamont, Michèle, and Virág Molnár. 2002. "The Study of Boundaries in the Social Sciences." *Annual Review of Sociology* 28(August): 167–95. https:// doi.org/10.1146/annurev.soc.28.110601.141107.

Lamont, Michèle, and Patricia White. 2009. *Workshop on Interdisciplinary Standards for Systematic Qualitative Research: Cultural Anthropology, Law and Social Science, Political Science, and Sociology Programs.* Washington, D.C.: National Science Foundation. http://www.nsf.gov/sbe/ses/soc/ISSQR_workshop _rpt.pdf.

Landale, Nancy S., Jessica Halliday Hardie, R. S. Oropesa, and Marianne M. Hillemeier. 2015. "Behavioral Functioning among Mexican-Origin Children: Does Parental Legal Status Matter?" *Journal of Health and Social Behavior* 56(1, March): 2–18. https://doi.org/10.1177/0022146514567896.

Lareau, Annette. 2011 *Unequal Childhoods: Class, Race, and Family Life.* Berkeley: University of California Press.

Latour, Bruno, and Steve Woolgar. 1986. *Laboratory Life: The Construction of Scientific Facts.* Princeton, N.J.: Princeton University Press.

Laub, John H., and Robert J. Sampson. 1993. *Crime in the Making: Pathways and Turning Points through Life.* Cambridge, Mass.: Harvard University Press.

———. 2003. *Shared Beginnings, Divergent Lives: Delinquent Boys to Age 70.* Cambridge, Mass.: Harvard University Press.

———. 2020. "Life-Course and Developmental Criminology: Looking Back, Moving Forward." *Journal of Developmental and Life-Course Criminology*: 6: 158–71. https://doi.org/10.1007/s40865-019-00110-x.

Lawson, Kenneth. 2015. "Police Shooting of Black Men and Implicit Racial Bias: Can't We All Just Get Along." *University of Hawaii Law Review* 37: 339. http:// hdl.handle.net/10125/66072.

LeCompte, Margaret D., and Judith Preissle Goetz. 1982. "Problems of Reliability and Validity in Ethnographic Research." *Review of Educational Research* 52(1, Spring): 31–60. https://doi.org/10.3102/00346543052001031.

Lee, Jennifer, and Frank D. Bean. 2007. "Reinventing the Color Line: Immigration and America's New Racial/Ethnic Divide." *Social Forces* 86(2, December): 126. https://doi.org/10.1093/sf/86.2.561.

Lee, Jennifer, and Min Zhou. 2015. *The Asian American Achievement Paradox.* New York: Russell Sage Foundation.

Legewie, Nicolas. 2013. "An Introduction to Applied Data Analysis with Qualitative Comparative Analysis." *Forum Qualitative Sozialforschung (Forum: Qualitative Social Research)* 14(3, September 29). https://doi.org/10.17169/fqs-14.3.1961.

Lenski, Gerhard. 2013. *Power and Privilege: A Theory of Social Stratification.* Chapel Hill: University of North Carolina Press.

Levine, Kenneth J. 2021. "It's Okay to Change Your Mind: You Do Not Need to Vote the Same Way Twice." *American Behavioral Scientist* 66(3, March): 376–89. https://doi.org/10.1177/00027642211009277.

Levinson, David. 2005. *Community Colleges: A Reference Handbook.* Santa Barbara, Calif.: ABC-CLIO.

Lewis, Oscar. 1961. *Children of Sánchez: Autobiography of a Mexican Family.* New York: Random House.

Lewis, Tyson, and Elizabeth Vazquez Solórzano. 2006. "Unraveling the Heart of the School-to-Prison Pipeline." In *Reinventing Critical Pedagogy: Widening the Circle of Anti-Oppression Education,* edited by César Augusto Rossatto, Ricky Lee Allen, and Marc Pruyn. Lanham, Md.: Rowman and Littlefield.

Lieberson, Stanley, and Freda B. Lynn. 2002. "Barking Up the Wrong Branch: Scientific Alternatives to the Current Model of Sociological Science." *Annual Review of Sociology* 28(August): 1–19. https://doi.org/10.1146/annurev.soc.28.110601.141122.

Light, Audrey. 1999. "High School Employment, High School Curriculum, and Post-School Wages." *Economics of Education Review* 18(3, June): 291–309. https://doi.org/10.1016/S0272-7757(99)00007-2.

Liu, Jia-Lin. 2022. "Face, Race, and Legality: How Class Origins and Cultural Practices Matter among Transnational Undocumented and Mixed-Status Chinese Families." PhD diss., International Education, New York University.

Lobo de la Tierra, Albert. 2016. "Essentializing Manhood in 'the Street': Perilous Masculinity and Popular Criminological Ethnographies." *Feminist Criminology* 11(4, October): 375–97. https://doi.org/10.1177/1557085116662313.

Longazel, Jamie. 2013. "Subordinating Myth: Latino/a Immigration, Crime, and Exclusion." *Sociology Compass* 7(2, February): 87–96. https://doi.org/10.1111/soc4.12018.

López, Gustavo, and Jens Manuela Krogstad. 2017. "Key Facts about Unauthorized Immigrants Enrolled in DACA." Washington, D.C.: Pew Research Center, September 25. https://www.pewresearch.org/fact-tank/2017/09/25/key-facts-about-unauthorized-immigrants-enrolled-in-daca/.

Lopez, Mark Hugo, Ana Gonzalez-Barrera, and Jens Manuel Krogstad. 2018. "More Latinos Have Serious Concerns about Their Place in America under Trump." Washington, D.C.: Pew Research Center, October 25. https://www.pewresearch.org/hispanic/2018/10/25/more-latinos-have-serious-concerns-about-their-place-in-america-under-trump/.

Lopez, Mark Hugo, Jeffrey S. Passell, and D'Vera Cohn. 2021. "Key Facts about the Changing U.S. Unauthorized Immigrant Population." April 13. Washington D.C.: Pew Research Center.

Louie, Vivian. 2012. *Keeping the Immigrant Bargain: The Costs and Rewards of Success in America.* New York: Russell Sage Foundation.

Lu, Wei Ting. 2013. "Confucius or Mozart? Community Cultural Wealth and Upward Mobility among Children of Chinese Immigrants." *Qualitative Sociology* 36(3): 303–21. https://doi.org/10.1007/s11133-013-9251-y.

Lundman, Richard, and Robert Kaufman. 2003. "Driving while Black: Effects of Race, Ethnicity, and Gender on Citizen Self-Reports of Traffic Stops and Police Actions." *Criminology* 41(1, February): 195–220. https://doi.org/10.1111/j.1745-9125.2003.tb00986.x.

Luthra, Renee, Roger Waldinger, and Thomas Soehl. 2018. *Origins and Destinations: The Making of the Second Generation.* New York: Russell Sage Foundation.

Luyt, Russell, and Don Foster. 2001. "Hegemonic Masculine Conceptualisation in Gang Culture." *South African Journal of Psychology* 31(3, August): 1–11. https://doi.org/10.1177/008124630103100301.

MacDonald, John, and Jessica Saunders. 2012. "Are Immigrant Youth Less Violent? Specifying the Reasons and Mechanisms." *Annals of the American Academy of Political and Social Science* 641(1): 125–47.

MacKenzie, Kathleen, Geoffrey Hunt, and Karen Joe-Laidler. 2008. "Youth Gangs and Drugs: The Case of Marijuana." *Journal of Ethnicity in Substance Abuse* 4(3/4): 99–134. https://doi.org/10.1300/J233v04n03_05.

Mackey, Kathleen, Mary Louise Arnold, and Michael W. Pratt. 2001. "Adolescents' Stories of Decision Making in More and Less Authoritative Families: Representing the Voices of Parents in Narrative." *Journal of Adolescent Research* 16(3, May): 243–68. https://doi.org/10.1177/0743558401163001.

MacLeon, Jay. 2008. *Ain't No Makin' It: Aspirations and Attainment in a Low-Income Neighborhood.* Boulder, Colo.: Westview Press.

Mader, Nicole, Clara Hemphill, and Qasim Abbas. 2018. "The Paradox of Choice: How School Choice Divides New York City Elementary Schools." New School Center for New York City Affairs, May. https://static1.squarespace.com/static/53ee4f0be4b015b9c3690d84/t/5aecb1c3352f537d3541623b/1525461450469/The+Paradox+of+Choice.pdf.

Mahler, Sarah. 1995. *American Dreaming: Immigrant Life on the Margins.* Princeton, N.J.: Princeton University Press.

Mahoney, James. 2000. "Path Dependence in Historical Sociology." *Theory and Society* 29(4, August): 507–48. https://doi.org/10.1023/A:1007113830879.

———. 2001. "Beyond Correlational Analysis: Recent Innovations in Theory and Method." *Sociological Forum* 16(3, September): 575–93. https://doi.org/10.1023/A:1011912816997.

———. 2004. "Comparative-Historical Methodology." *Annual Review of Sociology* 30(August 11): 81–101. https://doi.org/10.1146/annurev.soc.30.012703.110507.

Mahoney, James, and Rodrigo Barrenechea. 2019. "The Logic of Counterfactual Analysis in Case-Study Explanation." *British Journal of Sociology* 70(1, January): 306–38. https://doi.org/10.1111/1468-4446.12340.

Mahoney, James, and Gary Goertz. 2004. "The Possibility Principle: Choosing Negative Cases in Comparative Research." *American Political Science Review* 98(4, November): 653–69. https://doi.org/10.1017/S0003055404041401.

March, Artemis. 1982. "Female Invisibility in Androcentric Sociological Thought." *The Insurgent Sociologist* 11(2, April): 99–107. https://doi.org/10.1177/089692058201100212.

Marcia, James E. 1980. "Identity in Adolescence." In *Handbook of Adolescent Psychology*, edited by Joseph Adelson. New York: Wiley.

Markert, John. 2010. "The Changing Face of Racial Discrimination: Hispanics as the Dominant Minority in the USA—A New Application of Power-Threat Theory." *Critical Sociology* 36(2, March): 307–27. https://doi.org/10.1177/0896920509357526.

Marrow, Helen B. 2009. "Immigrant Bureaucratic Incorporation: The Dual Roles of Professional Missions and Government Policies." *American Sociological Review* 74(5, October): 756–76. https://doi.org/10.1177/000312240907400504.

———. 2011. *New Destination Dreaming: Immigration, Race, and Legal Status in the Rural American South*. Palo Alto, Calif.: Stanford University Press.

Martin, Patricia Yancey. 1998. "Why Can't a Man Be More Like a Woman? Reflections on Connell's Masculinities." *Gender and Society* 12(4, August): 472–74. https://doi.org/10.1177/089124398012004008.

Massey, Douglas S. 1995. "The New Immigration and Ethnicity in the United States." *Population and Development Review* 21(3, September): 631–52. https://doi.org/10.2307/2137753.

———. 2007. *Categorically Unequal: The American Stratification System*. New York: Russell Sage Foundation.

———. 2020. *New Faces in New Places: The Changing Geography of American Immigration*. New York: Russell Sage Foundation.

Massey, Douglas S., Camille Z. Charles, Garvey F. Lundy, and Mary J. Fischer. 2003. *The Source of the River: The Social Origins of Freshmen at America's Selective Colleges and Universities*. Princeton, N.J.: Princeton University Press.

Massey, Douglas S., and Kristin E. Espinosa. 1997. "What's Driving Mexico-U.S. Migration? A Theoretical, Empirical, and Policy Analysis." *American Journal of Sociology* 102(4, January): 939–99.

Mathema, Silva. 2017. "Keeping Families Together: Why All Americans Should Care What Happens to Unauthorized Immigrants." Washington, D.C.: Center for American Progress, March 16. https://www.americanprogress.org/issues/immigration/reports/2017/03/16/428335/keeping-families-together/.

Matsuda, Mari J., Charles R. Lawrence III, Richard Delgado, and Kimberle Williams Crenshaw. 2018. *Words That Wound: Critical Race Theory, Assaultive Speech, and the First Amendment*. New York: Routledge. (Originally published in 1993.)

Matsuda, Kristy N., Chris Melde, Terrance J. Taylor, Adrienne Freng, and Finn-Aage Esbensen. 2012. "Gang Membership and Adherence to the 'Code of the Street.'" *Justice Quarterly* 30(3): 440–68. https://doi.org/10.1080/07418825.2012.684432.

McAdams, Dan P. 1985. *Power, Intimacy, and the Life Story: Personological Inquiries into Identity*. Homewood: Dorsey Press.

———. 1993. *The Stories We Live By: Personal Myths and the Making of the Self.* New York: William Morrow and Co.

———. 2006. "The Redemptive Self: Generativity and the Stories Americans Live By." *Research in Human Development* 3(2/3): 81–100. https://doi.org/10.1207/s15427617rhd0302&3_2.

McAdams, Dan P., Ann Diamond, Ed de St. Aubin, and Elizabeth Mansfield. 1997. "Stories of Commitment: The Psychosocial Construction of Generative Lives." *Journal of Personality and Social Psychology* 72(3): 678–94. https://doi.org/10.1037/0022-3514.72.3.678.

McAdams, Dan P., Ruthellen Josselson, and Amia Lieblich, eds. 2006. *Identity and Story: Creating Self in Narrative.* Washington, D.C.: American Psychological Association.

McBeth, Mark, and Donna Lybecker. 2018. "The Narrative Policy Framework, Agenda, and Sanctuary Cities: The Construction of a Public Problem." *Policy Studies Journal* 46(4, November): 868–93. https://doi.org/10.1111/psj.12274.

McCann, James A., and Michael Jones-Correa. 2020. *Holding Fast: Resilience and Civic Engagement among Latino Immigrants.* New York: Russell Sage Foundation.

McDermott, Monica, Eric D. Knowles, and Jennifer A. Richeson. 2019. "Class Perceptions and Attitudes toward Immigration and Race among Working-Class Whites." *Analyses of Social Issues and Public Policy* 19(1, December): 1–32. https://doi.org/10.1111/asap.12188.

McDonald, Seonaidh. 2005. "Studying Actions in Context: A Qualitative Shadowing Method for Organizational Research." *Qualitative Research* 5(4, November): 455–73. https://doi.org/10.1177/1468794105056923.

McFadden, Mark G. 1995. "Resistance to Schooling and Educational Outcomes: Questions of Structure and Agency." *British Journal of Sociology* 16(3): 293–308. https://doi.org/10.1080/0142569950160302.

———. 1996. "'Second Chance' Education: Accessing Opportunity or Recycling Disadvantage?" *International Studies in Sociology of Education* 6(1): 87–111. https://doi.org/10.1080/0962021960060105.

McFadden, Mark G., and J. C. Walker. 1997. "Resistance Theory." In *International Encyclopedia of Sociology of Education*, edited by Lawrence J. Saha. London: Pergamon Press.

McGrew, Ken. 2016. "The Dangers of Pipeline Thinking: How the School-to-Prison Pipeline Metaphor Squeezes Out Complexity." *Educational Theory* 66(3, June): 341–67. https://doi.org/10.1111/edth.12173.

McKnight, Abigail. 2015. "Downward Mobility, Opportunity Hoarding, and the 'Glass Floor.'" Social Mobility and Child Poverty Commission research report. London: London School of Economics, Centre for Analysis of Social Exclusion (CASE), June.

McNulty, John E., Conor M. Dowling, and Margaret H. Ariotti. 2009. "Driving Saints to Sin: How Increasing the Difficulty of Voting Dissuades Even the Most Motivated Voters." *Political Analysis* 17(4, Autumn, special issue): 435–55. https://doi.org/10.1093/pan/mpp014.

Mehta, Clare M., Jeffrey Jensen Arnett, Carlie G. Palmer, and Larry J. Nelson. 2020. "Established Adulthood: A New Conception of Ages 30 to 45." *American Psychologist* 75(4): 431–44. https://doi.org/10.1037/amp0000600.

Meiners, Erica R., and Maisha T. Winn. 2010. "Resisting the School to Prison Pipeline: The Practice to Build Abolition Democracies." *Race Ethnicity and Education* 13(3): 271–76. https://doi.org/10.1080/13613324.2010.500832.

Menjívar, Cecilia. 2014. "The 'Poli-Migra': Multi-Layered Legislation, Enforcement Practices, and What We Can Learn about and from Today's Approaches." *American Behavioral Scientist* 58(13, November): 1805–19. https://doi.org/10.1177/0002764214537268.

———. 2021. "The Racialization of 'Illegality.'" *Daedalus* 150(2): 91–105. https://doi.org/10.1162/daed_a_01848.

Menjívar, Cecilia, and Leisy J. Abrego. 2009. "Parents and Children across Borders: Legal Instability and Intergenerational Relations in Guatemalan and Salvadoran Families." In *Across Generations: Immigrant Families in America*, edited by Nancy Foner. New York: New York University Press.

———. 2012. "Legal Violence: Immigration Law and the Lives of Central American Immigrants." *American Journal of Sociology* 117(5): 1380–1421. https://doi.org/10.1086/663575.

Menjívar, Cecilia, Leisy Abrego, and Leah Schmalzbauer. 2016. *Immigrant Families*. Cambridge: Polity Press.

Menjívar, Cecilia, and Andrea Gómez Cervantes. 2016. "The Effects of Parental Undocumented Status on Families and Children." American Psychological Association, CYF News, November. https://www.apa.org/pi/families/resources/newsletter/2016/11/undocumented-status.

Menjívar, Cecilia, and Daniel Kanstroom, eds. 2014. *Constructing Immigrant "Illegality": Critiques, Experiences, and Responses*. Cambridge: Cambridge University Press.

Menjívar, Cecilia, and Olivia Salcido. 2002. "Immigrant Women and Domestic Violence: Common Experiences in Different Countries." *Gender and Society* 16(6, December): 898–920. https://doi.org/10.1177/089124302237894.

———. 2006. "Liminal Legality: Salvadoran and Guatemalan Immigrants' Lives in the United States." *American Journal of Sociology* 111(4, January): 999–1037. https://doi.org/10.1086/499509.

Merton, Robert K. 1938. "Social Structure and Anomie." *American Sociological Review* 3(5): 672–82.

———. 1984. "Socially Expected Durations: A Case Study of Concept Formation in Sociology." In *Conflict and Consensus: In Honor of Lewis A. Coser*, edited by Walter W. Powell and Richard Robbins. New York: Free Press.

———. 1987. "Three Fragments from a Sociologist's Notebooks: Establishing the Phenomenon, Specified Ignorance, and Strategic Research Materials." *Annual Review of Sociology* 13(1): 1–28. https://doi.org/10.1146/annurev.so.13.080187.000245.

Merton, Robert, and Pitirim Sorokin. 1937. "Social Time: A Methodological and Functional Analysis." *American Journal of Sociology* 42(5, March 1): 615–29. https://doi.org/10.1086/217540.

Messerschmidt, James W. 1997. *Crime as Structured Action: Gender, Race, Class, and Crime in the Making*. Thousand Oaks, Calif.: SAGE Publications.

———. 2019. "The Salience of 'Hegemonic Masculinity.'" *Men and Masculinities* 22(1, April): 85–91. https://doi.org/10.1177/1097184X18805555.

Messerschmidt, James W., Patricia Yancey Martin, Michael A. Messner, and Raewyn Connell, eds. 2018. *Gender Reckonings: New Social Theory and Research.* New York: New York University Press.

Messerschmidt, James, and Michael Messner. 2018. "Hegemonic, Nonhegemonic, and 'New' Masculinities." In *Gender Reckonings: New Social Theory and Research,* edited by James W. Messerschmidt, Patricia Yancey Martin, Michael A. Messner, and Raewyn Connell. New York: New York University Press.

Messner, Michael A. 1997. *Politics of Masculinities: Men in Movements.* Lanham, Md.: AltaMira Press.

———. 2011. "The Privilege of Teaching about Privilege." *Sociological Perspectives* 54(1, March): 3–13. https://doi.org/10.1525/sop.2011.54.1.3.

Metis Associates. n.d. "Determining the Impact of Going to College Early." https://www.metisassociates.com/case-studies/determining-the-impact-of-going-to-college-early/.

Migration Policy Institute. n.d. "Deferred Action for Childhood Arrivals (DACA) Data Tools." https://www.migrationpolicy.org/programs/data-hub/deferred-action-childhood-arrivals-daca-profiles (accessed January 5, 2023).

Mills, C. Wright. 1959. *The Sociological Imagination.* Oxford: Oxford University Press.

Minnite, Lorraine C. 2010. *The Myth of Voter Fraud.* Ithaca, N.Y.: Cornell University Press.

Misra, Jordan. 2019. "Voter Turnout Rates among All Voting Age and Major Racial and Ethnic Groups Were Higher than in 2014." Washington, D.C.: U.S. Census Bureau, April 23. https://www.census.gov/library/stories/2019/04/behind-2018-united-states-midterm-election-turnout.html.

Mitchell, J. Clyde. 1983. "Case and Situation Analysis." *Sociological Review* 31(2, May): 187–211. https://doi.org/10.1111/j.1467-954X.1983.tb00387.x.

Mollenkopf, John. 2013. "Dimensions of Immigrant Political Incorporation." In *Outsiders No More? Models of Immigrant Incorporation,* edited by Jennifer Hochschild, Jacqueline Chattooadhyay, Claudine Gay, and Michael Jones Correa. Oxford: Oxford University Press.

Moore, Joan W., and Alfredo B. Cuéllar. 1970. *Mexican Americans.* Hoboken, N.J.: Prentice-Hall.

Morgan, Stephen L. 2013. *Handbook of Causal Analysis for Social Research.* New York: Springer.

Morgan, Stephen L., David B. Grusky, and Gary S. Fields. 2006. *Mobility and Inequality: Frontiers of Research in Sociology and Economics.* Palo Alto, Calif.: Stanford University Press.

Morgan, Stephen L., and Christopher Winship. 2007. *Counterfactuals and Causal Inference.* New York: Cambridge University Press.

Morrill, Calvin, and Michael Musheno. 2018. *Navigating Conflict: How Youth Handle Trouble in a High-Poverty School.* Chicago: University of Chicago Press.

Moss, Philip, and Chris Tilly. 1996. "'Soft' Skills and Race: An Investigation of Black Men's Employment Problems." *Work and Occupations* 23(3, August): 252–76. https://doi.org/10.1177/0730888496023003002.

Munns, Geoff, and Mark McFadden. 2000. "First Chance, Second Chance, or Last Chance? Resistance and Response to Education." *British Journal of Sociology of Education* 21(1): 59–75. https://doi.org/10.1080/01425690095162.

Murguia, Edward, and Rogelio Saenz. 2002. "An Analysis of the Latin Americanization of Race in the United States: A Reconnaissance of Color Stratification among Mexicans." *Race and Society* 5(1): 85–101. https://doi.org/10.1016/j.racsoc.2003.12.006.

Murguia, Edward, and Edward E. Telles. 1996. "Phenotype and Schooling among Mexican Americans." *Sociology of Education* 69(4): 276–89. https://doi.org/10.2307/2112715.

Murray, Charles. 1984. *Losing Ground: American Social Policy, 1950–1980.* New York: Basic Books.

Myers, Dowell. 2007. *Immigrants and Boomers: Forging a New Social Contract for the Future of America.* New York: Russell Sage Foundation.

Nadal, Kevin L. 2014. "A Guide to Responding to Microaggressions." *CUNY Forum* 2(1): 71–76. https://www.massmed.org/Patient-Care/Health-Topics/Antiracism,-Diversity,-and-Equity/A-Guide-to-Responding-to-Microaggressions/.

Nadal, Kevin L., Yinglee Wong, Marie-Anne Issa, Vanessa Meterko, Jayleen Leon, and Michelle Wideman. 2011. "Sexual Orientation Microaggressions: Processes and Coping Mechanisms for Lesbian, Gay, and Bisexual Individuals." *Journal of LGBT Issues in Counseling* 5(1): 21–46. https://doi.org/10.1080/15538605.2011.554606.

National Academies of Sciences, Engineering, and Medicine. 2015. *The Integration of Immigrants into American Society,* edited by Mary C. Waters and Marisa Gerstein Pineau. Washington, D.C.: National Academies Press.

National Committee to Preserve Social Security and Medicare (NCPSSM). 2017. "Immigration Reform and Social Security." Washington, D.C.: NCPSSM, May 12. https://www.ncpssm.org/documents/social-security-policy-papers/immigration-reform-and-social-security.

National Immigration Law Center. n.d. "Immigration Reform and Executive Actions." https://www.nilc.org/issues/immigration-reform-and-executive-actions/.

Neckerman, Kathryn M., Prudence Carter, and Jennifer Lee. 1999. "Segmented Assimilation and Minority Cultures of Mobility." *Ethnic and Racial Studies* 22(6): 945–65. https://doi.org/10.1080/014198799329198.

Newton, Lina. 2008. *Illegal, Alien, or Immigrant: The Politics of Immigration Reform.* New York: New York University Press.

New York City Comptroller. 2020. "The Economic Impact of NYC Nonprofit Organizations." New York: Office of the New York City Comptroller, July 2. https://comptroller.nyc.gov/reports/the-economic-impact-of-nyc-nonprofit-organizations.

New York City Department of Education. 2006. "NYC Secondary Reform: Selected Analysis." Parthenon Group. https://www.classsizematters.org/wp-content/uploads/2013/05/parthenon-2006.pdf.

———. 2018. *Additional Ways to Graduate: High School Diploma and Equivalency Programs, 2017–2018.* https://www.schools.nyc.gov/docs/default-source/default-document-library/other-ways-to-graduate-english.

New York City Public Schools. n.d. "Young Adult Borough Centers." https://www.schools.nyc.gov/enrollment/other-ways-to-graduate/young-adult-borough-centers.

Nichols, Walter. 2013. *The DREAMers: How the Undocumented Youth Movement Transformed the Immigrant Rights Debate.* Palo Alto, Calif.: Stanford University Press.

Nix, Justin, Bradley Campbell, Edward Byers, and Geoffrey Alpert. 2017. "A Bird's Eye View of Civilians Killed by Police in 2015." *Criminology and Public Policy* 16(1, February): 309–40. https://doi.org/10.1111/1745-9133.12269.

Nobles, Jenna, and Christopher McKelvey. 2015. "Gender, Power, and Emigration from Mexico." *Demography* 52(5): 1573–1600. https://doi.org/10.1007/s13524-015-0401-6.

Noddings, Nel. 1999. "Two Concepts of Caring." *Philosophy of Education,* 36–39. https://uwethicsofcare.gws.wisc.edu/wp-content/uploads/2020/03/Noddings-Two-Concepts-of-Caring.pdf.

———. 2002. *Starting at Home: Caring and Social Policy.* Berkeley: University of California Press.

Noe-Bustamante, Luis, Antonio Flores, and Sono Shad. 2019. "Facts on Hispanics of Mexican Origin in the United States." Washington, D.C.: Pew Research Center, September 16. https://www.pewresearch.org/hispanic/fact-sheet/u-s-hispanics-facts-on-mexican-origin-latinos/.

Nolan, Kathleen. 2011. *Police in the Hallways: Discipline in an Urban High School.* Minneapolis: University of Minnesota Press.

Nsangou, Ashly, and Lauren Dundes. 2018. "Parsing the Gulf between Africans and African Americans." *Social Sciences* 7(2): 24. https://doi.org/10.3390/socsci7020024.

Núñez, D. Carolina. 2010. "Fractured Membership: Deconstructing Territoriality to Secure Rights and Remedies for the Undocumented Worker." *Wisconsin Law Review* 817(July 21). Last modified September 1, 2020. https://ssrn.com/abstract=1646497.

Oboler, Suzanne. 1995. *Ethnic Labels, Latino Lives: Identity and the Politics of (Re)presentation in the United States.* Minneapolis: University of Minnesota Press.

Oesterle, Sabrina. 2013. "Pathways to Young Adulthood and Preventive Interventions Targeting Young Adults." In Institute of Medicine and National Research Council, *Improving the Health, Safety, and Well-Being of Young Adults: Workshop Summary.* Washington, D.C.: National Academies Press.

Okamoto, Gina D. 2003. "Toward a Theory of Panethnicity: Explaining Asian American Collective Action." *American Sociological Review* 68(6, December): 811–42. https://doi.org/10.2307/1519747.

Okamura, Jonathan Y. 1981. "Situational Ethnicity." *Ethnic and Racial Studies* 4(4): 452–65. https://doi.org/10.1080/01419870.1981.9993351.

Okigbo, Karen Amaka. 2021. "Not So Black and White: How Second-Generation Nigerian-Americans Decide Whom to Marry." PhD diss., Sociology Department, CUNY Graduate Center.

O'Neill, Susan E., and Kenneth J. Sher. 2000. "Physiological Alcohol Dependence Symptoms in Early Adulthood: A Longitudinal Perspective." *Experimental and Clinical Psychopharmacology* 8(4, November): 493–508. https://doi.org /10.1037//1064-1297.8.4.493.

Osgood, D. Wayne, E. Michael Foster, and Mark E. Courtney. 2010. "Vulnerable Populations and the Transition to Adulthood." *The Future of Children* 20(1, Spring): 209–29. https://doi.org/10.1353/foc.0.0047.

Pager, Devah. 2003. "The Mark of a Criminal Record." *American Journal of Sociology* 108(5, March): 937–75. https://doi.org/10.1086/374403.

Pallmeyer, Rebecca R., and Dan P. McAdams. 2018. "Second Chances in *The Wire*: Perspectives from Psychology and the Judiciary." *University of Chicago Legal Forum* 2018(9): 193–212. https://chicagounbound.uchicago.edu/uclf /vol2018/iss1/9.

Parker, Keith P., Komanduri S. Murty, A. Lakshminath, and Dora O. Tilles. 2018. "Using Microaggression Theory to Examine U.S. Voter Suppression Tactics." *Negro Educational Review* 69(1–4): 101–23, 142–43.

Pascoe, C. J. 2007. *"Dude, You're a Fag": Masculinity and Sexuality in High School.* Berkeley: University of California Press.

Passel, Jeffrey S., and D'Vera Cohn. 2009. "A Portrait of Unauthorized Immigrants in the United States." Washington, D.C.: Pew Hispanic Center, April 14. https://www.pewresearch.org/hispanic/2009/04/14/a-portrait-of -unauthorized-immigrants-in-the-united-states/.

Pastor, Manuel, Jared Sanchez, and Vanessa Carter. 2015. "The Kids Aren't Alright—But They Could Be: The Impact of DAPA on Children." Los Angeles: University of Southern California, Dornsife Center for the Study of Immigrant Integration (CSII), March 11. https://dornsife.usc.edu/eri/publications/kids -arent-alright-dapa-impact/.

Patler, Caitlin, Jorge A. Cabrera, and Dream Team Los Angeles. 2015. *From Undocumented to DACAmented: Impacts of the Deferred Action for Childhood Arrivals (DACA) Program Three Years Following Its Announcement.* Los Angeles: UCLA Institute for Research on Labor and Economics. https://www.chicano .ucla.edu/files/Patler_DACA_Report_061515.pdf.

Patler, Caitlin, Erin Hamilton, Kelsey Meagher, and Robin Savinar. 2019. "Uncertainty about DACA May Undermine Its Positive Impact on Health for Recipients and Their Children." *Health Affairs* 38(5, May): 738–45. https://doi.org /10.1377/hlthaff.2018.05495.

Patler, Caitlin, Erin R. Hamilton, and Robin L. Savinar. 2020. "The Limits of Gaining Rights while Remaining Marginalized: The Deferred Action for Childhood Arrivals (DACA) Program and the Psychological Wellbeing of Latina/o Undocumented Youth." *Social Forces* 100(1, September): 246–72. https://doi.org/10.1093/sf/soaa099.

Patler, Caitlin, and Whitney Laster Pirtle. 2018. "From Undocumented to Lawfully Present: Do Changes in Legal Status Impact Psychological Wellbeing among Latino Immigrant Young Adults?" *Social Science and Medicine* 199(February): 39–48. https://doi.org/10.1016/j.socscimed.2017.03.009.

PayScale. 2024. "Average Construction Foreman Hourly Pay in New York, New York." https://www.payscale.com/research/US/Job=Construction_Foreman /Hourly_Rate/c144b3f7/New-York-NY.

Pease, Bob. 2002. "(Re)Constructing Men's Interests." *Men and Masculinities* 5(2, October): 165–77. https://doi.org/10.1177/1097184X02005002003.

Perlmann, Joel, and Roger Waldinger. 1997. "Second Generation Decline? Children of Immigrants, Past and Present—A Reconsideration." *International Migration Review* 31(4, December): 893–922. https://doi.org/10.1177/019791839703100405.

Perlmann, Mark. 2007. "A 'Giant of Record.'" *The American Economist* 51(2, October): 25–32. https://doi.org/10.1177/056943450705100205.

Pessar, Patricia R., and Sarah J. Mahler. 2003. "Transnational Migration: Bringing Gender In." *International Migration Review* 37(3, September): 812–46. https://doi.org/10.1111/j.1747-7379.2003.tb00159.x.

Pettigrew, Thomas F., and Linda R. Tropp. 2008. "How Does Intergroup Contact Reduce Prejudice? Meta-Analytic Tests of Three Mediators." *European Journal of Social Psychology* 38(6, September/October): 922–34. https://doi.org/10.1002/ejsp.504.

Pettigrew, Thomas F., Linda R. Tropp, Ulrich Wagner, and Oliver Christ. 2011. "Recent Advances in Intergroup Contact Theory." *International Journal of Intercultural Relations* 35(3, May): 271–80. https://doi.org/10.1016/j.ijintrel.2011.03.001.

Philbin, Morgan M., Morgan Flake, Mark L. Hatzenbuehler, and Jennifer S. Hirsch. 2018. "State-Level Immigration and Immigrant-Focused Policies as Drivers of Latino Health Disparities in the United States." *Social Science and Medicine* 199(February): 29–38. https://doi.org/10.1016/j.socscimed.2017.04.007.

Phinney, Jean S. 1989. "Stages of Ethnic Identity Development in Minority Group Adolescents." *Journal of Early Adolescence* 9(1/2, February): 34–49. https://doi.org/10.1177/0272431689091004.

———. 2006. "Ethnic Identity Exploration in Emerging Adulthood." In *Emerging Adults in America: Coming of Age in the 21st Century*, edited by Jeffrey J. Arnett and Jennifer L. Tanner. Washington, D.C.: American Psychological Association.

Pincus, Fred L. 1980. "The False Promise of Community Colleges: Class Conflict and Vocational Education." *Harvard Educational Review* 50(3): 332–61. https://doi.org/10.17763/haer.50.3.y733663386302231.

Pittman, Cassi L. 2011. "Ethnicity/Race." In *Encyclopedia of Consumer Culture*, edited by Dale Southerton. Thousand Oaks, Calif.: SAGE Publications.

Platt, Lisa F., and Alexandra L. Lenzen. 2013. "Sexual Orientation Microaggressions and the Experience of Sexual Minorities." *Journal of Homosexuality* 60(7): 1011–34. https://doi.org/10.1080/00918369.2013.774878.

Polkinghorne, Donald. 1988. *Narrative Knowing and the Human Sciences*. Albany: State University of New York Press.

Polletta, Francesca. 1998. "'It Was Like a Fever . . .': Narrative and Identity in Social Protest." *Social Problems* 45(2, May): 137–59. https://doi.org/10.2307/3097241.

Polletta, Francesca, Pang Ching Bobby Chen, Beth Gharrity Gardner, and Alice Motes. 2011. "The Sociology of Storytelling." *Annual Review of Sociology* 37(August): 109–30. https://doi.org/10.1146/annurev-soc-081309-150106.

Pope, Nolan. 2016. "The Effects of DACAmentation: The Impact of Deferred Action for Childhood Arrivals on Unauthorized Immigrants." *Journal of Public Economics* 143(98, November): 114. https://doi.org/10.1016/j.jpubeco.2016.08.014.

Portelli, Alejandro. 2018. "Living Voices: The Oral History Interview as Dialogue and Experience." *Oral History Review* 45(2): 239–48.

Portes, Alejandro. 2016. "International Migration and National Development: From Orthodox Equilibrium to Transnationalism." *Sociology of Development* 2(2, June): 73–92. https://doi.org/10.1525/sod.2016.2.2.73.

Portes, Alejandro, and Patricia Fernández-Kelly. 2008. "No Margin for Error: Educational and Occupational Achievement among Disadvantaged Children of Immigrants." *Annals of the American Academy of Political and Social Science* 620(1, November): 12–36. https://doi.org/10.1177/0002716208322577.

Portes, Alejandro, and Rubén Rumbaut. 2001. *Legacies: The Story of the Immigrant Second Generation*. Berkeley: University of California Press.

Portes, Alejandro, and Min Zhou. 1993. "The New Second Generation: Segmented Assimilation and Its Variants." *Annals of the American Academy of Political and Social Science* 530(1, November): 74–96. https://doi.org/10.1177/0002716293530001006.

Powell, Brian, Laura Hamilton, Bianca Manago, and Simon Cheng. 2016. "Implications of Changing Family Forms for Children." *Annual Review of Sociology* 42(July): 301–22. https://doi.org/10.1146/annurev-soc-081715-074444.

Pratt, Michael W., Mary Louise Arnold, and Kathleen Mackey. 2001. "Adolescents' Representations of the Parent Voice in Stories of Personal Turning Points." In *Turns in the Road: Narrative Studies of Lives in Transition*, edited by Dan P. McAdams, Ruthellen Josselson, and Amia Lieblich. Washington, D.C.: American Psychological Association.

Prince, David, and Davis Jenkins. 2005. "Building Pathways to Success for Low-Skill Adult Students: Lessons for Community College Policy and Practice from a Statewide Longitudinal Tracking Study." New York: Teachers College, Columbia University, April. https://ccrc.tc.columbia.edu/media/k2/attachments/pathways-success-low-skill-adult.pdf.

Pujol, Jesús, Pere Vendrell, Carme Junqué, Josep L. Martí-Vilalta, and Antoni Capdevila. 1993. "When Does Human Brain Development End? Evidence of Corpus Callosum Growth to Adulthood." *Annals of Neurology* 34(1, July): 717–75. https://doi.org/10.1002/ana.410340113.

Puszyk, Monika. 2016. "Families of Non-Heterosexual People with Children—Among Old Answers and New Questions." *Studia Humanistyczne AHG* 15(4, December): 7–19. https://doi.org/10.7494/human.2016.15.4.7.

Pyrooz, David C., and Gary Sweeten. 2015. "Gang Membership between Ages 5 and 17 Years in the United States." *Journal of Adolescent Health: Official Publication of the Society for Adolescent Medicine* 56(4, April): 414–19. https://doi.org/10.1016/j.jadohealth.2014.11.018.

Ragin, Charles. 2008. *Redesigning Social Inquiry: Fuzzy Sets and Beyond*. Chicago: University of Chicago Press.

Ragin, Charles, and Howard Becker. 1992. *What Is a Case? Exploring the Foundations of Social Inquiry*. Oxford: Oxford University Press.

Ragin, Charles C., Joane Nagel, and Patricia White. 2004. "Workshop on Scientific Foundations of Qualitative Research." Summary of the proceedings of the "Scientific Foundations of Qualitative Research" workshop, National Science Foundation, Arlington, Va., July 11–12, 2003.

Ragland, Cathy. 2003. "Mexican Deejays and the Transnational Space of Youth Dances in New York and New Jersey." *Ethnomusicology* 47(3, Autumn): 338. https://doi.org/10.2307/3113938.

Ramakrishnan, S. Karthick, and Irene Bloemraad. 2008. *Civic Hopes and Political Realities: Immigrants, Community Organizations, and Political Engagement.* New York: Russell Sage Foundation.

Reber, Sarah, and Chenoah Sinclair. 2020. *Opportunity Engines: Middle-Class Mobility in Higher Education.* Washington, D.C.: Brookings Institution.

Reeser, Todd. 2011. *Masculinities in Theory: An Introduction.* London: Wiley.

Reeves, Richard. 2017. *Dream Hoarders: How the American Upper Middle Class Is Leaving Everyone Else in the Dust, Why That Is a Problem, and What to Do about It.* Washington, D.C.: Brookings Institution Press.

Reifman, Alan, and Sylvia Niehuis. 2022 "Extending the Five Psychological Features of Emerging Adulthood into Established Adulthood." *Journal of Adult Development* 30: 6–20. https://doi.org/10.1007/s10804-022-09412-9.

Remler, Dahlia K., and Gregg G. Van Ryzin. 2014. *Research Methods in Practice: Strategies for Description and Causation.* Thousand Oaks, Calif.: SAGE Publications.

Rendón, María G. 2019. *Stagnant Dreamers: How the Inner City Shapes the Integration of Second-Generation Latinos.* New York: Russell Sage Foundation.

Reskin, Barbara. 2003. "Including Mechanisms in Our Models of Ascriptive Inequality." *American Sociological Review* 68(February): 1–21. https://doi.org/10.1007/1-4020-3455-5_4.

Rhodes, Jean. 2004. *Stand by Me: The Risks and Rewards of Mentoring Today's Youth.* Cambridge, Mass.: Harvard University Press.

Ridgeway, Cecilia L. 2011. *Framed by Gender: How Gender Inequality Persists in the Modern World.* Oxford: Oxford University Press.

———. 2014. "Why Status Matters for Inequality." *American Sociological Review* 79(1, February): 1–16. https://doi.org/10.1177/0003122413515997.

———. 2019. *Status: Why Is It Everywhere? Why Does It Matter?* New York: Russell Sage Foundation.

Ridgeway, Cecilia, Kristen Backor, Yan Li, Justine Tinkler, and Kristan Erickson. 2009. "How Easily Does a Social Difference Become a Status Distinction? Gender Matters." *American Sociological Review* 74(1, February): 44–62. https://doi.org/10.1177/000312240907400103.

Rihoux, Benoît, and Charles C. Ragin. 2008. "Introduction." In *Configurational Comparative Methods: Qualitative Comparative Analysis (QCA) and Related Techniques.* Thousand Oaks, Calif.: SAGE Publications.

Rios, Victor M. 2009. "The Consequences of the Criminal Justice Pipeline on Black and Latino Masculinity." *Annals of the American Academy of Political and Social Science* 623(1, May): 150–62. https://doi.org/10.1177/0002716208330489.

———. 2011. *Punished: Policing the Lives of Black and Latino Boys.* New York: New York University Press.

Riosmena, Fernando, and Douglas S. Massey. 2012. "Pathways to El Norte: Origins, Destinations, and Characteristics of Mexican Migrants to the United States." *International Migration Review* 46(1, March): 3–36. https://doi.org/10.1111/j.1747-7379.2012.00879.x.

Rivera-Batiz, Francisco L. 1999. "Undocumented Workers in the Labor Market: An Analysis of the Earnings of Legal and Illegal Mexican Immigrants in the United States." *Journal of Population Economics* 12(1): 91–116. https://doi.org/10.1007/s001480050092.

Roberts, Bryan. 1995. "Socially Expected Durations and the Economic Adjustment of Immigrants." In *The Economic Sociology of Immigration,* edited by Alejandro Portes. New York: Russell Sage Foundation.

Robinson, Gregory, John McNulty, and Jonathan S. Krasno. 2009. "Observing the Counterfactual? The Search for Political Experiments in Nature." *Political Analysis* 17(4, Autumn, special issue): 341–57. https://doi.org/10.1093/pan/mpp011.

Rocque, Michael. 2015. "The Lost Concept: The (Re)emerging Link between Maturation and Desistance from Crime." *Criminology and Criminal Justice* 15(3, July): 340–60. https://doi.org/10.1177/1748895814547710.

Rocque, Michael, Chad Posick, and Helene R. White. 2015. "Growing Up Is Hard to Do: An Empirical Evaluation of Maturation and Desistance." *Journal of Deviance and Life-Course Criminology* 1(4, December): 350–84. https://doi.org/10.1007/s40865-015-0018-x.

Roediger, David R. 1991. *The Wages of Whiteness: Race and the Making of the American Working Class.* London: Verso.

Rojas-Flores, Lisseth, Mari L. Clements, J. Hwang Koo, and Judy London. 2017. "Trauma and Psychological Distress in Latino Citizen Children Following Parental Detention and Deportation." *Psychological Trauma: Theory, Research, Practice, and Policy* 9(3, May): 352–61. https://doi.org/10.1037/tra0000177.

Romero, Mary. 2006. "Racial Profiling and Immigration Law Enforcement: Rounding Up of Usual Suspects in the Latino Community." *Critical Sociology* 32(2/3, March): 447–73. https://doi.org/10.1163/156916306777835376.

Rose, Mike. 2012. *Back to School: Why Everyone Deserves a Second Chance at Education.* New York: New Press.

Rosenfeld, Michael J. 2010. "Nontraditional Families and Childhood Progress through School." *Demography* 47(3, June): 755–75. https://doi.org/10.1007/s13524-012-0170-4.

Roth, Wendy D. 2012. *Race Migrations: Latinos and the Cultural Transformation of Race.* Stanford, Calif.: Stanford University Press.

Roth, Wendy D., and Alexandra Martin. 2021. "The Role of Skin Color in Latino Social Networks: Color Homophily in Sending and Receiving Societies." *Sociology of Race and Ethnicity* 7(2, April): 175–93. https://doi.org/10.1177/2332649220940346.

Roy, Kevin M., and Dan P. McAdams. 2006. "Second Chances as Transformative Stories in Human Development: An Introduction." *Research in Human Development* 3(2/3): 77–80. https://doi.org/10.1080/15427609.2006.9683362.

Royster, Deirdre A. 2007. "What Happens to Potential Discouraged? Masculinity Norms and the Contrasting Institutional and Labor Market Experiences of Less Affluent Black and White Men." *Annals of the American Academy of Political and Social Science* 609(1, January): 153–80. https://doi.org/10.1177/0002716206296544.

Ruggles, Steven, Sarah Flood, Matthew Sobek, Danika Brockman, Grace Cooper, Stephanie Richards, and Megan Schouweiler. 2023a. "IPUMS USA: Version 13.0 Census 1990, 5%." Minneapolis, Minn.: IPUMS. https://doi.org/10.18128/D010 .V13.0.

———. 2023b. "IPUMS USA: Version 13.0 Census 2000, 5%." Minneapolis, Minn.: IPUMS. https://doi.org/10.18128/D010.V13.0.

———. 2023c. "IPUMS USA: Version 13.0 American Community Survey 2010, 5%." Minneapolis, Minn.: IPUMS. https://doi.org/10.18128/D010.V13.0.

———. 2023d. "IPUMS USA: Version 13.0 American Community Survey 2020, 5%." Minneapolis, Minn.: IPUMS. https://doi.org/10.18128/D010.V13.0.

Rumbaut, Rubén G. 2005. "Turning Points in the Transition to Adulthood: Determinants of Educational Attainment, Incarceration, and Early Childbearing among Children of Immigrants." *Ethnic and Racial Studies* 28(6): 1041–86. https:// doi.org/10.1080/01419870500224349.

———. 2008. "The Coming of the Second Generation: Immigration and Ethnic Mobility in Southern California." *Annals of the American Academy of Political and Social Science* 620(1, November): 196–236. https://doi.org/10.1177 /0002716208322957.

Rumbaut, Rubén G., and Walter A. Ewing. 2007. "Special Report: The Myth of Immigrant Criminality and the Paradox of Assimilation: Incarceration Rates among Native and Foreign-Born Men." Washington, D.C.: American Immigration Law Foundation, Immigration Policy Center, Spring. https:// www.americanimmigrationcouncil.org/sites/default/files/research/Imm%20 Criminality%20%28IPC%29.pdf.

Rumbaut, Rubén G., and Golnaz Komaie. 2010. "Immigration and Adult Transitions." *The Future of Children* 20(1, Spring): 43–66. https://doi.org/10.1353 /foc.0.0046.

Ruszczyk, Stephen. 2015. "Undocumented Youth Living between the Lines: Urban Governance, Social Policy, and the Boundaries of Legality in New York City and Paris." PhD diss., Sociology Department, CUNY Graduate Center.

Sakuma, Amanda. 2014. "Undocumented Workers Are Keeping a Key Benefit Program Afloat." *MSNBC*, August 12. https://www.msnbc.com /msnbc/undocumented-workers-are-keeping-key-benefit-program-afloat -msna388136#53366.

Sampson, Robert J. 2008. "Rethinking Crime and Immigration." *Contexts* 7(1, February): 28–33. https://doi.org/10.1525/ctx.2008.7.1.28.

———. 2012. *Great American City: Chicago and the Enduring Neighborhood Effect.* Chicago: University of Chicago Press.

Sassen, Saskia. 2001. *The Global City: New York, London, Tokyo.* Princeton, N.J.: Princeton University Press.

Savelli, Lou. 2005. *Gangs across America and Their Symbols.* New York: Looseleaf Law Publications.

Schippers, Mimi. 2007. "Recovering the Feminine Other: Masculinity, Femininity, and Gender Hegemony." *Theory and Society* 36(1): 85–102. https://doi.org/10.1007/s11186-007-9022-4.

Schneider, Eric C. 1999. *Vampires, Dragons, and Egyptian Kings: Youth Gangs in Postwar New York.* Princeton, N.J.: Princeton University Press.

Schoenfeld, Heather. 2016. "A Research Agenda on Reform: Penal Policy and Politics across the States." *Annals of the American Academy of Political and Social Science* 664(1, March): 155–74. https://doi.org/10.1177/0002716215601850.

Schrock, Douglas P., and Michael Schwalbe. 2009. "Men, Masculinity, and Manhood Acts." *Annual Review of Sociology* 35(August 11): 277–95. https://doi.org/10.1146/ANNUREV-SOC-070308-115933.

Schudde, Lauren, and Sara Goldrick-Rab. 2015. "On Second Chances and Stratification: How Sociologists Think about Community Colleges." *Community College Review* 43(1, January): 27–45. https://doi.org/10.1177/0091552114553296.

Scott, Dylan. 2017. "Orrin Hatch Just Made the Republican Agenda Startlingly Clear." *Vox*, December 5. www.vox.com/policy-and-politics/2017/12/5/16733784/senate-tax-bill-orrin-hatch-chip.

Settersten, Richard A., Jr., Frank F. Furstenberg Jr., and Rubén G. Rumbaut, eds. 2005. *On the Frontier of Adulthood: Theory, Research, and Public Policy.* Chicago: University of Chicago Press.

Sewell, William H. Jr. 1992. "A Theory of Structure: Duality, Agency, and Transformation." *American Journal of Sociology* 98(1): 1–29.

Sheftel, Mara Getz. 2023. "Immigrant Wealth Stratification and Return Migration: The Case of Mexican Immigrants in the United States during the Twentieth Century." *Demography* 60(3, June 1): 809–35. https://doi.org/10.1215/00703370-10693686.

Shih, Howard, and Peiyi Xu. 2013. "Asian Americans in New York City: A Decade of Dynamic Change, 2000–2010." New York: Asian American Federation, April. https://dataspace.princeton.edu/handle/88435/dsp01b5644v67v.

Sigona, Nando. 2012. "'I Have Too Much Baggage': The Impacts of Legal Status on the Social Worlds of Irregular Migrants." *Social Anthropology* 20(1): 50–65. https://doi.org/10.1111/j.1469-8676.2011.00191.x.

Singer, Audry, Nicole Prchal Svajlenka, and Jill Wilson. 2015. "Local Insights from DACA for Implementing Future Programs for Unauthorized Immigrants." Brookings Metropolitan Policy Program. Washington, D.C.: Brookings Institution, June 4.

Small, Mario Luis. 2009a. "How Many Cases Do I Need? On Science and the Logic of Case Selection in Field-Based Research." *Ethnography* 10(1, March): 5–38. https://doi.org/10.1177/1466138108099586.

———. 2009b. *Unanticipated Gains: Origins of Network Inequality in Everyday Life.* New York: Oxford University Press.

———. 2011. "How to Conduct a Mixed Method Study: Recent Trends in a Rapidly Growing Literature." *Annual Review of Sociology* 37(August): 55–84. https://doi.org/10.1146/annurev.soc.012809.102657.

———. 2017. *Someone to Talk To: How Networks Matter in Practice.* New York: Oxford University Press.

Smeeding, Timothy, Robert Erikson, and Markus Jäntti. 2011. *Persistence, Privilege, and Parenting: The Comparative Study of Intergenerational Mobility.* New York: Russell Sage Foundation.

Smilde, David. 2007. *Reason to Believe: Cultural Agency in Latin American Evangelicalism.* Berkeley: University of California Press.

Smith, Dorothy. 1987. *The Everyday World as Problematic: A Feminist Sociology.* Boston: Northeastern University Press.

Smith, Robert C. 2005. "Racialization and Mexicans in New York City." In *New Destinations for Mexican Migration*, edited by Ruben Hernandez Leon and Victor Zuniga. New York: Russell Sage Foundation.

———. 2006. *Mexican New York: Transnational Worlds of New Immigrants.* Berkeley: University of California Press.

———. 2008. "Horatio Alger Lives in Brooklyn: Extra-Family Support, Intra-Family Dynamics, and Socially Neutral Operating Identities in Exceptional Mobility among Children of Mexican Immigrants." *Annals of the American Academy of Political and Social Science* 620(1, November): 270–90. https://doi.org/10.1177/0002716208322988.

———. 2014. "Black Mexicans: Operating Identities, Conjunctural Ethnicity, and Long Term Ethnographic Research." *American Sociological Review* 79(3, June): 517–48. https://doi.org/10.1177/0003122414529585.

———. 2016. "What's a Life Worth? Ethnographic Counterfactual Analysis, Undocumented Status, and Sociological Autopsy." *Ethnography* 17(4, December): 419–39. https://doi.org/10.1177/1466138116636899.

———. 2017. "'Don't Let the Illegals Vote!': Epithetic Stigma and Contested Latino Political Integration." *RSF: The Russell Sage Foundation Journal of the Social Sciences* 3(4, July): 148–75. https://doi.org/10.7758/RSF.2017.3.4.09.

———. 2019. "The Hawthorne Effect in Ethnography." Paper presented to the American Sociological Association meetings, New York, August 12.

———. 2022. "Advancing Publicly Engaged Sociology" (Eastern Sociological Society Presidential Address). *Sociological Forum* 37(4, December): 926–50.

———. 2023a. "Introduction to the Special Issue: Advancing Publicly Engaged Sociology." *Sociological Forum* 38(S1, September): 930–53. https://doi.org/10.1111/socf.12901.

———. 2023b. "Will DACA Recipients Return to Their Birth Countries if DACA Is Ended?" *Journal on Migration and Human Security* 11(4, December): 1–20. https://doi.org/10.1177/23315024231199713.

———. 2024. "Doing Community and Institutionally Engaged Work and Promoting Immigrant Well-being While Building a Research Career." *American Behavioral Scientist.* https://doi.org/10.1177/00027642241229539.

Smith, Robert Courtney, and Andrés Besserer Rayas. 2022. "How Traffic Stops Impose a Racial Hierarchy and a Mexican Driver Tax on Immigrant Families." Paper presented at the American Sociological Association meeting, Los Angeles, August 5–9.

Smith, Robert Courtney, Andrés Besserer Rayas, Daisy Flores, Angelo Cabrera, Guillermo Yrizar Barbosa, Karina Weinstein, Maria Xique, Avery Guidicessi, Michelle Bialeck, and Eduardo Torres. 2021. "Disrupting the Traffic Stop to Deportation Pipeline: The New York State Greenlight Law's Intent and Implementation." *Journal on Migration and Human Security* 9(2, June): 94–110. https://doi.org/10.1177/23315024211013752.

Smith, Robert Courtney, Caitlin Patler, et al. 2019. "Amici Curiae Brief of Empirical Scholars in Support of Respondents. Supreme Court of the United States.

Three Consolidated DACA Cases (18-587, 18-588, 18-589)." https://www
.supremecourt.gov/DocketPDF/18/18-587/118236/20191004172647483
_18-587%20Amicus%20Brief%20of%20Empirical%20Scholars%20in%20
Support%20of%20Respondents.pdf.

Smith, Robert Courtney, Don J. Waisanen, and Guillermo Yrizar Barbosa. 2019. *Immigration and Strategic Public Health Communication: Lessons from the Seguro Popular Healthcare Project.* Abingdon, U.K.: Routledge.

Smith, Robert Courtney, Guillermo Yrizar Barbosa, and MIDA Team. 2019. "Databrief: Why and How a Greenlight Law Will Reduce Preventable Harm to U.S. Citizen Children in New York State." New York: Baruch College, Marxe School of Public and International Affairs, March 9. https://greenlightny .files.wordpress.com/2019/04/revised-databrief-greenlight-campaign-nys -3-9-19-with-county-specific-states-4-15-19.pdf.

Smith, Robert Courtney, Guillermo Yrizar Barbosa, Cesar Zuniga, and MIDA Team. 2022. "Policy Cracks and Organizational Bridges in Promoting DACA: The Collaborative University–Immigrant Organization–Consular Approach in the Mexican Initiative on Deferred Action (MIDA) in New York State." Draft paper, Marxe School, Baruch College, CUNY.

Solórzano, Daniel, Walter R. Allen, and Grace Carroll. 2002. "Keeping Race in Place: Racial Microaggressions and Campus Racial Climate at the University of California, Berkeley." *Chicana/o Latina/o Law Review* 23(1): 15–111. https:// doi.org/10.5070/C7231021142.

Solórzano, Daniel, Miguel Ceja, and Tara Yosso. 2000. "Critical Race Theory, Racial Microaggressions, and Campus Racial Climate: The Experiences of African American College Students." *Journal of Negro Education* 69(1/2, Winter /Spring): 60–73.

Somers, Margaret R. 1994. "The Narrative Constitution of Identity: A Relational and Network Approach." *Theory and Society* 23(5, October): 605–49. https:// doi.org/10.1007/BF00992905.

Stanton-Salazar, Ricardo D. 2001. *Manufacturing Hope and Despair: The School and Kin Support Networks of U.S.-Mexican Youth.* New York: Teachers College Press.

Suárez-Orozco, Carola. 2017. "Conferring Disadvantage: Behavioral and Developmental Implications for Children Growing Up in the Shadow of Undocumented Immigration Status." *Journal of Developmental and Behavioral Pediatrics* 38(6, July/August): 425–28. https://doi.org/10.1097/DBP .0000000000000462.

Suárez-Orozco, Carola, Mona M. Abo-Zena, and Amy K. Marks. 2015. *Transitions: The Development of Children of Immigrants.* New York: New York University Press.

Suárez-Orozco, Carola, and Marcelo M. Suárez-Orozco. 2001. *Children of Immigration.* Cambridge, Mass.: Harvard University Press.

Suárez-Orozco, Carola, Marcelo Suárez-Orozco, and Irena Todorova. 2010. *Learning a New Land: Immigrant Students in American Society.* Cambridge, Mass.: Belknap Press of Harvard University Press.

Suárez-Orozco, Carola, and Hirokazu Yoshikawa. 2013. "Undocumented Status: Implications for Child Development, Policy, and Ethical Research." *New

Directions for Child and Adolescent Development 2013(141, Fall): 61–78. https://doi.org/10.1002/cad.20043.

Sue, Derald Wing, Christina M. Capodilupo, Gina C. Torino, Jennifer M. Bucceri, Aisha M. B. Holder, Kevin L. Nadal, and Marta Esquilin. 2007. "Racial Microaggressions in Everyday Life: Implications for Clinical Practice." *American Psychologist* 62(4, May/June): 271–86. https://doi.org/10.1037/0003 -066X.62.4.271.

Sun, Ken Chih-Yan. 2021. *Time and Migration: How Long-Term Taiwanese Migrants Negotiate Later Life.* Ithaca, N.Y.: Cornell University Press.

Swidler, Ann. 1986. "Culture in Action: Symbols and Strategies." *American Sociological Review* 51(2, April): 273–86. https://doi.org/10.2307/2095521.

Swidler, Ann, and Jorge Arditi. 1994. "The New Sociology of Knowledge." *Annual Review of Sociology* 20(August): 305–29. https://doi.org/10.1146 /annurev.so.20.080194.001513.

Telles, Edward. 2014. *Pigmentocracies: Ethnicity, Race, and Color in Latin America.* Durham: University of North Carolina Press.

Telles, Edward, and Vilma Ortiz. 2008. *Generations of Exclusion: Mexican Americans, Assimilation, and Race.* New York: Russell Sage Foundation.

———. 2012. "Racial Identity and Racial Treatment of Mexican Americans." *Sociology of Race and Ethnicity* 4(1, April). https://doi.org/10.1007/s12552 -012-9064-8.

Telles, Edward, and Christina A. Sue. 2019. *Durable Ethnicity: Mexican Americans and the Ethnic Core.* New York: Oxford University Press.

Terriquez, Veronica. 2014. "Dreams Delayed: Barriers to Degree Completion among Undocumented Community College Students." *Journal of Ethnic and Migration Studies* 41(8, October 30): 1–22. https://doi.org/10.1080/13691 83X.2014.96853.

Tetlock, Philip E., and Aaron Belkin. 1996. *Counterfactual Thought Experiments in World Politics: Logical, Methodological, and Psychological Perspectives.* Princeton, N.J.: Princeton University Press.

Thomas, William I., and Dorothy S. Thomas. 1928. *The Child in America: Behavior Problems and Programs.* New York: Alfred A. Knopf.

Tilly, Charles. 1997. "Contentious Politics and Social Change." *African Studies* 56(1): 51–65. https://doi.org/10.1080/00020189708707860.

Timmermans, Stefan, and Iddo Tavory. 2012. "Theory Construction in Qualitative Research: From Grounded Theory to Abductive Analysis." *Sociological Theory* 30(3, September): 167–86. https://doi.org/10.1177/0735275112457914.

Toomey, Russell B., Adriana J. Umaña-Taylor, David R. Williams, Elizabeth Harvey-Mendoza, Laudan B. Jahromi, and Kimberly A. Updegraff. 2014. "Impact of Arizona's SB 1070 Immigration Law on Utilization of Health Care and Public Assistance among Mexican-Origin Adolescent Mothers and Their Mother Figures." *American Journal of Public Health* 104(S1, February): S28–S34. https://doi.org/10.2105/AJPH.2013.301655.

Townsend, Barbara K. 2000. "Rationales of Community Colleges for Enrolling Reverse Transfer Students: A Second Chance for Whom?" *Community College Journal of Research and Practice* 24(4): 301–11. https://doi.org/10.1080 /106689200264088.

Tran, Van C. 2015. "More than Just Black: Cultural Perils and Opportunities in Inner-City Neighborhoods." In *The Cultural Matrix: Understanding Black Youth*, edited by Orlando Patterson, with Ethan Fosse. Cambridge, Mass.: Harvard University Press.

Treschan, Lazar. 2010. "Latino Youth in New York City: School, Work, and Income Trends for New York's Largest Group of Young People." Policy brief. New York: Community Service Society, October. https://smhttp-ssl-58547.nexcesscdn.net/nycss/images/uploads/pubs/LatinoYouthinNYCOct2010.pdf.pdf.

Treschan, Lazar, and Apurva Mehrotra. 2013. "Young Mexican-Americans in New York City: Working More and Earning Less." New York: Community Service Society, March. https://smhttp-ssl-58547.nexcesscdn.net/nycss/images/uploads/pubs/Mexican%20Youth%20Report%20FINAL.pdf.

Trouille, David. 2021. *Fútbol in the Park: Immigrants, Soccer, and the Creation of Social Ties*. Chicago: University of Chicago Press.

Trouille, David, and Iddo Tavory. 2019. "Shadowing: Warrants for Intersituational Variation in Ethnography." *Sociological Methods and Research* 48(3, August): 534–60. https://doi.org/10.1177/0049124115626171.

Tyson, Karolyn, William Darity Jr., and Domini R. Castellino. 2005. "It's Not 'a Black Thing': Understanding the Burden of Acting White and Other Dilemmas of High Achievement." *American Sociological Review* 70(4, August): 582–605. https://doi.org/10.1177/000312240507000403.

Umaña-Taylor, Adriana, Stephen Quintana, Richard Lee, William Cross Jr., Deborah Rivas-Drake, Seth Schwartz, Moin Syed, Tiffany Yip, and Eleanor Seaton. 2014. "Ethnic and Racial Identity during Adolescence and into Young Adulthood: An Integrated Conceptualization." *Child Development* 85(1, January/February): 21–39.

U.S. Census Bureau. 2000. "Decennial Census." https://www.census.gov/data/datasets/2000/dec/microdata.html.

———. 2010. "American Community Survey 2006–2010." https://www.census.gov/programs-surveys/acs/microdata/access/2010.html.

———. 2021. "American Community Survey 2017–2021." https://www.census.gov/programs-surveys/acs/microdata/access/2021.html.

U.S. Citizenship and Immigration Services (USCIS). 2017. "Approximate Active DACA Population: Country of Birth (as of September 4, 2017)." https://www.uscis.gov/sites/default/files/document/data/daca_population_data.pdf (accessed January 4, 2020).

U.S. Elections Project. n.d. "Voter Turnout Demographics." https://www.electproject.org/election-data/voter-turnout-demographics.

Valdés, Guadalupe. 1996. *Con Respeto: Bridging the Distances between Culturally Diverse Families and Schools: An Ethnographic Portrait*. New York: Teachers College Press.

Valencia, Richard R., ed. 1997. *The Evolution of Deficit Thinking: Educational Thought and Practice*. London: Routledge.

Valentín-Cortés, Mislael, Quetzabel Benavides, Richard Bryce, Ellen Rabinowitz, Raymond Rion, William D. Lopez, and Paul J. Flemin. 2020. "Application of the

Minority Stress Theory: Understanding the Mental Health of Undocumented Latinx Immigrants." *American Journal of Community Psychology* 66: 325–36. https://doi.org/10.1002/ajcp.12455.

Valenzuela, Angela. 1999. *Subtractive Schooling: U.S.-Mexican Youth and the Politics of Caring.* New York: State University of New York Press.

Vaquera, Elizabeth, Elizabeth Aranda, and Roberto G. Gonzales. 2014. "Patterns of Incorporation of Latinos in Old and New Destinations: From Invisible to Hypervisible." *American Behavioral Scientist* 58(14): 1823–33. https://doi.org /10.1177/0002764214550293.

Varsanyi, Monica W. 2005. "The Rise and Fall (and Rise?) of Non-Citizen Voting: Immigration and the Shifting Scales of Citizenship and Suffrage in the United States." *Space and Polity* 9(2): 113–34. https://doi.org/10.1080/13562570500304956.

———, ed. 2010. *Taking Local Control: Immigration Policy Activism in U.S. Cities and States.* Stanford, Calif.: Stanford University Press.

Varsanyi, Monica, Paul G. Lewis, Doris Provine, and Scott Decker. 2012. "A Multilayered Jurisdictional Patchwork: Immigration Federalism in the United States." *Law and Policy* 34(2, April): 138–58. https://doi.org/10.1111/j.1467 -9930.2011.00356.x.

Vasquez, Jessica M. 2010. "Blurred Borders for Some but Not 'Others': Racialization, 'Flexible Ethnicity,' Gender, and Third-Generation Mexican American Identity." *Sociological Perspectives* 53(1): 45–71. https://doi.org /10.1525/sop.2010.53.1.45.

Vasquez-Tokos, Jessica, and Kathryn Norton-Smith. 2017. "Talking Back to Controlling Images: Latinos' Changing Responses to Racism over the Life Course." *Ethnic and Racial Studies* 40(6): 1–19. https://doi.org/10.1080/01419870 .2016.1201583.

Vertovec, Steven. 2006. "The Emergence of Super-Diversity in Britain." Working Paper 06-25. University of Oxford, Centre on Migration, ESRC Policy, and Society. https://www.compas.ox.ac.uk/wp-content/uploads/WP-2006-025 -Vertovec_Super-Diversity_Britain.pdf.

———. 2007. "Super-Diversity and Its Implications." *Ethnic and Racial Studies* 30(6): 1024–54. https://doi.org/10.1080/01419870701599465.

———. 2022. *Superdiversity: Migration and Social Complexity.* London: Routledge.

Vickerman, Milton. 1999. *Crosscurrents: West Indian Immigrants and Race.* Oxford: Oxford University Press.

Virgin, Vicky, and Robert Warren. 2021. "Mapping Key Determinants of Immigrants' Health in Brooklyn and Queens." New York: Center for Migration Studies of New York, February. https://cmsny.org/wp-content/uploads /2021/02/Mapping-Key-Health-Determinants-for-Immigrants-Report-Center -for-Migration-Studies.pdf.

Vygotsky, L. S. 1978. *Mind in Society: The Development of Higher Psychological Processes.* Cambridge, Mass.: Harvard University Press.

Wagner-Pacifici, Robin. 2010. "Theorizing the Restlessness of Events." *American Journal of Sociology* 115(5, March): 1351–86. https://doi.org/10.1086/651299.

Waldinger, Roger. 1999. *Still the Promised City? African-Americans and New Immigrants in Postindustrial New York.* Cambridge, Mass.: Harvard University Press.

Waldinger, Roger, and Cynthia Feliciano. 2004. "Will the New Second Generation Experience 'Downward Assimilation'? Segmented Assimilation Re-assessed." *Ethnic and Racial Studies* 27(3, May): 376–402. https://doi.org/10.1080/01491987042000189196.

Warner, Nathan. 2014. "On the Same Page: The Strong Teacher Professional Community at the Heart of a Good New York City Public Middle School." PhD diss., Sociology Department, CUNY Graduate Center.

Warren, Robert, and Donald Kerwin. 2015. "Beyond DAPA and DACA: Revisiting Legislative Reform in Light of Long-Term Trends in Unauthorized Immigration to the United States." *Journal on Migration and Human Security* 3(1): 80–108. https://doi.org/10.1177/233150241500300104.

Waters, Mary C. 1999a. *Black Identities: West Indian Immigrant Dreams and American Realities*. Cambridge, Mass.: Harvard University Press.

———. 1999b. "Sociology and the Study of Immigration." *American Behavioral Scientist* 42(9, June): 1264–67. https://doi.org/10.1177/00027649921955029.

———. 2001. "Growing Up West Indian and African American: Gender and Class Differences in the Second Generation." In *Islands in the City: West Indian Migration to New York*, edited by Nancy Foner. Berkeley: University of California Press.

Watson, Tara. 2014. "Inside the Refrigerator: Immigration Enforcement and Chilling Effects in Medicaid Participation." *American Economic Journal: Economic Policy* 6(3, August): 313–38. https://doi.org/10.1257/pol.6.3.313.

Way, Niobe, and Lisa Chen. 2000. "Close and General Friendships among African American, Latino, and Asian American Adolescents from Low-Income Families." *Journal of Adolescent Research* 15(2, March): 274–301. https://doi.org/10.1177/0743558400152005.

Weber, Amanda, Shelly-Ann Collins, Tracy Robinson-Wood, Elda Zeko-Underwood, and Bianca Poindexter. 2018. "Subtle and Severe: Microaggressions among Racially Diverse Sexual Minorities." *Journal of Homosexuality* 65(4): 540–59. 10.1080/00918369.2017.1324679.

Weber, Max. 1946. "Science as a Vocation" [1918]. In *From Max Weber: Essays in Sociology*, translated and edited by Hans H. Gerth and C. Wright Mills. New York: Free Press.

———. 1949. *Max Weber on the Methodology of the Social Sciences*, translated by Edward A. Shils and Henry A. Finch. Glencoe, Ill.: Free Press.

Weinberg, Dana, and Jessica Dawson. 2021. *From Anti-Vaxxer Moms to Militia Men: Influence Operations, Narrative Weaponization, and the Fracturing of American Identity*. Washington, D.C.: Brookings Institution.

Weis, Lois. 2019. *Between Two Worlds: Black Students in an Urban Community College*. London: Routledge. (Originally published in 1985.)

Wessendorf, Susanne. 2013. "Commonplace Diversity and the 'Ethos of Mixing': Perceptions of Difference in a London Neighbourhood." *Identities* 20(4): 407–22. https://doi.org/10.1080/1070289X.2013.822374.

———. 2014. *Commonplace Diversity: Social Relations in a Super-Diverse Context*. London: Palgrave Macmillan.

Westrope, Elizabeth. 2018. "Employment Discrimination on the Basis of Criminal History: Why an Anti-Discrimination Statute Is a Necessary Remedy." *Journal of*

Criminal Law and Criminology 108(2, Spring): 367–97. https://scholarlycommons
.law.northwestern.edu/jclc/vol108/iss2/5.

Willis, Paul. 1977. *Learning to Labor: How Working-Class Kids Get Working-Class Jobs*. New York: Columbia University Press.

Winders, Jamie. 2013. *Nashville in the New Millenium: Immigrant Settlement, Urban Transformation, and Social Belonging*. New York: Russell Sage Foundation.

Winham, Donna M., and Traci L. Armstrong Florian. 2015. "Nativity, Not Acculturation, Predicts SNAP Usage among Low-Income Hispanics with Food Insecurity." *Journal of Hunger and Environmental Nutrition* 10(2): 202–13. https://doi.org/10.1080/19320248.2014.962779.

Winship, Christopher, and Stephen L. Morgan. 1999. "The Estimation of Causal Effects from Observational Data." *Annual Review of Sociology* 25(1, August): 659–706. https://doi.org/10.1146/annurev.soc.25.1.659.

Wood, Wendy. 2019. *Good Habits, Bad Habits: The Science of Making Positive Changes That Stick*. New York: Farrar, Straus & Giroux.

Yim, Sejung Sage. 2021. "Latinos in Brooklyn: Demographic and Socioeconomic Transformations in Sunset Park/Windsor Terrace and Bushwick, 1990–2017." Latino Data Project Report 93. New York: Graduate Center City University of New York, Center for Latin American, Caribbean, and Latino Studies.

Yoshikawa, Hirokazu. 2011. *Immigrants Raising Citizens: Undocumented Parents and Their Children*. New York: Russell Sage Foundation.

Yoshikawa, Hirokazu, Carola Suárez-Orozco, and Roberto G. Gonzales. 2016. "Unauthorized Status and Youth Development in the United States: Consensus Statement of the Society for Research on Adolescence." *Journal of Research on Adolescence* 27(10): 1–16. https://doi.org/10.1111/jora.12272.

Yrizar Barbosa, Guillermo. 2020. "Papers, Places, and Pinatas: Immigrant Social Mobility in Mexican New York." PhD diss., Sociology Department, CUNY Graduate Center.

Zerubavel, Eviatar. 2006. *The Elephant in the Room: Silence and Denial in Everyday Life*. Oxford: Oxford University Press.

Ziliak, Stephen T., and Deirdre N. McCloskey. 2007. *The Cult of Statistical Significance: How the Standard Error Costs Us Jobs, Justice, and Lives*. Ann Arbor: University of Michigan Press.

Zong, Jie, Ariel G. Ruiz Soto, Jeanne Batalova, Julia Gelatt, and Randy Capps. 2017. "A Profile of Current DACA Recipients by Education, Industry, and Occupation—Fact Sheet." Washington, D.C.: Migration Policy Institute, November. https://www.migrationpolicy.org/research/profile-current-daca -recipients-education-industry-and-occupation.

Zucker, Robert A. 2008. "Anticipating Problem Alcohol Use Developmentally from Childhood into Middle Adulthood: What Have We Learned?" *Addiction* 103(1, May): 100–108. https://doi.org/10.1111/j.1360-0443.2008.02179.x.

Zúñiga, Victor, and Rubén Hernández-León. 2005. *New Destinations: Mexican Immigration in the United States*. New York: Russell Sage Foundation.

═ Index ═

Tables and figures are listed in **boldface**.

adulthood: early, typical events in, 18; established, as term, 307n37; middle, 307n37

African Americans: masculinity in, 197, 198, 199; perception of racial discrimination, 126–27. *See also entries under* Black

American dream, immigrants and, 47, 66, 69–71, 82, 123, 181, 259, 283, 285, 289

Asian immigrants, 142–43, 233. *See also* Chinese immigrants

assimilation theories, 7–8, 115, 137, 171

Biden administration, 38

Black fraternities, Mexican college students and, 121

Black friends, and upward mobility, 4, 8, 24, 27, 103, 106, 121–22, 236–38, **237**, 280–81, 352n35

Black Lives Matter movement, 26, 261

"Black" schools: advantages and disadvantages of, 86–87, 88–90, **89**; Black models of achievement in, 2, 4, 24, 87; and changed attitudes about Black people, 95; counterfactual analysis in choice to attend, 92–94, **93**, 94–95, **96**; and crime, 103; fear of, 21, 83, 86–87, 94–95, 99, 102, 107, 324n42; meaning of "Black," 1, 87; successful Mexicans' attendance at, 1–2, 4, 8–9, 21, 58, 84, 94–95, 102, 107, 128, 131, 133

Black students: changed attitudes about, 95; conflicts with, 97–99

Category Changers: case studies, 3–4, 59–61, 99–108, 246–48; definition of, 3; immigrant family bargain and, 51, 55, 59–60, 64, 81; income over time, 77–81, **78**, **79**, **80**, **329n35**; increased success with changed status, 7, 8–9, 56, 77, 111, **329n35**; as living counterfactual cases, 38–39, 91, 99–108, 278–79; mentors and, 138; passing advantages to next generation, 52, 65; U.S. immigration policies and, 40

children, having: change of behavior and, 171, 177; success and, 110, 124, **329–30n35, 332–35n38**

Chinese immigrants, **13**, 14, **14**, 15, 22–23, 41, 42, 56–57, 86, 106, 142–43, 173, 233, 275, 284, 357n52

City University of New York (CUNY), promotion of immigrant mobility, 45, 172, 263, 269–70, 282, 354–55n15

classic assimilation theory, 24

college graduate rates: immigrant family bargain and, **322n40**; of second-generation Mexicans in U.S. *vs.* New York City, 9, **10–11**, 14; of U.S.-born Mexicans *vs.* other U.S.-born groups, **13**, 13–15,

14, 394–94nn24–26; of U.S.- *vs.* foreign-born Mexican migrants, 9–12, **12**

College Graduates ideal type, characteristics of, 17–18

community support for mobility, for Mexican *vs.* Chinese immigrants, 56–57

conduct and decisions of student, impact on success, 108–11, **326–28n34**, **329–30n35**, **332–35n38**

conjunctural ethnicity theory, 43, 90,112, 229

counterfactual analysis, 90–91; Category Changers as living counterfactuals, 38–39, 91, 99–108, 278–79; ethnicity as heuristic device and, 229; intrafamily learning and decision reruns, 91, 94–97, **96**, **97**, 101, 107; lack of, in choosing school, 97–99, **98**; matched proxy cases in, 91, 92–97, **93**; overview, 91; second-chance mechanisms and, 193

criminal justice system: excessive punishment of non-White offenders, 191; increasing focus on punishment, 169–70

criminal justice system second-chance mechanisms, 193; for citizens only, 169, 174, 184–92, 193; gangs and, 184–85, 188–89, 190, 191; prosecutorial discretion and, 190–92, 193; success of, 187–92, 193; 2007 Second Chance Act, 172; types of, 169; for undocumented immigrants in New York City, 182, 183; and upward mobility, 169, 174; youthful offender (YO) status, 168, 172, 187–90, 193, 345n21

culture: ethnicity's acquiring of meaning and, 43–44; and mobility, 41–44, 45, 232–33

culture of poverty theories, 7, 24

CUNY. *See* City University of New York

Deferred Action for Childhood Arrivals (DACA): and breaking of association of Mexicans with illegality, 141–42; Chinese immigrants and, 142–43; criminal record and, 183; documents provided by, 3, 7, 38, 39, 140, 141; driver's licenses and, 38, 140, 141, 158, 160, 161; eligibility, 38, 61, 144; emotional benefits of, 166; family immigration tensions and, 161–62, 166; fear of revocation, 140, 151, 162, 167; fewer-than-expected applicants for, 144, 343n19; freedom to travel and, 145, 160–61; hiding of immigration status prior to, 146–49, 151–53, 161; immigrant family bargain and, 145, 147, 157, 166; impact on NYCOMPers, 145–62; legal efforts to end, 144–45; mentors and, 138; number of Mexicans in, 143; NYCOMPers' ongoing fears despite, 147, 151; obstacles to applying for, 161, 163; and overseas travel, 156–57; quasi-legal status provided by, 139–40, 144, 157; removal of obstacles to upward mobility, 38, 139–40, 141, 145, 147, 149–50, 155–58, 159–62, 166–67, 177, 178–79; research on impact of, 140–41; status resets provided by, 157; study participants and, 308n43; as temporary enforcement policy, 143–44; types of immigrants not helped by, 162–66; undocumented immigrants' fear of registering for, 3, 64, 163–64; and undocumented status turned into private matter, 140, 145, 151, 156, 166

deportation: assistance in avoiding, 48, 131; for criminal offenses, 144, 174, 183, 192, 193; DACA protection from, 3, 7, 38, 144, 158, 161; driver's licenses and, 142, 143, 170, 263; and family separation,

47–48; as federal law, 170, 283; federal reach into local institutions and, 264; New York's refusal to cooperate with ICE, 170, 182, 263, 268; and self-esteem, 74; of those without criminal records, 264; threat of, as obstacle to normal life, 3, 65–66, 158, 159–60, 183, 190, 194, 205–6, 263–64, 292; traffic stops and, 26, 143, 158, 234, 292; undocumented's constant fear of, 205–6

discrimination, reports of, in research, 26

diversity: of New York City, 271, 284; ongoing increases in, 284

Dreamer movement, 26, 71, 145–46, 148, 282–83, 290

driver's licenses for undocumented: in California, 142; DACA and, 38, 140, 141, 158, 160, 161; in New York, 170, 263; New York State Greenlight Law, 170, 315

educational second-chance programs: for citizens, 185–86; in New York City, 173; success of, 174, 185–86; types of, 173; undocumented youths and, 168, 174, 176, 178, 179–83, 192–93

education attained: immigrant family bargain and, 75–76, **319–20n36, 320n38**; mentors and, **339n31**; planful thinking and, 88, 104, 110–11, 285, **326–28n34, 332–35n38**; racial attitudes and, 108–9, **326–28n34**; school quality and, 108–11, **326–28n34, 329–30n35, 332–35n38**; student conduct and, 108–11, **326–28n34, 329–30n35, 332–35n38**; for U.S.- *vs.* foreign-born Mexican migrants, **304n20**. *See also* college graduate rates

Enriquez, Laura, 28–29, 141, 142, 150, 234

ethnic cultures, lazy stereotypes of, 229, 232–33

extracurricular second chance programs, 169, 175–76, 192

Flores, Ed, 198, 216, 226

friends: bad influences, and "avoid Mexicans" strategy, 1–2, 87, 95, 97, 101, 109; picking to enhance future prospects, 231–32, 235

friends, race/ethnicity of: NYCOMPers' three friendship strategies, 238–39; and upward mobility, 229, 231–32, 236–40, **237**. *See also* Black friends; Whites, NYCOMPers relationships with

gang: benefits of membership, 212; negative mentors and, 118; pressure to join, 205; prevalence of, 1; second-generation Mexicans and, 281; targeting of good kids, 205, 207–8

gang involvement: and drinking alcohol, 348n43, 349n49; impact on adult outcomes, 214–25, **349n60**; number of NYCOMPers with, 214; types of involvement with, 214–15

gang masculinity: as analytical ideal type, 196; case study of, 209–14; characteristics of, 196; conceptions of social time in, 201–2; family and friends' pushback against, 200; and immigrant family bargain, 196–97, 277; impairment of upward mobility, 194–95, 209–14, 225, 278; later-life regrets, 200; research on, 195; time use and, 201–2, **203–4**

gender, success and, 110, **329–30n35, 332–35n38**

glass floor of wealthy families, 53, 56, 86, 192, 280

Gonzales, Roberto, 29, 63, 140, 171, 233–34

Guerrero-Rippberger (Guerrero-Mustafa), Sara, 31, 34–37, 274, 296–97

High Fliers ideal type: Category Changers as, 101–8, **107**; characteristics of, 18; immigrant family bargain and, **319–20n36**, **322n40**; mentors and, 127–33; school quality and, 108–9, 110, **326–28n34**, **329–30n35**; student behavior and, 108–9, **326–28n34**; views on race and, 108–9, **326–28n34**
Holdaway, Jennifer, 13–14, 171, 275
Horowitz, Adam, 43, 230, 233
hypermasculinity, 198, 199, 226. *See also* gang masculinity; perilous masculinity
hyperselected mobility theory, 22–23

immigrant family bargain, 4; Category Changers and, 100; college graduate rates and, **322n40**; DACA and, 145, 147, 157, 166; failure of, family tensions and, 57; family strategies and, 54–57; gang masculinity and, 196–97, 277; grim realist parents, 66–69; High Fliers and, **319–20n36**, **322n40**; high stakes of, 54–55; and life success, 5, 8, 50, 58, 61, 125; Mexican mobility masculinity and, 197, 277; NYCOMP family settlement patterns and, 274; obligations on all generations, 55; older siblings and, 52–53, 55–57, 58, 59–61, 66–67; opportunities for Mexican *vs.* Chinese immigrants, 56–57; and tensions in mixed-status families, 71–75; transnational families and, 316n1; and upward mobility, 205–6, 276, 277, 280, 285; U.S. immigration policy and, 80
immigrant family bargain, legal status and, 3, 4, 49–57; case studies,

57–75; statistical analysis of family history and outcomes and, 75–76, **319–20n36**, **320n38**, **321n39**, **322n40**
immigrants' rights movement, 145–46
immigrants' success, benefits to U.S., 286
Immigration Reform and Control Act (IRCA), 3, 8, 39, 52, 119, 124, 138, 253
income: immigrant family bargain and, 75–76, **319–20n36**, **321n39**; legal status and, 77–79, **78**, **79**, **80**, 81–82, **319–20n36**, **321n39**, **323n41**; mentors and, **339n31**; for NYCOMP participants *vs.* New York census data, 80–81; racial attitudes and, 108–9, **326–28n34**; school quality and, 108–11, **326–28n34**, **329–30n35**, **332–35n38**; student conduct and, 108–11, **326–28n34**, **329–30n35**, **332–35n38**
intergenerational mobility, research on, 27–28
IRCA. *See* Immigration Reform and Control Act

jail time, and change of behavior, 168, 171, 181–82, 187, 191, 193, 200
Jiménez, Tomás, 26, 43, 230, 232, 233

Kasinitz, Phil, **10–11**, 13–14, 85, 171, 275

Lee, Jennifer, 22–23, 27, 230, 233, 312–13n118
legal exclusion theory, 8, 115, 137, 171
legalization of undocumented, as good policy, 262, 285, 290–93
legal status: current difficulty getting, 38, 40; DACA and, 139–40, 144, 157; desire for, as evidence of respect for U.S. law, 40; IRCA and, 3, 8, 52, 119, 124, 253; needed reforms in, 6; passing advantages to next generation, 52–54; unequal access to, as civil rights issue, 261–62;

upward mobility and, 1, 4, 5–6, 29, 39, 109–11, **326–28n34, 329–30n35, 332–35n38**. *See also* Category Changers; immigrant family bargain, legal status and

legal status, lack of. *See* undocumented status

life courses: of families, 54; of individuals, 53–54

Louie, Vivian, 27, 41, 115, 137, 265–66, 280, 282

marriage, early, upward mobility and, 124–25

masculinity: in African American males, 197, 198, 199; positive forms, value of programs promoting, 226; research on, 198–99; "urban drinker" model of, 206, 208; *"yo mando"* model of, 213. *See also* gang masculinity; hypermasculinity; Mexican mobility masculinity

mentors: access to, via public transportation, 276; author as, 47, 137–38; *vs.* brokers, 337n10; case studies, 119–33; conflict in school and, 133–34, **339n32**; duration and depth of mentoring and, 134. **340n33, 135**; educational second-chance programs and, 185–86; formal *vs.* natural, 117, 133; former mentees as mentors, 122; good, characteristics of, 117, 118–19; lack of legal status and, 8, 136, 138, **341n38**; mentee's missed opportunities and, 129–30; minorities' move into White-dominated fields and, 115; negative, 118, 133–34, **340n35, 341nn37–38**; in New York public schools, 117; peers as, 117–18, 133–34, **339n32**; race/ethnicity of, 118, 137; statistical analysis of effects, 133–36, **339–41nn31–38**; students with hard life circumstances

and, 134–36, **340n35, 341nn37–38**; types of help given by, 116–17, 138; as under-researched, 115, 137; upward mobility and, 1–2, 5–6, 9, 21, 28, 35, 44, 70, 86, 95, 102, 105, 107–8, 112, 114–16, 136, 265–66, 282, 286; in work life, 122, 125–27, 253

Mexican ethnicity, meaning of: change over life course, 230, **237**, 239–40, 243–59, 281; common stereotypes in 1990s-2000s, 228; and counterfactual thinking, 229; diversity of New York City and, 271, 284; as heuristic tool, 228, 229; real-world significance of, 234; rise of Mexican mobility culture and, 260; as status *vs.* identity, 227–28, 234–35, 243–59, **244**; in upward *vs.* downward mobility, 230–31, 233, 259, 269; variation by place, 271–72, 281

Mexican immigrants: anti-Black attitudes in, 88, 95, 102; and gendered power, 195; low status of, 206; and racialized illegality, 29–30, 141–42, 151–54

Mexican mobility culture: community organizations and, 282; community-wide sharing of information and, 275, 281–82; emergence of, 262, 279–85; meaning of Mexican ethnicity and, 260; in New York City, 6, 16, 112, 138; undocumented status and, 284–85

Mexican mobility masculinity: as analytical ideal type, 196; case study, 202–209; characteristics of, 197; conceptions of social time in, 201; first- and second-generation versions of, 197; immigrant family bargain and, 197, 277; mentors attracted by, 208–9; positive effect on upward mobility, 194–95; and success despite disadvantages, 205–209, 225, 278; time use and,

202, **203–4**; and turn from gang activities, 217–18; and upward mobility, 281

Mexican students, stereotypes of: as handicap, 106; origin of "poor student" stereotype, 87–88; and surprise at success, 120, 337n18

minority cultures of mobility, 27, 279–80, 283

Mollenkopf, John, 13–14, 171, 275

New York City: decoupling of "mainstream" and Whiteness in, 235–36; number of Mexicans in, 236, 352n33; pro-immigrant economy in, 268–69; superdiversity of, 271, 284

New York City and State programs: Greenlight Law, 170, 315; inclusive policies for undocumented, 4, 170, 172, 263–64, 266–70, 283; legal status and, 5; New York Dream Act of 2019, 146; programs supporting Mexicans' mobility, 138; role in NYCOMPers' success, 111–13; U.S. immigration policies and, 263, 264; viability in other jurisdictions, 263

New York City Children of Migrants Project (NYCOMP): analytical leverage of, 30–44, 278–79, 297–98; author's positionality, 47, 313–16n130; capture of effects of U.S. immigration policies, 37–40; "code all cases and processes" approach in, 301; contributions of, 18–20, 40–44, 225–26; data analysis, 34–37, 46–47, 298–99, 300, 311n102; data set, 302; emergent theme approach, 298; extended time of data gathering, 33–34, 37–38; framework for explaining mobility, 44–48; goals of, 295; history of project, 297; key findings, 4, 5–6; long-term case development, 36–37, 299; methodology, 5, 296, 299–300, 301;

mixed-method research and, 36; number of fully developed cases, 21, 307–8n42; sample for, 4; as strategic research site, 16, 20; terminology in, 46; time periods of data collection, 324n42

NYCOMP. *See* New York City Children of Migrants Project

Obama administration, 3, 38, 143–44, 145–46

Okigbo, Karen, 23, 127, 233, 317–18n20

origins and destinations theory, 8, 26

Ortiz, Vilma, **10–11**, 14–15, 25, 26, 264–68, 272, 275–77, 354n6

outcome categories, ideal, 17–18, 306–7n36, **307n36**; predicted *vs.* actual, for NYCOMPers, 18, **19**. *See also* High Fliers ideal type

parents of NYCOMPers: abuse by, 103, 129, 174, 175, 179; blocking of children's advancement, 179; data gathered on, 32–33; demographics of, 22–23, 26; undocumented, immigrant family bargain and, 64–65

participants in NYCOMP (NYCOMPers), 8; author's interaction with peers of, 350n66; demographics of, 20–22, 23–24; legal status over time, 38–39, **39**; number jailed or arrested, 199–200; places of origin, 27, 272, 355n26; selection of, 20–21, 31–33

Patler, Caitlin, 28–29, 140–41, 234

perilous masculinity, 199–201

planful thinking, and upward mobility, 5, 88, 104, 110–11, 285, 286, **326–28n34**, **332–35n38**

police involvement, adult outcomes and, 215

policy recommendations to promote mobility, 285–87, 290–93; activism for legalization and, 290; anti-immigrant sentiment and, 289–90;

government assistance for all
immigrants, 285–86; government
review of social media platform
algorithms, 289; legalization of
undocumented Americans, 262,
285, 290–93; *vs.* structural change,
261, 285, 287; tax code changes, 286;
universal approaches, value of,
289–90; U.S. epistemic crisis and,
261, 287–90
priming, 141, 143
problematic Mexicans theory, 7, 17,
24, 225, 231, 262

race, attitudes about: impact on
success, 108–9, **326–28n34**;
interaction with other groups and,
231
racial exclusion theory, 7, 25–26, 81,
111, 137, 171, 225–26, 231, 262, 1115
racial injustice, structural change
and, 261
racialized illegality, 29–30, 141–42,
151–54
reactive ethnicity, 7, 24, 232
Rendón, María, **11–12**, 25, 31, 43, 86,
111–13, 137, 218, 225–26, 264–69,
273, 274, 276–78, 355n27
research and theories on outcomes
of Mexican immigrants, 7–8,
22–30, 41
retrospective reframing of life events,
171–72
Ridgeway, Cecilia, 43, 233–34, 248

school: leaving due to family need,
2–3, 8, 50, 62–66, 163–64; police
in, 169–70, 173; quality, impact
on success, 108–11, **326–28n34**,
329–30n35, **332–35n38**; racialized
illegality in, 153–54. *See also*
educational second-chance
programs
schools, better, outside neighborhood:
advantages and disadvantages
of, 86, 88–90, **89**, 102; Category

Changers as counterfactual cases
on, 99–108; counterfactual analysis
in selection of, 92–97, **93**, **96**, **97**;
factors in choice of, 86–87; future
income and, 84; gang masculinity
and, 211–12; intrafamily learning
and decision reruns, 91, 94–97,
96, **97**, 101, 106; lack of adequate
guidance and, 104; and New York's
school choice system, 275; students'
choice of, 83–85; successful
Mexicans' attendance at, 1, 4,
8–9, 25; and upward mobility,
280–81, 282
schools, local zoned: advantages
and disadvantages of, 86–87,
88–90, **89**; funneling effect and, 86,
88, 90, 93, 99; gangs and, 84, 88,
97–100, 122, 175–76, 180–81, 205,
206–7; honors/special programs,
86, 88, **89**; lack of counterfactual
analysis in selection of, 97–99, **98**;
marginal quality of, 86; Mexican
settlement patterns and, 87–88;
need to address deficiencies in,
112; parents' preference for, 86–87;
students' concerns about, 83–84;
upward mobility despite, 205–209;
wide range in quality of, 85
schools in New York City: IDs for
undocumented, 268; policies
promoting student mobility, 275;
ways to gain admission to, 85–86
Second Chance Act of 2007, 172
second-chance mechanisms: case
studies, 175–92; for citizens only,
168–69, 170, 174, 192; in New York
City and state, 172–83; research
on, 171–72; scientific justifications
for, 172–73; success of, 170, 192–93,
286; undocumented youths'
discouragement and, 168, 192;
upward mobility and, 169, 174,
266; as wise public policy, 169–70,
171. *See also* criminal justice system
second-chance mechanisms;

educational second-chance programs; extracurricular second chance programs

second-generation advantage theory, 7, 23, 42

Secure Communities program, 29

segmented assimilation theory, 7, 23, 24, 41–42, 232

segregation, 312–13n118

settlement patterns: as context for mobility, 43, 85–90, 113, 230, 262, 270–74; and mentors, 118, 137; and perception of Mexican immigrants, 122

Social Security, undocumented workers and, 292–93

Spanish language fluency, as career asset, 187, 227, 256

status, research on, 233–35

step-ups: avoiding, through school choice, 100; reasons for, 206; response to, and upward mobility, 37, 92–94, 95, 194, 195, 208, 215; targeting of good kids, 205

Suárez-Orozco, Carola, 28–29, 137, 140–41

taxes, undocumented immigrants and, 165

Telles, Edward, **10–11**, 14–15, 25, 26, 42–43, 264–68, 272, 275–77, 354n6

time use, 201–2, **203–4**

Trump administration, 38, 144, 162

two-way assimilation theory, 7, 23, 42

Undocumented and Unafraid campaign, 290

undocumented status, **319–20n36**, **322n40**; academic second-chance programs and, 174, 176, 178; as accident of birth, 71; as barrier to upward mobility, 2–3, 5, 6, 19–20, 153–55, 158–60, 161–62, 164–65, 173, 177, 178; changed meaning of, 282–83; discouragement and, 3, 63, 73, 90, 168, 179–83; educational

or career success despite, 68–69, 70–71, 73–74; immigrant family bargain and, 50–57, 61–75; increased impact since 1990s, 29–30, 38, 312n111; and magical thinking, 69–71; as master status, 65–66, 139, 157, 166, 234, 292; as more likely in older children, 316n3; number of people, 144; passing as documented, 141, 143, 146–49; passing of disadvantage to next generation, 52–53; and racialized illegality, 29–30, 141–42, 151–54; renting of apartments and, 160; research on impact of, 28–30, 51; romantic life and, 150–51, 158, 161, 167; and stigma, 72, 141. *See also* deportation

upward mobility in U.S., 16–17

upward mobility of NYCOMPers: behaviors promoting, 44, 280–81; case studies, 1–2; conditions promoting, 17; as contrary to most theories, 20–31; created roads of, 27; culture and, 6, 232–33; decline in U.S. upward mobility and, 16–17; framework for explaining, 44–48; job types and salaries, 269; large increase in, 14–15; legal status and, 44–45; and "mainstream" culture concept, 42; New York City and State policies and, 44; New York City public transportation and, 44, 276; participant expectations and, 15; place and, 270; salient factors in, 266, 285–86; in second generation Mexicans in New York City, 6, 15; social location of Mexicans and, 44; undocumented status as barrier to, 2–3, 5, 6, 19–20, 153–55, 158–60, 161–62, 164–65, 173. *See also* college graduate rates; income

upward mobility of NYCOMPers *vs.* comparable groups studied, 111–13, 264–78; community-wide sharing of information and, 275, 281–82; dynamic of settlement and incorporation and, 266–67, 270–74; generalizability of NYCOMP results, 263; identification of salient factors in, 266; immigrant family bargain and, 276, 277; influence of place on, 283–84; levels of community violence and, 276–78; New York City and State programs and, 266–70; New York City public transportation and, 44, 276; U.S. immigration law and, 272

U.S.-born Mexican teenagers in U.S.: academic outcomes in, 230; increased number *vs.* foreign-born, 16, 230, 281, **305n30**

U.S. immigration policies: *vs.* American values, 65, 74, 82; and crushing of young dreams, 179; direct effect on legal status public relations participants, 40; harsh penalties for undocumented immigrants' crimes, 170, 174, 183; immigrant family bargain and, 80; mobility for undocumented and, 81–82; New York City and State programs and, 263, 264; NYCOMP design and, 37–40; periods of, 37–38; recommended changes in, 285–86; as structural legal violence, 47–48; trumping of inclusionary efforts, 65. *See also* undocumented status

values, American: and immigrant support, 286–87; legalization of undocumented and, 290–92; and magical thinking by immigrants, 69–71; *vs.* U.S. immigration policies, 65, 74, 82

Waters, Mary, 13–14, 127, 171, 275

Whiteness, as decoupled from "mainstream" for NYCOMPers, 232–33, 235–36, 245–50, 260, 283

Whites, NYCOMPers relationships with: and Mexicanness as identity or status, 243–59, **244**; minimal contact, 9, 87, 245–50; patterns over time in, 240–43, **241**; substantive, from childhood or high school, 254–57; substantive, throughout life, 257–59; through early transition to adulthood, 250–52; through upward mobile transition to adulthood, 252–54; and upward mobility, 230, 235–36, **237**, 238–39, 240–43, **241**, 259–60

women's college graduate rates for U.S.-born Mexicans *vs.* other U.S.-born groups, 13, **14**, 15

youthful offender (YO) status, 168, 172, 187–90, 193, 345n21

Zhou, Min, 22–23, 24, 230, 233, 312–13n118